The Cambridge Companion to

GRAND OPERA

．．．．．．．．．．．

EDITED BY
David Charlton
Royal Holloway, University of London

CAMBRIDGE
UNIVERSITY PRESS

PUBLISHED BY THE PRESS SYNDICATE OF THE UNIVERSITY OF CAMBRIDGE
The Pitt Building, Trumpington Street, Cambridge CB2 1RP, United Kingdom

CAMBRIDGE UNIVERSITY PRESS
The Edinburgh Building, Cambridge, CB2 2RU, UK
40 West 20th Street, New York, NY 10011-4211, USA
477 Williamstown Road, Port Melbourne, VIC 3207, Australia
Ruiz de Alarcón 13, 28014 Madrid, Spain
Dock House, The Waterfront, Cape Town 8001, South Africa

http://www.cambridge.org

First published 2003

Printed in the United Kingdom at University Press, Cambridge

Typeface Minion 10.75/14 pt   *System* LATEX 2$_\varepsilon$ [TB]

A catalogue record for this book is available from the British Library

ISBN 0 521 64118 7 hardback
ISBN 0 521 64683 9 paperback

The Cambridge Companion to Grand Opera

In this fascinating and accessible exploration of the world of grand opera, a team of operatic scholars and writers examines those important Romantic operas which embraced the Shakespearean sweep of tragedy, history, love in time of conflict, and the struggle for national self-determination. Rival nations, rival religions and violent resolutions are common elements, with various social or political groups represented in the form of operatic choruses. The book traces the origins and development of a style created during an increasingly technical age, which exploited the world-renowned skills of Parisian stage-designers, artists and dancers, as well as singers. It analyses in detail the grand operas of Rossini, Auber, Meyerbeer and Halévy, and discusses Wagner, grand opera in Russia, the Czech lands, Italy, Britain and the Americas. It also includes an essay by the renowned opera director David Pountney.

DAVID CHARLTON is Professor of Music History at Royal Holloway, University of London. He has published *Grétry and the Growth of Opéra-Comique* (Cambridge, 1986), *E. T. A. Hoffmann's Musical Writings: Kreisleriana; The Poet and the Composer; Music Criticism* (Cambridge, 1989) and, most recently, *French Opera, 1730–1830* (2000).

Cambridge Companions to Music

Contents

Part IV • Transformations of grand opera

Illustrations

Contributors

M. Elizabeth C. Bartlet, a specialist in eighteenth- and nineteenth-century French opera, has edited Rossini's *Guillaume Tell* for the critical edition of his oeuvre, published a monograph on the staging of grand opera, and written widely on music during the Revolution, Consulate and Empire (including a two-volume book on Etienne-Nicolas Méhul). She serves on the editorial committee for the Rameau *Opera Omnia* and her editions of *Platée* and *Dardanus* are forthcoming in this series.

Matthias Brzoska, Professor of Musicology at the Folkwang-Hochschule, Essen (Germany), is editing Meyerbeer's *Le Prophète* for the new critical edition of the composer's stage works. He is author of *Die Idee des Gesamtkunstwerks in der Musiknovellistik der Julimonarchie* (1995), and co-editor of a three-volume *Geschichte der Musik* for Laaber (2001).

David Charlton is Professor of Music History at Royal Holloway, University of London. His most recent books are *French Opera 1730–1830: Meaning and Media* and *Michel-Jean Sedaine (1719–1797): Theatre, Opera and Art* (co-edited with Mark Ledbury).

Marina Frolova-Walker studied musicology at the Moscow Conservatoire, receiving her doctorate in 1994. She lectures at the Faculty of Music, University of Cambridge, and is a Fellow of Clare College.

Thomas Grey is Associate Professor of Music at Stanford University. He is author of *Wagner's Musical Prose: Texts and Contexts* (1995) and editor of *Richard Wagner: Der fliegende Holländer* (2000), as well as the *Cambridge Companion to Wagner* (forthcoming).

Diana R. Hallman, Associate Professor of Musicology at the University of Kentucky, centres her research in nineteenth-century opera, French grand opera and the music of Fromental Halévy. She is author of various articles, and of *Opera, Liberalism, and Antisemitism in Nineteenth-Century France: The Politics of Halévy's 'La Juive'* (2002); her next book will be *Fannie Bloomfield Zeisler: American Virtuoso of the Gilded Age*.

Sarah Hibberd is a research fellow in the Department of Music, Royal Holloway, University of London. She is currently working on representations of historical figures on the Parisian lyric stage during the July Monarchy.

Steven Huebner has taught at McGill University, Montreal, since 1985 and is the author of *The Operas of Charles Gounod* (1990) and *French Opera at the Fin de Siècle: Wagnerism, Nationalism and Style* (1999).

Hervé Lacombe is Professor of Music at the University of Rennes 2 (France), and specialises in nineteenth-century French music. His *The Keys to French Opera in the Nineteenth Century* was published in 2001, and the extended study, *Georges*

Bizet: Naissance d'une identité créatrice (Fayard, 2000), won the Prix des Muses for biography and the Prix Bordin of the Académie des Beaux-Arts.

Fiamma Nicolodi is Professore ordinario de Drammaturgia musicale at the University of Florence (Italy). She has worked on composers from Rossini and Meyerbeer through to Dallapiccola and Berio, published on symbolist music-theatre, musical nationalism, and music in the fascist era; she is currently director of the *Lessico musicale italiano* (LESMU).

James Parakilas is the James L. Moody, Jr. Family Professor of Performing Arts at Bates College (Maine), where he chairs the Music Department. He has written *Ballads Without Words: Chopin and the Tradition of the Instrumental Ballade* (1992) and, with collaborators, *Piano Roles: Three Hundred Years of Life with the Piano* (2000).

David Pountney has been an international opera director for thirty years as well as spending ten years each as a member of Scottish Opera and then English National Opera. He has also written numerous opera translations from several languages, as well as original opera librettos for Stephen Oliver, John Harle and Maxwell Davies.

John H. Roberts is Professor of Music and Head of the Music Library at the University of California, Berkeley. He wrote his doctoral dissertation on the genesis of Meyerbeer's *L'Africaine* and has published widely on Handel, particularly his borrowing from other composers.

Herbert Schneider teaches musicology at the Universität des Saarlandes at Saarbrücken (Germany). His main fields of research are French music and theory from the seventeenth to the end of the nineteenth centuries, and the musical relations between Germany and France.

Jan Smaczny is Hamilton Harty Professor of Music at Queen's University, Belfast. He has written extensively on many aspects of Czech music and, chiefly, on the life and works of Dvořák.

Mary Ann Smart, Associate Professor of Music at the University of California, Berkeley, is author of 'Bellini' and 'Donizetti' in *New Grove/2* and editor of the critical edition of Donizetti's last opera, *Dom Sébastien*. Her recent book *Resonant Bodies* examines music and gesture in repertory between French grand opera of the 1830s and Wagner's *Ring*.

Marian Smith was educated at Carleton College and the University of Texas, and received a doctoral degree in musicology from Yale University. She is Associate Professor of Music at the University of Oregon and author of *Ballet and Opera in the Age of Giselle* (2000), which was awarded the de la Torre Bueno Prize.

Nicholas White is Lecturer in the Department of French at the University of Cambridge and Official Fellow of Emmanuel College. He is author of *The Family in Crisis in Late Nineteenth-Century French Fiction* (1999) and co-editor of *Scarlet Letters: Fictions of Adultery from Antiquity to the 1990s* (1997). His edition of Mauldon's translation of Huysmans's *Against Nature* won the 1999 Scott Moncrieff Prize.

Simon Williams is Professor of Dramatic Art at the University of California, Santa Barbara. He is the author of *German Actors of the Eighteenth and Nineteenth Centuries* (1985), *Shakespeare on the German Stage* (1990) and *Richard Wagner and Festival Theatre* (1994).

Preface

This Companion is about nineteenth-century opera of a certain large-scale type; it provides a survey, arranged thematically, which contains more information about its subject than any previous publication in English. Yet the operas considered here are mostly different from those within, for example, Eric A. Plaut's *Grand Opera: Mirror of the Western Mind* (Chicago, 1993). The association between 'grand opera' and large material resources is an essential aspect of our definition here, one which in fact takes French opera as its focus, though not as its boundary. The core of our repertory is characterised in the 1954 edition of *Grove's Dictionary* under 'Grand opéra', which says:

> A *grand opéra* is a nineteenth-century French type . . . [containing] a
> serious, often tragic subject of an epic or historical nature, the use of the
> chorus in action, the inclusion of a ballet, at least one spectacular scene
> with elaborate writing for the solo and choral voices in concert and
> (normally) division into five acts . . .

In Part I we investigate several of these resources, and also offer new interpretations concerning the wider significance of grand opera, which played no small part in the cultural consciousness of its age. (In the view of many, it stood at the top of a particular artistic hierarchy.) However – and crucially – the present Companion is not just about French opera. The impact of Parisian grand opera on composers in every developed country was enormous; consequently, for example, Donizetti and Verdi came to work in Paris, and their work is duly considered within. The same impact was translated into further works, in several different countries, so that the term 'grand opera' for us consciously reflects the reality that the French model and its many non-French derivatives were, for a half-century, ubiquitous and dominant. Their dominance was not uniform, and was heaviest during the years up to 1870; yet they continued to be dominant. Wagner and *verismo* did not dislodge them until very late, and they co-existed with 'Italian opera' as a mainstream type. To help to demonstrate this point, our authors have supplied information at the end of each chapter in Part III showing how rapidly grand operas of French origin were to be seen, sometimes in adapted forms, throughout the operatic stages of the world.

In Part IV the wider evolution of grand opera as a genre is explored. After the particular case of Wagner in Chapter 16, this is shown through various national studies. Non-French opera traditions are covered in Chapters 17 to

20, detailing (within the constraints of allowable space) the assimilation of French works in these respective countries, but at the same time exploring the less well known range of native operatic creations.

Our phrase 'grand opera' differs from the traditional use of the term, which was generalised. Thus *The New Grove Dictionary*, 2001 edition (hereafter *New Grove*/2), offers no entry for 'grand opera' and the reasons are not hard to divine, if one is familiar with the way the term has developed. (More on this debate will be found in Chapter 1 below.) The 1954 article in *Grove* naturally took older usage into account:

> [*Grand opéra*]: A term with a definite meaning in French, unlike the English 'grand opera', which is not its equivalent and is useless for classification, since it is loosely used to mean simply serious as distinct from comic opera.

And former American usage of 'grand opera' was similarly vague, or sweeping: my old libretto of Puccini's *Tosca*, issued by Charles E. Burden at Steinway Hall, New York, price 35 cents, is headed: 'Grand Opera by the Boston-National Grand Opera Company, A National Institution' – which, at the same time, neatly illustrates the way that such operatic terms can simultaneously apply to (i) a genre, (ii) a theatrical company, (iii) a building, and (iv) an institution. Indeed the French phrase *grand opéra* evolved over two centuries ago through just such a loose web, centred on the Paris Opéra.

Perhaps a transitional period of meaning was reached in 1945, at least for England, when for the first time the State began to give regular subsidy to the main London opera companies and subsequently took over Covent Garden. In an appraisal entitled 'The Opera in Britain' (1948) our phrase occurs only once: 'For grand opera, a large cast, chorus and symphony orchestra are required, besides a full-sized opera house, with production and decor in keeping'.[1]

Nevertheless, since this Companion is about a multi-media genre it contains many types of information that may not be apparent from the chapter titles. Here is a location-note showing where various important themes are discussed:

Terminology, genre and definitions: Chapters 1, 10 and 15

French laws, censorship, budgets, salaries: Chapter 2

Survey of plots: Chapter 3

Musical forms: Chapters 10 (duets), 13, 14 and 16

Orchestration: Chapter 13

Staging and production: Chapters 4, 8 and 18

Contracts between artists and the Opéra: Chapter 14

The relation of grand opera to society and politics is something that many chapters deal with: particular case-studies are found in Chapters 4, 9, 11 and 13.

The international appeal of grand opera is reflected in the different ways that different nations actually think and write about the topic. A key aspect of this Companion's design lies in the invitation to scholars from different countries and critical traditions to participate, writing (originally) in four different languages. This itself has made for an implicit dialogue on current grand opera research and clarifies international perceptions of the topic. Most of our contributors have already written book-length studies on aspects of grand opera. In this general connection Christopher Smith's role as translator of three of these chapters must be mentioned, together with those of Deirdre O'Grady and Tim Carter for the fourth: it cannot be stressed too strongly that their generosity and painstaking work has brought to this book the benefit of rare linguistic and musicological skills.

Constructing grand opera has often previously involved the apposition of Auber, Meyerbeer and Halévy to other composers such as Verdi, Wagner and Musorgsky. This Companion offers an opportunity to re-evaluate that construction by widening the total picture, emphasising operatic re-creation and reception as such. The choice of illustrations has been made with a view to suggesting how grand opera was absorbed into wider culture and its artefacts; further analysis of this comes in Chapter 2. Thus the mixed media of our illustrations and images are intended to carry due weight in the appreciation of their 'content'.

In mentioning 're-creation', special attention must be drawn to David Pountney's essay, Chapter 8, which shows that the actual praxis of re-creation forces one to face a host of vital contextual issues; the essay serves also to remind British readers that their own national experience of grand opera in recent years compares but sporadically with the range and vitality of foreign experience: both productions considered here were created for Vienna. As the genre approaches its 200th anniversary it deserves to be increasingly revived and reinterpreted in the opera house.

Information tables will be found in several chapters, and a general chronology at the head of Chapter I. It was decided, in general, not always to include detailed opera plots. That information is, after all, usually found by appropriate reference to other books or on-line sources (*Kobbé's Opera Book, The New Grove Dictionary of Opera* (henceforth *Opera Grove*), *The New Penguin Opera Guide* etc.) and, besides, there was too much else to write about. Instead, our authors have approached the matter of narrative in a number of ways, keeping the reader informed of those plot elements which are essential to know in order to understand their current argument.

Note
1 [anon.], 'The Opera in Britain', *Planning*, 15/290 (8 November 1948), 147–62, here 156.

Acknowledgements

First and foremost I should like to thank all contributing authors and transla-
tors for their exceptional goodwill, patience and forbearance in the interests
of this common endeavour. Second I should like to thank the Research
Committee, Department of Music, Royal Holloway, for granting a research
leave in 2001; and third Patricia Scholfield for her partnership in keeping a
complicated show on the road.

For various words of wisdom and advice imparted in the course of
this volume's development I owe thanks to several friends and acquaintances: Mike Ashman, Beth Bartlet, Geoffrey Chew, Francesca Chiarelli,
John Deathridge, Jan Hart, Janet Johnson, Barry Millington, Karin Pendle,
Philip Reed, Clive Scott, Anastasia Siopsi and Nicholas White.

For equally generous help with ascertaining or obtaining various sources
and information, I am most grateful to Diana Bickley, Gunther Braam,
Rodolfo Caesar, my father A. W. F. Charlton, Roberto Duarte, Mark Everist,
Sarah Hibberd, Kostas Kardamis, Michel Noiray, Margaret Oliver, Cécile
Reynaud, Rodrigo Cicchelli Velloso and Nicole Wild.

Christina Fuhrmann is owed especial thanks for allowing us to have
rapid access to her completed doctoral dissertation concerning operatic
adaptations at Covent Garden, and allowing us to make use of her research.

The particular help and the generous counsel of Robert Ignatius Letellier
played an important part in the volume and is acknowledged with many
thanks.

Jean-Louis Tamvaco went out of his way to make available both information and many special pictorial sources, and this considerable generosity
made the enhanced scope of the iconographical content of this project possible. Other essential help in this area was kindly provided by Bettina Porpaczy,
and her colleagues Mss Sedivy, Tremmel and Maly at the Vienna Staatsoper.

The contribution to the volume of Christopher Smith (formerly Reader
in French and a colleague of mine at the University of East Anglia) extends
beyond the translator's authority and sympathy evident in the three chapters
he prepared: in the course of this work he clarified numerous points of fact
and detail. Our debt to him is extensive and my thanks cannot be too warmly
expressed.

Abbreviations

Grove Opera   *The New Grove Dictionary of Opera*, ed. Stanley Sadie,
4 vols. (London: Macmillan, 1992)

New Grove/2   *The New Grove Dictionary of Music and Musicians*, 2nd edn, ed.
Stanley Sadie, 29 vols. (London: Macmillan, 2001)

Paris Opéra,   The most important of the French lyric theatres, and the oldest,
or Opéra   established by letters patent in 1669. Its official titles included:
Académie Royale de Musique (1815–48); Théâtre de la Nation
(1848–50); Académie Nationale de Musique (1850–51);
Académie Impériale de Musique (1851–54); Théâtre Impériale
de l'Opéra (1854–70); Théâtre National de l'Opéra (1870→).
From 1821 to 1873 the Opéra occupied the Salle Le Peletier (see
Figs. 4 and 5), which burned down on 28–29 October 1873. The
new house designed by Charles Garnier in 1861 was begun the
same year and opened on 5 January 1875.

Chronology

	Events and operas in France	Events and operas outside France
1799	Napoleon becomes First Consul	
1804	Napoleon crowns himself Emperor	
1807	*La Vestale* (3, Spontini; Jouy)	
1809	*Fernand Cortez* (3, Spontini; Jouy, Esmenard)	
1815	Napoleon defeated and exiled: Louis XVIII restored to the throne	*Ivan Susanin* (2, Cavos; Shakhovskoy)
1817	*Fernand Cortez* revised version (3, Spontini; Jouy)	
1821	Death of Napoleon on St Helena; new Paris Opéra, rue Peletier, opens	Greek war of independence (to 1829); revolution in Piedmont crushed by Austria
1824	Death of Louis XVIII; accession of Charles X; Rossini becomes director of Théâtre Italien	Death of Lord Byron
1825	*Il crociato in Egitto* (2, Meyerbeer; Rossi) (prem.: Venice, 1824)	
1826	*Le Siège de Corinthe* (3, Rossini; Balocchi and Soumet)	
1827	*Moïse et Pharaon* (4, Rossini; Balocchi, Jouy); Hugo, *Cromwell*	
1828	*La Muette de Portici* (5, Auber; Scribe)	
1829	*Guillaume Tell* (4, Rossini; Jouy, Bis)	
1830	July Revolution: abdication of Charles X: succession of Louis-Philippe; censorship lifted; Véron succeeds Lubbert as Opéra director	Greece declared independent; Belgium proclaims independence
1831	*Robert le Diable* (5, Meyerbeer; Scribe); Chopin arrives in Paris; Hugo, *Notre-Dame de Paris*	Polish uprising suppressed by Russia; revolutions in Parma, Modena, Papal States, crushed by Austria
1832		Deaths of Walter Scott and of Goethe
1833	*Gustave III* (5, Auber; Scribe)	
1834		*The Mountain Sylph* (2, Barnett; Thackeray), London
1835	*La Juive* (5, Halévy; Scribe); reintroduction of censorship follows assassination attempt on the king	*Askold's Tomb* (4, Verstovsky; Zagoskin), St Petersburg
1836	*Les Huguenots* (5, Meyerbeer; Scribe, Deschamps)	*A Life for the Tsar* (5, Glinka; Rozen, Sollogub, Kukol'nik, Zhovovsky), St Petersburg
1837		*Fair Rosamond* (4, Barnett; C. Z. Barnett, Shannon), London; *Joan of Arc* (3, Balfe; Fitzball), London
1838	*Guido et Ginevra* (5, Halévy; Scribe)	
1839	*Le Lac des fées* (5, Auber; Scribe, Mélesville)	
1840	*La Favorite* (4, Donizetti; Royer, Scribe and Vaëz); birth of Zola	

	Events and operas in France	Events and operas outside France
1841	*La Reine de Chypre* (5, Halévy; St-Georges)	
1842	Death of Cherubini	*Ruslan and Lyudmila* (5, Glinka; Shirkov and others), St Petersburg; *Rienzi* (5, Wagner), Dresden
1843	*Dom Sébastien* (5, Donizetti; Scribe) *Charles VI* (5, Halévy; C. and G. Delavigne)	*Der fliegende Holländer* (3, Wagner), Dresden; *The Bohemian girl* (3, Balfe; Bunn), London
1844		*The Daughter of St Mark* (3, Balfe; Bunn), London
1845		*Leonora* (3, Fry; J. R. Fry), Philadelphia; *Tannhäuser* (3, Wagner), Dresden
1847	*Jérusalem* (4, Verdi; Royer and Vaez)	*Esmeral'da* (4, Dargomïzhsky; Hugo [trans. Dargomïzhsky and others], Moscow
1848	February Revolution: abdication of Louis-Philippe. Louis-Napoléon elected president of the Second Republic. Dramatic censorship lifted (until 1850)	Revolutions in Italy, Germany, Austrian Empire, Poland; Wagner supports insurrection in Dresden and subsequently lives in exile in Switzerland until 1860
1849	*Le Prophète* (5, Meyerbeer; Scribe)	
1850	*L'enfant prodigue* (5, Auber; Scribe) Death of Balzac	*Genoveva* (4, Schumann), Leipzig; *Lohengrin* (3, Wagner), Weimar
1851	*Sapho* (3, Gounod; Augier); Louis-Napoleon seizes power	Great Exhibition, London
1852	Second Empire proclaimed (2 Dec.), led by Napoleon III	
1852	*Le Juif errant* (5, Halévy; Scribe, St-Georges)	
1854	*La Nonne sanglante* (5, Gounod; Scribe and Delavigne)	Crimean War (to 1856); France acts as international power broker
1855	Exposition universelle *Les Vêpres siciliennes* (5, Verdi; Scribe and Duveyrier)	Accession of Tsar Alexander II
1857	Baudelaire, *Les Fleurs du mal*	
1858	*La Magicienne* (5, Halévy; St-Georges)	
1859	*Herculanum* (4, David; Méry and Hadot) *Faust* (5, Gounod; Barbier and Carré) (Théâtre Lyrique version). War in northern Italy.	*Catalina di Guisa* (3, Paniagua y Vasques; Romani), Mexico City Darwin, *On the Origin of Species*
1860		*Kroatka* (4, Dütsch; Kulikov), St Petersburg; *Lurline* (3, Wallace; Fitzball), London
1861	*Tannhäuser* (3, Wagner) (Opéra version); work begins on the new Paris Opéra designed by Garnier	Emancipation of Russian serfs Death of Cavour, architect of Italian unification; death of Scribe. Victor Emmanuel II proclaimed King of Italy
1862	*La Reine de Saba* (5, Gounod; Barbier and Carré); French intervention in Mexico (to 1866); Hugo, *Les Misérables*	Prague: Provisional Theatre opened
1863	*Les Troyens* Acts III–V (Berlioz) at Théâtre Lyrique	*Judith* (5, Serov; Serov and others), St Petersburg; second Polish revolt
1864	Death of Meyerbeer	
1865	*L'Africaine* (5, Meyerbeer; Scribe) (edited by Fétis)	*Tristan und Isolde* (3, Wagner), Munich; *The Templars in Moravia* (3, Šebor; Sabina), Prague; *Rogneda* (5, Serov; Serov and others), St Petersburg

	Events and operas in France	Events and operas outside France
1866		*The Brandenburgers in Bohemia* (3, Smetana; Sabina), Prague; war between Prussia and Austria
1867	*Don Carlos* (5, Verdi; Du Locle and Méry)	
1868		*Lejla* (4, later 5, Bendl; Krásnohorská), Prague; *Mefistofele* (5, Boito), Milan; *Dalibor* (3, Smetana; Wenzig), Prague; *The Hussite Bride* (5, Šebor; Ruffer), Prague
1869	*Faust* (5, Gounod: with added ballets: Opéra version); Verlaine, *Fêtes galantes*	*Das Rheingold* (1, Wagner), Munich
1870	Franco–Prussian war; French defeated at Sedan; collapse of Second Empire; founding of Third Republic	*Il Guarany* (4, Gomes; Scalvini, D'Ormeville), Milan; *Bretislav* (5, Bendl; Krásnohorská), Prague; *Die Walküre* (3, Wagner), Munich. Italian army occupies Rome, which is then incorporated within the Kingdom of Italy. Birth of Lenin
1871	Paris Commune (March–May)	Proclamation of German Empire (Reich); Bismarck governs German Empire to 1890. *Aida* (4, Verdi; Ghislanzoni), Cairo
1873		*The Maid of Pskov* (4 then 3, Rimsky-Korsakov), St Petersburg; *Fosca* (4, Gomes; Ghislanzoni), Milan
1874		*Boris Godunov* (4, Musorgsky), St Petersburg; *La Gioconda* (4, Ponchielli; Boito), Milan. Russian Populist students try to incite peasantry
1875	Inauguration of the new Paris Opéra designed by Garnier	*Demon* (3, Rubinstein; Viskovatov, Maykov), St Petersburg; *Makkavei* (*Die Maccabäer*) (3, Rubinstein; Mosenthal), Berlin [St Petersburg, 1877]; *Mefistofele* [revised] (4, Boito), Bologna
1876		*Der Ring des Nibelungen* (Wagner): as a cycle, Bayreuth; *Vanda* (5, Dvořák; Beneš-Šumavský and Zákrejs), Prague
1877	*Le Roi de Lahore* (5, Massenet; Gallet)	*Samson et Dalila* (3, Saint-Saëns; Lemaire), Weimar
1878	*Polyeucte* (5, Gounod; Barbier and Carré)	
1879	Anti-clericalism movement increases in France	*Maria Tudor* (4, Gomes; Praga, Boito, Zanardini), Milan; *Neron* (4, Rubinstein; Barbier), Hamburg
1880	*Aïda* (4, Verdi; French translation by Du Locle and Nuitter)	*Don Giovanni d'Austria* (4, Marchetti; D'Ormeville), Turin; *Il figliuol prodigo* (4, Ponchielli; Zanardini), Milan
1881	*Le Tribut de Zamora* (4, Gounod; d'Ennery and Brésil)	Tsar Alexander II assassinated. *The Veiled Prophet of Khorassan* (3, Stanford; Squire), Hanover [in German]; *Orleanska deva* (*The Maid of Orleans*) (4, Tchaikovsky), St Petersburg; *Libuše* (3, Smetana; Wenzig), Prague; *Blaník* (3, Fibich; Krásnohorská), Prague; *Hérodiade* (3, later 4, Massenet; Milliet, Hartmann and Zanardini), Brussels
1882	*Françoise de Rimini* (5, Thomas; Barbier and Carré)	*Dimitrij* (4, Dvořák; Červinková-Riegrová), Prague

	Events and operas in France	Events and operas outside France
1883	*Henry VIII* (4, Saint-Saëns; Détroyat and Silvestre)	*Dejanice* (4, Catalani; Zanardini), Milan. Prague: National Theatre rebuilt
1884	Huysmans, *A rebours*	*Sigurd* (4, Reyer; du Locle and Blau), Brussels; *Mazeppa* (3, Tchaikovsky; Burenin, rev. Tchaikovsky), Moscow; *The Bride of Messina* (3, Fibich; Hostinský), Prague
1885	*Le Cid* (4, Massenet; d'Ennery, Gallet and Blau)	*Marion Delorme* (5, Ponchielli; Golisciani), Milan German expansion in Africa begins
1886	*Patrie!* (5, Paladilhe; Gallet and Sardou)	*Khovanshchina* (5, Musorgsky, completed by Rimsky-Korsakov), St Petersburg *Gwendoline* (3, Chabrier; Mendès), Brussels
1889		*Lo schiavo* (4, Gomes; Paravicini), Rio de Janeiro
1890	*Ascanio* (5, Saint-Saëns; Gallet)	*Prince Igor* (4, Borodin), St Petersburg
1891		*Les Troyens* (5, Berlioz), Karlsruhe; *Ivanhoe* (3, Sullivan; Sturgis), London
1892		*Mlada* (4, Rimsky-Korsakov), St Petersburg; *Cristoforo Colombo* (5, Franchetti; Illica), Genoa; *Nydia* (5, Fox), London
1893	*Thaïs* (3, Massenet; Gallet)	*I Medici* (4, Leoncavallo), Milan
1894	*Frédégonde* (5, Saint-Saëns; Gallet)	
1896	Dreyfus case re-opened	*Hedy* (4, Fibich; Schulzová), Prague
1897		*Pampa* (3, Berutti; Borra), Buenos Aires. Czech language in Bohemia granted equality with German
1897/8		*Sadko* (3 or 5, Rimsky-Korsakov), Moscow
1898	Zola, 'J'accuse'	
1899	Dreyfus pardoned	*Yupanki* (3, Berutti; Rodriguez Larreta), Buenos Aires
1900		Russian Socialist Revolutionary Party founded. King Umberto of Italy assassinated
1901		*Os saldunes* (3, Miguéz; Neto), Rio de Janeiro
1902		*Servilia* (5, Rimsky-Korsakov), St Petersburg
1903		Russian Communist Party founded
1904		*Armida* (4, Dvořák; Vrchlický), Prague
1905	Separation of Church and State	
1907		*Legend of the Invisible City of Kitezh* (4, Rimsky-Korsakov), St Petersburg

1 Introduction

DAVID CHARLTON

There is no more astonishing evidence of the power of grand opera than *A Life for the Tsar*, first given at St Petersburg in 1836. Glinka's extraordinary genius was able to exploit most of the elements we still recognise in the genre: historical crisis, a personal tragedy, regional character (focused through musical local colour), active choruses, dance, and political imperatives refracted from the distant past towards the composer's present. Yet in 1836 grand opera was still a new phenomenon, originating in Paris. Glinka's opera clearly demonstrates that this genre rose to worldwide importance in the decade following Beethoven's death in 1827. Alongside contemporary advances in piano music – Chopin, Liszt, Schumann – grand opera was probably the most significant musical development of the 1830s and 1840s.

Because of its various musical challenges and Tsar-centred narrative, Glinka's opera was harder to export than those grand operas showing more nuanced leading figures, but the fact remains that this masterpiece dates from the same year as the more widely exported *Les Huguenots* by Meyerbeer. Had Carl Maria von Weber lived longer and written German equivalents to *A Life for the Tsar*, the 'map' in Table 1.1 would have required less emphasis than it presently does.[1] As this book shows, the genre of grand opera (taken as a nexus of properties: dramatic, formal, vocal) was sufficiently powerful to continue developing in time and space: through the 1840s and beyond, and across an increasing number of countries.

In Table 1.1, dividing opera history into fifty-year intervals, grand opera's dominance is seen as part of the increasing globalisation of opera: the multiplication of genres seems to reflect a shrinking world (one that has known industry, advertising, railways and mass media for 150 years now), as well as to express it psychologically.

Lyric theatre history can be defined by place and stage tradition, rather than by composer: by certain styles of acting and singing, and the delivery of the sung or spoken text. As the world industrialised, national types travelled faster, finding audiences further away. From Table 1.1 we can guess why Wagner was affected by grand opera (before and after 1850 – see Chapter 16) and how Gluck's reform operas played their role in the evolution of the same genre.

In this chapter, themes relevant to the present book are introduced through a discussion of particular topics, with special mention being made

Table 1.1 *A simple 'map' of the opera world*

Dates	Dominant types	Places of origin and export
1600–1650	Monteverdi etc.	Mantua, Venice, Rome
1650–1700	Cavalli to Scarlatti: evolution of opera seria and Lully's *tragédie en musique*	North and South Italy→ southern Europe and Paris
1700–1750	Opera seria; comic intermezzo	Italy→ rest of Europe/S. America
1750–1800	Reform (French-influenced) opera; opera buffa, dramma giocoso	Italy and France→ wider Europe and Americas
1800–1850	Dialogue opera (French and German); **grand opera**; 'Italian opera'	France, Germany, Italy→ world
1850–1900	Opéra-lyrique; Wagnerian types; 'Italian opera'; operetta	France, Germany, Italy→ world

(The table does not show the gradual emergence of given types during the years preceding their appearance in the middle column, or the corresponding decline of dominant types during succeeding decades.)

of recent research. Useful shorter orientations for grand opera have been written by Dennis Libby in *History of Opera* (New Grove Handbooks), by M. Elizabeth C. Bartlet in *New Grove/2* ('*Grand opéra*') and by Janet L. Johnson, whose 'The Musical Environment in France' is found in *The Cambridge Companion to Berlioz*. Single-composer issues in grand opera studies include new critical editions of the music of major composers (most recently Meyerbeer and Rossini); various composer monographs (e.g. Diana Hallman on Halévy); and in-progress documentary publications such as Robert Ignatius Letellier's English translation of Meyerbeer's diaries and journals, or Berlioz's music criticism (issued in French).[2] The expansion of knowledge about historical staging techniques is epitomised in an important chapter by Karin Pendle and Stephen Wilkins. This and other writings are individually listed in the select Bibliography at the end.

One special factor lies behind all work on grand opera: that of language. German has been the language of the majority of post-war articles and books. This was quantified when in 1987 Anselm Gerhard published a complete classified bibliography of grand opera research.[3] Of 276 items listed, *c.* 21 per cent were published in French, *c.* 28 per cent in English and *c.* 40 per cent in German. There is now an unavoidable and problematic time-lag in assimilation, since important and numerous writings by, for example, Heinz Becker, Sieghart Döhring, Herbert Schneider, Michael Walter and Matthias Brzoska have for the most part not been translated; Jürgen Schläder's 1995 history of the nineteenth-century duet is not even referred to under 'Duet' within *New Grove/2*.[4] Although we have translations of Carl Dahlhaus's comments on grand opera within both his *Nineteenth-Century Music* and *Realism in Nineteenth-Century Music*,[5] the major exception that proves the language rule is Mary Whittall's translation of Anselm Gerhard's *Die Verstädterung der Oper* (1992) as *The Urbanization of Opera* (1998), a study which is mentioned many times in the present Companion.

Genre

As Herbert Schneider emphasises in Chapter 10, the phrase *grand opéra* was never used systematically as a genre description by the French. But that does not signify that it had no meaning. Hervé Lacombe, for one, has clarified such meanings for French opera, teasing out the way that reference books approached terminology.[6] Generic descriptors are important because they traditionally help define audience expectation in terms of a work's ambitions, tone, relation to earlier works, relation to foreign traditions, balance or distribution between text and music, and possibly a connection with an institution. Of course this is not an exact science and it is essential (guided by Shakespeare) to be able to laugh at genres, especially when Polonius announces the players in *Hamlet*.[7] The writer Pierre Nougaret used 'grand opéra' in 1768 when referring to all-sung operas (which by legal imperative could be seen in Paris only at the Opéra), and also when referring to works characterised by 'marvels, variety, theatrical splendour', including ballets.[8] Fifty years later the musical dictionary *Encyclopédie méthodique* (1818) constructed the phrase along the same lines.[9] 'Grand opera' there is defined by the space itself (the Paris Opéra as theatre, providing luxury, patronage and a certain image) and, by extension, as comprising any work accepted for performance in that space by that company – whether historical, tragic or even comic – and sung throughout. In other words 'grand opera' was endowed with consistent meaning more by reason of the institution promoting it than by the dramatic content of the work.

After the defeat of Napoleon in 1815 the restored monarchy was keen to maintain subsidy for 'official' theatres (alongside a licensing system for new ones), so the Paris Opéra was maintained *de facto* as the place where the 'grandest' category of theatre could be seen.[10] The French continued to use *grand opéra* as a phrase to refer to any opera sung from end to end (as distinct from opéra comique) or, generically, evincing a certain elevation of tone.[11] In the following chapter Hervé Lacombe quotes in detail from the directorial schedule of the Paris Opéra, showing that *grand opéra* was enshrined legally as a term while remaining, necessarily, loosely defined. Continuity with past genres was seen in the schedule as important, i.e. the grandeur of *tragédie lyrique*. But a *grand opéra* could, technically, be written in one or two acts only, as well as in three, four or five acts. However, the die had been cast by Auber's *La Muette de Portici* (five acts) and Rossini's *Guillaume Tell* (four acts).

In any case, the Romantic age had no respect for genre as such. Gounod's *Faust* (1859) deserves mention for its immense popularity and yet ambiguity of genre. With five acts, a tragic heroine, a chorus and obviously elevated tone, this opera nevertheless began as part of a different line of French works, closely modelled on single works of literature. It was premiered at the Théâtre-Lyrique and contained some scenes in spoken dialogue. By 1869 it had moved into the camp of grand opera, both physically and generically: having lost its dialogues and gained recitatives, it was received into the bosom of the Paris Opéra where it now sprang a ballet (and some other music): its medieval setting and strongly etched choral writing happily echoed grand opera tradition, while its subject-matter resolutely remained faithful to Goethe's drama of individuals.

There is another facet: it is useful to recall the penchant of the nineteenth century for the word 'grand', whether as a sign of belief in progress and expansion, or of value as inhering in size: see p. 298. Berlioz published a *Grand traité d'instrumentation* and a *Grande messe des morts*, Francesco Berger a *Grande Fantaisie brillante sur l'Opéra Masaniello* and Chopin a *Grande polonaise* for piano and orchestra. Or perhaps we are simply dealing with a by-product of the advertising industry.

The evolution of grand opera in the 1820s

Opera historians have been uncovering the 1820s, a complex decade, and one already finely described by David Kimbell in respect of Italian opera.[12] 'The Age of French Romanticism' is still being defined in properly musical terms. Recent foundation opera studies include Janet Johnson's work on the Théâtre Italien, on Rossini and on Stendhal; Mark Everist's articles on the origins of Meyerbeer's *Robert le Diable* and the French version of Weber's *Euryanthe*; and dissertations by Maribeth Clark, Sarah Hibberd, Michael Mitchell, Cormac Newark and Ben Walton (see Bibliography on p. 470). All recent studies acknowledge (explicitly or otherwise) Karin Pendle's path-breaking publications on Scribe and French opera, and her work on the influence of popular theatres on grand opera,[13] as they also rely on Heinz and Gudrun Becker's work on Meyerbeer and Michael Walter's and Anselm Gerhard's work on the same composer and on Spontini.

In this volatile decade Louis XVIII died, Charles X was crowned (1825) and Victor Hugo, Eugène Delacroix, Hector Berlioz, Stendhal, Lamartine, Rossini, Saint-Simon, Benjamin Constant, Mme de Staël, Géricault, de Vigny and others were at some stage active in the capital. Charles Kemble's company brought Shakespeare in English to Paris in 1827. Giacomo Meyerbeer arrived in Paris in 1826: his diaries show that in January 1827 he met the writers Scribe, Castil-Blaze, Sauvage, the singer Giuditta Pasta and composers Cherubini and Boieldieu. Amid a mushrooming of newspapers and journals François-Joseph Fétis founded the *Revue musicale* in the same year and the work of the earlier German Romantic writers and philosophers first came to notice in their pages. There emerged 'by about 1827 or

1828 . . . a relatively coherent and self-conscious set of "Romantic doctrines". This was, in short, the period of what has long been termed *la bataille romantique*.'[14]

The evolution of grand opera at the same point in the 1820s contains a yet more international element, however: a freshness and breadth of outlook that Walter Scott startles us with when in Chapter 4 of his novel *Rob Roy* (1818) its protagonist announces:

> I was born a citizen of the world, and my inclination led me into all scenes where my knowledge of mankind could be enlarged.

Following his death in 1824 at Missolunghi, Greece, Lord Byron's substantial literary popularity had been boosted in Europe, amid fervent popular support for the Greek War of Independence by which Turkish rule was ended in 1827. As Mark Everist well puts it, 'The Greek War of Independence was as much a part of cultural life in European intellectual circles in the 1820s as the Spanish Civil War in the 1930s or the war in Vietnam in the 1960s and 70s.'[15] Not by chance was Christian–Muslim conflict depicted in two pre-grand operas of these years: Meyerbeer's *Il crociato in Egitto*, dating from 1824 and mounted in Paris the following year; and Rossini's *Le Siège de Corinthe* (1826) at the Paris Opéra. We must try and account for the important effect of these Italian works.

Their most important ancestor was an opera written by Gaspare Spontini (1774–1851), one of many Italian-born composers forming part of French tradition: a historical opera on the conquest of Mexico entitled *Fernand Cortez* (1809). It is, coincidentally, one of the few French operas of the period to have been recorded since the advent of compact discs (Accord 206612, conducted by Jean-Paul Penin), and it is fortunate that this recording consists of the opera's extensively revised version of 1817. This version continued to hold the stage, and was practically the only all-sung French opera originating from 1810–20 to be a lasting success: it gained 248 performances which stretched into the 1839–40 season.[16] Much later, in the nationalistic 1870s, when the new home of grand opera, the Palais Garnier opera house, was nearly finished, *Fernand Cortez* was memorialised by that institution's librarian and historian, Théodore de Lajarte. He referred to *Cortez* as 'the germ of grand opera' by reason of its 'elevated dramatic feeling', with 'startling oppositions of strength and tenderness', not to mention its spectacular elements.[17] Further, it painted the exotic Mexicans in strong visual and musical colouring and it opposed two cultures and two religions (Aztec/Christian) with a cross-cultural love-match at the centre (Cortez the conqueror loves and is loved by Amazily), while also remaining faithful to the outlines of history.

If all this anticipates grand opera, so does the ethos of historically accurate staging, which Lajarte's evidence proves as having been in place: the following letter of 17 May 1809 contains a report from the *Cortez* scene-painting workshop:

> Four painters were brought in from the start of May and have been tracing and applying ink to the stencils. One of them is employed to conduct research in the Imperial libraries to become familiar with the type of monuments in Mexico in the days of Cortez, especially for the type of ships and the design of weapons at that time. He has discovered Charles V's portrait and hopes to locate that of Cortez. M. Ciceri, landscape painter, retained by the Opéra, is commissioned to go to the Botanical Garden *every day*, to sketch trees and plants of Mexican origin . . .[18]

Even this was not the first documentation of French costume research in action, for eleven years before, the press reported of Dalayrac's *Primerose* that 'the costumes are of 13th-century style; sumptuous and numerous, they were copied from the Bibliothèque nationale with exactitude'.[19]

In 1809 the appearance of Ciceri's name was significant: his career came to dominate scene-painting in the 1820s and early 1830s (see below). Lajarte's evidence for *Cortez* also shows that fourteen horses and riders were contracted to appear in the opera (costing 6,000 francs for each of the first six nights).

Much more deserves our notice in *Fernand Cortez* and there is a great deal to enjoy in Dennis Libby's dissertation 'Gaspare Spontini and his French and German Operas' (Princeton University, 1969): no other full-length study is available. Libby showed how frequently Spontini's solos and duets are cast in slow–fast forms inherited from the old century but especially associated in the new one with Italian opera and grand opera (see Chapter 10 below). He also notices that in 1817 Spontini tended to prune shorter arias and duets so that 'The omission of these [1809] pieces from the 1817 version shifts the emphasis, already strong in the original, still more toward the side of the chorus and ensemble and away from solos, particularly in Acts I and II' (*ibid.*, 163). Such tendencies were noticed later in grand opera's first phase in a telling comment by Hector Berlioz:

> Today, everything tends towards massed musical forces. See at the Conservatoire concerts how unfavourably vocal or instrumental solos are greeted . . . At the Opéra, even in new works, solos get fewer every day: I know plenty of people who cannot tolerate arias in whatever shape or form.[20]

In the year 1824, Rossini settled in Paris and became musical director at the Théâtre Italien. But the following extract from a forgotten 1824 pre-grand opera by Rodolphe Kreutzer (*Ipsiboé*) reveals that the ground had been tilled already: a positive desire both for dramatic novelty and the assimilation of Italian (Rossinian) musical particulars is most notable:

> For a long time now, most literary journals accuse *tragédie lyrique* of being out of step with current taste and musical progress in France . . . In fact [operatic] tragedy cannot offer the things demanded by music: sudden transitions, abrupt and frequent oppositions. Italian scores have greatly influenced us; we are no longer happy with well-declaimed phrases and a few expressive arias – we want *morceaux d'ensemble*, *finales* and so on.[21]

Music, it seems, was seeking a new voice to match advances in literature or painting. But to be successful, everything in an opera must work together, and *Ipsiboé* proved unequal. A much more prominent step was taken in *Il crociato in Egitto* (compact disc: Opera Rara ORC 10, conducted by David Parry). Derived from a French *mélodrame* (only recently identified: see note 15) this opera gave new life to Italian forms and to choral and orchestral writing, as well as foregrounding religious division and historical sources and colour. Sieghart Döhring has written memorably of its importance for the 1820s:

> If Meyerbeer went [from his native Germany] to Italy to learn, it was during that time that he became a teacher. *Crociato*, whose profound traces have long lain unnoticed in the Italian opera between Bellini and Verdi, shows that Meyerbeer finally found, in the idiom of an alien genre, his own musical language and personal style. With the world-wide success of this single opera, he rose to become the leading composer of Italian opera after Rossini.[22]

Indeed the general proximity of opera to *mélodrame* must never be forgotten, for Romantic theatre owed it a comprehensive debt which is often obscured by our unfamiliarity with the French originals, though was famously exposed in Peter Brooks's study *The Melodramatic Imagination*.[23] Sarah Hibberd explores more of these connections in Chapter 9 below, especially visual ones: for grand opera's desire for visual authenticity essentially rested on the way popular Revolution theatre expanded its visual resources. Consider this report from February 1799 which interpreted that cult in terms of excess:

> 'On "Scenic" Plays [*pièces à décorations*]': Our theatres seem to compete in spending the most money on sets and costumes: if it continues, this abuse will hasten the decline of dramatic art still further . . . Heaven, hell, settings apt for all genres, costumes apt for all climates, blazing buildings, shipwrecks, people snatched into the air, tournaments, hand-to-hand combat, mounted combat, etc.: we have seen everything.[24]

However, *mélodrame* at this time was a fiercely moralistic as well as stagey genre, and it remains to be seen whether grand opera's new use of the tragic ending also derives from it. Tragic endings in opera were not unknown (Cherubini's 1797 *Médée* is a rare and monumental example) but when in 1826 Rossini's *Le Siège de Corinthe* used one, it transformed the effect of the cross-cultural conflict in opera. Rossini's work centres on the Turkish-Muslim defeat of one of the last strongholds of the Christian Eastern Empire of Byzantium in 1458, by Sultan Mehmed II.[25] There was obvious political urgency to this theme at a moment when for the first time since 1461 the definitive Greek struggle for independence was in progress: the tragic ending amounted to an aesthetic statement as shocking as Delacroix's analogous canvases *Scenes from the Massacres at Chios* (1824) or *Greece Expiring on the Ruins of Missolunghi* (1826). Betrayed by the fact that she has been wooed by Mahomet (= Mehmed) himself in disguise, the Greek heroine Pamira kills herself as the work ends and Corinth goes up in flames: she will not survive the defeat of her people. This important opera (seen 103 times up to 1844), Rossini's first to be staged at the Paris Opéra, was followed by *Moïse et Pharaon*, *Le Comte Ory* (a fine comedy) and *Guillaume Tell* (described in Chapter 14).

In another respect, too, *Le Siège* is a turning-point, for Rossini had been brought to the capital specifically to reform French singing not just with younger artists but by more generally imposing Italian principles of voice-production. This revolution had itself been prepared for at the Théâtre Italien, Paris's most fashionable venue, under Rossini as musical director. But the Opéra actually shared its management with the Théâtre Italien from 1818 until 1827 and so links were particularly close for much of the 1820s, as Janet Johnson has pointed out: 'The two theatres were to be deeply and mutually conditioned by an alliance that for nearly ten years provided a unique institutional arena for the interaction of French and Italian operatic traditions'.[26] And she cites Edouard Robert, the Italien's joint director from 1830 to 1838, drawing up in 1832 a balance-sheet which is essential for understanding the origins of grand opera:

> From the artistic point of view the Théâtre Italien works powerfully towards musical progress in France. It cannot be denied that it has served as a model for French composers, by reason of the character of its melodies, its ensembles, its finales and musical development in general which, previously, was found to such a notable degree only in the Italian school . . .
>
> Had Paris not had its Théâtre Italien, Rossini, Meyerbeer and others would probably never have composed for the Opéra. And has not the singing of [Manuel] Garcia, [Gaetano] Crivelli, [Nicola] Tacchinardi and [Giovanni] Rubini, [Luigi] Lablache, [Caterina] Barilli, [Henriette]

Sontag, [Giuditta] Pasta, [Maria] Malibran and [Giuditta or Giulia] Grisi, had a powerful influence on the success of our French artists? Mme [Laure Cinti-] Damoreau, M. [Nicolas] Levasseur, Mme [Gosselin-] Mori, have sung at this theatre. [Adolphe] Nourrit can be regarded as a pupil of the Italian school, since he was finally taught by Garcia. Most of the Opéra's orchestral musicians have worked at the Théâtre Italien, which has constantly acted as a nursery for the former institution.[27]

We saw earlier how the tragic arrangement of personal relationships in *Le Siège de Corinthe* exists within a plot which has notable similarities with Spontini's *Fernand Cortez* (which Rossini admired and conducted in Naples): invasion and defeat of a less powerful culture by a more powerful one, and a cross-cultural love theme. But by analysing the individual dynamics, an essential difference between the two operas is shown up. Scott L. Balthazar's method, expressed in the concept of 'love-triangles', has been derived from a range of theatre research.[28] Indeed this helps all the better to explain why Pamira's tragic end acted as a catalyst in grand opera's development, and fructified nineteenth-century opera in general:

Type 1: 'false triangles': the lovers feel helplessness, confusion and misery; this is the earlier, eighteenth-century pattern of Metastasio and *opera seria*. No infidelity occurs, for the lovers 'realise that their problems originate elsewhere', for example through social rank. Because in Spontini's opera Cortez and Amazily's mutual love is threatened by her physical safety alone (in the first version, especially) or only indirectly through the Aztecs' possible reprisals, it conforms on the personal level to an older-fashioned pattern.

Type 2: 'misconstrued triangles': again, no infidelity occurs, this time because 'the subject of the rivalry is blameless, having ended previous affairs, or been forced into an unwanted betrothal', but at the same time 'exonerating information is absent or ignored and infidelity is presumed'; 'a misconstrued love-triangle multiplies and intensifies conflicts . . . increasing the justification for a tragic ending' but also allowing reconciliation. This is the pattern of *Il crociato in Egitto* where two triangles operate: both can be resolved because the central lovers are secretly married (the Egyptian Palmide and the Christian knight Armando).[29] Plots in this category, showing even aggression and physical pain, had been used in French dialogue opera for a long time,[30] so it was hardly surprising that Paris criticism dismissed the plot of *Il crociato* as 'uncommonly absurd' and unworthy of current taste.

Type 3: the 'true triangle': in which, by an unwanted tie of alternative marriage or some other loyalty, the main lovers are 'irrevocably estranged' making reconciliation or happiness 'impossible'. Think of *Romeo and*

Juliet, so admired in 1827 Paris, as well as *Le Siège de Corinthe* or, later, Verdi's *Don Carlos*. Grand opera prefers this level of personal conflict, sometimes writ large against opposing social or religious movements. One would have to say that Meyerbeer's 1831 *Robert le Diable* resembles Type 2, but it is focused exceptionally upon familial rather than sentimental ties of loyalty, and evokes Faustian struggle rather than History.

History, politics

Conceived and born in a liberal era, grand opera's messages of religious, social and erotic freedom were often too strong for censors outside France: Nicholas White and Simon Williams effectively provide us with responses in this book to Carl Dahlhaus's observation, 'grand opera was always political'.[31] On the other hand, different generations naturally differ in their approach to hermeneutics. Matthias Brzoska in Chapter 11 presents recent thinking on Meyerbeer's engagement with theories of human progress as such. Sarah Hibberd's reading of Auber's *La Muette de Portici* (1828) recounts in Chapter 9 the meticulous way that Scribe's libretto evolved so as to inscribe politics at every structural level of the drama. Research by Herbert Schneider here and in Chapter 10 on *La Muette* illuminates a work universally known and famously admired by Wagner, yet which does not find mention in Dahlhaus's *Nineteenth-Century Music*, first issued in 1980. Evidence of wide familiarity with Auber's opera is found in various chapters following, including 18 and 20, and this evidence points to an essential vitality born out of a spirit of liberalisation in France. Although the July Revolution was still some time away,

> Towards the end of Charles X's reign, particularly under the liberal ministry of Martignac, a greater laxity crept into the functioning of the censorship. Plays and operas centring on popular heroes and national uprisings, such as Delavigne's *Marino Faliero* (1829), which so impressed Stendhal's Julien Sorel, and Auber's *La Muette de Portici* . . . were allowed with some misgivings and shown with great success . . . There remained only two subjects still considered strictly taboo: plays evoking the memory of the Napoleonic era, and plays portraying a former monarch.[32]

This and other grand operas can be seen as part of an active theatrical critique of society, the best of whose products went on to provide inspiration up to the end of the century. Music history in the years following 1980 was to look more carefully at grand opera structure, its social context and reception history. Maybe there was no direct connection, but Patrice Chéreau's influential staging of Wagner's *Ring* cycle in 1976 at Bayreuth was predicated on the belief 'that [its] mythological setting . . . heightens rather than diminishes the social and historical dimensions of the work', causing Chéreau to depict elements of the industrial revolution, such as the Rhine as a hydroelectric dam, and emphasising 'the extent to which the work was conceived as a political allegory', as Barry Millington puts it ('Chéreau' in *New Grove*/2). In 1980, as in 1830, the thinking public's image of itself naturally found current concerns expressible through the metaphorical languages of art, served by the use of historical fiction. An important difference is that in the 1830s these enriched languages were adopted in earnest not simply by makers of opera but by professional historians themselves in order to represent the past as newly inclusive and newly realistic. 'It could be said that the idea of the people [bound] together the virtues of the erudite historian and the visions of the prophet, the novelist and the rhetorical militarist'.[33] Not just 'the people' but also their struggle for self-determination occupied many minds. No better place to understand this exists than the historical novels of Walter Scott, whose totally new style and approach captivated all readers from about 1817. His novels have numerous connections with opera, something to which Stendhal presciently drew attention in *The Life of Rossini* (1824) with his memorable and extended comparison between Rossini's orchestral writing and Scott's descriptive techniques.[34] The musicologist Ludwig Finscher, writing in the 1980s, re-explored similar links.[35] The way that Scott foregrounded social groups is easily seen in *Rob Roy* (1818), for example, where he makes the oppositional consciousness basic to the mind of the narrator (and thereby the reader). Indeed it is Francis Osbaldistone's Northumbrian nurse who imbues this model within Francis's receptive young ears:

> Now, in the legends of Mabel, the Scottish nation was ever freshly remembered with all the embittered declamation of which [she] was capable . . . And how could it be otherwise? Was it not the Black Douglas who slew with his own hand the heir of the Osbaldistone family the day after he took possession of his estate . . .? All our family renown was acquired, – all our family misfortunes were occasioned, – by the Northern wars. Warmed by such tales, I looked upon the Scottish people during my childhood as a race hostile by nature to the more southern inhabitants of the realm . . .[36]

and to this distinction will be added the Protestant–Catholic divide, constantly present in various ways, and made more vivid at one point by Scott's historical detailing of ancient anti-Catholic laws, albeit amusingly placed in the mouth of a pettifogging official who is addressing the novel's striking young Catholic heroine, Die Vernon:

– good evening ma'am; I have no more to say, – only there are laws against
papists . . . There's third and fourth Edward VI, of antiphoners, missals,
grailes, processionals, manuals, legends, pies, portuasses, and those that
have such trinkets in their possession, Miss Vernon; and there's
summoning of papists to take the oaths . . .[37]

This detailing and archaic language exactly correspond to a pervasive search
for historical immediacy in other fictional spheres at the time, for example
easel-painting or indeed grand opera, both of which employed the idea of
'local colour' for this purpose; such a technique is obvious here in Scott both
in the weird vocabulary and in the speaker's grotesque character. Sectarian
religious and social conflict was never far from the grand opera agenda, as
Chapter 5 amply explains.

In the post-Chéreau search for the 'mentalities' and force-fields surrounding grand opera Jane Fulcher published *The Nation's Image* in 1987
and Anselm Gerhard completed in 1985 the thesis that would eventually
become *The Urbanization of Opera*.[38] Fulcher sought to uncover 'the emergence of the [Paris] Opéra as a politically contestatory realm', analysing
the power and control over art in the institution itself and the ways that
the public's reaction fed from both the operas and the political forces in
play at the time. Her book brings together work on theatre economics, the
production details and various documents of reception as revealed in the
press reviews, squarely facing the reality that opera texts do not reside solely
in the libretto, score, production-book or visual effects, but in the theatre,
before an audience. In Fulcher's translated extracts from reviews we can
read the engagement between French politics and grand operas set in the
past, the operas being seen as mediated, performative historical texts in
themselves.

Disagreements with Fulcher's book arose not least from her view that
the Opéra after 1852 'was a tightly, indeed a rigorously controlled institution, run more or less directly by officials or bureaucrats of the French
state . . . [T]he aim of this control was to ensure a certain kind of theatre.'[39]
Hervé Lacombe, in Chapter 2 below, asserts the distance between artists
and officials, denying that the former were 'the spokesmen of the State',
employed to create propaganda.

Gerhard's *The Urbanization of Opera* was yet more culturally centred
than Fulcher's study, but far more concerned with social and existential
questions than party allegiances; we might even claim him as a precursor
of musicologists now linking arms with 'urban historians' who publish in
the journal *Urban History* or books like *The Cambridge Urban History of
Britain*.[40] His was, however, so comprehensive a project that it is not possible to encapsulate it except in remembering its scope: an avowed attempt

to produce a totally new and valid perspective of grand opera. Gerhard's technique is to weave together a series of enquiries into opera's perceptual and material nature. Grand opera, he says, already betrays a modern sensibility – its dramaturgy anticipates the cinema, its great contrasts correspond to life-impressions in the modern city; its ambiguities result from cultural tensions with which we can identify today. Encompassing even terroristic violence, the opera crowd or chorus can sometimes allegorise the public assemblies that condition political change. For example in an 1844 journal article Gerhard finds proof that Meyerbeer's *Les Huguenots* 'reflected nineteenth-century fears' at a moment when street crime was rife: it contains the sentence, 'Every intimate evening party ends [nowadays], as the fourth act of *Les Huguenots* begins, with the blessing of weapons' (*Urbanization*, 231).

But historical opera in France related to public understanding of history at a deeper level too, by containing the illusion of cause and effect. Gerhard's enquiry into such operatic texts typically looks outside conventional operatic sources in order to gain a stronger foothold and alights upon a mid-eighteenth-century best-seller by A. R. Richer which 'showed' how great human events arose from 'little details multiplied'.[41] One can actually see this thesis displayed in a pre-grand opera in 1783 which set out to dramatise, using history, how crucial events are brought about by the actions of common people and not the traditional rulers usually depicted. This was *Péronne sauvée*, seen briefly at the Paris Opéra and set by the composer Dezède. The librettist, Billardon de Sauvigny, took as subject the known figure of Marie Fouré, a baker's wife, who at a critical moment in history (in 1536) acted with quick-witted courage to save her town from the English invader.[42] Sauvigny's preface explains his purpose: to show that 'the greatest events have always been the effect of little causes multiplied'.

Once it was accepted that such elaborations of narrative complexity were possible in opera, the way lay open for the Romantics to emulate the colour and sweep of Scott's novels, for example, or to re-create his effects of insecurity, of not being in control, of being part of a larger picture (social and geographical): again *Rob Roy* provides a convenient example. In Chapter 16 Francis Osbaldistone is suddenly informed by Die Vernon of highly disturbing news:

> 'Have you heard from your father lately?' 'Not a word,' I replied . . . 'That is strange . . . Then you are not aware that he has gone to Holland to arrange some pressing affairs which required his own immediate presence?' 'I never heard a word of it until this moment.'

Here, as in contemporary opera, the audience may 'know' more than the characters do, just as in reading a history book we sympathise with past dilemmas but also enjoy all the benefits of knowledge gained in hindsight. The protagonist of grand opera may well be tricked, but the reasons must fit into the broader scheme. In 1823 the great Italian writer Alessandro Manzoni published an essay about the need for drama to forget classical convention and become 'the work of the historian'. Historians, he says, like any dramatist or novelist, should allow audiences 'to understand, between the events shown, the connections of cause and effect, of anteriority and consequence'. Both types of writer 'must, so to speak, sort out the events in order to attain a unity of perspective'.[43]

However, it is one thing to identify such techniques but another to interpret their reception in practice: thus the debate raised by Jane Fulcher's book has continued, and reviews of Gerhard's book produced analogous questions.[44] In a recent short study Mary Ann Smart concludes that no straightforward correspondences may be drawn between 'history lessons' in grand opera, and the public's reactions: the effects of stage presentation, and indeed of sheer chance occurrence, were yet more decisive.[45]

Recent research

The location of grand opera within cultural perspectives is proceeding in diverse ways: at one extreme, work on race and gender, at the other, work on statistics and institutions. A simple example of the rewards of further investigation is that of role-types. Recently a start has been made on thinking about the cross-dressed phenomenon of the 'page', whose presence in grand opera was preceded by cross-dressed pages in other stage genres, when set in the Middle Ages. In 1790s opéra comique Mlle Carline had acted a prominent page-role in *Primerose* (mentioned earlier); in the ballet-pantomime *Alfred le Grand* (1822: see Fig. 10) Mlle Bigottini at the Opéra was cast as Olivier, 'young page' to the English king. Heather Hadlock duly notes that Meyerbeer's *Les Huguenots* Act II contains a doubly voyeuristic example of this female-as-young-male convention, where Urbain's function is 'to conduct the adult man [Raoul de Nangis, but obviously the audience too] into a forbidden female realm'.[46] Admittedly there were purely vocal reasons for including the type, for which the excellent level of detail in Jean-Louis Tamvaco's new study concerning performers (see note 57 below) provides some insight. (Page-roles in 1836–38 were particularly taken by Louise Flécheux and Dolorès Nau, who were rivals; less expectedly, Rosine Stoltz took the page-role of Ascanio in Berlioz's *Benvenuto Cellini*.) Nevertheless an 1851 caricature in *L'Illustration* (see Fig. 1) sharply reduces the convention to upper-class ogling, as purporting nothing more than a kind of demeaning entertainment act.

Beau page! mon beau page!
quell' culott' vous portez!

Figure 1 'Handsome page! my handsome page! what a shapely costume!': one of a set of operatic caricatures drawn by Marcelin, featured in the weekly news-magazine, *L'Illustration*, on 22 November 1851.

Great nineteenth-century singers have continued to generate some re-evaluation of the hoary myths and hazy photographs by which we remember legendary names. Foundation studies in the 1980s investigated the interpretations of the singers themselves.[47] Mary Ann Smart's scrutiny of Rosine Stoltz formed a noted contribution to the debate on 'voice' in past operas.[48] Alan Armstrong looked at two tenors in their effect on evolving grand opera[49] while Meyerbeer's *L'Africaine* inspired two very different investigations of its exotic, mythical and formal aspects.[50] Race, religion and orientalism were addressed by James Parakilas in 1993[51] and Mark Everist in 1996, issues that also informed Cormac Newark's scrutiny of Halévy's *La Juive*.[52] Sarah Hibberd has related grand opera to phenomena such as the notion of Scotland, the supernatural, staged mime and the burgeoning Faust legend.[53]

As opera redefines its role in the electronic age, so the institutional details of earlier operatic culture may be moving again towards the centre of

DE PARIS. 343

BRANDUS ET Cie, 87, rue Richelieu. — ÉDITEURS, — **TROUPENAS ET Cie,** 40, rue Vivienne.

LE PROPHÈTE,

Opéra en 5 actes. — Paroles de M. SCRIBE. — Musique de

Giacomo Meyerbeer.

La Partition pour Piano et Chant, édition de luxe, ornée du portrait de Meyerbeer, net : **40 fr.**
La Partition arrangée pour **Piano** seul, format in-8°, net : **10 fr.** | **La Partition** arrangée pour **Piano à 4 mains**, net : **25 fr.**

TOUS LES MORCEAUX DE CHANT DÉTACHÉS

Arrangés avec Accompagnement de Piano par GARAUDÉ,
ET AVEC GUITARE PAR CARCASSI.

MORCEAUX POUR LE PIANO SUR LE PROPHÈTE.

BENEDICT. Fantaisie brillante	4	» net.
BURGMULLER. Grande valse brillante	3	» net.
DREYSCHOCK et PANOFKA. Duo pour piano et violon	4	» net.
DUVERNOY. Op. 182, fantaisie (moyenne force)	2	50 net.
Stephen HELLER. Op. 70, caprice brillant	3	» net.
Jacques HERZ. Arrangements des quatre airs de ballet et de la Marche du sacre, cinq suites, chaque	3	» net.
Id. LES MÊMES, arrangées pour piano à quatre mains, par *Ed. Wolff*, cinq suites, chaque	4	» net.
KRUGER. Op. 19, fantaisie brillante sur la Pastorale et la Marche du sacre	3	» net.
LECARPENTIER. Deux bagatelles (109e et 110e), chaque	2	» net.
Id. Op. 141, fantaisie à quatre mains	3	» net.
N. LOUIS. Op. 184, fantaisie dram. p piano et violon.	4	» net.
OSBORNE. Op. 78, fantaisie brillante	3	» net.
ROSELLEN. Op. 114, grande fantaisie brillante	4	» net.
Id. LA MÊME, à quatre mains	4	» net.
A. TALEXY. Op. 20, fantaisie brillante	3	» net.
Charles VOSS. Op. 101, grande fantaisie dramatique	4	» net.
Ed. WOLFF. Op. 158, grand duo a quatre mains	4	» net.
WOLFF et BÉRIOT. Duo brillant pour piano et violon	4	» net.

2 quadrilles par MUSARD, pour piano, à 4 mains et orchestre.
1 quadrille par LECARPENTIER, id.
1 quadrille par STRAUSS, id
Valses par ETTLING, pour piano, à 4 mains et orchestre.
Polka par PASDELOUP, id.
Redowa par PILODO, id.

LEE. Op. 53. Fantaisie dramatique pour violoncelle avec accompagnement de piano	4	» net
WALCKIERS. Op. 87. Quatre fantaisies pour flûte, seule	3	» net.
WALCKIERS. Op. 88. Fantaisies pour flûte avec accompagnement de piano	4	» net.
MOHR. Trois pas redoublés et une marche pour musique militaire, chaque	2	50 net.

LES AIRS ARRANGÉS

POUR MUSIQUE MILITAIRE, en 2 suites, par MOHR. | POUR 2 VIOLONS ET VIOLON SEUL, par N. LOUIS. | POUR 2 FLUTES ET FLUTE SEULE, par WALCKIERS. | POUR 2 CORNETS ET CORNET à pistons seul, par GUICHARD.

POUR PARAITRE INCESSAMMENT, DES MORCEAUX SUR LE PROPHÈTE,
par Ad. Adam, Beyer, Cramer, Ernst, Hunten, Liszt, Prudent et Schubert.

La grande partition et les parties d'orchestre du PROPHÈTE sont à la disposition des théâtres de France, et seront expédiées dans l'ordre des demandes.

Figure 2 Press advertisement in *Revue et Gazette musicale de Paris* for numerous derivatives of a grand opera, offering a large variety of instrumental combinations, down to two cornets, and arranged in a variety of musical forms: fantasias, marches, waltzes, suites, more straightforward arrangements. See Chapter 16, p. 325 and 327, n. 15, for information about Richard Wagner's short-lived role in preparing this type of publication.

interest: cultural imperatives are, after all, not so hard to relate to power-centres, patronage and financial exigency. John Drysdale's new thesis is a fiscal and legal re-evaluation of the Paris Opéra during the later Restoration and under Dr Véron: while not the first archival analysis of the economics of grand opera (the work of Dominique Leroy and Yves Ozanam[54]) Drysdale's work points a bright and revealing searchlight at the murky foundations of an obstinate institution unwilling to cope with reform, let alone

Table 1.2 *Separate editions of music and text deriving from Auber's* La Muette de Portici.

Full score editions, deriving from a single set of plates: 2

Type	France	Austria/Germany	UK/USA	Italy	Other
Piano scores (with or without vocal parts)	8	40	12	8	2
Librettos	36	76	28	24	23 (in 8 languages)
Collected excerpts	5 (1 Belgian)	5	3	1	1
Arrangements of the overture	11	65	50	4	8

Printed vocal arrangements with newly translated or composed texts (all countries): *c*. 215
Printed instrumental arrangements including fantasias, pots-pourri, dances, counting all combinations of players: *c*. 532.

revolution.[55] Through its analysis of Véron's methods, it suggests (paradoxically) how he did more to swell audiences and his own income than than he did to forward grand opera as a genre. He implemented ideas already tried unsuccessfully or merely suggested, and he was obliged to obey the spirit, if not always the letter, of his State-ordained schedule (or *cahier des charges*: see the next chapter). Equally revealing is Drysdale's meticulous unpeeling of Ciceri's *de facto* monopoly as chief scene-painter in the 1820s, and the relatively peripheral role of the new staging-committee set up in 1827. All this inevitably makes Véron's predecessor, Emile Lubbert, a more fascinating creature.

Because audience access remained on a privileged social level, grand opera was diffused to others by various manifestations of the mass market, plus excerpts given in concerts or salons: sheet-music or piano-vocal scores for the home, band-arrangements for the street, virtuoso arrangements for piano celebrities, simpler ones (or 'reminiscences') for the modest amateur (Fig. 2). In Herbert Schneider's extraordinary 1994 catalogue of the works of Daniel Auber,[56] we now have the *prima facie* evidence to plan very different future histories of grand opera, centring on these arrangements: their availability, price, poetic or functional nature, parodic content and ability to suggest an interpretation of the operas. To list the sheer numbers of surviving editions, especially those deriving from representative popular operas, is truly sobering: see Table 1.2.

The sheer impact of Auber's music, therefore, resonated far and wide beyond the many theatres where his operas were acted and sung, attaining perhaps the status of popular music in our sense of a universally known musical object specifically distributed and promoted by commercial interests.

At the very source of this network the Paris Opéra was and remains a place of cultural fascination, a 'machine' or 'great empire' to use some early metaphors. Most notable among recent publications is an edition of a manuscript journal kept in secret by an administrator at the Opéra between 1836 and 1838, with some subsequent entries: *Les Cancans de l'Opéra: Chroniques de l'Académie Royale de Musique*.[57] For those who read French, a substantial resource has been released, a kind of spy-hole optic on the day-to-day moralities and scandals of the 'machine' but also a wealth of assorted information on musicians, finances, preparatory stages of new operas, with set-piece descriptions of life in the theatre: its studios, technical resources, rehearsals, music copying, chorus, cashiers and those – like the Halévys, and the journal's author, Louis Gentil – who actually resided within the building. The high quality and rarity of the illustrations in this publication deserve special notice, as does the level of biographical annotation.

Grand opera re-created

We have defined grand opera as a set of French works, a collection of adaptations of them, and as a repertory produced in response to them in various countries. The scope of this Companion permits essays on some but not all these countries. Those not covered include Germany (see note 1); New Zealand, for which Adrienne Simpson has published an account;[58] and Greece, for which research is starting to amass details of operatic performances and composers unmentioned in *Grove Opera*, like Iossif Liberalis (1820–99), Nikolaos Metaxas (1825–1907) and Pavlos Karrer (1829–96).[59] Just as the identity of grand opera in France was subtly modified in the second half of the century, including by what Steven Huebner calls 'heightened sensitivities to nationalism' (Chapter 15), so the importance of the genre to other countries will have been tied up with their own political aspirations. In France, says Huebner, 'the defenders of grand opera celebrated its national characteristics'. But the way in which each country understood its own situation *vis-à-vis* grand opera themes remains to be fully explored. In the Czech lands (see Chapter 18) the opera competition sponsored by Count Jan Harrach in 1861 made sure that entries 'should be based on the history of the lands of the Czech crown'. In Russia (see Chapter 17) 'French grand opera always enjoyed the special attentions of the censor', and even the title of *La Muette de Portici* was disguised in order, it was hoped, to quell any possibility of social unrest being inspired. Since grand opera frequently depicted localised groups of people in choruses, musicological tales presumably remain to be told about the way that various adapters constructed their notions of the exotic Other, faced with such pressures. All this simply bears upon the point made at the start of this Introduction: that opera from less familiar traditions must be taken into account in order to arrive at a more appropriate view of the music history of which it forms a part.

PART ONE

The resourcing of grand opera

2 The 'machine' and the state

HERVÉ LACOMBE

'A machine so complicated as the [Paris] Opéra is like a maze: only people with long and profound acquaintance with the house can find their way through it.' So wrote J.-T. Merle in *De l'Opéra* in 1827. The truth is that no artistic enterprise before the creation of cinema could match grand opera in complexity; no mode of artistic production was comparable with what this theatre offered in uniting all the material and human factors that make up an operatic production, and to create the conditions necessary for its performance. It is no denial of the importance of creativity to assert that grand opera was the product of technology, albeit in a very wide sense of the term.

Grand opera[1] developed and became a significant factor in European culture thanks to the power of this technology. For a more comprehensive understanding of this particular variety of opera, it is therefore necessary to describe the 'machine' in all its economic and political ramifications (that is to say, its ramifications in Parisian life and its relations with the French state) and also its cultural and moral ramifications (especially with censorship). In the nineteenth century, opera became the vehicle for both aesthetic and moral values indissolubly linked with the environment from which they sprang. Grand opera was born and grew up within a particular historical, institutional and legislative situation. While concentrating on the period of the blossoming of the genre, which corresponds with the reign of Louis-Philippe (between the Revolutions of 1830 and 1848), our analysis of the conditions of its production and creation will endeavour to bring out relationships with earlier and later periods. The same 'machine' allowed grand opera to endure throughout the nineteenth century; some works simply took their place within the traditions of the genre (despite adaptations to new tastes, which will be discussed later, in Chapter 15), but the repertory was shaped by certain key works, shown in Table 2.1, and their creators.

Institutional mechanisms

The Paris Opéra was an institution inasmuch as it partook of social structures established by law and custom. Its nature was defined within a legislative

Table 2.1 *The central repertory of French grand opera*[a]

Opera title	Sample total number of Parisian performances	Date of relevant statistic
La Muette de Portici (1828)	489	1882
Robert le Diable (1831)	751	1893
La Juive (1835)	500	1886
Les Huguenots (1836)	1,000	1903
Le Prophète (1849)	573	1912
L'Africaine (1865)	400	1888

[a] Statistics for the period 1890–1910 are found on p. 301.

framework; it can be fully understood only in the general context of theatre legislation. It had to fulfil two cultural functions: serving the public interest at home, and promoting a certain image of France in Europe.[2] This was the justification of the large subsidies that it received and the controls under which it operated. In the course of the nineteenth century its role was ever-changing: sometimes it functioned as if it were a museum charged with preserving the nation's musical heritage, and sometimes it was the nursery of the modern world's loftiest creations. It was when it sought to play the latter role that it created grand opera. The institutional framework was restrictive in that it determined the conditions in which opera was created and performed, yet it could also be dynamic, for it provided special artistic conditions and functioned as a place where various powers and creative drives could interact.[3]

The legal foundations of the Opéra were laid down by Napoleon. By the decree of 8 June 1806 all theatrical activity was placed under state control, and the Opéra, the Comédie-Française and the Opéra-Comique were each allotted their specific repertory. On 25 April 1807 the Minister of the Interior promulgated regulations for the theatres, establishing a hierarchy in Paris. The Opéra, the Comédie-Française (to which the Odéon was linked), the Opéra-Comique and the Théâtre de l'Impératrice (later Théâtre Italien) were designated 'grand theatres'. The other authorised theatres became 'secondary theatres', and by a decree of 29 July 1807 they were restricted to four in number, though many others were to open in Paris in the course of time.[4] The 1807 regulations also defined the type and genre of entertainment permitted at each of the various institutions, only the Opéra being allowed to mount productions wholly in music, and ballets 'in the noble and gracious style'. Later on, these general limitations were to be specified more exactly – and sometimes modified even during his period of control – in each director's *cahier des charges*. This schedule detailed his managerial obligations, in return for which the state granted him subsidies and his licence (or '*privilège*') to operate at his own financial risk and for his own profit, if he succeeded in making any. The first holder of this type of schedule was Louis-Désiré Véron (1798–1867), a young ex-doctor who had gone into business, first with a patent medicine and then by founding the *Revue de Paris* in 1829.

It is worth quoting more explicitly from these documents (see p. 455, n. 37). In 1831, clause 8 of Véron's schedule laid down that 'no dramatic genres other than those hitherto designated for this house may be performed at the Opéra. First, *grand opéra* and *petit opéra*, with or without ballet; secondly, ballet-pantomime.' Véron was supposed to put on the following new works in each year of his directorship: one *grand opéra* (in either three or five acts); one ballet of similar dimensions; two *petits opéras* in either one or two acts; and two ballets, of similar dimensions. The wording of Duponchel's schedule, dated 15 August 1835, specified 'First, *grand opéra*, with orchestrally accompanied recitative, in one, two, three, four or five acts, with or without ballet; secondly, ballet-pantomime in one, two, three, four or five acts' (clause 21). Only at the end of the century was the Opéra, under Eugène Bertrand's directorship in 1891, theoretically allowed to stage musical performances of every sort: 'all types of opera and ballet may be performed on stage at the Opéra'. Following the line of thought that had regulated French opera since the seventeenth century, both a particular genre and its institution were, then, linked and circumscribed by decree and regulation. In its drafting of directors' schedules the government was furthermore guided by financial concerns – the desire to maintain and improve the building and its equipment, which were the property of the state – and artistic and political concerns: the desire to sustain the reputation of France's premier theatre.

On 6 January 1864 a decree of Napoleon III announced that the theatre industry henceforth was free: 'any individual may build and run a theatre, provided due declaration is made to the Ministry of our Fine-Arts Household and the Paris Prefecture of Police'. It declared that 'those theatres which appear more particularly worthy of encouragement may be granted subsidies, either by the state or the local authorities'. Clause 4 of this decree also jettisoned the former legislative notion linking specific theatres with particular types of theatrical entertainment: 'dramatic works of any genre, including plays which have fallen into the public domain, may be performed in any theatre'. Censorship was, however, re-established, and control of the subsidies indispensable for the production of major works meant that only the Opéra was able to mount grand operas regularly. Léon Carvalho (1825–97) had tried to bring grand opera to the Théâtre-Lyrique in 1863 with shortened performances of Acts III to V of Berlioz's *Les Troyens* (under the title *Les Troyens à Carthage*, complete with a specially designed prologue), and also offered works of intermediate type, with new modes of expression (e.g., Gounod's *Faust* with spoken dialogue in 1859). His efforts did not, however, meet with success.

Grand opera, or the product of a crisis

Grand opera emerged in the wake of a crisis that was both aesthetic and institutional. On the one hand the Opéra at the end of the 1820s was in the throes of an aesthetic dispute following the impact of Rossinian vocal styles and operatic forms on the French repertory; on the other it was riven by politico-administrative disputes linked to the instability of its management, various abuses, rising fees for singers and poor financial management. Matters were being made worse by the lack of any great personality capable of renewing the repertory. Under the Restoration (1815–30) the Opéra's expenditure fluctuated between 1,264,251 francs (in 1822) and 1,782,663 francs (in 1829). There was uncertainty about the best means of facilitating decision-making within the institution. Ought responsibility to be concentrated in one man's hands or be shared? Should the Opéra be run directly by the state or should management be entrusted to an individual? Vicomte Sosthène de La Rochefoucauld, director of the Department of Fine Arts from 28 August 1824, was himself criticised. The conflict between those favouring and those opposed to the way the Opéra was being run was reflected in pamphlets published anonymously in Paris in 1828–29.[5]

As early as the start of the nineteenth century the Académie Impériale (later Royale) de Musique, as the Opéra was properly known, had appeared antiquated and unattractive by comparison with the smaller secondary theatres that had, under intelligent management, successfully responded to new tastes and the aspirations of a wider public. On 11 January 1816, in a letter to Comte de Vaublanc (briefly Minister of the Interior), Comte de Pradel, director of the Royal Household from 1815 to 1820, remarked on the poor voices and inadequate delivery of the sung text now encountered at the Opéra.[6] He went on to make a revealing comparison that touched on moral, aesthetic, political and financial issues:

> For a long time the people who really care about the arts and morality have
> been appalled by the almost frightening state of prosperity that the
> secondary theatres in Paris have come to enjoy. The Comédie-Française
> and the Académie Royale are often empty while the Variétés and the
> Ambigu-Comique are crowded out. The losses suffered by the major
> houses are growing even larger on account of the almost excessive number
> of these secondary theatres, not to mention the smallest Parisian theatres.
> To me it seems appropriate to impose at least a heavier tax on the
> secondary theatres, thus making them contribute to the support of an

institution whose mission is to bring back to the truly national theatres decent themes that offer so much of value to the progress of the arts and good writing.

The problem was plainly one of competition, and it was made all the more acute because of the relationship between the government and the two major institutions whose failings were felt to tarnish its image. In addition, the authorities did not wish to be associated with something that appeared old-fashioned. The notion of competition may be noted even in a censorship document dated 13 March 1827 about the French version of Rossini's *Mosè in Egitto*:

> New sections have been added, as well as some of the miracles worked by Moses during his sojourn in Egypt and at the moment of his flight. The crossing of the Red Sea comes from an old melodrama played at the Théâtre de la Gaîté. We shall see whether the Académie Royale de Musique will again fail in this new struggle against the Boulevard theatres.

(It did fail: see Chapter 14, p. 268).

This makes it easier to understand the ambiguous relationship between grand opera in its early days and the theatrical styles of the Boulevard theatres. The project of giving the Opéra a new style of stage-setting led to the formation in 1827 of a Staging Committee, the *Comité de mise-en-scène*, to co-ordinate the various production departments. The role of Ciceri, the great scene-painter whose work is shown in Chapter 4, was crucial. Solomé, who had won a reputation at the Théâtre Français, was stage manager from September 1827 to June 1831, and Duponchel was in charge of props and sets from January 1829 to June 1831. This team gradually brought together the technical means needed to carry out new ambitions.[7]

Against the need to attract the public by drawing on fashionable themes, and accepting the inheritance of the tremendous advances in dramaturgy and stage representation being pioneered by the secondary theatres, had to be balanced the need to preserve a certain grandeur in the themes dealt with at the Opéra. Grand opera managed to bring the liberal middle classes and the 'spirit of the age' within its walls, thanks in large measure to the dramatic skills of Eugène Scribe (1791–1861). In *La Muette de Portici*, he borrowed the role of Fenella from the mimodrama (described in Chapter 9), thus linking movement and mime closely with plot; he took from Daguerre's dioramas the idea of accurate stage-setting (see Chapter 4); from melodramas came the eruption of Vesuvius, and from vaudevilles came the liveliness of the ensemble scenes. Grand opera was to be inscribed in society as experienced by the bourgeoisie, not, as *tragédie lyrique* had previously been, outwith reality in a world of heroes and marvels that accorded better with aristocratic dreams.

An inspection report by the Department of Fine Arts in 1829 is testimony to official satisfaction at the aesthetic renewal brought about by Rossini and by the Staging Committee:

> the sustained success of Rossini's works, of our male and female singers who have been trained on good [i.e. Italian] principles, the ever-increasing size of audiences, are clear proof that the musical revolution determined upon by Monsieur de La Rochefoucauld and carried out by maestro Rossini, with the assistance of Monsieur Lubbert [see Table 2.2], was timely and urgent . . . The splendour of the spectacle is wedded to the delights of the music. The historical and architectural accuracy of both scenery and costumes truly conveys us to where the action takes place.

Not long after, with *Robert le Diable*, there was a more or less conscious desire to absorb the great intellectual developments of the age (see Chapter 11), in this instance a certain type of Romanticism that combined, against a medieval background, the struggle between good and evil, the melodramatic themes of paternity, religious sentiment and so on.

Administration and personnel[8]

Throughout the Restoration the administrative organisation of the Opéra comprised three layers: the minister for the Royal Household; a ministerial official charged with oversight of the Opéra; and the Opéra's management. Political events hastened changes at the Opéra. After the 1830 July Revolution and the accession of Louis-Philippe (the 'bourgeois king') administrative arrangements for the Opéra were altered. By an Order of 26 August 1830 the Minister of the Interior appointed a 'commission to examine the present state of the theatres in Paris, with regard to both legislation and literary and financial administration'. The government's financial concerns were shown when on 30 January 1831 the Minister of the Interior set up a new commission to look into the receipts and expenses of the Académie Royale de Musique. A Royal Ordinance of 25 January 1831 made it plain that the institution was no longer linked with the Royal Household but fell, like the other so-called royal theatres, within the sphere of the Secretary of State for the Interior (see Table 2.2). The tax on the secondary theatres (decree of 13 August 1811) from which the Opéra benefited – it received, for example, 188,000 francs from the theatre tax in 1828, over and above a subsidy of 850,000 francs – was discontinued by Royal Ordinance on 24 August 1831.

The new form of management by a private contracting-director – the 'financially interested arrangement' – was a form of public service franchise.

Table 2.2 *Overseeing authorities and directors of the Opéra from 1827 to 1870*

Overseeing authority	Director or administrator (date of start of duties)
State Enterprise (1827–31)	
Royal Household (1815–30) then Minister of the Interior (decree of 25 January 1831)	Emile Lubbert (July 1827)
Enterprise franchised to a contracting-director (*directeur-entrepreneur*) (1831–54)	
Minister of the Interior, then Minister for Commerce and Public Works (17 March 1831–4 April 1834), then Minister of the Interior (4 April 1834 to 1848)	Louis Véron (1 March 1831)
	Henri Duponchel (1 September 1835)
From 12 May 1839 the premises placed under the Ministry of Public Works	Duponchel and Édouard Monnais (1 December 1839)
	Léon Pillet, Duponchel and Monnais (1 June 1840)
	Pillet (1 June 1842)
	Pillet, Duponchel, Nestor Roqueplan (August 1847)
	Duponchel and Roqueplan (30 November 1847)
	Roqueplan (21 November 1849)
Minister of State (decree of 14 February 1853)	
State Enterprise (1854–66)	
Imperial Household (decree of 28 June 1854) July 1854–April 1866	Roqueplan (1 July 1854)
	François-Louis Crosnier (11 November 1854)
The decree of 16 December 1860 places the Opéra once more under the Minister of State, without, however, removing it from the Civil List with respect to financial responsibility for running costs	Alphonse Royer (1 July 1856)
	Emile Perrin (20 December 1862)
Enterprise franchised to a contracting-director (1866–70)	
	Emile Perrin (1 May 1866)

La Rochefoucauld had been thinking of this system as early as 1827. In exchange for a subsidy, the director undertook to observe a schedule (the *cahier des charges*) that had been negotiated with the ministry exercising general oversight, and the Opéra became a commercial enterprise under a director who was appointed by the minister and who then managed the institution for his personal profit. The aim was to avoid the budgetary and administrative difficulties that had arisen from arrangements in place under the Restoration while at the same time ensuring that the Opéra lost nothing of its splendour. Directors acted in the name of the government and on its behalf. The foundations of this new system for running the Opéra were laid between July 1830 and February 1831, and apart from two intervals, from 1854 to 1866 and from 1870 to 1871, the system was to endure until 1939.

The 1830 Revolution provided the state with the opportunity of casting off the enormous burden of running the Opéra. Furthermore, the image that the incoming régime sought to create would have accorded ill with an Opéra subsidised by the civil list and under royal protection. The July Monarchy was conforming to the prevailing mood of liberalism in setting up this financially interested arrangement. Political régimes in France continued to determine the way the Opéra was run, as was to become clear with developments under the Second Empire. Imperial authoritarianism was reflected in direct management between 1854 and 1866, and liberalism in the Second Empire by franchising the Opéra to private enterprise between 1866 and 1870, while a period of control by the performers themselves in 1870–71 corresponded with the spirit of the Commune.

Dr Véron – who as director of the *Revue de Paris* had in 1829 met various writers (Scribe included) and composers – was appointed as the first contracting-director of the Opéra; with the help of the banker Alexandre Aguado (1784–1842) he was able to put up a substantial financial guarantee. His schedule, dated 28 February 1831, stipulated in its first clause that 'The management of the Académie Royale de Musique, otherwise known as the Opéra, shall be entrusted to a contracting-director who shall run it for a period of six years at his own risk, peril and expenses subject to the following obligations, clauses and conditions'. Véron was living proof that the bourgeois influence had penetrated even the world of opera houses.[9] In the six volumes of his *Mémoires d'un bourgeois de Paris* he related in detail the story of his life, and his account of the considerations that led him to choose the directorship is revealing, even if a little improved in the telling. 'The July Revolution was the triumph of the bourgeoisie, a victorious bourgeoisie that wanted to lord it and be entertained; the Opéra will become its Versailles, and it will throng there to replace the aristocrats and princes lately driven into exile.' He went on: 'this plan to make the Opéra both brilliant and popular appeared to me to have great prospects after the July Revolution.' Véron's policies paid off, and are reflected in a letter of 28 October 1833 to the Minister of Commerce from the divisional head in the Ministry of Fine Arts, reminding him that there were two principles behind seat pricing at the Opéra: on the one hand the aim was to maintain the character of the house as one 'intended for the better class of society', but on the other it was to make it accessible to 'the middle classes'.[10]

The financial problem for the Paris Opéra lay in the virtual impossibility of balancing the demands for luxury against the constraints of a budget that tended to limit and control production costs which were being inflated by the birth of a 'star system'. Throughout its long life the Opéra had been a vast drain on finance. The demand for a balanced budget came up against the demands for art and theatrical spectacle. Véron, first of the financially interested directors, was the only one ever to make a profit. (On 30 June 1854 the contracting-director Nestor Roqueplan (1805–70) went bankrupt, with a shortfall of 900,000 francs; the decision was taken to liquidate the Opéra's debts, and the house was brought under the responsibility of the Minister of the Imperial Household: see Table 2.2.) Véron's subsidy came in tangible form (lease of the auditorium and its equipment) and in money. During his first year he received an exceptional subsidy of 810,000 francs, but this was reduced subsequently, being set between 1836 and 1852 at 620,000 francs *per annum*. Voting this subsidy often provoked lively parliamentary debate. Apart from all disbursements for maintenance, staff salaries and production expenses, the director was obliged to subtract from receipts the Poor Tax (which was not discontinued until 1938), and he also had to pay royalties to authors and composers.

In the financial management of the Opéra heed had to be paid to every smallest detail, for the scale of the productions ratcheted up expenses. In *L'Envers du théâtre* (Paris, 1873) J. Moynet cites the example of character make-up for the choruses and extras in *L'Africaine*: the cost was 128 francs 75 centimes for each performance, that is, 12,875 francs for a hundred. Production expenses were sometimes very high. Those for *La Juive* amounted to 134,004 francs: 6,179 francs for copying music, 69,769 francs for costumes and props, and 58,056 francs for scenery. For *Les Huguenots*, total expenditure came to 109,076 francs: 8,000 francs for copying music, 35,202 francs for costumes and props, and 65,874 francs for scenery. Table 2.3 shows how singers' salaries went up between 1831 and 1836, and to these must be added the *feux*, a sort of appearance bonus for each performance. Reputation and length of service at the Opéra were factors that came into the equation, with drastic effect. The chorus went up from fifty-nine singers (costing 70,150 francs) in 1831 to eighty-two (costing 82,750 francs) in 1836. The principal dancers, on between 10,000 and 1,000 francs, were paid less than the leading singers, twenty-eight dancers receiving a total 186,200 francs in salary in 1836. The consequences of the general underpayment for the female *corps de ballet* were dire (see the end of Chapter 6). In the same year, 1836, 106,200 francs were paid to the eighty-one instrumentalists. Individual salaries varied between 2,000 and 800 francs, with four exceptions. The famous flautist Tulou received 3,000 francs and the oboist Brod 2,300 francs, in comparison with just 600 francs to Duret junior (cymbals) or 300 francs to Dauverné junior (triangle). François-Antoine Habeneck, the violinist-director of the orchestra, received 8,000 francs a year between 1831 and 1836.

In the 1848–49 season the great tenor Gilbert Duprez, who was required to give six performances a month, earned 3,000 francs a *month*, with a bonus of 500 francs for each extra appearance. Pauline Viardot, the first Fidès in *Le Prophète*, had a special clause drawn up as follows: 'price and salary will be settled amicably by the arbitration of M. Meyerbeer' (for the background

Table 2.3 *Increases in singers' salaries, 31 May 1831 to 1 June 1836*

Singer (status) Voice type	Salary for 31 May 1830	Salary for 1 June 1836
	Gentlemen	
Nourrit (leads) 1st tenor	10,000	25,000
Lafont (leads) 1st tenor	2,000	20,000
Dupont (stand-in) 2nd tenor	10,000	8,000
Wartel (understudy) 2nd tenor	X	6,000
Raguenet (understudy) 2nd tenor	X	6,000
Ferdinand Prévos (stand-in) 1st baritone	7,200	7,200
Massol (stand-in) 1st baritone	7,200	7,200
Bernadet (understudy) 2nd baritone	X	3,000
Levasseur (leads) 1st bass	10,000	25,000
Dérivis (stand-in) 1st bass	X	15,000
Prévost (stand-in) 2nd bass	8,000	4,500
Serda (stand-in) 2nd bass	X	8,000
Martin (understudy) 3rd bass	X	1,200
Trévaux (understudy) 3rd tenor	2,400	3,300
	Ladies	
Dorus-Gras (leads) 1st first soprano	X	25,000
Falcon (leads) 1st first soprano	X	25,000
Jawureck (leads) 2nd first soprano	9,000	10,000
Flécheux (stand-in) 2nd first soprano	X	4,000
Nau (understudy)	X	3,000
Gosselin-Mori (leads) 1st contralto	7,200	7,200
Laurent-Grandidier (understudy) 2nd contralto	7,200	7,200
Cayot (understudy) 3rd first soprano	X	1,500

Source: Archives nationales, AJ[13] 181. Figures do not include *feux* (appearance bonuses for each performance).

to this, see Chapter 7). In 1850 the tenor Gustave Roger cost the Opéra 50,000 francs, and Pauline Viardot 54,000. In 1870 the principal singers alone received total fees of 500,000 francs.

In the 1830s receipts of 8,000 francs for a performance were reckoned excellent. This sum included both tickets sold 'at the door' and season tickets, the latter amounting, between 1835 and 1869, to more than 25 per cent of the total take.[11] The first supplement to Véron's schedule (30 May 1831), as also to that of Duponchel in 1835, laid down that the director was not entitled to raise the price of seats without authorisation. Up until 1833 the price of amphitheatre and gallery seats was 8 francs, if purchased in advance, and 6 francs on the night. The *Relevé Général de la Salle* or daily seating summary, which was printed in the 1860s and used for each performance, shows how the auditorium was parcelled out into seats at various prices (see Figs. 3 and 4). The director was also obliged to make arrangements for those with free entry or entitled to special rates, for example, on occasion, the claque, a part of the institution that will be discussed presently. The July Monarchy government broke with the precedent that had tended to turn the Opéra into a society drawing room. Edmond Cavé (1794–1852), who was secretary of the Opéra Commission, wrote on this subject in his report of 20 May 1831; his conclusion was that 'since the Opéra auditorium has space for only 1,900 people, if all those who are allowed free entry exercised their privilege on the same evening, the house would certainly be full'. This explains why free entry came to be restricted.

Véron divided up the staff of the Opéra into three groups: (a) stage staff (musicians and dancers, wardrobe, scenery, machinery and props); (b) house staff (safety, lighting, claque, ticket checkers and usherettes etc.); (c) administration. The *cahier des charges* specified the minimum composition of the orchestra, chorus and *corps de ballet*, the sizes of which were to match the institution's pretensions. Véron was required to have at least sixty-six chorus singers, seventy-nine instrumentalists and a conductor. Between 1831 and 1848 the actual number of principal dancers fluctuated between twenty-four and thirty; the *corps de ballet* between seventy-five and 113; and the size of the orchestra between eighty-one and eighty-seven (see Table 2.4), to which must be added such possible reinforcements and also onstage musicians required for any particular work; the choruses were made up of between fifty-eight and eighty-three singers. Conservatoire pupils studying singing added extra weight to the chorus on occasion, for example in *Robert le Diable*. With such forces, which included a number of leading performers who were both outstanding and prepared to innovate, grand opera emerged to profit from the co-operation between an outstanding dramatic craftsman (Scribe), remarkable scene-painters, and composers such as Auber, Halévy and Meyerbeer.

The in-house staff also included the singers' official physicians, the many suppliers of necessities as well as such staff as firemen and *gendarmes* to guarantee safety; the total number of the latter (Table 2.5) is testimony to the particular importance of the Opéra. At 'extraordinary' performances, such as the first three of any new work, further *gendarmes* were drafted in (e.g., thirty-one at the Opéra, thirteen at the Théâtre Français and at the Feydeau, twelve at the Vaudeville, twenty-two at the Théâtre Italien).

THÉÂTRE IMPÉRIAL
DE
L'OPÉRA

RELEVÉ GÉNÉRAL DE LA SALLE

REPRÉSENTATION du   186

	STALLES D'AMPHITHÉÂTRE.	STALLES D'ORCHESTRE.	PLACES DE PARTERRE.	PLACES DE BAIGNOIRES.	PLACES de 1res LOGES		PLACES de 2es LOGES		PLACES de 3es LOGES		PLACES des 4es et 5es LOGES et Amphithéâtre.	TOTAL.	OBSERVATIONS.
					de face et d'Avant-Scène.	de côté.	de face et d'Avant-Scène.	de côté.	de face.	de côté.			
Nombre de Places................	133	220	311	86	94	108	118	120	90	156	350	1786	
Location à l'année...............													
— au jour.................													
— supplémentaire..........													
Billets vendus au bureau...........													
Billets donnés numérotés..........													
Billets donnés sans numéro........													
Billets des auteurs													
Entrées personnelles..............													
Service du parterre..............													
CONCESSIONS ET SERVICE.													
Loge du Ministre d'État..........				4								4	
— du Préfet.................							6					6	
— du Commissaire de police.....								6				6	
— du Conservatoire											6	6	
Stalle de l'officier de paix.........		1										1	
— de l'officier de sapeurs		1										1	
— du médecin de service	1											1	
TOTAUX......													
Suppléments à ajouter............													
— à retrancher..........													
TOTAUX DÉFINITIFS.....													

Vu par l'Inspecteur du Contrôle et de la Salle,   *Dressé et certifié par le Chef du Contrôle,*

Paris. — Typ. Morris et Comp. — N° 68

Figure 3 Daily seating summary designed for use at Paris Opéra performances in the 1860s. It shows categories of subscribers (those by the year and those coming on fixed days); box-office sales; numbered/unnumbered free seats; seats for 'authors' (presumably including composers); those having a personal right of entry, and so on, totalling 1,786 places.

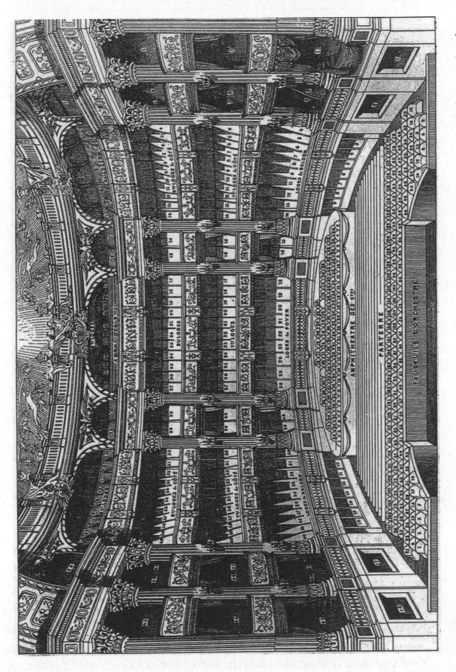

Figure 4 Perspective seating-plan of the Paris Opéra, Salle Le Peletier (1821–73). The seating areas can be correlated with the categories of seats (and numbers of places) seen along the top horizontal axis of the plan in Fig. 3.

Table 2.4 *Numbers of orchestral players at the Paris Opéra*

Instrument	1825 (Source: Opéra, PG 698)	1836 (Source: Archives nationales AJ[13] 181)
I[st] violins	12	12
2nd violins	12	12
Violas	8	8
Cellos	10	10
Basses	8	8
Flutes	3	3
Oboes	3	3
Clarinets	3	3
Bassoons	4	4
Horns	4	4
Trumpets	2	4
Trombones	3	4
Timpani	1	1
Harps	1	2
Bass drum	0	1
Cymbals	0	1
Triangle	0	1

Table 2.5 *Safety staff in Parisian theatres in 1829*

Theatre	Number of safety staff
Théâtre de l'Opéra	24
Théâtre Français	9
Théâtre Italien	17
Théâtre Feydeau	9
Théâtre de l'Odéon	7
Théâtre de Madame, later Gymnase-Dramatique	7
Théâtre du Vaudeville	7
Théâtre des Variétés	7
Théâtre des Nouveautés	7
Théâtre de la Porte Saint-Martin	8
Théâtre de la Gaîté	7
Théâtre de l'Ambigu	7
Théâtre du Cirque Olympique	7

Source: Archives nationales AJ[13] 187

Other controls

The government had at its disposal many control mechanisms. Early in 1831 a Commission was appointed to oversee the Opéra and the Conservatoire; it was made up of political figures, among them the Duc de Choiseul. Since Véron did not take over until 1 June 1831, this Commission ran the Opéra until that date. Afterwards it had the more limited role of advising the minister. It checked that obligations under the director's schedule were being fulfilled, writing a report on each new work, as well as an annual appraisal. The essential elements of the genre were to be spectacle, luxury and striking effects. Of *Gustave III*, the Commission wrote on 26 March 1833 that 'this opera conforms entirely to the type of work that should be performed in the Académie Royale de Musique. The ballets are sumptuous, and the scenery is lavish, creating an admirable impression. The management must be congratulated on the quality of the production . . .; nothing has been stinted that can achieve visual impact and win over the audience.' Relations between Véron and the Commission often became strained, however. According to Véron, the minister was even jealous of his success.

Louis Gentil (1782–1857) was appointed as controller of the theatre's equipment with effect from 28 September 1831. He was to remain in post until 1848, serving at the same time as a source of information about the Opéra for the head of division in the Ministry of Fine Arts.[12] On 20 August 1835 the Minister of the Interior had appointed a royal commissioner whose duty was checking on the fulfilment of the director's schedule. When Véron's reign gave way to that of Henri Duponchel (see Table 2.2) a Royal Ordinance of 31 August 1835 created a new Special Commission for the Royal theatres under the Duc de Choiseul, to replace the earlier body.

After five years during which it was officially lifted, general censorship was re-established in France in 1835 by the law of 9 September, under the same conditions as during the Restoration. Discontinued again in March 1848, it was again reinstituted in July 1850 and maintained until 1906, apart from a short period in 1870. As well as the censors, there was an inspector of theatres whose duty was to keep an eye on productions, and the Commissioner of Police had to check that new works had been passed by the censor. Between 1835 and 1848, no fewer than 8,330 dramatic texts, intended for every sort of theatre, were submitted to the censors;[13] not one of the works that were banned belonged to the Opéra's repertory. With rare exceptions, censorship of the Opéra centred on religious issues. Bringing the clergy or religious customs and ceremonies on stage would attract the censor's attention and sometimes be forbidden if resemblances with contemporary practices were too close. Though the distancing implied by opera meant, in the view of the censors, less moral or political impact than in ordinary plays, any overlap of a plot with contemporary affairs was, however, noted. The report of 9 May 1826 authorising the performance of Rossini's *Le Siège de Corinthe* dwelt on parallels with the war currently being waged in Greece, which, according to one censor, should ensure that the work would be received 'with great enthusiasm'.

Though the Opéra was subject to strict control, grand opera cannot be reduced simply to propaganda: the librettists and composers were not the spokesmen of the state. It is the reception of a work of art that determines its ideological impact, as is shown by a comparison between Carafa's opéra comique *Masaniello* of 1827 and *La Muette de Portici*.[14] Where Scribe was

Figure 5 General view from the wings during an interval at the Paris Opéra drawn and engraved c.1844 by Edouard Renard and Henri Valentin. Vertical supports (*mâts*, or 'masts') stand ready to take the tall painted flats of scenery (*fermes*) already being manoeuvred into position. Vast under-stage spaces and machinery also allowed flats to be wheeled sideways. On the far right, a technician arranges gas lights contained within two suspended battens. Top-hatted male subscribers exercise their privilege to chat with female performers.

clever with *La Muette de Portici* was in leaving many ambiguities and taking attention away from the revolutionary hero Masaniello to concentrate rather upon Fenella and the love story. The censors expressed general satisfaction, asking only for the removal of a few lines such as 'Le peuple est maître' ('The people are sovereign').

A social mechanism

Unlike arts such as painting or literature, drama requires bringing together, in a single place, the constituents of a work that does not really exist save in production by the mediation of sound and visual images, and its per-formance before the public. This temporal and spatial simultaneity – the 'here and now' of theatrical production and its reception by an audience – partially explains why this art form is, to an exceptional degree, dependent on society. The direction of an opera house involves first the production team and everything that is required for the performance, secondly adver-tising, and thirdly arrangements for the receiving of the public. The opera house brings these three functions together in three spaces: the stage, the bill-board and the auditorium. Advertising, which used to involve posting bills on the outside walls of the auditorium, was almost totally taken over during the nineteenth century by the press, and publicity became a busi-ness. Crowd responses, which were always regarded by the authorities with apprehension, could become worrying when posters were misleading, not displayed widely enough or else were over-explicit. For instance, at the time of the long-awaited first performances of *Le Prophète* in 1849, the Prefect of Police forbade posters announcing that since all the boxes and stalls had already been taken up, no tickets would be on sale to the general public.

Improving facilities for the public had become a matter of importance. The Opéra always mounted public performances three or four days a week (see Table 6.1, p. 94). Véron made a start by refurbishing the boxes in order, as he put it, 'to suit better the means and economical habits . . . of the new bourgeois court that was going to replace the one formerly gathered around Charles X'. While improving interior decoration and lighting, he sought to provide 'luxury and pleasure at reasonable prices'. The auditorium of the Le Peletier opera house – home of the Académie de Musique from 1821 to 1873, when it was accidentally burnt down on the night of 28–29 October – possessed an exceptional acoustic and was, according to contemporaries, 'a Stradivarius of a building'.[15] (Fig. 5.) Véron turned it into a sort of club for season-ticket holders, who alone were allowed entry backstage and into the ballerinas' green room. When in 1840 the Prefect of Police expressed the desire to ban such backstage visits, Duponchel, the current director, was furious: a measure like that could jeopardise the success of his next production. The tradition of including ballet in grand opera was in part aesthetic (grand opera was a union of all the arts), in part institutional (see Chapter 6) and in part social, for the ballerinas found rich admirers among the season-ticket holders.

In the age of grand opera social considerations often counted as much as aesthetic ones. People went to the Opéra for the artistic spectacle, but equally for the spectacle of themselves as reflected in the mirrors installed in the public spaces and found gratification in both gazing at others and being gazed at in the auditorium, which remained lit during performances right up until the early twentieth century, when André Messager (1853–1929) ended the practice, though not without many protests. This social narcissism was sometimes carried to such an excess as to allow the two spectacles to mingle together, as when members of the public – in costume – took to the stage during the Act V ball scene of Scribe and Auber's *Gustave III*.[16]

Up until the early twentieth century the Claque, otherwise ironically known as the 'Applause Department' or the 'Success Guarantee Service', served as a link between the stage and the public. Some members of the claque who were required to pay for their seats (which were, however, re-served for them), could choose which performances to attend and had more freedom over what response they cared to show. Enquiries were made into the operation of the claque, and attempts were made to ban it, but to no avail. If some thought it despicable, others judged it essential because it could direct attention to the best passages and draw the best out of the per-formers. The famed leader of the claque, Auguste Levasseur – universally known as Auguste – was active from the early 1820s until his death in 1844. He would decide with the Opéra management what was needed for any par-ticular performance. He took his remuneration in tickets which he then sold on, and also received tickets and cash from performers. In Roqueplan's time as director, the appointment of the leader of the claque or 'chef du service du parterre' ('Head of Pit Services') was a ministerial decision, and David Cerf was the first one appointed in this way. Meyerbeer's devoted friend Louis Gouin, for his part, ran a parallel claque, paid for with tickets handed over by the composer. He gave Meyerbeer a full account of his tactics. For instance, when Véron was putting on *Gustave III*, Gouin tried to puff *Robert le Diable* so that patrons should not neglect it for Auber's rival opera.

Such practices were but one aspect of a huge effort to ensure commercial success; others include granting privileges to the season-ticket holders and maintaining good relations with the press. Véron was one of the first to divine the importance of the fourth estate and make use of advertising. He likewise appreciated, in the spirit of modern communications, that getting himself, as director, talked about would have the positive effect of bringing the Opéra before the public eye. All publicity was good publicity, and the traditional Opéra balls also played their part in keeping up the fascination that all society felt for the Opéra, the source of pleasures artistic and otherwise, the place where the best people met and socialised. The institution's extraordinary hold over minds and attitudes at the time can only be explained by the combination of French centralisation with metropolitanisation, which sucked the nation's energies towards the capital and inflated the tendency for fashion and taste to be dictated by Parisians. The Opéra supported, besides, a luxury industry occupying a significant place in the economy (see Fig. 6). Ladies' fashions and coiffure, the jewellery trade, restaurants and cafés all owed something to opera in general, which also attracted many foreigners to Paris. Finally, vocal melodies and dance tunes first heard in various productions, not to mention innumerable arrangements, 'reminiscences', fantasies and medleys, became an important factor in music publishing, salons and the programming of concerts, as is evident from the advertisement illustrated in Fig. 2 (p. 16). A wide range of 'merchandise' reflected the productions and stars of the Opéra, like those of other nineteenth-century theatres.[17]

Deeply rooted in a basically capitalist society yet profiting from major state support, grand opera occupied an ambiguous position where several superimposed functions intersected. These were political and ideological, aesthetic and industrial. The Opéra was a machine for creating pleasures, dreams and symbols, just as much as for producing a marketable commodity.

Making symbolic impressions

The success and the image of grand opera cannot be reduced to a single political, administrative or artistic policy; they derived too from the fact that significant works emerged for a particular public at a certain moment in the history of taste and sensibility when the themes treated were in accord (in ways that were not always foreseen) with contemporary events. Grand opera staged, in various historical disguises, the birth of its own age, i.e. the Revolution, the terrible struggles that accompanied it, the fight for liberty against oppressors and for people's right to self-determination. This art lent dramatic form to society's deepest feelings, which had been given fresh urgency by the major events of the 1830 and 1848 Revolutions. It showed history in action and reflected the most frightful panorama of modern times, by representing all the horrors of fanaticism, endless disorder, massacres and war. Perhaps, by implication, it showed too the necessity of a form of order that is assured by the state. Grand opera may even have provided an

Figure 6 One of a pair of luxurious porcelain vases made in Paris by the Darte brothers around 1834, at the height of grand opera's first phase. They incorporate copies of well-known lithographs. One bears the image of Maria Malibran, who specialised in Italian opera; the other – above – after Vigneron's portrait, bears the image of Laure Cinti-Damoreau (see Chapter 7), leading singer in *Guillaume Tell*, *La Muette de Portici*, *Robert le Diable*, etc.

imaginary space between sovereign and nation, thus producing a cathartic release of psychological tension or else creating a link between government power and the audience's political awareness. Typically, its heroes are tossed hither and thither by events, even if, like Masaniello in *La Muette de Portici* and Jean in *Le Prophète*, they believe for a moment that they can control them. Grand opera showed a society that thinks in class terms, where the people become an active force and, thanks to the chorus, finds its own form of representation. Taking up an idea from Ernest Renan's 1882 lecture *Qu'est-ce qu'une nation?* we might say that this art form corresponded to the desire to 'accomplish great things together'. It gave special life to the idea of the nation. Memories of shared ordeals, an awareness of history and the representation of the past made grand opera the expression of a collective identity, subsuming the genre within the orbit and ideology of nationalism. Furthermore Scribe was clever enough to write librettos that satisfied bourgeois sensibilities while deriving inspiration from various other dramatic forms that had been well received. Thus, thanks to its aesthetic strength and its occasional fortuitous contemporary relevance, this art form helped provide the bourgeoisie with a 'common emotional bond', a 'shared dream', as André Malraux terms it in *La Tentation de l'Occident*. Society at large responded to the music, images and emotions produced and given full expression by this great machine. Often a reflection of literature, grand opera is itself reflected in literature, as a 'social marker' and also as a point of visual reference and as a pattern for emotions and sometimes for thought.

A virtual obsession with period and regional accuracy in scenery and costumes, the desire for realism, the variety and contrast in scenes and also in the musical means employed, all combined to give the impression of mastery over what was real and what might be real, effectively like an industrial process capable of producing wealth, and a comparable display of social power. French opera was testimony to the march of progress and to the idea that knowledge could grow exponentially. On the Opéra stage bourgeois society 'ennobled' its property through the symbolic metamorphosis of its riches. Luxury became an institutionalised aesthetic category: clause 4 of Véron's schedule laid down that 'the contractor shall maintain the Opéra in the state of splendour and luxury befitting this national theatre'. Eclecticism was affirmed as an aesthetic principle. To paraphrase Pierre Larousse's *Grand Dictionnaire universel du XIXe siècle*: 'Slowly, and to meet modern needs better, opera is becoming an enormous machine, an historical epic, a kind of drama incorporating all genres – sacred music, ballet music, concert pieces, *romances* and barcaroles'.[18] Great efforts were made to bring on stage the totality of the world, both people and nature. This mirrors the new power of the bourgeoisie, which was linked to its economic capabilities rather than to social rank or the influence of the aristocracy. The Opéra operated as a device for harnessing the riches and energy of the time, revealing in a number of exceptional works, as has been shown by Anselm Gerhard, changes related to developments in the modern metropolis.[19]

The Académie de Musique was also a sort of enchanted domain, in which France took pride because it offered the possibility of transcending foreign art. In 1872, Charles-Ernest Beulé defended the Opéra and its subsidy in a National Assembly speech that was greeted with applause (*Journal officiel*, 20 March 1872). Its hyperbole is revealing. Looking back over the history of the house he remarked:

> In the course of the nineteenth century, since the true and full development of French opera, the Opéra has produced a miracle, the sight of which has made Italy and Germany turn pale. France has taken their geniuses [Rossini and Meyerbeer] and made them Frenchmen . . . Our Opéra has made them greater than they were before.

The fortuitous coming together of all these factors and forces – human, institutional, administrative, economic, political, social and historical – in the productive 'machine' that was the Académie de Musique, allowed grand opera to emerge and endowed it with a symbolic importance (or as Pierre Bourdieu has it, '*un capital symbolique*'[20]) that was unique in its day, both in France and elsewhere.

Translated by Christopher Smith

3 Fictions and librettos

NICHOLAS WHITE

The verses which the librettist writes . . . are really a private letter to the composer . . . They must efface themselves and cease to care what happens to them.[1]

It is a cliché to observe that opera, and perhaps in particular grand opera, is a composite venture, and that it is from this very hybridity that its strengths are fashioned. One need only peruse the range of 'resources' discussed in Part I of this Companion to see that grand opera generates a form of cultural force-field in which otherwise disparate skills are focused in the service of a particular production (and a particular product which hopes to exceed the proverbial sum of its parts). If this is true of performance arts in general, then to the theatrical arts here we must add the musical faculties of orchestration and singing. Indeed, it is hard to resist the sense that these faculties are at the core of a cultural product to which the visual and the textual contribute but which they do not dominate.

One can imagine how the story of the relationship between grand opera and its textual complement, the libretto, might be idealised as a harmonious marriage of equal partners; purely aesthetic criticism would explore how the libretto supports or underpins the project of staging a particular opera. It would, however, probably be a mistake to claim that it is largely in such textual frameworks where we find the most conspicuous innovations of grand opera, innovations which might lead us to recall, for more than purely historical reasons, the merits of an essentially nineteenth-century genre as the twenty-first begins. This tension between words and music has a long history, of course, which is set into dramatic relief by Salieri's *Prima la musica et poi le parole* (1786) and Strauss's *Capriccio* (1942). Examples abound of the derision and contempt with which words for music have often been condemned: such as the observation in Act I scene 2 of Beaumarchais's *Le Barbier de Seville* that 'nowadays, what's not worth saying, you sing'; and Joseph Addison's quip in *The Spectator* in 1711 that 'nothing is capable of being well set to Musick that is not nonsense'.[2]

It would be wrong, however, to think that there is little that is particular and characteristic in the librettos around which grand operas are plotted. On the contrary, many of those operas which were intended for the Paris Opéra around and after the July Revolution of 1830 draw a link between the two senses of the French term 'histoire' by grounding their *story* (or plot) in specific incidents often located in medieval or Renaissance *history*.

Although the politics behind such evocations may be complex,[3] the least
that one can say is that many such representations do share a fascination
for those crisis moments at which questions of nationhood come to the
fore. Such a fascination needs to be contextualised in terms of European
nationalism and Romantic historicism (whose taste for the Middle Ages
was epitomised by the publication of Jean Froissart's fourteenth-century
chronicles in the *Chroniques nationales* series of Alexandre Buchon), but its
particular forms are usually the result of negotiation with those we might
term the capitalists and managers of grand opera (directors, state sponsors
and censors) and in particular negotiation between composer and librettist.
The way in which this composite cultural product assembles different talents
invites us to reconstruct the interpersonal relations upon which grand opera
depended, and it is in the light of such a history of cultural production that we
should temper any temptation to idealise grand opera as an unproblematic
union of the arts.[4] It would often be wise to write 'negotiation' in ironical
quotation marks, not least when the composer felt sufficiently powerful
as to override the goals of the librettist by either prescription or a kind
of artistic 'promiscuity' in which a dissatisfied Giacomo Meyerbeer, for
example, might turn to other writers to find the satisfaction he desired or, as
in the case of *Le Prophète* and *L'Africaine*, ask the librettist himself, Eugène
Scribe, to 'show the outline to our mutual friend, Germain Delavigne'.[5]
Other composers such as Wagner and Berlioz would rely on their own
multiple talents to write librettos as the notion of composer as dramatist
developed during the course of the century. Moreover, in the words of Brian
Trowell:

> It is important to remember that a libretto is addressed in the first place to
> the composer, and that the convenience of an audience or critic is only a
> secondary function . . . It should not necessarily be assumed that the words
> always preceded and inspired the musical setting, or that, particularly in
> the texts of arias, the poet had an entirely free rein, as if he were writing
> verse for its own sake.[6]

In any event, it is to the libretto that we must turn if we wish to find the
site of grand opera's poetry and plotting, even if that poetry should not be
overrated and those plots were subject to pragmatic alterations in keeping
with musical imperatives. Louis Véron, the director of the Paris Opéra from
1831 to 1835, argued that,

> It has been thought for a long time that there was nothing simpler than
> writing an opera libretto. That is a great mistake in literary criticism. An
> opera in five acts can come to life only if it has a very dramatic plot,
> involving the great passions of the human heart and powerful historical
> factors. This dramatic plot must, however, be capable of being taken in
> through the eyes, like the action of a ballet.[7]

As Didier van Mœre reminds us, 'Far from smiling at librettos as we often do today, criticism of the time was most pernickety on this matter'.[8] But it is important not to forget the problematic status of the libretto as poetic narrative, given in particular the hierarchy of contributions within the composite frame of the operatic product. As much as the music and language may aim at mutual enhancement, the music may be said to hold sway, not least in the mind of the audience who may well have some difficulty in following the intricacies of the plot and may indeed only display a limited interest in its detours and complexities.

This tension between contributing art forms in the production of opera (and here we must also include theatrical staging and dance, as well as the business of opera houses) is reflected in critical as well as popular responses to that product. Just as each contributor to an opera may have vied for some sort of influence within that hierarchy, so different critical traditions may be tempted to inflate the centrality of their own particular interests. Clearly the libretto fashions a narrative form in which certain musical and theatrical procedures are invited (e.g., certain types of staging on a grand scale). Textual and in particular literary criticism might as well avow, however, that plot and language (or what might be termed the performance of language) are probably not the source of the ultimate emotional power of grand opera. Indeed, although there are characteristic types of grand opera plot, it would be an error to see in the aesthetic texture of their language any great poetic innovations. It is not only artificial to isolate librettos from the rest of the operatic product, it is also painful to do so, for they are often rather blunt textual instruments intended to convey a plot, sometimes in rather basic terms, and to allow for the repetitions and inflected variations of song. We may at moments be tempted to sympathise with the Venetian Signora B's stipulation that nobody should bring a libretto into her box, even at the première. As Stendhal tells us in a reference to 'the sinful indiscretion of reading the libretto' in his *Life of Rossini*, she would have a summary of forty lines prepared and then during the performance be informed in four or five words of the theme of each aria, duet, or ensemble.[9]

Operatic narratives do not necessarily read well as poetry, fashioned as they often are with the broad brushstrokes of simple rhyme schemes and commonplace rhetoric. In the words of Théophile Gautier, 'The verses in librettos are rather mediocre, it is true; but we don't hear them and the music lends wings to the most lame and transfigures the most shapeless into sylphs or cupids.'[10] But these very limitations might invite a reading of them which is attuned to their cultural rather than purely literary resonance. The modern reader might best conceive of this relationship by drawing a contrast between, on the one hand, the ultimately supportive (if also animating and amplifying) role of the text in opera where music is to the fore, and on the other, the role of the *backing* track in film where plot, and thus the text, come to the fore. In both cases, though, the mediations of language are focused by the different types of immediacy offered by musical and visual pleasures. This tension between collaborators also stages the conflict between, on the one hand, burgeoning Romantic notions of individual genius (or the cult of authorial power allegorised as the 'aristocracy of the spirit') and, on the other, the manifestly collaborative nature of a project so vast as opera.

Nevertheless, the plot lends the music a narrative shape and creates patterns of character identification which compel the audience in its tracking of musical shapes and forms. Indeed, the role of language can be dynamic rather than merely vehicular, and the site of such dynamic interaction is of course in song. At the level of reception, it should also be noted that audiences may have been more aware of the historical (*Charles VI*) and cultural (*Les Troyens*) models than today we might imagine. These are some reasons why opera in particular may lend itself not merely to an account of its many components but also to a scholarly approach which is in itself composite or – to use the terminology of modern humanities research – interdisciplinary.

The most prolific author of grand opera librettos was undoubtedly that 'well qualified supplier'[11] Eugène Scribe (1791–1861), though this was by no means the only area of the performance arts where his considerable industry paid high dividends.[12] By 1820 'the inevitable Scribe'[13] had become the most popular playwright in Paris. We may find in grand opera a reflection of a number of the concerns of Romantic writing, not least in a desire to authenticate this otherwise 'extravagant art' by grounding its plots in historical particulars rather than what were perceived to be the abstractions of neoclassical culture. This dependence on the illuminating exemplarity of local colour found its most eloquent advocacy in Victor Hugo's preface to *Cromwell* (1827: see p. 59). In spite of a keenness for such authenticating specificity, Scribe did not preen himself on the narcissistic cult of Romantic subjectivity. If he had not been born with the name Scribe, it would have had to have been invented for him, as his view of his craft was in no small degree artisanal.[14] According to Karin Pendle:

> The constant use of ellipses and the almost complete lack of true poetry in Scribe's verses, the use of a single language and a single manner for all characters in all situations, indeed the presence of actual grammatical errors in his writing, did not sit well with the [critics].[15]

More recently, Herbert Schneider has stressed the practical side of this approach: 'Scribe's work during rehearsals and his strict control over the first performances after the première were both valued and feared.'[16] He made even the younger Meyerbeer effect multiple changes to *Robert le Diable*, such

Pourquoi les étrangers ont-ils si bien compris l'opéra de
M. Scribe ? — Parce qu'ils ne savent pas le français.

Figure 7 *Question*: 'Why do foreigners understand Scribe's opera so easily?' *Answer*: 'Because they don't know French!' Drawn by Marcelin for *L'Illustration*, 12 January 1856.

was his sureness of touch after twenty years writing plays, *mélodrames*, and vaudevilles. He was, in Patrick J. Smith's phrase, 'a story planner and scene-and-act organizer',[17] who created librettos by astutely merging elements taken from disparate sources.

Rather than imagining himself to be a solitary Romantic genius, alone in his ivory tower (as Gérard de Nerval was to characterise his generation in *Sylvie* (1853)), Scribe was willing and able to work with others in the very writing of librettos themselves, hence the green-eyed jibe heard in the dispute over his subsequent election to the Académie française, 'We shouldn't give him a chair but a bench!'[18] His complete works are dedicated 'To my collaborators', and in particular to those fellow writers with whom he worked 'en société' (to borrow his own phrase, though Scribe seems to have been the dominant contributor in such collaborations[19]). From the very beginning French grand opera librettos were conceived of not as immutable expressions of a particular Romantic *génie* but as malleable responses to the needs of the Paris Opéra and its composers, not least Auber, Halévy, Meyerbeer and Verdi. Contracts permitting, the latter were not averse to altering certain texts which Scribe and his collaborators had generated, as for instance in Rossi's reworking of the character Marcel in *Les Huguenots*, written for Meyerbeer.[20] Grand opera librettos were not well-sealed artefacts; with neither the aura of the Romantic classic nor the autonomy of the 'well-made work' associated with Scribe's own spoken drama, they served rather than dictated the process of production and performance.

Although such a demystification of the text might suggest that its status is somehow subliterary, we should not conclude that the poetry and plotting of the text were uninfluential in terms of the audience's experience. On the contrary, Scribe's sense of the particularity of operatic staging meant that in spite of literary influences he would not base librettos on a drama so directly and with as few changes as Desriaux made in his version of

Voltaire's *Sémiramis* for Catel (1802). Whereas his opéras comiques usually took a novel, drama or other literary plot as their foundation, the influence of literature on his grand operas was diluted in a freer association involving various fictional works and historical 'facts'.[21]

In order to categorise the dramatic effects which underpin this achievement, critics as diverse as Smith and Anselm Gerhard still rely on the six characteristics defined in a thesis now almost half a century old: (i) the delayed-action plot in which obstacles come to the fore (see p. 169); (ii) the acceleration of suspense and action; (iii) the alternating focus on and fortunes of hero and antagonist; (iv) the logical order of climactic scenes; (v) the spectators' awareness of a central misunderstanding or *quiproquo*; and (vi) the reproduction in individual acts of the general delayed-action structure.[22] To these, Scribe's operas integrate the chorus as the natural allies of one or both sides, for as Schneider observes, 'opposition between different social or philosophical groups was at the root of Scribe's plots.'[23]

Amidst the many collaborative successes they enjoyed, Scribe worked on two grand opera librettos for Daniel-François-Esprit Auber (1782–1871): *Gustave III* (1833), whose full-blown plot as an *opéra historique* was borrowed by Verdi in *Un ballo in maschera*, and *La Muette de Portici* (1828) with Germain Delavigne (1790–1868), often cited as the first grand opera.[24] Set, with the obsessive geographical and historical specificity of much grand opera, on 15 and 16 March 1792 in Stockholm, *Gustave III* turns on the cross-fertilisation of the love plot (between the composer-king and Amélie, the wife of his best friend Ankastrœm) with the unjust cabal against the king. Just as the king has renounced his transgressive desire, the 'historical magic' of Arvedson's prediction is fulfilled as Ankastrœm shoots him (see the jacket illustration). This theme of revolt echoes *La Muette de Portici* which is based on the events narrated in Raimond de Moirmoiron's *Mémoires sur la révolution de Naples de 1647*, when the people of Naples rose against their Spanish oppressors (and also on the 1631 eruption of Mount Vesuvius). This sets a tragic pattern for grand opera in which the ultimate price of national struggle is death (see Chapter 9). The play begins on the wedding day of Elvire and Alphonse, son of the Spanish viceroy, and Scribe triggers his characteristic delayed-action plot by the mimed account (shown in Ex. 9.1) of Alphonse's seduction of Fenella, her month-long imprisonment by the Viceroy, and her escape. The plot begins once Elvire has already come to Naples to be married and Masaniello has already started to dream of overthrowing the Spanish. A concern for national, ethnic and religious distinctions underpins the libretto written by Scribe for Jacques-François-Fromental Halévy's (1799–1862) *La Juive* (1835) which is set in Konstanz (Constance), Switzerland, in 1414 and recounts the tragic love of the Christian, Léopold, who disguises himself as a Jew in order to see his beloved Rachel, only for her anti-Christian, social rather than biological father, Eléazar, to reveal when it is too late that she was not born a Jewess at all, but the daughter of the very Cardinal de Brogni who has condemned her. Only in sacrificial death is apotheosis possible. Four of Halévy's other grand operas were set in Renaissance or medieval Europe: *Guido et Ginevra* (1838), *La Reine de Chypre* (1841, with a libretto by Georges Henri Vernoy de Saint-Georges (1799–1875)), *Charles VI* (1843, libretto by Casimir (1793–1843) and Germain Delavigne), and *Le Juif errant* (1852). In *La Juive*, as in *Guido et Ginevra*, the well-being of romance depends upon a paternal authority which wavers between tyranny and wisdom. Only a blessing by Ginevra's lost-and-found father, Médicis, can legitimate her passion for Guido. Scribe's 'spring-loaded' plot for *La Juive* follows sensations and revelations with moments of horrified reaction, often expressed as a grand static ensemble, the *pezzo concertato* of Italian tradition. Though the most obvious point of comparison may well be Lessing's 1779 drama of toleration, *Nathan der Weise*, critics have from the start been tempted to map the figure of Eléazar back to Shylock and Rachel to Rebecca from Scott's *Ivanhoe*. Certainly the influence of the historical novel as embodied by Scott pervades grand opera's attention to history as a process, while comparable motifs include the widowed Jewish father, 'the love affair spanning the cultural divide, and a scene centred on the woman's imminent execution'.[25] The ideal of toleration is brought into relief by a depiction of fanaticism comparable with representations of Saint-Bris (in Meyerbeer's *Les Huguenots*), the Anabaptists (in the latter's *Le Prophète* (1849) which is set in the sixteenth century around the seizure and occupation of Münster by John of Leyden), and the priest of Brahma in Meyerbeer's *L'Africaine*.

One of the most testy yet fruitful relationships developed by Scribe involved him in the composition of librettos for Giacomo Meyerbeer (1791–1864). As we have seen, the collaboration became more difficult with the passing years. Meyerbeer's creative ideas regularly preceded the casting of the libretto, since Scribe would be offered dummy texts with prosodic models carrying rhymes for him to follow. The cautionary function of these models, or *monstres* (monsters), is perhaps best understood in terms of its Latin etymology, *monere*, to warn. Certainly it was the music which appears to have balanced the more grotesque elements in *Robert le Diable* (1831) written by Scribe and Delavigne jointly in 1825–27 as a three-act opéra comique, and reworked in 1829–31 into the five-act form which would become typical of grand opera.[26] Like Max in *Der Freischütz*, Robert is tempted by magic in the pursuit of his beloved, the princess Isabelle. In its stretching of the bounds of plausibility it recalls Gothic novels such as Ann Radcliffe's *Mysteries of Udolpho* and M. G. Lewis's *The Monk* (later reworked by Scribe as *La Nonne sanglante*), but it was the very prevalence of this literary mode which helped to fashion an audience amenable to such dark extravagance. Equally the figure of Bertram recalls Charles Maturin's tragedy, *Bertram* (1816), whilst operatic influences include Weber's *Der Freischütz* and Mozart's *Don Giovanni*.

One of the most conspicuous choices of historical setting is to be found in *Les Huguenots* (1836) which is constructed around the Catholic massacre of Huguenots in Paris on the night preceding the feast of St Bartholomew, 24 August 1572, and thus returns to the theme of cohabiting rivals, whose difference is religious. Here as elsewhere librettist and composer signed a contract to cement the project. Whereas *Le Prophète* is a historical opera based merely on suggestions drawn from descriptions of the events themselves,[27] *Les Huguenots* is filtered through a novelistic conception of history. For not only did Scribe work on Emile Deschamps's model, but he also considered other paradigms, not least Mérimée's *Chronique du règne de Charles IX* (1829), as well as Hérold's opéra comique based on the same source, *Le Pré-aux-Clercs*. Although Mérimée's melding of politico-religious violence and love plot does not offer the problems of scale imposed by other potential models of historical narrative such as Scott's and Dumas *père*'s, Scribe still telescopes his material using the delayed-action plot not only for the drama as a whole but also for individual acts. Rather than borrowing the array of Mérimée's characters, Scribe absorbs their dominant traits into a tighter range of individuals, bracketing out prominent historical figures such as Coligny and foregrounding the romance of Raoul and Valentine rather than the events of political history themselves.[28]

It would be simplistic to find in historical references some absolute marker of authenticity, for as Roland Barthes explains in his analysis of Balzac's technique of keeping historical figures such as Napoleon in the background of *La Comédie humaine*, 'it is precisely this meagre importance which confers on the historical character his *exact* weight in reality: this meagreness is the measure of authenticity.'[29] In fact, Mérimée's own account contains within Chapter 8's 'Dialogue between the reader and the author' a parodic self-distancing from the very assumptions of historical fiction about psychology and causality, inviting his reader in Byronic terms merely to 'suppose this supposition'.[30] Such a foregrounding of the process of cultural confection at the expense of claims to historical referentiality is completed by the very incompleteness of the ending: 'Did Mergy find consolation? Did Diane take another lover? I leave this decision to the reader, who, in this way, will always finish the novel as he pleases' (450). In parodying the genre of historical fiction as much as he indulges in its fetishising of the past, Mérimée is ironically not so distant from the self-conscious artifice of grand opera.

As with Halévy's *La Juive*, a post-Enlightenment discourse of religious toleration permeates *Les Huguenots* in a plot shape which is common to a number of grand operas. In conflicts between factionalism and romance, the cross-wires of personal and official affiliations (be the latter by blood, race, political or religious creed) lead to the sacrifice of the romantic connection. Even if it is true that 'Scribe's plays and operas are always well controlled and methodically carried out, no event occurring unexpectedly or without purpose', we should beware the conclusion that 'his characters are their own masters, moving in accordance with their own wills or plans, seldom subject to external control whether from human or superhuman sources. In this lies one of the essential differences between Scribe and the Romanticists.'[31] Among nine parallels between Walter Scott's novels and the world of opera, Jerome Mitchell locates the 'leading character who finds himself caught in the middle; he cannot . . . support either side because he has ties on both sides; he *wavers* . . . he himself has little control over what happens to him.'[32]

So general is the tragic schema present in *Les Huguenots* that it would be ridiculous to suggest that it is unique to grand opera, and its particular inflections in different operas mean that it might be misleading to reduce it to a 'Romeo and Juliet complex'. Nevertheless this structure of contrary imperatives (namely, the heart versus the rationale of official ties to collective groupings of church, party or family) facilitates the representation in the *grosse Szene* (or grand scene) of major historical moments in all their epic breadth, whilst implying the particularity of each person embodied in the chorus as crowd. The use of the group scene in Act III, for instance, allowed for the serial evocation of the simultaneity of the crowd which could not help but resonate in the echo chamber of post-revolutionary historical memory. In Act V's typically melodramatic scenario of delayed recognition, Saint-Bris only realises when it is too late that he has ordered his troops to fire on his own daughter who has renounced her faith in order to marry her beloved.

Though Scribe's personal writings convey an anti-authoritarian and anti-clerical liberalism, his pragmatic relativism made him suspicious of all absolute creeds and thus ambivalent on the topic which necessarily underpinned most reflections on history in nineteenth-century France: revolution.[33] In *Le Prophète* Scribe's Jean is something less than the mad fanatic: he dreams of his coronation but joins the Anabaptists in response to Oberthal's cruelty; and his fiancée Berthe's presence in Münster draws him there. The fact that such devotion is 'a far-cry from the real and enthusiastically polygamous John' reveals Scribe's dramatic wish to contrast two forms of idealism, one amorous and the other religious.[34]

As Edward Said has famously shown, the colonial project of nineteenth-century France amplified the cultural interest in exoticism, and Meyerbeer's

L'Africaine shares this tendency to fix otherness from the perspective of Western eyes.[35] Though the idea was first conceived in 1837, the opera was not premiered until 1865 after the composer's death: it was left to François-Joseph Fétis to supervise the final alterations to the work. That tendency, which Said discusses, to homogenise the exotic is evident in this bizarre title for an opera whose heroine is the Indian princess Sélika. Again the path of love links hegemonic (Portuguese) and dominated (Indian) groups in a way which reflects the structure of colonial power even though Vasco da Gama's shipwrecked crew is massacred by the Indians. The tragic chain of desire runs thus: Nélusko (whose ballad 'Adamastor, king of foul storms'[36] suggests Scribe's reliance on the sixteenth-century epic penned by Luis de Camões, *Os Lusíadas*) loves his fellow captive, the princess, who loves the European explorer Vasco, who in turn feels passionately about Inès. The European couple is released by Sélika to return home once their mutual passion is evident, while Nélusko joins Sélika in death by inhaling the poisonous perfume of the manchineel tree.

Scribe worked with Charles Duveyrier on Verdi's *Les Vêpres siciliennes* (1855: now more familiar as *I vespri siciliani*). As in the case of Wagner, grand opera allowed the composer to conjure with a theatrical framework which would bear more significant fruit later, though Verdi complained about the enormous five-act length required by French grand opera. Like *Don Carlos*, Verdi's opera drew on post-classical European history. This tale (set in Palermo in 1282 and already fictionalised in Lamothe-Langon's novel, *Jean de Procida*) recounts the efforts by Sicilians to dislodge their French invaders and is indeed reflected in the feuding between Scribe and Verdi which was discussed in the newspapers, and not swept under the carpet so as to present an apparently effortless product to the public. The libretto was adapted from a text on which both Halévy (for a brief spell in 1838) and Donizetti (intermittently but at some length from 1839) had worked without success. Verdi made it clear that he disliked the libretto which he said would offend the French because they are massacred at the end, and would offend the Italians because of the depiction of the treacherous behaviour of Sicilian patriots.

For however distant it might seem, medieval and Renaissance history offered a set of analogies by which the French audience of the second quarter of the nineteenth century could reflect upon the turbulent history of its own country in the wake of the Napoleonic Wars, especially the alternation of republican and imperial régimes inaugurated by '1789 and all that'. Grand opera does not suggest that we merely learn *about* history, but rather that by implication and analogy we might learn *from* it.[37] Or in Lindenberger's words, 'The continuity between past and present is a central assertion in history plays of all times and styles'.[38] Such an operatic version of history is defined in terms of those crisis moments in which the very existence of a nation may be put in jeopardy ... or in which the nation itself may not yet exist. As Gary Schmidgall argues, '[the composer] and the librettist must search for moments in literature – call them lyric or explosive or hyperbolic – which permit them to rise to an operatic occasion', or in other words 'moments of expressive crisis' or 'nuclear moments in which potential musical and dramatic energy is locked'.[39] The precarious nature of national identity and security which underpins such dramatic possibilities also facilitates a form of counterfactual hypothesis particular to grand opera:

> Earlier works present history as a straightforwardly closed book, whether
> in background or foreground. Grand opera with a public political interest,
> however, comments upon history, repeatedly, through the dramatisation
> of opposition groups acting within a given society. The illusion is created,
> by the usual suspension of disbelief in the theatre, that history could have
> been different. Thus the spectator must consider why it was not different,
> and can analyse history as something in the making. The processes of
> power themselves are under scrutiny.[40]

Such moments abound in Gioacchino Rossini's *Guillaume Tell* (1829), set to a text co-authored by Victor-Joseph Etienne de Jouy and Hippolyte Louis Florent Bis and inspired by the dramatic model of the early Schiller play *Wilhelm Tell*[41] in its account of the birth of the Swiss nation in the thirteenth century. Like *La Muette de Portici*, it reflects the revolt of an oppressed people against dictatorial foreign rulers. As Guillaume utters emblematically, 'All unjust power is fragile'. Once again we see factional conflict traversed by the bonds of love, though the ending resists its full potential for tragedy since the Swiss triumph and the Austrian Mathilde, whose brother Gesler is killed by Tell but who still loves the Swiss Arnold, finds refuge in the latter's arms. The personal and the political are not merely parallel plots which interweave in the dramatic dilemma of contrary affiliations to desire and duty but also mutually underpinning drives in the bid for secure identity. Family happiness, so Guillaume notes, can only be based on national integrity: 'A slave has no wives, a slave has no children!' Otherwise, 'there is no longer a fatherland' ['patrie'] (the connotation of paternity in the term 'patrie' signalling the metonymical relation between the traditional family and full nationhood). Here as elsewhere it is most productive to read the model neither as a slavishly transposed master-plot nor as an opportunistically stolen gem whose shine is dimmed, but instead as the name of a narrative field in which history and legend meet in ways which invite subsequent nuances and simplifications by librettists. The problematic quality of the original libretto by Jouy led to the revision by Bis. In the words of Jules Janin, 'If they ever decided to award a prize for the most dull production,

Messieurs Jouy and Bis would share the crown'.[42] Even afterwards changes had to be made by Armand Marrast and Adolphe Crémieux, as well as the composer himself. Still, the success of *Guillaume Tell* showed how older techniques might simply be reformed in the light of recent trends, even if its structure lacks the tightly constructed cohesion of a Scribean libretto.

A French version of that myth of national origins is encoded in Halévy's *Charles VI*. Suzanne Citron suggests how 'liberal and national history in the nineteenth century incorporates the imaginary constructed around the Frankish kings: Clovis, Charlemagne (annexed), Hugues Capet, this is already "France". Substituted for the Trojan myth, this myth of gallic origins spatialises continuity . . . The predestination of France is inscribed in the soil, it is geographical.'[43] Halévy's cautionary tale echoed themes witnessed in Népomucène Lemercier's banned 1820 play, *La Démence de Charles VI* (*The Madness of Charles VI*) and other fictions (see p. 245). Here critical interest lies not merely in the finessing of sources for the libretto written by the Delavigne brothers, but in the elucidation of a cultural mood attuned to the resonances of this tale. The crisis runs thus: can Odette (a fictional conflation of Odette de Champdivers and the Maid of Orleans) cure the mad king Charles so as to inspire revenge against the perfidious Albion? At first the king does not recognise his own son. Indeed his madness is exemplified by his confusion of terms in the metonymy linking family and state which we have already considered in the context of *Guillaume Tell*: 'He is right to call me father, all Frenchmen are my children'. By the end of the opera political and biological paternity are realigned as Charles dies confident in the belief that his son will lead the rebellion against the English: 'Your old king is dying . . . Long live the king!'

Odette uses the image of Charlemagne (the first king Charles after whom all others would be judged), found on a playing card turned over by Charles VI, as a model to inspire him. Indeed, inasmuch as such examples of grand opera offer cautionary tales of nationhood (and in this case invite censorship), they are also inspirational at a number of levels, breathing life (hence the etymology: *in* + *spirare*) back into the national past. As Odette tells the king, her father, Raymond, is 'guardian of these vaults, where your ancestors the kings sleep; he will watch over their tombs'. In other words it is his symbolic role to protect the heritage of the nation as a set of historical models to which the modern age must aspire. We find here a Janus-like gesture which promises to save the nation by such necromancy, raising the spirits of former heroes as Odette does when she leads French troops into the Eglise Saint-Denis in Act V scene 2, and by Charles passing on the beacon of national sovereignty to the Dauphin. Such an inspirational gesture might be said to emblematise the project of French grand opera in general, which breathes new life into the body of the nation and its shaping narratives.

The undermining of such hard-won national security by the moments of peripeteia provided by history sometimes finds expression in the disruption of formal ceremonies such as the malediction and excommunication which are imposed on Wagner's Rienzi as he enters the church expecting to be greeted by the *Te Deum*. Herbert Lindenberger sees in opera's oaths, curses, prayers, waltz interludes, marches and friendship-vow duets a 'ceremonial character, by means of which we are meant to feel ourselves overwhelmed by forces larger than ourselves'.[44] The irony is that even the confident staging of national identity and grandeur which such ceremony embodies is liable to interference by the historical process. In other words, the *mise en abyme* in such a staging of the theatre of state does not hold in the face of the *coups de théâtre* of events.

Indeed, in its tendency to depict history on an epic scale, the librettos imposed a considerable burden on the process of staging. As such it is worth asking just how grand could grand opera afford to be? At the opposing pole to the pared-down elegance of the neoclassical unities lay the threat that *histoire* as plot might acquire the potential formlessness of history itself. (The sprawling Romantic 'plays', Victor Hugo's *Cromwell* (1827) and Alfred de Musset's *Lorenzaccio* (1834), were actually aimed at a reading audience rather than stage production.) The libretto for Berlioz's *Les Troyens*, authored largely by the composer himself on the basis of books 1, 2 and 4 of Virgil's *Aeneid* (though Horace and Ovid are also footnoted), returns to Classical subject matter out of fashion in grand opera, due in no small part to the influence of a Romantic concern for the history of the second millennium AD. It nevertheless foregrounds the by now familiar force of the past. Enée is haunted by four spectres from his Trojan encounter: Priam, Chorèbe, Cassandre, and Hector – whose widow finally yields to Pyrrhus as he later reminds himself, Dido and, not least, the French public via an echo of Racine in Act IV. It also ends with a characteristic vision of a fractious and fractured future: Anna and Dido foresee the end of Carthage and the immortality of Rome, 'our sons against our sons', as we hear the first cries of the Punic War. The opera's function in the reconsolidation of a fabricated narrative of French nationhood which antedates the nineteenth century emerges from Citron's demystificatory prose: 'This tale is woven from textual sources intended to exalt the memory of the Frankish kings . . . in a mystical continuity going back to Clovis, whilst attributing to them prestigious Trojan origins.'[45]

The opera was not produced in its full five-act form until twenty-one years after the composer's death (in Karlsruhe, over two evenings, in German). The Paris Opéra failed it, and an unintended split was made. Acts III to V were premièred as *Les Troyens à Carthage* at the Théâtre Lyrique in 1863, and the first two acts, given the title *La Prise de Troie*, did not appear in France until 1891, in Nice. Though the music is audacious, the language and structure of the libretto are less so; nevertheless the perceived significance of the libretto in its own right is underlined by the fact that Berlioz gave apparently successful readings of it before the good and the great of the Parisian cultural world.[46] In addition to that characteristic garnering of considerable forces including off-stage bands, Berlioz himself was aware that he had produced a 'Shakespeareanised Virgil'. Indeed, the Romantics' estimation of Shakespeare is visible not only in the influence of Lorenzo and Jessica's evocation of 'In such a night' from *The Merchant of Venice* on the love duet in Act IV (where Berlioz claimed merely to have 'edited' Shakespeare 'who is the real author of the words and music'[47]) but also in the mixture of genres, the wide geographical range of the action and the sharp juxtaposition of contrasted scenes (which reflects the techniques of *mélodrame* too). The growth of *mélodrame* on the French stage, from the late eighteenth century on, also exerted an influence in its use of historical and supernatural subjects, thrilling horror plots and all the attendant stage effects.[48]

The double life of librettos as both springboards to performance but also as texts in their own right allowed librettists to use the publication of their texts as a means of authenticating their project in terms of the literary and historical sources they used, not least by means of considerable footnotes. Even though the experiences of the opera-going public might not be directly affected by such bids at self-authentication, Berlioz for instance was keen to use such notes to articulate the cultural modelling left implicit in performance, explaining in Act V Dido's apparently mythical vision of her avenger Hannibal in a historical note which explains the Ancients' belief in such foresight on the verge of death. Such otherwise excessive gestures can be understood as a kind of mortgaged textual authority. Scribe himself had begun to add such notes in *Gustave III*, citing John Brown's *The Northern Courts* (see p. 181) and the composer-king's opera *Gustave Wasa*. In the case of Scribe, moreover, the *Œuvres complètes* allowed the librettist to publish his own text even if it were at odds with the version ultimately used for performance, the prime instance being the differences between his and Meyerbeer's versions of the text for *Les Huguenots*. In a gargantuan footnote which would look more at home in a doctoral thesis than a libretto Scribe also explains how *Les Vêpres siciliennes* 'unfortunately has no relation to Casimir Delavigne's version',[49] a five-act tragedy which appeared at the Odéon in 1819. Instead of literary sources, Scribe piles up historical references to Fazelli, Muratori and Giannone . . . but only in order to counter 'those who will as usual blame us for ignoring history', and to prove that he realises the fictitious nature of the tale of Jean de Procida's organised revolt. As in Mérimée's version of the St Bartholomew's Eve massacre, the fascination centres on the mysterious forces by which a 'general revolution' emanates from sudden manifestations of popular displeasure without concerted planning and clearly delineated causes. Scribe uses historians in order to justify his recourse to myth by suggesting that it is the very formlessness of historical events and their very unfathomability which invite the licence of artists.

Berlioz was certainly not the only composer to write his own libretto for grand opera; nor was he the only composer to aspire to a verbal poetry which might do justice to his musical achievement. Wagner's *Rienzi* (first performed in Dresden in 1842) borrows its setting in mid-fourteenth-century Rome from literary sources. The composer (who was to theorise the importance of the libretto as poetic focus rather than parenthetical adjunct in *Oper und Drama*[50]) knew Bulwer-Lytton's quite epic novel of 1835, *Rienzi, the Last of the Roman Tribunes*, which had been translated into German by Bärmann (from whom he borrows directly in his evocation of the battle hymn in Act III scene 3, as he states in a footnote). In this cautionary tale the fickle people turn on their champion who is ultimately joined in death by his sister, Irene, and her beloved Adriano (who has already conveyed the sense of fatalism we have observed above in *Gustave III* in his anticipation of misfortune). The influence of Mary Mitford's 1828 tragedy, *Rienzi*, can also be seen in Wagner's condensation of Rienzi's two careers as tribune and senator into one (just as Rienzi absorbs any personal life into his political function with the words 'Rome will be the name of my bride!'). Such conflation in Mitford's 'beautiful Tragedy' is actually criticised in Lytton's preface to his first edition in a manner which reveals by implication the challenge facing grand opera as it, too, attempts to overcome 'the advantage possessed by the Novelist of embracing all that the Dramatist must reject'.[51] As we have seen, grand opera often constructs history in terms of its moments of inauguration and crisis, but here it resists the myth of an end to history, as the equation of political 'Freiheit' (freedom) with the 'Friede' (peace) of narrative stasis evoked in Act II by the Friedenboten (messengers of peace) is displaced by the nobles' appropriation of the same vocabulary of antithesis, 'Frechheit' (impudence) and 'Schmach' (ignominy), which motivated popular revolt in the opening act. The names attached to particular roles may change but the conflict borne of desire (political as well as sexual) remains, as the opera closes in flames and darkness. As we read in Lytton's cautionary appendix, 'the moral of the Tribune's life, and of this fiction, is not the stale and unprofitable moral that warns the ambition of an individual: – More vast, more solemn, and more useful, it addresses itself to nations.'[52]

4 The spectacle of the past in grand opera

SIMON WILLIAMS

Shifting perspectives

Among the most long-lasting cultural effects of the French Revolution was a sense among the population of Europe of separation from its past. By and large, the eighteenth century experienced continuity with the past, in particular an affinity with the values of classical civilisation, but after the depredations of the Revolution and the Napoleonic Wars, 'all that had gone before seemed to belong to a world forever lost'.[1] The consequence of this alienation from the past was not, however, the embracing of an exclusively modernist culture. On the contrary, at no time in European history have the forms, styles, and modes of the past been so assiduously cultivated as they were in the hundred years following the Revolution. In all phases of artistic activity, the past was recaptured and preserved, partly to deny its loss, partly to escape from the realities of contemporary life. The nineteenth century also identified with history periods that either offered parallels to unstable aspects of its own social and political life or reflected values important to contemporary society.

The historicist tendency that so characterises post-revolutionary culture had already begun to reveal itself in eighteenth-century Europe in, for example, the pre-Romantic movements of Gothicism in England and *Sturm und Drang* in Germany. In Paris too there were signs in the latter half of the eighteenth century that theatres were beginning to break away from the conventions of classical scenography in the cause of greater realism.[2] It was, however, only during and after the Revolution that freedom from the restraints of a primarily classical culture gave birth to a variety of novel theatrical genres that captured the imagination of the popular audiences filling the auditoriums of the new theatres. In this vigorous theatrical renaissance, the public desire to be imaginatively transported to past ages and exotic locales was catered to most completely through the production of *mélodrame*. The most salient figure among purveyors of *mélodrame* in post-revolutionary Paris was the prolific Guilbert de Pixérécourt (1773–1844) whose immensely popular plays, while sparse in dialogue, rudimentary in characterisation and short on ideas, were visually scintillating and thrillingly plotted. He and his designers were adept at constructing, often in the most minute detail, a variety of imaginary historical *milieux*, in particular the eerily preternatural world of popular Romanticism, the Gothic environment of ruined abbeys and castles, dreary forests, precipitous mountains and horrendous dungeons.

Parisians' taste for visual stimulation and total immersion in an environment different from their own was satisfied by other means as well. In 1809, the early pioneer of photography, Louis Daguerre (1789–1851), began his career by painting for public display panoramas of famous cities. Later, in 1822, he opened the immensely popular 'Diorama', a circular theatre of scenery alone. Here, through the subtle blending of a double surface of painting with light, he represented romantic landscapes and historic places 'with every artifice to fool the audience into believing that what they saw before their eyes was the size of life and just as real'.[3] The appetite for realistic illusion was so great that total realism in design became a precondition for the success of a production. As Victor Hugo put it in his seminal preface to *Cromwell* (1827), an essay that defined the new Romantic theatre in opposition to epigonic classicism:

> Nowadays we are beginning to realise that being exact with respect to location is one of the first elements of reality. The characters who speak or act are not the only ones who leave a faithful imprint of the action engraved in the spirit of the spectator. The place where this or that catastrophe occurred becomes a terrible and inseparable witness of the tragedy; and the absence of this type of silent character detracts from the completeness of the drama in the grandest scenes of history.[4]

By all accounts, the Opéra was slow to adapt to the changing theatrical tastes of post-revolutionary France. Instead, classicism prevailed. By the early nineteenth century, the company was sinking into a state of serious decline and it had to be reanimated as a place of cultural prestige by the efforts of Napoleon, who restored its pre-eminence. In the first twenty years of the century, its repertory was composed largely of operas that either dated from pre-revolutionary times or recalled the ambience of that period. Ballets became, once again, a leading attraction and the operatic emphasis fell increasingly on works explicitly or otherwise designed to impress foreign visitors.[5] By and large, staging was expensive but dull, with perspective sets that were starting to be broken up by practicable scenery (three-dimensional objects) but still designed on principles that fundamentally had not altered since the sixteenth century. Change, however, was in the air. For two decades after the Revolution, the Opéra was housed in the National Theatre on the Rue de la Loi. In February 1820, however, the company was forced to move when the theatre was demolished as a consequence of the Duc de Berry, heir-presumptive to the throne, being assassinated on its steps. After brief sojourns in the Salle Favart and the Salle Louvois, in August 1821 the Opéra settled in a theatre specially built for it in the Rue Le Peletier (see Fig. 4). Here, a large auditorium and an immense stage, measuring 26 metres deep by 33 metres wide, presented the company with physical dimensions considerably more expansive than any among which they had previously performed.[6] Fortunately, the Opéra already had on its staff designers capable of taking advantage of the greater space. Pierre Ciceri (1782–1868), who was to be the most influential of all Romantic scene designers, had been working with the company since 1805 and by 1816 had risen to the rank of chief designer, a position in which he was joined briefly in 1820 by Daguerre himself. Both men had already acquired notable reputations as designers for the boulevard theatres, and as the hold of the antiquated repertory relaxed, they were able to introduce fresh scenic styles. Their single most successful collaboration was the design for *Aladin* (1822), a fairy-opera of scant musical significance, but with sets that were praised by one critic as 'a veritable kaleidoscope, which constantly changes form and colour'.[7]

The visual experience

The new theatrical space and, it has been argued, growing concern among its state sponsors that the Opéra should not be 'remote, [or] a fossilised institution alienated from modern France',[8] led to increased attention to visual spectacle as the potentially most appealing aspect of operatic production. In 1827, a Staging Committee to oversee the *mise-en-scène* was established, charged with ensuring that the highest standards of design and staging were maintained in production on the Opéra's stage. The committee was charged too with maintaining an appearance of opulence that was considered only fitting for the premier theatrical and musical institution of the country. Under Dr Véron (see Chapter 2, pp. 35, 41) the *cahier des charges* continued this same imperative. Accordingly, the two decades that followed saw a striking reversal in the company's fortunes. The grandeur and detail of the historically concrete spectacle with which it presented its major operatic offerings drew large audiences, while the careful alignment of scenic production with the specifics of vocal and orchestral music achieved a unity of theatrical elements that was unprecedented. As spectacle came more and more to the fore in the Opéra's priorities, the sheer logistics of planning necessitated at least eighteen months' lead time for any major production and endless rehearsals once work on it had begun. The various elements of the production, ranging from the assemblage of massed choric singers and extras, through the coordination of scenery and costumes, to the correlation of stage action with the tempi adopted by the orchestra and conductor, could only be achieved with a single individual at the helm. Although at this stage in theatre history the conception of a director as the ultimate authority on all matters relating to staging and interpretation was rudimentary at best, the exigencies created by spectacular production made such a figure necessary. Throughout the high period of grand opera, from *La Muette de Portici* in 1828 to *Le Prophète* in 1849, one individual above all others executed this function at the Opéra, Henri Duponchel (1794–1868). Duponchel had trained as a designer, but expanded his skills to devising and coordinating the spectacle that contributed so greatly to the success of grand opera.[9]

Under Duponchel's direction, the historical period in which the action of the opera was set would be scrupulously researched. The widest variety of characteristic styles of architecture, landscapes, costumes, and particulars of folk-life from different times and locales were incorporated into production in order to gratify audiences' demand for complete scenic illusion. The ultimate truth of theatrical performance was conceived to lie mainly in the apparent wholeness with which specific historical times and geographical locations were reconstructed and in the perceived accuracy of their myriad details. As Jean Moynet, a scene-painter who provided the most complete account of the stage production of his time, put it:

> The modern stage is able to accomplish almost perfect settings . . . Today, the cooperation of all the fine arts has become necessary to theatrical production . . . The audience, now of greater number, is composed of all classes of society. Their knowledge of archaeology is more exact. Today's audiences would find ridiculous the conversations and actions of ancient Assyrians done in a French palace of the seventeenth century. It is necessary . . . to observe actuality and truthfulness in costumes and properties . . .

Later he argued, as Victor Hugo had done in 1827, that local colour should emanate from the living heart of a work:

> Under the influence of Romanticism, the study of local colour became a necessity. One no longer contented oneself with the 'approximate' or old devices which had served until then. It was necessary . . . to substitute even greater fidelity in historical costuming for the bizarre accoutrement conventionally accepted. The theatre was asked to make its characters live in the actual environment in which they had lived. Dramatic artists researched zealously promoting this movement by allying themselves to truthfulness in costuming.[10]

So crucial was staging to the success of an opera that it came to be regarded as integral and unalterable an aspect of the finished work as the score and libretto. Many productions at the Opéra were marked by the publication of a staging manual (*livret de mise-en-scène*, or *livret scénique*) that recorded, usually in painstaking detail, the blocking of characters, the disposition of the chorus, the topography of the sets, and the specifications of the costumes, often down to the most minute detail (see Fig. 12, p. 81).[11] The prime readership for the *livrets* were provincial and foreign opera houses, eager to stage the latest Parisian hits, and to do this literal reconstruction of the original staging, sets, and costumes was a precondition for success. The impact of the visual aspects of production could be so overwhelming that they could become the *raison d'être* for the performance as a whole. Indeed, by the 1830s, emphasis on the visual was so marked that several moments in the unfolding of the operas' plots could only be understood by careful attention to staging. The eye became as important an organ of interpretation as the ear.

So, even if the music was mediocre, the libretto weak, and the action un-involving, spectacle could carry one away. As Théophile Gautier, the leading critic of French Romantic theatre commented, it is the designer 'who pro-vides local colour to so many works that are lacking it, and more than once he has managed to make us forget the action because of décor that is infinitely superior to the work'.[12] Gautier also observed that no expense should be spared on décor or costumes. 'The costumes, the scenery should always be treated with great care at the Opéra', he wrote. 'This splendour has much to do with its success and it is there above all where meanness would be disas-trous: at the Opéra prodigality is the better economy'.[13] Prodigality served as a powerful lure to draw audiences to the Opéra and as the institution's financial resources were greater than those of any other theatre, spectacle flourished here more than anywhere else in Paris. Expenditures on sets in-creased vastly during the July Monarchy. In the early decades of the century, scenery at the Opéra would be recycled whenever possible, so no production was individually designed. Even *La Muette de Portici* in its first production boasted only two completely original sets, but as the audience's appetite for visual novelty increased each production was given a totally new design and expenditures multiplied rapidly. So, while the settings of a new production early in the century would average around 18,000 francs, grand opera was more demanding of resources. Rossini's *Guillaume Tell*, the first new pro-duction to be designed from scratch, cost 30,000 francs. Despite Véron's extensive cost-cutting and battles with his political masters, 58,000 francs were spent on *La Juive* (1835), an opera that required the most sumptuous and detailed reconstruction of medieval life.[14] His successor, Duponchel, expended nearly 66,000 francs on scenery for *Les Huguenots* in 1836 (see p. 29).

Public approval of an opera depended as much upon variety as upon realistic illusion. Opera production in France had never been as subject to the unity of place as was the more classically orientated spoken the-atre; even so, the action of recent operas had been relatively circumscribed

La palette du décorateur.

lui parvient manuscrite, de son acte. En tout cas, il se pénètre bien de son sujet, le rumine une huitaine de jours et crayonne ensuite un croquis. Présenté au directeur de théâtre, le croquis est rarement accepté tel quel; on le remanie de concert, on l'arrête définitivement, et le vrai travail commence.

Il ne suffit pas, en effet, pour le décorateur, d'imaginer l'ensemble d'un décor; avant de construire, la maquette, qui est la réduction à trois centimètres...

Figure 8 The art of the theatrical scene-painter, here mixing colours on a giant palette. Canvases for flats or backdrops were likewise painted on the floor. Various flats are seen stacked against the wall. Drawn by an anonymous artist for *L'Illustration*, 24 February 1894.

and centred around a single geographic location. Grand opera joined in the sense of physical freedom that had so energised popular theatre earlier in the century. Even though the exigencies of plots might still require some unity of place in the settings, even single geographical locations were represented from as wide a variety of viewpoints as possible. *La Muette de Portici*, set in the comparatively exotic locale of mid-seventeenth-century Naples, has a stage playing time of about two and a half hours. In the course of the action we travel to many different locales, from the palace of the Spanish viceroy to a fisherman's hut on the beach at Portici, from the market place in Naples to gardens that imaginatively include Vesuvius within their purview. The settings of this opera and of *Guillaume Tell*, designed by Ciceri after a journey to Switzerland and Italy specifically for the purpose, constituted a veritable tour of Europe's most scenically spectacular country. Many grand operas demonstrated greater freedom in the setting of the action. Meyerbeer's *Les Huguenots* moves from the French countryside into Paris, *Le Prophète* ranges broadly over the landscape of the Low Countries and Westphalia, while his posthumously produced *L'Africaine* moves from Lisbon to an African country that resembles Madagascar. As the century progressed, composers and librettists felt themselves less and less restricted by any unity of place.

Among the designers of grand opera from the late 1820s through to the middle decades of the century, Ciceri and his various pupils were the most prominent. They abandoned the ubiquitous single perspective for *trompe l'œil* paintings of Romantic landscapes and historical scenes, and in so doing opened up scene painting to previously unsuspected horizons.[15] In the earliest years of grand opera, including the first productions of *La Muette de Portici, Guillaume Tell,* and *Robert le Diable,* Ciceri was the sole designer for the Opéra and all sets were constructed under his direction or in his privately-owned *atelier,* or workshop. But once Véron took over the directorship, he was minded to cede commissions to other *ateliers,* not least because of pressure from Ciceri's own pupils. From henceforth operas were designed not by a single artist, but each act by a different artist with each set being constructed in the *atelier* with which that artist and his speciality were associated. During the high period of grand opera production, in the 1830s and 1840s, one saw the work of Charles Cambon (expert in painting architectural sets and interiors), Auguste Caron, Edouard Despléchin (expert in landscape and effects of light on water), René Philastre and Charles Séchan (expert in romantic contrasts) as much as Ciceri's. The necessity of achieving visual unity in any given production meant that freedom to develop an individual style of design was limited. Nevertheless, records indicate that audiences were aware of the contributions of individual designers and even acknowledged these in their applause.

The work of the stage designer was so arresting that it struck contemporaries as having been raised to the level of an art in itself. Richard Wagner retained lifelong admiration for French expertise, which he sought for the 1845 *Tannhäuser.* From the sketches, lithographs and maquettes that are the sole visual record of these productions today, it is clear that standards of draughtsmanship were of the highest.[16] (Fig. 9.) In contrast to the generic nature of sets prior to the 1820s, scenic design at the Opéra grew more varied in subject matter, the Romantic settings of the action providing the scene designers with freedom and challenges that were previously unparalleled. The early work of Ciceri has the balance and clarity associated with the painting of Jacques Louis David and still has about it an aura of formal grandeur associated with the Napoleonic period. But his later work, and that of his contemporaries, has at times a serenity reminiscent of the paintings of Caspar David Friedrich, while in the urban landscapes of cities, from ancient Rome to Sweden in the eighteenth century, parallels can be detected with the paintings of such groups as the Nazarenes. Grandeur is not the prime quality of these settings, rather they are distinguished by charm of locale and period. But when the sets themselves were filled with unruly crowds, they looked exciting enough, bringing forth comparisons to the turbulent, crowded canvases of Eugène Delacroix, the leading French painter of the Romantic period.[17] (Fig. 10.)

Figure 9 Ciceri, set design drawn for Act I of *Sapho, tragédie lyrique* in three acts, music by Reicha (1818). The classical landscape and balanced composition are offset in mood by the ruined temple and violent boulders, and above all by lighting. The libretto specifies that 'it is still night-time' and 'the sea is rough'. Furthermore, 'a beacon (stage right), which is starting to fade, projects an uncertain light'. Ciceri has eliminated a modern-looking lighthouse and substituted a glow from behind the right-hand trees.

Oddly enough, this transformation in stage production was neither caused nor assisted by radical changes in the technology of the stage. The opening productions at the Salle Le Peletier still employed single perspective sets, but as the repertory modernised, so too did physical elements in the design. Daguerre's youthful experiments led to the adoption of a panorama at the back of the stage in place of the usual backdrop or shutters: *Guillaume Tell* had one in 1829. In the 1830s the Opéra made more use of the technique, already ubiquitous on the boulevards, of building practicable sets that both allowed the action to take place on several physical levels and provided three-dimensional scenery, additional to the type already constructed in two dimensions alone. 'Fermes', flats of an irregular shape, with the centre often cut away to allow for novel entrances or unusual perspectives, were also introduced. Furthermore, over the years a variety of traps were installed on the stage, including the famous 'English trap', which allowed ghostly figures to slide through walls or rise through floors in an eerily diagonal ascent. But in the first half of the century there was little change in the machinery of the theatre, which led to problems in manipulating the scenery. The new design and construction of the sets meant they could not be changed by the old pole and drum system. Instead, scenery had to be

Figure 10 Ciceri, set design drawn for Act III scene 6 of *Alfred le Grand*, ballet-pantomime in three acts, music by Gallenberg and Dugazon (1822). The setting is in Somerset (England) and portrays the camp of invading Danes. King Alfred (*r.* 871–99), disguised as a harp-carrying shepherd, spies on the Danes and finally leads the English to victory over them. Visual detail researched and portrayed by Ciceri was set in a stage space suggesting practicable scenery and irregular groupings of actors across an ambitiously varied landscape. A 'Note historique' leaves the reader of the libretto in no doubt that the work is to be understood as a parable about good kingship and national unity.

moved by a cumbersome system of counterweights, winches and machines with multiple pulleys, chariots, and rollers adapted from the pole and drum but not coordinated into a new configuration. Vast numbers of stagehands were therefore required to change the unwieldy sets and, to accommodate them, long intervals became standard at the Opéra.

The only major technical innovation occurred in the area of lighting. In the first two decades of the century, the stage was lit mainly by Argand lamps, oil lights that cast a steady light upon the stage, but were smoky and unpleasant. In 1822, gas lighting was installed for the production of *Aladin, ou la Lampe merveilleuse*. Audiences were fascinated by the way in which this allowed for rapid changes of light over the whole stage, from 'mysterious dusk . . . to . . . dazzling light'.[18] As gas fitments could be placed not only as footlights but in overhead battens and at various points in the wings, the stage space could be illuminated uniformly (see Figs. 5, p. 36, and 14, p. 105). When required, variations in the density of light could also be made between separate areas of the stage. Limelight, which allowed characters or scenic areas to be highlighted, was invented in 1826 but not used at the Opéra until mid-century: see Fig. 11, p. 68. Although electric arc light was first seen at the Opéra in 1846 and, in a notable experiment, was employed to represent a spectacular sunrise in the first production of Meyerbeer's *Le Prophète* (1849), it was not placed into general use until the 1880s. From 1822 on, indication of differences in the places and times of the action became more refined as subtler variations in the quality and density of light on stage became progressively more possible. Furthermore, light could imperceptibly influence the mood of audiences, an effect that grew in strength during the middle decades of the century as the light in the auditorium gradually diminished until, by the early 1900s, audiences sat in complete darkness. Light, as well as the new sets, increasingly made the stage into its own world. One witness of this was Carl Baermann, after seeing *Les Huguenots* in 1839:

> Duprez was quite outstanding, totally involved in what he is doing, full of imagination. On the whole the scenery is simply amazing. The chateau in Act II especially is depicted with endless verisimilitude much enhanced by the new mode of excluding the side-wings, and the use of gas lighting, which gives the clarity of daylight.[19]

Embodied experience

While Gautier had expressed some doubts about the quality of the dramatic and musical material the designer had to work with, in the case of grand opera, the basic material was more likely to have been a stimulus than an obstacle to the visual imagination. Grand opera introduced on to the stage of the Opéra popular modes of theatrical representation and used them to corporealise music of a grandiosity and action of a tragic dimension that the boulevards could never equal. The elevated aura of the Opéra's classical tradition and the idea of dramatic action as a chronicle that incorporated the fate of nations were translated into the vigorous theatrical language of the populace. This involved, however, a crucial shift in emphasis at the heart of the opera. Invariably aristocratic characters and rulers were central to the action of the opera seria or *tragédie lyrique* of the *ancien régime*. These figures did not disappear from the operatic stage, but they were placed among characters from less privileged social strata. Furthermore, decisive forces that influenced the course of the action no longer originated in the ruling classes, nor were they controlled by them. Moreover, such forces were no longer subject to the blandishments of individual heroic will. Instead, fate was invested more in the process of

Figure 11 Final scene of *La Muette de Portici*, revived in Paris in 1863 and drawn by Godefroy Durand for *L'Illustration* in January of that year. Fenella remains the focus of attention, fainting as she learns of the death of her brother Masaniello. Seconds later she grasps princess Elvire's hand (seen already outstretched), rushes up the flight of steps, and destroys herself in Vesuvius's lava-flow. The décors, by Charles-Antoine Cambon and Joseph Thierry, were new. The costume designs remained those of Hippolyte Lecomte (1828): see Fig. 19. Neapolitan men, seen on the right, wear the Phrygian cap and are halted by Spanish guards. Performances of *La Muette* had tailed off in the 1850s but this new production had fifty-two performances in 1863 alone.

causation or, if it were to be seen as unpredictable and arbitrary, in the demands of the ubiquitous crowd, represented on stage by the vastly augmented chorus.

The world of grand opera was therefore broader than that of *tragédie lyrique*, a phenomenon instantly apparent in the wider horizons and multiple perspectives of its sets. In place of the relatively limited number of characters in late eighteenth-century opera, grand opera employed a cast of Shakespearean proportions, not to mention the chorus, which, as a prime articulator of the forces that circumscribe historical action, had a greatly enlarged role in all grand operas. The power of the crowd to determine public affairs was depicted in many ways: by insurrections, which are central events in several grand operas; by moments of mass resolve, often centred around the singing of a communal prayer or swearing of an oath; by social rituals; and by celebrations in the open spaces of cities, which involved much use of local colour in the costumes and props (see the next chapter). For example, the procession that climaxes Act I of Halévy's *La Juive*, among the most celebrated spectacles in the canon of grand opera, requires a minimum of 250 personnel not counting the chorus, which sings as the procession advances.[20]

The dangerously unpredictable violence that is a characteristic of much grand opera dominates *La Muette de Portici*, the first grand opera to enjoy widespread popularity in Europe.[21] The subject matter, revolutionary disturbances in Naples under the popular leader Masaniello, had already been dramatised on the boulevards. Ciceri's sets, which recaptured both the poetic landscape and the teeming urban world of Naples in the seventeenth century, exemplified the love of local colour that was to be so common a feature of grand opera. It gave identity both to the people and to the historically determining forces they embody. In *Muette* the crowd has a constant presence. In the opening act, during the wedding of Elvire and Alphonse, it is seized with awe at the ceremony but, more importantly, surges with resentful anger around the rigorously disciplined troops that materialise the oppression of Spanish rule. Later, in vivacious tableaux of city life, we see the crowd at the harbour and in the market-place at Portici (see Ex. 17.1a, p. 356). In the final act, the crowd's energy has turned dangerous, which leads to the murder of its erstwhile leader. In the memory of Richard Wagner, this was a thrilling experience:

> The recitatives shot lightning at us; a veritable tempest whirled us on to the chorus-ensembles; amid the chaos of wrath we had a sudden energetic cry to keep our heads cool, or a fresh command to action; then again the shouts of riot, of murderous frenzy, and between them the affecting plaint of anguish of a whole people lisping its prayer.[22]

The increased attention to spectacle had a fundamental impact upon the composition of the operas themselves. With attention divided between individual characters and the broader world of which they are a part, the action acquired a tableau-like quality, in which the momentum generated by conflict between individuals is lessened and a stage-world that depicts the relationship of the individual to a potentially idyllic society is substituted. Take, for example, Rossini's *Guillaume Tell*. The main function of the opening act is to celebrate the oneness of humans with nature in a Rousseauist paradise. That oneness is violated by the forces of political oppression, the brutal incursion of Gesler's troops who burn the peasants' cottages and devastate the natural beauty of the landscape. The ultimate goal of the opera will be to regain this paradise. The setting, designed by Ciceri, emphasises harmony between humanity and nature, centring on two chalets nestled between a river in the foreground and the mountains in the distance. From the start, the staging has a static quality. Children are at play, villagers at work. The initial effect, one of an unfolding tableau, is augmented as the act progresses. Villagers process on to the stage carrying their instruments of work, vegetables, and flowers, prior to preparing for a pastoral wedding. Initially each character in the extensive cast expresses her or his feelings not as a component of a linear action but as an element in a mosaic, in a picture of a whole larger than any single individual. In the middle of the act the wedding with processional and ballet serves as an epitome of the idyllic, innocent environment. No character stands out musically from the *milieu* of the stage.[23] Even Arnold, whose inner struggle between love and patriotism is to form a major strand of conflict as the drama develops, does not express himself in a formal aria, but in accompanied recitative followed by a duet with Tell. Little is done in the first act to establish him as a major character. The action only begins an hour after the curtain rises with the onslaught of the brutal Austrian troops. The result is that for the rest of the opera the audience is engaged less with the fate of individual characters, more with the contrast between the pastoral life of the Swiss peasants and the oppression of the forces ruling them. As the action progresses, individuals as representative of different aspects of Swiss and Austrian society come to the fore, but the symbolic quality of the dramatic action, as established by the tableau of the opening act, prevails. The most memorable dramatic climaxes are not ones in which character confronts character. Rather they are realised in spectacular scenic effects, such as the gradual daybreak at the end of Act II, or in mass scenic events like the Rütli oath, or the confrontation between the Swiss and Austrians in Act III, in which Tell's heroism plays surprisingly little part, and in the concluding celebration of the union of nation and nature.

Guillaume Tell, unlike the Schiller play on which it is partly based, is an optimistic work reflecting values that, by the time of the opera's première, in 1829, were dated, something sensed by no less a person than Rossini himself, who abandoned his career in opera immediately after composing it. In its idealised fusion of nationalism and nature, *Tell* looks back to the earlier years of Romanticism, to a time in which social harmony might have seemed an attainable goal. However, in the strongest phase of European Romanticism, the only phase in which French culture fully participated, Rossini's optimism appeared naive. More to the taste of the public was the cynical worldliness of Byron and the alluring blend of eroticism and blasphemy that gave a unique frisson to the Gothic world of his poetry. This taste was catered to superlatively in *Robert le Diable* by Meyerbeer (see Chapter 11). Here, once again, dramatic characters are incorporated into the spectacle, though not this time as representatives of social forces, nor as pawns in the flux of political struggle, but as agents of a powerfully drawn ambience of ghostly intrigue and sexual despair. The décor of *Robert le Diable*, the last opera to be designed solely by Ciceri and heavily dependent on the atmospherics that Daguerre had pioneered in his dioramic theatre, seamlessly complemented Meyerbeer's score, which is rich with poignant, harrowing melodies and represents with no little depth and subtlety varying degrees of emotional trauma. *Robert le Diable* provided the Opéra with the most notorious moment in its history, when, during the celebrated scene at the end of Act III, Robert searches for a magic branch that will restore him to Isabelle, whom he wishes to marry. Eugène Scribe, the librettist, and Meyerbeer had first imagined the goal of his search to be Mount Olympus and were all for staging it with a ballet of shepherdesses and amoretti. Duponchel, however, persuaded them to set it in a medieval cloister, to a ballet performed by the ghosts of nuns who recreated in dance the irregular sexual acts they had committed in their lifetime. The result was a scandal and, predictably, a popular success. The scene combined to perfection the Byronic strains of Gothic decadence and sexual prurience:

> We are in an abandoned monastery. The walls are in ruins. On the silent tombs stand white statues. The mysterious rays of the moon light up the sad interior with pale clarity. All of a sudden, music can be heard. The creatures on the tombs raise themselves to their full height, the immobile statues return to movement and life. A crowd of mute shades glides through the arches. All these women cast off their nuns' costume, they shake off the cold powder of the grave; suddenly they throw themselves into the delights of their past life; they dance like bacchantes, they play like lords, they drink like sappers. What a pleasure to see these light women dancing in the middle of this doubtful light.[24]

The unsettling atmosphere intensified by unusual backlighting, the suggestiveness of the ballet, the resourceful use of the English trap, and the articulation of the fantasy world of the supernatural through concrete historical detail (the set was based on a cloister still standing today) made *Robert le Diable* one of the most popular operas of the nineteenth century.

Despite its inordinate success, few attempts were made to repeat the potent mix of *Robert le Diable*. In actuality, most grand operas were set in precisely specified periods of history that provided sites for dramatic confrontations highlighting the fragility of the individual's plight when caught up in historically momentous conflicts. For the audience of the time, however, such conflicts were far from being merely historical; they reflected, albeit indirectly, the volatile political circumstances of contemporary France where social and economic inequalities were still all too common a feature of society and revolutionary outbreaks constantly threatened. Civil violence and the damage it caused both to the individual and to the social fabric was the central theme of Meyerbeer's *Les Huguenots*. This is not a unified, harmonious world, which can be represented either literally or metaphorically in a single perspective. Multiple sets materialise the differences and divisions in a world torn by irreconcilable conflict between Catholics and Huguenots. The action covers a wide range of social territory, from the chateau of a Catholic count, to the country palace of the Queen, to Paris, where the last three acts are divided between the apartments of the aristocracy and the streets where brutality reigns. Social divisions, the cause of the conflict, are reflected in the changing scenes, at times even within a single set. For example, in Act III, the setting of the Pré-aux-Clercs, a meadow by the bank of the Seine, includes two taverns, one patronised by city folk, the other by the Huguenots, both of which lie adjacent to a Catholic church. As the intrigue of frustrated love and violated honour unfolds, emotional tensions between the characters implicate their religious differences. Played out against the precisely choreographed movement of dancers, gypsies, students, and townspeople moving between the symbolic areas of the set, the tension of the private intrigue is felt as a product of the broader social world. As the private action unfolds it is sensed as an epitome of the public world and the characters are understood as helpless victims of impersonal historical forces, even though those forces have been initially represented as emanating from themselves. The spectacle of the stage represents the conflict of the central characters projected onto a plane beyond that of the individual.

One of the most distinct contributions made by grand opera to the development of theatre was its introduction of specific experience on to the operatic stage. This process can be measured through the changes an opera of a different genre underwent when it was adapted to the requirements of the Opéra stage. For example, Donizetti's *Poliuto* was initially intended for the Naples Opera, but was banned due to the religious nature of the work. Eager to make his mark in Paris, Donizetti adapted it in collaboration with Scribe, and *Poliuto* was transformed into *Les Martyrs* (see Chapter 14). The changes were fundamental and sufficient to make two very different operas. *Les Martyrs* is substantially longer than *Poliuto*, for the length of a grand opera generally complemented the grandeur of its physical conception. Salvatore Cammarano's libretto for *Poliuto*, based on Corneille's *Polyeucte*, is about a Roman officer who converts to Christianity and is martyred for his beliefs. When Scribe reconfigured it, the logical workings of cause and effect were brought more to the fore. Scribe simplified the interestingly ambivalent triangle between Poliuto, his wife, Pauline, and her rejected suitor, Severo, in the first opera to craft a more conventional situation centred on the conflict between love and duty in the second. Notably he expanded the opportunity for spectacle, as Chapter 14 describes. *Poliuto* ends with the hero and his wife simply leaving their prison for the arena where they will be torn to pieces by the lions; in *Les Martyrs* the same action is scenically more specific. It begins with Pauline begging her father, the governor, to save Polyeucte's life. He refuses and she joins her husband in prison where she determines to die with him. From here they pass into the arena itself and the final curtain descends as the lions are about to be released. This sequence, resonant with biblical allusions, embodies in visual terms the spiritual passage of the characters from the quotidian world through a valley of darkness into a field of light, which stands for what Scribe and Donizetti clearly conceived of as the glory and release of death.

Towards alienation

Grand opera developed the art of theatrical spectacle a decade or two prior to the great productions of historical drama and opera that were staged by Charles Kean (1811–68) in London and Franz von Dingelstedt (1814–81) and the Duke of Saxe-Meiningen (1826–1914) in Austria and Germany. But so substantial was the work of Ciceri and Duponchel in grand opera and so widespread their influence, that they have as much claim to be regarded as precursors in the technical development of the modern theatre as do their later English and German counterparts.

Grand opera also initiated a dramatic theme that would be of central concern to spoken theatre later in the nineteenth century. The greatest irony attaching to grand opera as it was produced in Paris in the 1830s and 1840s was that audiences were drawn by the magnificence of the spectacle and vast resources were accordingly devoted to it. However, the rise of spectacle heralded the decline of the heroic individual. Most characters central to the action of grand opera – Masaniello, Robert, Valentine and Raoul in *Les Huguenots*, and Jean (John of Leyden) in *Le Prophète* – have their share of weakness and passivity and are either ignorant of the nature of the social and political world in which they find themselves, or corruptible by it. Ironically, the lavishness invested by the Opéra in the spectacle of power implied complicity in the values of power because it was intended to reify the Opéra as a national institution. But while the spectacle was impressive, even intimidating, the fragility of the emotionally labile individual tended to catch the sympathy of the audience and so cast the forces animating the spectacle into a negative light. In this regard, it is possible to see in the work of Auber, Halévy and Meyerbeer a first instance of one of the most persistent conflicts in modern drama, that of the individual pitted against the forces of an impersonal society, which has little concern for the integrity and freedom of human beings.

This was a theme to be taken on by the heirs of grand opera as it moved beyond the confines of Paris. In the heyday of Parisian grand opera, individual characters stood no chance of resisting or even having an impact upon the historic forces in which they were involved. The forces embodied in the spectacle prevailed, indeed the most spectacular effects of the complete production were usually reserved for the cataclysmic demise of the leading characters. The violated Fenella throws herself into the lava of Vesuvius at the end of *La Muette de Portici*, the lovers Valentine and Raoul are slaughtered in a withering fusillade in the final scene of *Les Huguenots*, Eléazar and Rachel in *La Juive* are ceremoniously boiled in oil, while virtually all characters, including the chorus, meet their end in the spectacular explosion of Münster palace at the end of *Le Prophète*. Wagner, who owed much to a genre he professed to despise, would resolve the conflict between the individual and the spectacular world by elevating the individual to a heroic status so that the spectacle became a metaphor for his own fate. While Brünnhilde is destroyed in the cataclysm that ends *Götterdämmerung*, it also glorifies her. Verdi took another path entirely. He retained the fallible and broken individual at the centre of his operas, though he invested this figure with firmer contours and a more vibrant inner life than did his predecessors. He sustained the public world of spectacle, even though his characters withdraw progressively from it. In so doing, Verdi extended the central theme of grand opera, but, as his career progressed, the implication of authority and oppression in the act of spectacle became increasingly emphatic. This leads to the crowning irony of grand opera. There is one work that stands today in the popular imagination as the supreme celebration of spectacle, of the spirit of grand opera itself, *Aida*. To this day, audiences pack the opera house drawn by the alluring sight of temple dances and the stirring extravaganza of the triumphal scene. But these occur only in the first half of the opera. *Aida*'s most affecting music and action occur in the second half and they are dedicated to representing the rejection of this world. Spectacle is progressively reduced until it is notable solely by its absence; the priests who condemn Radamès do not do it in view of the audience, they are heard in an off-stage chant only. The opera concludes with the voices of Aida and Radamès soaring from the grave above the lachrymose chant of Amneris and her companions. In the contrasts between ecstatic sounds of Verdi's greatest duet, Amneris' lament, and the stilled bodies of the temple dancers, we can hear the death-knell of grand opera. It was a knell that Auber and Meyerbeer had already rung, albeit unwittingly, in Paris, several decades before.

5 The chorus

JAMES PARAKILAS

The chorus puts the 'grand' into grand opera. In Act III of *Les Troyens*, when Berlioz moves the action from Troy to Carthage, he establishes the grandeur of Carthage by joining a supplementary chorus to the regular house chorus, so that there are 'two or three hundred voices, men, women, and children' to sing the National Song, 'Gloire, gloire à Didon' (Ex. 5.1). Beyond sheer size of chorus, it can be choral complexity that makes grand opera grand, as in the third-act finale of *Les Huguenots*, when the Catholic newly-weds, Valentine de Saint-Bris and the Comte de Nevers, are joined by dancing gypsies and a five-part mixed chorus of wedding guests as they make their way from the bank of the Seine on to a festive wedding boat, where a band is playing for them. These festive sounds make themselves heard against the very different sounds of the ongoing sectarian dispute emanating from the shore: the solo voices of the Catholic queen and of Valentine's disappointed Huguenot suitor Raoul and the choral voices of seigneurs of both faiths, as well as Catholic students (a two-part chorus of tenors) and Huguenot soldiers (a two-part chorus of basses) (Ex. 5.2).

These two numbers push the resources even of grand opera to their limits. Berlioz was dreaming, and he knew it: in the score of *Les Troyens* (a work he composed with no promise of performance) he allowed in a footnote that 'the supplementary chorus is not obligatory'. And even the score of *Les Huguenots*, which Meyerbeer wrote to order for what he called the 'immense resources' of the Paris Opéra, shows where a cut was made to the Act III finale in the original Paris production. Nevertheless, it was just those 'immense resources' of the Paris Opéra – and the immense effects that Meyerbeer and other composers achieved with them – that put dreams of choral grandeur into the head not only of Berlioz, but of composers from Rio to St Petersburg. If what springs to most people's minds today at mention of the term 'grand opera' is the triumphal scene of *Aida* or the coronation scene of *Boris* rather than any number from an opera written for Paris, that is still a tribute to the powerful impact made by the choral forces of the Paris Opéra four decades before those two operas were written.

Choral grandeur had a long tradition in Paris. From the mid-seventeenth century to the end of the 1780s, the French monarchy displayed its glory in an opera house whose choral as well as balletic and scenic effects no other

Example 5.1 Berlioz, *Les Troyens*, Act III scene 2, 'Chant national': 'Glory to Dido, our beloved queen'.

house could rival, while the Italian opera that dazzled the rest of Europe staked everything on the splendour of the solo voice.[1] When Paris became the centre first of a world-shattering revolution and then of Napoleon's militant imperial order, the nation's foremost opera house already had a chorus in place ready to step to the footlights in new roles embodying the power of a people to liberate itself and to form an invincible state.[2] Through endless changes of régime in the wake of the Revolution, the French government maintained the choral resources of the Paris Opéra on a scale that no other opera house in Europe could match. By the beginning of the grand opera period, around 1830, the Paris Opéra chorus numbered sixty or seventy; in 1836 – the year of the première of *Les Huguenots* – it numbered eighty-two. In the same year, by contrast, only five German opera houses could muster choruses of fifty to sixty; St Petersburg had a chorus of forty-eight; and the San Carlo in Naples – the great rival of La Scala among Italian houses – had a mere thirty-six.[3]

Numbers alone do not tell the whole story. In the 1830s and 1840s the choristers of the Paris Opéra, trained at their national Conservatory, could read music and learn difficult parts, while Italian choristers were generally untrained and learned their notes by rote. Furthermore, Italian choristers were badly-paid part-time singers who were rehearsed just enough to be able to hold their parts as they stood stock-still in a line, while the Paris choristers were full-time professional musicians who learned intricate blocking and

Example 5.2 Meyerbeer, *Les Huguenots*, Act III, finale: antiphonal and contrapuntal play shown between spatially separated ensembles.

movements as well as long and difficult musical parts by rehearsing each new work for months. (Berlioz at least had the self-restraint to imagine his hundreds of supernumerary choristers seated in tiers.) Furthermore the staging of such complex scenes as the wedding-boat finale in *Les Huguenots*, involving hundreds of singers, dancers and instrumentalists on a sectioned stage, relied on two innovations of the 1820s: the appointment of a *metteur en scène* to organise the staging, and the introduction of gas stage lighting,

Example 5.2

[Stage ensemble together with main orchestra]

which allowed the chorus to command attention while strolling, cowering, rioting or marching around the full extent of the stage.[4]

Other opera houses began to catch up with Paris in choral forces from the 1840s on, for the simple reason that their audiences demanded to see the grand operas that were the sensation of Paris. In fact, Parisian grand operas were designed for export. At the time a work was first produced in Paris, the materials needed to produce it elsewhere would be published: the full orchestral score (a form of publication rarely found except in France) and – because the Paris staging of a grand opera was as much a part of its 'text' as the score – the staging manual, or *livret de mise-en-scène*, which mapped every movement of the soloists, chorus and supernumeraries, in word and diagram, against the appropriate lines of the libretto (Fig. 12). Faced with the challenges that these publications spelled out, opera houses invested in new resources. In 1855, when La Scala first produced Meyerbeer's *Le Prophète*, its chorus suddenly swelled to one hundred members.

The composition of choruses changed along with their size. The Paris Opéra chorus was largely male: the seventy-six choristers in 1837 divided as twenty-nine sopranos, twenty-seven tenors and twenty basses. Those proportions permitted the unbalanced divisions of the chorus that the actions of Parisian grand operas required. In the scenes calling for the fullest resources of the house, a mixed-gender chorus representing a general population (in the Act III finale of *Les Huguenots* it is the wedding guests) is usually shown threatened by, or in contention with, or at least contrasted with, an all-male chorus representing a smaller, but power-wielding group: soldiers, priests, monks or retainers (in this case the Catholic students and Protestant soldiers). Opera houses in Berlin, Prague, Vienna and elsewhere that had largely female or evenly balanced choruses in the 1830s not only increased the size of their choruses as they attempted the new French repertory, but in doing so changed the balance within those choruses to a preponderance of men.[5]

The power of the people

With the chorus, as Simon Williams writes in his essay above, grand opera depicts 'the power of the crowd to determine public affairs', whether in riots, moments of mass resolve, social rituals or civic celebrations. It may seem that no musical subtlety is involved in rendering this power of the crowd: the librettist and composer just let the largest group of singers on stage throw their vocal weight around until they get what they want. In fact, one of the glories of grand opera – and one of its great contributions to the resources of world drama – lies in the endless musical variety and expressiveness with which the chorus is used to map the relationships and processes of mass political power.[6] The music of the quarrelling students and soldiers in *Les Huguenots*, for instance, makes clear that neither group is capable of routing the other at this point; they assault each other in evenly matched answering phrases. But even in their stalemate they demonstrate a terrible power: these very same phrases, by interrupting the wedding party, intruding on it, and distracting it from its celebratory singing, show how

Collection de Mises en Scène, rédigées et publiées par M. L. PALIANTI.

Propriété pour tous pays. — Réimpressions ou traductions interdites.

N°

LA
JUIVE

OPÉRA EN CINQ ACTES

De M. E. SCRIBE
MUSIQUE DE F. HALEVY

Représenté pour la première fois à Paris, sur le Théâtre de l'Opéra, le 23 février 1835.

ACTE PREMIER.

DÉCOR.

— Rideau de fond représentant la ville de Constance. —

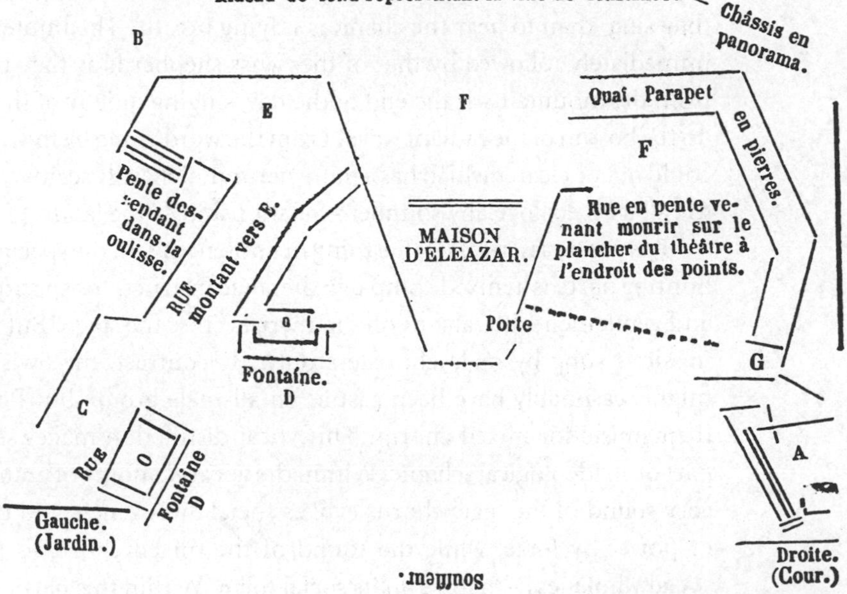

Un carrefour de la ville de Constance en 1414. — A droite A, le portail d'une église. On y monte par six ou huit marches de pierre. — La maison d'Eleazar, à l'angle d'une rue, fait face au public. — On y entre par le côté. — D. Fontaine.

INTRODUCTION.

Au lever du rideau les portes de l'église sont ouvertes.—Quelques groupes de femmes occupent les premiers plans.—Quelques-unes sont assises sur les marches de l'église.—

Figure 12 Page from a *livret de mise-en-scène* detailing scenery of all kinds, breaking up the stage space, and mentioning the backcloth ('Rideau de fond') being fitted as a 'Châssis en panorama', a curved frame which would heighten the illusion of reality. Other diagrams typically show exact positioning of soloists and choral subgroups.

small groups that pursue their quarrels at all costs can destroy the rituals (like weddings) by which a society assures its continuity.

Choral groups in grand opera may 'determine public affairs' in the sense that they take control of the stage by force of voice or arms: in the final act of *Les Huguenots*, for instance, when the Catholics have tired of trying to outshout the Huguenots, they exterminate them. But even a scene-setting chorus may 'determine' the outcome of the dramatic struggle in the sense that it shows the spectators where they will be justified in investing their sympathies. At the opening of the second act of Rossini's *Guillaume Tell*, for instance, two choral groups sing in succession, each bathing itself in the 'local colour' of the Swiss countryside and thereby claiming the right to control the destiny of that place. But the two groups make very unequal claims on the sympathies of the audience. First to appear is a hunting party of the Austrian overlords, exulting in treating nature as brutally as the audience has already seen them treat their Swiss subjects. Is there any greater pleasure, they sing, than to hear the chamois's dying breath? The hunters' chorus is immediately followed by that of the Swiss shepherds as they return home from the mountains at the end of the day, singing quietly of the sun fleeing 'to the bosom of the radiant wave'. From the words sung by the two groups, it could not be clearer which has a more natural – it hardly seems anachronistic to call it an ecologically sounder – relationship to the land.

The music asserts the same thing in its own way. To the spectators' eye the hunting party is a mixed company: the stage instructions specify that 'ladies and gentlemen with falcons on their wrists cross the stage'. But the hunters' music is sung by male choristers only. By contrast, the Swiss shepherds might reasonably have been cast as an all-male group, but Rossini writes their music for mixed chorus. This vocal distinction makes sense only as part of an ideological scheme. Within the vocal economy of grand opera, the very sound of the male chorus evokes social divisiveness and the assertion of power by force, while the sound of the mixed chorus is the voice of social wholeness – 'nature' in its social form. Within this particular opera – concerned from its overture to its nature-worshipping final tableau with the relationship of politics to the natural world – this scene, in its contrasts of sound as well as of sentiment, shows the Austrians to be as alienated from nature as the Swiss are at one with both nature and themselves.

The moral terrain of almost every grand opera is mapped in this way by divisions of the chorus that represent opposed nations, social groups or political factions; the individual characters then define their positions and their dilemmas by the ways they orientate themselves on the map that these groups delineate. In *Guillaume Tell*, for instance, the contrasting choruses of the Austrian hunters and Swiss shepherds set the stage for the Habsburg princess Mathilde to appear alone, having broken free of her hunting

Example 5.3 Rossini, *Guillaume Tell*, Act I, chorus and ensemble: 'Heaven, adornment of the world'.

[Orchestral accompaniment omitted]

companions, and in the aria 'Sombre forêt' (see p. 276) to cloak herself in the tranquil sounds of nature, aligning herself implicitly with the Swiss shepherds and thereby letting the audience know that though she is the highest-born Austrian character in the opera, her heart will soon carry her over to the cause of the Swiss. Equally, in the first act of the opera, when Arnold, torn between his patriotic feelings as a Swiss and his love for Mathilde, sings phrases at odds with the hymn being sung by all his fellow villagers ('Ciel, qui du monde es la parure', shown in Ex. 5.3), he is revealing his need for the severe test of character that will occupy him for two acts until he finds his way back into accord with his people.

Not that a chorus representing 'the people' in grand opera could itself be counted on to manifest a stable political position. In the eighteenth century the bourgeois court of public opinion (or the 'public sphere' as it is now called) first made its presence felt on the stage in an inert, if powerful, form: when a Count Almaviva or a Don Giovanni is required to show what Thomas Jefferson had recently called 'a decent respect to the opinions of mankind', there is little question of what those opinions might be. But grand opera was born, a couple of revolutions and half a century later, in the era of electoral politics, and its choral forces dramatise the political order of that era, ruled by the endless fluctuations to which popular opinion and action were prone. In fact, once the chorus had 'entered the narrative level of the principals',[7] as David Charlton has put it, opera could hardly have been dramatic at all if that chorus were not just as subject to changes of heart as any individual. Accordingly, though the chorus defines the political landscape within which the soloists act, the actions of the soloists are to a considerable extent devoted to manipulating and mobilising the opinions of a chorus that is by no means sure of its political intentions. In *Guillaume Tell*, for instance, the Swiss display no uniform courage in defence of their liberty.

Passive in more than one encounter with their feared Austrian rulers, they require Tell's exhortations and especially Tell's heroic example to galvanise them into action.

A contest for the direction of public opinion is characteristically at the heart of the grand opera plot, and the 'immense resources' of the opera house are pressed into enacting it. Auber's *La Muette de Portici*, the work of 1828 that set the terms for the development of the genre, is built entirely around the fluctuations of political opinion and loyalty that drive an insurrection against Spanish rule in seventeenth-century Naples. In the first number of the opera (the chorus 'Du prince, objet de notre amour'), the Neapolitan people complaisantly pay tribute to their foreign rulers; in the second act the protagonist Masaniello rouses his fellow fishermen to rebel against Spanish rule; in the third the people rise in revolt; in the fourth they hail Masaniello as their new ruler; and in the final act, left leaderless by Masaniello's death, they succumb once more to the Spanish forces. Though the contest over public opinion does not take the same course in every grand opera, certain types of choral scene or number appear in opera after opera to mark the stages and turning-points of the contest. The remainder of this chapter is devoted to an examination of these types.

Conspiracy scenes

In *La Muette de Portici*, the crucial mobilisation of opinion occurs through the sequence of musical numbers that occupies most of the second act. At the beginning of the act Masaniello counsels the fishing community (women included) in coded language and the lulling rhythms of a barcarole ('Amis, la matinée est belle') to keep their discontent quiet until the moment for revolt is ripe. The chorus signals its acquiescence by repeating the final phrases of each verse of his song; the process of persuasion could have no simpler or clearer musical representation than that. Next, Masaniello meets with his friend Piétro, and the two sing a martial duet (see Ex. 10.1) swearing death to the hated enemy – a tenor–baritone pledge-duet on the model that Verdi would follow in *La forza del destino*, *Don Carlos* and *Otello*. Then in the finale of the act, Masaniello calls back the fishermen (men only now) and leads them – at times phrase by phrase – in a revolutionary oath. When their wives and children arrive on the scene, Masaniello orders the men to keep the revolt secret even from them; men and women then join in a second barcarole, whose words celebrate the charms of singing a barcarole, though in some passages the men return to their theme of revolt even while singing in the same innocent-sounding phrases as the women (Ex. 5.4). By framing the entire act in barcaroles, Auber creates an enormous and complex musical structure that deftly conveys both the spreading of the Neapolitans'

Example 5.4 Auber, *La Muette de Portici*, Act II, finale: 'Let us sing the barcarole, to sweeten our brief leisure. Let us join forces against our enemies.' The words of this last sentence were added to the score and appear in neither the censor's MS libretto nor the published libretto of 1828.

conspiracy from one and then two leaders to a whole mass of followers and the wrapping of that conspiracy in the secrecy of feigned innocence.

The conspiratorial oath, which converts a relatively private political grievance into a mass commitment to action, is a commonplace of grand opera, with roots in French revolutionary drama (see n. 2) and imitations in Wagner's *Rienzi*, Verdi's *Ernani* and many other works spun off from the Paris grand opera tradition. In general, it is a musical sequence of gathering forces and mounting excitement that conveys the process by which conspirators find the courage for a dangerous enterprise in their solidarity with each other. Beyond that, however, there is no single model of musical form or dramatic effect at work among even the examples in the central repertory of grand opera. The 'Conjuration' in Act IV of *Les Huguenots*, for instance, differs from its immediate predecessors, the second-act conspiracy in *La*

Muette and the Rütli oath in *Guillaume Tell*, in that this conspiracy – of Catholics to slaughter defenceless Huguenot men, women and children – is designed to provoke a response very far from sympathetic. The audience's sympathies are attracted instead to three figures who stand to the side in the oath-taking: the chief conspirator's daughter, Valentine; her Huguenot lover Raoul, who observes the scene from a hiding place; and her Catholic husband Nevers, a man of honour who is expected to join in the conspiracy but declines.

His resistance in particular determines the musical shape of this con-spiracy scene, a giant rondo formed around three verses of the song 'Pour cette cause sainte' ('For this holy cause'). The first verse is sung as a solo by the Comte de Saint-Bris, the chief conspirator, calling on Nevers and other Catholic noblemen to take up arms under his command; as he repeats the second half of the verse, the others interject their responses, supportive from most of the noblemen, horrified from Valentine and Nevers. After Nevers refuses to join the others in swearing to take part and is consequently placed under guard – and as the stage fills with Catholics enlisted from every class – he proclaims his resistance to the conspiracy by singing a new verse of Saint-Bris's song, but to words very much his own: 'Ma cause est juste et sainte!' ('My cause is just and holy'). This time, when those present are all (except for Valentine) opposed to what the soloist is saying, their interjections begin before he has even finished his first phrase. When he finishes his verse, he is led away and Valentine leaves the stage, so that in the remaining sections of the scene there is no one on stage who might speak up in opposition to the horrible plan being launched. After orders have been given and monks have blessed the conspirators' weapons (see Ex. 11.1), the entire company of conspirators, whipped into a frenzy of bloodthirstiness, sings a third and final verse of 'Pour cette cause sainte' to Saint-Bris's original words, at full voice, in unison, and this time with no rejoinders of any sort. The effect is both thrilling – as conspiracy scenes always are when the accumulation of conspiring voices reaches its peak – and frightful: not just because this cause, unlike those of other conspiracy scenes, is anything but holy, but also because the return of music that had previously provoked such strong opposition, now heard in a totally unchallenged version, chillingly reminds the audience of how the voices of conscience have been silenced.

Processional and ceremonial scenes

If conspiracy scenes are choral scenes that exclude anyone not commit-ted to the cause, processional and ceremonial scenes are the opposite: the supremely inclusive moments of grand opera. In general, these are occasions when the people of a nation are brought together, often in a sacred space, to join with their religious authorities in affirming or celebrating the legitimacy of their secular authorities: the arrival of the Holy Roman Emperor at the Council of Konstanz in Act I of Halévy's *La Juive*; the coronation scenes in *Le Prophète*, *Boris Godunov* and Tchaikovsky's *The Maid of Orleans*; the Carthaginian festival in Act III of *Les Troyens*; the *auto-da-fé* scene in *Don Carlos*; the triumphal scene in *Aida*. What makes these scenes impressive is that the illusion of a whole nation on stage is created, not simply by huge numbers (the already large chorus, which usually plays the bystanders, supplemented by even larger numbers of marching supernumeraries), but by representatives of every estate and group of the society. The differentiation of these types is more the work of the costumer than of the composer. In 1835, when *La Juive* was first produced, Paris was agog at its opening procession scene: religious of several orders, clergy including sumptuously robed cardinals, hundreds of soldiers in real armour that had been cast for the production (Donizetti, who was present at the première, meant it when he wrote of this scene, 'It's not illusion, it's reality'[8]), and finally the Holy Roman Emperor with his attendants, all filing past a populace that was itself differentiated by sex, age, occupation and religion. The composer's role in such a scene was to unite all the groups into a single body, through the sound of a march sequence, and into a single voice that affirms the legitimacy of the nation's leaders through shouts of praise and sacred-patriotic hymns: 'Hosanna, Hosanna, gloire à l'Empereur!' in *La Juive*, 'Le voilà, le Roi Prophète! le voilà, le fils de Dieu!' in *Le Prophète*, 'Uzh kak na Rusi tsaryu Borisy, Slava!' in *Boris*, 'Gloria all'Egitto, ad Iside che il sacro suol protegge!' in *Aida*.

The affirmation may not be given willingly. In the processional scene that leads into the coronation scene of *Le Prophète*, for instance, the burghers of Münster curse the Prophet (Jean) and his soldiers under their breaths whenever they are not being cowed by the proximity of those soldiers into shouting praise to both him and them. This device was imitated in the *auto-da-fé* scene of *Don Carlos* as well as the first scene (just preceding the coronation scene) of *Boris Godunov*. In each case the signs of discontent among the people just before the pageantry is underway set the stage for an unexpected intrusion at the height of the pageantry that challenges the legitimacy and undermines the authority of those being praised and anointed.

It is the presence of the chorus – of the people – that makes these intrusions turning-points in each opera. In a private setting, it would hardly change the course of events for Fidès to recognise the Prophet Jean as her son, for the enslaved Aida to discover her father among the newly captured Ethiopians, for Joan of Arc's father to call her a sorceress, or for the guilt-ridden Tsar Boris to report that his soul is in mourning. But when these announcements are made at authority-affirming public ceremonies, it makes all the difference to the course of the drama how the announcement – or the announcement along with the challenged ruler's response – plays with the crowd. At occasions designed to make the solidarity of the ruled with their rulers seem irresistible, a single voice asserting that the rulers are not who or what they claim to be suddenly exposes instead the tense imbalance between the power of the rulers, who are few but defended by force, and that of the ruled, who are unarmed but many. In the wake of a hymn of praise that united the full chorus and all the soloists on stage, the audience now hears a complex debate in which the solitary voice of a ruler or leader is posed against the doubting or pleading or rebellious massed voice of the populace.

These moments when public ceremonies veer towards political chaos, like conspiracy scenes, tend to grow in musical force as they proceed. Interrupted ceremonies, though, generate tensions not found in conspiracy scenes: tensions about which side the loudest voice – that of the chorus – will weigh in on and what impact that voice will have. In the *auto-da-fé* scene of *Don Carlos*, the challenge to King Philip's authority is issued in the first place by the solitary voice of his son, Don Carlos, presenting six delegates of the Flemish people to make a plea that he knows his father does not want to hear. They in turn, speaking up for their people, set off the public debate that eventually draws in everyone on stage. They have an effect, then, like one of those solitary characters – Fidès or Joan of Arc's father – who bring a ceremony to a halt with their unwelcome words. What is more, the Flemish delegates sing their plea ('Is this the final hour for your Flemish subjects?') to a melody that sounds as if it should issue from a single voice: a rhetorical utterance in which steadily descending phrases suddenly surge upward, plain ones are capped with flourishes, and calm exposition leads to insistent pleading (Ex. 5.5). The remarkable thing is that this melody, in this situation, is sung by six basses in unison. It is typical of grand opera, actually, for a composer to experiment with sonority, and especially with the scale of sound production. This passage is nevertheless remarkable in that instead of working at the extremes of his resources, Verdi found a novel sonority in between two of them, the solo voice and the chorus – dissolving for an astonishing and affecting moment that basic distinction between the individual and the mass on which the musical vocabulary of grand opera apparently depends.

The delegates need their combined voices especially for the competition of overlapping sonorities that they set off: by the time they come to repeat their plea, they have to hold their own against both the hostile sound of the king, whose solitary voice is reinforced by a vocal bodyguard of six bass

Example 5.5 Verdi, *Don Carlos*, Act III scene 2, ensemble and finale: six Flemish deputies plead with the king to restore their country's peace and security.

friars, and the supportive sound of the king's other subjects, soloists and chorus, who crowd the stage. The upshot is characteristic of such moments of interrupted ceremony: the ruler, standing his ground against his challengers and his people, retains his control of the situation and his power. Public opinion, in raising its voice against the ruler, seems simply to expose its powerlessness. But the moment has nevertheless revealed a chasm in the political order that will need to be resolved, by means not yet foreseeable at this mid-point of the opera, before the work can be brought to a close.

Hymns of the true believers

The choral scenes considered here so far make it evident how pervasive hymns are in the expressive repertory of the grand opera chorus, whether they take the form of hymns to God (like the *a cappella Te Deum* heard from within Konstanz Cathedral that raises the curtain on *La Juive*) or patriotic anthems (like the 'national songs' in *Les Troyens* and *Aida*) or even hymns to nature (like the shepherds' chorus in Act II of *Guillaume Tell* and the final chorus of that opera). The hymn deserves consideration in its own right, however, for the special role it plays in one sub-set of the grand opera repertory: the crucial set of works that treats the theme of denominational strife. These include *La Juive*, *Les Huguenots*, *Le Prophète* and *Don Carlos* (all set during the Reformation or in comparable periods just earlier or later); Donizetti's *Les Martyrs* (his reworking for Paris of his own *Poliuto*, dealing with the persecution of the early Christians); and in the Russian repertory Musorgsky's *Khovanshchina* (dealing with what nineteenth-century Russians looked back on as their version of the Reformation). That the history of Christianity, and in particular the Reformation, provided such an important stock of plots for grand opera can be attributed to the fact that the religious strife of the Reformation offered nineteenth-century dramatists one of the few close historical models for the ideological political strife of their own era, the model of a society in which different denominations, or parties, of believers vie with each other for the allegiance of every member of the society and consequently for power over the society as a whole. The model, that is, related to those societies in Europe in the wake of the French Revolution where a person's political identity was no longer fixed at birth, but was a matter of choice and therefore susceptible to conversion.

In many of the operas that enact stories of religious strife, each side in the struggle – or at least the minority or oppressed side – is identified by its own hymn or hymns. The performance of such a hymn does not necessarily mark a decisive stage in the drama, as the conspiracy or ceremonial scene does; rather, the hymn may appear at several points in the opera, performing a somewhat different function each time. It may even appear in the overture, as the Lutheran hymn 'Ein' feste Burg' does in *Les Huguenots*, so that it becomes an emblem for the story as a whole (just as it is invariably the martyred minority that gives an opera of this kind its title). Donizetti did Meyerbeer one better by embedding in his overture to *Les Martyrs* a largely *a cappella* performance of the oppressed Christians' hymn by a chorus behind the curtain, so that the hymn seems both to belong to the action and to stand outside it. 'Ein' feste Burg' stands outside the drama of *Les Huguenots* in yet another sense: in both words and music it is an authentic Protestant hymn, if not an authentic Huguenot one. Its authenticity as a hymn may have added to its credibility as a denominational marker; the choice of a hymn from the wrong denomination, and in particular from a non-French denomination, may have been calculated to avoid both censorship and controversy in the nation for which the opera was created. Likewise Halévy could model phrases of his Seder music in Act II of *La Juive* rather closely on Jewish chants without fear of the censor, but he avoided any specific reference to the music of the established church in his *Te Deum* for Act I;[9] and Musorgsky in *Khovanshchina* respected the rules forbidding representation of the Orthodox clergy and its music, but sent his Old Believers to their deaths singing a reworked version of an authentic Old Believer hymn.[10]

A hymn, like a national anthem, unites a group – turns a crowd into a chorus – at the same time as it marks that group off from others. However, national anthems like 'Gloire, gloire à Didon' in *Les Troyens* or 'Gloria all'Egitto' in *Aida* tend to be sung at moments when the people of a nation think they can celebrate their nationhood undisturbed. Denominational hymns, by contrast, can act more like battle hymns, sung by the believers in the face of threats from rival groups. In Act I of *Les Huguenots*, for instance, 'Ein' feste Burg' is sung by Raoul's aged retainer, Marcel, to recall his young master to the Huguenot fold when he finds him carousing with a group of Catholic noblemen. While Marcel is singing it (making as striking a musical effect in a solo performance of a hymn as the six Flemish delegates in *Don Carlos* make in their joint 'solo' plea), Raoul explains to his Catholic companions that among Protestants this is 'the protector-song that we always sing at a moment of danger'. In Act I of *Le Prophète* the three Anabaptist militants use their hymn 'Ad nos ad salutarem undam' to punctuate the recruiting 'sermon' in which they persuade the peasants of Dordrecht to rise up against their oppressive lords; at the end of the number the peasants join with them in a powerful unison rendering of the hymn. The scene as a whole is therefore like a conspiracy scene in its accumulating power around a single theme. In Act I of *Khovanshchina* the Old Believers, members of a sect that refuses to accept either the religious reforms of the established Orthodox church or the political authority of any of the competitors for secular power, announce that they will sing a 'Song of Renunciation of This World', but the unaccompanied hymn ('Bozhe vsesil'nïy': see Ex. 5.6) that the men of the sect then perform – in an artificial 'religious' style that owes at least as much to previous grand opera as to any Russian sacred tradition – shows a militant involvement in, rather than a renunciation of, the politics of this world: as they sing the words 'Vanquish the Antichrist's powers to tempt us!' they turn to the Kremlin, letting everyone – including the audience – know what enemy they are pursuing. In all these cases the hymn is directed both inward and outward: inward in that it bolsters the resolve of the singers and of any true or potential believers who hear them, outward in that it puts the singers' enemies on notice of their power and determination.

At the end of each of these operas, the members of the minority denomination may still be singing a hymn, even (in *Les Huguenots*) the same identifying hymn, but their ambitions for power on the national stage

Example 5.6 Musorgsky, *Khovanshchina*, Act I, chorus, 'Bozhe vsesil'nïy': 'Almighty God, drive the words of the Crafty One from us!'

Meno mosso – mistico

appear defeated. In fact, they face extinction at the hands of their enemies. In this circumstance, the members of the group create an utterly ambiguous dramatic impression, depending on whether they are viewed as directing their hymn singing outwardly or inwardly, at their enemies or themselves. For operatic Huguenots or Old Believers or early Christians (in *Les Martyrs*) to acknowledge their beliefs to others by singing an identifying hymn is suicidal: their enemies seize on the identification as a pretext to slaughter them (or, in the case of *Khovanshchina*, to threaten them to the point that they burn themselves to death). But at the same time, the singing of the hymn supplies the community of singers with the solidarity that they need more than ever before to retain their faith while facing their deaths. Accordingly, the spectacle of a minority religious community going to meet death with its hymn on its lips seemed, to audiences in an age when the civil rights of religious minorities were widely debated rather than universally accepted, both an admirable display of unshakeable conviction and a horrifying example of fanaticism. In larger political terms, nineteenth-century opera-goers found in that spectacle a disturbing test of their feelings about any concerted resistance to the power of the people, as that power was embodied in the new and by no means established principle of majority rule. The chorus in grand opera, by singing the steadfast hymns of true believers as much as by shouting a whole people's uncertain praise of its rulers, allowed nineteenth-century audiences to recognise the irresolvable dissonances of their own political order.

6 Dance and dancers

MARIAN SMITH

My first conference with the director of the Grand Opéra showed me that the introduction of a ballet into *Tannhäuser*, and indeed in the second act, was considered a *sine qua non* of its successful performance. I couldn't fathom the meaning of this requirement . . .[1]

Thus Wagner begins his account of *Tannhäuser*'s rough treatment at the hands of the Parisians. His well-publicised frustration over the director's insistence that a ballet be added to this work, and his bitterness over the opera's rude reception by the ballet-mad Jockey Club, might lead one to believe that all ballet in Parisian opera of his day was imposed artificially from without. Yet it makes far more sense to regard the French insistence on creating ballets within grand opera as nothing more than an extension of the well-entrenched Baroque custom of mixing dancing and singing (in various proportions) within a single work. Indeed, opera and ballet had always gone hand in hand at the Opéra.

Ballet's vital role at the Paris Opéra in the nineteenth century was far from restricted, however, to the dances that were woven into grand operas. The same great ballet-masters who created choreographies for operas also created independent ballet-pantomimes, dramatic pieces from which singers were excluded, and which told a complete story in dance and mime. Without understanding ballet-pantomime, we cannot fully understand the role of dance in grand opera, because the latter absorbed so many elements from the former. Such narrative works had first appeared at the Opéra in the eighteenth century after a handful of reform-minded choreographers, such as Gasparo Angiolini and Jean-Georges Noverre (already active in London, Vienna, and elsewhere), had insisted that ballet could flourish not only in opera, but as a self-sufficient dramatic genre.[2] A series of successful ballet-pantomimes (for example *Psyché*, 1790; *La Dansomanie*, 1800; *Paul et Virginie*, 1806; *Clari*, 1820; *La Sylphide*, 1832; and *Giselle*, 1841) created at the Opéra by its first-rate choreographers, composers, librettists, dancers, set designers and machinists proves the wisdom of the reformers' foresight.[3] Yet, in spite of the obvious autonomy of the ballet-pantomime, nobody at the Opéra during the period under scrutiny here had conceived the notion of presenting exclusively these independent pieces throughout an evening. Ballet-pantomimes were always performed before or after opera, and continued to be so until well past the mid-nineteenth century. A check-list of titles will be found in the Appendix to this chapter.

Table 6.1 *The performance schedule at the Paris Opéra, January 1843*

Sunday 1	*La Reine de Chypre* (5-act opera by Halévy with ballets)
Monday 2	*Le Guerillero* (2-act opera by Ambroise Thomas), *La Jolie fille de Gand* (3-act ballet-pantomime, music by Adam)
Wednesday 4	*La Favorite* (4-act opera by Donizetti with ballets)
Friday 6	*Le Dieu et la bayadère* (2-act opera by Auber; a singer and a dancer in leading roles); *La Sylphide* (2-act ballet-pantomime, music by Schneitzhoeffer)
Sunday 8	*La Juive* (5-act opera by Halévy with ballets)
Monday 9	*Le Vaisseau fantôme* (2-act opera by Louis Dietsch); *Giselle* (2-act ballet-pantomime, music by Adam)
Wednesday 11	*La Muette de Portici* (5-act opera by Auber, with ballet-dancer in mimed leading role)
Thursday 12	Benefit performance for pension fund
Friday 13	*Le Guerillero* (as above); *La Jolie Fille de Gand* (as above)
Monday 16	*La Reine de Chypre* (as above)
Wednesday 18	*Le Philtre* (2-act opera by Auber); *Giselle* (as above)
Friday 20	*La Favorite* (as above)
Sunday 22	*Les Huguenots* (5-act opera by Meyerbeer with ballets)
Wednesday 25	*Le Vaisseau fantôme* (as above), *La Gipsy* (3-act ballet-pantomime, music by François Benoist, Thomas and Marc-Aurèle Marliani)
Friday 27	*Le Serment* (2 acts of the 3-act opera by Auber), *La Gipsy* (as above)
Monday 30	*Guillaume Tell* (3 acts of the 4-act opera by Rossini[a], with ballets)

[a] It was not uncommon for operas to be presented only in part. For instance, the last act of Auber's *Gustave III*, with its popular ball scene, was often performed by itself; so was Act III of Rossini's *Moïse*.

Thus did the Paris Opéra offer both singing and dancing at every performance. Table 6.1 shows this by reproducing the schedule for January 1843.

What were the artistic ramifications of throwing together, under one roof, so many creative artists expert in both opera and ballet, and having singers and dancers perform together on a regular basis; of having the choreography, sets, costumes and machines of opera and ballet-pantomime designed by precisely the same people; of having the librettos and scores of ballet-pantomime created by artists experienced in both genres? For representative examples, one might name the composers Adolphe Adam and Ferdinand Hérold, who were particularly adept with ballet and opéra comique, or the librettists Eugène Scribe and Vernoy de Saint-Georges, who between them supplied librettos for more than twenty operas and ballet-pantomimes at the Opéra during the July Monarchy.[4]

Perhaps the most obvious consequence was that ballet-pantomime and opera had a great deal in common. For example, both favoured complicated plots, and usually set their action in Europe and its colonies in the medieval and early modern periods. They relied on many of the same devices and situations, such as nobles appearing in disguise, a man loving a woman above his station, and so forth. They made frequent use of on-stage or off-stage musicians and featured either the *corps de ballet* or the chorus quite prominently, populating the Opéra's stage with the same types of minor characters: peasants, pilgrims, soldiers, courtiers, penitents, masquers and huntsmen, to name only a few. Both tended to switch frequently between styles and moods – from noisy festive celebrations to poignant soliloquies or from sedate gatherings to rancorous confrontations, unfolding in such a way as to afford the audience plenty of variety in mood, pacing and musical style. Both featured sets and costumes designed to look 'authentic' down to the last detail. Both consisted of dramatic action punctuated with danced segments. Both made use of spectacle, and tended to feature magnificent processions and breathtaking special effects, such as the flying sylphides in *La Sylphide*, the instantaneous transformation of flowers into flame-breathing reptiles in Aumer's ballet-pantomime-féerie *La Belle au bois dormant*, the eruption of Mt. Vesuvius in Auber's *La Muette de Portici* or the burning lake of Hell in the ballet-pantomime *Le Diable amoureux* (see p. 107 for details). Characters in both types of work, too, engaged in monologues and conversations (whether in sung speech or in mime), and audiences could buy librettos that explained what was going on. Opera librettos laid out all the sung words, with a few stage directions; ballet-pantomime librettos provided detailed, scene-by-scene descriptions of the action, occasionally quoting the actual words or sentences that the characters were supposed to be 'saying' through gesture.

Personalities and dance styles

Grand opera and ballet-pantomime at the Opéra also deployed many of the same dancers, their ballet roles drawing from a single pool of high-ranking soloists and *corps de ballet* dancers. Lise Noblet (1801–52), for example, a leading ballerina of the 1820s and 1830s known for her great lightness, the elegance in her poses, and the voluptuous quality in her movements, appeared in the most important ballet-pantomimes of her day, assuming, for instance, the title roles in the ballet-pantomimes *Cendrillon* and *Clari*, as well as creating unnamed solo roles in operas, grand or otherwise: Rossini's *Le Siège de Corinthe* (choreographed by P. Gardel), his *Guillaume Tell* (Aumer), Ginestet's *François Ier à Chambord* (A. Vestris), Meyerbeer's *Robert le Diable* (P. Taglioni), Auber's *Gustave III* (P. Taglioni), Cherubini's *Ali-Baba* (Coralli), Mozart's *Don Giovanni* (Coralli) and Halévy's *La Juive* (P. Taglioni). She also created the role of Fenella, the 'mute girl' in *La Muette de Portici*, which owed no small part of its great acclaim to her exquisite miming. Indeed, as we shall see in Chapter 9, this role calls for no dancing at all.

Lucien Petipa (1815–98) found himself one of the few male dancers whose fame approached that of his female counterparts in Paris during the heyday of grand opera, for the *danseur* had been pushed aside in favour of the

Figure 13 Lise Noblet had been appearing at the Opéra professionally since 1819; here, wearing the attributes of irrationality, she dances the role of La Folie (madness, eccentricity) in Auber's *Gustave III*. Drawn by Wattier, engraved by Mme König, 1833.

danseuse in French choreography (though he maintained his powers in Italy and Denmark[5]). After making a début in Donizetti's *La Favorite* in 1841, Petipa created roles in the operas *La Reine de Chypre* (1841, choreographed by Mazilier) and *L'Ame en peine* (Flotow, 1846, choreographed by Coralli), and the ballet-pantomimes *Giselle* (1841, Coralli and Perrot), *La Jolie fille de Gand* (1842, Albert), *Le Diable à quatre* (1845, Mazilier), *Paquita* (1846,

Mazilier) and *Betty* (1846, Mazilier). As the Opéra's ballet-master from 1860 to 1868, Petipa contributed choreography to the operas *Sémiramis* (the 1860 production of Rossini's opera), *Tannhäuser* (1861), *La Reine de Saba* (1862), *Don Carlos* (1867) and *Hamlet* (1868).

Marie Taglioni (1804–84), perhaps the most famous ballerina of the nineteenth century, astonished audiences with her highly individual style (developed painstakingly under the tutelage of her father, Philippe Taglioni), marked by a lightness that seemed to challenge the laws of gravity. Historians have focused mainly on her ethereal qualities in the title role of *La Sylphide* and her breakthrough *pointe* technique (to dance *en pointe* – 'on point' – is to dance on the extreme tip of the toe). This technique seems to have begun in ballet shortly before 1820. At first, no special point shoes existed; the modern point shoe (with toes stiffened with glue) began to appear in the 1860s. Taglioni was also well-beloved for her great skills in 'national' or 'character' dance, a sort of theatricalised folk dance (discussed below) that was tremendously popular in ballet well into the twentieth century;[6] her gypsy dancing in *La Gitana*[7] caused great sensations in St Petersburg and London. At the Opéra, she created leading roles in the ballet-pantomimes *La Sylphide* (1832), *Nathalie* (1832), *La Révolte au sérail* (1833) and *La Fille de Danube* (1836) (all choreographed by her father), and in Auber's opera-ballet *Le Dieu et la bayadère* (1830), which is discussed later. She also created important solo roles in the grand operas *Guillaume Tell* and *Robert le Diable*, where she danced as Héléna, the mother superior in Act III, eliciting ecstatic responses: see p. 346.

Later dancers of 'superstar' status at the Opéra, however, instead of joining the regular casts of new operas, confined most of their opera performances to their own débuts (which required presentations in three separate works) and guest appearances. In this manner dancers added new interpretations to established grand operas. Fanny Elssler (1810–84: see Fig. 18, p. 155), for example, gave a début performance at the Opéra in *Gustave III* in 1834, and went on to a brilliant career at the Opéra (and across Europe and in North America), gaining particular fame for her character-dancing (especially the *cachucha*, a Spanish dance calling for a highly flexible torso and the use of castañets) and her superb miming. Charles de Boigne's account of her *cachucha* is reproduced on p. 106 below. Of her 1837 rendering of Fenella in *La Muette de Portici*, Théophile Gautier wrote as follows:

> rejected by the guards of the chapel where her seducer's marriage is taking place, she sits down on the ground and lets her head fall into her hands as she dissolves into a flood of tears. She could have been a figure by Bendemann, the painter of *Jeremiah*, or one of the Trojan women of Euripides. She was as beautiful as an antique statue. Her Neapolitan

costume, which was completely authentic and severe, fell in large austere
folds that were incomparably stylish . . . Mlle Fanny plays her role without
any show of coquetry towards the audience, concentrating entirely on her
desperate situation . . .[8]

Possessed of 'strength, lightness, suppleness and an originality of style
which placed her at one bound between Elssler and Taglioni',[9] Carlotta
Grisi (1819–99) made her début performance at the Opéra with Lucien
Petipa in *La Favorite* in 1841, went on to create title roles in Adam's *Giselle*
and *La Jolie fille de Gand*, Bergmuller's *La Péri* and Louise Bertin's opera
La Esmeralda (first given in 1836), and also distinguished herself as a fine
character-dancer. Lucile Grahn (1819–1907), the 'tall, slender, loose-jointed
and well formed'[10] Danish ballerina whose lightness rivalled that of
Taglioni, made one of her first Opéra appearances in *Don Giovanni*, found
much success in the title role of *La Sylphide* among many other ballets, and
later, while serving as ballet mistress at the Munich Court Opera from 1869
to 1875, helped Wagner with some of his opera stagings (e.g., *Das Rheingold*
and *Die Meistersinger von Nürnberg*), and choreographed the Bacchanale
scene in *Tannhäuser*.[11] These dancers, like many others, performed in opera
houses outside Paris (e.g., in the French provinces and abroad), in ballet-
pantomimes, operas and in short divertissements, many of them in the
character-style, that shared the bill with opera. Jules Perrot and Carlotta
Grisi were particularly famous for their 'character' divertissements, including a *zapateado* and an 'original *Tarantella* directly imported from Naples'.[12]
Equally popular was the *Pas de quatre* choreographed by Perrot for Taglioni,
Grisi, Grahn and the great Italian ballerina Fanny Cerrito, the première
of which took place between the acts of Donizetti's *Anna Bolena* at Her
Majesty's Theatre in London in 1845.

Clearly, audiences often went to the opera house for the multiple pleasures afforded by singing and dancing – often by celebrity performers – just
as they often did in the eighteenth century. Moreover, they were familiar with
the three distinct styles of movement in the dancer's vocabulary: narrative
pantomime; classical (or academic) dance; and 'character' dance, as mentioned above. Some sense of the contrast between 'classical' or 'academic'
dance (based on codified steps, movements and positions, and sometimes
copying classical statues) and 'character' dance (based on folk dance) may
be gained by reading these comparisons by Théophile Gautier, dating from
1830 and 1839:

A woman who appears . . . to pose before your opera glasses in the glare of
eighty footlights with no other purpose than to display her shoulders,
bosom, arms and legs in a series of attitudes that show them off to best
advantage seems amazingly impudent if she is not as beautiful as [the

Graces] . . . Dolores [Serral] and [Mariano] Camprubí have nothing in common with our own dancers. They have a passion, a vitality and an attack of which you can have no idea . . . There is nothing mechanical in their dancing, nothing that appears copied or smacks of the classroom . . .[13]

[At the time of her début] we explained how superior were [Dolores Serral's] suppleness, vivacity and Andalusian passion to the geometrical poses and the right-angled *écarts* of the French school. At that time people of taste found [her dancing] bizarre, alien, incompatible with the traditions of good schooling and the rules of good taste. The very mention of the word *cachucha* made wigs stand on end and set the [pocket violins] of ballet-masters screeching.[14]

Ballets in operas

Every four- or five-act opera at the Paris Opéra featured at least one ballet, sometimes called a divertissement, created by one of the Opéra's ballet-masters and usually featuring both solo and ensemble choreography. No fixed rules dictated where these ballets were placed within the opera. More-over the ballets themselves, like vocal numbers, were subject to alteration, and were sometimes shortened if deemed less than stageworthy. They were also subject to the tastes of the ballroom (see below), so that their steps were sometimes re-choreographed to accommodate the talents of débutants or visiting dance luminaries. Thérèse Elssler, Fanny's sister, made her début as dancer and her own choreographer in a *pas de deux* in the ball scene of *Gustave III* in 1834, for example; Lola Montez danced *L'Ollia* and *Las Boleras de Cadiz* in the ball scene of *Don Giovanni* during a brief sojourn in Paris in 1844.

Certain rules, however, did apply to the operatic ballet. First, because of fairly strict ideas about verisimilitude, the dancing was always externally diegetic, that is, perceived as actual dancing by other characters. Operatic ballets therefore were designed to arise naturally from the action (celebrations of battle victories, or masked balls, for instance). The dancers, more-over, were always of a type supposed likely to dance in real life (gypsies, slave girls, peasants celebrating weddings, ball-goers, hired entertainers). One observer noted the consequent analogies between social and theatrical dance, connections which are discussed in more detail below.

> It is the same on stage as it is at our society balls; the attention there is concentrated on the dancers. One doesn't ever pay attention to the grandmothers and the old men, because they aren't dancing at all. And if they did dance, they would be ridiculous. To make the heroes of modern history jump around is utterly contrary to illusion. Serious medieval topics lend themselves even less to *pirouettes* and *entrechats*.[15]

Table 6.2 *Rationales for dancing and divertissements in selected grand operas (relevant act is indicated in brackets)*

1829	*Guillaume Tell* (I)	Village wedding celebration
	Guillaume Tell (III)	Tyrolean peasants are forced to dance during festivities celebrating Austria's dominion over Switzerland
1831	*Robert le Diable* (II)	Dances are performed at a tournament
	Robert le Diable (III)	Ghostly nuns dance by moonlight in an attempt to lead Robert into temptation
1833	*Gustave III* (I)	A ballet-master conducts a dance rehearsal for Gustave's opera *Gustaf Wasa*
	Gustave III (V)	A masked ball is given at the royal palace
1835	*La Juive* (I)	Onlookers dance spontaneously as the emperor and victorious soldiers march into the city of Konstanz
	La Juive (III)	Léopold's victory over the Hussites is celebrated
1836	*Les Huguenots* (III)	Roving gypsies dance spontaneously on the banks of the Seine
	Les Huguenots (V)	The wedding of Marguérite de Valois and Henri de Navarre is celebrated
1838	*Guido et Ginevra* (I)	At a village festival, Diana the huntress is honoured
1840	*Les Martyrs* (II)	The new proconsul, Sévère, is honoured
1840	*La Favorite* (II)	Victory over the Moors is celebrated
1843	*Dom Sébastien* (II)	Zayda's homecoming is celebrated
1844	*Marie Stuart* (III)	A masque is performed in honour of Marie (Queen of Scots)
1849	*Le Prophète* (II)	Villagers dance at Jean's inn
	Le Prophète (III)	Ice-skaters bring supplies to the Anabaptists' camp and then entertain the soldiers by dancing
1855	*Les Vêpres siciliennes* (II)	Sicilian peasants dance the tarantella; among them are brides-to-be, whom French soldiers kidnap
	Les Vêpres siciliennes (III)	A ballet ('The Four Seasons') is performed for the Duke of Palermo

Wagner's complaints notwithstanding, librettists rationalised the ballets carefully so that they would fit into the opera's story, even if they did not usually figure in the main action of the opera (see Table 6.2). Some ballets, of course, did help drive the opera's narrative forward: angry insurrectionists are spurred on by events taking place during the ballets in *Les Vêpres siciliennes* Act II and *Guillaume Tell* Act III; the morally indecisive title character faces a terrible temptation in the ballet of *Robert le Diable*, Act III. Yet even ballets taking place during respites from the main action could function dramatically. Some could reflect by analogy a crucial aspect of the plot: thus the masque performed as a divertissement for the title-character in Louis Niedermeyer's 1845 opera *Marie Stuart* – a depiction of Esther triumphantly replacing the fallen queen Vashti – echoed Queen Mary's hopes in her struggle with Queen Elizabeth. Some could exert dramatic irony, as in *Les Huguenots* Act V, a gay celebration which, unknown to its revellers, would come to a ghastly conclusion. Ballets of the light-hearted variety could also counterbalance the heavy, often bloody, scenes upon which so many grand operas relied – the skaters' ballet in *Le Prophète* provides in this way a happy (though dramatically relevant) respite from the growing tensions generated by John of Leyden's rise to power.

Example 6.1 Jean-Madeleine Schneitzhoeffer, 'Ecossaise' from *La Sylphide*, edited from a manuscript orchestral part.

By presenting 'character' dance, moreover, an operatic ballet could help set the locale in a convincing manner. This was no trifling achievement: a chief attraction of these works was their ability to transport audiences to distinctive places by using as much seemingly realistic detail as possible. Gautier's assessment of Fanny Elssler's tarantella in the ballet-pantomime *La Tarentule* (1839), music by Casimir Gide, gives some sense of the audience's strong association of movement vocabulary with locale, and indeed, the potency of the belief that movement style was essential to one's place of birth (akin to Herder's conviction that 'Climate, water, air, food and drink, they all affect language . . .'[16]):

> Mlle Elssler . . . dances a tarantella which gladdens and excites you. In turn coquettish, fiery, witty, she portrays with wonderful intelligence that ardent character which is found only on the volcanic soil of Italy . . .'[17]

Dancers in opera would thus serve as an extension of the elaborate *mise-en-scène*, providing living, moving scenery which further sharpened the audience's sense of utter removal from its everyday life to an unfamiliar place. And composers frequently contributed to the effect by supplying dance music tailor-made to evoke the locale in question. Dance music, as Pietro Lichtenthal wrote in his musical dictionary of 1826, 'must be characteristic and analogous to the locale where the action takes place, thus the dance airs of the Indians, the Scots, the Hungarians must have the character of the music of their countries . . .'[18] Example 6.1 shows a stylised Scottish dance from 1832.

Mixing mute and sung roles at the Opéra

Dancers regularly appeared in operas, but in three works created around 1830 they were actually cast in principal roles, playing opposite singing characters. In *La Muette de Portici* the mute peasant girl's tragic love affair with Alphonse, the viceroy's son, plays its part in the popular insurrection against the Spanish in the Naples of 1647. In Auber's *Le Dieu et la bayadère* a mute Hindu temple dancer falls in love with a mysterious stranger who is being persecuted by a cruel despot; in *La Tentation* (officially styled a 'ballet-opéra'), a spectacular retelling of the Temptation of St Anthony, the four principal roles are equally divided between singers and dancers.[19] In order to maintain standards of verisimilitude, some of the silent characters' gesturing was carefully rationalised, whereas such precautions were deemed unnecessary in the ordinary ballet-pantomime: thus, Auber's *bayadère* had newly moved to a foreign country and could comprehend but not yet speak its language; his mute girl of Portici was assumed to have been silenced by 'a terrible event' (see Chapter 9 n. 22).

Though the hybrid approach to casting taken in these popular works is not typical of the Opéra's output during the whole age of grand opera, it is nonetheless noteworthy, for it helps demonstrate further the Opéra's responsiveness to trends in the Boulevard theatres, which had often featured mute characters alongside singing (and sometimes speaking) ones in the casts of vaudevilles, *mélodrames* and pantomimes in the 1820s: some are mentioned in Chapter 9.[20] The influence of opéra comique upon these mixed-cast works is also apparent, silent characters having featured therein for some time. Hybrid casting also demonstrates that ballet and opera characters – who, after all, shared the Opéra's stage at every performance – were comfortably capable (occasionally, at least) of face-to-face 'conversations', in which phrases of sung recitative alternated with mime accompanied by pantomime music. Consider, for example, the dialogue in Example 6.2 between princess Elvire and Fenella, in which the latter is asked to identify her betrayer. In this case the rhythm of the pantomime music offers the syllabification and expression of the text that the silent character is conveying

Example 6.2 Auber, *La Muette de Portici*, Act I scene 5: Fenella mimes: 'He who deceived me . . . he who gave me this scarf . . . he who betrayed me . . .' Elvire: 'Well? Who is the guilty one?' Fenella (pointing): 'It is he!'

in gesture ('C'est lui' ['It is he']), a musical tracing of unspoken text. This technique was often used in ballet-pantomime.

Later, as the ballet-pantomime gave way to more abstract danced works, and ballet characters broke away from the practice of conveying specific words, they ceased to share a language with opera characters. So subsequent opera-ballets (e.g., Rimsky-Korsakov's *Mlada* (1892) and Stravinsky's *Le Rossignol* (1914)), though few in number, tended to cast ballet dancers as other-worldly spirits, or birds, or shades; as creatures incapable of and uninterested in language, instead of as flesh-and-blood humans who readily communicated with characters who intoned language. Yet, clearly, it still made sense around 1830 at the Opéra to create ballet characters who shared a language with singing characters. The strong presence of mute characters at the Opéra – appearing every night in ballet or ballet-pantomime and often using elaborate gestures to convey ideas – helped make this sort of mixed casting feasible.

Between ballet and the ballroom

The close connections between prevailing social-dance customs and theatrical ballet can scarcely be overstated. Most obviously, the music composed for ballet at the Opéra sounded quite like that encountered in the ballroom: a chain of dances, in a variety of dance metres, often simply and regularly phrased, with prominent melodies and light accompaniments, often closing out with a *galop*. Particular melodies frequently migrated from the Opéra to the ballroom and parlour, often in the form of quadrille arrangements. In fact, 'Most Parisians almost always dance an opera before they see it', observed one critic.[21] In this spirit, public dance events could be rendered 'theatrical', bringing them closer to staged dance and imparting to ordinary people a vivid sense of participation in the action depicted in an opera. Maribeth Clark has unearthed a marvellous example of this: music from *Les Huguenots* arranged as a quadrille and played at a summer dance garden entertainment in 1836, in which fireworks were set off during the final figure, mimicking the violent closing scene of the opera. An eyewitness described the experience of the public dance thus: 'the bandstand, the pavilion, the trees, all are enveloped at the same time in a rapid explosion, the flames of which take on different colours successively while one hears firearms sounding from all directions.'[22]

It is probable that even the choreography of the on-stage ensemble dances, as opposed to the more virtuosic *pas de deux* and *pas de trois*, was closer in skill level to social dance of the era (which required instruction and entailed fairly complicated ballet steps) than we generally acknowledge.

Consequently, it is hardly surprising that audience members occasionally tried to make their way to the stage and join in the *galop* of the ball scene in Act V of *Gustave III*, so accustomed were they to throwing themselves into the fray under similar conditions in social-dance settings.

Not even the more virtuosic steps devised for the soloists in these divertissements, however, would have struck an audience as being the exclusive province of theatrical dance. For it was customary in ballrooms for professional ballet dancers to perform specially choreographed divertissements, sometimes entailing abstract numbers such as 'The Four Seasons', or 'The Four Quarters of the World', in which each season or region would be represented in a solo *pas*. Choreographers then transferred this custom to the stage by including such variations as entertainments for fictional noble dinner guests, for example, 'The Four Seasons' performed for the Duke of Palermo in Verdi's *Les Vêpres siciliennes*. So the Opéra's spectators were likely to find even in these abstract operatic ballets a point of reference from their own personal experiences, instead of seeing them, as we might do today, as stylised and slightly puzzling intrusions.

The character-dances that so frequently cropped up both in ballet-pantomime and in operatic ballets also constituted a vital part of the social-dance scene in Paris. They were eagerly executed by everyday Parisians, who flocked to amateur dance studios for instruction after the wild success in 1834 of four visiting Spanish dancers (Dolores Serral, Mariano Camprubí, Manuela Dubiñon and Francisco Font) recently hired at the Opéra both for its carnival balls and in *La Muette de Portici*. Their performances were 'brilliant, alive, poetic, strongly coloured, captivating, full of charm, seduction, passion and fire'.[23] Character-dances were frequently included in hired ballroom entertainments as well. Elssler and Taglioni, for example, danced a variety of them at an Opéra ball during Carnival season in 1834/35:

> the great success obtained at the last Carnival [i.e. the appearance of the four Spanish dancers in January 1834] gave rise to the idea of seeking a new success with an array of national dances of the different peoples of Europe, and in some local dances from our southern provinces. Thus we will see [at a Carnival ball] the execution, by the top ballet dancers of the Opéra, led in turn by Mlles Taglioni and Elssler, of the *pas styrien*, the mazurka, the bolero and the fandango from Andalusia, Neapolitan tarantellas and dances of the Languedoc region, *las Treias* and *lo Chibalet* . . .[24]

Voyeurism and ballet

Ogling the *danseuses* at the Opéra – sometimes through 'cannon-sized' binoculars[25] – was a favourite Parisian sport, practised unabashedly by

Un habitué de l'Opéra.)

Figure 14 'A regular at the Opéra' (anonymous artist, November 1844): as a season-ticket holder he is permitted to go backstage and stands in the wings. Other images similarly published in *L'Illustration* show regulars sitting in their boxes, armed with even bigger binoculars.

the Jockey Club and other men, and frequently mentioned in the press. Théophile Gautier memorialised the phenomenon thus:

> And how attentive everyone is! Look at them levelling and focusing their binoculars, not those light country binoculars that fit into a jacket pocket, but large military binoculars, twin monsters, optical howitzers that will make future generations think we were a race of giants![26]

Even the gauzy below-the-knee Romantic tutu, the costume of sylphs and Wilis which is often read today as a symbol of purity, served quite the opposite purpose in some nineteenth-century erotic literature, as Tracy C. Davis has pointed out.[27] 'National' costumes, too, could strike the spectator as erotic. Consider this description of Fanny Elssler's *cachucha* by Charles de Boigne:

> Those swayings of the hips . . . those provocative gestures, those arms
> which seemed to reach out for and embrace an absent being, that mouth
> which asked to be kissed, the body that thrilled, shuddered, and twisted,
> that seductive music, those castañets, that unfamiliar costume, that short
> skirt, that half-opening bodice, all this, and, above all, Elssler's sensuous
> grace, lascivious abandon and plastic beauty were greatly appreciated by
> the opera-glasses of the stalls and boxes . . .[28]

In any case, the managers of the Opéra capitalised on the sex appeal of the *danseuses* by admitting members of the Jockey Club and selected male patrons (deputies, peers, upper ministerial employees, journalists, 'in a word . . . all the people whose relationships could be useful or at least agreeable' to the Opéra director[29]) to the *foyer de la danse*, the warm-up studio where the female dancers stretched their bodies before curtain-up. In this cosy space, wealthy and powerful men could make the acquaintance of their favourite *danseuses*, flirtations sometimes playing themselves out in more private venues under a system of 'prostitution légère'.

Indeed, many female dancers found prostitution ('légère' or otherwise) tempting because, without outside income, many of them were too destitute to pay for food, fuel and lodging.[30] Of the many dancers at the Opéra, only the 'premier sujets' were paid well. So inadequate were the *corps* dancers' salaries, in fact, that many of them suffered from malnutrition. (Most dancers at the Opéra came from the lower classes or from theatrical families and, sadly, were accustomed to such harsh working conditions.) As Julie Daubié's famous study of poor women in France (*La Femme pauvre au XIXe siècle*, 1869) had concluded, during the mid-nineteenth century women could not achieve financial independence even when working full-time, because they were so terribly underpaid. That women working on the stage had an opportunity to attract patrons, and hence increase their income, was widely recognised. Daubié even accused powerful French government officials of habitually expending government funds 'supporting the arts' by patronising actresses and dancers, and accused dance teachers of telling their young female students: 'Your art consists of poses and provocations which should have a powerful effect on the senses of the spectators'.[31]

Yet, no matter how repugnant the Opéra's overt salesmanship of the *danseuse*'s sexuality, it need neither obscure the practical reasons for their sometime prostitution, nor suggest (as it did to Wagner) that ballet at the Opéra was meritless as art. For dancing and pantomime were as crucial to the Opéra's success as was singing. And if we wish to recapture from our distant vantage point some sense of the spectators' experience at this house during the age of grand opera, and their generally warm regard for dance, it is crucial to recognise not only the prestige conferred upon ballet by long-standing French tradition, and the dramatic power of ballet-pantomime (a genre well appreciated by the Opéra's audience), but the close kinship between ballet and social dance – a kinship which could make the ballet divertissements within grand opera familiar, accessible and welcome.

Appendix 6.1 *Select list of ballet-pantomimes in alphabetical order, showing genre, number of acts, librettist/author, composer/arranger and choreographer. Anonymous authorship is, by tradition, credited to the choreographer.*

1829	*Belle au bois dormant, La*	Ballet-pantomime-féerie, 4; Eugène Scribe, Ferdinand Hérold, Jean Aumer
1846	*Betty*	Ballet-pantomime, 2; Joseph Mazilier, Ambroise Thomas, Mazilier
1823	*Cendrillon*	Ballet-féerie, 3; Scribe, Fernando Sor, Albert [pseud. of François-Charles de Combé, also known as François Decombe]
1820	*Clari, ou la Promesse de mariage*	Ballet-pantomime, 3; [?], various composers arr. Rodolphe Kreutzer, Louis Milon
1800	*Dansomanie, La*	Ballet-pantomime, 2; [?], Etienne-Nicolas Méhul, Pierre Gardel
1840	*Diable amoureux, Le*	Ballet-pantomime, 3; Jules-Henri Vernoy de Saint-Georges, François Benoist/Henri Reber, Mazilier
1845	*Diable à quatre, Le*	Ballet-pantomime, 2; Adolphe de Leuven, Adolphe Adam, Mazilier
1839	*Gipsy, La*	Ballet-pantomime, 3; Saint-Georges, Benoist/Thomas/Marc-Aurèle Marliani, Mazilier [each composer wrote one act]
1841	*Giselle, ou les Wilis*	Ballet fantastique, 2; Théophile Gautier/Saint-Georges, Adam/Friedrich Burgmüller, Jean Coralli/Jules Perrot
1838	*Gitana, La* [St Petersburg]	Ballet, 3; Philippe Taglioni; Hermann[?] or Johann Philip Samuel Schmidt, Taglioni
1842	*Jolie fille de Gand, La*	Ballet-pantomime, 3; Saint-Georges, Adam, Albert
1832	*Nathalie, ou la Laitière suisse*	Ballet, 2; [?], Adalbert Gyrowetz/Michele Carafa, Taglioni
1846	*Paquita*	Ballet-pantomime, 2; Paul-Henri Foucher, Edouard Deldevez, Mazilier
1806	*Paul et Virginie*	Ballet-pantomime, 3; [?], R. Kreutzer, Gardel
1843	*Péri, La*	Ballet-fantastique, 2; Gautier/Coralli, Burgmüller, Coralli
1790	*Psyché*	Ballet-pantomime, 3; [?], Miller [Ernest Louis Müller], Gardel
1833	*Révolte au sérail, La*	Ballet-féerie, 3; [?], Théodore Labarre, Taglioni
1832	*Sylphide, La*	Ballet-pantomime, 2; Nourrit, Schneitzhoeffer, Taglioni
1839	*Tarentule, La*	Ballet-pantomime, 2; Scribe, Casimir Gide, Coralli

7 Roles, reputations, shadows: singers at the Opéra, 1828–1849

MARY ANN SMART

'The devil who steals Peter Schlemihl's shadow'

In an 1841 puff piece on the soprano sensation of the moment, Sofia Loewe, Henri Blaze de Bury related that Giacomo Meyerbeer had recently become so infatuated with Loewe's voice that he had gone religiously to hear her sing in Berlin, hiding himself behind the curtains of a *loge* and noting down details of her technique, hoping to cast her in his next opera. Blaze de Bury concluded:

> Meyerbeer is made so: he travels around the world in search of beautiful voices; as soon as he encounters one he copies it into a notebook, and thus he constructs in his imagination a dream cast for his next opera . . . Do you not find that there is something fantastic in this manner of collecting sopranos, tenors, and basses? Meyerbeer cuts out a beautiful voice for us, no more or less than that devil who steals Peter Schlemihl's shadow on a moonlit night, folds it up and hides it away in his wallet.[1]

The vaguely sinister image of the composer scribbling furiously in the obscure depths of his opera box is given an extra uncanny tinge by the allusion to Peter Schlemihl, a folk character immortalised in an 1814 novella by Adalbert Chamisso, who sells his shadow (in reality, his soul) to the devil in exchange for limitless wealth.[2]

Of course composers of opera had always 'collected' and reanimated great voices, and Blaze de Bury could easily have focused on more positive aspects of this assembly of a 'dream cast', emphasising the dialogue, exchange and renewal that also inform transactions between singer and composer. Blaze de Bury's choice of the more sinister image of Meyerbeer as shadow-stealing demon perhaps betrays a peculiarly French unease with opera's reliance on singers to bring its scores to life. For the French, steeped in an illustrious tradition of spoken drama, vocal display and the dominance of singers had long been marked as foreign and decadent. The stylistic opposition between French and Italian vocal styles was neatly exemplified in the divide between the two chief Parisian operatic venues. Virtuosic singing was associated with the Opéra's chief competitor, the Théâtre Italien, and especially with the wildly successful Rossini operas performed there. On the other hand, the works written for the Opéra – even those by Rossini

Example 7.1a Meyerbeer, *Les Huguenots*, Act IV, grand duo. Raoul has just pulled Valentine over to the window and shown her the bloody victims already in the road: 'Raoul! they will kill you! Ah! have pity!'

Example 7.1b Halévy, *La Juive*, Act V, finale. Rachel: 'Ah! father, I'm scared! their mournful prayers fill me with icy fear!' Eléazar: 'My God, what should I do?'

himself – asserted their distance from the Italian style by granting singers less leeway, and by emphasising dramatic force and precise declamation over vocal display.

This preference for an operatic style closely resembling speech is reflected in reviews and in the pamphlets chronicling the careers of the Opéra's singers, which tend to downplay qualities of agility and tonal beauty in favour of the affecting delivery of individual lines of highly charged poetry. Berlioz provides an extreme example in his *Memoirs* when he harks back nostalgically to soprano Cornélie Falcon's manner of pronouncing a single phrase from Meyerbeer's *Les Huguenots*; the words he singles out, 'Raoul! ils te tueront!', occur in the middle of a recitative, and are recited on a monotone (Ex. 7.1a).[3] Similarly, accounts of mezzo-soprano Rosine Stoltz's early career attribute her ascent from provincial theatres to prima donna at the Opéra to the intensity with which she delivered another string of repeated notes, from Halévy's *La Juive*: her rendition of Rachel's dying plea 'Mon père, j'ai peur!' (a chain of chest E♭'s) in the opera's last act (Ex. 7.1b) so captivated Adolphe Nourrit when he partnered Stoltz in a Brussels performance that he lobbied for a contract for her at the Opéra.[4]

This is not to say that the singers employed by the Opéra did not enjoy an 'Italianate' status as celebrities. Even in Paris, a word from a singer was sometimes enough to influence crucial compositional decisions, and there is no doubt that the theatre's economic fortunes were directly dependent on its ability to retain a stable of star performers. If in practical terms the position of French singers differed little from that of their Italian counterparts, the critical discourse that surrounded them was quite different – no less laudatory, perhaps, but more prescriptive and often tempered with defensiveness against the foreign threat. The music conceived for these stars of the Opéra might be seen as marking out a middle ground between French and Italian tendencies, and between catering to singers and the desire to tame them. Amid a wealth of often conflicting evidence, we shall focus on a handful of moments when singers were particularly influential in shaping the Opéra's repertory and reputation, listening in turn to both the music written for them and to the words written about them.

Women of few words

Anxieties about the power of the singer are neatly reflected in the work usually counted as the first grand opera, Daniel-François-Esprit Auber's *La Muette de Portici* (1828). As we see in Chapter 9, the opera centres around a mute girl, a role calling for elaborate powers of pantomime and played by the ballerina Lise Noblet at the first performance. Auber's mute Fenella was an instant hit, but in aiming to capitalise on *La Muette*'s huge success the Opéra could hardly imitate the popular theatre of the time by spinning out a series of works around the gimmick of the mute character.[5] Instead, the role of Fenella effectively metamorphosed into what became one of grand opera's stock characters: a humble young woman, no longer mute, but reticent; who demonstrates her virtue and sincerity by singing primarily in syllabic style and strophic forms. The type was elaborated in the most successful operas of the next decade, but this association between virtue and vocal simplicity did not altogether banish pleasure in the soprano voice from grand opera. As if to placate audiences who demanded both Rossinian vocal *jouissance* and serious declamation worthy of the Comédie-Française, grand opera began to enforce a strict division of labour between the soprano character who *acts* and one who *sings*. Fenella's demure descendants – Alice in *Robert le Diable*, Valentine in *Les Huguenots*, Rachel in *La Juive* – are almost always complemented by high-born women who sing melismatically, exhibiting the *hauteur* and decadence denied their more maidenly counterparts, and often marked as vaguely unsympathetic or threatening. *La Muette*'s Elvire, Isabelle in *Robert*, Eudoxie in *La Juive*, and Marguerite de Valois in *Les Huguenots* are all aristocrats – and in plot terms, 'other women' – who express

Example 7.2 Louis-Sébastien Lebrun, *Le Rossignol* (*The Nightingale*), Philis's aria 'Toi qui nous plaît'.

themselves in elaborate coloratura, their arias placed in unabashedly public contexts.

None of these exhibitionistic princesses is overtly identified as foreign, but contemporary audiences must have noted that three of the four roles were created by a singer with an Italian name – one who, moreover, had made her name singing down the street at the Théâtre Italien, in the popular productions of Rossini that had aroused both fanatical enthusiasm and anxiety for the patrimony of French vocal music. Born in Paris as Cinthie Montalant, the prima donna Laure Cinti-Damoreau (1801–63) – see Fig. 6 (p. 40) – Italianised her name early in her career in a bid for publicity. After signing on at the Opéra in 1826, she sang the first performances of Rossini's *Le Siège de Corinthe* (Pamyra) and *Guillaume Tell* (Mathilde), but before that her art was displayed in Louis-Sébastien Lebrun's opera *Le Rossignol* (1816), whose most famous number was a bravura duet with solo flute (Ex. 7.2).[6] This '*oiseau*' idiom was to remain Cinti-Damoreau's speciality, a style that Meyerbeer imitated and enhanced in *Les Huguenots* in the elaborate *fioriture* and the mimicry of nature sounds within Marguerite de Valois's showpiece aria, 'O beau pays de la Touraine' (Ex. 7.3). Sung while the queen looks at herself in a mirror and set against a decadent background of bathing beauties and voyeurism, the aria perfectly captures the heady combination of seduction and risk attached to Italianate singing in the grand operas of the 1830s.

Cinti-Damoreau left the Opéra in a contract dispute before she could première the role Meyerbeer had conceived for her, but her replacement as Marguerite, Julie Dorus-Gras (1805–96), shared many of these implicitly

Example 7.3 Meyerbeer, *Les Huguenots*, Act II, Marguerite's air: 'O beautiful region of Touraine'.

Italianate qualities: flawless technique, a rather wooden acting style, and a mechanical correctness that Charles de Boigne compared to that of an instrument.[7] In an 1840 book dedicated to Rossini and transparently designed to champion Italian influences at the Opéra, the Escudier brothers celebrated Dorus-Gras as a 'truly French' artist who, following

Example 7.3

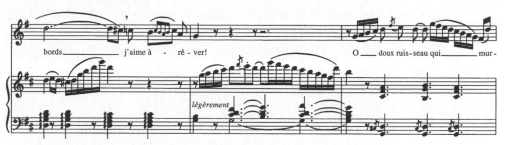

Cinti-Damoreau, proved that the French language was not – as had always been thought – fundamentally hostile to ornamental singing. However, their belief that the opposites could be reconciled was a minority position.[8] As we have seen, the Opéra itself, at least by way of the scores it produced, advocated a different sort of *juste milieu*, building the opposition between French and Italian styles into its plots (and its casting) in such a way that audiences could enjoy the diversion of Italianate ornament while their moral sympathies were firmly fixed on the more purely 'French' singer of the pair.

During much of the 1830s, these sympathies were transfixed by the chief exponent of such domestic heroines, the irresistible Cornélie Falcon (1812–97). Falcon created the roles of Valentine and Rachel, and displaced Dorus-Gras as the public's favourite Alice: when Meyerbeer heard her in the latter part for the first time he declared his opera to be finally 'complete'.[9] As the Opéra's universally loved *ingénue* – perhaps the only singer of the time to maintain a reputation for chastity – Falcon barely needed to open her mouth to bring the role of Valentine to life. What was not communicated by the music Meyerbeer had written for her would be supplied by spectators' memories of seeing Falcon in the other roles with which she was associated, or by anecdotes about her off-stage life, which journalists mingled freely with those of her characters. Just as film stars today can carry their personas with them from one role to the next, Falcon's reputation for virtue and modesty inhabited and ennobled any character she portrayed.

Although she was on stage for only a brief five years, Falcon achieved the status of myth well before her untimely retirement in 1837. Her 1832 debut at the age of eighteen as Alice was an early public-relations triumph, attended by 'le tout Paris', including (among many other celebrities) Auber, Berlioz, Halévy, Rossini, Maria Malibran, Giulia Grisi, Alexandre Dumas, Honoré Daumier and Victor Hugo.[10] Falcon quickly became the Opéra's top star, by 1835 earning an unprecedented 50,000 francs per year, more than three times as much as her colleagues Dorus-Gras and Cinti-Damoreau, and well ahead of the 30,000-franc salary of her teacher, the tenor Adolphe Nourrit (cf. Table 2.3, p. 30).[11] Falcon's short sojourn on the stage was so memorable that her name has survived into the present as the label for an entire category of singer: the 'falcon', a dramatic soprano with a rich lower register and a somewhat restricted range on top, as contrasted with the lighter, soubrette soprano roles named for another singer of the past, the 'dugazon'.[12] A description recorded by Castil-Blaze soon after Falcon's debut can perhaps help to account for the delirious enthusiasm Falcon inspired, and for the persistence of her memory as a nostalgic ideal of vocal expression:

> Her voice is a strongly characterised soprano, with a range of two octaves
> extending from b to d''', and resonating at all points with an equal vigour.
> A silvery voice, with a brilliant timbre, incisive enough that even the
> weight of the chorus cannot overwhelm it; yet the sound emitted with such
> force never loses its charm or its purity. Mlle Falcon attacks the note
> boldly, sustains it, grasps it, and masters it without effort, giving it the
> inflection most suitable for the sentiment she wishes to express. Full of
> soul, with a rare musical intelligence, and a perfect accord between her
> gestures and the melody she sings – these are the precious qualities we have
> noticed in this young artist.[13]

Such descriptions can give a general sense of a voice, but the terms of approval tend to be generic, phrases like 'silvery voice' or 'full of soul' occurring in connection with one successful singer after another. A more precise sense of Falcon's style can be deduced from the music Halévy wrote for her in *La Juive*, particularly the unusual Act II *romance*, 'Il va venir' (Ex. 7.4). As we have seen, Berlioz was dazzled by Falcon's way with recitative in *Les Huguenots*, and Halévy mines this same strength by injecting an exceptional amount of fragmented declamation into the set piece itself. Although nominally in ternary form, the *romance*'s outer sections are dominated by short, uneasy bursts of declamation depicting Rachel's fear and trembling ('Il va venir... Je me sens frémir'), with melodic continuity entrusted mainly to the French horn. As the soprano gradually begins to shape a melody of her own (at 'd'une sombre et triste pensée'), Halévy exploits both Falcon's gift for

Example 7.4 Halévy, *La Juive*, Act II, Rachel's romance: 'He will come! and I seem to shiver with fear!'

sharply etched attacks and the extraordinary ease with which she must have shifted between chest and head voices. Subsequent phrases build by small leaps to $g\flat''$, then g'', and finally through a seventh to a quiet $a\flat''$ before subsiding to the cadence. These repeated gestures suggest that Falcon excelled at delicate high notes, but also that she may have had trouble making a smooth transition across her break around a' and $b\flat'$.[14] As here, much of the music written for Falcon avoids stepwise motion across this break, just as much of it dwells on the G above the staff, as if she sounded particularly ravishing there.

If Falcon's debut was fairy-tale-like, the circumstances of her vocal decline were no less astonishing. Suddenly during a performance of Louis Niedermeyer's *Stradella* in 1837, she opened her mouth and nothing but noise came out: Berlioz described hearing 'raucous sounds like those of a child with croup, guttural, whistling notes that quickly faded like those of a flute full of water'.[15] She experimented with a variety of remedies, from a sojourn in the warmer climate of Italy to a Hoffmannesque regimen of singing inside a glass bell, presumably intended to enhance her natural resonance. Despite all efforts, though, a comeback attempt in 1840 was disastrous.[16]

Theories about the source of Falcon's vocal collapse range from the quasi-scientific to the sensational: among them are the ill-effects of beginning to sing in a large opera house before her body was fully mature, an attempt to force her natural mezzo-soprano into a higher tessitura, the taxing style of Meyerbeer's music, and sheer nervous fatigue perhaps brought on by romantic troubles. What is certain is that Falcon's particular affliction, the fact that her career ended in a kind of noble *muteness*, resonated particularly well with the persona that had been built up for her in the press, and perhaps also with the qualities the Paris public wished to see and hear from their leading performer of the quiet heroines who symbolised 'French' virtues and 'French' vocalising.[17]

After her retirement, Falcon lived on for a half-century as a virtual recluse in the Chaussée d'Antin, within a stone's throw of the Opéra. Camille Bellaigue told of visiting her shortly after the première of *Carmen* to play her some of Bizet's music on the piano: he claimed that although she had not heard any music at all since 1840, she was immediately able to grasp the beauties of the new work.[18] Bellaigue aimed to invest the unforgettable Falcon with timeless aesthetic instincts, and perhaps also to hint at the ageless appeal of French music. But it is impossible to contemplate this odd encounter without also reflecting that, even in her prime, Falcon would have been neither able nor willing to play Bizet's entirely new type of heroine – a wilful woman who, careless of virtue and anything but reticent, explodes into exhibitionistic song and dance at the slightest provocation.

Tenors as trumpets

If any male singer approached Falcon's legendary status, it must have been her teacher Adolphe Nourrit (1802–39), first interpreter of the roles of Arnold (*Guillaume Tell*), Masaniello (*La Muette*), Robert and Raoul (*Les Huguenots*). While celebrations of Falcon tended to focus on her chastity and generosity, or on her affecting acting style, Nourrit is acclaimed first of all for his creative contributions to the works he premièred. Meyerbeer once wrote to Nourrit of what he called '*our Huguenots* – because you have done more for it than its authors', Donizetti used similar language about his 1838 opera *Poliuto*, and Halévy credited Nourrit with writing the words for the central tenor aria in *La Juive*, 'Rachel, quand du Seigneur'.[19] As with Falcon, Nourrit's mythology derives partly from the way his career ended – all the more so because that end was intimately connected with changes in vocal technique and audience taste. In 1837 Nourrit was virtually chased off the stage of the Opéra by the arrival of Gilbert-Louis Duprez (1806–96), the first tenor to sing up to *c″* in full chest voice. Dismayed by his waning popularity, his voice failing, Nourrit took refuge in Italy where he hoped both to strengthen his voice and to discover a more sympathetic public. When this did not happen, suffering increasingly from symptoms of paranoia, he threw himself to his death from a Naples balcony.[20]

Duprez's cataclysmic introduction of the '*ut de poitrine*' is something of an anomaly in the history of singing. Unlike the shadowy 'lost' voices preserved only in memoirs and partisan journalistic verbiage, this change is concrete, precisely dateable to 17 April 1837, and even to a specific passage in Arnold's cabaletta in the last act of *Guillaume Tell*.[21] The moment is widely credited with definitively altering perceptions of the tenor voice. But what exactly changed, vocally and dramatically, when Duprez so violently upstaged Nourrit in 1837?[22]

One effect of Duprez's innovation concerned dramatic verisimilitude and archetypes of masculinity. Accustomed as we are today to the blaring tones of a Pavarotti (or even a Caruso), we might guess that Duprez's ringing, fully embodied high notes would inspire librettists and composers to create a new kind of tenor lead, more forceful, active – in short, more convincingly *masculine*. But in fact the movement was nearly in the opposite direction. Where the roles associated with Nourrit (with the possible exception of the naive and passive Raoul in *Les Huguenots*) tended emphatically towards the heroic and the revolutionary, those conceived for Duprez were likely to be defined more by love-interest than by political conviction. Masaniello and Arnold, both originally Nourrit roles, are revolutionaries above all, and both use their highest notes as clarion calls to action: Masaniello sings a rabble-rousing duet with baritone studded with exuberant high notes ('Mieux vaut

Example 7.5 Rossini, *Guillaume Tell*, Act I, duo of Arnold and Tell: 'Mathilde, treasure of my soul, must I renounce my love? O fatherland, to you I shall sacrifice my love and my honour!'

mourir': see Ex. 10.1, p. 175) while Arnold specialises in leaps of sixths and sevenths, triumphantly laying claim to the Swiss landscape in an imitation of Alpine yodelling (Ex. 7.5). In contrast, the roles conceived for Duprez (see Table 7.1) are surprisingly restrained in their use of the newly forceful high notes, instead exploiting the warmth and breadth of tone for which Duprez was noted.[23] Each of the three arias Donizetti composed for Duprez delivers one or two high c''s in its final phrase, but the real heroism in each

Table 7.1 *Roles premièred by Gilbert-Louis Duprez*

Florence, Teatro della Pergola	
1833	Donizetti, *Parisina* (Ugo)
1834	Donizetti, *Rosmonda d'Inghilterra* (Enrico II)
1835	Donizetti, *Lucia di Lammermoor* (Edgardo)
Paris, Opéra	
1838	Halévy, *Guido et Ginevra* (Guido)
1838	Berlioz, *Benvenuto Cellini* (Cellini)
1839	Auber, *Le Lac des fées* (Albert)
1840	Donizetti, *La Favorite* (Fernand)
1840	Donizetti, *Les Martyrs* (Polyeucte)
1841	Halévy, *La Reine de Chypre* (Gérard)
1843	Halévy, *Charles VI* (Duke of Bedford)
1843	Donizetti, *Dom Sébastien* (Sébastien)
1847	Verdi, *Jérusalem* (Gaston)

Example 7.6 Donizetti, *La Favorite*, Act IV, Fernand's cavatina: 'Purest angel, whom I found as in a dream'.

involves tessitura. Both 'Mon seul trésor' (*Les Martyrs*, 1840) and 'Ange si pur' (*La Favorite*, 1840) float around an axis of e'', stretching up to f'', g'' and even a'' within their basic melodic compass (Ex. 7.6). No wonder Duprez's voice was already beginning to shred by 1840.

Similarly, the passage in which Duprez unveiled the momentous '*ut de poitrine*' must have invested the singer with quite different varieties of heroism. In the cabaletta 'Amis, amis' from Act IV of *Tell*, a rebel leader inflames his followers through sheer vocal energy. Like much of Arnold's other music, the cabaletta is propelled by martial rhythms, stiffened by trumpet and French horn doublings and arpeggiated surges up to that top c'' (Ex. 7.7).[24] As performed by Nourrit, one can imagine that it sounded pure, ringing, and somehow idealistic; however, it was probably the sheer vocal muscle Duprez brought to the scene that made it a prototype for countless later tenor cabalettas and for the figure of the defiant rebel-tenor, typified by Verdi's Manrico with his famous cabaletta 'Di quella pira' (*Il trovatore*, 1853).

Example 7.7 Rossini, *Guillaume Tell*, Act IV, Arnold's air: 'Follow me! let us overcome the murderous monster!'

Just as Nourrit and Duprez escape type-casting along gender lines (at least in terms of gender as we understand it today), the discourse of national difference that surrounded the rivals was equally slippery – although no less vigorous for being confused. Both were French by birth, and Nourrit was embraced as a homegrown talent in a fairly uncomplicated way. The case of Duprez, though, presented both a challenge and an opportunity to journalists determined to decline vocal technique along national lines. Italophilic critics like the Escudiers would gleefully recall Duprez's 'first' Paris debut, an 1825 performance of Rossini's *Barbiere* at the Odéon, when his voice had been so weak that – as one witness put it – listeners had to observe a religious silence in order to hear it.[25] These writers insisted that only ten years of study and apprenticeship in Italy, where Duprez had created several important roles for Donizetti (including Edgardo in *Lucia di Lammermoor*), could have produced the sublime ability Duprez exhibited on the Opéra stage by the late 1830s.

Champions of French training, on the other hand, gave full credit for Duprez's success to his first teacher, Alexandre-Etienne Choron, whose school for religious music had also trained mezzo-soprano Rosine Stoltz and (briefly) the tragic actress Rachel. While the professors of voice at the Conservatoire (source of most of the Opéra's singers) were sometimes criticised for treating the voice as if it were just another orchestral instrument, Choron's pedagogical system was aggressively anti-operatic, rooted in a careful declamation and simplicity of line inherited from the eighteenth-century Neapolitan school and from the German chorales he used as teaching tools.[26] As the inventor of a reading method for children based on sensitivity to the sounds – the unique 'voice' – of the French language, Choron's patriotic credentials were unimpeachable, and his voice students accordingly were recognised above all for their declamation of recitative.[27] Where Nourrit and his generation had delivered recitative in a style halfway between reciting and singing, Duprez pioneered a more lyrical delivery in full voice that closed the gap between recitative and aria, injecting new life into the French poetry but also perhaps bringing it closer to the song-based Italian aesthetic.[28]

If Nourrit and Duprez can be 'read' as cultural icons in the same way that the pair Falcon and Cinti-Damoreau can, Duprez must occupy the ground of the *juste milieu*, melding French and Italian virtues, while Nourrit would represent the '*français pure laine*', famed for his depictions of patriots on stage and destroyed off-stage by his banishment from France and the dispossession he suffered in Italy. Such, at least, is the story told by Fromental Halévy, whose affectionate memoir of Nourrit reports that shortly before his suicide the singer described himself as an 'exile', lamenting that

> art requires freedom, and I am not free. I am an alien, an exile! [Here in Italy] I speak a language that is not my own, and my audiences hear a language that is not their own.[29]

Elaborating the patriotic elements of the tale, Halévy traces Nourrit's vocal problems back to the 1830 Revolution. In those heady days, Nourrit apparently strained his voice by singing the Marseillaise from the barricades and by rushing from one theatre to another, determined to play Masaniello at the Opéra and sing revolutionary songs at the popular theatres in a single evening. Like so many stories about singers, this one may contain no more than a grain of truth, but Halévy's picture of Nourrit striving to turn his voice into a trumpet of the July Revolution and exhausting himself in the process offers an aurally vivid contrast to the established idea of the high tenor as 'weak' or effeminate.

'The banter of an Amazon'

The last two singers I shall focus on are less of a matched pair – neither rivals like Nourrit and Duprez, nor foils like Falcon and Cinti-Damoreau. Rosine Stoltz (1815–1903) and Pauline Viardot (1821–1910) never sang together – their careers at the Opéra did not quite overlap – and although both were technically mezzo-sopranos, they sang very different types of roles. Their public personas, too, were worlds apart, with Stoltz demonised in the press as the quintessential selfish diva while Viardot was idolised as that rare singer who placed the good of the work as a whole above the imperatives of her own ego. These two opposites may share only a single attribute, but it is an important one for my purposes: their idiosyncratic voices and dramatic gifts inspired profound changes in the kinds of roles written for women at the Opéra.

Like Duprez, Rosine Stoltz was trained by Alexandre Choron, and she must have learned his lessons well – at least if we can believe the anecdote about her conquest of Nourrit and of a contract at the Opéra through a single line of recitative in *La Juive*. But where Duprez had supplemented his early training with further lessons and performances in Italy, Stoltz studied only with Choron before making early debuts in Belgium and then at the Opéra (1837), perhaps without perfecting her voice. She was regularly praised in reviews for the intensity of her acting, her declamation and her vivid gestures, but the purely technical aspects of her voice seem to have been less secure, and critics often complained of lack of agility and unevenness of timbre across her range.

On the personal level, too, Stoltz was controversial, accused of using unfair techniques against her rivals and of profiting from a romantic liaison with the Opéra's director, Léon Pillet. She is remembered today mostly for the role attributed to her in the onset of Donizetti's madness. According to an oft-retold anecdote, Donizetti's mental illness first manifested itself after a rehearsal of *Dom Sébastien*. Stoltz protested violently at having to stand idle on stage during the baritone's *romance* and insisted on cuts; the distraught Donizetti obliged but, the story goes, was never quite the same again. It is now known that Donizetti's illness was a result of long-dormant syphilis, and the tale is revealed as one of those fictions that collect around divas, perhaps in reaction against the influence they can exert during the compositional process.[30]

The roles conceived for Stoltz were shaped equally by her talents and her deficiencies, both on and off the stage. She refused to share the stage with any other principal soprano, thus almost single-handedly making obsolete the convention of paired lyrical and virtuosic female leads. Her two-octave range (roughly from *a* to *a''*), impressive low register and facility with large leaps between the extremes of her range were best suited to roles that emphasised fire and decisiveness over either the demure or ornamental attributes of the previous generation of grand opera heroines. In an 1842 letter Donizetti described Stoltz as a 'Joan of Arc' type, and imagined casting her as Hélène in *Le Duc d'Albe*, in what he called 'a role of action, of a type perhaps quite new in the theatre, where women are almost always passive'.[31] Although *Le Duc d'Albe* never reached the Opéra stage, the 'Joan-of-Arc' persona can be perceived in the two roles with which Stoltz was most closely associated, the title role in *La Reine de Chypre* (1841) and Léonor in Donizetti's *La Favorite* (1840). A substitute cabaletta Donizetti wrote for Stoltz in *La Favorite* sums up many of her strongest qualities: its jagged contours with sharp shifts between extremes of range, extended passages in the low register and short phrases in a mostly syllabic style create the impression that Donizetti exploited her weaknesses as well as her strengths to maximum dramatic effect.[32]

Having begun with the image of Meyerbeer surreptitiously surveying one singer from the depths of his *loge*, it seems only fitting to conclude with his obsession with another. While Meyerbeer was haunting Sofia Loewe's Berlin performances, he was also tracking Viardot, scheming to cast her as Fidès, the spurned mother of the fraudulent Anabaptist prophet Jean, in *Le Prophète* (1849). Viardot's rich voice and musical intelligence were more than enough to justify Meyerbeer's interest, but it is tempting to speculate that he may also have recognised in her a mirror of his own stylistic eclecticism, an ability to shift easily between national styles. As her early piano teacher Franz Liszt put it, Viardot transcended 'her Spanish origin, French upbringing, and German sympathies', to unite 'the charm of the [southern school] with the substance of the [northern] in a happy eclecticism', ultimately proving that 'art prefers to name its fatherland of its own free will'.[33]

Viardot's father and sole voice teacher, Manuel Garcia, the most successful vocal pedagogue of his generation, was renowned for instilling both force and facility in his pupils, and his female students in particular (including Viardot's older sister, Maria Malibran, 1808–36) stood out for the 'double' character of their voices, combining a rich contralto register with a soprano extension and often juxtaposing the two extremes to great effect, sounding at once 'brilliant and severe'.[34] Viardot made good use of this family trait, which also seems to have allowed her to essay Italian and French styles with equal success. Her London and Paris debuts in 1838 and 1839 concentrated on Rossini – Desdemona (also Malibran's most successful role), Rosina in *Barbiere*, and *La Cenerentola* – and throughout her career she excelled in *bel canto*, while also gradually expanding her repertoire to encompass both more modern and more classical styles. Rather than prompting a completely new kind of heroine as Stoltz had, Viardot in a sense brought together in a single body the characteristics of grand opera's traditional contrasting sopranos – high and low, lyric and dramatic, Italianate and declamatory. In one 1847 performance Viardot even enacted the symbolic demise of that convention, when she sang the roles of both Alice and Isabelle in *Robert le Diable* on the same evening.

Strictly speaking, this was no more than an accident – the soprano scheduled to sing Isabelle was ill – yet the story of that 1847 performance is told and retold as an emblem of Viardot's versatility, her capacity to be all things to all composers.[35] For Viardot was also that rare creature, a *female* singer who enjoyed full and friendly collaboration with composers, her input welcomed by Meyerbeer, Gounod, Berlioz, Saint-Saëns, all of whom designed roles with her in mind. She is widely credited (although in the absence of clear documentation) with contributing much to the score of *Le Prophète*, and she had a substantial part in shaping both Gounod's *Sapho* (1851) and Berlioz's 1859 reworking of Gluck's *Orphée*, both roles she premièred.[36] Viardot even exerted influence on roles she never sang, such as Dido in Berlioz's *Les Troyens* (1858/1863) and Dalila in Saint-Saëns' *Samson et Dalila* (1877).[37]

The Garcia family pedigree probably encouraged composers to place their trust in Viardot, but at least as important must have been her unusually broad musical training, which, in addition to serious piano study with Liszt, included composition lessons with Antoine Reicha. Viardot's own compositions, produced steadily throughout her career, are confident and original, showing an impressive ability to meld traditional vocal forms and adventurous harmonic and timbral effects.[38] Just as Viardot inspired and influenced young composers, who actively sought her advice and enshrined her in their mezzo-soprano heroines, Viardot also collected a wide circle of literary friends and admirers, many of whom seemed equally eager to depict her unique personality in prose. The copious memoirs of Viardot's social and family life often convey the impression that she inspired affection and awe in equal parts. The awe is echoed in Saint-Saëns' vivid, if not entirely flattering, description:

> Her voice was tremendously powerful, prodigious in its range, and it overcame all the difficulties in the art of singing. But this marvellous voice did not please everyone, for it was by no means smooth and velvety. Indeed, it was a little harsh and was likened to the taste of a bitter orange. But it was just the voice for a tragedy or an epic, for it was superhuman rather than human. Light things like Spanish songs and Chopin mazurkas, which she used to transpose so that she could sing them, were completely transformed by her voice and became the banter of an Amazon or a giantess.[39]

Clearly, we have come a long way from the docile persona of Falcon, or the bird-like Cinti-Damoreau. The diversity of the roles Viardot played, as well as the multiplicity of images in her many factual and fictional portraits, raise the suspicion that she was somehow resistant to the 'typing' that constrained most singers, her talents spilling far beyond any single dramatic or vocal category.[40] In light of Blaze de Bury's charge against Meyerbeer as a thief of singers' shadows, it seems significant that the composer cast Viardot in a role that had few antecedents on the nineteenth-century stage – that of a *mother* – and that in doing so he 'stole' only *part* of her voice, building up and challenging her talents for dramatic declamation while ignoring almost completely the florid Italian style on which she had built her fame.[41] And because the overwhelming success of *Le Prophète* came quite early in Viardot's long career, it seems likely that Meyerbeer's Fidès also helped to 'invent' Viardot, shaping the singer she became in the following decades.

Of course, certain aspects of the role of Fidès were shaped by Viardot's existing vocal talents as much as by Meyerbeer's more abstract dramatic concept. The role's remarkably wide tessitura exploited her impressive two-and-a-half octave range, and its emphasis on firm diction and attack similarly highlights a style in which all Garcia's students were considered exceptionally gifted. But reciprocally, Meyerbeer also perhaps helped to define Viardot's style, especially the ability to build emotional intensity through chains of short, gasping, recitative-like phrases which later became a hallmark of her style.

Meyerbeer himself commented on the 'unprecedented tragic heights [Viardot attained] both as a singer and as an actress' in the cathedral scene of Act IV, and it is there that his vocal writing for Fidès seems most personal and most moving.[42] The 'Complainte de la mendiante', in which Fidès enters the cathedral as a destitute seeking alms (Ex. 7.8), relies on detached articulations and phrases gapped with rests to create a sense of pathos and physical weakness. Each of the melody's first two phrases begins with a falling-fourth sobbing figure perfectly matched to the prosody and affect of the plea 'donnez' ('give'). As the number unfolds, this three-note motif returns in a variety of guises, rising and falling, and in the final phrases of the *couplet* is stretched out to a tritone, on repetitions of the word 'hélas!' (bars 25, 27, 29).[43] But the *tour de force* of the cathedral scene is Fidès' lament after Jean has refused to recognise her (Ex. 7.9), a blend of righteous outrage and self-questioning ('Qui je suis? moi!') that plays beautifully on Viardot's 'double voice' and on her aptitude for vibrant, detached attacks. After a recitative-like opening based on another gasping three-note motif, the number climaxes with a series of pulsating figures in chest voice ('And you, you denied knowing me!': bars 23–6) which are finally swept away by a soaring cadential phrase in the upper range (bar 29): 'Ungrateful one!'

Example 7.8a Meyerbeer, *Le Prophète*, Act IV: Fidès, exhausted, is led to the front of the stage: the 'Lament of the Mendicant' follows. (See also Ex. 12.3.)

The role of Fidès may have been a unique invention when *Le Prophète* was first performed in 1849, but the character had an important legacy, initiating a series of mezzo-soprano and contralto roles that aimed to extend Viardot's unique combination of force and lyricism into a recognisable vocal type. The influence of Meyerbeer's Fidès on Verdi's conception of the gypsy-mother Azucena in *Il trovatore* (1853; Paris 1857) is often noted; and although this memorable pair hardly managed to launch a vogue for operatic mothers, the numerous gypsies and other exoticised women who populate late nineteenth-century French opera can be counted among their offspring.[44] But no female role of the next few decades came close to spanning the stylistic extremes Viardot had commanded. Indeed, among this late generation of 'othered' heroines, the division between sopranos who sang like birds (Leïla in *Les Pêcheurs de perles*, Mignon, Lakmé) and those who embraced a less florid style (Carmen, Dalila) was, if anything, more solid than it had been even in the midst of the Opéra's agonistic sparring with Rossini in the 1830s.

In other words, while the story told here might seem to outline a progression from singers like Falcon and Cinti-Damoreau, narrowly identified with clear vocal and dramatic archetypes, to the new force of the heroines created by Rosine Stoltz and beyond to Viardot's far more versatile profile, the history of singers at the Opéra is more properly told as an expansion

Example 7.8b The 'Lament of the Mendicant', continuation

of possibilities followed by a rapid return to archetypal casting, with some new archetypes added along the way. Even for men, the spectrum of roles available by the later nineteenth century was one-dimensional compared to the interesting tension between vocal force and passivity played out by both Nourrit and Duprez. The reasons for this were many. The formation after mid-century of a body of repertory works established a fixed set of vocal traits as requirements for *any* soprano, or tenor, or baritone, since all singers had to be able to sing Rachel or Valentine or Arnold while also appearing in newly composed roles. This reliance on a standard repertory shifted the onus of innovation away from composition and on to performance, throwing a new emphasis on the 'technology' of vocal performance, on the spectacular high notes and mechanistic roulades that could inject a

Example 7.9 Meyerbeer, *Le Prophète*, Act IV, finale: Fidès, denied by her son, reacts with shock.

sense of 'event' into even the thousandth performance of *Guillaume Tell*. But as always when singers are concerned, practical factors tell only part of the story: a character as memorable as Fidès is created above all by the collision of forceful temperaments, by a sort of 'chemistry' that arises in the collaborations and negotiations between the 'shadow-stealing' composer and 'his' singers.

PART TWO

Revaluation and the twenty-first century

8 Directing grand opera: *Rienzi* and *Guillaume Tell* at the Vienna State Opera

DAVID POUNTNEY

Directing grand opera in the early twenty-first century is somewhat like being required to remake *Ben Hur* for an art-house budget. The essence of the aesthetic of grand opera was rooted in the fact that it was a commercial enterprise, designed with a lavish sense of the spectacular to flatter the newly rich bourgeoisie, for whom the pompous splendours of theatres like the Palais Garnier were created. It took the aristocratic art form *par excellence*, transformed it into a celebration of conspicuous consumption, and trumpeted the dominance of new money in its natural home at the heart of the newly industrialised city. Garnier's fantastic building, and the construction of the Avenue de l'Opéra, remind us today of the luxury that clothed grand opera during and after the Second Empire, though it is revealing that the home of opera, once an adjunct of the Court, has now become a traffic island.

The parallels with Hollywood are apt, and especially the Hollywood of escapist fantasy and spectacle of the 1930s and 1940s. It is significant for instance that the main achievements of grand opera are scenic and structural as much as musical. There are probably only two true musical masterpieces which can be correctly attributed to the genre – *Guillaume Tell* and *Don Carlos* – although it is clear that neither *Les Troyens* nor even the libretto of *Götterdämmerung* is free of its influence. But otherwise, the massive works of Meyerbeer, Spontini, Halévy and even Wagner which fit into this category are currently remembered more for their achievements of technical innovation, if not also excess. As with the Hollywood blockbuster, the special effects come to seem more and more to dominate the content.

Thus we have in *Robert le Diable* the first instance of a moonlit scene – the ballet of dead nuns – being lit from above, i.e. from where the moon would actually be. The signal for the massacre of St Bartholomew's Eve in *Les Huguenots* was given by bells hung, for the first time, in the roof of the theatre. This attention to detail about scenic and spatial effects would of course percolate through into more profound areas of the repertory. The exquisite evocation of the hunt in Act II of *Tristan und Isolde* is a stunning artistic response to what had become a stock cliché. But in pre-grand opera works scenic events are given pretty short shrift musically. The collapse of the statue of Baal in *Nabucco*, for instance, elicits from Verdi nothing more than a rapid descending scale. This is more or less the same technique to be found in Handel's *Serse* (*Xerxes*) where the collapse of the bridge across the Hellespont occasions nothing more than a brief flourish. It is interesting to reflect how different Wagner's treatment of the final scene of *Götterdämmerung* would have been if he had composed his libretto straight away instead of waiting for twenty years. The realisation of the musical potential of such important scenic moments is probably the key contribution of grand opera style.

A director might well, then, feel slightly reverential towards grand opera, for it naturally follows that it was with the scenic and spatial demands of the genre that the seeds were sown which would eventually lead to the invention of the opera director – surely a type high on Hans Keller's list of 'phoney professions'.[1] This was the era, for instance, in which production-books first become common (see Fig. 12, p. 81). Publishers like Ricordi insisted on sending out these detailed records of the positioning of singers, chorus, extras, descriptions of props and scenery, along with the musical material, in recognition of the fact that the commercial success of a new work was now also linked to the grandeur and effectiveness of its visual as well as musical realisation. Initially, this realisation was in the hands of a stage-manager: there was no interpretative function at work here. That element, if it existed at all, was in the hands of the librettist and conductor. But the scale and intricacy of the stagings that became a fashionable and necessary ingredient of grand opera occasioned the practical demands that would lead to the invention of the director.

The roots of the recognition of the value of scenic effect were, however, more serious than the mere cynical need for spectacle. It is an idea rooted in Romanticism which suggested that the visual ambience of landscape and weather was an integral part of the mood and meaning of existence. This is clear when we compare different works by Rossini whose career straddles such a wide range of styles. The storm in the *Barber of Seville* has no inner psychological meaning. It is simply an excuse for orchestral bravura: an imitative exercise in musical colour in the tradition of Vivaldi. By the time we get to *Guillaume Tell*, however, the storm, despite employing essentially similar musical devices, has become an integral part in the argument of the drama. The heroic Tell, a man of the soil at home in his native landscape, is undaunted by nature's fury. Indeed he is able to exploit it to fashion his escape from his enemies, at the same time magnanimously saving their lives. The alien conquering foreigners are helpless in the face of outraged nature: Tell revels in it.

In pictorial terms too it is Romanticism with its fascination for the untamed, rugged landscapes of 'pure nature' – something that Shakespeare would have called a 'desert' or 'wilderness' – which drives the quest in grand opera for ever more realistic and detailed evocations of extravagant location. Of course, Baroque opera had also had its grottoes, its lonely islands and its forests populated by savage beasts. But these remained purely backdrops, and it was extremely rare for the music itself to pay any attention to location. The essence of Romanticism was however to be inside nature, so that the characters of *Guillaume Tell*, for instance, do not simply perform in front of their Swiss mountains, they are shown to exist within them. Indeed, the first twenty minutes of *Guillaume Tell* do almost nothing other than evoke the idyllic rural existence of the Swiss protagonists and, crucially, this evocation is not merely pictorial but also musical. The location is at the heart of the motivation of the drama and Rossini paints an exquisite Arcadian musical tableau to establish the essential rightness of the peasant existence and therefore, by implication, the justice of their struggle against the Austrian conquerors.

Nature equals love in this Romantic vision, and hence the classic plot structure of grand opera contains the inevitable conflict between politics, or the State, and passion, or Nature. The State is represented by the city, and hence the balancing pole of extravagantly detailed evocations of Nature was the equally extravagant representation of the citadels of power. Since the inherent function of grand opera was to massage the ego of the newly powerful urban *haut bourgeois* it was inevitable that the State should be shown in dimensions of immense grandeur: this was, after all, the aristocratic and monarchic world which the rentier had conquered. Grand opera became, and indeed remains therefore the home of fantasy architecture as displayed, for example, in Séchan's 1849 design for the crypt of Münster Palace in *Le Prophète*, Act V, or Delannois' monumental staircase designed in 1833 for *Gustave III*.

There existed already in France, since shortly before the 1789 Revolution, a tradition for the design of superbly unbuildable public buildings: the designs of Etienne-Louis Boullée and Claude Nicolas Ledoux contain many fascinating and inspiring examples of this, which remain invaluable image-banks for directors and designers! Grand opera provided the format in which such fantasies, albeit much more vulgar and less sophisticated, could be given quasi-three-dimensional reality. 'Quasi' is important because for all its pomp and magnificence this remains a painted world, but one which by the clever separation of planes within the picture could contain three-dimensional platforms and staircases to accommodate the proliferating masses of chorus, ballet and extras demanded to puff up the conventional grand opera evocation of State power.

To reiterate: the crucial difference was that this grandiosity did not remain purely pictorial: it spilled over into the music, where it found expression in increasingly lavish and extended marches, processions, grand entrances, all furnished with grandiose ceremonial music often making use of extensive batteries of stage musicians. These were, however, the decorative extras in the musical language of grand opera: the real meat lay in the development of the vast, concerted ensemble, which was the musical form that brought the conventional scene of State power to its spectacular conclusion, as in the *auto-da-fé* scene in *Don Carlos* and the Triumphal March scene of *Aida*. Wagner liked to distance himself from the commercial vulgarity of this tradition, but nonetheless there are passages in *Tannhäuser* and *Lohengrin* which clearly show its influence, and the middle act of *Götterdämmerung* with its summoning of the vassals and subsequent marriage processions is clearly a grand opera conception even if, by the time he came to compose it, Wagner's music had evolved way beyond such conventions. But the Wagner work which practically defines the grandiose, urban world of State power as seen through the conventions of grand opera, is *Rienzi*.

In this early work we find the young Wagner desperate for commercial success and trying to outdo even the already extended limits of musical and theatrical scale that grand opera permitted. It lasted over seven hours in its original form, and is built up of a succession of colossal ensembles, each preceded by bombastic and violently militaristic entrances, marches, oaths and ceremonies. The rise and fall of the demagogue Rienzi is portrayed in music of unashamed, bullying, hectoring hysteria, breaking off only to descend into equally unabashed sentimental religiosity. The whole work is driven by an overwhelming energy – an awesome synergy between the vaunting ambition of its protagonist and its composer. And, inevitably, the setting of ancient Rome gives the work the perfect setting for the fantasy architecture of power. Boullée and Ledoux lead directly to Albert Speer; Rienzi leads directly to Hitler, who, reminiscing about a performance he heard in Linz in his adolescence, remarked: 'In jener Stunde begann es' – 'It began in that moment'.

Rienzi is clearly a grotesquely lopsided work, because Wagner's obsession with depicting the rise and inevitable betrayal of the revolutionary Rienzi – like all Wagner's leading characters, an allegory of himself – meant that he forgot or, at that stage in his life, was unable to develop in any significant way the essential conflicting theme of love. Crucially, the thing that saved grand opera from merely being a propaganda platform for the *nouveaux riches* was that there was a conflict at its very heart, and this conflict forms the basis of the drama of all successful examples of the genre.

Romanticism was itself a prescient reaction to the impending triumph of the industrial revolution. At the moment when the practice and profit of manufacture assumed dominance over the material world, romanticism sought refuge in unblemished Nature. Thus the celebration of the power of the *nouveaux riches* was simultaneously tinged with regret at the destruction it provoked. Hence the insistent thematic conflict between love and politics, passion and reason, the imperatives of the state and the demands of the individual – timeless themes of dramatic content – became in grand opera the dominant issue. But like all clever commercial packages, grand opera was even more adept at flattering its audience than one might at first suppose. For alongside the flattery of its power by spectacles of conspicuous consumption it also convinced its audience that they were sensitive beings who could weep in sympathy with the catalogue of rebellious lovers which the medium provided. There was, however, a harsh proviso: the sympathy and the tears were conditional on the fact that the lovers die before they are able to do anything seriously to disturb the status quo. This rigid convention applied even to works that actually defied the conventions of grand opera. Only thus could the wealthy rentier take his daughter to *La traviata*: he visited women such as Violetta himself after supper, and so joined in as a participant in the glamorous parties and gay flirtations. As a father he could sympathise with Père Germont, and could depart happy that the bitter ending had imparted to his daughter, if not to him, a sound moral lesson. In this, as in so many areas, the modern parallel for the *mores* of a successful commercial art form like grand opera is the classic Hollywood blockbuster, whose manipulation of themes of emotional actuality (thus far and no further!) combined with glamour and spectacle, learned all there was to learn from grand opera.

Grand opera toyed with revolutionary politics much as it toyed with prostitutes, allowing it just enough space to titillate the audience with a glimpse of the terrifying possibilities of the revolutionary mob without ever going so far as to actually celebrate anything so destructive as radical politics. Nonetheless, the grand ceremonial scene of State power such as the *auto-da-fé* scene in *Don Carlos* is matched in the tradition of grand opera by the appearance of the revolutionary mob, repetitively so in *Rienzi*. These were reminders of a very real preoccupation for the nineteenth-century *bourgeois*: revolutionary movements spread through Europe in 1830, 1848 and the 1870s, so that no generation was entirely free from the fear that the mob might dispossess it of its opulent villas and heavy furniture. Nonetheless, Romanticism preached individual and national independence: at the heart of grand opera was a similar paradox that intrigued, titillated and excited its audience, a heady recipe for successful commercial art.

I have emphasised at some length the political, social and cultural roots of grand opera because it is impossible for a director, given the perhaps dubious task of reheating this sometimes slightly stale porridge, to begin without considering what it was originally for and how that purpose might function in a modern theatrical context. This is not because I necessarily insist upon the idea of updating works when devising contemporary representations of them, but I do insist upon the fact that the eyes, ears and experiences of the audience have updated themselves so that the whole notion of so-called 'authenticity' in this area becomes illusory. To take one prime example: an art form whose primary underlying purpose was to reassure its audience could encompass many conflicts and contradictions, but not necessarily irony. Today, however, no audience can be expected to listen to, say, the Soldiers' Chorus from *Faust* without simultaneously tapping their feet and squirming into the convenient intellectual refuge of an ironic smile.

Irony often found it hard to penetrate the painted decorative façade that was grand opera. In considering an almost superhumanly bombastic work such as *Rienzi*, where could one turn for a visual style which would avoid the ridiculous without itself ridiculing the work, and which would allow the piece to speak without, God help us, actually reaffirming its message? As always, given that a production is a temporary realisation of a two-dimensional object – a score, in three dimensions, on a stage – location is critical. In this case, the commission was from the Vienna State Opera.

Rienzi was an historical figure of the fourteenth century, but a 'wrinkled tights' version of this story could only be ridiculous. In Vienna of all places, a deliberate linkage of Rienzi with Hitler, or perhaps more pertinently with Mussolini, would be crass: the resonance of the politics of Rienzi, with its echoes of the Saint-Simonian doctrine of the 'genius leader' and the irrational surrender of the 'ordered mass' (*foule ordonnée*) to his leadership needed no emphasis from me, and the mere sound of its relentless marches would conjure in that audience sufficient memories of, if not nostalgia for, the Nazi rallies at which they were indeed played.

The solution in this particular case was to choose the most threatening option, that of locating Rienzi in the near future as a warning of the undying power of demagoguery and political manipulation. The costumes for the masses, by Marie-Jeanne Lecca, created an image of a conformist urban proletariat, whilst the two rival families of 'nobles' whose warring creates the destabilised political climate in which Rienzi's cry for 'order' can find its response were characterised as rival gangs adopting the deliberately anachronistic attributes of the German student guilds, or duelling societies, which still exist today.

The scenic conception (designer Robert Israel) brought us up against one of the fundamental practical difficulties of reinterpreting grand opera for the modern stage: money. As I have said, the extravagant excess of grand opera – *szenische Pracht* in Wagner's words – was a painted world. Such a world on the stage has been aesthetically impossible since Wagner's interpreters, T. W. Adorno and Edward Gordon Craig, insisted that the stage was a three-dimensional space in which action must move in a three-dimensional plane. But the transition from painted to sculptural scenery has enormous consequences for cost and stage technique. Built objects obviously cost more, and take longer to move. The 'grandeur' of grand opera must therefore inevitably be circumvented, even at such a lavish establishment as the Vienna State Opera, and this process of 'circumvention' almost involuntarily involves a process of commentary which very quickly introduces its own element of irony. To take a generic example, if we render a 'Royal Palace' as a single golden wall which might turn to reveal a sculpted, rocky reverse side, this might serve as a typical scenic alternation between 'Palace' and 'Mountainside'; indeed it might even be an elegant and evocative solution to these two locations. But the very abstract simplicity of this solution itself points a mocking finger at the entire overblown structure of grand opera. And in case one might wonder whether it might not be better simply to revert to the painted scenery for which the work was conceived, then one must confront the fact that in the accelerated world of images – a much more rapidly changing language than the aural one of music – anachronistic 'quotation' could appear equally ironic, if not simply lazy.

In our case, the solution for *Rienzi* was a massive, concrete apartment block with a balcony, but here and there with fragments of ancient Roman detail, as if the building had been plastered over some earlier ruin, as indeed has happened in Rome down the centuries. This provided the location for our conformist mass of the *Volk*, and the ideal speech-making podium for Rienzi. On the other hand, his quarters were a more specific Roman pastiche, echoing his historical characteristic – the real Rienzi was a collector of Roman antiquities. The idea reached its climax in the setting for his famous prayer, in which he moved between a large collection of Roman statues – clearly power had enabled him to loot on a substantial scale – some hardly out of their crates. This chimed in with the development of his costume, which began identically with that of the people but gradually acquired more and more inflated echoes of Rome's Imperial past, as his hubristic rise to power gathered pace. (Fig. 15.) He died encased in golden armour which collapsed in the final moments, revealing nothing but dust.

The final ingredient of the design conception was its most important and its most dangerous: kitsch. The massive concrete structure gave the design the scale and weight which were inherent in Wagner's epic conception, and when it disintegrated as Rienzi led his people into destruction, it became an appropriate symbol for the 'musical mass-pathos' ('musicalisch-massenhaften Leidenschaftlichkeit') which Wagner saw as intrinsic to 'grosse Oper'. But Wagner was also trying to do something else in this opera, for which this alone was too dark, too brutal and too epic: he was attempting to match, indeed outdo, the musical brilliance of grand opera. Wagner invested the musical realisation of *Rienzi* with the unashamed extravagance

Figure 15 *Rienzi* at the Vienna Staatsoper, directed by David Pountney in December 1997. Stage design was by Robert Israel, costumes by Jean-Marie Lecca.

and tasteless exaggeration of a Las Vegas hotel, with much the same effect: one can be simultaneously repelled and fascinated, but the sheer scale finally bludgeons a degree of awe as well as a smile. Only the self-consciously deliberate and unabashed use of kitsch could match this musical egomania, giving it the hedonistic exuberance it demands, without insulting or perhaps pandering to the audience by suggesting that it should be taken entirely too seriously. The tone was set by the front cloth – an extravagant array of pink roses and Roman weaponry – through which Rienzi and his beloved sister could be seen dreaming together, perhaps of their destined greatness and destruction, rather as Hitler described his hill-top reverie after witnessing a performance of *Rienzi*.

This element also gave us the clue to solving the next inevitable conundrum for the director of a grand opera: what to do about the ballet? If you can embrace kitsch, you can embrace the ballet. There is no point in doing to *Rienzi*, or indeed any other grand opera, what Cosima Wagner and Julius Kniese did: cut out everything that seemed superfluous, in the vain hope that what would be left would be a 'music drama' in the Wagnerian sense. Grand opera is built around carefully balanced moments of display, both scenic and musical, and ballet is an intrinsic part of its obligation to entertain. The positioning of the ballet, allowing particularly the late-coming male consumers to view in quasi-artistic action the limbs that they hoped to consume after the performance is one of the more questionable ways in which grand opera mirrored the needs and tastes of its audience, but there is no point in reviving these pieces if one seeks to hide from that.

In the particular case of *Rienzi*, the ballet shows Wagner simultaneously following and breaking the conventions of grand opera. He breaks convention by placing the ballet in the finale to Act II rather than its traditional placing in Act III, and further removes it from its role as pure divertissement by using an extraordinary pantomime to give the ballet dramatic function and coherence. This pantomime, possibly suggested by a similar device in Halévy's *La Juive*,[2] is a dramatic rendering of the Rape of Lucretia with the music designed precisely to follow the actions of the three principals: Lucretia, her husband Collatinus and her rapist, Tarquinius. This is acted out in front of Rienzi as part of a lavish victory celebration and is clearly intended as a piece of political agitprop supporting Rienzi's agenda by showing a virtuous Roman woman despoiled by an arrogant aristocrat, much as the opera itself begins with the abduction of Rienzi's sister, thus falling into line with a long tradition of using atrocities against women as inflammatory war propaganda. Wagner's stage-directions run alongside the music, which is therefore mimetic and functions rather as would a pianist accompanying a silent film.[3] This was indeed the reference we sought to pick up, initially attempting to make a special silent film to run with a shortened version of the music, and when that proved too expensive, choosing the option of a series of highly posed, glossy 'stills' of the kind frequently used to publicise Hollywood films, each image having the impact of a bill-board poster. This also obviated the problem which was already evident in some form to Wagner when he cut the pantomime in Dresden for the want of three convincing performers, namely that three small figures on a large stage will have great difficulty in matching the scale of their mime to the impact of the orchestra: blown up to triple life size, these images ideally matched the epic scale of the music as well as capturing the tawdry use of such images for cheap political effect, a device which showed that kitsch can pack a considerable punch.

Figure 16 *Rienzi* at the Vienna Staatsoper: choreography was by Renato Zanella.

The original pantomime continued with the prescient and ominous stage-directions given to Brutus as he surveys Lucretia's corpse after her suicide:

> With a heroic gesture, upon which the others are surprised, Brutus raises his sword heavenwards with both hands and swears the downfall of the tyrant . . . they all likewise swear upon the sword to punish and destroy tyranny.

Wagner here uses the techniques of ballet-pantomime, described in Chapter 6. In our case, a brief text was displayed on a final 'still', the words serving to 'motivate' the colossal sequence of ballet-numbers which follows, each one showing more and more aspects of Rienzi's military power like a Red Army May Day parade. The music for these sequences is as banal as any routine ballet music is, but as so often in this work banality achieves a kind of effect disproportionate to its quality simply by virtue of the awesome self-confidence of its energy and scale. Naturally we were not able to perform it all, but brought the sequence to a dramatic climax by bringing ninety small children on to the stage performing a relentlessly repetitive ballet of simple flag movements. Costumed in little uniforms overprinted with blue skies and with wigs of golden curls they made a mass effect which was again both as kitschy as the music and as horrifying in its scale, especially with its echoes of the mass gymnastics of 1930s rallies. It should be added that one of Wagner's greatest convention-busting inspirations in this work is the conclusion of the ballet sequence, building relentlessly towards a thumping cadence which never arrives because it is abruptly interrupted by the assassination attempt on Rienzi. The beginning and end of this ballet sequence are thus woven into the dramatic content of the work to excellent effect.

The final problem confronting any director of grand opera is not unique to this type of opera, but is present in *Rienzi* on an extended scale: the staging of the grand, concerted ensemble. As with the transition of taste and fashion from painted to sculptural scenery, this 'problem' is more the result of evolving theatrical taste than an inherent difficulty in the genre. The concerted ensemble (*pezzo concertato*), to which each act was supposed to build, was never intended as a scene of action: once the forces had been laboriously manoeuvred on to the stage, there would be little room for, and certainly no expectation of, further movement within the scene. However, modern taste has limited tolerance for such extended, static tableaux and the director must attempt to have a few cards up his sleeve which will maintain a sense of dramatic and visual momentum without creating impossible difficulties for the musical co-ordination of these large numbers. In the case of *Rienzi*, with such ensembles coming at the ends of Acts I, II and III, the pressure is certainly on to maintain a level of invention for the third. This ensemble describes the return of Rienzi's now exhausted troops from yet another victory over the nobles, but this time at horrifying cost. The ensemble begins with an awesome processional entry complete with brass band, proceeds through Baroncelli's lament for the Romans killed in the battle, Adriano's discovery of his dead father, and climaxes, somewhat improbably, with Rienzi once again able to rouse the people to impassioned fervour and belief in his cause. The scenic device which gave the possibility of movement and visual development to this ensemble were the giant bins which rumbled on during the initial procession, opened to disgorge ominous quantities of 'body bags' and, in the final stretto, became ghoulish altars on which ghostly women and children created tableaux of saccharine religious kitsch, an indication of the illusory nature of the euphoria which Rienzi succeeds in whipping up in this, the final ensemble before the total collapse of his régime.

It will be clear from all the above that the director's task in dealing with a work like *Rienzi* is not only to grapple with the problems of the genre of grand opera – its meaning, its scale, and its particular ingredients of ballet, ensemble and musical virtuosity – but also how particularly to deal with an immature, unbalanced and only partially successful work. In the case of *Guillaume Tell*, however, we are dealing with a mature masterpiece, a work of exceptional taste, delicacy, sophistication and refinement. Moreover, *Tell* fully inhabits the conventions of grand opera and exploits them with unerring appropriateness. This makes it stand out from Verdi's examples, particularly *Don Carlos*, which although technically a grand opera, is an exercise in dramaturgy specific to Verdi rather than to the genre. *Guillaume Tell* is an extremely demanding test for a director, posing the question of whether the conventions of grand opera can, in such a case, be translated into modern stage language without irony; whether, in fact, a director can find a way to release the superb qualities in this magnificent work.

Tell celebrates the identification of Romanticism with liberty, and hence is one of the benchmark works in a long tradition of celebrating national independence through the medium of opera. This tradition came to have such a hold on the nineteenth-century imagination that no nation could decently equip itself for independence unless it acquired, along with a flag and a possibly reinvented language, an indigenous operatic repertory, a compulsion which reached its apogee in the Khedive of Egypt's commission to Verdi to write an opera on an Egyptian theme. Rossini was, however, too subtle a man to indulge in the rampant political hysteria which runs through *Rienzi*: for him, the justness of the Swiss cause lay in the rustic, natural nobility of Tell's character and its reflection in the landscape he inhabited. Thus the opera poses for the director and designer the most acute technical problem of modern stage design: the representation of nature.

This has become doubly difficult in the case of famously dramatic landscapes such as the Swiss mountains because the mechanical reproduction of images of such landscapes has moved them irrevocably into the world of the picturesque. Even when confronted with the real thing, one frequently has the sensation of wishing to reach out and see if the poster will peel off the wall. Direct representation, even if feasible, must invoke involuntary irony here even more swiftly than in the case of urban monuments. Equally, elegant abstraction introduces an element of artful contrivance which militates precisely against the desired effect of unadorned, truthful nature. Neither may the issue be in any way ducked: Rossini devotes the first twenty minutes of the work solely to the evocation of a rural idyll, so that when it is evoked again in the final ensemble of the work there is a true sense of resolution and of paradise regained.

The solution which the designer, Richard Hudson, and I came up with was a miniature landscape, beautifully carved out of wood, including houses and trees. This landscape rose up into mountains at the back, and could accommodate people, though obviously not too many, because of its contours. The evening began with a vision of this landscape in its entirety, the people posed on and around it. Gradually, during the long opening sequence, this landscape, made up of several independent trucks, moved apart and came

Figure 17 *Guillaume Tell* at the Vienna Staatsoper, directed by David Pountney in October 1998. Stage design and costumes were by Richard Hudson, choreography by Renato Zanella.

together again, creating different acting spaces for the chorus in their sequence of songs and rural rituals. However, although the opening sequence does represent a rural idyll, it is an idyll under threat from the Austrian conqueror, and hence this fragmentation also suggested that the idyll was vulnerable, and indeed the entire landscape was never seen complete again until the final image of the opera. For the interior scenes, there were no actual interiors of typical Swiss farmhouses which, again, could too easily slide towards unintended kitsch, but slightly larger small-scale models of these houses, exquisitely carved, which served as furniture for the principals. This miniaturised world was, however, contrasted with the paired father- and mother-figures in the piece: Tell's mother and Arnold's father. These small but important roles were treated as archetypal parental figures, who each sat upon huge wooden dolls representing their ritual identities.

From this beginning, an opposing vision of the world as seen from the Austrian perspective naturally followed. Gesler, the Austrian governor, had a model of the Swiss landscape, again miniaturised, but this was enclosed in a glass table as though a collector's specimen. And when the action moved to the urban seat of his authority, the miniature landscape of the peasants was straddled by a giant red metallic bridge: a balcony from which authority could dominate and terrorise.

It is one of the tragedies of *Guillaume Tell* that it is now only really famous for the absurd military music which follows the slow introduction to the overture. People forget that the overture begins with an elegiac cello solo which shows up the following military rataplan for all its intentional banality. It also points up the significance of dealing with the question of ballet in these works since this famous piece of music actually comes from the third-act ballet depicting the Austrian conquerors. Rossini's wit and enigmatic sense of the absurd is here deliciously close to the spirit of Shostakovitch, another composer who, for quite different reasons, kept his cards close to his chest and constantly leaves us wondering if his irony is intentional or not.

There are in fact two major ballet sequences in *Guillaume Tell*, and both merit serious attention. It is notable that whereas in *Rienzi* Wagner created a logical dramaturgical envelope for his ballet and then proceeded to fill it with musical trash, Rossini is content for his ballet to appear as if it were a conventional divertissement, but fills it with music of exquisite quality. The first, breaking convention by appearing already in the first act, brings to a climax the sequence of choruses evoking the idyllic life of the peasants in their mountain landscape. It opens with a theme which has become, through countless excerpts, the other instantly recognisable musical idea from the opera. In fact it is an idea of great delicacy, implying wit: a cheeky humour somehow laced with tension. From this we derived the idea that the Swiss might have been forbidden by the Austrian occupiers to use their ethnic costumes and ceremonies, a common reaction by an imperial power to provoke unruly natives. The British government for instance forbade the use of Highland dress and the Gaelic language in the Scottish Highlands following the '45 rebellion, and this practice has been constantly emulated all over the world. Rossini's music lent itself brilliantly to a display of mischievous, defiant humour as the dancers brought more and more of their treasured ethnic costumes into the open, and then, as the music became increasingly confident and rumbustuous, used pieces of captured Austrian costume and military paraphernalia to make fun of their conquerors.

The ballet in the third act occurs at an altogether more serious point in the drama, and is set in the Austrian garrison where the Swiss population is effectively being held prisoner. It again begins with touching delicacy, the ballet built up around a *sotto voce* Swiss folk song. This immediately suggested that the prisoners were being forced to 'perform' their native music and dances under conditions of terrifying duress. Again the poignant delicacy of this opening section is deliberately contrived by Rossini to point up the brilliant banality of the famous military rataplan which follows, in which Gesler first of all paraded mechanical toy soldiers which marched in time to the music, and then unleashed a mock battle of explosions in the 'captive' landscape enclosed in its glass case.

Rossini himself may have found it unnecessarily didactic to insist upon a coherent dramatic content for his ballets. On the other hand, the imagination and quality of the music he did provide easily stir the imagination to find ways to integrate these divertissements into the overall dramaturgy of the evening. It is clear that his instinctive theatrical talent would not permit him to write music that could be inappropriate to the situation, even if he did not choose to spell out how that might be realised.

Guillaume Tell also has its extended concerted ensembles: these are handled with a much surer sense of proportion than those in *Rienzi*, and consequently never seem forced in their length. In any case, Rossini himself builds them around situations of genuine dramatic movement: the destruction of Tell's village by Austrian troops at the end of Act I, the swearing of the oath at Rütli, and the famous scene of the shooting of the apple are all scenes which need strong and carefully crafted staging by the director, but have no need of 'invented' action to justify or redeem them. In other words, the conventions of grand opera when handled by a master with an instinctive theatrical sense prove no more difficult to realise for the contemporary stage than any other dramatic convention. It is not the convention which is the problem, but the imagination with which it is used by the composer.

The same applies regarding the very considerable musical element of virtuosic display in *Tell*. Wagner attempts a certain amount of this in *Rienzi*, but the results tend to be clumsy and embarrassing. Rossini on the other hand makes a simple decision to characterise the 'noble' lovers, Arnold and Mathilde, with this element of musical brilliance, and binds the language of Tell himself to a noble, earthy simplicity. Thus with one simple stroke the virtuosic element becomes a part of the feverish emotional instability of these two typical romantic figures, each torn by the conflicts between their love and their duty. The demands of Rossini's vocal display may be a daunting burden for the two singers, but with this deft piece of musical and dramatic characterisation he has turned it into a psychological gift for the director. The latter's only problem here will be to discover whether any singer, confronted with the technical demands of the music, has either breath or brain left to give attention to dramatic detail.

Rossini showed that it was possible to take a form created out of a commercial imperative and fill it with genuine and serious dramatic content which can only give a director pleasure to handle. Much of the rest of the genre inspires, in me at least, the same kind of ironic affection that we commonly reserve for those magnificent edifices of Hollywood high camp; although, as the makers of *Gladiator* showed, if you are sufficiently unembarrassed and have the sheer nerve to go for scale, display and unabashed sentimentality, then grand opera will provide you with a glittering and spectacular vehicle.

PART THREE

Grand operas for Paris

9 La Muette and her context

SARAH HIBBERD

The 'first' grand opera, *La Muette de Portici*, has been remembered since its première in 1828 for its revolutionary sentiments: the depiction of a violent but unsuccessful revolt in seventeenth-century Naples, resonant with the events of 1789. Two years later it was performed following the successful July Revolution in Paris[1] and it apparently sparked the Belgian revolt against the Dutch in the same year, which resulted in the independence of Belgium.[2] Thereafter it was regularly recognised in France as a symbol of national spirit, during such events as the 1870–71 Franco-Prussian War. At this same moment, Wagner famously associated the opera with subsequent political events, recalling how '[*La Muette*], whose very representations had brought [revolts] about, was recognised as the obvious theatrical precursor of the July Revolution, and seldom has an artistic product stood in closer connection with a world-event'.[3] More than a century after Wagner, Jane Fulcher commenced her book on the political role of opera in nineteenth-century Paris with an assessment of *La Muette* as a dangerous and seditious work with a populist message.[4]

Yet, in spite of the undoubted turbulence in Paris in 1828, it was not the political aspect of the opera that exercised its first audiences and critics, but rather its mute heroine.[5] This is shown not only by the reports of the Opéra's literary committee and by newspaper reviews, but also by the unprecedented response of various state-funded and commercially run theatres in the city. Mutes danced across the stage of every significant theatre in Paris within four months of the première: Dalayrac's 1806 opéra comique *Deux mots* was revived at the Odéon and the Opéra-Comique; a *mélodrame*, three vaudevilles, a *pantomime-dialoguée* and two parodies were staged at the secondary theatres. On any night in April or May 1828 one could find at least three or four of these works being performed.[6]

Significantly, none of these dramas exploited the opera's most ingenious facet: the symbolic link between mute heroine and oppressed people. Instead, various silent but highly expressive and articulate female characters were at the centre of firmly non-political works. This easy transference of the heroine's affliction to a range of genres underlines the fact that *La Muette* was itself an eclectic work that drew on techniques of physical gesture, orchestral narration, tuneful melody and thematic recollection that characterised those same genres. On one level it is possible to step back from the political subject of *La Muette* altogether and understand the heroine simply as a product of her broad theatrical context. Conversely, one can trace the influence of the musical and dramatic syntax used to portray her through works by such composers as Wagner and Verdi.[7]

A new kind of plot

The work's première on 29 February 1828 was recognised by critics as a momentous night for the Opéra. 'For a long time enlightened critics have thought that alongside the old *tragédie lyrique* it was possible to have a more realistic and natural drama which might suit the dignity of this theatre'.[8] The welcomed novelty and realism of *La Muette* were most obviously apparent in its subject. It had moved away from the Opéra's usual domain of Classical mythology and medieval history, to the sort of more modern setting that was becoming increasingly popular in the novels of Walter Scott and others. Another fundamental departure in *La Muette* that contributed to this 'more realistic and natural drama' was its expansion from the usual three acts to five, and the structural developments inherent in such a change. As the librettist of *Guillaume Tell*, Etienne de Jouy, had already acknowledged in his 1826 *Essai sur l'opéra français*:

> Division into five acts seems to me most suitable for any opera that would reunite the elements of the genre: that is, a *drame lyrique* where the dramatic focus were combined with the marvellous; where the nature and majesty of the subject allowed, or even demanded, the addition of attractive festivities and splendid civil and religious ceremonies to the natural flow of the action, and consequently needed frequent scene changes.[9]

Jouy emphasised that rather than increasing the aggregate number of verses, or complicating the plot, such a development was needed 'to expand the action, to increase the interest, to establish opposites and contrasts for which music and decoration are eager'.[10] Indeed, although its story is relatively simple, the five acts of *La Muette* allow space for the plot to unfold on two other levels: the realisation of the drama in the *mise-en-scène*, and the integration of dance and pantomime into the action. This five-act structure was thus a crucial element in the transformation of the genre.

La Muette tells the story of Tomas Aniello (Masaniello), a fisherman who led the Neapolitans in rebellion against the ruling Spanish in 1647. The opera also focuses on the fate of a fictional mute fishergirl, Fenella, Masaniello's sister, who has been seduced and abandoned by Alphonse, the son of the Spanish Viceroy. The curtain rises on the preparations for

Alphonse's marriage to his socially more suitable love, the Spanish princess Elvire. After the ceremony, to Elvire's horror, Fenella identifies Alphonse publicly as her seducer, and then escapes in the resulting confusion. In Act II Masaniello swears to avenge his sister (albeit he is ignorant of the seducer's identity), and this provides the impetus to call the rebels to arms against the Spanish oppressors. Act III sees Alphonse and Elvire uneasily reconciled and determined to help Fenella but, as Spanish soldiers dispatched by Alphonse pursue Fenella, the people in the market-place rise up, defeat the soldiers and go in search of the Viceroy. In Act IV, Masaniello deceives his rebel companions by helping Fenella when she begs him to protect Alphonse and Elvire from the mob. We see, as it concludes, the people celebrating their preliminary victory and acclaiming Masaniello, while his comrades plot against him. In the final act the Spaniards regain control, and Masaniello, temporarily recovered from a poison that his companion Piétro has given him, leads the people again; he dies saving Elvire from the rebels. Vesuvius erupts as if in divine judgement and a despairing Fenella leaps into the lava.

The Masaniello legend was well known throughout Europe in the eighteenth and early nineteenth centuries.[11] The first adaptation to appear on the French stage was Michele Carafa's opéra comique *Masaniello, ou le Pêcheur napolitain* (with a libretto by Lafortelle and Moreau de Commagny), first performed with considerable success just two months before *La Muette*, on 27 December 1827. With *La Muette de Portici*, however, the librettists Eugène Scribe and Germain Delavigne introduced a mute character into the Masaniello legend for the first time. One of Scribe's early biographers tells us that Scribe took the idea from Dalayrac's opéra comique *Deux mots*, which he saw with Auber,[12] but Walter Scott's *Peveril of the Peak* (1822) also appears to have been an important influence. In the preface to this novel, Scott tells us that he in turn took the inspiration for his deaf and dumb Fenella from Goethe's shy (but speaking) gypsy, Mignon, in *Wilhelm Meisters Lehrjahre* (1795–96). As does Scribe's heroine, Scott's deaf and dumb Fenella bridges both the social divide in the story (she is a gypsy in love with a nobleman) and the personal and public elements of the story: although driven by her unrequited love for the young hero, Julian, she is also, we eventually discover, at the centre of the political machinations of the plot.[13]

The linking of the personal and the political is developed further in *La Muette* by integrating Masaniello's personal motivation with political events. Certain fictional versions of the legend written in the 1820s similarly move towards such assimilation. In his novel, A. J. B. Defauconpret depicts the leader of the revolt as being in love with Isabella, the daughter of the Viceroy.[14] This relationship not only interweaves social classes and nationalities, but also intensifies the political implications of the plot because Masaniello's personal feelings for Isabella are always presented as secondary to his duty to the people. In George Soane's five-act play (Drury Lane, 1825) Masaniello is torn between his wife, Lorina, and a Spanish noblewoman, Olympia. These personal preoccupations have an interesting, if indirect, effect on the political course of the play.[15]

In *La Muette* a gradual entwining of personal and public motivations to create the mechanism of the drama – and cement the relationship between the protagonists and the choruses – can be traced in four developing versions of the libretto, written between 1825 and 1827.[16] In the earliest draft, Fenella and Alphonse love each other, but are prevented from marrying by their social difference (she is engaged to Masaniello's comrade Piétro, and Alphonse to Elvire); there is no organic connection between their story of doomed love and that of the 1647 Revolution. But in the final version, Fenella has been abandoned by Alphonse before Act I; her story provides the catalyst for the rebellion, and Fenella herself comes to symbolise the powerlessness of the rebels, her death underlining their final defeat.

This focus on the personal in the depiction of public events was reinforced variously. Perhaps most importantly, dramatic irony encouraged the audience to recognise the modernity of the characters' actions, and identify with them. One of the clearest examples of this appears to have been inspired directly by Soane's play, and features in every draft of the libretto. Soane's Masaniello appears at the end of Act II on horseback in a procession of people who are shouting 'Long live Masaniello!' while the jealous Count Manfred and Duke d'Arcos accuse him of trying to trick the people. This clearly parallels the still more ironic – and similarly visual – climax to Act IV of the opera, when Masaniello also appears on horseback. While the Neapolitans sing 'Célébrons ce héros' ('Praise to the hero!'), Piétro and others plot his downfall, and Fenella looks on anxiously.[17]

A fundamental irony also accompanies Elvire's appearance in the first act of the opera when she promises to aid Fenella, so that trust is established between the two women before they realise their opposing personal and political positions. Equally, the fact that Masaniello never knows that Fenella's seducer is Alphonse means that he can be persuaded to help him, and thus bring about the failure of the revolt and his own death. Irony also serves to intensify the (inevitably) tragic situation by focusing on the impossibility of a resolution of the private and political dilemmas of Fenella and Masaniello.

An important feature of the libretto is its concision, linked to this piling on of irony. One can trace through the earlier drafts the gradual elimination of material that is not directly concerned with the characters of Fenella and Masaniello.[18] For example, in the second draft Elvire is more prominent: Piétro mentions how he has killed her after the wedding ceremony, but she appears in Act V, pale and trembling, in blood-stained clothing, and asks

Fenella for her help. In a state of shock the two women act out a sort of trance scene, with Fenella translating visually the emotional desperation expressed vocally by Elvire before effectively coming to her senses and saving Elvire, as Piétro and his companions arrive.[19] In spite of its dramatic potential and its satisfying mirroring of Act I scene 4, when Fenella obtains Elvire's protection, this scene is removed from the third draft of the libretto, and in the final version Elvire exists dramatically to underline the hopelessness of Fenella's love for Alphonse.

Further consolidation of the plot can be seen in the evolution of Fenella's relationships: in the first three versions of the libretto she is Masaniello's daughter and engaged to Piétro, which thus adds another level of rivalry and jealousy to the story, and a mirror-image to the royal engagement. But by the final version Alphonse's ties to Elvire are the only impediment to his union with Fenella – and a presumably younger, more vital Masaniello is recast as Fenella's brother. Other secondary relationships are also eliminated, notably the crowd's (misplaced) trust in Alphonse in the first draft of the libretto, which serves only to complicate matters further and provide a reason for the rebels to turn against Masaniello. Finally, Masaniello's political feelings, the focus of the earlier drafts of the libretto, are increasingly presented only in conjunction with his determination to avenge Fenella. An example of this shift occurs in what was to become one of the most popular numbers in the opera, the Act II duet between Masaniello and Piétro 'Mieux vaut mourir'. In the first draft there is no mention of Fenella, either in the number itself or in the immediately preceding and succeeding scenes. However, in the second – and all subsequent – versions the scene opens with Masaniello fearing for Fenella's safety, and the words 'Songe à ma sœur [fille] arrachée à mes bras' ('Imagine my sister [daughter] torn from my arms!') are introduced before the final section of the duet. Fenella is thus evoked as the music rises to its high point, so that the vengeance of the people and the fate of Fenella become inseparable from this point onwards.

An unusual feature of the libretto, present in its earliest draft and closely bound to the integration of private and public dramas, was its tragic ending. During the first decades of the nineteenth century serious operas ended happily (as they traditionally had done) and dramas featuring mute characters would return the voice at the end of the work, as part of the happy ending.[20] Typically, the return of a heroine's voice was linked to a resolution of the trauma that had caused its disappearance in the first place, such as the return of a father, son, brother or lover – or any combination of these – believed to be dead. (This is akin to earlier operatic 'psychodramas' experienced by unbalanced heroines – such as Dalayrac's Nina – who recover their sanity following the return of a loved one.[21]) Muteness, like madness or other trance phenomena, was thus presented as a transitory female condition. In Fenella's case, however, the circumstances that might allow a return to domesticity do not exist. We do not know how or why she lost her voice, but in any case, with Alphonse married to Elvire, there is no chance that Fenella can be reunited with him.[22] When her brother is reported dead, it seems there is no longer any way for her to achieve domestic happiness – and regain her voice. Moreover, as Anselm Gerhard notes, 'careful reading of the libretto reveals that in her love affair with Alphonse she has undoubtedly lost what counted as the one essential criterion of feminine innocence according to the moral double standards of the nineteenth century'.[23] In such a reading, the only option for Fenella is therefore death, and her silence is elevated to a symbol of the hopelessness of both her own situation and that of the people.

As Jouy had predicted in 1826, the French expansion of the opera libretto from three to five acts involved increased dramatic effect rather than an extension of the text.[24] Indeed, the libretto of *La Muette* is remarkably short – significantly shorter than the texts of other grand operas.[25] We shall now see how the directness and concision of the libretto – and its arresting conclusion – were transposed to the visual effects and the music, and how all three contributed to the clarity of the mute's expression and to the political urgency of the opera.

Sight and sound: Fenella

In the 1820s mime was generally seen at the Opéra only in ballet-pantomime, and the conventional symbolic gestures of this repertory were introduced into an opera for the first time in *La Muette*.[26] But perhaps more obvious and direct an inspiration for *La Muette*, given Scribe and Delavigne's experience, was the sort of mime used in spoken genres at the secondary theatres, particularly in *mélodrame*. Mime was used in such works for both speaking and silent characters. Expressive gestures and tableaux were used regularly at moments of climax to convey emotions and passions more directly – and concisely – than was possible in speech; visual symbols, *mise-en-scène* and atmospheric music helped to clarify such expression.[27] But a genuinely mute (often male) figure was also frequently found at the heart of a *mélodrame*, where difficulty in communicating provided a source of tension as his or her innocence was questioned and finally understood. The inspiration for such mute characters is generally recognised as being Jean-Nicolas Bouilly's *comédie-historique L'Abbé de l'Epée* (1799) for the Théâtre Français, based on the life of a famous historical character, who invented sign language and founded an institution for the deaf and dumb.[28] A young deaf and dumb orphan, Théodore, whose inheritance the Abbé helps to recover, is

Figure 18 Fanny [Franziska] Elssler (1810–84), Viennese by birth, was the daughter of Joseph
Haydn's amanuensis, Johann Elssler. Her career began in 1825. Later she was a *protégée* of
Robert Gallenberg, director of the Vienna Opera and composer of *Alfred le Grand* (see Fig. 10).
As Fenella in *La Muette de Portici* (Vienna, Kärntnertortheater, 1832, pictured here) she scored a
triumph and became world-famous thereafter. Gautier's description of her subsequent Parisian
performances is translated in Chapter 6. Fenella is shown here just after the moment portrayed
in Fig. 11: according to the libretto, 'Vesuvius begins to throw out smoke and flame and
Fenella, arriving at the top of the terrace, considers this frightening sight. She stops, removes
her scarf, throws it towards Alphonse, lifts her eyes to heaven, and jumps into the abyss.'
(Drawn by Schroeder and engraved by A. Geiger for *Bilder zur Theaterzeitung*)

at the centre of the play. In this work, and in the *mélodrames* that followed,
either a speaking character would translate the mute's pantomime, or the
gestures would have a simple metaphorical significance in themselves. In
Pixérécourt's *mélodrame Le Chien de Montargis* (1814), for example, the

mute Eloi, falsely accused of murder, tries to defend himself in a court scene. We do not need to understand what he is actually trying to communicate, and simply understand his complicated gestures as metaphor rather than literal translation.[29]

Although the gap between thought and expression was the dramatic point of such scenes, and a crucial element in most early nineteenth-century depictions of mutes (including Walter Scott's Fenella), it was a technique rejected by Scribe and his contemporaries in the 1820s. Fenella's muteness has no bearing on the plot, and it is no obstacle to her communication with the other characters in the opera. Moreover the mute heroines in similar works of 1828 share with Fenella this greater lucidity.[30] Such attention to articulate expression was part of an increased public interest in the state of muteness in the 1820s. Although the Abbé de l'Epée had opened the first publicly funded institute for deaf-mutes in France in 1755, training teachers who established schools throughout Europe, it was not until the first decades of the nineteenth century that, with the efforts of his pupil the Abbé Sicard, widespread concern for deaf-mutes became apparent among the general public. By 1828, numerous books and newspaper articles highlighting concerns about deaf-mutes in the community had been published. Interest was shown in educating and communicating with them in various types of sign language, reports were produced and efforts were made to help them partake in cultural life.

In December 1827 an article appeared in *La Pandore*, reporting on a meeting of deaf-mutes, and showing interest in how they communicated:

> When, instead of passion, it is words that one wants to communicate, the language of natural signs becomes so detailed and long, often even evasive and confused, that it is better to abandon dramatic pantomime and resort to conventional alphabetical or elliptical signs.[31]

In the theatre, too, emotion could be communicated with force and immediacy (as evidenced by Pixérécourt's mutes), but factual narrative, which was frequently Fenella's chosen mode of expression, presented more of a challenge.

Contemporary and modern commentators alike have signalled the function of music in bridging this interpretational gap between thought and gesture in narrative. An early review of *La Muette* noted:

> A mute woman who has many things to say in the work says them and expresses them with the greatest clarity, since the words, contained in the orchestra, are most intelligible to the audience.[32]

And the critic Joseph d'Ortigue observed thirty-five years later that music was more important than gesture in communicating Fenella's thoughts:

> I am not talking here of gesture and mime . . . voice and words are given to
> her through the orchestra. How touching, expressive, passionate and full
> of sensitivity are the speeches that she performs, thanks to the orchestra![33]

So in precisely what way does the music clarify Fenella's gestures? It works
on a number of levels (word-painting; suggesting atmosphere; as bearer of
reminiscence motifs; and by alluding subtly to other works) all in partnership with a lexicon of simple, gestural expressions. These were combined
in order to convey the two types of expression noted above: emotion and
narrative. As Marian Smith has noted, most of Fenella's miming occurs in
scènes, recitatives, ensembles and finales (rather than arias), flexible forms
that were more accommodating to her type of expression and that allowed
a singing character to confirm the meaning of her gestures.[34] Nevertheless,
one of the most innovative and successful scenes in *La Muette* is Fenella's
description of her imprisonment and escape in Act I scene 4, which unfolds
more like an aria, with only occasional interjections from a singing character (see Ex. 9.1). As with mutes in early nineteenth-century *mélodrames*,
great tension derives from the urgency of her predicament. Yet unlike her
predecessors, Fenella is perfectly understood by Elvire, and apparently by
the audience, without any spoken translation. Certainly we are aware of the
outline of her story, since Alphonse explains it to his companion Lorenzo
in the first scene of the opera; and the Spanish soldier Selva describes her
imprisonment and escape to Elvire as Fenella runs on stage. However, the
score – which in some ways replicates the highly atmospheric orchestral
passages that accompanied Pixérécourt's mutes[35] – is also packed with musical metaphors that clarify the detail of events and produce the illusion that
her muteness does not impede her communication. A pounding march
rhythm accompanies her description of the soldiers taking her away, and
a sequenced descending flourish in the bassoons and strings represents a
key being turned and a bolt shot on her prison door. When she 'narrates'
her escape effected by knotting her sheets together, a slithering scale in the
flutes and clarinets decorated with a pattern of chromatic triplets in the
violins gracefully accompanies her descent from the window. The atmospheric agitated passage that brought her on stage reappears at the end of
the pantomime, returning us to the present; unsurprisingly, the episode
has been compared to the similarly efficient technique of the cinematic
flashback.[36]

  The dramatic sophistication of this scene becomes more evident when
compared with earlier drafts of the libretto. In the first, three-act version,
part of the story appears much later in the opera (in II.10) in a conversation
with Alphonse during which she explains that there is a conspiracy against
him. They declare their love for each other, and then Fenella helps him to

Example 9.1 *La Muette de Portici*, Act 1 scene 4: Fenella's mimed 'narration' to Elvire.

[SELVA] took her away by force.

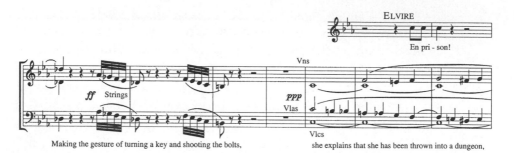

Making the gesture of turning a key and shooting the bolts,   she explains that she has been thrown into a dungeon,

where she prayed, sad and thoughtful, plunged into sorrow,   when suddenly the idea came

to her to escape from her slavery; pointing to the window, she indicates that she attached her sheets to it,

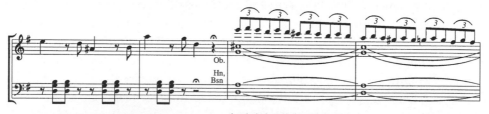

that she let herself slide to the ground,

that she thanked the heavens [etc.]

escape out of the window before the conspirators arrive. In other words, the unfolding of threatening events in the original draft was later recast as Fenella's narration of her own recent escape. This immediacy of her expression is closely bound to her more developed role at the heart of the drama seen in later drafts, rather than to that of bystander to political events, as in the first version.

Familiar melodies are also used to decode Fenella's expression. Orchestral quotation of borrowed songs and opera arias was a common technique in both popular theatre and ballet-pantomime, and it was an important feature of all the other 1828 works featuring mute heroines: the meaning of their gestures was conveyed through the words that came to the viewer's mind when a particular tune was played by the band. (The technique is still alive in popular culture and advertising, of course.) In *La Muette*, however, Fenella does not 'recall' the texts of other works; rather, motifs from within the opera are summoned and developed, a technique familiar from both opéra comique and Weber's mature works.[37] For example, in a scene with Masaniello in Act II, Fenella pours her heart out in gestures supported by musical quotation (see Ex. 9.2 and Fig. 29, p. 415). Much of what she has to 'say' is known to the audience, which transfers its knowledge unconsciously to Masaniello, whose responses confirm for the audience the meaning of her gestures. When Fenella indicates that she is unable to marry her love, as he is a nobleman, she is accompanied in the wind and violins by the dotted quaver motif from the first Spanish chorus 'Du Prince objet de notre amour'. The string melody that follows, when Fenella adds that he is already married, is a minor-mode transformation of the Spanish chorus sung at the wedding ceremony. Masaniello, however, does not realise the beloved's identity.

In addition to the recalling of words, a more subtle reminiscence technique is employed to suggest a recurring moral quality. Rather in the manner of Weber's thematic web in *Der Freischütz*, in which the presence of evil is evoked through the diminished-seventh chord that signals Zamiel's first appearance, Auber evokes Fenella's piety by means of a texture that reappears in different guises at strategic points in the opera. The texture first appears in her Act I pantomime (see Ex. 9.1, bar 9): a static figure in the strings, incorporating chromatic passing notes and a descending chromatic line in a prolongation of a C major chord, accompanies her prayers and thoughts of Alphonse. The mood of this passage is evoked in 'O Dieu puissant', a Spanish chorus that follows Fenella's pantomime, in which the people bless Alphonse and Elvire at their wedding ceremony: the (tonic) C pedal returns, supporting the characteristic dactylic rhythm (Ex. 9.3a). Although the melodic and harmonic content is quite different, the proximity of the two static passages, in a generally fast-moving score, suggests a striking recurrence of mood that implies a dramatic link between Fenella's thoughts

Example 9.2 *La Muette de Portici*, Act II scene 4: Fenella's mimed 'narration' to Masaniello.

But as for marrying her, he is too well-born.

no further hope, that he is married to another.

of Alphonse and the choral blessing of the marriage. In the Act III finale the choral prayer 'Saint bien heureux' evokes a similar mood: this time the voices are unaccompanied, but the number again centres on a tonic (E♭) pedal and opening dactylic pulse, and recalls the rhythm and melodic contour of 'O Dieu puissant' (Ex. 9.3b). Finally, Fenella's prayer for her brother immediately before his death, in the last scene of the opera, is a direct quotation of 'Saint bien heureux'; the theme is heard in octaves in the wind over an urgent tremolando string accompaniment, this time in D♭ (Ex. 9.3c).[38] These four passages each accompany prayer and suggest calmness in the midst of turmoil. On each occasion they precede an important moment in the action, and emphasise a suspended moment of time – a dramatic pause – before the action accelerates.[39] The stasis suggested by a tonic pedal and calmness evoked by a gently lilting rhythm add definition to the advance of the drama and establish Fenella's piety at its centre.

Example 9.3a *La Muette de Portici*, Act I, chorus 'O powerful God, protecting God'.

Example 9.3b *La Muette de Portici*, Act III, finale: chorus, kneeling in prayer: 'Blessed saint, whose divine image'.

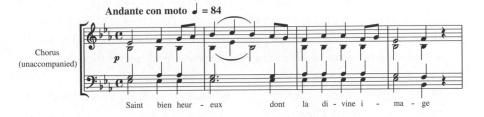

Example 9.3c *La Muette de Portici*, Act V, finale: Masaniello is dragged off; Fenella stares after him; she returns to the side of the stage and prays to heaven for his protection.

The public sphere

One of the most unusual and striking features of *La Muette* is the way in which it embraces the visual techniques of popular theatre, transposing the personal to the public dimension.[40] This is most evident in its apocalyptic finale. The *mélodrame Le Monstre et le magicien*, an 1826 adaptation of Mary Shelley's *Frankenstein*, concludes with the monster's revenge on his creator. This takes place during a violent storm and is subsumed into a final horrific tableau of death and disaster following the massacre of a band of outlaws. The despair of the main characters and various onlookers is mingled with hints of the supernatural and the force of nature, a typical combination in popular drama of the time. Another *mélodrame*, Pixérécourt's *La Tête de mort, ou les Ruines de Pompeïa* (1827), presented a similarly cataclysmic finale in which the despairing main characters and a group of bandits pursued by soldiers are all engulfed by the molten lava of Vesuvius. Again, the tableau not only translates the emotional state of the characters in visual terms, but also intensifies and ultimately subsumes the drama: 'The red glow with which everything has been infused, the terrifying noise of the volcano, the screams, the agitation and despair of the characters, each of these elements contributes to . . . a horrible tableau that one might justly compare to Hell'.[41]

The final scene of *La Muette* presents a similar sublimation of Fenella's emotion and the horror of the people in a visual tableau. Yet modern critics have been generally disappointed by this conclusion, focusing narrowly on the music, and in particular on the 'unremarkable' passage that accompanies Fenella's suicide.[42] Indeed, when merely *listening* to this final scene the music accompanying the heroine's leap passes us almost unnoticed. However, the visual aspect and wider musical significance of the scene – its '*Don Giovanni*' undertow – are crucial to its drama. Striking minor ninths (in root position) mark Masaniello's departure with his men. Fenella first prays for her brother, recalling a theme from Act I as she comes full circle in her predicament. With Vesuvius grumbling in the background, minor elevenths and the eerie timbre of the tam-tam herald the appearance of Elvire, the first to arrive with news from the fighting. Tension mounts as the narrative is passed to each new character arriving on stage. The sense of inevitability is increased by the pull of chromatic bass lines and Fenella finally learns that her brother has died (see Fig. 11, p. 68). D minor semiquaver scales and arpeggios build to the entry of the simple descending chromatic theme; Fenella throws a last tender glance towards Alphonse. The theme is repeated, and a series of sequenced descending wind and violin figures accompanies Fenella as she looks up to the sky and finally throws herself into the lava. The clouds lift and the erupting volcano melodramatically reflects Fenella's release and the discharge of dramatic affect. Alphonse and Elvire cry out, and the people pray that this sacrifice has appeased God's anger; the tam-tam that accompanies the prayer seems to confirm the divine dimension of the punishment. As in *La Tête de mort*, the personal and the political are subsumed in the lava in the final horrific tableau:

> Everyone moves about with the greatest fright . . . mothers carry their children; men support their wives; some fall to the ground, others lean on the colonnades . . . those who come across the terrace die on the steps; the terror in the characters' every movement cannot be overemphasised.[43]

Fenella's leap is thus effectively supplanted by the tableau and the chorus prayer; swirling D minor scalar quavers continue, underpinning the static line of the prayer and the orchestral conclusion to the opera. Rather than a lack of dramatic skill on Auber's part, as has been suggested, these final moments represent the visual and musical transference of Fenella's anguish to the people as she and they lose all hope.

This close relationship between personal and public drama, presented visually, permeates the entire opera. Each act concludes with a tableau in which the action is reviewed; the choruses and principal characters present a sort of summarising picture in which the concerns of individual characters are momentarily highlighted by visual means and mirrored by external forces. The finale of Act I seems in some ways to anticipate that of Act V: after Fenella identifies Alphonse as her seducer, with a dramatic *fortissimo* exclamation in the orchestra, her flight passes almost unnoticed musically as the moment becomes subsumed into the mass panic of the other characters and opposing choruses. Individual scenes are played out amidst the confusion: a group of people prevents the soldiers from pursuing Fenella; then soldiers surround the people and point their guns at them; meanwhile Alphonse tries to lead Elvire away, but she looks at him contemptuously and instead joins the noblewomen.

In such scenes, then, Fenella's voice is not represented simply by her gestures and her descriptive music. Her emotion and despair become transferred to all elements of the opera: sublimated, siphoned into *mise-en-scène* and chorus, making her physical presence redundant.[44] Symbolic of the hopeless rebels, Fenella effectively embodies the action of the entire opera, and ultimately her body is the locus of its resolution. She is seduced and abandoned by Alphonse, as the people are 'seduced' and abandoned by Masaniello; her gestures provide the impetus behind every action in the opera, those of Elvire, Alphonse and the Spanish, and those of Masaniello and the rebels. The language of grand opera lies not merely in its music or text, but in the combined effect and the interaction of all its elements, not least the visual. With the clarity of Fenella's gestures extended to the broader canvas of the *mise-en-scène*, the opera itself thus became visually legible.

Music

An equally important feature of the opera in communicating the resolve of the people – the implications of which could not have been anticipated by the censors – was the sense of forward propulsion generated by the music. If the concision of the libretto and the clarity of the *mise-en-scène* – in part inspired by more popular genres – contributed to the opera's urgency, Auber's distinctive 'élan' and 'esprit' were also part of a more direct idiom than that usually encountered at the Opéra in the 1820s.[45] As Wagner was to recall forty years later, the striking success of the opera was in part due to Auber's 'popular' style, 'his thrusting down to the roots of the genuine folk-spirit', which served both to clarify the drama and to reflect the mood of the time.[46]

Given Auber's expertise as a composer of opéra comique, at a time when the genre was absorbing the influence of (Rossinian) Italian opera, it is not surprising to find that *La Muette* bears the marks of these genres. In common with the opéras comiques written by Scribe and Delavigne with Auber in the 1820s, *La Muette* features short-breathed forms with simple lyrical melodies, and a prominent role for the chorus.[47] Two such numbers defining the sentiments and musical language of the Neapolitans are presented in Act II. The lilting barcarole 'Amis la matinée est belle' (see Ex. 5.4, p. 85) is sung by Masaniello and the fishermen; it will later be recalled in Act V both by Piétro (who sings his own barcarole) and by Masaniello in his delirium, to dramatic – even ironic – effect. The rousing patriotic duet delivered by Masaniello and Piétro, 'Mieux vaut mourir', embodies the revolutionary spirit of the opera (see Ex. 10.1, p. 175) and made a strong political impact on audiences in 1828 and beyond. As well as its inspiring text, the duet's animated musical style was influential, so that its swearing of fraternal loyalty (albeit doomed) anticipated such later nineteenth-century duets as 'Mon compagnon' in *Don Carlos*. A high, 'heroic' range in the tenor part (rising to a B in the final line, on the word 'daring') and varied pacing and play between the voices contributed to its energy and rallying effect. Such simple, affective numbers to precipitate action served – as was recognised at the time – to underline the popular spirit of the drama.[48]

The political urgency and sentiments of the opera were further emphasised by the prominence of the chorus – divided into various Spanish, Neapolitan, and male and female groupings. It is present for most of the opera and engages in the action, often opposing or supporting principal characters rather than behaving simply as a group of onlookers. Thus, the finale to Act IV is launched with one part of the chorus proclaiming Masaniello their hero, with the march 'Honneur et gloire'. It is joined by Piétro and a second chorus of fishermen, who interject their contrasting contempt for Masaniello's actions. Dividing the chorus has the effect of polarising the drama, using *fortissimo* declarations in dotted notes and strong rhythms that recall the confrontational dynamic of revolutionary song, even in places where the words evoke less inflammatory emotions.

Auber employed another traditional technique: the use of musical styles to identify social and national traits of the two groups of characters. Alphonse and Elvire sing Italianate numbers (the libretto evoking the elevated language of Classical tragedy), and Spanish dances (a Guaracha and a Bolero) are presented during their wedding celebrations in the Act I ballet. By contrast, Masaniello, Piétro and the fishermen sing popular strophic numbers such as the barcarole, while a southern Italian folk-dance, the

Figure 19 Costume designs (1828) in the Bibliothèque de l'Opéra for *La Muette de Portici*, drawn by Hippolyte Lecomte (1781–1857). The male Neapolitan dancer wears a Phrygian cap and plays the castañets, traditional in performing the tarantella, seen in Act III of the opera. Pencil indications show that his tunic buttons were little spherical bells. The female figure's costume, labelled 'Chœurs' (one of twenty-eight made) is exceedingly detailed; but at a cost of 25 francs this costume was far less expensive than many others. The opera's costume-bill as a whole totalled almost 13,000 francs.

Tarantella, is performed in the Act III ballet in the market place. Thus the political opposition on which the opera is built extends to the musical language in quite simple and stark terms.

In addition to the influence of opéra comique, some numbers reveal Auber's absorption of Rossinian musical style, notably the static ensembles and choruses in which rhythm and repetition overwhelm thematic development for dramatic effect. (To this successful absorption, Fétis bore witness: see p. 180.) The chorus in Act III 'Au marché', a number that helps to establish the local colour of the village market, is a particularly good example of this. It is essentially a choral patter-song: the words are repeated in a mesmerising stream, and the whole number seems to acquire its own momentum as the beats of the time signature are blurred: see Ex. 17.1, p. 356.

Furthermore, the ensemble in Act IV scene 7 ('Je sens qu'en sa présence'), when Alphonse and Elvire find themselves face-to-face with Masaniello and Piétro, contrastingly recalls Rossini's 'stupefaction' ensembles. Time seems momentarily suspended as a horn (supplemented by bassoons and a trombone) delicately – and slightly eerily – weaves around the voice of Masaniello, who is joined by Piétro, Elvire and finally Alphonse, each presenting their own thoughts. Aggressive interjections of the fishermen, who share Piétro's sentiments, give way to the contemplative, almost trance-like, unaccompanied voices of the ensemble group. Finally, the spell is broken as the orchestra returns and Fenella reminds her brother of his promise to spare Alphonse and Elvire.

Commentators have wrongly criticised Auber for his failure to delineate character and psychological conflict through the music.[49] In a sense the charge is irrelevant. We have seen how the stark juxtaposition of vivid moods and characterisations (including dances), underpinned by an urgent rhythmic impulse, serves to increase the political urgency of the drama. But beyond that, Fenella's piety and the highly expressive quality of Masaniello's accompanied recitatives are musical achievements that constantly impress the hearer. Nor must Auber's wide-ranging orchestral skill be forgotten.

Conclusion

La Muette presents an ambiguous political message. On one hand the Neapolitan revolt is distanced from its associations with France and shown to be both pointless and distasteful in its violence. But on the other hand, popular insurgence in the face of unjust oppression is evoked in a particularly vivid manner.[50] The interweaving of personal and political themes and the nature of the visual and musical perspectives of the opera appear to have undermined its politically 'safe' libretto. This uneasy balance between authoritarian legitimacy and heavy revolutionary symbolism perhaps reflected the anxiety of the authorities, torn between liberal and ultra-royalist extremes in the years before the events of July 1830. Indeed it probably helps to explain why the opera was adopted for both populist and patriotic purposes in the nineteenth century, as was suggested at the beginning of this chapter.

The ambiguous implications of the opera are in many ways embodied by Fenella. Her ubiquitous role in the opera – embracing national and class divisions as well as representing the oppressed – can be seen as a variation on that of Marianne, the silent emblem of the Revolution.[51] As a symbol both of the Republic and of Liberty, Marianne's shifting political significance often conflicted with broader interpretations, a paradox mirrored by *La Muette*'s fluctuating significance through the nineteenth century.[52] Ultimately, however, the visual, textual and musical inspirations for *La Muette* came from popular genres, and the resulting idiom of the opera must surely have contributed to the populist interpretation of the work favoured by the majority of commentators. As Wagner recognised in 1871, Auber's 'popular' musical language – his 'certain *excess*' – perhaps stood in the way of his subsequent acceptance as a composer of 'serious' opera.[53] In spite of the longevity of *La Muette* and its influence on nineteenth-century opera, it was remembered chiefly as a work that captured the popular spirit of its age.

There were 505 performances at the Paris Opéra up to 1882. The work was seen (usually in translation) throughout central and northern Europe immediately after its Paris première, reaching London in 1829.[54] Two years later it was produced in New York, in both English and French, and in 1832 it reached Italy, from where it travelled to the further reaches of Europe, including Russia and Scandinavia. In the 1840s and 1850s it arrived in Australia and South America. It was particularly popular in England, Germany and America, where many editions of the libretto and score were published, along with numerous excerpts and arrangements of numbers, notably the patriotic duet sung by Masaniello and Pietro, 'Mieux vaut mourir' (see Table 1.2, p. 17). *La Muette*'s popularity waned after World War I, but in 1953 it was revived in Berlin in a production that apparently foregrounded the revolutionary overtones.[55]

10 Scribe and Auber: constructing grand opera

HERBERT SCHNEIDER

Scribe and the term 'grand opera'

As we saw on p. 3, 'grand opera' is not a generic term with secure historical credentials. Since William Crosten's book *French Grand Opera: An Art
and a Business* (1948) it has gained currency in musicology for a not very
precisely definable subspecies of nineteenth-century opera that is French
and influenced by France. From the late 1820s, long before the emergence of the generic paradigm, librettists and composers did, according
to Anselm Gerhard, use the term to 'characterise individual works', but not
very systematically.[1] In 1803, for instance, when Henri Berton dedicated his
Aline, reine de Golconde to Pierre-Alexandre Monsigny, he referred to the
ageing Monsigny's 1766 setting of the same libretto as follows: 'With your
tuneful songs you enriched the poem *La Reine de Golconde*, grand opera'.[2]
In fact, the older work had been designated as a *ballet héroïque* and as an
opéra. Critics of Auber's operas at their first performances did not use the
generic label 'grand opera'; nor did Scribe and Auber when their works were
printed. It is, however, found in a number of Scribe's manuscript librettos
for five-act operas such as *Le Prophète*[3] and *Noëma* (intended for Meyerbeer and containing elements that were reused in *L'Enfant prodigue*),[4] for
four-act operas such as *Dom Sébastien* (set by Donizetti), for one-acters
such as *La Tapisserie* or for the adaptation of Auber's opéra comique *Le
Cheval de bronze* as a three-act opera-ballet for the Opéra.[5] In a letter to
Auber in 1847 Scribe used the term with reference to *L'Enfant prodigue*
(1850):

> It is with [this libretto] that I think I shall have done least badly in grand
> opera, for it brings together everything that I am always looking out for –
> generally in vain – in a work of this sort. A subject with variety and
> offering opportunities for music, ceremonies, dance, spectacle, scenery
> and a grand setting, all these are there for you! And for me, there is
> something that is interesting and even original, which may seem surprising
> with this particular story.[6]

In his *Mémoires* of 1853–55, Louis Véron (see Chapter 2) used the phrase
grand opéra to refer to the major productions during his period in charge
at the Opéra.[7] In 1855, on the other hand, Castil-Blaze was still applying
the term in his history of opera in France to all the operas performed at the

Paris Opéra, without by any means restricting it to those in the five-act form that later came to be accepted as a defining characteristic of the genre.[8]

Usage was just as vague outside France. For example, in a letter to Scribe of 22 November 1832 the management of the Berlin Opera House requested a libretto for a 'grand opera in three or five acts with ballets and choruses', for setting by Mendelssohn.[9] In German the term 'grand opera' was used in the nineteenth century for both the Paris Opéra's current repertory and Gluck's Parisian *tragédies lyriques*.

In our own time, Gilles de Van has accepted a general consensus that places the birth of grand opera in the period between *La Muette de Portici* in 1828 and *Robert le Diable* in 1831. Determinant factors in his view are both the heritage of *tragédie lyrique* and Romantic demands for an 'all-inclusive presentation of social realities': these contrary forces led to 'the oscillation between a higher unity, never before achieved in opera, and gigantic rag-bags'.[10] De Van compares Scribe's dramatic manner with that of Italian operas: he takes from Stanton (see p. 48) the expression 'delayed-action plots', describing them as a means for holding back the conflict, 'fragmenting the action and revealing essentials only as the action moves forward'.[11] For him, a major characteristic of grand opera is the balance between documentary realism (even with acts of gross brutality) and episodes in divertissements or tableaux that are calculated to please, yet are integrated within the sphere of 'social action'. He distinguishes three main types of tableau (scenic, dramatic and 'act tableaux'[12]) and suggests that affinities between grand operas and novels may be detected in Scribe and Auber's *Le Lac des fées* and *L'Enfant prodigue*, in endeavours to create a 'social totality wherein collective destinies and individual fates are interwoven and influence one another. In terms of theatrical aesthetics, the social plot may be said to add a novelistic dimension to dramatic tension.'[13]

After Rossini's *Guillaume Tell* and Meyerbeer's *Robert le Diable* Scribe and Auber created, with *Gustave III, ou Le Bal masqué* (27 February 1833), a work whose musical and musico-dramatic features have been undervalued up until the present, although it held the stage for a considerable period, especially outside France. The subject of *Le Lac des fées* (1 April 1839) does not stand in the mainstream of grand opera, though supernatural elements were not excluded from other grand operas.[14] Even here, Scribe took pains over historical authenticity, for example in the Twelfth Night festivities in Cologne. With *L'Enfant prodigue* (6 December 1850) Scribe and Auber broke new ground with a biblical theme (something which had not been used in opera for a considerable period), and one in which mythology and legend are employed to resolve historical issues. Auber's counterparts to the 'historical' *Guillaume Tell* and *Robert le Diable* are, then, two works that do not measure up to the usual definition of grand opera. Though *Le Lac des fées* has spectacular scenes offering opportunities for various sorts of local colour, this opera, like *L'Enfant prodigue*, does not have the great central scene in which private and public conflict reach their climax. In both, the plot ends with the happiness of individuals.

The librettos

Véron's appreciation of Scribe's grand opera librettos touches on two works devised for Auber (for it was not possible for him to comment on *L'Enfant prodigue* in his *Mémoires*):

> It has been thought for a long time that there was nothing simpler than writing an opera libretto. That is a great mistake in literary criticism. An opera in five acts can come to life only if it has a very dramatic plot involving the great passions of the human heart and powerful historical factors. This dramatic plot must, however, be capable of being taken in through the eyes, like the action of a ballet. The choruses must play an impassioned role and be, so to speak, one of the interesting characters in the action. Each act must offer a contrast in scenery and costume and, above all, in carefully prepared situations. One of the drawbacks of *Guillaume Tell* is a certain sameness in scenes, sites, views and costumes. Scribe's *La Muette*, *Robert le Diable*, *Gustave*, *La Juive*, *Les Huguenots* and *Le Prophète* offer this richness in ideas and then great dramatic situations in a variety of stage settings as demanded by the poetics of a five-act opera. When it is a question of the most enormous theatre with a stage allowing fourteen levels in depth, an orchestra of more than eighty musicians, a chorus of nearly eighty men and women, eighty extras, not to mention the children and a team of sixty scene shifters, the public expects and demands a lot from you. It is a dereliction of duty if such vast resources are employed only for opéras comiques and vaudevilles. I say without fear of contradiction that Scribe is, of all dramatic authors, the one who understands opera best. He is first-rate in his choice of subjects, he is outstanding in the creation of situations that are both interesting and musical, in accord with the particular talents of the composer concerned. Without admiring the over-heated *La Juive* so much as Duponchel [Véron's successor as director of the Opéra, 1835–42], I have always found in the scenarios offered to me by Scribe excellent motivations for novel and varied settings, and ingenious reasons for all those expenses that are justly demanded from the manager of the Opéra.[15]

Even in 1886 Ernest Legouvé declared in a critical appreciation of Scribe that his librettos fell into a completely new category:

> Before him, the repertory of the Opéra consisted of virtually nothing, with the glorious exception of *La Vestale*, save ancient tragedies such as

Table 10.1 *Textual modifications during composition and production*

Printed libretto	Number of text lines	Subtractions/additions in each act of score
La Muette de Portici	779 (S: 743)	IV.1 cut (−36 lines)
Gustave III	1,546 (S: *c.* 1515)	II (+95 new lines, −11); III (−25, +8); IV (−51, +10); V (−59, +10)
Le Lac des fées	1,466 (S: *c.* 1241)	I (−32, +10); II (−79, +24); III (−87, +22); IV (−77, +20); V (−26)
L'Enfant prodigue	1,246 (S: *c.* 1107)	I (−52, +12); II (−56, +23); V (−80, +14)

Iphigenia, Alcestis, Œdipus and the rest – always the same ones, of course – refashioned as librettos. These were taken up time and again by different composers, and librettists were left with little more than some credit for elegant versification. What does Scribe bring? Real poems. *Le Prophète, Les Huguenots, La Juive, Robert, Guido et Ginevra* and *Gustave* are subjects that were quite unknown before Scribe. With them he has become, if we take the word *poet* in its ancient sense, one of our *greatest lyric poets*.[16]

The process of setting a libretto to music in France did not cause the separate identity of the poetic text to be forgotten, and librettos were usually published independently as literary artefacts. In conception and in the demands implied by a line count, Scribe's librettos for Auber's grand operas are extremely varied. The proverbial concision and compression of plot in *La Muette de Portici*, as compared with other works, is reflected in the line count of the printed libretto. The libretto as separately printed for the première of *La Muette de Portici* largely coincides with what is set to music in the printed score, apart from omissions from Act IV scene 1.[17] As Auber's other scores reveal significant deviations of this type in places, the figures in Table 10.1 for the total number of lines of text published in separate printed librettos are supplemented by the figures (preceded by 'S' in brackets) for the actual number of lines set to music in the scores.[18] *Robert le Diable*, by comparison, contains 1,100 lines, a total closer to that of *La Muette de Portici* than of Auber's other grand operas.

In the following discussion, considerations of space preclude full accounts of the origins of the librettos or of the different versions that, as in the case of *La Muette de Portici*, we can document with holographs and published copies.[19] The deviations, which are sometimes significant, between printed librettos and what is found in the scores can have the most varied motivations. (Gerhard's statement that 'the printed versions generally correspond to a very late stage in the production of the work and Scribe evidently took no responsibility for the very last changes' is too sweeping.[20])

Unusual care was taken over the libretto for *Gustave III*, whose plot is better known to us today from Verdi's setting, *Un ballo in maschera*. Nonetheless, during composition and doubtless during rehearsals significant changes

were introduced. The separately printed libretto contains several decisive
variants concerning plot motivation and its political significance, characterisation and dramatic technique. In this instance the censors cannot be
held responsible for the changes, because French operas were not subject
to censorship at the time when *Gustave III* was first performed. A few of
the more important changes deserve mention. In the score the conspirator
is Count 'Warting'; before the première and in the musical sources he is
called 'Ribbing'. In Act I scene 1, line 7 of the libretto runs 'Thou whose
yoke oppresses Sweden', but in the score the rigour of royal government is
transposed into the past ('Thou whose yoke weighed heavy on Sweden'),
thus showing present-day rule more positively. In the libretto (lines 48–
52) the king, who is overwhelmed by affairs, 'prays' for solace in the arts,
but this is cut. On the other hand, the king's dramatic intentions in the *Gustav
Wasa* rehearsal scene are made a good deal clearer in the score. (Following
history, Auber's Gustave III is represented as having drafted the libretto for
his own opera *Gustav Wasa*, which is seen in rehearsal.[21]) The libretto has
the announcement, 'A masked ball in fancy dress / With fresh new costumes /
That is fine'. In the score, the 'Air de danse' in Act I scene 3 bears the head-
ing 'Sommeil' (dream sequence). The king's sung words then explain the
pantomime: 'Fatigue overwhelms him, he falls asleep / The Spirit of Sweden
and sweet dreams / Reveal to him the country's glorious future'. A few bars
later the king voices his criticism: 'No, that is not the way I want that scene
to go'. During the second *air de danse*, designated a 'Dalecarlian wedding',[22]
the king has to turn aside from his artistic endeavours: 'Orders to sign;
leave us'. These additions, probably made during rehearsals, can best be
accounted for as part of the dramatic working-out of the king's own opera
rehearsal scene. Scribe, who was very actively involved in the production,
would not have rejected such developments, even if the idea had come from
Auber.

The C minor *couplets* in Act II, which are not given as in the printed
libretto, become more dramatic, since Auber has the chorus sing the refrain.
In Act III scene 2 (after line 362) a passage was added in which Amélie,
Arvedson the fortune-teller and Gustave together pray for help.

Particularly large cuts were made in *Le Lac des fées*. Mostly it was a
matter of abbreviating recitatives and ensembles. As regards content this
meant, for instance, that dramatic force – which Auber strove to achieve by
musical means with the greatest possible concentration – was increased by
numerous extra choral interventions (in I.3, II.9 and 13, III.1 and IV.8) and
by reducing the amount of detail, for example in the Act III finale. Auber
cut Scribe's repetitions and extended vocal ensembles in order to speed up
the plot and sharpen conflicts.[23] In Acts III and IV of *L'Enfant prodigue* cuts
and additions more or less cancel one another out.

Table 10.2 *Disposition of numbers in grand operas*

Title	Arias/ couplets	Duets	Ensemble	Scène	Introduction	Finale	Chorus	Dances
La Muette	5; 3C	2		2	1+aria	3; 1+C	6	3
Gustave III	4; 4C	4	5	4	1	3; 1+C	6	8
Le Lac des fées	5; 3C	2	3	3	1	3; 1+aria	7	5
L'Enfant prodigue	8; 5C	3	1	6	1	2	13	7

Musical organisation

In Auber's works the musical sections are consecutively numbered and clearly distinguished from one another. To an ever-increasing extent individual figures who are on stage participate in the solo numbers with interjections, responses and so on, as do many others, either by joining in ensembles or as the chorus. Auber also created larger scene-complexes that he generally designates as 'scène', with or without such additions as 'scene and chorus'; these on occasion, as in *La Muette de Portici*, cover informal ensembles. In other words, 'scène' can mean dialogue in recitative as well as pieces involving soloists, ensembles and even chorus. Many romances are included among those numbers which are in strophic form: the latter appear in Table 10.2 as '*couplets*' (denoted by 'C'), this being the French generic term for strophic vocal items.

Few finales or introductions include formal solo numbers; in Table 10.2 they appear as 1+C or 1+aria and should be counted as extras in the resultant figures. The choruses often take part in free-standing numbers sung by the soloists and always participate in introductions and finales. *La Muette de Portici* and *Le Lac des fées* show the closest relationship between solos, ensembles and chorus. Scribe and Auber created the most ensembles and major scene-complexes in *Gustave III*, but its subject also offered fewer possibilities for choral participation. In a period when the demands of the musical scenes were increasingly determining the shape of opera plots Auber remained true to himself in *L'Enfant prodigue*. On the one hand he linked several relatively brief closed forms with simple recitatives in a rather old-fashioned way, thus no doubt maintaining his natural affinity with opéra comique. On the other he pioneered, for instance, duets that were precursors of the modern dialogue duet. The fact that in his grand operas he did not adhere to the Meyerbeerian prototype but went his own way is no cause for disparagement. Véron, for instance, often mentions Auber, Halévy, Meyerbeer, Adam and Rossini without picking out any one of them as the towering figure: plainly he accepted each for his own qualities and individuality.

Table 10.3 *Textual and musical form of 'Mieux vaut mourir'*

Masaniello 'Mieux vaut mourir que rester misérable' (abab)	[Next quatrain not set to music: cdcd]	Dialogue between Masaniello and Piétro 'Me suivras-tu?' (efef)	First quatrain repeated, followed by 'Amour sacré de la patrie' sung à 2 (ghgh)	Dialogue between Masaniello and Piétro 'Songe au pouvoir'(ijij)	Stanza 1 repeated but sung à 2: 'Plutôt mourir que rester misérable'	'Amour sacré de la patrie' repeated, sung à 2.

Formal issues: duets

The dramatisation of duets in the nineteenth century is no less widespread than the dominance of Rossini's five-part duet form, which became (with local variants) a staple resource of French grand opera.[24] For ease of comprehension the following Italian terms are used for the five sections of large-scale duets: *scena*, *tempo d'attacco*, cavatina,[25] *tempo di mezzo* and cabaletta. The type is regularly found in Auber's earlier grand operas. Scribe's favoured verse-form is the alexandrine, often in alternation with decasyllabics for recitatives, with octosyllabics for longer fixed forms, and shorter lines, generally hexasyllabics, for cabalettas. Scribe does not abide by any strict typology in the choice of lines. For other duets, for example 'Mieux vaut mourir' in Act II of *La Muette de Portici*, the only alternation is between octosyllabics and decasyllabics.

On the other hand, the textual form of 'Mieux vaut mourir', the first duet (186 bars) in *La Muette de Portici*, was designed not in five-part form but as a sort of rondo, described later by Meyerbeer as being 'in the French manner'.[26] It is sung by Masaniello and Piétro just following the revelation that Fenella is still missing: Masaniello, assuming his sister has been violated, swears vengeance. In Table 10.3, the rhyme-scheme is indicated by bracketed letters.

Following the second dialogue section, Auber composed the final sections afresh, so that whereas 'Amour sacré de la patrie' (the words were borrowed from *La Marseillaise*) is first sung in the dominant, A major, it finally resounds in the tonic, D. In the whole duet, Auber departed from Scribe's pattern and handed the leading role over to Masaniello, thus changing the logic of its content. This is enhanced musically through a famous effect: redisposition of the vocal parts in the final section causes Masaniello to sing the theme 'Amour sacré' in the upper tenor register, a tone higher than when it was heard the first time (Ex. 10.1a and 10.1b).

Opening Act III is a passionate duet for Alphonse and Elvire ('N'espérez pas me fuir': 50 lines of text and 242 bars), in five Italianate sections.[27] Elvire angrily forces her husband to agree to find Fenella, and almost resolves to

Example 10.1 *La Muette de Portici*, Act II, duo of Masaniello and Piétro, 'Mieux vaut mourir': 'Sacred love of fatherland, give us daring and pride'.

(a)

(b)

leave him. The opening reveals conflict as Elvire reproaches Alphonse with betraying her love (Allegro agitato recitative, then B♭, $\frac{4}{4}$ Allegro moderato in vocal dialogue, modulating to G minor): this corresponds to a *scena* and *tempo d'attacco*.[28] Then comes Elvire's self-accusation (G minor, $\frac{6}{8}$ Andante), the cavatina section. Next, Alphonse's admission of guilt leads to a dialogue with Elvire (Allegro moderato) and finally reconciliation in a cabaletta (B♭, $\frac{2}{2}$ Allegro vivace). In the first Allegro moderato, the voices sing a pronounced melody in turn, as in Italian examples. But later, the orchestral motif accompanying their dialogue resumes in the 'Tempo di mezzo' after the Andante, where the music explores new tonal regions of E♭, C minor and D. The resulting closed form for the first section of the *tempo di mezzo* is distinctly unusual. Furthermore, in the Andante (cavatina) the composer links two eight-bar passages (solo, then duet) without formal repeat: here Auber changed his earlier, more Italianate plan.[29] The cabaletta is more orthodox in formal respects. Thus the duet conforms in general with the norms of the extended Italian duet.

In *Gustave III* a series of duets involving the three principals focuses dramatic progress towards a revelation of infidelity and the fall of the prince. The first (Act I, 'O Gustave, ô mon noble maître', 44 lines of text and 206 bars) is an encounter between Gustave and Count Ankastrœm, whose wife Amélie is secretly loved by the king. Basically formed as a five-section extended duet, its cabaletta continues directly from the *tempo di mezzo*; the latter (as with the preceding example) is musically linked through orchestral figuration

Example 10.2 Auber, *Gustave III*, Act III, duo of Gustave and Amélie: 'I cannot survive without you, this intoxicating love drives me mad'.

and sense of development with the *tempo d'attacco*. An Andante con moto ('Par sa seule présence') serves as slow section. The second (Act III, 'Calmez votre frayeur', 63 lines of text with significant deviations between score and printed libretto; 210 bars) foregrounds Gustave and Amélie in a highly volatile duet of the same type (Ex. 10.2 shows the cavatina section).

Act IV opens with the most dramatic duet in the opera, Ankastrœm and Amélie's 'D'une épouse adultère'; described as 'Duo and Cavatina', it comprises 76 lines of text and 233 bars. The piece begins in D minor with an emotionally fraught forty-four-bar instrumental Allegro vivace that serves, unusually, as both *entr'acte* and ritornello for the first section of the duet. In the first section (cast in hexasyllabics) Ankastrœm threatens to kill his wife while, in a plea punctuated by many pauses, she denies adultery and finally convinces him. In her cavatina she asks her husband to let her once more see their son, who will close her eyes when she is dead. Following a slower thirteen-bar passage (octosyllabics) Ankastrœm, moved by this plea, decides – as the pair sing together – to kill the king instead of his wife. Like the opening section, Amélie's loosely ternary cavatina is in D minor, Auber's 'tragic' key. In the final twenty-one bar section (octosyllabics) for both singers Auber modulates into D major, signalling triumph, but the tempo is still slow. There is thus no *tempo di mezzo* or ordinary cabaletta.[30]

Gustave and Amélie's final duet is included within the 'Scène, couplets, chœur, duo et final' concluding Act V; it is fully integrated in the dramatic progression of the through-composed scenes. Though the tempo is unchanged throughout, the duet passes through Eb minor (Amélie's appeal to Gustave to leave the ball), D minor (Gustave realises that she it was who wrote the letter of warning), E major (she again refers to the threat to his life, he realises that he has lost her love for ever), then an ensemble of sixteen bars and dialogue (forty-eight bars) in which Gustave proclaims Ankastrœm's appointment to the governorship of Finland as well as what he appreciates must be his separation from Amélie, thus ending his misdeeds. This dialogue is briefly interrupted by the chorus, and ends with Gustave's murder by Ankastrœm.

The plot of *Le Lac des fées* is much less than familiar today. A group of German students discovers a 'swan-lake' in the Harz mountains; when the swans change into fairies, Albert falls in love with Léïla. As they bathe, Albert (in fact already engaged to Marguerite) takes Léïla's veil, but this deprives her of immortality. She is thus forced to work (at an inn) for Marguerite, who jealously dismisses her upon noticing Albert's feelings. Rodolphe, a wealthy aristocrat, proceeds to flirt with both women. Albert's savings are stolen during the Cologne Twelfth Night festival, and, unable to repay the money-lender Issachar, he is imprisoned. Eventually Marguerite resolves the situation by retrieving the lost veil: Albert returns it to Léïla, and its power releases her from enforced betrothal to Rodolphe.

The two duets in *Le Lac des fées* present a total and unexpected contrast in approach. Act II no. 8 ('Ah, jamais l'on n'a vue / Est-ce toi, réponds-moi' sung by Albert and Léïla) is actually in strophic form sung by Albert, Léïla simply linking the strophes in a ten-bar codetta that returns at the end, the voices now together.[31] A fairy chorus joins in with the next duet, 'Asile modeste et tranquille', opening Act III. This shows the idyll in the student's garret: Léïla is weaving cloth and Albert copying music in order to pay off his debts to Issachar. With 206 lines of text (whole sections of which display differences between score and published libretto) and 463 bars of music, it is quite exceptional by comparison with other such designs in Auber. The idyll is first disturbed by Léïla's worries about their debts and then by Albert's breaking of his promise and confessing to her about his love. Léïla calls on the fairies for help. Finally Albert admits that he has stolen her veil and thus prevented her escape back to fairyland; nonetheless, he now returns it. He simply cannot believe it when she does not accept the veil, deciding to stay on earth with him.

As the foregoing reveals, this is a duet in which dialogue is paramount. It does, however, also contain musical development, though it has few closed sections and follows no preordained form. One section is in the form of a free three-part canon ('Asile modeste'). This unorthodox duet amalgamates several elements of the plot and constitutes the dramatic climax of the emotional debate between Albert and Léïla. Auber dispenses with tonal symmetry, opening in E♭ major, moving to sections in A minor, C major, C minor, E♭ major and concluding in B♭ major. He eschews any attempt to give the duet even token unity, for example by returning to one of the earlier thematic motifs at the end of the duet. Here Auber prepared the way for the modern dialogue duet.

L'Enfant prodigue (*The Prodigal Son*) tells the parable narrated in St Luke's Gospel, chapter 15. This opera saw a new element: the integration of duets within a larger musico-dramatic context, featuring the avoidance of final double bars and closing tonic cadences. Instead, the following sections are seamlessly linked through a new modulation. It is true that Auber does not abandon the number system, but he avoids strict differentiation between numbers, thereby participating in the contemporary trend that favoured a gradual departure from fixed and traditional forms. Having lost their outward connection with Italianate five-part form, the duets consist of uninterrupted movements divided by changes of tonality rather than by changes of tempo or metre. The opera itself portrays the experiences of Azaël in the city: gambling, love, the Mysteries of the temple of Isis. Ruined, and with no choice but to become a shepherd, he returns home where Jephtèle, his cousin and lover, still remains.

The three duets in *L'Enfant prodigue* differ greatly in form and weight. 'Au sein des plaisirs' (Act I no. 4) is a tenor–bass duet whose 50 lines of text are set in 216 bars of music; it contains the discussion between Ruben and his son, Azaël, who is consumed with longing to see the distant city of Memphis. A single Allegro section, it starts in C major but concludes in E♭ major. The father correctly recognises his son's desire to get away from home and in his twenty-bar strophe warns Azaël against idle dreams. Azaël then sings the same musical strophe, but in E♭ major, obsessed by the dream of quitting the constrictions of his father's house. Their opposing views are presented by the two voices in E♭ minor, leading to a dialogue section (from B major to G major). Finally, the voices sing together in E♭ in a cabaletta-like section but the music side-steps to G major at the close when Jephtèle enters with the words 'Consentez-y, mon père' ('Agree to it, father, let him leave!').

The duet 'D'où viennent ces cris de vengeance?' (Act III, no. 17: soprano and bass, 73 lines of text in 124 bars of music) is devoted to a violent confrontation between Jephtèle, the sacrifice of whom is demanded by the mob, and Bocchoris, the priest of Isis. There are no parallel strophes; an initial Andante section juxtaposes both voices (E♭ major, $\frac{12}{8}$), as Jephthèle's despair counters Bocchoris' vain reassurances. In the single remaining

Allegro this dialogue is taken up again (brief sections in C, A♭ and G major) before a cabaletta-like section of sixty-four bars for both voices, whose climactic tonic preparation of E♭ resolves instead on to B major.

The third duet, 'Quelle morne douleur' (Act V, no. 25, 'Romance and Duo' for soprano and tenor), uses only thirty-seven of Scribe's text lines, set to fifty-eight bars of music. Jephtèle meets Azaël, who has come to grief while abroad and is now returning home exhausted. Only after their twinned romances is a duet form assumed. It starts with a dramatic Allegro moderato in dialogue, when the cousins recognise each other. Auber links this with the Act I duet (no. 4) through a reprise of an earlier triadic motif: Azaël remembers his father's scorn. Though brief, the later duet is completely integrated in the dramatic framework and may also be regarded as foreshadowing the modern dialogue duet.

La Muette de Portici: structure and reception

Politics at the end of the Restoration are clearly reflected in Carafa's *Masaniello* (see p. 151), Auber's *La Muette* and other works: the Neapolitan fisherman is the embodiment of hopes for a new revolution. Despite the possibilities of compromise expressed in its final chorus, *La Muette* was interpreted in the nineteenth century as a revolutionary opera, thanks especially to the Act II duet already analysed, and the finales of Acts II and III. In Masaniello's mad scene, a dramatic episode of a type much appreciated at the time, Auber alluded to earlier numbers, particularly 'Courons à la vengeance' and Masaniello's two barcaroles. Using a host of recurring ideas throughout, the composer created a network linking music and drama that is underpinned by his overall tonal structure. Scribe's alternation of crowd scenes and those for individuals forms another pointer to future developments. The intensification of musical tension up until the last finale can be compared to that of Mozart's *Don Giovanni*, already well-known in France. Both focus on the key of D minor, as their plots finally unravel.

In press reports of the day, stress was placed on Auber's capacity for *vérité de couleur*, the depiction of local colour:

> From the moment the curtain rises you can smell the southern breeze: you
> are at Naples, Portici, at the centre of that marvellous gulf. Do Ciceri's
> scene painting and his Mediterranean create this illusion? No, it is the
> composer who transports you to the foothills of Vesuvius with tunes that
> are lively, cheerful and passionate too.[32]

F.-J. Fétis praised the dramatic structure of the acts in respect of their content:

> In this work, in which the first act alone appears a little too long, interest
> never flags. In each act the scenes are deftly arranged to lead up to a finale

that is effective and tableaux that have different colours . . . The
interspersing of melodrama with singing will displease only those who do
not understand instrumental music. Besides, this role for a mute woman is
an innovation in opera. It brings variety, and in an age where novelty is
what is chiefly demanded it would ill become us to complain when the
creators have combined in a single work the advantages of both opera and
ballet . . . The music is very varied, ranging from barcarole to hymns and
from the sweetest tones to the most forceful . . . Frankly abandoning the
style of Rossini and reverting to the style that is his own, Auber has, with
La Muette de Portici, placed himself in the foremost rank of French
musicians.[33]

Reviewing a revival of *La Muette de Portici* in 1837, Théophile Gautier
mentions among the reasons for the public's enthusiasm for the piece 'the
desire to judge what Auber's music would produce after such grand and
solemn scores as those of *Les Huguenots*, *Guillaume Tell* and *La Juive*'.[34]
Though Gautier admits that some of the audience came for Auber's music,
he accounts for the continued popularity of the opera by reference to the fact
that Duprez took the role of Masaniello, that Fanny Elssler played Fenella
and that Lise Noblet performed *El Jaleo de Jerès*, a 'pas espagnol'.

The Act II Masaniello–Piétro duet was the outstanding example of an operatic number that exerted a particular political effect. Nineteenth-century
French periodicals especially mentioned when it was sung at political
meetings.

In Richard Wagner's view French music reached its 'highest climax' in
La Muette de Portici, 'a national work of the sort that each nation has only
one of at the most'.[35] As for the character of the work, Wagner opined:

This tempestuous energy, this ocean of emotions and passion, depicted
most vividly and shot through with the most individual melodies,
compounded of grace and power, charm and heroism – is not all this the
true incarnation of the French nation's recent history? Could this
astonishing work of art have been created by any composer other than a
Frenchman? – It cannot be put any other way – with this work the modern
French school reached its highest point, winning with it mastery over the
whole civilised world.

Gustave III ou le Bal masqué: origins and character

The political situation in the early 1830s and the interest the French took in
the character of Gustavus III of Sweden and his reign account for the choice
of subject, a choice linked with the threat to Louis-Philippe's government
in the 1830s – the silk-weavers' revolt in Lyons in 1831, the riots on 5 and
6 June 1831 (at the time of General Lamarque's funeral) and the attempted
Legitimist *coup d'état* the same year.[36] Romantic dramas such as those of

Victor Hugo, first produced around the same time, likewise exerted a decisive influence on many aspects of subject and dramaturgy. (As already noted, the subversive libretto of *Gustave III* was not subject to censorship at this time.)

Scribe's major source for his libretto was J. Cohen's *Les Cours du Nord* published in Paris in 1820. This was a translation, with hitherto unknown material added, of John Brown's *The Northern Courts*, first issued in Edinburgh two years earlier.[37] Scribe largely based his plot on this historical account. It also probably prompted the inclusion of personal conflicts arising from the love affair between Ankastrœm's wife and the king. The following table summarises under rough headings similarities and differences between Brown–Cohen and Scribe's libretto. Only divergences are noted in the right-hand column:

	Brown–Cohen	Scribe–Auber
Characters	Gustavus as patron of the arts, well-read and an opera-director. Magnificent settings and costumes.	
	Ankastrœm, captain, in opposition to the king, since the king was responsible for the loss of his fortune.	Ankastrœm, minister, at first friend of Gustave; becomes his enemy because of the king's love for his wife, Amélie.
	Armfelt, Count Horn, Ribbing, conspirators. The king is ruler, though opposed.	
	Tensions between king and Armfelt as exponent of the new political forces.	Political conflicts between king and nobles.
	The people of the Swedish province of Dalecarlia and their character.	Presented in ballet.
Dynasty under threat	No recognised heir to the throne. The Queen-Mother spreads rumours of the king's impotence. Only after a long separation and a reconciliation are sons born.	Supposed motivation of the king's affair with Amélie. There is no Queen in the opera. Omitted.
Plot	A letter warns the king of an assassination attempt.[38] Gustavus is not alarmed, but hesitates to go to the ball. Ankastrœm is his political counsellor.	The political conspiracy is in progress from Act I.[39] Ankastrœm becomes the king's deadly enemy for personal reasons.
	An air pistol is the murder weapon.	A pistol is used.
	Gustavus does not die until the day after the assassination.	Gustave dies in the Opera House ballroom.

In the first printed edition of his libretto Scribe published an excerpt from an essay with the title *Relation de la mort de Gustave III extraite de l'ouvrage de M. Coxe sur la Suède*.[40] Its wording is identical with the Brown–Cohen volume. As both of William Coxe's historical accounts of the Scandinavian lands came out before the king's assassination in 1792 (see n. 36), this statement, which may have been inserted by the libretto's publisher, could just be a mistake. With the exception of the new character Amélie, Scribe took from John Brown all the names, including that of Arvedson, the 'sibyl' or fortune-teller.[41]

According to Véron, Rossini was invited to set the libretto, but declined:

> The Revolution of 1830 was most generous in its dealings with Rossini. Yet despite his contract he obstinately declined to write for the Opéra after the popular triumph of *Robert le Diable*. His state pension of 6,000 francs a year was none the less officially guaranteed. As director of the Opéra I personally offered him a bonus for a five-act opera of 100,000 francs over and above his royalties and his pension. Nothing could overcome the composer's resistance. I had even asked Scribe to draft a five-act opera scenario for advance submission to Rossini. The great man came over to Scribe's apartment for a reading of the libretto for *Gustave*; he made some jottings, observing that the great Act IV 'conspirators' scene' was the most important part of the score. But once his pension had been sorted out and guaranteed, Rossini told me I could do as I pleased with Scribe's scenario.[42]

Further comments by Véron make it clear how the opera was staged in 1833:

> Scribe went to Auber, his old friend and former collaborator. The libretto was read, for a second time, to this prolific and intelligent composer. Auber accepted the libretto of *Gustave*, but the subject appeared to him perhaps too dramatic to be musical. Act V with the masked ball inspired him to write tunes for the dances and the *galop* that were most original, lively and charming. The Act II crowd scenes were turned into choruses that were full of verve and jollity. A little role for a page was entrusted to Mademoiselle Jawureck, and it carried all before it. The dramatic role of Ankastrœm's wife was sung by Mademoiselle Falcon. In the first four acts the scenery and costumes certainly did the situations or the music no favours. The principals wore wigs. Powdered and in Louis XV costumes, the performers were ill at ease, finding it hard to express powerful emotions . . .
>   In Act V – the masked ball – Duponchel and I did our best to compensate for the unfortunate consequences of which we were well aware and for the mistakes over costumes and scenery earlier on. Nothing was neglected to make the ball scene a brilliant spectacle: the quadrilles were as varied as could be and the most brilliant fancy dress added novelty and comic originality. The opulent scenery was set up so as to provide space for hosts of people; innumerable candelabra illuminated the stage brilliantly. The whole of Act V was regal and worthy of the Opéra.[43]

Gustave is the victim of an assassination plan that runs through the whole plot from Act I like a scarlet thread; it is mounted by his opponents who oppose the king's reforms and the constitution he has introduced. Scribe was plainly conscious of the political significance of his subject, to which he added a second, personal conflict in the love affair. *Gustave III* is, after *Robert le Diable*, the third grand opera in which the greatest stress lay on scenery and staging, particularly the ball scene, in the course of which some three hundred people thronged the stage, with more than a hundred taking part in the sensational *galop*. Romantic Gothicism was reflected in the spectacular Act III night scene in the executioner's field outside the gates of Stockholm, where the king's assignation takes place with Amélie.

The turbulence of the revolt is also found in a score that reflects a distinct overall conception, though individual numbers vary considerably in quality. The ball theme is presented in various aspects – high-spirited, enjoyable, and solemn. All this is especially linked with the page Oscar up until the king's death, with the suspense felt by Amélie, who has discovered that her husband and the conspirators are planning assassination, and the triumph experienced in anticipation by the conspirators, who are looking out for their chance to strike. The presence of the ball theme during the last three acts serves in many ways as a preparation for its apotheosis and perversion in the murder at the end of the opera. It emerges in the Act IV trio, the meeting of the conspirators with Ankastrœm. In the quintet closing Act IV the emotional states of the various characters at the ball are expressed. In long *parlante* passages, when conversation is sung against the background of continuous orchestral music, Auber anticipates four eight-bar phrases from the unusual *galop* in its minor-mode form, adopting numerous different formal patterns. The juxtaposition of fear, pleasure and desire for revenge, the combination of vocal virtuosity, Amélie's asides and the collective declamation by the three male voices, all have as background the *galop* that will ring out afresh as the apotheosis of the ball. *Parlante* technique, in the three reprises of the E♭ minor dance, again plays a decisive role in the Allegro of Gustave's aria 'Sainte amitié'.

Despite all the musical innovation in his score, Auber was aware of the weaknesses of his work. In a letter to Scribe on 13 October 1860 he excused himself by reference to the shortage of time – the score was completed between December 1832 and February 1833 – and the great pressure on time during rehearsals:

> During rehearsals I was so rushed. I was allowed so little time for thought that the music suffered. I am sorry about this for the sake of the libretto, which deserved better.[44]

In a remarkable, if somewhat partial, study of the ball scenes in Verdi's operas, Stefan Kunze unfortunately neglected to draw attention to the influence of Scribe and Auber.[45] It may be seen in Verdi's work even before *Un ballo in maschera* (based on *Gustave III*: 1859) and indicates he had studied the operas of Scribe and Auber. First, his ball scenes are linked with disasters. They exploit a discrepancy between festivities and tragic events as they are taking place. In Hugo's play *Hernani* of 1828, as in Verdi's *Ernani* sixteen years later, Act V begins with festivities during which the tragic conclusion is reached. Ball scenes are not just the background to murder: they make it possible. Scribe must have known *Hernani*, yet the historical event of the murder of Gustavus during a ball at the Stockholm Opera House was provided directly by the subject that was chosen. Second, Verdi uses the *galop* as ballet music in *Ernani* and *Rigoletto*, like Auber in *Gustave III*; as in the latter, he also uses a minuet in *Rigoletto* as an aristocratic social dance. Third, Verdi's ball scenes are presented as tableaux that form a closed frame for the tragic ending of the plot. Fourth, with the exception of the minuet, the ballet music represents the 'music of the present day, irrespective of historical accuracy in scenery and costume'.[46] Kunze also passes over without comment the influence of the great *parlante* scenes in *Gustave III* on similar episodes in *Macbeth*, *La traviata* and other operas.[47]

Gustave III was seen 168 times in Paris, but only sporadically from 1840 to its last showing in 1853. It was successfully produced in Germany (Leipzig, 1834 etc.), Austria and England (see Chapter 20). In Vienna invented names were given to the historical personages, the king was changed into a duke who is saved at the eleventh hour by the fortune-teller, and the plot was relegated to the sixteenth century. When Verdi decided to set the libretto anew, he had difficulties with the censorship: in Antonio Somma's libretto the action is set in the English colonies in America at the end of the seventeenth century.

Le Lac des fées (The Fairy Lake)

Le Lac des fées (1 April 1839) was announced in *Le Ménestrel* on 23 September 1838 as *La Reine des fées*, then, on 28 October 1838, as *La Sœur des fées*, with its main role (Léïla) intended for Maria-Dolorès-Bénédicta-Joséphine Nau. Scribe and Mélesville (pen-name of Duveyrier) were responsible for the libretto, the basis of which provoked various conjectures. *Le Ménestrel* of 7 April 1839 reported that the librettists had put about the rumour that the plot was based on a German ballad. It added:

> This German ballad is, however, remarkably similar to *La Fille de l'air*, one of the most gracious plays from our Boulevard du Temple. It is true that the Académie-Royale, that great lady, does not wish to admit that it takes anything from the Folies-Dramatiques. Filch from a compatriot, and a working class one at that. But my dear!

The account of the plot in *La France musicale* is still more ironical and sarcastic.[48] Its downright denial of a 'German' source may have had political motivation. In his summing up, the anonymous author emphasises that:

> the libretto required every sort of music – the vaporous and the fantastic, comedy and wit, drama and passion. The composer takes on the same variety of styles. The music of *Le Lac des fées* is dreamy and mystic in Act I;

it is lively and gay, with verve and 'agudezza' [*sic*] in Act II; and full of warmth and glamour in Act III; throughout Act IV, which will be one of the composer's chief claims to fame, it is dramatic; and in Act V it is calm and considered.

Travel literature about the Harz was very popular and, like the chronicles and histories, it included mythological material. Scribe may have become aware of this thanks to Heinrich Heine's *Reisebilder* (Hamburg, 1826–34). As regards its theme, *Le Lac des fées* also has connections with other French works of a Romantic cast, such as *Le Sylphe d'or*, *La Fille du Danube*, *La Sylphide*, *La Peau d'âne* and *Les Pilules du diable* in which a good fairy generally appears as the foil to more or less wicked humans. Similarities in plot with *La Fille de l'air*, a three-act fairy play by the Cogniard brothers and Raymond that had been running at the Folies-Dramatiques with great success since 1837, amount, despite the views expressed in *Le Ménestrel*, to no more than a few common traits:[49] like Léïla, the fairy Azurine leaves the celestial realms and at the end of the play sacrifices her immortality in order to marry a witless peasant lad from Basse-Bretagne, one of the 'accursed denizens of the terrestrial globe'. In contrast to the libretto by Scribe and Mélesville, *La Fille de l'air* is full of mordant social and political criticism. All mankind is mocked for its follies and superstitions, as is the new Romantic intellectual elite:

> clever fellows from down there, Romanticists . . . that is a French word I can't make head or tail of . . . they used to go in for the black dogs, for storms; they wanted to overturn everything, striving today to cast down the idol that they had set up only the day before.[50]

Love is ridiculed, as are Romantic predilections for the irrational, the 'night-side' and the 'Wilis'.[51]

Scribe, on the other hand, strove to show a social and imaginary world in all its facets. This is revealed by his stage directions for each act: 'a round lake surrounded by tall rocks'; 'the garden of a large inn'; the students' lodging in an old building; Cologne's central square decorated for Twelfth Night; a Gothic chamber in Rodolphe's castle and a heavenly plain amidst the clouds. Scribe and Auber develop a contrast characteristic of grand opera, that between the private sphere (the idyll of student lodgings in Cologne) and the great public tableau, the indoor scene (based on the prints and paintings of Lucas van Leyden, Cranach, Dürer and Burgkmair[52]), and of the Cologne festivities in Act III (with processions and phantasmagorias, centaurs and chimeras, Bacchantes, with Bacchus, Silenus and 'a thousand and one other monstrous fantasies').[53] Links are made too with the social reality of the period, for instance through the conflict between the nobility and the military as well as students and the common people, and the forced marriage planned for Léïla and Rodolphe. Much interest was taken in the third-act ballet with 'the attempt at mythological renewal' in a bacchanal 'in the ancient manner' with ballerinas in tiger and panther skins.[54]

Among further conflicts that give the work its own dramatic force, and make any complete differentiation from grand opera appear doubtful, are the following:[55] the longing of the grasping Issachar, 'a damnable usurer, a veritable second Shylock',[56] to be able to gain complete dominance over the freedom, the blood and thus the life of Albert; Albert's madness (Act IV) and the attempt to murder him which is foiled by Léïla; and the latter's threatened marriage to Rodolphe. The combination of widely different tableaux makes the greatest demands on staging, while the work remains virtually a rag-bag of clichés.[57] In the last act, panorama technology was plainly called into use for the transformation from the fairies' celestial realms through the gradual appearance of the horizon, a mountain peak, the town with its church-towers and finally Albert's garret. In his music Auber tries to reproduce various aspects of this reality, such as the characterisation of the fairy realm using the timbre of the mélophone (invented in 1837), or the town crier in the Act III street scenes.

La France musicale was positive in its judgement of the music ('Like every great artist, Auber has a gift for . . . being popular without vulgarity')[58] while Blaze de Bury, on the other hand, pronounced a tight-lipped condemnation: 'The fantastic is just wretched childish foolery designed to justify the scene-designer's art'.[59] Théophile Gautier's discussion was half-ironic, half-enchanted, evoking Goethe's *Faust* and Heine's *Reisebilder*.[60] Albert's decision to leave Marguerite for Léïla has less to do with her beauty than with the endeavour of this dreamy idealistic student to achieve union with the higher spirits. Gautier, while stressing how Auber's achievement was debated among his colleagues in the years before the première of *Le Lac des fées*, rated him a 'composer of exceptional merit':

> He has a style of his own, which is, in our view, the first quality of any
> artist. This style, it is true, does not perhaps possess all the severity that is
> desirable, but it has a clear-cut quality and is easily recognisable: an Auber
> phrase is not a phrase by anyone else, and no one could mistake that.
> There is an abundance of motifs and melodies, which is rare in this period
> of *anti-music* in which everyone tries to surprise the ear, rather than charm
> it, and nimble-fingered performers show off impossible difficulties
> without worrying in the least about feeling, grace, or passion, about
> pleasure which is, in a word, the only and the true object of art.[61]

In Gautier's view the music of *Le Lac des fées* is completely apt for its subject with its elegance, its lightness and its dream-like character, with the result that in its five acts there is no tedium.

Le Lac des fées received thirty performances at the Opéra. Typical of its reception outside France was the way it underwent curious adaptations in which arrangers played fast and loose with it in order to make it popular in different countries.[62] The first German performance, at Leipzig on 30 December 1839, used a close translation. But on 10 November 1839 *Le Ménestrel* reported as follows on performances of the English version at Drury Lane:

> The public may have thought it was Auber's opera. Not at bit of it: it was, as the poster put it, simply Auber's music adapted 'to the taste of the British public'. This misbegotten version scored a brilliant success. The audience did not hear twenty notes of the original score, but people thought they were listening to a work by Auber and that was enough to keep them happy. Bully for them![63]

The opera was very well-received in England and in Russia when adapted as a romantic ballet. In the King's Theatre, London, a ballet by Antonio Guerra was performed with Auber's music arranged by the conductor Jean-Baptiste Nadaud. The lead was danced by Fanny Cerrito. Marie Taglioni scored a great success in St Petersburg in *Der See der Zauberinnen* in 1840–41. The choreography was by Philippe Taglioni, and Auber's music was arranged by F. Keller. The opera was performed in Berlin's Royal Opera House on 13 October 1840; the translation was the work of Carl Blum, and Paul Taglioni (Marie's brother) was responsible for the choreography. Another free adaptation, with the title *Le Voile enchanté*, opened in Vienna at the Josephstädter Theater, clocking up 126 performances in less than six months:

> Many changes have been made to the French composer's music. Here and there songs with words referring to purely local matters have been introduced, and these are greeted with roars of laughter. The scenery and costumes are magnificent, and the ballets have been devised with taste. At the end of the final act the hero is seen going down the Danube in a boat; the river banks, from Vienna to Linz, make a magical panorama.[64]

L'Enfant prodigue (*The Prodigal Son*)

In his search for historical authenticity, the librettist used not only the Bible (quoting verbatim from a French translation of the parable of the Prodigal Son) but also turned to historical sources. When the mob demands a human sacrifice in order to avert a natural catastrophe (Act III), Scribe refers to the following three sources: Joseph-Toussaint Reinaud's *Extraits des historiens arabes* (1829), Voltaire's *Philosophie de l'histoire* (1765) and Claude-Etienne Savary's *Lettres sur l'Egypte* (1785). In a note to Act II scene 3 Scribe mentions a contemporary custom with roots in patriarchal times: 'The bull Apis is one of the incarnations of Osiris, the god of agriculture. Such no doubt, though its high antiquity is not suspected, is the basis of a ceremony still performed in nineteenth-century France, that of "parading the Fattened Bull".' The detailed description in the stage-directions (II.4) of the ceremonies of the cult of Isis links in, of course, with the ambition to create 'historical colour'. Even Véron thought this was getting out of hand: 'Staging in our theatres, whether large or small, is every day developing beyond all measure: the theatrical arts are recruiting even archaeologists in the search for more accuracy in costumes.'[65]

With its luxurious exotic scenery, however, the staging of the opera excited general admiration. Maurice Bourges included extra information that pays special tribute to Scribe's 'incontestable revelations about the secret private life of Ancient Egypt's priests', found 'on the four faces of the Egyptian obelisk in the Place de la Concorde . . . precious hieroglyphs, where he has read everything that he shows us [and] managed to reveal the secrets of Isis and the mysteries of Memphis.'[66] Bourges expresses himself in more impassioned vein about Auber's music, though in the sort of terms that had been applied to it far earlier:

> As always there is a profusion of elegant and easy ideas, with lively rhythms that carry you away, are easy on the ear and linger in the memory; always the same distinction in the musical patterns, the same attractive accompaniment and orchestral colour, always this supreme art that carries its erudition lightly. Does not this ability to please constitute the greatest form of artistry? That is not all, [for] the style is so varied, so colourful and so supple that it seems to have taken on fresh vigour. We have been struck by the power of several scenes where expressive force is allied with melodic charm.

Among many details in his second article, which is devoted to musical analysis, Bourges drew attention to the 'particular characterisation' of Ruben and Jephtèle that is maintained throughout the whole opera, the thoroughly tragic tone of Act III and the inexpressible dejection and sorrow expressed in the cantabile 'J'ai tout perdu, Seigneur' near the end of Act IV.[67]

Translated by Christopher Smith

11 Meyerbeer: *Robert le Diable* and *Les Huguenots*

MATTHIAS BRZOSKA

Robert le Diable

The origins of *Robert le Diable*

Meyerbeer came to be considered one of the foremost composers in Italy towards the end of the 1820s, especially after the international triumph of his Italian opera *Il crociato in Egitto* (Venice, 1824; Théâtre Italien, Paris, 1825). Goethe, for instance, did not think anyone but Meyerbeer could set his *Faust* to music: 'Mozart should have composed *Faust*. Meyerbeer would perhaps be capable; but he would not touch anything of the kind; he is too much engaged with the Italian theatres.'[1] Not surprisingly, Meyerbeer attracted the interest of the French too; since Piccinni's time down to the era of Spontini and Rossini they had always been able to attract the leading Italian operatic composers. Though initial contacts with Meyerbeer had been made by the director of the Paris Opéra in 1823, it was Guilbert de Pixérécourt, at that time director of the Théâtre Royal de l'Opéra Comique, who in 1826 offered him a commission for a three-act opéra comique. Because Pixérécourt relinquished his post the year after, nothing came of the plan. But this marked the start of intense collaboration between Meyerbeer and Eugène Scribe, who was to remain the composer's chief librettist for the remainder of his life.

The original libretto of what was to become the nineteenth century's most frequently performed and highly rated opera, given at the most far-flung theatres, was the fruit of collaboration between Eugène Scribe and Germain Delavigne, who was responsible for the first sketches. He borrowed the title *Robert le Diable* from a Breton legend well known since the eighteenth century thanks to its inclusion in 'la Bibliothèque bleue' (cheap blue-covered books sold by hawkers) and through a host of subsequent *mélodrame* and vaudeville adaptations. None of these sources, however, provided all the details taken up by the librettists. Among various literary sources, the most significant was *Das Petermännchen*, a novel of 1791 by Christoph Heinrich Spieß. Henri de Latouche's translation, *Le petit Pierre*, had appeared as recently as 1820.

Scribe and Meyerbeer met for the first time on 4 July 1826, and the libretto was completed by 1 April 1827. During the summer the composer set most of this first version to music.[2] He stopped composing after Pixérécourt's resignation in August 1827 and the resulting crisis at the Opéra-Comique since he could no longer be confident about the availability of singers. Not until August 1829 did Scribe, Delavigne and Meyerbeer agree to refashion the work for the Opéra, in five acts, with seven scene-settings. The contract with Emile Lubbert, the director of the Opéra, was signed on 29 December 1829, and Meyerbeer was able to hand over his new score on 26 May 1830. The July Revolution and the change of director at the Opéra meant further delays. On 1 March 1831 Louis-Désiré Véron became 'contracting-director' of the Opéra – henceforth run as a private enterprise, albeit still with considerable government subsidies. Véron resolved to press on with this project inherited from his predecessor and make his first main production as magnificent and dazzling as possible.[3] On 1 April 1831 Aimé-Simon Leborne, the Opéra's copyist, was ordered to complete the preparation of vocal and orchestral parts that had been under way since 27 November 1830.

In spring 1831 Meyerbeer resumed work on the score, putting it into its final form. Apart from the substitution of recitatives for spoken dialogue, many changes were required because the solo parts had been reallocated and also because the conventions of the Opéra had to be observed. Meyerbeer completely altered Act III, for instance, in order to introduce a grand ballet scene – the Ballet of the Nuns. He also added another dance episode in Act II and the final scene in the cathedral. On the other hand, he cut the duet for Bertram and Robert, originally intended for Act I. Among role changes, the most important was the alteration of Bertram's, originally conceived as a mainly speaking part for Auguste Huet, a favourite Opéra-Comique actor who was a poor singer. At Lubbert's suggestion, Meyerbeer turned it into a major bass role for Nicolas-Prosper Levasseur. He also refashioned the role of Robert, at first intended for Louis Ponchard, for the Opéra's leading tenor, Adolphe Nourrit.

Rehearsals for chorus and soloists started in June 1831, those for orchestra on 8 October. Meyerbeer, as always, kept a close eye on the production, taking a personal interest in many details of staging and orchestral effects, supervising rehearsals for the soloists and modifying the score to suit them. Véron had recruited a team of the era's finest theatrical specialists. Henri Duponchel was in charge of the production, in association with Nourrit and Scribe. Pierre-Luc-Charles Ciceri designed the settings and Philippe Taglioni was responsible for choreography. In addition to Nourrit and Levasseur, the best soloists available were employed. Julie Dorus-Gras took the role of Alice, Laure Cinti-Damoreau that of Isabelle, and Marcelin Lafont that of Raimbaud. The prima ballerina Marie Taglioni played Héléna (the Mother Superior) for six performances, to be succeeded by Louise Fitzjames (who danced the role 232 times).[4]

Philosophical and aesthetic ideas

The première took place on 21 November 1831. The opera's extraordinary and unprecedented success cannot be accounted for without a summary of current aesthetic ideas about opera. Since the 1820s, particularly in so-called 'prophetic' circles (such as the Saint-Simonians or the neo-Catholic movement[5]) aiming at social reform, many dreamt of an 'art of the future' comprehending all the arts and linking all their effects in a single master-piece, a *Gesamtkunstwerk* (total work of art), so to speak, before the term was coined. It should express the development of history from which would emerge the new society of the future, and provide a faithful image of modern man's metaphysical condition. In his *Nouveau Christianisme* (1825) Saint-Simon elaborated a new religion in which all the arts would have their part to play: 'In order to produce . . . the most powerful and most useful action, all the means and resources the arts can offer must be combined'.[6] This idea was developed and refined by Saint-Simonians whose influence in artistic circles in the 1830s must not be underestimated. Joseph d'Ortigue, music critic of the neo-Catholic daily *L'Avenir* and, in musical matters, spokesman of the paper's founder, Félicité-Robert de Lamennais, looked forward to a similar fusion of the arts in a reform of opera. He recognised the first signs in Rossini's *Guillaume Tell*. As regards composition, he looked forward especially to a combination of Rossini's vocal style with the instrumental technique that had been admired in Beethoven's final works, above all the Choral Symphony and the late quartets.[7]

Robert le Diable met these ideas of an 'art of the future' in three essentials. It offered meticulously developed dramatic action in a production that combined all the arts in order to create an unprecedented stunning totality of musical and dramatic impression. Secondly, it presented a theme that was received as emblematic of modern man. Thirdly, Meyerbeer's score combined virtuoso singing – the legacy of his Italian operas – with the scrupulous integration of musical motifs, harmony and orchestration. All that was missing was the expression of the sort of philosophy of history found in Pierre-Simon Ballanche's *Essais de palingénésie sociale* (1827–29). Meyerbeer and Scribe would take this up in their subsequent historical operas, for which *Robert le Diable* offered in the meantime a metaphysical foundation in its conception of mankind.

Consequently, on the première of *Robert le Diable*, d'Ortigue could salute Meyerbeer as the messiah of modern art:

> Finally, eager to return to his own identity, and finding there an inevitable solution; and furthermore convinced that the two schools that had in turn commanded his allegiance would sooner or later give way to the irresistible movement which was becoming apparent around them, he preserves

everything deserving to survive this dual dissolution. Boldly he goes
forward towards the developments that open up before him, straight away
taking his position at the crossroads where Italian song and German
orchestration have to meet. Thus that union takes place which the author
of this article now ventures to congratulate himself on having announced,
the union of the vocal style created by Rossini and the instrumental
manner developed by Beethoven and applied to dramatic music by Weber.[8]

Fétis was just as enthusiastic, making similar points, if less emphatically:

> The score of *Robert le Diable* is not only Meyerbeer's masterpiece; it is a
> also a remarkable work within the history of music. Full of fresh, newly
> discovered touches, it extends the domain of picturesque music . . . Equally
> satisfying for its expression as its melodic charm, remarkable for its stylistic
> variety, this work seems to me to unite all the qualities needed to establish
> a composer's reputation unshakeably. It certainly places Meyerbeer at the
> head of the present-day German school, making him its leader.[9]

Musical and dramatic structures

The conception of the principal role derives from the vacillating or
'Hamletic' hero, met with at this time on Italian and French stages, for
instance in the roles of Armando (Meyerbeer's *Il crociato in Egitto*), Anaïs
(Rossini's *Mosè in Egitto*) and Arnold (*Guillaume Tell*). But this model has
been fundamentally altered to allow the emergence of a type of role quite
unprecedented in opera. Robert is not, like his predecessors, merely the
prisoner caught in a conflict that is tragic but essentially exterior to his personality – between love and honour, love and patriotism or just two loves.
Instead, he bears the germ of the conflict within his very being. Born of
a liaison between a devil who would drag him down to Hell and a saintly
mother who strives for his redemption, his soul comprehends the dual facets
of humanity so far as to be incapable of opting between them. The resolution
to the conflict does not, in fact, stem from some decision, but rather from
the hero's simple failure to make a choice. What, in the dramatic system of
a Scribean well-made play, would be the hero's 'obligatory scene' (*scène à
faire*)[10] – the Act V trio that is the plot's culmination – is in fact its theatrical
negation. Robert remains motionless between Alice (his mother's messenger) and Bertram (his devilish father), symbols of opposing metaphysical
forces; the resolution is brought about by the simple running-out of time
that is allowed to Bertram to complete his diabolical seduction.[11]

No less unusual than the conception of the opera's principal character
is that of the representatives of the two forces between which Robert is
torn. Derived from the typical role of the simple peasant girl, Alice is little
more than a theatrical figuration of heavenly power. The symbol of this is

Robert's mother's will that she is charged to deliver to the hero. Bertram, on the other hand, has all the advantages of the wicked, apparently possessing from the outset everything requisite for his designs. But Bertram has one unusual and shocking trait that certainly has its counterpart in Romantic literature but was nonetheless new and disturbing in opera. Bertram does not try to destroy Robert because the infernal powers require him to. He does so because he loves his son Robert so much that he prefers to lead him astray and take him down into Hell rather than save him and suffer eternal separation from the sole being he has ever loved.

Such confusion of feelings produces an ambivalence in the representation of evil that, in the eyes of contemporaries, was typical of modern man. Heine saw in Robert the expression of 'the moral uncertainties of these days'[12] and in the musical analysis of *Robert le Diable* that is the key to *Gambara* (1837, one of the so-called 'Etudes philosophiques' in the *Comédie humaine*, now available in translation[13]) Balzac saw in Robert a modern conception of mankind, tossed between wanting 'to be' and 'not to be'. To even better effect than in these literary responses, the enigmatic nature of the trio is shown in a picture of 1835 by François-Gabriel Lépaulle (Fig. 20). It depicts Robert, standing motionless and staring, as if facing some superhuman test, between Alice, the forefinger of whose left hand points up to heaven, and Bertram, who draws him urgently towards hell.

This dualistic metaphysical view of mankind takes on a further psychological dimension by the representation of good and evil with reference to paternal and maternal aspects. This 'parental' psychology was apparently an idea of Meyerbeer's. While working on *Robert le Diable* he conceived the paternal role for Bertram and brought out its dramatic significance, which Scribe's first libretto had passed over. He did much the same in his next operas too with the roles of Marcel and Fidès.

In order to stage this pattern of opposing forces Meyerbeer needed a new musico-dramatic style to convey the fatal inevitability of this metaphysical idea. The dramatic method obviously echoed Scribe's concept of the 'well-made' play.[14] The basis of the plot is a crucial misapprehension disclosed only to the spectators: Bertram is none other than the satanic father of Robert, who knows him only as a companion-in-arms. Each act presents one complete episode, the conclusion of which also implies the exposition of the next. Scene divisions follow a principle of alternating shallow stage settings and deep ones. Local colour is based on a similar contrast between the diabolical and the heavenly with a common background in the world of chivalry.

But the working-out of this dramatic style was completely fresh. Meyerbeer and Scribe brought this about essentially by a new approach to time as represented on stage and by a musical system that gave structure to time

Figure 20 Painting (in the Musée de la musique, Paris) of Levasseur, Nourrit and Falcon in the Act V trio from *Robert le Diable*. The artist, François-Gabriel Lépaulle (1804–86), specialised in operatic personalities. The fallen angel Bertram has informed his beloved son Robert that if Robert does not sign a pact by midnight, Bertram will be eternally separated from him. Alice has just confirmed that Robert may marry Isabelle unopposed, and now prays for his protection. Bertram will then produce a parchment for Robert to sign, while Alice produces the last will and testament of Robert's mother.

and place. The opera portrays the events of a single day, during which there is a constant decrease in the length of imagined time occupied by each of the seven tableaux.[15]

Act I: deep stage setting, exterior: the knights' encampment on the shore at Palermo offers a broad picture of early morning, setting a scene of medieval chivalry at the time of the Norman conquest of Sicily (1091–1194). Meyerbeer uses musical means to give form to this spectacle. The ballad sung by Raimbaud ('Jadis régnait en Normandie') narrates the opera's central myth: the engendering of Robert duke of Normandy by a devil. Variations in harmony, orchestration and dynamics are used to bring out demonic aspects between successive strophes (*couplets*) and the refrain. Meyerbeer gives force to this plan by subverting the music for the strophes more and more radically, until its phrases are grotesquely perverted in the final strophe. These 'affective variations' convey increasing terror as Raimbaud unfolds his tale.

The structural function of the ballad is of even greater significance. According to the principles of the well-made play, spectators must be informed about the misapprehension at the heart of the action long before the characters on stage can possibly guess it. On first meeting Raimbaud in scene 5, Alice recognises in his face the image of the fallen angel she had seen in a picture back home in Normandy. Though Robert manages to calm her emotions, the audience hears confirmation of Bertram's diabolical nature in orchestral quotations of the ballad theme. Music thus acquires an autonomous dramatic function. The basic facts about the misapprehension are not stated in so many words in the libretto; instead they are conveyed solely in music. In his later operas Meyerbeer went on to develop this technique, and Wagner derived his *Leitmotif* system from it. The ballad makes an obvious reappearance in Act V when Bertram reveals his identity to his son, in a declaration of paternal love that is at the same time the last and greatest of his temptations.[16]

The orchestration of the demoniacal coloration – essentially represented by horns, bassoons and timpani in dark-toned mixtures – serves as a *Leitklang* (i.e. recurring timbre) throughout the opera. Even on its own, it is specific enough to convey the nature of the characters.

Act II: a shallow setting, interior: morning to midday. Isabelle, princess of Sicily, is in a palace hall. Isabelle's aria, a women's chorus and a love duet for Isabelle and Robert establish feminine aspects of chivalry, in contrast to the men's voices in Act I. When, during Act II with its rather bright, high-pitched vocal colour, the Prince of Grenada's herald appears, his coming from 'another' world is signalled by 'diabolical' orchestration – bassoons, horns, trombones and ophicleide – long before there is any reference to the fact in the libretto. Likewise, when in the Act II finale the Prince arrives to challenge Robert in the tournament, the 'other-worldly' setting of his theme for, of all things, three solo timpani underpinned with *pizzicato* double-basses, indicates his character as a fantastic spectre long before the libretto adds confirmation. In the same finale the dramatic exploitation of the passage of time also makes its first impact. Robert, who has been led astray by the spectre in the depths of the forest, does not appear at the tournament, and frustrated expectations of his arrival accumulate dramatic tension.

It is, however, in the first tableau of Act III (deep setting, exterior: a rocky landscape in afternoon) that the passage of time becomes a genuine dramatic device. Bertram engages in direct confrontation with demons who, in an off-stage cavern, set him an imperative time-limit: by midnight he must have won his son's soul. The force of the scene comes from a symbolic interior conflict. After Bertram has, in the course of a comic duo, had little difficulty in taking Raimbaud away from considerations of hell, his confrontation with

Alice serves as theatrical counterpart to the demonic meeting. The heavenly domain represented by Alice is once again given visual form by means of a theatrical symbol: facing the grotto that is supposed to be the entrance to the underworld stands a cross to which Alice clings during her meeting with the wicked Bertram. Meyerbeer takes pains to expand theatrical space with music. Though the demons remain invisible, their voices are amplified and distorted by the megaphones used by the off-stage chorus. The musico-dramatic device requires listening on three levels: off-stage chorus (demons from another sphere), soloists on stage (the realistic level of the plot) and orchestra (storm music, etc.). Each different, these modes of expression help make up a gripping totality of all the musico-dramatic elements that interact and reinforce one another. All that is missing is dance and pantomime; they will be present in the next tableau (deep setting, interior: the ruined nunnery after sunset).

This scene, in which the nuns are summoned from their graves, showed off the utmost skills and most highly developed staging techniques of the time. Here the opera becomes just moving image, of the sort that nowadays we meet only in the cinema. Film aesthetics are revealed in the representation of the central theme in purely visual terms, without recourse to language, simply through pantomime and dance. After a ghostly bacchanale Héléna, the Mother Superior, seduces Robert into stealing the mystic branch from Saint Rosalie's tomb, a talisman conferring power and immortality. We experience a host of visual impressions. The will-o'-the-wisp effects at the opening of the scene, the metamorphosis of the accursed nuns into beings of flesh and blood, the bluish tinge of the gauze-tinted lighting that was a mystery that baffled theatrical research until modern times, all remained secrets of the production of this opera.[17] Meyerbeer had been able to devise music that caught the character of this scene, a mixture of the fantastic, the lascivious and the uncanny. According to Berlioz, the 'Nuns' Resurrection', particularly the employment of bassoons on their own within a narrow range in their middle register was 'the most prodigious invention in modern dramatic music'.[18] The dramatic integration of the ballet and of pantomime to give visual form to the central episode in the plot is a high point in this fusion of the arts into a Romantic *Gesamtkunstwerk*.[19]

In Act IV (shallow setting: the Princess's apartments in late evening), the traditional 'tableau vivant' is used to dramatic effect. Robert approaches the Princess with the talisman that causes all to fall asleep and remain motionless. Meyerbeer reveals how well he can exploit both orchestral techniques that his contemporaries considered borrowings from the German school, and also Italianate coloratura singing. As regards the meaning of the drama, the act constitutes the hero's moment of expiation, a notion central to the philosophical systems of those days and an essential inner precondition of the hero's final redemption. Though in possession of the talisman that confers power over Isabelle, Robert breaks it. Isabelle's famous cavatina ('Robert, toi que j'aime'), a plea for mercy and the dramatic motive for the hero's conversion, is placed here.

The last act (first tableau: shallow setting, the entrance to Palermo Cathedral just before midnight) finally brings on stage the redemption of the hero who, vacillating to the last, remains unable to reach a decision. Here the simple passage of time can be felt as a dramatic force in itself. Quoting the dictum of a future director of the Opéra, Anselm Gerhard calls this typical principle of Meyerbeer's dramatic style a 'dramaturgy of suspense'. The extreme tension comes from the fact that the passage of time on stage remains the sole dramatic principle while the events of the plot seem to be suspended by the balance between conflicting forces.[20] Here Meyerbeer brings in 'heavenly' coloration. Up until this final scene this had been deliberately under-represented through Alice's simple peasant nature. Now it becomes a dramatic force capable of confronting the powers of darkness. Meyerbeer turned to two musical devices. Off stage he has an organ which, supposedly pealing out from behind a tapestry in the cathedral, reminds Robert of the chanting he knew as a boy and makes him stagger each time he is about to sign the diabolical pact proposed by Bertram. This extraordinary effect – for this was one of the first organs installed in a theatre – gave theatrical expression to heavenly power, which serves as dramatic motivation for Bertram's final effort to win over his son, by revealing his identity. The second device representing celestial powers was the positioning of two keyed-trumpets in the prompter's box, in order to produce the effect of a voice from another world when Robert finally reads his late mother's will.

Two entries in Meyerbeer's pocket diary – on 28 October 1831 and, for the London production, on 21 April 1832 – reveal that he intended to give visual effect to Bertram's final collapse by showing the selfsame picture of the archangel Michael ejecting Satan from paradise that Alice had described on first meeting Bertram (I.5).[21] This over-explicitness emphasises once again Meyerbeer's aim to combine all the arts to express the idea behind his work and, with musical and scenic reminiscences, to give the opera internal unity. The happy ending is given visual form in a very brief final tableau, inside the cathedral, with Robert about to marry Isabelle.

International reception; later changes

At the Paris Opéra alone, *Robert le Diable* was performed 758 times up until 1893, a record beaten only by *Les Huguenots* and Gounod's *Faust*, which ran there for nearly a century longer. For the London production

(Meyerbeer was there from 19 April to 26 May 1832) he wrote for Nourrit an extra aria, which has not survived, and brought in a few alterations that are partially preserved in the Schlesinger full score.[22] For the Paris revival of 30 November 1838 Meyerbeer added at the start of Act II a new aria for Nourrit's successor, Giovanni (or Mario) Matteo di Candia; this aria was rediscovered and sung by Chris Merritt in New York in 1988. After Paris and London performances, the opera was soon heard in all the capitals of the world: Berlin (1832), Vienna and Copenhagen (1833); New York, Budapest, St Petersburg and Amsterdam (1834); Prague and Bucharest (1835); Basle and Calcutta (1836); then, in the years up to 1854, Warsaw, Lisbon, Stockholm, New Orleans, Florence, Barcelona, Odessa, Rio de Janeiro, Helsinki, Batavia, Zagreb, Malta, Mexico City and in Melbourne in 1866, not to mention numerous provincial productions.

Les Huguenots

Origins of the opera

Soon after the triumph of *Robert le Diable*, Meyerbeer and Scribe started looking for a new project. After discussing a number of ideas they decided to work on an historical opera, at first called *Léonore ou la Saint-Barthélemy*. For his first version of the libretto Scribe relied mainly on Prosper Mérimée's historical novel *1572: Chronique du règne de Charles IX*, published in 1829. On 23 October 1832 a contract was agreed with Véron, but Meyerbeer was not happy with Act I of the libretto. It seemed to him 'elegant and full of wit, but lacking the historical colour that would be particularly important in this work'.[23] This marked the beginning of a series of disagreements between the collaborators that resulted not only in a complete revision of the original libretto but also the emergence of a new relationship between librettist and composer. In earlier centuries the function of the composer had generally been to set to music, within a few short months, a libretto already written to commission by the librettist. After *Les Huguenots* writing an opera became a process requiring lengthy consideration by equal partners, if not, as in the case of Berlioz and Wagner, the composition of libretto and music by the same person. Developing an opera was to become the work not of a few months, but years, on occasion even decades. Scribe deserves respect for the flexibility with which throughout his career he met his partner's demands. That was unprecedented. The vast majority of their joint projects never, in fact, saw the light of day, and the five that were not abortive were often completed only after long periods of painful and distressing conflict.

With *Les Huguenots* the creative effort led finally not just to a revision of the libretto, but also to a completely fresh dramatic concept of historical opera. Döhring calls it 'a form combining the epic and the dramatic'.[24] At the outset Meyerbeer undertook historical studies of sixteenth-century music in search of period colour.[25] But he became more and more dissatisfied with Scribe's libretto, especially with Marcel's role, which provided essential links with the historical colour of the Wars of Religion. Scribe made him a mere servant. 'Your treatment of Marcel did not match the musical idea of the role that I sketched for you', wrote Meyerbeer.[26] In September 1833 the composer cancelled the contract with Véron, paying him, on 30 September, the stipulated indemnity of 30,000 francs. The next day he set off for Italy where he immediately got in touch with Gaetano Rossi, his former Italian librettist. Between October 1833 and April 1834 Meyerbeer wrote most of the opera, new passages of libretto being provided by Rossi in Italian, in accord with the composer's musical requirements. In this revision the most considerable element was the introduction of the Lutheran chorale 'Ein' feste Burg ist unser Gott'. Associated above all with Marcel, it serves throughout as an emblem of the period. On his return to Paris on 31 August 1834 Meyerbeer, with Scribe's agreement, had all the new Italian passages translated by Emile Deschamps. A new contract with Véron, who handed back the indemnity of 30,000 francs, was signed on 29 September 1834.

Despite all this many more changes were made before the première. Mostly they reflected criticisms by the producer, Duponchel, and observations by the censor, who prohibited the on-stage appearance of Catherine de Médicis in the scene with the 'Consecration of the Swords'. Among smaller alterations, the most notable was the revision, at Nourrit's suggestion, of the central section of the Act IV duo. It became one of the most admired parts of the opera. The change of management at the Opéra, with Henri Duponchel taking over on 1 September 1835, occasioned no delays. Chorus rehearsals started on 2 June 1835; the first rehearsal with sets took place on 6 October. Meyerbeer, who invariably wrote far too much music for what was then regarded as an opera of normal length, was obliged to make big cuts right up until the last moment. Even on 10 January 1836, four weeks before the première, he had to shorten the score by some three-quarters of an hour. Among others things he deleted a whole scene from the start of Act I, with an account of the attack on Coligny and a monologue by Marcel, intended to explain the paternal aspects in this character to whom Raoul's father is supposed to have entrusted the care of his son. Meyerbeer's letters make it plain that he regretted most of these omissions. Though the version of the opera in general use appears to have the authority of the Schlesinger score published shortly after the première, future editors of a critical edition, established without reference to constraints encountered on first performance, ought to restore the opera to its original state.[27]

The première of *Les Huguenots* at last took place on 29 February 1836. The cast included Julie Dorus-Gras (Marguerite de Valois), Cornélie Falcon (Valentine), Marie-Louise Flécheux (the page, Urbain), Adolphe Nourrit (Raoul de Nangis), Nicolas-Prosper Levasseur (Marcel) and Jacques-Emile Serda (Saint-Bris).

Philosophical and aesthetic ideas

It is not surprising that Scribe and Meyerbeer turned to a historical subject which took as its theme a period that was attracting much attention in various contemporary systems of the philosophy of history. In his *Palingénésie sociale*, Ballanche had announced a philosophical system that explained mankind's progress in terms of successive decline, expiation and regeneration. This pattern of endlessly recurrent fall and rebirth would lead mankind in the course of history towards the perfection foreseen by Providence. This historical interpretation derived from the trauma of the Revolution, which was accounted for as an ordeal inflicted on society by God in expiation of earlier excesses. Various schools took up and popularised these notions. In this profoundly neo-Catholic perspective, the Wars of Religion obviously served as a paradigm of history's palingenetic development. In his *Palingénésie musicale*, d'Ortigue laid down the succession of periods as follows: 'Catholicism, reform and regeneration are the three great forms that are reproduced in all manifestations of thought'.[28] Accordingly the palingenetic moment of reform, of which the Reformation and the Wars of Religion are a historical model, is central to mankind's development. Assuming an expiatory function, it will lead it to regeneration at the price of martyrdom as required by the divinity.

Thus the Opéra, in treating, from Halévy's *La Juive* onwards, Reformation themes, was simply following fashions current in intellectual circles. A dramatic problem particular to opera arose, however. Opera springs from conflict that is given expression by soloists and is the plot's core and motivation. What, on the other hand, was essentially modern in these new concepts in the philosophy of history was precisely a denial of the importance of the individual in historical developments, explanations lying rather in societal forces rather than the conduct of individuals, whether rulers or slaves. Historical opera capable of reflecting these views demanded a new dramatic style to relate the history of societies, expressing the autonomous forces of social movements by abandoning the practice of concentrating on a plot dominated by the fate of the soloists. This, in short, was the task Meyerbeer set himself for the rest of his life. In *Les Huguenots* he developed a drama of the masses as a whole, setting it within an epic panorama; in *Le Prophète* he took up the perspective of the individual at odds with a social movement; and in *L'Africaine* he turned to a global picture as he applied his vision of the Reformation to the process of colonialisation.

Dramatic and musical structures

Meyerbeer adopted essentially two approaches to the problem of expressing his conception of truly historical opera. In the first place, he uses grand tableaux to provide epic panoramas of the period and convey its colour while setting aside the musical presentation of a conventional plot. Secondly, he uses dramatic devices for presenting the passage of time and creating suspense, which give expression to the independent development of historical events springing from group antagonisms. As regards composition, the technical correlatives of this dramatic manner are montage and collage. Meyerbeer works like a film director, casting light by means of music on details of a visual scene, or sometimes creating a total auditory impression, with all the possible gradations of linked dissolves.

Act I: shallow set: Touraine, a chamber in the Comte de Nevers's castle. The act provides a general historical depiction of the French nobility's opulent and gallant way of life in 1572. Traditional plot elements scarcely figure, though the Protestant noble, Raoul de Nangis, sings a Romance to his Catholic hosts about the beauties of a woman he recently rescued. A conversation between Nevers and Valentine is not even shown on stage; it is only observed by the knights while taking place off stage. Raoul recognises Valentine as the lady with whom he has fallen in love, and so from now on thinks that she is in love with Nevers, when in reality the Queen, Marguerite de Valois, has requested her to break off her engagement with Nevers; this provides the plot with its central misapprehension. For the moment, attention is hardly drawn to this essential element, and the arrival of the Queen's page Urbain with the delivery of a mysterious invitation to Raoul introduces a new dramatic development that attracts the attention of characters and spectators alike.

Great pains are, however, taken to create the sixteenth-century knightly atmosphere and the tensions within this society just before the St Bartholomew's Eve massacre. In particular the gallant and profane atmosphere is suddenly altered by the sectarian and military coloration of the Lutheran melody sung by Marcel (Raoul's servant), who is scandalised by the impiety he sees. Though respecting the chorale tune, Meyerbeer gives it a majestic and fanatical accent by inner contrasts in instrumentation, with *fortissimo* bassoons, horns, trumpets, trombones and ophicleide set off against *pianissimo* flutes, oboes and clarinets. The orchestration becomes stranger still when Marcel launches into a Huguenot battle-song. The staccato notes of the piccolos, thrown into relief by bass drum, cymbals, bassoons and double-basses, create the background of distorted sounds of combat while the voice, harsh of tone but singing old-fashioned figures, creates an image of the veteran warrior's religious fanaticism. This challenge by the Huguenot servant is not, at the time, taken seriously by the Catholic knights. Yet Meyerbeer's contrasting coloration, further tinted in recitative by a neo-Baroque type of accompaniment, is a first inkling of the concept of the 'troubled idyll'. This creates the impression of disturbance by historical events that individuals will in the course of the opera be shown less and less capable of controlling. For the moment, the page's ingratiating aria with a wealth of coloratura brings out the alternative coloration of the idyll that is going to be established on stage in the next act.

Act II: deep set; gardens in front of the Château of Chenonceaux. Once again the tableau depicts a huge historic panorama with few plot details. It includes a bathing scene, not without its touch of eroticism, a dance episode, amorous conversation, an entry for the knights and so on. In a word, the Queen's court is presented as an artificial paradise (see Ex. 7.3, p. 112). By means of elegant virtuosity in the use of women's voices, adeptly chosen instrumentation and musical progressions that have an old-fashioned accent, Meyerbeer creates a lightness of style with something of rococo mannerism about it. The aim of this court is to draw back from religio-political issues and take refuge in love and luxury, which for Marcel is plain impiety. Only at the end is the plot advanced. To give her own marriage to the Protestant Henri de Navarre the wider effect of bringing peace to France, Marguerite de Valois wishes to marry Valentine, her lady of honour, to the Protestant Raoul. But this attempt to alter the course of history by means of a conventional personal intrigue is a failure. For Raoul such a marriage would be a disgrace: still under the misapprehension that Valentine is Nevers's mistress, he refuses her hand. This personal delusion sparks animosity that immediately takes on political dimensions. The Queen can hardly calm the affronted Catholic knights, and bloodshed is only just avoided. The extreme fragility of the artificial paradise is shown by the dramatic device of the 'troubled idyll', and the political powerlessness of the Queen becomes plain in her failure to control the spat at court.

In contrast to the first two tableaux which show the higher social echelons, the third-act tableau (deep set; Paris, Pré-aux-Clercs beside the Seine) brings the whole of society on stage. Here communities are literally brought face to face. On one side of the stage is an inn frequented by Catholic students, and on the other a tavern where Huguenot soldiers are drinking, while a chapel stands centre stage. By successive collage and simultaneous montage Meyerbeer brings into musical confrontation the stage areas allocated to the different parties. Litanies chanted by Catholic women and then the cries of furious Catholic people first interrupt and next combine with the chorus of Huguenot soldiers. Tension between the groups is about to burst out into fighting when suddenly gypsies turn up and distract everyone's attention with singing and dancing.

In narrative terms this is not part of the plot and has even less connection with the earlier scenes; it is an epic panorama that stages purely social movement. It makes us aware of tensions beneath the situation on stage. The consequence is to give force to the passage of time. It is clear that the catastrophe is coming nearer every moment as tension mounts between the groups. The plot is, however, integrated into this scene. Hiding in the chapel behind a pillar, Valentine has heard her father, Saint-Bris, plotting against Raoul; he plans to have him killed by his men in the course of a duel. Valentine warns Marcel, who, launching into the chorale while the fighting continues, calls on the Huguenot soldiers in the inn for help. The plotting Catholics, for their part, cry out to the students in the inn. Once more tension is about to turn into general strife, when, again, catastrophe is postponed, this time by the arrival of the Queen on her way back from Touraine. She explains Act I's misunderstanding to Raoul. A moment later he is driven to public despair: Valentine is unmasked as his recent saviour, but has that same morning married Nevers. The marriage procession is expected. Meyerbeer develops the dramatic device of suspense with a double chorus. During the happy and brilliant wedding chorus, the Catholic and Protestant groups go on threatening each other, and the Queen has difficulty in keeping them from one another's throats (see Ex. 5.2, p. 78).

Act IV (shallow set: an apartment in Nevers' Parisian mansion) stages the plot hatched on the wedding-night. The Catholic nobles, at Catherine de Médicis' behest, are going to slaughter the Protestants during the festivities for the wedding of Marguerite de Valois and Henri de Navarre. When Nevers speaks out against this cowardly plan, Saint-Bris's men take him prisoner. In a sombre ritual the conspirators swear on their swords, which have been blessed by monks. Meyerbeer gives this famous 'Consecration of the swords' a dark, sombre coloration with harmonic progressions that were very advanced in using apparently unrelated chords a third apart (Ex. 11.1), and low-pitched instrumentation (bassoons, horns, trumpets, trombones and ophicleide). Raoul, who had come secretly to explain himself to Valentine, has heard everything from a side-room. He wishes to go at once and warn his friends, but Valentine bids him stay so that his life will be spared. This provokes one last suspension of the action, that creates an extremely tense sensation of time slipping away before the concluding catastrophe. In

Example 11.1 Meyerbeer, *Les Huguenots*, Act IV: 'All those present draw their swords and daggers: the monks bless the arms'. 'Pious blades! holy swords, soon to be drenched in impure blood.'

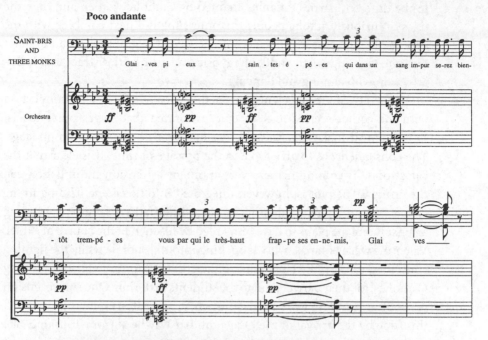

deepest distress Valentine forgets herself and the obligations of nobility: she allows herself a declaration, which means that Raoul must leave at once. According to Carl Dahlhaus, this 'Cavatine – Andante amoroso du Duetto' deserves to stand as the epitome of one type of 'musical culture' of its age (paired opposite Beethoven).[29] The tune is perfectly balanced, in exemplary classical form, accompanied only by chords (as *piano* as possible) and gentle woodwind harmony. This music seems, at a moment of danger and extreme misfortune, to descend from heaven as the expression of boundless bliss unattainable here below.

This utopian moment is interrupted by an off-stage happening that brings Raoul back to reality. A bell sounds the tocsin (see Ex. 7.1a, p. 109). Raoul tears himself from Valentine's embrace to warn the Protestant nobles gathered for the wedding celebrations at Henri de Navarre's Parisian mansion (Act V, first tableau: deep set, apartments in the Hôtel de Nesle). Bursting in on a brilliant ball, Raoul, in blood-stained garments, warns the Protestants. (This tableau recalls the dramatic device of the 'interrupted ceremony'.) During the ballet the bells can sometimes be heard, and the audience recognises the signal for killing to start.

In the next tableau (deep set: a graveyard, with a Protestant church rear left and, right, a grille opening on a crossroads) Meyerbeer uses musical movement to convey the autonomous sweep of historical events. As in

Robert le Diable, the musical form selected is a trio, but whereas the earlier trio creates an impression of time passing as the only dramatic force, here time is given dynamic strength. To this end Meyerbeer uses the Lutheran chorale to structure the scene. It is incorporated many times into the musical form, and on each occasion the speed is quickened so that at the end the melody fragments. The foreground is reserved for three major characters (Raoul, Valentine and Marcel), at the back the massacre of the Huguenots can be seen, and the final confrontation between the major characters and their murderers will take place centre stage. At first, Protestant women and children are seen taking refuge in the church at the back. Valentine offers Raoul her life if he will convert to Catholicism; she is free now, for Nevers has perished while protecting his Protestant guests. Raoul, however, will not betray his Protestantism and desert his co-religionists. Valentine then decides to remain with him and embrace Protestantism. The lovers ask Marcel to unite them with a solemn blessing which will serve as a marriage ceremony. At this moment the Lutheran chorale is heard being sung for the first time within the church. To the accompaniment of a solo bass clarinet – an instrument only recently developed by Sax – Marcel invites the couple to exchange vows. The chorale is heard again, but on this occasion it is suddenly interrupted by hordes of murderers who burst into the church and start to strike down the women and children. In the face of the murderers' fierce and brutal chorus, the victims shout out the chorale again, in greatly speeded-up form. This time it is brutally interrupted by arquebus fire. A moment's silence tells the major characters, who have witnessed the massacre from the front of the stage, that the last of the Protestants have been slain and that they will themselves soon have to face death. At this moment of agony they are carried away by a heavenly vision that reveals the martyrs' paradise opening before them. Just as they too start singing the chorale the audience sees the murderers straining to open the grille between them and their victims. As the grille is forced and physical contact is made between murderers and victims, the latter take up the melody once more: its opening motif is repeated in sequence and finally becomes doubled in speed. When the final massacre takes place, the tune is broken up; furthermore, the chorus of murderers likewise takes up its motivic fragments. Originally established as the musical emblem of an age, the chorale comes to symbolise, in its acceleration and final destruction, the conviction that the course of historical events is developing a dynamism of its own that ultimately will destroy not only the Protestant victims but likewise their Catholic murderers. The very brief final scene (deep set; the Paris quays) does no more than give visual expression to this interpretation of history. The mortally wounded Raoul is being given last succour by Valentine when her father, Saint-Bris, orders his companions to open fire on the group. Only too late does he realise the innocent victim is his own daughter, who expires before his eyes. A final entry brings the Queen on stage; powerless, terrified and ruined, she sees the mangled corpse of her favourite lady-in-waiting.

Success in Paris; international reception; later alterations

There can be no doubt that, at an ideological level, Meyerbeer voiced in *Les Huguenots* a fervent attack on religious fanaticism and inhuman intolerance. It is no less true that thanks to the techniques of montage and collage he discovered a musico-dramatic style to express on the operatic stage the modern historical conception that events are not the work of heroes but result rather from socio-economic forces. Neither aspect was completely understood during Meyerbeer's lifetime; perhaps only after the twentieth century, with its global catastrophes, can we see just how radical Meyerbeer is. For his own part, he was well aware of the modernity of his techniques and the implications of his theatre. During the first Paris run of *Les Huguenots* he wondered whether the public would appreciate the modern aspect. 'The part of Marcel is better than any of the music – *Robert* included – that I have written in my whole life. I don't know whether he will be understood. At first he probably won't be, I fear.'[30] After *Les Huguenots* he spoke of intending to 'complete my dramatic system with a third opera', which is fairly clear testimony to his regarding his successive works as steps in a coherent and logical argument – a prefiguration of the tetralogy.

The success of the opera in Paris was of a new type. Expecting above all else an opera, not a philosophical debate, the public remained totally surprised and amazed when confronted by the epic images that made up the first three acts. Act IV alone won the opera its success, one that became more and more pronounced with each performance. *Les Huguenots* was to be the first opera to be performed a thousand times at the Opéra, reaching this total on 16 May 1906 (and 1080 by 1914). Earlier operas had experienced either success or failure, but *Les Huguenots* gave rise to debate. 'Do not imagine', wrote Meyerbeer after the triumph, 'that there is not a lot of criticism at the theatre and in drawing rooms, even though the success in the theatre has been immense and unanimous. Many dislike the aesthetic aspect of my style of writing, either in part or in general . . .' However, 'even those who do not care for this opera say that it is one of the most significant musical productions of recent years.'[31]

International success soon followed. By 1878 the opera had been performed in Cologne, Leipzig, The Hague, Brussels, Munich, Basle, Budapest, New Orleans, Vienna, Lvov, Prague, Florence, Stockholm, Berlin, London, Odessa, New York, Copenhagen, Havana, St Petersburg, Helsinki, Riga,

Batavia, Lisbon, Barcelona, Dublin, Madrid, Warsaw, Algiers, Sydney, Rome, Mexico City, Istanbul, Malta, Buenos Aires, Cairo, Rio de Janeiro, Christiania (Oslo), Bucharest and Zagreb, as well as in various provincial theatres. Censors, especially in Catholic countries, often raised objections to the libretto. Sometimes considerable alterations were made, so that in Munich in 1838 the opera became *Die Anglikaner und Puritaner*, as it did too in Florence in 1841. Until the 1848 Revolution two versions were played in Vienna – *Die Gibellinen in Pisa* and *Die Welfen und die Gibellinen* – while in Rome in 1864 it was given as *Renato di Croenwald*. Clearly these alterations spoiled the dramatic style of an opera of which the basis was essentially the musical coloration of the Reformation period.

Translated by Christopher Smith

12 Meyerbeer: *Le Prophète* and *L'Africaine*

JOHN H. ROBERTS

Le Prophète

As he put the finishing touches on the vocal score of *Les Huguenots* in May 1836 Meyerbeer was already anxious, as he told his wife, to begin work as soon as possible on a third grand opera 'in order to plant my dramatic system . . . on indestructible pillars'.[1] Initially Scribe proposed an opera dealing with the career of John of Leyden, the infamous Anabaptist leader of Münster, but eventually this idea was rejected, probably because of the unsuitability of the principal roles to the current company at the Opéra.[2] Instead, in May 1837, Meyerbeer commissioned Scribe to write the libretto of an opera called *L'Africaine*, a sprawling romantic tale set in Spain and darkest Africa with an intervening act on the high seas.[3] Meyerbeer may have started composing the music, but if so he came to an abrupt halt in the spring of 1838 after his friend Germain Delavigne warned him that the libretto was fatally flawed. His confidence badly shaken, the composer laid *L'Africaine* aside and in August signed a contract with Scribe for *Le Prophète*. Scribe's principal source was a passage in Voltaire's *Essai sur les mœurs*, recounting how in 1534 John (Jean) of Leyden (1509–36) established himself in grand style as prophet-king of Münster, espoused communism and polygamy, and withstood the attacks of his enemies until finally betrayed by his confederates. Around these bare facts the librettist wove an imaginary intrigue involving Jean's fiancée (Berthe), his mother (Fidès), three Anabaptist leaders who lead him astray (Zacharie, Jonas and Mathisen), and a lecherous nobleman who abducts Berthe (Oberthal). Laid out in four acts in deference to a short-lived fear that the Parisian public had tired of five-act operas, the libretto was soon rearranged in five acts, following the original plan of 1836.

Meyerbeer completed the finished score of *Le Prophète* in March 1841, but production of the opera was long delayed, primarily because of conflicts over singers. The company at the Opéra had sadly declined since its glory days in the mid-1830s. Gilbert Duprez, the tenor for whom the role of Jean had been conceived, had shrunk to a shadow of his former self, and there was also a major difference of opinion between the composer and the director of the Opéra, Léon Pillet, about the casting of the part of Fidès. Meyerbeer wanted the young Pauline Viardot; Pillet was determined to give the role to his mistress Rosine Stoltz, the reigning diva of the Opéra, whose singing Meyerbeer despised. In the end Meyerbeer agreed to accept Stoltz, but the tenor issue remained unresolved. Meanwhile he completed *L'Africaine* without orchestration in 1843. He would not consider having it performed at the Opéra before *Le Prophète*, however, because he believed the latter work to be far superior.

Finally in 1847 Pillet stepped down, and the new directors eventually came to terms with Meyerbeer and hired Viardot. Gustave Roger, a star of the Opéra-Comique, untested in grand opera, was selected for Jean. Before the rest of the cast could be chosen Meyerbeer undertook a major revision of the score, partly to accommodate the singers but also to improve or replace numbers with which he had grown dissatisfied, and major changes were likewise made in the libretto, partly with the secret assistance of Emile Deschamps.[4] Further extensive revisions and cuts followed during rehearsals. The first performance took place on 16 April 1849 with a cast that included Jeanne Anaïs Castellan as Berthe and Nicolas Levasseur, called out of retirement, as Zacharie. From the first the opera was an overwhelming success. Viardot was particularly admired as singer and actress, and Roger also won high praise. A spectacular production, including the first use of electricity at the Opéra for the rising sun at the end of Act III, helped ensure the triumph.[5]

After finishing the first version of *Le Prophète* in 1841 Meyerbeer frequently declared it the best thing he had ever written,[6] and the critics were nearly unanimous in acclaiming it at least the equal of *Les Huguenots*. Yet already at the time of the first performance there were private murmurs of dissent from such authorities as Berlioz and Jules Janin,[7] and when Richard Wagner published his bitter attack on Meyerbeer in *Oper und Drama* in 1852 it was *Le Prophète* that drew his most withering scorn. *Le Prophète* is indeed the most problematic of Meyerbeer's grand operas. It contains some of his most brilliant music and most dramatic scenes, but it also has many glaring weaknesses, and the overall effect is considerably less satisfactory than in *Les Huguenots*. To understand how the opera ended up as it did, it is necessary first of all to know something about Meyerbeer's outlook and inclinations at this point in his career.

Disinclined as he was to public pronouncements or artistic debate Meyerbeer never articulated what exactly constituted his 'dramatic system', but the operas themselves, together with his many written comments to Scribe, enable us to see more or less clearly that his primary aim was to make dramatic music as consistently 'characteristic' as possible. This approach resonates strongly with contemporary writing on local colour, such as Hugo's famous dictum that a dramatic author should seek above all to represent the characteristic, not the beautiful. But in Meyerbeer's case the seminal influence was probably his teacher Vogler, who had opined, in analysing his own opera *Der Kaufmann von Smyrna* in 1779, 'Writing beautifully is easy; expression is not too difficult; but only the genius of a great painter and the most practised brush can choose for each picture agreeable and natural colours that are peculiar only to it, and by themselves would be nothing'.[8] In attempting to realise this ideal Meyerbeer (inspired to some extent by Vogler's own methods) made extensive use of national, historical and topical styles and also relied heavily on tone-painting of physical phenomena, whether setting, stage movement, tone of voice or textual image. Certain topoi particularly appealed to him – the military (and its close allies the patriotic and the chivalrous), the religious, the amorous, and the horrible or sinister – and he tended to choose his subjects and shape his librettos so as to provide himself with plentiful opportunities for employing the associated musical colours. Along with Meyerbeer's fascination with musical representation went an apparent lack of interest in what for many composers of his time was the central task of the dramatic composer, expressing the emotions of the characters. In particular he had little feeling for the expression of personal suffering. Revealingly Henri Blaze de Bury, one of the composer's most worshipful apologists, admitted that 'sensibility is not exactly one of the characteristic traits of Meyerbeer; he uplifts, he stirs, but hardly has what we commonly call the gift of tears'.[9]

Meyerbeer's efforts to write the sort of grand musical drama that he obviously had in mind were also hampered by several other problems in his own personal and artistic make-up. First, even at the height of his fame he was tormented by fears of failure and sometimes went to extraordinary lengths to guarantee an overwhelming and lasting success. Believing that the key to public favour lay with the singers, he did everything he could to obtain the strongest possible cast and to use each singer to the greatest possible advantage. While this strategy certainly contributed to the success of his operas – and has no doubt been responsible for a number of their recent revivals – it did at times have negative side effects. Secondly, Meyerbeer was rather impractical. Scribe's grand opera drafts were always extremely wordy for a sung text, and although Meyerbeer often cautioned concision and pruned a lot of unnecessary verbiage himself, he invariably ended up composing vastly more music than could possibly be performed. The gradual realisation of this fact in the course of rehearsals then led to often brutal last-minute cuts that left permanent scars on the libretto and the music. On occasion he also overestimated the stamina of his principal singers, with similar results. Finally, Meyerbeer's compositional technique was decidedly uneven. He had a rich fund of appealing if somewhat short-breathed melody, commanded an increasingly rich harmonic vocabulary, and was a master of brilliant and novel orchestral effect. But he had very limited skill in thematic development and even less in contrapuntal combination, and he had a tendency to emphasise his deficiencies by attempting to demonstrate his prowess in these areas, particularly in large ensembles and overtures.

In addition to his own limitations Meyerbeer had also to contend with those of his collaborator. Skilful as he was as a theatrical craftsman, Scribe's particular talents were not well-suited to grand opera in five acts. A master of comedy, spoken or sung, he had little feeling for serious drama, and grand opera, being through-composed, offered limited scope for his great speciality, construction of an intricate plot. Even in Scribe's spoken comedies character was always subordinated to plot; in his grand operas the characters all too often emerged as vacuous, weak, base or inconsistent. This is particularly true of the later librettos. In his first five-act drama conceived originally for the Opéra, *Gustave III*, set by Auber in 1833, Scribe provided a well-crafted plot and voluminous historical documentation (see Chapter 10), and the librettos of *Les Huguenots* and *La Juive* also show signs of having been written with some degree of seriousness. But after 1835, perhaps as a result of the retirement of the demanding Louis Véron as director of the Opéra, he apparently became more cynical and careless as he moved closer to contemporary *mélodrame*. *Guido et Ginevra*, written for Halévy in 1836, teems with sensational horror and sentimentality and seems designed more as a succession of startling incidents (shown in Fig. 21 p. 241) than as the realisation of anything resembling a dramatic idea.[10] Most of Scribe's subsequent four- or five-act operas are of this kind. What the author himself thought of this portion of his output is indicated by a remark in his account book for 1841 about a dispute with Pillet over the fees for his librettos: 'I want to be paid for them according to what they bring in, that is to say a great deal. The present director only wants to pay for them according to what they are worth, that is to say very little.'[11]

Although Meyerbeer saw some of the shortcomings in the texts Scribe gave him and exacted endless revisions, he failed to recognise many other problems and sometimes created new difficulties in trying to remove old ones. He pressed Scribe to create distinctive character types, often providing detailed descriptions of what he wanted, yet his conceptions were usually essentially musical in origin, and he was quite capable of undermining a character in his efforts to enhance a role.

Before we consider *Le Prophète* in any detail a brief summary of the action is in order. Act I: the countryside near Dortrecht in Holland. Fidès has come to escort Berthe to Leyden for her wedding with Jean. Three Anabaptists arrive and rouse the peasants to overthrow their oppressors. Enter Oberthal, lord of the region, who has the Anabaptists arrested. Berthe catches his fancy, and when she and Fidès beg his permission for the wedding

212 John H. Roberts

he refuses and has them both taken off to his castle. Act II: The inn kept by Jean outside Leyden. He recounts to the three Anabaptists a dream in which he was crowned and hailed as messiah, then engulfed in blood. They tell him he can be king. No sooner are they gone than Berthe rushes in, fleeing from Oberthal. Jean hides her but, when Oberthal produces Fidès and threatens to have her killed, he hands Berthe over. The Anabaptists reappear and promise Jean that if he becomes their prophet he can have Oberthal killed. He agrees and reluctantly leaves his mother without saying farewell. Act III: The Anabaptist camp near Münster, in winter. Victory song of Zacharie. Skaters' ballet. Oberthal having been found wandering in the neighbourhood, the three Anabaptists try to recruit him before finally recognising who he is. Jean appears and refuses to go on because of all the bloodshed, but when he learns from Oberthal that Berthe is living in Münster he decides to attack the city. After quelling a rebellion among the soldiers, who have been defeated on a sortie ordered by Zacharie, he has a sudden vision of angels and leads his army off to Münster.

Act IV: A square in Münster. Unhappy bourgeois surrender their goods in response to the prophet's communistic decree. Fidès begs alms to say a Mass for her dead son. Berthe turns up, having escaped from Oberthal, but Fidès tells her (as she believes) that Jean has been killed on orders of the prophet. Berthe decides to assassinate the tyrant. Coronation of Jean in the cathedral of Münster. Fidès recognises him, but he forces her to deny him in order to save his life. Act V: A vault under Jean's palace. With the Emperor's forces advancing on the city the three Anabaptists decide to betray the prophet. Soldiers drag in Fidès, torn between rage and love. Jean comes to her, and she first chastises him, then leads him to repentance. They are about to leave when Berthe enters, hoping to kill the prophet. She is overjoyed to see Jean, but when she discovers he and the prophet are one and the same she stabs herself. In the final scene the prophet's followers are celebrating his coronation with a splendid banquet when, in the middle of his drinking song, his enemies burst in. He has the doors locked behind them and a series of explosions sets the palace ablaze. As it collapses around them Jean and Fidès, who suddenly emerges from the rubble, sing a final verse of his song, commending themselves to God.

It is not difficult to see why Meyerbeer chose to compose a grand opera on this subject. Particularly as recast under his direction in 1838 the scenario offered strong dramatic scenes and striking stage effects along with ample opportunity for the application of three of his favourite musical colourings, the military, the religious, and the sinister. Yet it was in some ways a dangerous choice. As the composer had seen already in 1836 the character of the drama tended towards more or less unrelieved gloom, and the role of Jean was potentially so large that it stood in danger of becoming unperformable.[12] He might also have worried (but apparently did not) that Scribe was hardly capable of doing justice to the complex and morally ambiguous figure of John of Leyden, and that such a story would also place heavy demands on his own limited powers of pathetic expression.

In his French operas Meyerbeer always endeavoured to give each score a distinctive overall colouring redolent of the setting and character of the dramatic action. Just as in *Les Huguenots* he had tried to suggest the ambiance of the Valois court by adopting a more pronounced French accent, so in *Le Prophète* he sought to evoke the Dutch and German settings with a subtle Teutonic inflection. The predominant atmosphere of fanaticism and violence was expressed by a consistently dark coloration, while a certain roughness and plainness of style served to characterise the peasants that make up most of the cast. Moreover, as some critics admiringly noted, Meyerbeer endowed *Le Prophète* with a grandeur surpassing even that achieved in *Les Huguenots*.[13] This is most apparent in the music associated with Jean and the Anabaptists, but the same aspiration can also be read in the large expressive gestures of Fidès and Berthe in Acts IV and V. The Coronation scene with its magnificent procession and march fit for a true king, in which a huge stage band engages in antiphonal exchanges with the enormous orchestra in the pit, set a new standard for grandeur in nineteenth-century opera.

No less than in *Les Huguenots* Meyerbeer attempted in various ways to suggest the historical milieu. Rather than borrowing an existing chorale as he had done in the earlier work he composed his own Anabaptist hymn, 'Ad nos ad salutarem undam', to which, as he explained to Liszt, he tried to give 'the colour of a song of the time'.[14] Like 'Ein' feste Burg' in *Les Huguenots*, it serves as the opera's principal recurring musical idea, appearing several times in Act I, in the recitative before the quartet in Act II, and in the *entr'acte* before Act V as well as in Jean's deleted prayer in Act III. In the Coronation scene the Anabaptists also sing a prayer for their king-prophet, 'Domine salvum fac regem nostram', cast in a suitably 'archaic' style.

Another source of historical colouring in *Le Prophète* is the music of Handel. Traces of this influence can perhaps be heard most clearly in Jean's *Hymne triomphal*, 'Roi du ciel', where an unmistakably Handelian melody and peroration lend biblical grandeur to the prophet's psalm-based rhetoric (Ex. 12.1) and in the probably parodistic roulades of Zacharie's *couplets* 'Aussi nombreux que les étoiles' (which Arthur Sullivan may have been spoofing in Arac's Handelian battle song 'This helmet, I suppose' in *Princess Ida*).[15] The square cut of some of the Anabaptists' other melodies and the touches of counterpoint in the quartet and the Act IV chorus of bourgeois point more subtly in the same direction. These allusions were by no means

Example 12.1 Meyerbeer, *Le Prophète*, Act III, no. 19, *Hymne triomphal*: 'King of Heaven and the angels, I will sing your praises, Like your servant David'.

accidental. When Meyerbeer was first working on the music of *Le Prophète* in late 1839 he had his Handel edition transported to Baden for his use, and in early 1840 he studied scores of *Joshua* and *Alexander's Feast*.[16] The primary idea seems to have been to lend the score an 'old German' colouring, somewhat as Wagner was later to do in *Die Meistersinger*, but Meyerbeer may also have seen Handel's style as an exemplar of the grandeur he was particularly striving for in *Le Prophète*.

The composer went to considerable lengths to evoke the rustic world to which Jean, Fidès and Berthe belong. The opening scene abounds in pastoral colouring, with two shepherds playing chalumeaux on stage and a chorus in $\frac{6}{8}$ time, full of drones and the simulated sound of windmills; and kindred effects pervade the *Valse villageoise* in Act II, the chorus of milkmaids in Act III and the skaters' ballet. Some of the music of the peasant characters also has a distinctly pastoral tinge, particularly Berthe's romance with Fidès in Act I, Jean's *Pastorale* in Act II, and the ensemble section 'Loin de la ville' in the Act V trio.

Meyerbeer boasted to his agent Gouin in 1847 that the part of Jean was 'the largest and the most important that has ever been written in the theatre for a tenor',[17] and despite the many curtailments it later suffered it remains an extraordinarily demanding and impressive role. One effective number follows another: Jean's dream (a free-form monologue emerging from recitative), the *Pastorale*, the quartet with the three Anabaptists, 'Roi

Example 12.2 Meyerbeer, *Le Prophète*, Act IV, finale: *L'Exorcisme*.

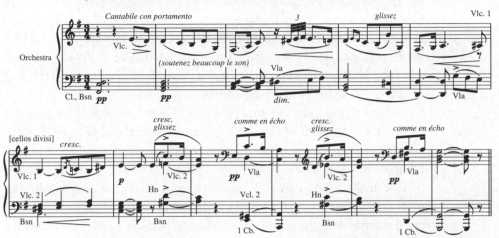

du ciel', his confrontation with Fidès in Act IV, their duet in Act V, and the *Couplets bachiques*. He has the manner of a visionary leader in his scene with the mutinous soldiers in Act III and 'Roi du ciel', where Meyerbeer told Scribe the prophet should be 'in a mystical ecstasy, half warlike, half religious'.[18] He speaks in the tender accents of a devoted lover and son in passages such as his farewell to Fidès in the quartet. Indeed Meyerbeer adopts exactly the same chastely loving tone whichever of the two women in Jean's life is in question and in Act III even uses the theme of his love song about Berthe, the *Pastorale*, to express his longing to see his mother.

The high point of Jean's role and indeed of the whole opera is the place in the Coronation scene where he pretends to perform a miracle by curing Fidès of her delusion that he is her son. First, in a luminously scored passage that quickly traverses a series of remote keys, he bids the 'sacred light' descend upon her. Then he fixes her with his gaze and forces her to her knees as the cellos play a melody of surpassing tenderness (Ex. 12.2). When he finally speaks his tone is cold and edgy, as he makes her affirm her love for her son and directs his soldiers to draw their swords; a sinuous solo contrabassoon, his only accompaniment, seems to depict his inner fear. But when he calls on the soldiers to kill him if he is indeed her son the cello melody comes back in greatly intensified form, and we know that he is appealing desperately to her love. He then poses the fateful question, 'Am I your son?' and she gives the required denial against a reprise of his initial incantation. There is some question as to how the central ritornello of this *Exorcisme* should be understood. Is Jean, as many have thought, exercising some sort of hypnotic power over Fidès, or is he simply trying to communicate his true feelings for her with a loving look? Meyerbeer's direction that Jean 'so fascinates her with his gaze that she falls involuntarily to her knees' might seem to favour the former interpretation. But in his published diary Roger, whose execution of this scene along with Viardot was universally admired, left no doubt of how they played it: 'It is the power of the gaze, it is the passage, visible only to the mother, from an imperious physiognomy to an expression of filial tenderness, that must bring about the so-called miracle . . . As soon as Jean, making a rampart with his arms as he lifts them to heaven, can direct a look of tenderness to his mother, she understands.'[19]

Despite all this excellent music the role of Jean is extremely problematic from a dramatic point of view, and the causes lie in the music as well as the text. We cannot be sure whether he is an impostor or a genuine visionary. He appears to throw in his lot with the Anabaptists in order to take revenge on Oberthal, an explanation he confirms to his mother in Act V ('Ah! c'est mon seul amour'), yet he recounts a dream in which (as it turns out) he accurately predicts the future, and in the Coronation scene, in virtually the only words we ever hear him say to himself, he seems really to believe he is the son of God ('C'est donc vrai, oui, je suis l'Elu, je suis le fils de Dieu'). We are likewise left to wonder whether he attacks Münster to rescue Berthe or because he sees a vision of angels. The great emphasis placed on Jean's love for Fidès and Berthe and the extreme tenderness of the music expressing his feelings for them also tends to undermine our belief in him as a military leader capable of conquering all Germany with an army of unruly peasants, especially since we get to see him in that role only once at the end of Act III.

Some of these problems were aggravated in the scaling back of the role for Roger in 1848–49.[20] As Meyerbeer had written it the part would probably have overtaxed Duprez in his prime, and Roger, though by all accounts a fine singer, did not have Duprez's former power and stamina. To make matters worse his overprotective wife attended all the rehearsals. Among the many casualties were two scenes with Jonas at the beginning of Act III, which showed Jean more or less clearly as a high-minded if troubled leader, and most of his prayer near the end of the act, reduced to its trumpet-laden coda.[21] Yet the changes made for Roger only compounded existing confusions arising out of Meyerbeer's attempt to impose on Scribe a different conception of Jean's character than the librettist originally had in mind. In the 1836 scenario Jean had been presented simply as an impostor who joined the Anabaptists solely for revenge. But when Meyerbeer finally accepted the subject in 1838 he requested that the prophet be portrayed as a true visionary:

> If he is an *impostor* he will only inspire disgust: if he makes himself an
> Anabaptist for vengeance because he had been robbed of his beloved, he
> will be excused but he will still not be interesting. I believe that he would

need to be an eccentric person, prey to dreams and visions, taken in by the doctrines of the Anabaptists whom he knows already.[22]

To please the composer Scribe planted in the text many references to Jean's piety and visionary tendencies, but he did not make any change in the basic plot. It was probably also Meyerbeer, wishing to maintain interest in Jean's love for Berthe, who persuaded Scribe to give it more prominence as a motive for his attack on Münster. The resulting contradictions seem to have passed unnoticed by the composer, who proceeded to write his conception of Jean's character into the music.

Jean's motivational muddle worried Pillet, who had something of a running battle with Scribe over the quality of his grand opera librettos.[23] After the *Prophète* text came into his hands in 1842 Pillet requested extensive changes, some of which are outlined in a fragmentary set of notes and drafts in the Scribe papers.[24] One of his principal concerns was obviously Jean's character, and he sketched out a plan under which he would have been represented as a conscious impostor but one who sincerely believes in the cause of delivering the suffering peasantry from oppression as exemplified by Oberthal. But the proposed changes were soon shelved as Meyerbeer and Pillet became embroiled in contractual disputes.

Giving a major role to an elderly mother was a bold step, and Meyerbeer sought to make Fidès a highly unusual figure. As he explained to Scribe in 1838 he envisioned her as an old woman, gentle and pious, speaking the naïve language of a simple peasant.[25] He did his best to give her a distinctive musical profile compounded of melodic and rhythmic simplicity, heavy accentuation, and low notes, extending as far down as *G*. He emphasised her faith in God with many references to the *religioso* style, and he graphically depicted her halting gait when she first appears in Acts I and IV. Yet for all the obvious care he put into her role, it frequently fails to attain the expressive heights to which he evidently aspired. This is partly because as drawn in the libretto Fidès often lacks the nobility and pathos one expects in such a figure. In the scene in Act II where Jean is forced to surrender Berthe to Oberthal, for example, she remains totally passive, and then, rather than seeking to comfort her son, blesses him for having loved her more than his fiancée. When she recognises Jean in the Coronation scene her primary reaction is rage at his refusal to acknowledge her rather than joy at finding him alive. A more serious problem, however, is that Meyerbeer was more successful at characterising Fidès as an old peasant woman than at expressing her profound sufferings. She makes a strong impression in Act I, especially in her comic babbling during her first recitative with Berthe, but her famous arioso 'Ah! mon fils' in Act II seems to be more a musical picture of her grief than its expressive embodiment, and Meyerbeer soars only when he reaches

Example 12.3 Meyerbeer, *Le Prophète*, Act IV, no. 21: *Complainte de la mendicante*. The continuation of this music is shown in Example 7.8(a).

his favourite religious topos at the words 'Que vers le Ciel'. The pantomimic instrumental introduction to her *Complainte* in Act IV (Ex. 12.3), which may have been in Wagner's ears when he wrote the desolate opening bars of Act III of *Tristan*, tellingly evokes the image of a crippled beggar woman, but the begging song itself is less convincing, especially as it turns more anguished in the second strophe. And her *couplets* in the Coronation scene, where she pours out her heart to Jean, are distinguished more by the imitation of her sobbing and shaking with rage than any real pathos (see Ex. 7.9, p. 128). Only perhaps when she is cursing the prophet in her *Imprécation* in Act IV and bringing Jean to heel in their duet in Act V – two situations that involve no pathetic sentiments on her part – does she become a truly compelling dramatic figure.

The role of Fidès also suffered from its transformation for Viardot in 1848–49. Meyerbeer had probably composed the part with her in mind in 1839–41, but she was then very young – only eighteen when he heard her sing at the Théâtre Italien in October 1839[26] – and her voice comparatively small. By the time Viardot was engaged to sing in *Le Prophète*, however, she had developed into a singer of considerable power as well as great agility, having successfully sung the Falcon roles of Valentine and Rachel. Since, moreover, she would be Meyerbeer's star attraction, he naturally wanted to exploit her extraordinary capabilities to the fullest. Accordingly he revised and expanded the entire part of Fidès, making it heavier and more elaborate vocally. He added a new solo scene for her in Act V, replacing one for Berthe, and transformed the earlier Berthe–Jean duet into a Fidès–Jean duet. These changes not only significantly altered the character of Fidès's role but created at certain moments a conspicuous tension between drama and vocal display. The complex and artificial cadenzas in the two duets with Berthe, dating from 1849, are dramatically inappropriate, as many commentators complained at the time, and the bombastic vituperations in the first recitative of her solo scene in Act V, like the dazzling acrobatics that follow in the cabaletta, seem improbable in the mouth of an elderly woman who under other circumstances has difficulty walking.

Strangely enough, much of Fidès's new music had originally been composed for other characters. The two principal set sections of her duet with Jean seem to have been taken from the old Berthe–Jean duet, though not without revision, and the *cavatine* in her solo scene must have been adapted from Selica's solo scene in the last act of *L'Africaine*, for the text is largely the same, and the detailed entries in Meyerbeer's diary of the period say nothing about his having composed a new setting.[27] In view of these borrowings it is remarkable that Meyerbeer managed to construct as coherent a musical character for Fidès as he did.

Berthe has generally been dismissed as a serious character, not entirely without reason. There are in effect two Berthes, the timid country girl we see in Acts I and II and the would-be assassin who suddenly emerges in Act IV – a problem Pillet had been particularly concerned to correct.[28] Meyerbeer's musical response to the former, seen in such numbers as the romance with Fidès in Act I, parts of their duet in Act IV, and the ensemble section of the trio in Act V, 'Loin de la ville', exude a sentimental sweetness that bespeaks his lack of affinity for the topos of pastoral innocence. Loss of her air in Act V and the ensuing duet with Jean robbed Berthe of her most important dramatic scenes. As a final indignity she acquired a showy and dramatically unjustified *cavatine* at the beginning of Act I, composed at the insistence of Castellan. Originally Berthe also had a protracted death scene, notable for its free form and imitation of gasping speech and for Meyerbeer's having briefly intended to assign a prominent role in it to the recently invented saxophone. It is a novel and attractive piece but would not suffice to rescue her from dramatic irrelevance.[29]

Cleverly drawn in Scribe's libretto, the three Anabaptist preachers are brilliantly realised in Meyerbeer's music. As he had already demonstrated with Bertram, Meyerbeer had a special knack for evoking evil, and we feel the Anabaptists' malevolent character from their first appearance on stage in Act I, accompanied by a characteristic combination of bassoons and horns. Their hymn not only contributes to local colour but aptly symbolises their sinister nature. The Anabaptists are also quasi-comic, an effect achieved largely through their exaggerated manner and further enhanced by their habit of singing as a trio; it may be significant that the one number sung by any of them alone, Zacharie's 'Aussi nombreux que les étoiles' in Act III, is the least effective part of their joint role. In the witty *Trio bouffe* they become overtly comic without losing any of their menace. Their other two principal numbers, the *Prêche anabaptiste* and the quartet with Jean in Act II, are no less memorable, particularly the *Prêche*, one of those long crescendos with which Meyerbeer could produce such stunning theatrical effect. After summoning the peasants with their hymn the Anabaptists take turns preaching with increasing vehemence, then work the crowd into a frenzy culminating in a thunderous rendition of the hymn, full of archaic fourths and fifths. In place of the last line of the hymn comes a hush as the peasants whisper 'Dieu signe l'arrêt' ('God signs their death warrant'), after which the orchestra erupts with a revolutionary march song that builds to a still more shattering climax. The effect could only be improved if Meyerbeer had been willing to go directly into the following recitative as Oberthal enters rather than bringing the movement to a full stop, presumably followed by prolonged applause. The stretta of the *Prêche* is one of several passages for the Anabaptists and their cohorts containing echoes of the type of military and patriotic music associated with the French Revolution, the other most notable examples being the moment in the quartet in Act II when Jean first joins the Anabaptists in song ('Oui, j'irai sous ta sainte bannière') and the climax of the chorus of mutinous soldiers in Act III ('Mort à l'imposteur, au faux prophète'). In each case the context is explicitly revolutionary. By a curious coincidence Meyerbeer composed the stretta of the *Prêche* to replace an earlier conclusion while the Revolution of 1848 was erupting around him in the streets of Paris.

Meyerbeer had a particular gift for writing characteristic choruses, and in *Le Prophète* he produced a succession of shining examples unmatched in his career. Especially remarkable are the opening chorus of Act III, 'Du sang, du sang', a picture of the Anabaptist hoard in full cry; the chorus of mutinous soldiers with its simulation of a roaring mob and exhilarating crescendo; and the almost pantomimic chorus of bourgeois, alternately hailing the prophet's soldiers and muttering defiance. Although most of these numbers are integral to the action, they function primarily as discrete vignettes, and the chorus does not generally become a significant player in the drama. The ballet music in Act III became famous long before Constant Lambert used it as the basis of his ballet *Les Patineurs*. Though suggestive of the peasant milieu, these dances were obviously designed to be eminently transferable to the nineteenth-century ballroom. To simulate the effect of ice-skating the dancers and some chorus members wore roller skates, an unusual though not unprecedented effect. This took place, be it noted, during the milkmaids' chorus, not the ballet itself.

It was Meyerbeer's intention to begin *Le Prophète* with a full-dress overture, but in his desire to produce an introduction that would set the scale for the grandiose drama to follow he seriously overreached himself, producing a piece that runs to 732 bars in its uncut version and contains an enormous amount of laboured and rather ineffective contrapuntal development.[30] It soon became apparent that this behemoth would have to be sacrificed along with many other parts of the opera, though it did reach publication in piano arrangements by Alkan. As a result of this debacle the opera opens with nothing more impressive than a brief agitation of the dominant that, as Johannes Weber observed, 'hardly has any significance other than to say to the audience, sit down and be quiet, if that is possible'.[31] Meyerbeer's technique again betrayed him in parts of the Coronation scene, particularly the big ensemble, akin to a Rossinian stretta, in which he attempted to develop ideas from Fidès's *couplets*, and the conclusion of the act following the *Exorcisme*. Here, he alternated in close succession the central idea of the ensemble, a partial paraphrase of the choral 'Domine salvum fac regem', and a third motif associated with the words 'Miracle, miracle'. It was a trick he had often tried before but rarely as boldly or as incoherently, and it is difficult to escape the impression that it arose primarily from his lack of contrapuntal skill.

Without question many of the cuts inflicted on *Le Prophète* during rehearsals did substantial harm. Not only was much fine music removed, but some of the surviving numbers were rendered significantly less effective. To mention only one example, the finale of Act I, in which Oberthal refuses to let Berthe marry Jean and then abducts her, lost so much of its music that it became decidedly scrappy and incoherent. A good deal of the opera's deleted music can be reconstructed[32] and will presumably appear in the forthcoming critical edition of the opera, and some conductors will no doubt be tempted to restore various earlier versions. But this should be done only with the greatest caution, since insertions in one scene can lead to excisions elsewhere, and those portions of the present score we could most easily do without are often the ones most likely to be regarded as indispensable by singers. It should also not be supposed that returning *Le Prophète* to something closer to its pre-rehearsal state can turn it into a satisfactory musical drama.

In a little over two years *Le Prophète* attained its 100th performance at the Opéra, and it long remained a staple of the Parisian repertory, reaching the 500 mark in 1898. The opera quickly conquered the capitals of Europe and soon made its way around the world. London saw it, with Viardot, already in July 1849, then Dresden, Vienna and Berlin early in 1850, in performances supervised by the composer. Meyerbeer's fears that it might be forbidden in some cities on account of its revolutionary content proved unfounded, though the Latin text had to be purged to satisfy the Viennese censor; Catholic authorities may have found the libretto less objectionable than that of *Les Huguenots* because the villains were Protestants. Within a year of the première *Le Prophète* arrived in New Orleans, going on to New York, Havana, Mexico, Buenos Aires, and Rio de Janeiro. As Meyerbeer had hoped, his third grand opera had won the same enormous popular success as its two illustrious predecessors.

L'Africaine (Vasco de Gama)

With *Le Prophète* safely launched on its triumphant course Meyerbeer soon began to think about *L'Africaine*, on which he had done no work since completing the unorchestrated score in 1843. Again he submitted the libretto to a trusted friend, Edouard Monnais, and again he received a negative verdict, but he evidently could not bring himself to give up on the opera, if only because the Parisian public had been anxiously awaiting it for so many years. Eventually Scribe undertook to rewrite the libretto, transforming it into a drama about Vasco da Gama's discovery of India. To accomplish this miracle the plot of the first two acts was largely reinvented, and even in parts of the three later acts where the action remained essentially unchanged the poetry was often replaced. The new libretto, entitled *Vasco de Gama*, was delivered to Meyerbeer in 1853, but after a few weeks' work the composer allowed himself to be distracted by other concerns. He did not return to the opera until 1857, when Scribe, irate over his having composed the opéra comique *Le Pardon de Ploërmel* with Barbier and Carré rather than setting *Vasco* or the three-act *Judith* that Scribe had written for him in 1854, threatened to take back both librettos immediately. From that time onwards *Vasco* remained the primary focus of Meyerbeer's creative life. When Scribe died in 1861, the composer lost no time in enlisting the help of the Berlin playwright Charlotte Birch-Pfeiffer in revising the libretto. He would set her German verses (unless he had already conceived the music on his own) and then have them translated by Joseph Duesberg, a German living in Paris. Preparations for performance had already begun when Meyerbeer suddenly died in Paris on 2 May 1864. To oversee rehearsals in his place and make whatever changes proved necessary the composer's widow selected François-Joseph Fétis, eighty-year-old patriarch of French musical scholarship and head of the Brussels Conservatory. Revisions in the text were carried out by Camille Du Locle, the future librettist of Verdi's *Don Carlos*, and a triumvirate of literary advisors appointed by Mme Scribe. The first performance on 28 April 1865, under the restored title of *L'Africaine*, was a tremendous success. Marie Sasse, reluctantly accepted by Meyerbeer for the role of Sélika shortly before his death, led a strong cast that included Emilio Naudin as Vasco and Jean-Baptiste Faure as Nélusko. The staging, if somewhat less sumptuous than Meyerbeer had hoped for, was well received, especially the realistic shipwreck at the end of Act III.

Although Meyerbeer had largely completed the score at the time of his death, it soon became apparent that it could not be performed as he had left it. As always he had composed far too much music, and there were numerous other problems to be resolved and interested parties to be reckoned with. On the whole Fétis and his colleagues did their job in a remarkably responsible way by the standards of the times, but inevitably in the absence of the composer the work turned out quite differently than it would have done had he lived to see it through the rehearsal process. Meyerbeer's autograph score survives largely intact,[33] and various other manuscripts help to trace the revisers' work. While the printed full score does not, as it claims, conform exactly to the original manuscript – as the main performing score for the final version it could hardly do that – it does contain most of the deleted music, and Fétis also published some of the same material in vocal score, accompanied by a preface explaining his revisions.[34]

The revisions cannot be described without first summarising the action of the final version. Act I: The Council Chamber of the Admiralty in Lisbon. Inès, an admiral's daughter, longs for the return of her beloved Vasco de Gama, who has sailed with Diaz on a voyage of exploration. Don Pédro, the man her father wants her to marry, reports that Vasco has died in a shipwreck along with Diaz. The Council assembles, but their deliberations are soon interrupted by the arrival of Vasco. He describes his escape and proposes to undertake a new voyage, offering in support of his plans two slaves of unknown race he had bought in Africa, Sélika and Nélusko. When the Council rejects his proposal, he defies them and is sentenced to prison. Act II: Vasco's prison cell. Sélika watches over her sleeping master, whom she secretly loves, and when Nélusko, who hates all Christians, attempts to kill him, she intervenes to save him. Vasco sketches a map of his intended route around Africa, but Sélika corrects him, revealing the existence of Madagascar. His tender expression of thanks leads her to believe he loves her in return. Next Inès comes to tell Vasco he is being released from prison. Seeing that she suspects him of betraying her with Sélika, he gives her the slave, but it is too late: she has already married Don Pédro, who, having stolen Vasco's plans, has received a royal commission for a voyage of his own.

Act III: Don Pédro's ship. Maritime choruses. Don Alvar cautions Pédro not to trust Nélusko, who is acting as their pilot. Nélusko persuades Pédro to change course, then entertains the sailors with a ballad about the sea-giant Adamastor. Having pursued them in another ship, Vasco now comes aboard and, for Inès's sake, tries to warn Pédro of the impending disaster, but Pédro refuses to listen and they start to fight a duel. Rescued by his men, Pédro orders Vasco arrested, but immediately a storm hits, the ship strikes a reef, and Nélusko's comrades come pouring over the side. Act IV: Outside a temple in Sélika's kingdom. Grand ceremonial scene with Sélika as queen. When everyone has gone Vasco comes in, marvelling at the beauty of the tropical scene. A chorus of sacrificers takes him prisoner, but Sélika persuades them to spare him by claiming that she had married him during her captivity out of gratitude for his saving her life. The high priest then has Sélika and Vasco go through a local religious ceremony that involves drinking a love potion. Left alone with Sélika, Vasco soon feels the effects of the potion, and they sing a passionate duet. But as the act ends he hears the voice of Inès singing in the distance. Act V: The queen's gardens. Sélika has just discovered that Inès has met Vasco, and, unmoved by her rival's protestations of his innocence, she orders that they depart together (Pédro is dead). Sélika tells Nélusko to meet her at the promontory overlooking the sea where the poisonous manchineel tree grows. In the last scene Sélika inhales the tree's deadly fumes and has a vision in which she is reunited with Vasco. Nélusko arrives just before she blissfully expires.

According to Fétis the massive cuts made in the score were necessitated not only by its immense length but also by the complexity of certain scene changes and what he perceived to be weaknesses in the libretto. In carrying out this surgery he displayed a high-minded attitude that did not always correspond with Meyerbeer's own. Where the composer had often shortened his numbers by small excisions and had indicated numerous possible abridgements of this kind in the score of *Vasco*, Fétis did his best to avoid internal cuts, preferring instead to remove entire pieces. He also had a tendency to protect uninspired expressive sections of the sort that Meyerbeer had often ended up eliminating from earlier operas. The largest cuts significantly altered the plot. In Act III, following Vasco's arrest, Sélika had forced Don Pédro to release him by threatening to stab Inès; then in revenge Pédro had ordered Nélusko to beat her or watch her killed, a choice from which he was delivered by the arrival of the storm. Fétis felt obliged to omit these scenes because they produced a poor impression in the theatre. Act V originally opened with a solo scene for Inès, including an attractive aria, 'Fleurs nouvelles', followed by a brief and inconclusive reunion with Vasco. At this point Sélika entered and began her tirade as in the final version while Vasco stood mutely by until finally dismissed with the words 'Qu'il s'éloigne à l'instant, je le veux!' ('He must withdraw immediately, I demand it!'). Fétis found the hero's ignominious exit ridiculous and in the end saw no other expedient than to remove him altogether.

If Fétis approached Meyerbeer's music with respect bordering on reverence, he had no compunction about tampering with the text, and he

encouraged his literary colleagues in revising it heavily. It was he who recommended changing the title, apparently above all because the public was
expecting an opera entitled *L'Africaine*. This had no basis in the existing
libretto, where Sélika was presented unambiguously as an Indian queen,
whose only African connection consisted in having been sold into slavery
on Madagascar after her boat was driven there by a typhoon. To justify
the resurrected title it seems to have been decided to make Madagascar her
kingdom while retaining all the trappings of the Indian milieu, but perhaps
deliberately this was never spelled out clearly in the text. For no obvious
reason the name of Sélika's faithful retainer was changed from Yoriko to
Nélusko, plucked from the same poem of Charles-Hubert Millevoye that
had served as Scribe's primary inspiration for the scene under the manchineel. There were also countless minor revisions in the text, many of which
precipitated alterations in the music.

The only real lacuna in Meyerbeer's score was the lack of ballet music,
which he had only begun to sketch. He had always intended that ballet should
play a unusually prominent part in *Vasco*, and he planned to compose three
dance sequences for the opera, one as part of a maritime divertissement in
Act III, a second after 'Nous jurons par Brahma' in Act IV, and a third enacting Sélika's dream after she falls asleep under the manchineel. To fill the gap
Fétis arranged two ballet movements from deleted numbers, but eventually
they were cut along with so much else. Otherwise outright additions were
few and unobtrusive: a few bars of ritornello here and there to allow more
time for the action on stage and a brief recitative for Nélusko preceding
the final chorus of Act III to convey information lost in a deleted middle
section. There were also many small changes in vocal lines (including the
interpolation of a high *C* in 'O paradis') and occasional tinkering with the
orchestration. By far the most harmful musical change involved the interpolation into the opera's final scene of an arioso for Nélusko and miniature
duet with Sélika, transplanted from the deleted scenes at the end of Act III.
This lamentable insertion, which arrests the action without offering much
compensating musical interest, was made at the behest of Faure while Fétis
lay ill shortly before the first performance.

The libretto that Scribe gave Meyerbeer in 1837 surely ranks as one
of the worst examples of his late grand opera style, diffuse, sensational,
improbable, and pointless. It is not surprising that Delavigne and Monnais
found it impossible, only that Meyerbeer failed to see how right they were.
Thanks to many successive revisions, in which the composer played a large
part, it improved greatly over the years, yet some of the original problems
remained, and each successive wave of changes brought new absurdities
and confusions. If it never became an entirely coherent drama, however,
the libretto finally set by Meyerbeer did have certain significant advantages

over that of *Le Prophète* from his point of view. Most importantly Sélika is a compelling dramatic figure, whose fate generally holds our interest as none of the characters in the preceding grand opera do. The action revolves to a great extent around love, one of the composer's favourite dramatic topoi, and there is less demand for expression of pathetic emotion. Not least, the settings exerted a stronger pull on Meyerbeer's imagination than those of *Le Prophète*, particularly the Indian milieu, which charmed him as thoroughly as had the Valois court in *Les Huguenots*.

Largely composed when the composer was between the ages of sixty-six and seventy-two, Meyerbeer's score has the characteristics usually associated with the artistic productions of old age. It is more refined in style, more delicate in feeling, and richly detailed. Particularly remarkable is the quality of dramatic speech in the recitatives and dialogue sections between set numbers; Meyerbeer had always excelled at this sort of writing, but in *L'Africaine* we find a new richness and flexibility that contributes considerably to the overall effect. Although he appears to have incorporated a small amount of music from his 1843 score in *Vasco de Gama* – we cannot be sure precisely how much because the earlier score is lost – no great stylistic discontinuity seems to have resulted.[35] What is most striking about *L'Africaine* is the richness of its melodic language. It has sometimes been suggested that the score is more Italianate than *Les Huguenots* and *Le Prophète*, and perhaps so, but its lyricism should be seen not as an evolutionary development of Meyerbeer's style but as a part of the overall colouring he adopted to reflect the Portuguese and Indian settings and an action dominated by love. Certainly he was not trying to characterise any particular group or milieu, for this lyrical warmth suffuses the entire score.

Meyerbeer was obviously enchanted by the Indian milieu, more precisely by the idea of an India remote in time as well as geography, since, as he explained to Scribe in another context, 'the English officers with their uniforms strike me as prosaic and anti-musical'.[36] He combed through numerous books in search of information about Indian customs and manners, and he added many characteristic details to the libretto. It was he who, with the help of Birch-Pfeiffer and Duesberg, produced the text of Sélika's *Air du Sommeil*, 'Sur mes genoux', with its references to lotus and a Bengali singing in the night, he who decided to begin Act IV with a *Marche indienne* accompanying a procession including bayaderes, jugglers, female warriors and elephants. Indian colouring was infused into the music primarily by evoking tropical heat and lush vistas, imitating fancied Indian manners and movements, and occasional exotic orchestral touches rather than by any attempt to suggest non-Western musical styles by modal inflections or the like. Meyerbeer introduced local colour of a different sort when he inserted Inès's *romance* 'Adieu, mon doux rivage' (originally 'Adieu, rives du Tage') in Act I, said to have been sung to her by Vasco on the night of his departure. The haunting opening section, which returns at the end of Act IV when Vasco hears Inès singing in the distance, has a strange colouring probably intended to indicate ancient origin; as Julian Budden has noted it seems to have served as Verdi's model for the Willow Song in *Otello*.[37] The maritime milieu in Act III was depicted in a series of choruses, patterned after the Pré-aux-Clercs divertissement in *Les Huguenots*. In an instrumental interlude cut before the first performance Meyerbeer went so far as to imitate an English hornpipe.

Sélika occupies a central position in the opera, almost justifying the posthumous change of title. Meyerbeer described to Scribe in 1852 precisely how he wanted her depicted: 'She must be made more a woman of her warm climate and painted with less European manners. Along with her innate virtues, she must be given the impetuosity and jealousy that the burning climate of her homeland inspires in the passions.' It is the 'continual combat between the impetuosity of her oriental blood and her ingenuous love that will furnish me with the musical colours to design her role'.[38] Despite this prescription neither Sélika's words nor her music are especially exotic, except in the supposed Hindu lullaby, 'Sur mes genoux'. She does, however, give ample expression to her love for Vasco, most notably in the middle section of the *Air du Sommeil*, their duet in Act II, and above all the love duet in Act IV, one of the high points of the score. This is an obvious pendant to the great duet in *Les Huguenots*, but now it is the woman, not the man, who owns the principal melody, and the lovers attain a greater sense of fulfilment as their passion finally subsides in a blissful coda. Dramatically the situation is somewhat questionable, since Sélika, having let Vasco drink a love potion, should hardly be so surprised at his sudden declaration of love – a *non sequitur* that had crept in when Meyerbeer and Birch-Pfeiffer introduced the potion to justify Vasco's abrupt change of heart. But such reservations must yield before the lyrical power of the music. Sélika is least satisfactory in her scene with Inès in Act V, though she gives a splendid exhibition of queenly temperament in the recitative and the first part of the duet before collapsing in their bathetic ensemble sections.

Sélika's crowning moment is of course her scene under the manchineel. The parallel with Dido, likewise deserted by a visiting hero, is inescapable, yet Scribe's heroine dies a very different death, in which as she becomes intoxicated by the fatal fumes she sees heavenly visions and forgets all her pain. It is probably for this reason that Meyerbeer succeeded as well as he did. He intended the scene to be vastly more extensive, a vocal and dramatic tour de force beyond anything he had ever done. In his final version it included a middle section and reprise in the *cavatine* 'La haine m'abandonne', a multi-part air 'O douce extase' after the second recitative, and a middle section

Example 12.4 Meyerbeer, *L'Africaine*, Act V, no. 21: *Grande scène du mancenillier*. The unison melody is played by clarinets, bassoons, violins and violas using exclusively the G string, and cellos.

for the waltz song, in which Sélika imagines being reunited with Vasco, leading to an abbreviated reprise of the waltz. This was to be followed by a ballet enacting Sélika's dream (never composed) and a celestial chorus, an abbreviated version of which is heard at the end of the opera. Inevitably this colossal scene-complex would have been greatly reduced before the opera reached performance, and Fétis seems to have salvaged the best sections.

Surprisingly, the part of the scene that produced the greatest impression at the time was the initial twenty-two bar ritornello, in which strings, clarinets and bassoons play an unaccompanied melodic line in unison – a real unison with no octave doubling (Ex. 12.4). Whether because of the unusual sonority or the emotional connotations this passage became an instant sensation.[39] Contemporary critics offered a variety of weighty interpretations of its meaning, but in view of Meyerbeer's inclination towards the literal and concrete he most likely conceived it as a piece of tone-painting illustrating Sélika's opening line, 'D'ici je vois la mer, immense et sans limite, ainsi que ma douleur' ('From here I see the sea, immense and without limit, like my sorrow'). The use of a waltz tune as the musical centrepiece of Sélika's dream puzzled and offended some commentators,[40] but they might have thought otherwise had they known that the scene was supposed to culminate in a ballet. Meyerbeer's scenario for this ballet closely parallels the vision described in the waltz song (the words of which he had written himself), and a purely instrumental version of the waltz would presumably have formed part of the planned ballet music.[41]

With Vasco, Meyerbeer came closer than ever before to creating a convincing heroic figure. His youthful ardour and chivalrous manner recall Raoul, but he has a steadier and more commanding voice, and in his entrance speech and final defiance in the Council scene he rises to impressive heights. Meyerbeer also gave Vasco some splendid love music, though we may regret that he has to lavish it on Sélika rather than the woman he really loves. It might further be objected that in some passages addressed to Sélika earlier in the opera – 'Mais parle donc' in the Council scene with its triply divided cellos or the ardent 'Combien tu m'es chère' in their Act II duet – Vasco's tone implies a nascent sexual interest that the composer surely did not intend to suggest. What deals a fatal blow to Vasco as a hero, however, is his desertion of Sélika in Act V. We may accept his preoccupation with his destiny – almost an occupational disease with nineteenth-century heroic tenors – even his making love to Sélika under the influence of a drug he has knowingly ingested. But that he should allow himself to be summarily dismissed by his new wife (as Meyerbeer had it) or simply disappear (as in Fétis's revision) is incompatible with the glory of a great explorer. After Scribe's death Meyerbeer began to worry about this point and had Birch-Pfeiffer and Duesberg prepare an alternative final scene in which Vasco returned to Sélika and she died in his arms, but there is no evidence that he ever set it.

Vasco's air 'O paradis' in Act IV is justly famous for the suave melody and evocative orchestral timbres of its first part. Yet it would be still more effective if performed as Meyerbeer wrote it. In the composer's version Vasco did not wander in inexplicably at liberty but was dragged in on his way to execution. A chorus of sacrificial priests brandishing axes intoned a bloodthirsty hymn, while the accompanying warriors struck their swords against their bucklers at the $\ominus$ sign (Ex. 12.5). Thus Vasco's exclamations of wonder over the tropical paradise were not so much the gloating of a greedy conqueror as the raving of a doomed man, and the choral interjections later in the air represented attempts by the priests to reassert control over their prisoner. The words Vasco sang were also quite different. Scribe's original text had been rich in visual images that Meyerbeer had deftly translated into music (Ex. 12.6), but the anonymous reviser replaced much of the specific imagery, transforming the illustration of light shining from afar ('Brilles au loin') into another expression of Vasco's overactive ego ('Tu m'appartiens'). Even Meyerbeer's orchestration suffered some modification, an English horn replacing the original bass clarinet in doubling the voice. Unfortunately the beauty of the first part of the air is not maintained in the second, where

Example 12.5 Meyerbeer, *L'Africaine*, Act IV, no. 14, *Chœur des prêtres sacrificateurs*: 'O sun that rises burning over us, You ask our swords for blood'.

Vasco, recovering from his rapture, tries to persuade his captors to let him tell his crew about his discovery before he dies, so that at least he will get the immortal fame he deserves. The insipidity of Meyerbeer's music, based in part on a sacred part-song composed in his student days, probably has less to do with the stupidity of the text than its pathetic character.

Nélusko is the most unusual character in the opera, a true successor to Marcel and Fidès. Meyerbeer instructed Scribe that he too should be given:

> warm language, coloured by oriental images, verse forms and special rhythms to distinguish him from the Europeans. As for his character, it is a mixture of hate, wickedness and irony against all Christians, and boundless devotion, a superstitious veneration for the royal blood of Celica [*sic*], and above all a secret delirious love for her, although he keeps it carefully hidden ... To give more reason to his hatred against Christians, and also because it would serve me for the musical colour, he must be a priest or monk of one of those numerous fanatical Indian sects.[42]

Example 12.6 Meyerbeer, *L'Africaine*, Act IV, no. 15, original words of Vasco's *Grand air*, 'O paradis': 'O gentle air, Splendid strand, Sky so blue, so limpid, By which my eyes are ravished, Shine from afar on this shore, With which I would have endowed my country.'

To depict this extraordinary personage musically Meyerbeer developed a distinctive colouring blending the savage, the diabolical and the religious. It is perhaps most tellingly displayed in the air 'Filles des rois', in Act II, which turns near the end into a free-form scene involving Sélika and Vasco, and in Act III. Nélusko's exchanges with Don Pédro and Don Alvar, partly excised before the first performance, show him at his most malevolent, and the ballad of Adamastor with which he entertains the sailors is one of the gems of the score, serving equally to characterise the evil other and to paint a picture of Camões' great sea-giant.[43] In the last two acts Nélusko is less prominent and less characteristic. Scribe seems to have been somewhat at a loss what to do with him once he had no more Christians left to persecute, and as usual Meyerbeer's inspiration failed him when faced with Nélusko's sufferings in his Act IV *cavatine* 'L'avoir tant adorée' or the transplanted arioso in the final scene. Only in two brief passages referring to the manchineel do we catch brief glimpses of the remarkable figure of the previous acts.

Though more a conventional villain than Nélusko, Don Pédro nonetheless is cleverly drawn in music. In his haughty response to Inès in the recitative before the trio in Act I, his pompous announcement in Act II that the king is sponsoring his voyage, or his self-satisfied reminder to Vasco in their Act III duet that they are on his turf Meyerbeer perfectly caught his offensive tone of voice. Inès never attracts much dramatic interest, being little more than a helpless victim. Like Berthe before her she never gets to sing a duet with the man she loves. Only once, at the end of Act II, does she take control of a situation, but it remains unclear why she should be sending Vasco off in search of glory when she is the one who is going away. Nonetheless she has some attractive music to sing, particularly when she is talking about love. In the Act I trio Meyerbeer seems to have construed her lament over the supposed death of Vasco as more loving than sorrowful, especially in the reprise with her father and Pédro where her melody expands and soars in much the same way that Sélika's does in the passionate middle section of her *Air du Sommeil*. Inès's farewell in Act II, nonsensical as it may be, drew from Meyerbeer one of his most sustained lyrical effusions. Here one senses the composer was less concerned with expressing her feelings than with evoking the scenes described in the text: Vasco sailing away, then returning to kneel at the tomb of his beloved whose voice whispers through the rustling branches while she awaits him in heaven.

Since the standard performing version of *L'Africaine* was never sanctioned by the composer, a good case can be made for revisiting some of the decisions of Fétis and his colleagues. Certainly he removed some pieces from the score that are far superior to some of those he chose to retain, and the presence of most of the deleted music in the printed full score would facilitate some judicious restorations pending the publication of the new critical edition. It would also be desirable to remove Nélusko's intrusive arioso from the final scene, and reinstate the chorus of sacrificial priests and the original words to 'O paradis', a hardship only for those rare tenors accustomed to singing it in French rather than Italian. The opening of Act V poses a special problem. Recent revivals in San Francisco and London have resurrected Meyerbeer's original version with Inès's *cavatine* and fleeting reunion with Vasco, but this makes for a long first scene of uneven interest at a time in the evening when an audience's patience can easily wear thin. A better solution might be to suppress the whole first scene, allowing Vasco's desertion of Sélika to be inferred from his realisation at the end of Act IV that Inès is still alive.

The last great success of French grand opera, *L'Africaine* was performed at the Opéra more than a hundred times during its first year and went on to establish itself firmly in the international repertory. Before the end of 1866 it had reached places as diverse as Madrid, New York, The Hague, St Petersburg, Sydney and Lemberg (Lvov). In Italy, perhaps because of its lyrical style, the opera was more rapidly accepted than any of Meyerbeer's earlier grand operas: see p. 389. Whereas *Le Prophète* had had to wait until 1852 for its Italian première, *L'Africaine* was performed in Bologna in November 1865, and by 1868 it had also been done in Florence, Genoa, Milan, Naples, Rome, Turin and Venice. Like *Le Prophète* it remained a popular favourite until fashion finally turned against the type of opera that both represented.

13 The grand operas of Fromental Halévy

DIANA R. HALLMAN

Fromental Halévy (1799–1862) established a strong but embattled reputation as a composer of grand opera, particularly through his first and most enduring work in the genre, *La Juive*. Although he wrote popular opéras comiques, two- and three-act operas, choral works, and the occasional ballet, Halévy's six five-act grand operas engendered the most prestige in his day, and played a substantial role in solidifying the genre. After the overwhelming success of *La Juive* in 1835, Halévy composed, with various collaborators, *Guido et Ginevra, ou la Peste de Florence* (1838), *La Reine de Chypre* (1841), *Charles VI* (1843), *Le Juif errant* (1852) and *La Magicienne* (1858). In the judgement of Richard Wagner, who was among the composer's partisans, the essence of Halévy's inspiration lay not in comic opera but in the 'pathos of high *tragédie lyrique*'.[1] Another writer, although disparaging of both composer and genre, viewed Halévy an ideal creator of grand opera, who 'gave himself body and soul to the *mise-en-scène*, the dramatic magnificence and the pomp, which he understands . . . better than anyone in the world'.[2]

Before *La Juive* propelled the thirty-five-year-old Halévy to critical acclaim and membership of the prestigious Académie des Beaux-Arts and the Légion d'honneur, his skills had been well nurtured and honoured at the Paris Conservatoire as both student and teacher, and as professional musician of the theatre. As accompanist at the Théâtre Italien from 1826,[3] then assistant *chef de chant* at the Opéra from 1829 to 1833 and, at the death of Hérold, main *chef de chant* from 1833 to 1840,[4] the composer learned invaluable lessons about vocal sonorities and capacities, operatic conventions and effective collaboration with singers. In his positions at the Opéra he helped prepare works by Rossini, Meyerbeer and Auber, and came into contact with the theatrical powers Véron and Scribe. It was to both director and librettist that Halévy appealed, in August 1833, for the opportunity to set Scribe's libretto for *La Juive*, previously offered to Meyerbeer.

La Juive

For his first endeavour at the Paris Opéra, Halévy joined a team of strong creative artists, from the well-proven Scribe and the stage director Duponchel to the choreographer Philippe Taglioni and conductor François-Antoine

Habeneck. Although Scribe (as we shall see in a moment) developed the opera's fundamental plot and text, Halévy and others helped to shape the drama as it moved from draft ideas to early performances. Léon Halévy (1802–83), the Classics scholar, essayist and dramatist, aided in libretto revisions as his brother scored the opera.[5] The tenor Adolphe Nourrit not only convinced the composer to create the role of Eléazar for him rather than the bass Levasseur, but reworked the text of his own central aria 'Rachel, quand du Seigneur' and suggested its placement at the end of Act IV; he is also credited with developing the *mise-en-scène*.[6]

At the heart of *La Juive*'s power and meaning is its socially and politically charged subject of religious conflict between Jews and Christians, a critique of religious-political intolerance largely aimed at the Catholic Church and past governments that had abrogated or curbed individual rights, including Jewish civil rights. Created after the July Revolution of 1830 had ended the Church–State alliance under the authoritarian king Charles X, the opera reflects liberal views within the July Monarchy and embodies personal ideologies of its librettist and primary collaborators. The Jewish characters, the goldsmith/jeweller Eléazar and his adopted daughter Rachel, clearly victimised by Catholic power, are shunned, vilified and condemned to death by Catholic officials and followers. The setting at the 1414 Council of Konstanz (Constance), a convocation that ended the papal schism but also executed religious reformers – see below – provided an ideal backdrop for the opera's subject. Like the St Bartholomew's Eve massacre appropriated by Scribe in *Les Huguenots*, the Council of Konstanz served as a Voltairean symbol defining religious oppression, one that resurfaced in the 1820s and 1830s when it became commonplace to denounce the tyranny of the Church and its power under the *ancien régime*. In *La Juive*, Scribe and Halévy toned down such denunciation by portraying Cardinal Brogni (the unwitting father of Rachel) sympathetically; indeed, he acts as foil to the mob's vicious attacks, even while Eléazar exhibits his own brand of intolerance and religious hatred. By comparison with the ghostly dancing of debauched nuns in *Robert le Diable* or the depiction of priests, bishops and popes as villains, murderers and Lotharios in satirical works appearing in Parisian theatres shortly after 1830, the anti-clerical elements of *La Juive* were veiled and equivocal, but still apprehensible. Nevertheless, one reviewer in the royalist paper *La Gazette de France*, who labelled the work 'Voltairean', found its treatment of Church history outrageous and particularly objected to the Act V depiction of the Council Fathers enjoying a 'great ceremony of boiling some Jews in a cauldron!'[7]

Scribe's Voltairean stance was not superficial, contrary to the opinion of many scholars who have viewed him as a practical, apolitical dramatist concerned with profits rather than reform or revolution – an understandable view, based on his success under different régimes as well as on his own testimony.[8] Many biographical statements, along with his works of the 1830s, challenge this given portrait. In Scribe's travel diaries of 1826–27, themes or symbols of religious intolerance recur as he expresses anti-authoritarian, anti-clerical sentiments common to liberals of his day. During a visit to Switzerland and Germany in July 1826 he noted down visual images and historical events associated with Konstanz, focusing on the 1415 Council's heresy trial and burning of the Bohemian religious reformer Jan Hus (1370–1415: see Chapter 18), author of theological treatises attacking traditional Church views. Obviously moved as he viewed the remnants of the trial and condemnation, Scribe described the stone block on which Hus kneeled when sentenced, the burning of his books, and the chair that bore him to the stake. While in Avignon, another historic seat of Catholic power and judgement, Scribe wrote at length of the Inquisition tribunal in the papal palace, describing the 'preparation room' where Inquisitors went 'to invoke the Holy Spirit, or, rather, the devil who inspires them', and of the torture chamber filled with instruments of cruelty.[9] Perhaps with these images in his mind, along with an awareness of their symbolic use in political debate, Scribe jotted down the word '*auto-da-fé*' (i.e. the burning of condemned heretics by the Inquisition) in a thumbnail sketch of nascent ideas for *La Juive*, and included the same term in an early version of the opera's title.[10]

In *La Juive* Scribe characteristically manipulates historical facts, compresses time and events, incorporates fictional characters and creates plot implausibilities in order to highlight the story of doomed love between the adoptive Jewess Rachel and the Christian prince Léopold (disguised as the Jewish painter Samuel) in the foreground, to intensify dramatic effect and propulsion, and to merge Romantic conventions with ideological meaning. Hus does not figure in the action, but he is referred to in the libretto, along with the Hussites, Bohemian supporters of the martyred reformer who are supposed, ahistorically, already to have been defeated by the fictional Léopold at the time of the Council's opening in Act I. Sigismund of Luxembourg (king of Hungary and Germany) was involved in the historical Council but is made Holy Roman Emperor in the opera, a role he fulfilled only in 1433; he makes a mute appearance on stage. In Scribe's most significant historical detour, he substitutes Jewish characters for Hus and another Council victim, the church reformer Jerome of Prague, in essence replacing one type of 'heretic' by another.[11]

As with many grand operas, *La Juive*'s opulent staging, intricate, well-researched costumes and historical aura enriched the work's serious subject matter even while it sometimes diverted attention from it.[12] Audiences, aroused by press reports of unprecedented expenditures, were awed by crowd scenes and processions featuring a sumptuously-dressed king and cardinal, live horses, armoured soldiers and the multi-hued, insignia-laden tunics, leggings and cloaks of banner-carriers, trumpeters, peasants, and clerics. Some critics found the *mise-en-scène* too distracting, with Berlioz complaining about the 'antimusical roar' that got in the way of the composer's inspirations.[13]

While Eléazar and Rachel are integral to the work's anti-authoritarian critique as they speak to the long history of Jewish persecution and to liberal concerns for religious and political freedom, their characters also reflect a paradoxical blend of literary and social associations. Scribe clearly draws on the stereotypes of the mercenary, persecuted Shylock and his beautiful daughter that were recast in such contemporary works as Scott's *Ivanhoe* (1820: translated the same year into French), one of the most widely read novels in France of its decade. The allusions to Jewish greed, vengefulness and 'fanaticism' in Eléazar (who sings of hating and duping Christians) touch on the stereotype, but they resonate further with anti-Semitic views still evident in early nineteenth-century France, well after the granting of civil rights to Jews after the 1789 Revolution and the winning of new social and legal provisions in the 1830s. The portrayal of Rachel, like that of Rebecca in *Ivanhoe*, carries elements of Orientalist exoticism – primarily through costuming – that fascinated contemporary readers and audiences, along with Christian-like traits that were modified as the work developed.[14]

Despite the fact that Halévy exhibited ambivalence about his own Jewish identity, his heritage and views undoubtedly coloured his work on *La Juive*. Along with his brother, an important articulator of progressive Saint-Simonian doctrine, he belonged to the first generation of 'emancipated' Jews who were educated in the institutions of France; both Halévys held liberal political views and believed in certain aspects of Jewish acculturation.[15] Although the composer partially distrusted orthodox Judaism, and referred to Eléazar as a 'juif fanatique', he maintained ties with the Reform synagogue and Jewish causes.[16] His portrayal of the Act II seder roughly corresponds with his later music for the synagogue and hints at first-hand experience, presumably through his father, a Talmudic scholar. Halévy probably influenced, or at least endorsed, libretto modifications that softened Eléazar's portrayal as Jewish usurer, along with the developing work's most significant alteration: the change from Scribe's original dénouement, in which Rachel accepted Cardinal Brogni as her real father and converted to Christianity. In the opera's tragic ending she is tried and executed as Léopold's illicit lover, remains a faithful adopted daughter and becomes a Jewish martyr.[17]

In *La Juive*, Halévy realised the new aesthetic of grand opera, enhancing Scribe's merging and contrasting of collective and intimate experience with music of dramatic force and a keen sense of pacing that features powerful large-scale choral scenes, skilled and innovative orchestration, striking *coups-de-théâtre*, varied uses of declamatory writing within set pieces, and characterisation of emotional depth alongside conventional figures. Acts I, III and V centre on mass scenes of celebration and confrontation, whereas II and IV focus on the characters' inner lives and emotions. Of the five acts, the first is the longest and the most thoroughly built on Jewish–Christian conflict. Enhanced by a stage set juxtaposing the Gothic cathedral of Konstanz and the turreted house and shop of Eléazar, a confrontational tone is immediately created in the clashing of an off-stage *Te Deum* (and organ introduction) with the on-stage celebrants' biting condemnations of the Jew, whom they resent for working on a Catholic feast day. Halévy heightens the tension of the scene's opening with agitated triplets in the strings and the pointed quaver repetitions, *sotto voce*, of the Catholic crowd. Following the celebratory chorus, 'Hosanna, plaisir, ivresse', and announcements of the Council's opening, the sound of Eléazar's anvil sets off a direct attack on the jeweller, intensified by official castigations and call for death.[18] The antagonism is quelled by Brogni's compassionate aria 'Si la rigueur', then suspended through Léopold's *sérénade* and three celebratory numbers leading up to the spectacular cortège. But in the finale the hostility reaches a fevered pitch with prolonged cries of punishment to the Jews, 'Au lac, oui, plongeons dans le lac', fomented by the history-laden reminder of Jesus evicting moneylenders from the temple, forcefully sung by the town provost Ruggiero. With rising fourths, detached choral syllables and their orchestral reinforcement, and Rossinian crescendo, Halévy admirably depicts the breathless anger of the enraged mob. Once again the crowd's emotion is diffused, to be followed by a celebratory chorus with four-part ensemble whose return to the *Te Deum* and *Hosanna* brings symmetry and closure to the act.

The opera's most poignant moments emerge in the depiction of the forbidden love of Rachel and Léopold (who comes to her as the painter Samuel), the conflicted love between Rachel and her adoptive father and the sincerity of Eléazar's faith, leading to and sharply contrasting with climactic dramatic shocks. In Act II, following the intimate seder scene and the introduction of the princess Eudoxie in the trio 'Tu possèdes, dit-on' (she is revealed as the wife of Léopold in Act III), Rachel emerges as a full-blooded woman, and dramatic soprano, in the *romance* 'Il va venir' (see Ex. 7.4, p. 115) and duo 'Lorsqu'à toi', where she expresses hesitancy, dread, anger and compassion in heightened declamation and full lyric writing. Poignant wind motifs and shifting textures mark her changing emotions. Sensing betrayal, she confronts Samuel/Léopold, pressing him to admit his identity. With the disguised prince's words 'I am a Christian', Halévy allows the orchestra to speak for the stunned Rachel in halting lines weighted with

Example 13.1 Halévy, *La Juive*, Act IV, recitative no. 19: 'I have condemned you to my eternal hatred'.

silence.[19] Rachel's enraged attack that begins the duet is felt immediately in octave leaps as she senses her dishonour before her father and God. While Léopold tries to soothe her, Rachel fears the consequences of their love, but soon capitulates and agrees to elope with him. Eléazar's interruption leads to the 'frozen' trio-finale,[20] in which emotional tension rebuilds in staggered levels after extended immobility: Eléazar reaches for his sword when he learns of Léopold's Christianity, and although Rachel's impassioned appeal mitigates his anger, he curses Léopold when the latter unexpectedly refuses to marry her.

The Eléazar–Brogni duet of Act IV, followed by Eléazar's celebrated 'Rachel, quand du Seigneur' as finale (at Nourrit's suggestion), intensifies the personal and religious enmity between Brogni and Eléazar. This composition, central to Eléazar's character, powerfully depicts the father's raging inner conflict as he shifts between animosity and loving paternal thoughts (Ex. 13.1). In expressing the latter, Halévy evokes pathos by means of the delicate orchestral accompaniment that underscores the progress of

Example 13.2 Halévy, *La Juive*, Act IV, air no. 19: 'Rachel, when the Lord's protecting grace placed your cradle in my trembling hands'.

Eléazar's self-confrontation in the recitative, and then through the haunting melody of the aria's F minor Andantino (Ex. 13.2). (Idelsohn identified this melody as the only truly Jewish melody in the opera.[21]) But, as Eléazar hears distant shouts of 'Death to the Jews', he reverts to a defiant stance in the cabaletta 'Dieu m'éclaire', and holds on to it until the opera's end, when he reveals Rachel's true identity to Brogni only as she plunges into the boiling cauldron.

Guido et Ginevra and *La Reine de Chypre*

In *Guido et Ginevra* and *La Reine de Chypre*, Halévy created works quite different in character from *La Juive*, the former to a libretto by Scribe and the latter by J. H. Vernoy de Saint-Georges. Both operas feature Italian settings and fated lovers. The story of *Guido*, which bears plot and character resemblances to *Romeo and Juliet*, is drawn from an Italian legend recounted in Etienne-Jean Delécluze's history, *Florence et ses vicissitudes* (1837), and

treated in Karl Spindler's serialised novel in *L'Europe littéraire*. Scribe's
setting in plague-ravaged Florence in the sixteenth century refers indirectly
to a famous contagion of 1348, but more topically to the 1832 cholera epi-
demic in Paris. Saint-Georges places *La Reine de Chypre*'s first two acts in or
near Venice, with views of the countryside and the city's canals, and the last
three in Cyprus. He adapted its subject from historical events surrounding
the negotiated marriage in 1469 of Catarina Cornaro (1454–1510) of Venice
to Jacques de Lusignan, king of Cyprus (*r.* 1460–73), her continued reign
after his death, and her resistance to aggressive threats from the Venetians.
Catarina and the French knight Gérard de Coucy have been betrothed – the
action begins on their wedding-day – but events of state conspire to deny
them happiness.[22]

The appearance of these two works strengthened Halévy's position as
grand opera composer. Although neither attained the distinction of *La
Juive*, both were commercially successful and critically acclaimed. Berlioz
lauded Halévy's *Guido* score for its effective use of local colour, particularly the Italian rural 'couleur villageoise', its sensitive orchestral treatment,
new harmonic touches, and musico-dramatic contrasts, as in the combination of three varied melodies sung by peasants, soldiers of fortune and
women praying.[23] Among the many numbers Berlioz admired were the
well-received *romance* of Guido in Act I, 'Pendant la fête', the chorus 'Vive la
peste' and the trio finale of Act V.[24] Of the *romance*, he noted the expressive
melody ideally written for Duprez, the 'suave', 'transparent' accompaniment
of sustained clarinets, low-register flutes, cello pizzicati and harp arpeggios,
and the melody's artful recall.[25] The intensely moving scene opening Act III,
with its split-stage depiction of a tomb beneath a cathedral interior (anticipating that of *Aida* by over thirty years), particularly impressed him. (See
Fig. 21.) He describes the monks' lugubrious, chant-like melody contrasted
with the nuns' off-stage ethereal melody, and Cosme de Médicis's anguished
a parte in his daughter Ginevra's tomb as the funeral ceremony takes place
above. Writing a few weeks after the première, Berlioz predicted that *Guido
et Ginevra* would become a glorious title of 'the French School'.[26]

Many critics judged *La Reine de Chypre* to be a more consistently well-
written work than *La Juive*: in addition to refined orchestration it explores a
rich harmonic palette. *Larousse* reflects the admiration of a number of writers in its praise of the composer's 'powerful expression', 'exquisite sensibility',
infusion of pathos and tenderness and intriguing use of recurring motifs.[27]
Richard Wagner, who was hired by Schlesinger to produce a piano-vocal
score, wrote four glowing articles about the composer and the opera in
the *Revue et gazette musicale*.[28] Among the numbers that impressed him
were the Act I *romance*, duet, and finale, and Act II opening (Ex. 13.3). Of
Gérard's *romance*, which begins the drama with an immediate focus on the

Figure 21 Memento of *Guido et Ginevra* (subtitled *The Florentine Plague*) by V. Adani: the artist has avoided any idealising (indeed, spelling mistakes in some captions provide an ironic commentary) and has emphasised the picaresque style of the tale. At the top (Act I) Florentine citizens in 1552 pray at a shrine to the Madonna. In the centre (Act III) Ginevra, abandoned for dead as a plague victim in the cathedral crypt, returns to life: marauding soldiers of fortune are scared off by her appearance and by the sound of angelic voices. At the end (Act V) the scene changes to the spectacular mountain village of Camaldoli: the plague has receded. Guido and Ginevra are reunited with her father, Cosme de Médicis, and a procession of thanksgiving winds down the hill.

Figure 22 Scene from *La Reine de Chypre* (1841) reproduced from a much later piano-vocal score published by the firm of Tallandier. Many illustrations in this edition focus on the figures forming the doomed 'triangle' of lovers (see Chapter 1 for 'triangles'). The way that the artist's style evokes the imagery of popular literature suggests a type of domestic performance prior to the advent of sound-recording, and the long-lasting appeal of more intimate narratives from grand opera.

Example 13.3 Halévy, *La Reine de Chypre*, opening of Act II.

central characters' intimate love, Wagner spoke of the 'nobility' and 'grace' of the melody of the final duet section and declamatory writing of a special type that he labelled Halévy's 'dramatic melody' (see Ex. 13.4). The Act I finale leads to the shocked and angry reactions of Catarina, Gérard and their wedding guests at the violent interruption of the celebration: the bride's father, on orders from the Venetian senator Mocénigo, must prohibit their marriage. These individual and collective responses realise a dramatic power in which 'all the passions are unleashed like a storm' (Wagner). The young composer commends Halévy for vividly expressing the 'violent emotions of the soul' as he captures the proud, forceful anger of Gérard's supporters through a gradual rhythmic acceleration.

To introduce the gondolier chorus that begins Act II, Halévy counterpoints a pizzicato quaver cello ostinato pattern against a wispy semiquaver motif in different winds and reiterated clangs of a tuned bell. Wagner calls this section 'one of the most original conceptions that ever issued from Halévy's pen'. For him, Halévy's local colour in this chorus captured the 'primitive character' of the gondoliers more truthfully than the barcaroles of 'modern' rhythms and 'piquant' harmonies fashionable in other operas.

Of the last three acts, Wagner spoke highly of many numbers, beginning with the opening drinking-chorus sung by Cypriot lords, and the *couplets* of Mocénigo (the sinister Venetian senator) in the following chorus. He admired the dramatic contrast of the final Gérard–de Lusignan duet in Act III, noting its pivotal role in turning the drama more sharply towards

Example 13.4 Halévy, *La Reine de Chypre*, conclusion of Caterina and Gérard's duo no. 2: an example of 'dramatic melody' as singled out by Richard Wagner.

tragedy. In Gérard's Act IV *air*, Halévy's depiction of the character's changing emotions moved Wagner, but the number he found the most sublime was the Act V quartet, in which the poisoned Cypriot king, de Lusignan, reacts with Catarina and Gérard to Mocénigo's treacherous plot to gain power. As Cypriots and Venetians battle in the finale, the dying king blesses the fated lovers, and Catarina leads the Cypriots in a cry for victory.

Charles VI: grand opera and French politics

Drawing its plot from French history, *Charles VI* represents Halévy's most blatantly patriotic grand opera. The story, set in the fifteenth century following the Battle of Agincourt, concerns the alliance formed by the French queen Isabelle de Bavière with her son-in-law, the English king Henry IV, and her attempts to cede to him the power held by her husband Charles VI (*r.* 1380–1422) and destined for her son Charles VII (*r.* 1422–61). Important to the tale are the fluctuating dementia of Charles VI, poignantly depicted in the Act II *scène et romance* of the king, and a touch of the supernatural in the Act IV ghost scene. It was a subject realised in several dramas of the 1820s, including the five-act tragedies *La Démence de Charles VI* (1820) by Népomucène Lemercier, *Charles VI* (1826) by La Ville de Mirmont, and *Isabelle de Bavière* (1829) by Lamothe-Langon. The opera's librettists Casimir and Germain Delavigne modelled their work on Lemercier's tragedy in plot and characterisation: 'Odelle', the young female companion to the king, becomes 'Odette' in the opera, for example.[29]

Like Lemercier's drama, which was destined for the Théâtre Royal de l'Odéon and refused authorisation by censors offended by the unorthodox depictions of king and queen, Halévy's *Charles VI* met with controversy: but in 1843 this was due to its blatant presentation of the British as enemies. It appeared only three years after France had been on the brink of war with England over the seizure of Syria, then an Ottoman province, by the Egyptian pasha Mehemet Ali. Louis-Philippe's government had supported Ali politically and financially, and when the British, fearing the expanded power of both Egypt and France in the Near East, took action to force out Ali, France prepared to retaliate. In July 1840 an agreement negotiated by the British foreign minister Lord Palmerston with Prussia, Austria and Russia, but excluding France, triggered an anti-British protest against this seeming renewal of the anti-French alliance of 1814. The French minister Adolphe Thiers reacted sharply with military preparations and threats of war: troops marched through Paris as volunteers lined up for recruitment. Louis-Philippe, however, sought compromise; he rejected Thiers' cries for war and formed a new foreign ministry headed by François Guizot, then ambassador to England, who supported the king's views. In July 1841, France resolved the Egyptian–Ottoman conflict by signing an agreement with England and the European powers who had joined in the 1840 negotiations.[30]

Franco-British relations remained shaky following this brush with war, and the conciliatory Guizot understandably wanted to avoid reigniting anti-British sentiments. As Nicholas White has written in Chapter 3, *Charles VI* is a 'cautionary tale' of nationhood typical of the way grand opera 'often constructs history in terms of its moments of inauguration and crisis' (p. 57); so close did it come to current national sensitivities that almost on the eve of the opera's première, Guizot and others connected with his ministry threatened to ban it and demanded textual alterations, even after the censors had authorised it.[31] (The censors' libretto indicates that after an initial 'provisional authorisation' signed by the Director of Beaux-Arts, Cavé – which predated modifications to be made at rehearsals – full approval by the Interior Minister, Duchâtel, only came on 10 March, five days before the première.[32]) Because of last-minute ministerial demands, Schlesinger was forced to reprint the libretto intended for public sale, without remuneration, after pulping the initial 8,000 copies that did not conform to the newly authorised manuscript.[33]

These ministerial intrusions brought a flurry of journalistic commentary. Reports about the extent of government action and its possible political causes varied, with some papers registering alarm that the censors and French ministers had tampered with the work. According to *La Gazette* and other papers, the most objectionable phrase to Guizot was the repeated 'War to the English!' in the opera's 'National Anthem' first sung in Act I by the old soldier Raymond, the Dauphin and chorus, and repeated in Act V; it was replaced by the more universal phrase 'War to the tyrants!'[34] Markings in the censors' libretto also suggest a cut of a reprise of the National Anthem in Act III, as well as condensation of belligerent scenes featuring the Dauphin and a crowd of students. But even with textual alterations in place, the chorus 'Guerre aux tyrans' remained central to the work's patriotic cast. Permeated with the spirit of the Marseillaise, it went on to become a chorus of opposition and patriotism outside the opera: it was often sung in political gatherings close to the time of the 1848 Revolution and appeared in an anthology of French patriotic songs that same year (see Ex. 13.5).[35]

Conventional musical references to battle and the hunt intensify the work's bellicosity, and the ambience of war even pervades the Act II card game (Duo des cartes), a number greatly admired by early audiences, in which Odette and the king re-enact the historic battles of France. Real war-cries within the drama's context begin with the words, 'O France, arme-toi tout entière' ('O France, take up your arms') in the Act III quartet

Example 13.5 Halévy, *Charles VI*, Act I no. 2, 'Chant national': 'War to the tyrants! never shall the English reign in France!'

sung by Odette, the Dauphin, the king and Raymond. At the end of the quartet appears a new tableau representing a historical view of Paris in earlier centuries. With its provocative depiction of the treacherous Isabelle celebrating with the English in 'the palace of French kings',[36] the scene undoubtedly aroused nostalgic and nationalistic sentiments, culminating in calls for effacing of wrongs 'in the oppressors' blood'. In Act V, French chevaliers, inspired by Odette as a symbolic leader cast in the image of Joan of Arc, prepare to attack the occupying English forces.

Contrasting with the predominant martial colour and action are the poignant depictions of the mental vacillations of Charles VI and the empathy of Odette as the king's devoted young companion. The king's madness is revealed from the drama's outset: the first reference, in a pensive G minor section of the opening chorus of sopranos, initiates the compassionate treatment of this weak and ageing ruler. Odette's words of pity for both king and son ('Malheureux fils, malheureux père!') are set off by Halévy with diminished chords and an expressive appoggiatura. In the Act II *Scène et romance*, Charles's confusion is evident as he weaves between concern for his own reason, longing for the once-beautiful Isabelle, memories of the battle that drove him to insanity and premonitions of the death of a king – forgetting momentarily that it is he who is king. Halévy vividly portrays Charles's mental state with dramatic pauses in his recitative and surprising harmonic and textural shifts. The king's reason seems to return in Act III no. 17, when he recognises his son, and in Act IV no. 23, when he curses Isabelle's treachery and the duke of Bedford. But it leaves him again in the ghost scene.

With the appearance of shrouded figures dragging chains, illumined by a 'fantastic lamp', ominous chromatic descending scales in winds and strings, diminished harmonies, funereal chants by a ghostly chorus, and forewarnings of murder by the spectres of dead soldiers, Halévy and his collaborators present a dark, lugubrious atmosphere. Contemporary reviewers noted Halévy's indebtedness to Mozart and Weber in this Shakespearean scene, which could be interpreted either as a digression to the supernatural or a representation of the delusions of a deranged king. Charles VI hears murmurings and sees figures from his past who warn him of his impending demise (the spectral chorus is accompanied by the full orchestra as well as off-stage trumpets and horns). In Act V, Charles once again sees his enemies clearly and, in the finale, spurs them to battle with a last refrain of 'Guerre aux tyrans'.

The majority of the press lauded *Charles VI* and reported on the impressive *mise-en-scène*, historically authentic costumes, effective numbers and interpretations. Henri Blanchard praised Halévy's 'deeply felt music', his 'experimental, rich, abundant, animated and dramatic orchestra', and 'distinguished' and melancholic melodies that lent appropriate colour to the subject.[37] Complaints did appear, among them that the opera was too long, with a première that reportedly lasted from seven o'clock to half-past midnight.[38] In the *Revue des Deux Mondes*, Henri Blaze vented against both composer and genre, downgrading grand opera to the 'category of stage-technicians and costumiers' and lamenting Halévy's persistence in writing 'never less than five acts'.

Le Juif errant and *La Magicienne*

Halévy's last two grand operas exploited the era's fascination with the supernatural to an even greater degree than *Charles VI*. In *Le Juif errant* (1852),

Scribe and his co-librettist Saint-Georges drew from the mysterious legend of the doomed Jewish wanderer Ahasvérus, variously treated by Edgar
Quinet in the epic poem *Ahasvérus* (1833); by Pierre-François Merville and
Julien de Mallian in the five-act *drame fantastique, Le Juif errant* (Ambigu-
Comique, 1834); and by Eugène Sue in a popular novel (1845) and drama
(1849).[39] Although diverging in plot and scope from these treatments, it
shares with them the integration of the metaphysical and historical as well
as the play of the 'two worlds' of Orient and Occident. In part to simplify
dramatically for the lyric stage, the opera avoided the widely panhistorical
action in Merville's and Mallian's drama, which began in Jerusalem on the
day of the death of Christ – the original place and time of the legend of
the artisan who denied Jesus a resting spot as he bore his cross to Calvary.
It also refrained from the weighty use of Christian imagery, biblical quotation, and demonic characters of this drama, or the emphatic philosophical–
political slant or allegorical breadth of Sue's novel. This latter work, an
anticlerical vehicle which targeted the Jesuits as 'false priests' bent on world
domination, portrayed the wandering Jew as a sombre, noble figure who
had suffered throughout time in the name of his Jewish descendants, the
downtrodden 'race of workers', but also for all humanity; Sue also topically binds his endless march with that of another mysterious traveller: 'Le
Choléra'.

Like Sue, Halévy and his librettists offered a compassionate depiction
of the divinely cursed *juif errant*, suggesting the weight of his guilt and the
sincerity of his repentance, the persecution that follows him and his progeny,
and the excessiveness of his punishment. They centre his travails in Anvers,
then Bulgaria, Thessalonica and Constantinople, in 1190, during the time
of the Crusades and of Baudouin I (1172–1205), count of Flanders and first
Latin emperor of Constantinople. Ahasvérus enters first in narrative, in the
plaintive *légende* of Act I (no. 2), sung by Théodora, a beautiful *batelière*,
or ferrywoman, and sister of Léon – both are related to the wandering Jew,
as later revealed. In the ballad's E minor sections, touched with funereal
figures, Théodora repeats the angel's order that had sealed Ahasvérus's fate
to seek in vain his own place of repose: 'Marche! Marche toujours'. At the
end of no. 5 of Act I, surrounded by lightning and gloom, the long-bearded
figure trudges on to the scene with stave in hand and without speaking,[40]
inducing fear in Ludger and his coterie of brigands, who are conspiring
to kill Baudouin's daughter. The sympathetic portrayal of this tragic figure
intensifies in the Act I *Scène et duo final*, in which, with heavy remorse,
he refuses a drink of water offered by Théodora, and tells of his relentless
journey. After Théodora discovers that Ahasvérus is her ancestor (her 'père'),
he is called by fanfares, thunder and lightning to move on, and they end Act
I with a regretful parting.

In Act II, Ahasvérus appears as a prophetic, almost divine figure who comes to save Irène (first identified as the sister of Théodora and Léon), from Ludger's bandits, her kidnappers. His revelation that Irène is in actuality Baudouin's daughter and destined to become the Impératrice d'Orient, is taken as a profanation of Nicéphone, the pretender to the throne. Ahasvérus is condemned to the stake, yet not even earthly death can allow him to escape his destiny: as fire surrounds him, a heavenly force extinguishes the flames. The weariness that this fate has brought him spills out in his recitative and aria of Act IV (no. 20), as he pleads with God to release him. He hopes for death, but in the final reckoning of Act V, as choruses sing of the fates of the 'chosen' and the 'damned' and the dead are called forth, his hope goes unrealised; from the distance an angels' chorus resounds, 'Marche toujours!'

At key moments in the drama, Halévy calls on expanded brass forces (see below) to signal *le juif errant*, to create the storms that swirl around him, and to depict the ultimate powers of the Last Judgement. He gives a repeated-note recurring motif on the words 'Marche toujours' to the Avenging Angel and to off-stage angels in Act IV (no. 22); it returns in Act V (no. 24). He also experiments with pitch associations, linking Ahasvérus and his fate with the pitches e–f♯. Both are repeated by Théodora as she recalls the angel's 'Marche' in her *légende*; Ahasvérus ascends from $f\sharp$ to a long-held e^1 as he reintroduces himself to Ludger in Act IV (no. 22); and the angels reiterate their command on repeated $f\sharp$'s.

Striking stage sets enhanced the fatalistic atmosphere, especially Joseph Thierry's tableau of temple ruins on the Bosphorus under moonlight and clouds for Act IV, and Edouard Despléchin's representation of the opening of hell beneath the shining peaks of heaven for Act V – a set so impressive that one critic boasted that the artist had 'surpassed Michelangelo'.[41] Eastern exoticism was realised in the dance of Ludger's harem of slaves from 'Asia, Georgia, Circassia' and in Cambon's depiction of the emperors' palace in Constantinople within Act III, which set the scene for more crowd-pleasing divertissements, including the dance of bees with Marie Taglioni as queen.

In a very different manner, supernatural elements combine with Christian ideology and historical allusions in *La Magicienne*, a work designated as 'half fantastic, half real' by one critic.[42] Like *Le Juif errant*, it is based on a popular myth, one appearing in numerous forms from the fourteenth to the nineteenth centuries,[43] and one also linked to the era of the Crusades in Saint-Georges's treatment. Appropriate for a setting of the myth, the opera fills the stage with fairies, wood nymphs, gnomes, and satanic figures with magical powers, and centres its story on the actions and transformation of Mélusine, a man-luring fairy-siren and sorceress. Rather than the metamorphoses of the fairy 'Mère-Lusine' of myth into a creature who is half-human, half-fish, Mélusine's transformation is ultimately a spiritual one. While she relishes her powers gained through a Faustian pact with the devil, or Stello (who also appears in the guise of a pilgrim in Act I), she is also unwillingly caught in his grip; she vows to fight him and believes that pure love can touch and save the soul that is not his. Through satanic artifice and deception she seduces the crusader Réné, and then calls forth evil spirits and a phantom to convince him of the infidelity of his fiancée Blanche, countess of Poitou, and to prevent their marriage. Yet it is Mélusine's love for Réné that begins to release her from the grasp of Stello, who also jealously loves her as he controls her. Stello tries to crush his opponent by revealing to Réné the true demonic identity of Mélusine, but her changing feelings pull her further away. The dichotomy between good and evil is most blatantly rendered in Act V, as the sorceress moves towards humanisation, conversion, and, finally, apotheosis: the defiant cries of Stello and his compatriots lose their effect as Mélusine vows to renounce 'le démon' forever and becomes Christian. She then dies in the arms of Blanche and Réné and symbolically ascends to heaven with the appearance of an illuminated cross and the choral singing of her 'return to God'.

In story, message and style, *La Magicienne* contrasts most sharply with Halévy's grand operas of the July Monarchy and the anticlerical leanings of *La Juive* (even if we remember Scribe's first thoughts about converting Rachel). The opera's blatant Christian religiosity speaks of changing values, perhaps reflecting the reconciliation of Church and State under the Second Empire. Although the composer uses elements similar to those found in earlier works, including reminiscence motifs drawn from Mélusine's *romance* of the Act I finale and the massive choral and orchestral forces of the Act III finale (see below), this work breathes more readily the air of opéra comique in its higher concentration on strophic numbers and its greater reliance on melodic and harmonic simplicity and textural clarity. Criticisms of it ranged from denigrating commentary in *Revue des Deux Mondes* to high praise by many reviewers, including Berlioz, while both Berlioz and Gounod expressed doubts about the work in private.[44]

Compositional style and vocal forms

Like Meyerbeer and other contemporaries, Halévy drew from French, Italian and Germanic operatic and symphonic traditions, leading critics then and now to label his work 'eclectic',[45] an adjective often used to describe the genre itself, but one that obscures the musico-dramatic coherence and power of his works. Although his integration of stylistic influences, reliance on conventional gestures and linking of set pieces can at times reveal a hurried composer at work, Halévy often succeeds in musically actualising the contrasts between intimacy and massed power sought after in the genre and meshing varying styles and moods into a convincing dramatic entity. At his best, as Wagner sensed in *La Juive*, Halévy imbues his writing with a visceral, emotional authenticity, in such impassioned collective responses as 'Au lac' and 'Sur eux anathème' of *La Juive*'s Acts I and III, or poignant, introspective expressions such as Eléazar's intensely moving Act IV *air*, Charles VI's despairing *romance*, or Guido's doleful music in Ginevra's tomb. The composer creates dramatic continuity through the integration of lyrical and declamatory writing; he often moves his dramas forward with affecting, well-paced gestures and mood-enhancing or psychologically revealing harmonies and instrumental colours.

Halévy begins his grand operas with either a short instrumental introduction or multi-sectional overture. Although he wrote both types for *La Juive*, the introduction was used for the première and most performances thereafter in Paris (the overture, which appears in vocal score editions but not in the first orchestral score, was first performed in October 1835).[46] In *Guido et Ginevra*, brilliant *tutti* bars move immediately to the melody of a choral prayer that returns in the fifth act. The overture of *La Reine de Chypre*, like *La Juive*'s introduction, begins softly and hesitantly, with falling diminished sevenths followed by passages of contrasting key, melody, rhythm, texture and orchestration. Themes from the drama proper, including the king's Act II *romance* and the National Anthem, are heard in the overture of *Charles VI*. Commonly framing each opera, and each act, are complex, multi-sectional choral numbers that incorporate ensemble and solo material, declamatory choral responses that spur the action forward, and sometimes the return of opening choral material, as happens in *La Juive*'s first act. Halévy also chooses non-choral beginnings (e.g., the *romance et duo* initiating *La Reine de Chypre*) or finales (e.g., the same opera's duet closing Act III, or the *air* closing *La Juive*'s Act IV). Reflecting the conventions explored in Chapter 5 above, his choruses range from celebratory, triumphal numbers that may feature divertissements to militaristic, hunting, drinking and prayerful choruses; some are solidly homophonic in four or five parts, often with piquant rhythms and voicings, and others contrapuntally treated, sometimes in the form of double, or even triple, choruses.

Halévy writes simple, tuneful, and affecting melodies – as in Léopold's *sérénade* or Eudoxie's *boléro* – that represent continuations of an Italianate aesthetic and often rely on square phrasing and cadential formulae. Yet he also creates melodic flexibility through extended and varied phraseology. Above all, his melodies are generally syllabic, but mixed with florid coloratura for aristocratic roles (e.g., Eudoxie and Isabelle de Bavière). Reviewers complained that his recitatives and arias resembled each other too closely,[47] and critics rarely thought melody to be his strength: much of it did not fit the *bel canto* ideal preferred by such critics as Castil-Blaze and his son Henri Blaze. As supporters of Rossini and the Théâtre Italien they (and others) condemned it as uninspired and unnatural. On the other hand Wagner admired the composer's 'dramatic melody' and emotionally intense declamatory style.[48]

The composer builds many of his multi-sectional *airs* and ensembles on French and Italian models, while he exhibits a progressive dramatic sense through manipulations of recitative–aria distinctions and also the integration of heightened recitative or *arioso* or *parlante* within set pieces. Whether solo aria or ensemble, Halévy creates varied structures through contrasts (of key, texture, tempo, metre, orchestration, lyrical and declamatory writing), symmetrical and asymmetrical phrasing, stable and unstable harmonic treatment, and cadential articulations. Rarely does the dramatic action remain static, but advances within or between lyrical sections (including restatements), at times with *coups-de-théâtre*. Cantabile–cabaletta aria divisions are reflected (e.g., Eléazar's 'Rachel, quand du Seigneur'), as well as the Rossinian duet prototype, described above in Chapter 10, found in the Eudoxie–Rachel Act III duet of *La Juive* and the Gérard–de Lusignan duet that ends the third act of *La Reine de Chypre*. Strophic forms appear, at times with choral or recitative interpolations between strophes or with other structural modification. Cavatinas, *romances* or individual aria sections are commonly ternary, for example the de Lusignan–Catarina *cavatine* of *La Reine*'s last act, but binary structures (e.g., Eléazar's Act II *cavatine*) are also found.[49]

Halévy's rhythmic treatment varies from banal, repeated figures with regularly accented downbeats, to elegant and novel choices.[50] However, concern for rhythmic consistency and vitality, along with Italianate leanings and interest in new types of versification for the sake of innovation, contributed to poor prosody in some set pieces.[51]

Although the composer's style is traditional in harmonic control and cadential structure, its harmonic language borders on the colourful and progressive. It exhibits a penchant for third-relations, often to signal dramatic disruption; for key-shifts a major or minor second away, which effect displacement and tension within, or between, sectional divisions; hints of chromaticism; diminished-, augmented-sixth and occasional augmented triads (e.g., within the recitative of *La Reine*'s Act I finale); and unprepared harmonies and unexpected melodic dissonances outside those used for local colour. Halévy finds many dramatic uses for diminished-seventh chords, often signalling and intensifying mood shifts or moments of confusion or horror. In *Guido et Ginevra* diminished harmonies permeate a blend of bassoons, horns and trumpets that speaks for Ginevra as she awakens in her tomb.

Halévy used recurring or reminiscence motifs sparingly but convincingly, for dramatic unity and reinforcement. The dying king recalls the words and melody of 'Triste exilé', first sung with his compatriot Gérard in Act III of *La Reine*; Charles VI's Act II *romance* is recalled before his Act IV ghost scene; the opera's patriotic National Anthem returns at the end, as we have seen; and when Guido enters Ginevra's tomb in Act III the orchestra recalls his Act I *romance*.

Orchestration; timbre

In response to the virtuosity of the Paris Opéra orchestra as well as developments in instrument construction, Halévy exploited enhanced ranges and colours towards effective musico-dramatic ends. Berlioz was only one of many admirers of the composer's powerful and nuanced orchestration, which features varied treatment of new and traditional brass instruments and colourful blends of woodwind timbres. While writing conventionally for the brass as harmonic and rhythmic supporters and in fanfares and horn calls, he also creates subtle and unusual dramatic effects; moreover he reinforces natural trumpets and horns in *La Juive* with valve trumpets and valve horns (this opera was among the first to exploit the resources of the latter). He calls for valve horns in seven of the twenty-two numbers, often using them to provide low notes unavailable on the two natural horns. More dramatic and innovative uses include the valve-horn doubling of Brogni's Act III malediction, and their unison blending with strings in the Act V march.[52] Halévy's treatment of valve trumpets includes the attention-seeking parallel-sixth ascent that opens the drinking-chorus of Act I, the doubling of solo vocal lines and instrumental bass lines, and blending of their low register with natural trumpets or with valve and natural horns.[53]

In most operas, Halévy's expanded brass section plays a vital role in creating a powerful sonority and building climaxes within choral numbers, particularly finales. *La Reine de Chypre* augments the sonic scope by calling not only for more brass, but also an additional (though optional) stage orchestra in Act III's *Chœur dansé* and in the procession of the queen's entourage in Act IV's *Chœur triomphal*.[54] The combined sound of this large group with the pit orchestra (and chorus) would have been massive, for both contained essentially the same winds, strings and percussion. In *Guido et Ginevra* Halévy blended the sound of the new valved soprano trombone, described by Berlioz as 'broad' and 'sonorous', with valve horns and trumpets in the Act II march;[55] he also introduced the mélophone in divertissements of the same act. The Opéra signed a contract with the instrument-maker Adolphe Sax in 1847, engaging him to provide special stage instruments (and

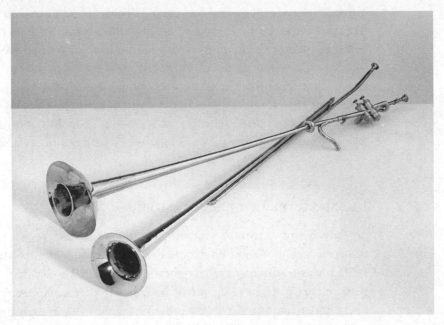

Figure 23 Two trumpets, now in the Musée de la musique, Paris, made by Adolphe Sax for grand operas, following his 1847 contract to supply various on-stage instruments and players to the Paris Opéra. The valveless trumpet can be dated to the 1876 performances of *Aida*. In 1847 Sax supplied on-stage saxhorns for Verdi's *Jérusalem*, mentioned in the following chapter.

players) for grand operas, past and future (see Fig. 23).[56] In *Le Juif errant*, Halévy experimented with saxophones as well as the newly developed family of saxhorns: in a supplementary brass group in the Act III finale he employed soprano, contralto, tenor, baritone, bass and contrabass saxhorns, along with valve cornets, trumpets (with cylinders), trombones, and ophicleide. For the 'Last Judgement' ending Act V, he adds soprano, tenor and bass saxophones to this extra brass contingent.

Contrasting with massive blocks of sound are moments of understated beauty, as in the poignant clarinet lines at the opening of the Eudoxie–Rachel Act IV duet, the cello melody in the following *scène* (emanating from Rachel's sacrificial gesture to save Léopold) and the cor anglais duet in Eléazar's famous *air*. In *La Reine de Chypre* Halévy creates a particularly delicate palette, with many passages for muted, sustained and *divisi* strings of three to four parts, pizzicato and tremolo effects, and chromatic writing with frequent markings of *con delicatezza* or *smorzando* (see Ex. 13.3). Halévy's use of the orchestra as dramatic agent is at its most exposed and refined in dramatic recitative and *arioso*, where unobtrusive hints of sound, interjections or full accompaniments punctuate singers' phrases and push the action forward. Conventional but impressive in his creation of tension and suspense are repeated bass patterns, sometimes sequential and chromatically inflected, quick scalar and arpeggiated figures, and drum rolls, fanfares, horn calls and bells that act as dramatic links or signals. Other transforming gestures can be as simple as a single unexpected pitch or harmony; the deftest gestures often reveal a shift in a character's mood or thought, as in the horn–bassoon chords that speak for Eléazar as he contemplates Rachel's fate prior to his Act IV *air* (Ex. 13.1). Halévy often intensifies introspective and revelatory moments with dramatic silences, as following Léopold's admission in *La Juive*'s Act II *romance* or Eléazar's discovery of the eloping couple.

Later performances and reputation

La Juive, a work central to the nineteenth-century Opéra repertory, continued to bring in solid audiences for decades following its première: in 1875, it was featured at the inauguration of the Palais Garnier;[57] its 500th performance came in 1886, and its last Parisian performances in 1933. The opera had a vigorous life in the provinces, appearing in early productions in Rouen, Lyon, Marseille, Toulouse and Aix-la-Chapelle, and on European stages in Leipzig, Berlin, Kassel, Frankfurt, Vienna, Brussels and Budapest.[58] An early adaptation was given on 16 November 1835 in London, followed by widely varied versions in that capital throughout the nineteenth century.[59] Leopold Damrosch introduced *La Juive* to New York's Metropolitan Opera on 16 January 1885, allowing an interpolation of 'Robert, Robert, toi que j'aime' from *Robert le Diable* by Marie Schröder-Hanfstängl.[60] After lapsing from the Met's turn-of-the-century repertory, it reappeared in a new production featuring Rosa Ponselle as Rachel and Enrico Caruso as Eléazar on 22 November 1919; it was performed regularly during the 1920s, with its fifteenth and final season of performances coming in 1935–36.[61]

Among Halévy's other grand operas, *La Reine de Chypre* and *Charles VI* had the longest performing lives. The former's 100th performance came in the reprise of 1854, when Rosine Stoltz returned as Catarina after her retirement from the Opéra;[62] it remained in the theatre's repertory until 1858, with a revival in 1877. In addition to performances in the provinces, including Bordeaux (1843) and Rouen (1844), it was given in Florence, Leipzig, Antwerp, Brussels, New Orleans, London and New York from 1842 to 1845, and in Vienna in 1858. *Charles VI* appeared in a new version at the Opéra in 1848, with alterations authorised by Halévy. Scenes 2 and 3 were cut from Act I and the *Chant national* shifted to Act III, somewhat mitigating the patriotic fervour that dominated the 1843 work. Act IV lost scenes 6–7, to end with the popular ghost scene.

Guido et Ginevra was performed in Amsterdam, The Hague, Antwerp, Hamburg, Berlin, Budapest, Brussels, Prague, Vienna and London from

1838 to 1845, and underwent significant alterations at the Paris Opéra, being reduced from five to four acts in 1840. Both *Charles VI* and *Guido* were revived in Paris in 1870, the former at the Théâtre Lyrique, the latter at the Théâtre Italien in Italian.

By the end of his operatic career, Halévy had moved from a position at 'the head of the young school of French composers', as Blanchard wrote in 1843, to the status of an admired, but often overlooked composer whose reputation had been partially eclipsed by Meyerbeer's more widely revered brilliance. In the year before his death, Halévy complained that his repertory was 'thoroughly sidelined' at the Opéra, remarking that *Guido*, for example, was left 'in the sack of forgotten [works]'.[63] Jealousy of the well-positioned composer was said to have motivated certain denigrators in Paris; the composer's role as acting director under Duponchel's directorship was but one which undoubtedly provoked adversarial feelings. Although Wagner's anti-Semitism did not seem to touch his views of Halévy, it is likely that some assessments were coloured by anti-Jewish sentiments. The novelist George Sand, privately applauding Pauline Viardot's decision not to sing in Halévy's *La Dame de pique*, referred to his music as 'the ugliest, most hook-nosed and most stupid music there ever was'.[64]

Halévy's work was inspired by many past masters, including his beloved teacher Cherubini, but also contemporaries such as Rossini, Meyerbeer and Auber. In turn, the operas of Donizetti, Verdi and Wagner, among others, bear his influence, something which is reflected in criticism of the day: a thorough assessment of his legacy, which can only be had through careful comparative study, lies in the future.

14 From Rossini to Verdi

M. ELIZABETH C. BARTLET

I hope to see you soon . . . when you will tell me all the news of the '*grande boutique*'.
VERDI TO LÉON ESCUDIER, 5 FEBRUARY 1869

Introduction

Verdi's publisher, Léon Escudier, nicknamed the Paris Opéra the '*grande boutique*' ('big shop', but with pejorative undertones), an appellation that the composer cheerfully adopted.[1] Of all the Italian composers who wrote for the Opéra during this period, Verdi had the most mixed feelings about the institution and the requirements for success. Yet even he felt obliged, at times against his inclination, to try to meet the challenge, and even after he no longer wished to compose for it, wanted to stay up-to-date about developments there.

Why was Paris, and specifically this theatre, such a magnet for *musiciens transalpins*, 'musicians from the other side of the Alps', as the French called them? Even before Spontini's arrival in 1803 (see Chapter 1) Antonio Sacchini and Antonio Salieri scored major triumphs in Paris before the Revolution; several of their works – notably *Dardanus* (1784) and *Œdipe à Colone* (1786) by the former, and *Tarare* (1787) by the latter – were performed well into the nineteenth century. Success in Paris after the Restoration of 1815 brought substantial financial advantages. Composers were assured of continuing honoraria for every performance at the Opéra (unlike the situation in Italy – not yet politically united – during the first half of the nineteenth century).[2] The thriving music publishing industry provided another important source of revenue, since resident composers' rights were protected by law.[3] The sheer size of the Opéra's establishment was an attraction and a challenge. Finally, Paris was the literary capital of Europe. French plays, whether at the government-supported Comédie-Française and the Odéon, or at the numerous boulevard theatres, intrigued Italian composers (and librettists): indeed, they were among the most important resources for nineteenth-century Italian opera.

What did the Opéra expect of the Italians? The principal three – Rossini (1792–1868), Donizetti (1797–1848) and Verdi (1813–1901) – were already stars before coming to Paris. All three had successes not only in Italy, but also in Paris at the Théâtre Italien and other lyric theatres before being invited to write for the Opéra, and all were willing to come to the French capital to supervise rehearsals of their operas.[4] (These are set out in Table 14.1 below.) The composers were offered unusually favourable terms. Rossini was promised (and ultimately received) a government pension in addition to full author's honoraria, even for adaptations of works written earlier, *Mosè* as *Moïse* and *Maometto II* as *Le Siège de Corinthe* (contrary to the theatre's own rules that dictated a 50 per cent reduction).[5] Indeed, the exceptions made for Rossini set a precedent for later composers (including Meyerbeer) and librettists (such as Scribe) to negotiate contracts in addition to the standard honoraria under Louis Véron and his successors. For Donizetti, the Opéra risked *Les Martyrs*, already forbidden by censorship in Naples for depicting saints' deaths.[6] Then in 1841 after the bankruptcy and closure of the Théâtre de la Renaissance, the administration jumped at the opportunity to acquire his *L'Ange de Nisida*, transformed it into *La Favorite*, and advanced it to the head of the rehearsal queue, again bending the rules.[7] Verdi, too, benefited from full author's honoraria for revisions of Italian operas and advantageous contracts.[8] When, during rehearsals for a revival of *Les Vêpres siciliennes*, the orchestra failed to follow his instructions, Verdi understandably took umbrage; to try to placate him, the administration sacked the conductor.[9]

Remembering the traditional reputation of Italians for singing and song, the administration counted on them to help train personnel in a more lyric and flexible vocal style. Rossini, Donizetti and Verdi had specific singers in mind when they composed for the Paris stage and had extensive rehearsals with them. Rossini insisted that Laure Cinti-Damoreau and Nicolas-Prosper Levasseur, whom he had already rehearsed at the Théâtre Italien, be assigned principal roles in his works at the Opéra. After the première of *Moïse* several critics credited the composer with greatly improving standards. As the *Gazette de France* wrote:

> The results [are] truly impressive . . . for what has been accomplished is nothing less than a lyric revolution accomplished in four hours by M. Rossini. Henceforth the *urlo francese* [the French howl] is banished for ever, and people will sing at the Opéra as they do at the Théâtre Favart [i.e. the Théâtre Italien].[10]

When first negotiating with the Opéra administration, Donizetti insisted that he have his choice among the leading singers and that three months of rehearsals (of three hours a day) be set aside for his work.[11] For *Les Martyrs* Donizetti worked closely with Julie Dorus-Gras and Gilbert-Louis Duprez, both of whom had previous experience in major roles in Rossini operas and in Italian singing style. Significantly, critics generally praised them.[12] *La Favorite* featured the veteran Levasseur, Duprez, Paul Barroilhet and, in the title role, Rosine Stoltz (see Chapter 7), who combined lyricism with an intense dramatic presence and earned an ovation from the public and most

Table 14.1 *Operas by Italian Composers at the Opéra, 1825–1880 (The titles of serious operas are given in bold.)*[a]

Title	Composer(s)/ Arranger	Librettist(s)	No. of Acts	Première at the Opéra	No. of performances at the Opéra to 1900[b]	Comments[c]
La belle au bois dormant	Carafa	Planard	3	2 March 1825	18	Autograph: *I-Nc*.
Le Siège de Corinthe	Rossini	Soumet, Balocchi	3	9 Oct. 1826	close to 100	Rossini's reworking of his *Maometto II* (della Valle), 2 acts, first performed at the Teatro San Carlo, Naples, 3 Dec. 1820. Autograph fragments: *F-Pn, F-Po, I-FOc*. Full score published by Troupenas (Paris); reprinted *Early Romantic Opera*, 14 (1980).
Moïse	Rossini	Jouy, Balocchi	4 [rev. 3]	26 March 1827	close to 150	Rossini's reworking of his *Mosè in Egitto* (Tottola), 3 acts, first performed at the Teatro San Carlo, 5 March 1818. Originally named *Moïse et Pharaon, ou le Passage de la mer Rouge*, but shortened to *Moïse* before the Parisian première. Autograph fragments: *F-Pn, US-NYp, US-STu*. Full score published by Troupenas (Paris); reprinted *Early Romantic Opera*, 15 (1980).
Le Comte Ory	Rossini	Scribe, Delestre-Poirson	2	20 Aug. 1828	over 350	Scribe revised and expanded his *comédie-vaudeville* of the same title in 1 act (première: Théâtre du Vaudeville, Paris, 16 Dec. 1816). Rossini borrowed from his score for *Il viaggio a Reims*, written to commemorate the coronation of Charles X (première: Théâtre Italien, Paris, 19 June 1825). Autograph fragments: *F-Po, B-Bmichotte*. Full score published by Troupenas (Paris); reprinted *Early Romantic Opera*, 16 (1980).
Guillaume Tell	Rossini	Jouy, Bis	4	3 Aug. 1829	close to 750	Rossini's last opera, it was performed in a 3-act version (revised by the composer) at the Opéra from 1831 to 1856; thereafter the 4-act version was re-established. Still in repertory after 1900. Autograph: *F-Pn*; autograph fragments: *F-Pn, F-Po*. Full score published by Troupenas (Paris); reprinted *Early Romantic Opera*, 17 (1980).
Ali-Baba, ou les Quarante voleurs	Cherubini	Scribe, Mélesville	4 + prologue	22 July 1833	11	Cherubini's last opera. He reworked four pieces from his score for *Kourkourgi*, unperformed but intended for the Théâtre Feydeau (1793). Autograph: *D-B*; autograph fragments: *F-Po*. Piano-vocal score published by Breitkopf & Härtel (Leipzig).
La Xacarilla	Marliani	Scribe	1	28 Oct. 1839	over 100	Full score published by S. Richault (Paris).
Les Martyrs	Donizetti	Scribe	4	10 April 1840	20	Donizetti reworked his score for *Poliuto* (Cammarano), 3 acts, intended for the Teatro San Carlo, but forbidden by the censor. Autograph: *I-Mr*; autograph fragments: *F-Pn*. Full score published by Schonenberger; reprinted *Early Romantic Opera*, 27 (1982).

Title	Composer	Librettist	Acts	Premiere	No.	Notes
La Favorite	Donizetti	Royer, Vaëz, rev. Scribe	4	2 Dec. 1840	over 650	Originally entitled *L'Ange de Nisida*, 3 acts, and intended for the Théâtre de la Renaissance. Revised and expanded for the Opéra after the Théâtre de la Renaissance closed. Still in repertory after 1900. Autograph fragments: *F-Pn, F-Po, I-Malfieri*. Full score published by Maurice Schlesinger (Paris); reprinted *Early Romantic Opera*, 28 (1982). (Piano-vocal score, arranged Wagner, also published by Schlesinger.)
Le Duc d'Albe	Donizetti	Scribe	4	unperformed	—	Donizetti began the score in 1839, but left it incomplete. Autograph fragments: *F-Pn, F-Po, I-Mr*. Scribe later revised his libretto for Verdi (see *Les Vêpres siciliennes* below). Salvi and others completed Donizetti's opera after his death; it had its première as *Il duca d'Alba* (in an Italian translation by Zanardini), 22 March 1882 at the Teatro Apollo, Rome. Piano-vocal score published by F. Lucca (Milan).
Dom Sébastien, roi de Portugal	Donizetti	Scribe	5	13 Nov. 1843	32	Donizetti's last opera. Autograph: *F-Pn*. Autograph fragments: *F-Po*. Full score published by the Bureau central de musique [L. Escudier] (Paris); reprinted *Early Romantic Opera*, 29 (1982).
Othello	Rossini, arr. Benoist	Royer, Vaëz	3	2 Sept. 1844	28	A reworking of Rossini's *Otello, ossia il moro di Venezia* (Berio di Salsa), written for the Teatro del Fondo, Naples (première: 4 Dec. 1816). Benoist's autograph fragments: *F-Po*. Piano-vocal score published Au Ménéstrel, Heugel & Fils (Paris).
Lucie de Lammermoor	Donizetti	Royer, Vaëz	4 [or 2]	20 Feb. 1846	close to 200	*Lucia di Lammermoor* (Cammarano) was written for the Teatro San Carlo, Naples (première: 26 Sept. 1835). The French adaptation was first performed in Paris at the Théâtre de la Renaissance, 10 Aug. 1839. Autograph fragments: *F-Pn*. Piano-vocal score published by L. Grus (Paris).
Robert Bruce	Rossini, arr. Niedermeyer	Royer, Vaëz	3	30 Dec. 1846	31	Niedermeyer reused the music from several Rossini operas, notably *Torvaldo e Dorliska* (Sterbini), 2 (première: 26 Dec. 1815, Teatro Valle, Rome), *Armida* (Schmidt), 3 (première: 11 Nov. 1817, Teatro San Carlo, Naples), *La donna del lago* (Tottola), 2 (première: 24 Oct. 1819, same theatre), *Bianca et Faliero, ossia il consiglio dei tre* (Romani), 2 (première: 26 Dec. 1819, Teatro alla Scala, Milan), *Zelmira* (Tottola), 2 (première: 16 Feb. 1822, Teatro San Carlo, Naples). Niedermeyer's autograph fragments: *F-Po*. Full score published by Troupenas (Paris).
Jérusalem	Verdi	Royer, Vaëz	4	26 Nov. 1847	33	Verdi reworked his score for *I Lombardi alla prima crociata* (Solera), first performed at Teatro alla Scala, Milan, 11 Feb. 1843. Autograph: *F-Pn*. Piano-vocal score published by the Bureau central de musique [L. Escudier] (Paris).

Table 14.1 (cont.)

Title	Composer(s)/ Arranger	Librettist(s)	No. of Acts	Première at the Opéra	No. of Performances at the Opéra to 1900[c]	Comments[b]
Louise Miller	Verdi	Alaffre, Pacini	4	2 Feb. 1853	8	Verdi reworked his score for *Luisa Miller* (Cammarano), 3 acts, first performed at the Teatro San Carlo, Naples, 8 Dec. 1849.
Betly	Donizetti, arr. Adam	Lucas	2	27 Dec. 1853	5	Adam arranged Donizetti's score for *Betly, ossia la capanna svizzera* (Donizetti), 1 act [later rev. in 2], first performed at the Teatro Nuovo, Naples, 21 Aug. 1836. Donizetti based the libretto on *Le Chalet* by Scribe and Mélesville (originally set by Adam, première: Opéra-Comique, Paris, 25 Sept. 1834). Adam's autograph fragments: *F-Po*.
Les Vêpres siciliennes	Verdi	Scribe, Duveyrier	5	13 June 1855	62	Scribe reworked his libretto, *Le Duc d'Albe*, mostly set by Donizetti (see above). Autograph: *F-Pn*. Autograph fragments: *F-Po*. Piano-vocal score published by L. Escudier (Paris).
La Rose de Florence	Biletta	Saint-Georges	2	10 Nov. 1856	5	Piano-vocal score published by Choudens (Paris).
Le Trouvère	Verdi	Pacini	4	12 Jan. 1857	over 200	Verdi reworked his score for *Il trovatore* (Cammarano [and Bardare]), first performed at the Teatro Apollo, Rome, 19 Jan. 1853. Piano-vocal score published by L. Escudier (Paris).
Roméo et Juliette	Bellini & Vaccai, arr. Dietsch	Nuitter	4	7 Sept. 1859	11	An adaptation for Acts I–III and opening of Act IV of Bellini's *I Capuleti e i Montecchi* (Romani), first performed at the Teatro La Fenice, Venice, 11 March 1830, and for most of Act IV of Vaccai's *Giulietta e Romeo* (Romani), first performed at the Teatro della Canobbiana, Milan, 31 Oct. 1825. (The substitution of Vaccai's final part for Bellini's setting first occurred 27 Oct. 1832 at the Teatro Comunale, Bologna.)
Sémiramis	Rossini, arr. Carafa	G. Méry	4	9 July 1860	35	An adaptation of *Semiramide* (Rossi), 2 acts, first performed at the Teatro La Fenice, Venice, 3 Feb. 1823. Carafa's autograph fragments: *F-Po*. Piano-vocal score published Au Ménestrel, Heugel & Fils (Paris).

Don Carlos	Verdi	F. J. Méry; Du Locle	5 [rev. 4]	11 March 1867	43	Autograph: *F-Pn*. Autograph fragments: *F-Po*. Piano-vocal score published by L. Escudier (Paris).
Aida	Verdi	Du Locle, Nuitter	4	22 March 1880	over 200	The opera in Italian (Ghislanzoni, after Mariette and Du Locle) had its première at the Cairo Opera, 24 Dec. 1871 (to celebrate the opening of the Suez Canal). It was first performed in Paris at the Théatre Italien (under Verdi's direction) 22 April 1876 in Italian and 1 Aug. 1878 in French. The Opéra took over the work after the closing of the latter theatre. Still in repertory after 1900. MS with autograph annotations: *F-Po*. Piano-vocal score published by L. Escudier (Paris).

Bibliographical sources: *Early Romantic Opera*, reprint series (New York: Garland, 1978–83)

Library abbreviations: *B-Bmichotte*: Brussels, Michotte private collection; *D-B*: Berlin, Staatsbibliothek zu Berlin Preussischer Kulturbesitz; *F-Pn*: Paris, Bibliothèque nationale; *F-Po*: Paris, Bibliothèque de l'Opéra; *I-FOc*, Forlì, Biblioteca Comunale Aurelio Saffi; *I-Malfieri*: Milan, Famiglia Trecani degli Alfieri, private collection; *I-Mr*: Milan, Biblioteca della Casa Ricordi; *I-Nc*: Naples, Conservatorio di Musica S. Pietro a Majella, Biblioteca; *US-NYp*: New York, Public Library at Lincoln Center, Music Division; *US-STu*: Palo Alto (CA), University, Memorial Library of Music, Department of Special Collections of the Cecil H. Green Library.

[a] Much information concerning the performance history in this table is derived from Théodore de Lajarte, *Bibliothèque musicale du Théâtre de l'Opéra: catalogue historique, chronologique, anecdotique*, 2 vols. (Paris: Librairie des Bibliophiles, 1878; repr. Hildesheim, 1969); Alfred Loewenberg, *Annals of Opera, 1597–1940*, and *Grove Opera*.

[b] The statistics have been established using those given by Lajarte and the manuscript *Journal de l'Opéra* in the Bibliothèque de l'Opéra. Unlike these two sources, the above table excludes partial performances. Totals over '75 performances are rounded off to the nearest 25 performances; thus 'over 150' means between 151 and 175 performances; 'close to 200 performances' means between 176 and 199 performances.

[c] For all operas important MS scores and performing materials still exist at Paris, Bibliothèque de l'Opéra (see Lajarte, *ibid.*). The score for Rossini's *Le Siège de Corinthe* is woefully incomplete and classed among the 'matériel' (orchestral parts) for this work. I do not cite them here, but, obviously, they are essential for the reconstruction of the Opéra performance tradition. On the other hand, I include reference to the contemporary published full scores and their modern reprints if any (if no full score was published, piano-vocal scores are given) and autographs in public collections (in the case of reworkings of operas originally written in Italian, only autographs and other sources pertaining to the French versions are cited). To date, only two operas have appeared in modern critical editions: Rossini's *Guillaume Tell*, ed. M. Elizabeth C. Bartlet, Edizione Critica delle Opere di Gioachino Rossini, sezione prima – opere teatrali; 39, 6 vols. (Pesaro: Fondazione Rossini, 1992 [*recte*: 1994]); and Donizetti's *La Favorite*, ed. Rebecca Harris-Warrick, Edizione Critica delle Opere di Gaetano Donizetti; 3, 2 vols. (Milan: Ricordi, 1997). (That of Donizetti's *Dom Sébastien, roi de Portugal*, ed. Mary Ann Smart, and Verdi's *Le Trouvère*, ed. David Lawton, will be published shortly. Others are in preparation.) Also, the piano-vocal score of Verdi's *Don Carlos*, ed. Ursula Günther and Luciano Petazzoni, 2 vols. (Milan: Ricordi, 1980) should be mentioned.

critics. Barroilhet went on to have a fine career at the Opéra, partly thanks to Donizetti's coaching and support. Like his compatriots, Verdi insisted on his choice of singers from among those in the employ of the Opéra, as well as the recruitment of others when the troupe did not satisfy his needs. Furthermore he coached them intensively, as the theatre's rehearsal records for *Les Vêpres siciliennes* prove.[13] And when his leading lady, the German singer Sophie Cruvelli, took off for a tryst with her lover Baron Vigier, plans for the première were put on hold – to the composer's extreme annoyance.[14]

Noting Italian successes in comedy, in works with exotic settings and in dance, the Opéra administration relied on the Italians to contribute to a broadening of the repertory at their theatre. Rossini's *vaudeville*-based *Le Comte Ory*, a pseudo-medieval farce, was the most successful. Adam's arrangement of Donizetti's *Betly*, a *dramma giocoso*, with the taming of an independently minded lass as its theme, did not please. Even more striking is that in these categories the Opéra was willing to stage works by riskier composers. Michele Carafa, an Italian prince, student of Cherubini's and friend of Rossini's, tried his hand at the Sleeping Beauty story, substantially revised, in *La Belle au bois dormant*. (The ballet version noted in Chapter 6, Appendix 1, was better received.) The failure of Cherubini's *Ali-Baba, ou les Quarante voleurs* (1833), even with its lavish sets, must have been a major disappointment to the seventy-three-year-old composer.[15] Marco Marliani, another Italian aristocrat and student of Rossini's (who died during the struggle for Italy's independence), was more fortunate in *La Xacarilla*, set in Spain with smugglers and their fence among the characters, and with a catchy 'recognition' song.[16] For *La Rose de Florence*, Emanuele Biletta, better known as a ballet composer (for Covent Garden), received praise for his melodies, but the work was more successful translated into Italian (Florence, 1875). Independent ballets (not in Table 14.1) constituted another genre to which Italian composers made significant contributions.[17]

Rossini, Donizetti and Verdi: a chronological overview

The Opéra came to rely on Rossini, Donizetti and Verdi for grand operas that, in addition to the works of Meyerbeer and the French, were the mainstay of their repertory for most of the nineteenth century and well into the twentieth. In fact the administration was determined to retain an Italian presence throughout this period, as Table 14.1 shows. The late 1820s belonged to Rossini. His comic opera *Le Comte Ory*, his two reworkings of Italian serious operas, *Moïse* and *Le Siège de Corinthe*, and above all his masterpiece, *Guillaume Tell*, continued to be performed frequently during

the next decades and after. By the late 1830s the administration, noting
the growing popularity of ballet in comparison to opera and wanting to
counterbalance this, turned to Donizetti. The early success of *Les Martyrs*
augured well, and the composer began work on Scribe's libretto for *Le Duc
d'Albe*. The Opéra administration preferred *La Favorite*. Indeed, the run of
Les Martyrs was cut short, probably because Duprez also starred in the new
opera and could not sustain both demanding roles at the same time.[18] The
acclaim for *La Favorite* earned Donizetti the reputation as Rossini's successor. Unfortunately, during the rehearsals of his last opera *Dom Sébastien*,
also with Duprez, the composer was already very ill (see p. 122).[19]

To ensure that the Italians still had a presence in the mid- to late 1840s,
the Opéra staged two Rossini operas, one a translation/adaptation (*Othello*)
and the other (*Robert Bruce*), a 'new' opera reusing music from several of
the composer's works, overruling protests from the director of the Théâtre
Italien.[20] The success for both was moderate.[21] Rossini's actual involvement,
though claimed by the Opéra, was minimal at most. In spite of opposition
from government overseers, the Opéra appropriated the French adaptation
of Donizetti's *Lucia di Lammermoor*, first performed in Paris at the Théâtre
de la Renaissance in 1839: *Lucie de Lammermoor* duly became a staple in the
Opéra's repertory. In addition the Opéra tried, without success, an adaptation of *Betly*.[22]

Seeking out a new Italian in the late 1840s and 1850s, the Opéra turned
to Verdi. The moderate performance run of his *Jérusalem* and the failure
of *Louise Miller* did not deter the administration from commissioning *Les
Vêpres siciliennes*. However, its *succès d'estime* prompted the Opéra again to
ask Verdi to revise one of his most popular works, *Il trovatore*: *Le Trouvère*
became a resounding success.[23] Then, while awaiting a new grand opera
from Verdi, the administration commissioned Pierre-Louis Dietsch, the *chef
de chant*, to revise Bellini's *Roméo et Juliette* (with the Vaccai substitution
in Act IV), and Carafa to adapt Rossini's *Semiramide* as *Sémiramis*: neither
stayed in repertory.[24] Verdi's masterpiece, *Don Carlos*, in several ways marks
the end of grand opera, or at least, new works in this genre that were written
for the Opéra.

Still, grand opera by Italians continued to please Parisian audiences:
Guillaume Tell and *La Favorite* remained in standard repertory there into
the twentieth century. One could argue that the title of the 'last grand opera'
to be given at the Opéra belongs to another work first written in Italian, but
based on a French scenario: Verdi's *Aïda*.[25] And, though the composer was
not involved with its production at this theatre, the French version proved
to be an enduring success, in fact Verdi's triumph there. It also marked the
close of a tradition more than two centuries old: looking to Italians for major
contributions to the new repertory at the Paris Opéra.

Their revisions of earlier works

The invited *maestri*, Rossini, Donizetti and Verdi, had similar strategies for making their Opéra début. All three chose to rework certain operas not yet familiar to Parisian audiences, which could benefit from the elaborate staging and resources offered by Paris. But in a way the process can be traced back further. It is no accident that Rossini's *Maometto II* and *Mosè* had their premières at the Teatro San Carlo in Naples and that Donizetti's *Poliuto* was written for this same theatre. These two composers dominated its repertory for over two decades. Verdi, too, had Neapolitan experience: though *I Lombardi* was for La Scala, *Luisa Miller*, for example, was first performed at the San Carlo, and *Il trovatore* was intended for it. Naples had strong French ties. Ruled by Napoleon Bonaparte's brother Joseph (1806–08) and then one of his generals, Joachim Murat (1808–15, married to his sister, Caroline), the city benefited from improvements in administration. In particular Murat enacted several policies (modelled on French practices) that greatly improved the financial position of the San Carlo, allowing the hiring of more singers (including Isabella Colbran, Rossini's first wife), dancers, orchestra players and other personnel, thus permitting the number of annual performances to increase substantially.[26] When the Bourbons returned to power, French administrative procedures were left in place. Indeed, royal family ties continued with the 1816 marriage of the duc de Berry, nephew of Louis XVIII, to Princess Maria Carolina of the Kingdom of the Two Sicilies. Just before Rossini's arrival, the composer most frequently commissioned for its new operas was Giovanni Simone Mayr, an admirer of French plays and operas who frequently used adaptations of these texts for his own works; he was also the teacher of Donizetti. Furthermore, French serious operas in translation had their Italian premières here, among them Sacchini's *Œdipe à Colone* (in 1808), Spontini's *La Vestale* (in 1811) and *Fernand Cortez* (in 1820, under Rossini's direction). Of all the cities in the peninsula Naples was culturally the closest to France. In addition to stunning vocal display, audiences there expected spectacle, dance, lavish sets and costumes, grand themes and extended tableaux, which incorporated several pieces often connected by orchestrally accompanied recitative – all influenced by the French model. Rossini and his successors met their demands.

Types of subject matter apt for grand opera travelled easily between Italy and France. With *Le Siège de Corinthe* (see Chapter 1) the choice was also topical.[27] *Moïse* capitalised on fashionable Egyptomania, a legacy of Napoleon's campaigns, and met requirements for a morally elevated theatre during the reign of Charles X. The setting of *Les Martyrs* is third-century Armenia during the oppression of the Christians, another working-out of the theme of religious persecution and sacrifice. Finally *Jérusalem*, set in the Holy Land at the time of the Crusades, tells a tale of treachery, of a hero wrongly accused of attempted murder, but of ultimate redemption. Leading French librettists and playwrights were involved (see Table 14.1): Etienne de Jouy was Spontini's favourite collaborator, Luigi Balocchi was 'poet' at the Théâtre Italien, and Alexandre Soumet a popular playwright; Donizetti worked with Scribe, while the dramatists Alphonse Royer and Gustave Vaëz had considerable experience as specialists in the adaptation of Italian librettos.

However, not even the grandest of Neapolitan operas fully met the requirements of the Parisian stage. So, revision and adaptation were necessary. Rossini, Donizetti and Verdi also had to learn to cope with setting the French language, whose inflections are so different from their native Italian. A detailed comparison of the originals with the new versions would be out of place here.[28] Nonetheless, some generalisations will help us understand these composers' approach to grand opera. First, there was the question of sheer size. Instead of the two or three acts common in Naples, four (or five) were preferred in Paris. Expansion was accomplished by an even greater emphasis on spectacle and dancing in divertissements or elsewhere, and by enhancing the dramatic role of the chorus. More generally, the *mise-en-scène* assumed a greater importance than in Italy: costumes, sets, acting, and movement – especially of massed groups on stage.[29] In addition to writing new pieces, composers reworked existing music, especially for soloists, into more extensive tableaux with major additions, even at the cost of violating accepted Italian formal procedures followed in the originals. At the same time, librettists sought to give the revisions greater dramatic logic by French standards.

Donizetti was well aware of the challenge. In writing to his teacher Mayr about the transformation of *Poliuto* into *Les Martyrs*, he noted:

> It is expanded into four acts instead of the original three and has been translated and adjusted for the French stage by Scribe. As a result, I had to redo all the recitatives from scratch, write a new finale for the first act, add airs, trios and characteristic dances as is customary here, so that the public cannot complain that the shape of the work is Italian, and in this the public is not wrong. French music and theatrical poetry have a *cachet* all their own, to which every composer must accommodate himself; . . . then between one statement of the cabaletta theme and the second, there is always some poetry which carries forward the action without the typical repetition of lines that our poets use.[30]

For Verdi, French rehearsal schedules were vexing, far different from the Italian situation in which he was accustomed to mounting an opera quickly.

He wrote to his father-in-law Antonio Barezzi on 1 November 1847, in the midst of rehearsals for *Jérusalem*:

> You will say to me: 'I know what an opera is'. No, no . . . You don't know, and no one knows unless he has attempted one here. An opera in Italy, however grandiose it may be, is as small as a solfeggio in comparison with a Mass. You cannot imagine the infinite number of tiny things which have to be done here, and which are so curiously annoying as to give the dead a fever. If I had imagined as much, I would have sent to the devil music, operas, Lombards and the lot. I hope that in a month from now I shall have gone on the stage, I say I hope, for another [problem] crops up every day.[31]

The following year after this experience Verdi reflected:

> You know that here one rehearses for six, seven or even eight months, and you might believe it's useless: I used to think so, but now that I have had experience I see how necessary it is, for a substantial part of the opera must be worked out during rehearsals on stage. Here the *mise-en-scène* is perhaps the most important element; many operas succeed because of it.[32]

By *mise-en-scène* Verdi and his French contemporaries did not mean simply costumes and sets, but rather how the entire presentation was visually (and musically) engaging the audience. It is worth recalling that the crossing of the Red Sea in Rossini's 1818 *Mosè*, which had apparently provoked laughter at its Naples première, also proved a challenge in *Moïse* in 1827 to the Opéra's *machiniste*: most thought it better handled on a boulevard theatre.[33] The Opéra's response to the situation (see Chapter 2) was to set up a Staging Committee including internal members and external theatre professionals: unsurprisingly, Rossini represented the musicians.[34]

All three composers and their collaborators (choreographers and librettists) recognised the special importance of ballet. Pressed for time in *Moïse*, Rossini reused dances from *Armida* (1817), an opera unfamiliar to the Parisian audience. For *Le Siège de Corinthe* he greatly expanded the role of the ballet by the insertion of wedding celebrations for Pamira and Mahomet. The divertissement, which dominates the second act, has a typically French structure: it originally consisted of five dances framed by two choruses (the first where the harem women view the forthcoming nuptials with enthusiasm; the second where the Turkish court prays for the Prophet's blessing).[35] Before the ceremony can be concluded, the Greeks attack.

Les Martyrs has its divertissement, also in the second act, during celebrations welcoming the new proconsul Sévère. Its *coup de théâtre* (see below) spurs the drama into a finale, which, like that in *Le Siège*, leaves the audience in suspense. More important in this opera are representations of religious rites, Christian and pagan, with the chorus an active participant: Pauline's offerings to Persephone at her mother's tomb, supported by her attendants ('Jeune souveraine'); Polyeucte's baptism and the Christians' hymn, both in Act I; the Armenian Roman citizens' offerings to Zeus ('Dieu de tonnerre') in Act III; their bloodthirsty call (with its powerful unison opening) to throw the Christians to the lions ('Il nous faut et des jeux et des fêtes'), and the Christians' final prayer (both Act IV). Where pageantry was an important element, many extras and the *corps de ballet* helped make the crowds impressive, as staging manuals and costume designs make clear.

The third-act divertissement in *Jérusalem* is reminiscent of that in *Le Siège*: it too takes place in a Middle Eastern harem, a fine excuse for voluptuous dancing, and is also interrupted by the arrival of Christians, in this case crusaders, again leaving the dramatic situation confused. Even more impressive is the scene newly written for Paris where the maligned hero Gaston is destituted of knightly honours in preparation for his execution:[36]

> The stage depicts Ramla's principal square. A dais draped in black on which an executioner's block has been placed dominates stage right. A march enters from stage left, and the people of Ramla turn to watch. The participants in the march (in order) are: a squad of sixteen soldiers in pairs; the legate's pages, also in pairs; the legate, the legate's priests, and his officers; Gaston and his squire Raymond carrying his master's banner; the executioner with his mace; preceded by the herald at arms, four officers – the first carries the black veil, the second Gaston's sword, the third his shield, the fourth his helmet; the crowd cries 'No pity!' and with his mace, one by one, the executioner destroys on his block the outward signs of Gaston's knightly status, despite his protests of innocence. The executioner then signals Gaston to mount the dais; when the disgraced knight reaches the first step the black veil is thrown over his head [the symbol of execution the next day]. The curtain falls quickly.

Verdi responded to the dramatic situation with an ensemble of exceptional power in which individuals are clearly delineated: Gaston pleading with his fellow knights for understanding, their rejection, his proud proclamation of his innocence before God, accompanied by his colleagues' call that justice be done.

In spite of these efforts and others, the press criticised many adaptations for being 'too Italian' dramatically.[37] Still, composers and librettists often made changes with a view to improving dramatic logic. In *Mosè* pharaoh's son had secretly married the Jewess Elcia, who was unrelated to the prophet; in *Moïse* he is merely infatuated with her and the heroine – renamed

Anaï – is now Moses' niece. The omission or redefinition of several characters allowed more development of the themes of love *versus* duty (to religion and to family) and exposed, it was thought, the perfidy of the Egyptian priesthood.[38] Dramatic verisimilitude also prompted the reordering of certain scenes: the miracle of the dispelling of darkness occurs not at the opening of Act I as in the Italian original, but that of Act II, after the pharaoh has reneged on his promise to let the Hebrews depart.

Poliuto had been based on Corneille's play *Polyeucte* (1643). As mentioned in Chapter 4, Scribe reworked Cammarano's libretto and brought it closer to the original play (well known to French audiences) with its emphasis on duty. Pauline has married Polyeucte, but in Act II her earlier love Sévère returns as the imperial proconsul in charge of suppressing Christianity; she lets slip that she still loves him, but swears that she intends to remain faithful to her husband. She is also caught between her duty as the Roman governor's daughter and as wife of a secret convert to Christianity. Polyeucte is torn between duty to his new religion and fellow Christians, and his love for Pauline. As in Gounod's 1878 version of the story (see next chapter) conflict is resolved in Pauline's conversion and the couple's martyrdom. The librettist also put on stage several highly dramatic events not in the play or only reported there, such as Polyeucte's baptism and his later overturning of pagan idols (Act III), well received by several critics.[39] The results had significance for Donizetti: the role of the high priest, for example, became a more minor one, whereas Félix, Pauline's father, gained in importance. Polyeucte's jealousy of his wife, introduced by Cammarano into *Poliuto*, disappears from *Les Martyrs*.

The transformation of *I Lombardi* into *Jérusalem* was even more extensive. Parisian audiences would have had problems with the complexity and morality of the original: two mortally opposed brothers; a patricide; a woman secretly Christian, though without our knowing why; and so on. In *Jérusalem* there are two lovers from opposing sides (Gaston and Hélène), an uncle with incestuous inclinations (Roger), his hired assassin, and a mistaken victim. Hélène's father, the comte de Toulouse, lives; and repentance and holy victory dominate the last scene.

All three composers adapted their melodies to suit the French language and French tastes. It is easy enough to find text-setting barbarisms in their début operas and to chart improvement over the years, but more interesting to examine their revisions of pieces taken over from Italian originals. Here there is a strong distinction to be made between procedures for women and for men. Parisian audiences generally admired and applauded ornamented passages when sung by the heroine,[40] but expected the men to be more restrained: the tenor had to have a flexible voice, but melismas in his part were comparatively few and strategically placed (for example, in expressions

Figure 24 The bass Adolphe-Joseph-Louis Alizard (1814–50) in the role of the villanous
Roger – disguised as a hermit – in Act II of Verdi's *Jérusalem* (1847). Alizard's career was
affected, especially in Paris, by his stoutness and shortness of height, though he was a regular
success in Brussels and Milan and had a magnificent voice.

of love); baritones and basses had almost none at all. Male *fioriture* in Italian
practice could still carry a heroic connotation inherited from the castrato
tradition; to the French, however, they sounded effeminate. This gender
distinction, already suggested in earlier works at the Opéra, such as those
by Spontini, was codified by Rossini and remained the norm for later grand
opera. He reduced ornamentation considerably in passages for baritones
and basses in leading roles. One brief comparison between *Maometto II* and
Le Siège de Corinthe illustrates his procedure (Ex. 14.1).

Donizetti continued the process in *Les Martyrs*.[41] The role of the villain,
Severo/Sévère (baritone), was revised in interesting ways, as his duet with

Example 14.1 Rossini, *Maometto II*, Maometto's aria 'Del mondo al vincitor' ('Leader of so many heroes') compared with *Le Siège de Corinthe*, Act I, no. 4, Mahomet's *air* 'Hommage, gloire, honneur' ('Leader of an unconquerable people').

Paolina/Pauline shows ('Il più lieto dei viventi'/'Par pitié'). Some sections were newly composed (besides *récitatifs*, which, as Donizetti noted, had to be made to fit the French language). In both versions of the duet after the introductory *récitatif*, the baritone expresses his unease, but the effect is quite different in each case (Ex. 14.2). *Poliuto* keeps the listener's attention focused on the vocal line with its well-placed melodic accents off strong beats, restrained ornamentation and continuous flow; the orchestral part is supportive. In *Les Martyrs* similar accents were heightened by a more declamatory setting and direct attacks after rests; the more active role of the orchestra, thematically and harmonically, adds to the tension, as do the shifting and unstable tonal underpinnings. Elsewhere, the composer often counted on Scribe to provide additional text needed when reducing the music's melismatic nature (Ex. 14.3). For these and, more generally, the soprano lines, Ashbrook noted: 'Since the fundamentally Italian contour and impetus of Donizetti's melodies protrude in the French version, the result is a queasy compromise of disparate styles.'[42] For *Les Martyrs* overall, the generalisation perhaps does not do the composer justice. Donizetti enhanced the more assertive musical language of men, increasing such emphasis through the bass role of Félix (replacing the tenor Felice of *Poliuto*), and through the smaller bass role of Callisthènes, the high priest.

Tenor roles were different. Donizetti's changes to the hero's part, in the several lyrical passages retained, are generally minor ones to accommodate French text (e.g., 'A Dio ti piego la fronte' / 'Que l'onde salutaire' in Act I of both operas). A relevant factor here is that Poliuto's part was originally written for the Naples début of Adolphe Nourrit, who had recently forsaken Paris. (Indeed the singer suggested the topic and the opera's banning was probably a factor in the depressed singer's suicide.) Later, Donizetti sought to please his new Polyeucte and wrote 'Si je t'aimais! . . . Oui, j'irai dans leur temple' especially for Duprez.

Example 14.2 Donizetti, *Poliuto*, Act II scene 2, duet between Paolina and Severo ('The happiest of humans when I returned here! I had hoped for supreme joy in our marriage'), compared with the equivalent duet in *Les Martyrs*, Act III scene 1 ('For pity's sake let me remain ignorant [of your new love]').

Rossini's *Guillaume Tell*

During the 1820s Rossinimania swept Paris.[43] His operas dominated the stage of the Théâtre Italien and, from 1826 on, that of the Opéra as well; his music and his position in the musical hierarchy were hotly debated in the

Example 14.3 Donizetti, *Poliuto*, same duet (continuation) ('Yes, a madman's dream!') compared with the equivalent passage in *Les Martyrs* ('the sweet image of a cloudless day which forecasts happiness!').

press and in pamphlets; and he was a favourite of the salons, including the duchesse de Berry's. After *Le Siège de Corinthe* one critic observed that 'this great composer owes it to his dazzling reputation to give us soon his setting of a [French] libretto for the lyric stage'.[44] Rossini finally responded with his first entirely original French opera, *Guillaume Tell*.[45] *Le tout Paris* stayed in the sweltering capital in order to attend the première; the theatre was sold out well in advance. *Tell* also proved to be his last. What is exceptional for an operatic swansong is that, while building on the composer's previous experiences, especially in Paris, it set new directions for French grand opera.

The composer again wanted to work with the veteran, Jouy. The librettist offered him *Le Vieux de la montagne*, a work whose main theme was religious intolerance and whose setting was the Near East, but after considering it for some time, Rossini rejected it, perhaps because it had too much in common with *Le Siège de Corinthe*. Then Jouy suggested *Guillaume Tell*, loosely based on Schiller's play, with borrowings from other treatments of the Tell legend.[46] His text, written several years before, required extensive revision, rearrangement and pruning to suit Rossini and the Opéra in the late 1820s; Hippolyte Bis, a rising star among playwrights, agreed to take on the task.[47] The result appealed to current tastes for the medieval, for a Romantic view of nature and especially the Swiss Alps (the administration even sent the designer Ciceri there to gain first-hand experience), and for supporting the underdog (here the Swiss are victorious over their Austrian oppressors, unlike the fate of the Greeks in *Le Siège*).

The overture sets the scene. Although the composer wrote out no programme, critics were quick to explain it in terms of one, and with minor variations their interpretations are congruent. Conceived in four sections, the overture opens with five solo cellos accompanied by five more, invoking the beauty of nature and profound solitude; soon a musical storm erupts (and a storm will be a major force at the fourth-act climax), but it dissipates, and the calm of the countryside and the harmony of the Swiss with their surroundings is evoked in a duet between flute and English horn (shepherd's pipes) playing a *ranz des vaches*, a traditional Swiss call to the cows. The concluding military *pas redoublé* anticipates the struggle of the Swiss and their valour.[48]

Rossini, Jouy and Bis placed special emphasis on the Swiss people; in a sense, they are the protagonists; through them, themes of resistance to oppression and a sympathy with nature have the clearest expression. They welcome a fine day, give thanks to God, celebrate village marriages with song and dancing, and at the urging of Melcthal resist the Austrians (Act I). They respond to Tell's call to revolt (finale of Act II) and at his instigation curse Gesler (finale of Act III); they answer Arnold's call to arms (opening Act IV); welcome the passing of the storm (in more than one sense) and the dawning of liberty (end of the opera). The chorus often takes on more than one character: Swiss sing against Austrians in the finales of Acts III and IV, but even more effective and challenging are the three male choruses representing men of the three Swiss cantons in the second-act finale (see below).

The eponymous hero does not have a solo aria, yet he dominates the opera dramatically: by his mutterings of discontent in the introduction, and doubts about the loyalty of Arnold, his young countryman; by his bravery in rescuing the shepherd Leuthold (all in Act I); by his challenge to Arnold's patriotism, and, with Walter Furst and Arnold, his rousing the Swiss men to revolt (Act II); by his refusal to bow to Gesler's hat and defiance of authority until his son Jemmy is threatened; his touching plea to Jemmy to hold still ('Sois immobile') while he shoots the apple from his head; his cursing the tyrant (Act III); his escape from captivity and well-aimed arrow killing Gesler (Act IV). What is equally important is that Tell and most other leading characters (Walter, Jemmy, Gesler, Hedwige) and minor ones (Ruodi, Leuthold, Rodolphe) interact with each other and with the choruses in dynamic, on-going situations. While traditional divisions (*récitatif*, duo, trio, finale, etc.) remain clear, Rossini's score matches the continuing action.

The lovers, Arnold (tenor) and the Austrian princess Mathilde (soprano), stand apart: she owes him her life, in a rescue from an avalanche. Early in Act II she presses him to prove his valour in Austrian service in foreign wars. Both participate in ensembles, and their Act II duet ('Oui, vous l'arrachez à mon âme') contains their mutual declaration of love. In addition, both have major arias, the only such examples in the opera. Significantly, these are the closest to Italian models in form and, especially Mathilde's, melodic style. Arnold's Act IV 'Asile héréditaire/Amis, secondez ma vengeance' is in typical *Cantabile* [*Andantino*]–*Cabaletta* [*Allegro*] form. It opens with his lyrical lament on his father's death, his most melismatic music in the opera and his only opportunity for a cadenza (carefully written out by the composer). Between it and the concluding section is a substantial dialogue between

Arnold and the Swiss men (they express their dismay at Tell's capture and their want of arms, whereupon Arnold replies that his father and Tell have anticipated this need), dramatically motivating the hero's call to arms during the Allegro. This – among other examples – set the model for later French operas: as Rossini originally composed it, the final section was in binary form, as was usual Italian practice, but the repetition was suppressed before the première. Since the Swiss readily agree to follow Arnold's lead, why repeat the demand?[49]

Originally Mathilde had two solos: a *romance* ('Sombre forêt, désert triste et sauvage', Act II) in which, alone, she confesses her affection for Arnold; and a grandiose *air* ('Plus notre amour, plus d'espérance') with a small part for Arnold in Act III: as there is no hope for their love, she urges him to flee Gesler rather than stay and avenge his father. He rejects the idea, and they part sadly. In 'Sombre forêt' Rossini took up a genre quintessentially French for over a century (popular in opéra comique since the days of Monsigny and Grétry). *Romances* were usually in strophic form, associated with simplicity and direct expression in the vocal line, and given a light, supportive accompaniment: here Rossini created a Gallo–Italian hybrid. It was one of the earliest in grand opera and became an important model for his compatriots writing for Paris and for Italy, as well as others. The accompaniment was more thoroughly worked out than usual and, while respecting the discreet spirit of the genre, Rossini gave a more extensive conclusion to the second stanza. 'Sombre forêt' has a slightly florid, 'Italianate' line, but it matches the French prosody quite well, even considering the numerous ornaments written in by Rossini. Cinti-Damoreau, the first Mathilde, recognised the special quality of this piece and added only restrained ornamentation (Ex. 14.4). Mathilde's *air* and the duet are more virtuosic and closer to Italian formal models.[50]

Nevertheless, the role of Mathilde posed problems for several critics, as did the length of *Guillaume Tell* at the première, which was close to four hours. It is significant that critics of *ultra* (extreme right Royalist) papers were the most bothered. According to one, the only reason for this 'banal' love intrigue was to allow Cinti-Damoreau to shine and at the end, he noted ironically, this princess deigned to become a Swiss peasant.[51] Another was more scathing:

> There is nothing more ridiculous than to see a princess jumping
> precipices . . . in order to see [her lover] . . . M. Jouy, in his *Fernand Cortez*,
> had already presented us a roaming princess in the character of Amazily
> who, in spite of her plumes and muslin dress, frequents barracks like a true
> canteen-keeper. In *Guillaume Tell* Mathilde is just as badly brought up and
> has the same morals. Assuredly, at the Opéra M. Jouy is fond of shameless
> hussies.[52]

Example 14.4 Rossini, *Guillaume Tell*, Act II scene 1, showing Cinti-Damoreau's embellishments in 'Sombre forêt, désert triste et sauvage', second stanza ('[You] who shine on my path, Ah! also be [my star and guide . . .] echo my secrets').

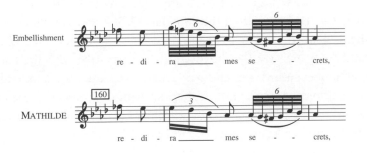

Still, the public adored Cinti-Damoreau and there was no question of eliminating Mathilde entirely. A compromise was found: Mathilde's *romance*, her duet with Arnold and her participation in the third-act finale were kept (she saves Jemmy from Gesler's wrath by invoking her royal rank), but the *air* and her presence in the fourth act disappeared in later performances, leaving the lovers' fate unresolved. While one may regret the musical suppressions (and few modern directors would make the same choices), the revisions do focus attention on the main themes: the heroism of Tell and the Swiss, and the fight against oppression.

What most impressed the audience at the première was the second act, especially the trio and finale. It opens with a chorus 'Quelle sauvage harmonie', hunters celebrating the chase, followed by a chorus of shepherds at a distance who welcome night as the end of a day's labour. Then follow Mathilde's scene (with the *romance*) and her meeting with Arnold (the duet). Tell's arrival with the patriot Walter Furst causes her to flee, and the drama abruptly shifts from tender avowals to the consequences of Gesler's tyranny. Tell takes Arnold to task for loving an Austrian, while Arnold angrily replies that his country no longer matters: he plans to seek glory in foreign climes. Then, in perhaps the most famous male trio in French opera ('Quand l'Helvétie est un champ de supplices'), Tell challenges Arnold's decision, and Furst adds grimly that one of Gesler's victims deserves better from him: Arnold guesses that the reference is to his own father.[53] He is overwhelmed by grief and wishes to die, but his companions insist he fight. Rossini responded with a flexible form closely matching the text. The trio starts in martial spirit; the announcement of Melcthal's death is in *récitatif*; Arnold's lament (with asides from the others) is an Andantino. The ensuing dialogue, again in *récitatif*, ends with the ringing declaration 'Either independence or death!' and sparks the final Allegro section in which all agree on vengeance, though Arnold's music stands out (see Ex. 7.5 for a comparable passage).

The finale is yet more dramatic. The three co-conspirators welcome the men of Unterwalden, Schwytz and Uri in succession. Each canton has a well-defined character but all are united by the password slogan 'Amis de la patrie!' ('Friends of the fatherland'). Tell and Furst seek to persuade them to revolt, but it is finally Arnold's intervention (recalling that his father's 'crime' was that he loved his country) that tips the balance. In a memorable oath chorus all swear to drive back the Austrians, ending with a curse (typical of the genre): 'If there are traitors among us, may the sun not shine on them, may heaven not hear their prayers, and may the earth refuse them burial'. A resounding call to arms concludes the act. Again, Rossini sought a musical translation for the shifting dramatic requirements with so much success that Berlioz proclaimed, and his confrères agreed, 'Ah, it is sublime!'[54]

Guillaume Tell re-evaluated the importance of interaction between principals and groups, but also provided one example of synthesis between French and Italian musical elements. The former predominate at key dramatic moments, but Rossini's Italian inflection is clear, especially in Mathilde's part. Most would agree with the critic of *Le Globe*: 'a new epoch has opened not only for French opera, but for dramatic music elsewhere'.[55]

Donizetti's *La Favorite*

In February 1840 Donizetti dominated Parisian opera houses:

> What! two major scores for the Opéra, *Les Martyrs* and *Le Duc d'Albe!* two
> others for the Théâtre de la Renaissance, *Lucie de Lammermoor* and *L'Ange
> de Nisida*! two more for the Opéra-Comique, *La Fille du régiment* and
> another whose title is not yet known [probably *Rita, ou Le mari battu*], and
> yet another for the Théâtre Italien [*L'elisir d'amore*] will have been
> composed or adapted in one year by the same author! M. Donizetti seems
> to treat us as a occupied country: it's a war of aggression. One can no
> longer say, 'the lyric theatres of Paris' but only 'the lyric theatres of M.
> Donizetti'![56]

But on 2 May 1840 the Théâtre de la Renaissance shut its doors for financial
reasons.[57] Shortly thereafter Donizetti wrote, '[Because of the closing] I
have lost *L'Ange de Nisida*, a three-act opera only suitable for it. *Ouff!*'[58]
Seemingly too ambitious for a boulevard theatre, not grandiose enough for
the Opéra, in French and in too Gallic a style to appeal to Italian theatres
(with potential censorship problems on religious grounds), he thought it
had no clear home. Yet *La Favorite*, transformed from *L'Ange de Nisida*,
became his triumph at the Opéra and his longest-lasting success there.[59] As
La favorita it conquered Italian opera houses as well. However, it came at
a cost to the librettists (see n. 7). They removed comic elements, changed
the scene from Naples to Spain (to take advantage of opportunities for local
colour not duplicating *La Muette de Portici*) and expanded the whole to four
acts with some new material in Act I and a divertissement for Act II. Music
was added or revised to suit the singers, especially Rosine Stoltz (Léonor)
and Paul Barroilhet (Alphonse XI, King of Castile).[60]

The origins of *La Favorite* as melodramatic theatre set a new model for
grand opera, closer to the later *drame lyrique*, since the complex emotions
and conflicts of three principals are the focus: while it did not supplant
the grandiose Scribe–Meyerbeer one it provided an alternative, anticipating
headier mixtures of love and religion in opera. The hero Fernand is a novi-
tiate of St James of Compostella; however, he idealises Léonor, leaves his
monastery and requests her hand in marriage, first proving himself in war:
he does not know that she is the king's mistress. In Act II a papal message
orders Alphonse to banish Léonor, whom he would prefer to marry, repu-
diating his wife. When the king cynically 'rewards' the valiant Fernand – to
whom he owes his victory over the Moors – with Léonor, the youth is mocked
by the court (Act III).[61] He is sorely tested when he finds he has married the
'favourite' and does what he believes is right in rejecting his honours and
new spouse. In the end he is reconciled with Léonor at her death.

A woman wronged by a man in power was hardly new at the Opéra: she had sisters, including Fenella in *La Muette de Portici* and the Sylphide in the ballet of the same name. What was new is the courtesan who finds true love, renounces riches for him and is faithful, though misunderstood, then repents and atones for her past sins by her death. For some critics, Léonor seemed too close to the boulevard theatre, *mélodrame*, or even Italian opera, and therefore unworthy of the *premier théâtre lyrique*.[62] Still, Léonor is surely an important precedent for (among others) Alexandre Dumas *fils'* novel (1848) and later play (1852), both entitled *La Dame aux camélias*, which became the source of Verdi's *La traviata*.[63]

The balance in *La Favorite* shifted from spectacular mass scenes to the confrontations and interactions of individuals. The chorus takes on a number of roles, but nearly all are supportive of the soloists. Monks begin the opera with a brief *hymne*, 'Pieux monastère' (accompanied in austere fashion mainly by violas, bassoons, cellos and basses), to establish the religious tone. In Act III the courtiers perform a typical choral function in celebrating the (off-stage) marriage of Fernand and Léonor. Only when stirred up by the courtier Don Gaspar do the knights begin to take on a strong collective character, resenting the honours the king has bestowed on the hero. Their refusal to welcome him after the wedding sparks the dramatic turning-point, but even when Fernand renounces his titles, breaks his sword and throws the fragments at Alphonse's feet, the drama is set as an intense, declamatory *récitatif*, vocal line accompanied by diminished-seventh chords (Ex. 14.5). The divertissement in Act II (the victory celebrations) is clumsily introduced from a dramatic point of view; yet Berlioz and other critics admired its music[64] and choreography.

The solo writing in *La Favorite* shows Donizetti's greater mastery of text-setting and French taste in general, but retains a decidedly Italian accent. Léonor's *air*, 'O mon Fernand' (Act III), is a case in point, where Donizetti chose in the opening section to emphasise Stoltz's mezzo-soprano range, common among Italian heroines, but still quite rare for French. A delicate orchestral accompaniment, featuring the harp, supports the vocal line which, while suave, is closely matched to French declamation. Its form is typically Italian, but by 1840 naturalised French: *cantabile–récitatif–cabaletta* (the latter in binary form, here with an extensive coda). The king's solo 'Pour tant d'amour' in the trio 'Fernand, devant lui paraître infâme' (also in Act III), is less florid than usual for a truly Italianate style, but retains features such as decorative figures with off-beat accents (Ex. 14.6).

The fourth act, confounding expectation, stunned the 1840 Parisian audience and critics: final acts were notoriously difficult to manage, and Rossini had substantially revised that for *Guillaume Tell*.[65] In a dignified chorus, the monks and pilgrims are digging their own graves: death will end this world's

Example 14.5 Donizetti, *La Favorite*, Act III, finale: Fernand repudiates Alphonse ('This dishonoured sword, which terrified our enemies, I break at your feet! For you are the king!').

Example 14.6 Donizetti, *La Favorite*, Act III, trio 'Fernand, devant lui paraître infâme': Alphonse's melancholy address to Léonore ('For such a love do not be ungrateful, when he will have only you for happiness').

sorrows. The choral unison writing and homophonic style (supported by an orchestra in which the winds function like an organ and the tremolo strings hint at the tension to come) give a sense of peace and stability. Balthazar welcomes Fernand back to the fold. Left alone, Fernand cannot help but think of Léonor: his ternary-form *romance*, 'Ange si pur' (borrowed from *Le Duc d'Albe*: see Ex. 7.6, p. 119), became one of the most popular solos in the opera, deceptively simple yet requiring a sensitive and nuanced performance. The finale returns to its religious mood as Fernand accompanies the father superior, novices and monks into the chapel. Distraught, the dying

Léonor comes in search of Fernand to implore his pardon: her *arioso*-like, intense *récitatif* and later interjections are in stark contrast to the choral *hymne* 'Que du Très-Haut la faveur t'accompagne' as the hero pronounces his vows. He leaves the chapel and finds Léonor. This highly dramatic and lengthy scene is treated with formal freedom musically matching the shifting moods. When Fernand urges flight, Léonor thinks of his salvation, and off stage the chorus repeats the *hymne*. The final twenty-six bars provide a brief, abrupt and unusual conclusion for a work on the stage of the Opéra. Parisians flocked to *La Favorite* in its first season and every year for decades to come.[66]

Verdi's *Don Carlos*

In the mid-1860s Verdi, with some reluctance, again agreed to compose something for Paris.[67] As early as 1850 Royer and Vaëz, the librettists of *Jérusalem*, had recommended an opera based on Schiller's play, *Don Carlos*. 'You have already drawn on Schiller for *Les Brigands* [*I masnadieri*, 1847] and *Luisa Miller* [1849]' they wrote, '*Don Carlos*, we believe, is a more vast and more poetic subject. It has great passion . . .'.[68] Verdi declined: he had misgivings about the theatricality of the subject and wanted the opportunity to work with Scribe. After some discussion *Les Vêpres siciliennes* was the result.[69]

After the fiasco of *Tannhäuser* (1861) and after Meyerbeer's death, Emile Perrin (see Table 2.2, p. 27) saw a new grand opera by Verdi as the best possibility to ensure the international prestige of his theatre.[70] At first rebuffed, Perrin continued to offer Verdi several subjects, among them Shakespeare's *King Lear*. This was set aside because of casting difficulties, and *Don Carlos* was chosen.[71]

As Vaëz had died in 1862 and Royer had retired, Perrin recommended Joseph Méry, who had worked with Félicien David and Jacques Offenbach, and Camille Du Locle, the director's young assistant and nephew. After producing a scenario whose general outlines pleased Verdi, Méry died. Turning the scenario into a libretto fell to Du Locle, though the composer insisted that it be shaped according to his wishes and needs. His initial reaction to the scenario was that:

> *Don Carlos*, a magnificent drama, is perhaps not spectacular enough. Furthermore, the idea to have Charles V appear is excellent, as is the Fontainebleau scene. What I should like, as in Schiller's play, would be a short scene between Philip II and the Inquisitor; the latter blind and very old . . . Further, I would wish a duet between Philip II and the marquis of Posa.[72]

Du Locle obliged. Verdi insisted on tightening up much dialogue, the introduction of some highly dramatic lines paraphrasing Schiller and on a thoroughgoing revision of the final act, following his own draft.[73] It would be fair to credit Verdi as one of the librettists. If Parisian taste for the spectacular was respected, Verdi's major concerns in *Don Carlos* were the psychological development of individuals, the tensions in their interrelationships (often triangular and intersecting) and, through these, the presentation of doomed love(s), frustrated desires for political liberty, and religious oppression.[74]

The opera opens in Fontainebleau about 1560 where the kind-hearted princess Elisabeth de Valois, who wishes to relieve French suffering from the privations of war, has allowed herself to be affianced to the Spanish Infante (the monarch's second son), Don Carlos. He meets her at first incognito, but soon reveals his identity and the pair express mutual love. It is short-lived: a messenger announces Elisabeth is to marry Philippe II, King of Spain, instead. The Elisabeth–Don Carlos–Philippe triangle gives rise to several of the most dramatic or poignant moments in the opera. In Act II Don Carlos seeks solace at the Yuste monastery. Later he confesses to his stepmother, to her horror, his continuing affection for her. Philippe becomes suspicious when he finds the queen unattended with the prince and publicly insults her. In the finale of Act III the king orders the prince's arrest, and in the opening of Act IV he realises with sorrow that Elisabeth has never loved him and anguishes over what is to be done with his son. At first reprieved, Don Carlos takes his leave of the queen, is surprised by his father and rearrested (Act V). In sum, the love between Don Carlos and Elisabeth is never fulfilled, affection between father and son is poisoned, and the queen is the hapless victim of duty. This triangle intersects with others. Princess Eboli, Philippe's mistress, smitten with love for Don Carlos but rebuffed by him, surmises the truth about the prince's feelings for his stepmother and betrays them to the king (Act III); overcome by remorse, she confesses to the queen, who orders her to choose between the convent and exile; before entering the convent, Eboli determines to rescue the now-imprisoned prince, and leads a revolt to free him (Act IV). The Eboli–Elisabeth–Carlos triangle is another example of frustrated loves, as well as treachery and repentance. The friendship between Don Carlos and Rodrigue, marquis de Posa, and the respect between Philippe and the latter form yet another triangle. As the prince's *confidant*, Rodrigue urges him to take up the Flemish cause and champion liberty, in part to distance himself from Elisabeth. With enthusiasm Don Carlos agrees. Later the marquis presents the Flemish case directly to the king: he is shocked, but then he admires Rodrigue's frankness to such an extent that he gives him free entry to the palace (Act II). When Philippe refuses the prince's demand for the governance of Flanders, Carlos rashly draws his sword; to defuse the situation, Rodrigue intercedes and disarms his friend (Act III). Later he incriminates himself as the heretics' supporter to spare the prince and dies victim on Philippe's orders (Act IV). Finally, the power of the Grand Inquisitor results from his ability to disturb Philippe's position in this triangle. He tries to force the king to surrender Rodrigue to the Inquisition, offering in return his support of Philippe's punishment of his son; saves the king from the mob bent on rescuing Carlos (Act IV); and in the last act insists on the prince's arrest. Significantly, the Grand Inquisitor as personification of religious intolerance commands the stage at key moments: in these his authority is seen as greater than the king's. However, there is a higher authority still: a voice from heaven welcomes the souls of those Protestants burnt at the stake on the condemnation of the Inquisition (Act III); and a monk, later revealed to be the ghost of Charles V, consoles and advises his grandson, Don Carlos (Act II), and rescues him (Act V).

Don Carlos is Verdi's richest score for the Opéra. We can discuss only three aspects here: first, the spectacular; second, musical translations of recurring dramatic themes; and third, musical interpretations of psychological conflict.

Escudier informed Perrin shortly after the composer had seen the initial scenario, '*Don Carlos* has captured [Verdi's] imagination . . . What worries him is the absence of one or two scenes where the staging will stun the public. He would like something unexpected, such as the skaters' scene in *Le Prophète* or that in the church, as a climax.'[75] After revision and elaboration the third-act finale surpassed the composer's hopes.[76] At the première the décors, costumes, movement of the masses on stage and special effects contributed to the impressive effect, but Verdi's music makes the scene thrilling. Framed by an E major march, the finale's keys, tempi and styles closely match the rapidly shifting moods of the drama. The people welcome their king with a joyous cry of triumph. The monks (six basses) entering escorting the heretics (E minor): *ppp* and in unison, the monks intone heaven's condemnation, the orchestral wind group in its low register sounding particularly ominous and funereal. The people return to celebration, and a stage band (Adolphe Sax's instruments dominate) dialogues with the orchestra. In hymn-like style the people prepare to welcome their king (C major). Philippe affirms his commitment to punish heretics, and his subjects praise him for his resolve (Eb major). A sudden speeding up, string tremoli and diminished-seventh chords warn us of danger as Don Carlos approaches to introduce the Flemish deputies (also six basses), whose lyrical style (Ex. 5.5, p. 89) is in strong contrast to the monks'. Philippe indignantly orders them dismissed (Ab minor). In an ensemble, monarch and monks are spokesmen for the Inquisition's judgement (usually in minor), while Elisabeth, Don Carlos, Rodrigue and the people support the deputies' plea for mercy

Example 14.7 Verdi, *Don Carlos*, Act I, duet between Elisabeth and Carlos 'Que faites-vous donc?', opening of the love-theme (the whole is sixteen bars long): 'What poignant and sweet emotions fill my soul! Ah! it's Carlos at my feet, a god brings him!'

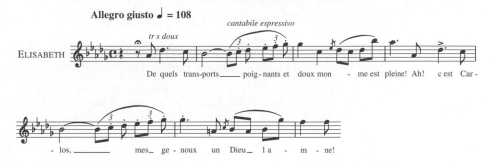

(usually in major). Carlos demands the governance of Flanders and, when his father rejects this, draws his sword, to the horror of all present. Rodrigue disarms his friend; in gratitude, the king awards him the title of duke. The E major march with chorus returns, but when the monks repeat their verdict during the *auto-da-fé*, a soaring voice from heaven, accompanied by harp and harmonium, welcomes the souls of the martyrs, while the Spanish praise God. The dénouement produces the unexpected element that Verdi required and the audience appreciated.[77]

Verdi's use of recurring themes is consistently tied to the drama. When characters repeat a text, then they repeat the music as well. More often, it is the situation that makes recall appropriate, and in these instances the orchestra takes on the role of presentation and implied interpretation. (In using musical themes to recall situations and emotions, Verdi drew on a rich history, Italian and French.[78]) Three cases merit particular attention. The doomed love of Don Carlos and Elisabeth has a motif derived from their Fontainebleau love duet; the friendship of the prince and Rodrigue, another from theirs in Act II; and even the monks of Yuste monastery repeat their opening chant from Act II at the close of Act V.[79] The latter reference underlines a dramatic parallel. In Act II they introduced an unidentified monk who subsequently tries to turn Carlos's thoughts to God; in Act V this monk proves to be the ghost of Charles V, who has just rescued the prince from the Inquisition. In the Fontainebleau scene when Carlos declares his love to Elisabeth, she makes clear in an expressive, lyrical melody that she returns his affection (Ex. 14.7). It dominates the concluding section of the duet where the pair swear eternal love. When the second part of Act IV opens with Don Carlos in prison, a solo oboe (accompanied by *tremolo* strings) cites the first four bars of Elisabeth's melody transposed to C major and modified to $\frac{3}{4}$ metre. The prince, though arrested for championing the Flemish cause, is possessed by his lost love. In the opening of Act V Elisabeth

Example 14.8 Verdi, *Don Carlos*, Act V scene 1, Elisabeth's *air* 'Toi qui sus le néant des grandeurs': 'France! noble country, so dear to me when young!'

weeps at her fate, but realises that for his sake the prince should leave. When her thoughts turn to the past the woodwinds reveal to us, even before her words do, what is in her heart (see Ex. 14.8). Elisabeth's counter-melody with its dramatic octave leaps downwards, its diminished seventh at 'pays' (i.e. her homeland), and the ethereal scoring, all refract the optimism of the original into the melancholic outcome.

The friendship of Rodrigue and Don Carlos, and their commitment to liberty, is fixed musically in the ensemble conclusion of their duet (Act II); united in their vow, they sing mainly in thirds and in the same rhythm: 'God, you inspire in our souls the same desire, the same noble love, the love of liberty! God, who has made our sincere hearts the heart of two brothers, accept our vow! We shall die while loving each other!' Three later citations deserve mention. In Act III Eboli has discovered Don Carlos' secret love for the queen. Rodrigue recognises the danger that this spurned, angry woman poses and begs the prince to commit any incriminating Flemish papers to him. Carlos hesitates, then hands them over. As the two embrace, the full orchestra proclaims their friendship in the coda, just before the finale begins. The prince subsequently surrenders his sword to the marquis – to the surprise of Elisabeth and the courtiers – but the friendship theme in the clarinets makes clear to the audience that Don Carlos's trust is well placed. In Act IV Rodrigue visits the prince in prison: he has used the papers to incriminate himself and turn suspicion away from his friend. Dying, he reminds Don Carlos that his destiny is to save Flanders, and the cornets provide a musical reminiscence of their affection, truly to death.

Scenes that make the strongest dramatic impression are often those that show characters in conflict (with themselves, or others, or in debate or even opposition). In these Verdi deployed interpretative melodies, flexible forms and expressive instrumentation. As dawn breaks in Act IV, Philippe in deep thought is seated 'as if dreaming' at his desk. In *arioso* style beginning in a monotone, the king bitterly remarks 'She [Elisabeth] does not love me!' Coming to his senses in *récitatif*, he regrets that restful sleep is no longer his (again in *arioso*). His *air* (*ABA'* in minor + two-part coda) is a sad commentary on the state of kingship: he will find peace only after death (lyrical *A* sections with broad, sweeping melodies) for, if the king sleeps, treason will have the advantage: his crown and his wife will be stolen (*B* section in declamatory style).[80] While the formal outlines are clear and well matched to the structure of the poetry, the separation between *récitatif* and *air* has disappeared: it is the entire monologue that forms the unit in spite of the variety of melodic styles and modifications in tempo. The orchestration sets the tone all through: desolate horns, bassoons and strings in octaves repeating the dominant (with acciaccaturas); later, an emphasis on woodwinds and strings, often muted, with a continuing cello presence, reinforces the mood.

The arrival of the Grand Inquisitor, blind and infirm, but determined, prejudiced and confident in his moral superiority, cuts short the king's contemplation. Bassoons, contrabassoon, cellos and basses, together with a 'death' motif in the timpani, sound particularly sinister.[81] Philippe wants from him absolution in advance if he has his son executed. Accompanied by trombones, bassoons and ophicleide, the Inquisitor assures him 'World peace is worth a rebellious son's blood', but he exacts a price: turn over to the Inquisition the marquis de Posa. Philippe cuts him short: Rodrigue is his surest advisor. The Inquisitor replies, 'why this man?' Losing his temper, the king retorts 'Silence, priest!' To this insult, the Inquisitor recalls Philippe to his duty; the king repeats that he will never surrender the marquis. But even a king can be hauled before the Inquisition: as the Inquisitor leaves, Philippe begs 'let there be peace again between us. . . . Let the past be forgotten!' Chillingly, the old man's final word is 'Perhaps!' (Ex. 14.9). In this struggle between Church and State, the orchestra informs us who is in control: it is the Inquisitor's motif that dominates to the last. The whole scene is an exceptional extended dialogue between two strong-willed individuals, not a conventional duet. They neither agree nor sing together. Their emotional reactions, especially the king's, run the gamut: hence the widely fluctuating tempi, melodic styles and dynamics, all reflected, supported and interpreted by the orchestra.[82]

Example 14.9 Verdi, *Don Carlos*, Act IV, conclusion of Grand Inquisitor's duet with Philippe II, showing the former's orchestral motif and the latter's concluding phrase, 'The king's pride yields before the priest's pride!'

In December 1866 his wife Giuseppina wrote to a mutual friend:

Don Carlos, if it pleases God and the tortoises of the Opéra, will receive its première at the end of January! Good gracious! How a composer is punished for his sins by having a work staged in that theatre with its machinery of marble and lead![83]

As it turns out, she was too optimistic by about six weeks. No fewer than 270 rehearsals, including eight dress rehearsals, were necessary – an unusually high number, even by the Opéra's 'tortoise' standards.[84]

Many factors contributed to the opera's mixed reception. Verdi's originality puzzled many at the Parisian première, even those hitherto among his most ardent supporters. They expected the tunefulness and clarity of *Le Trouvère* (the French version of *Il trovatore*) and were disappointed by the more dramatically intense vocal style and more thoroughly developed, 'symphonic' role for the orchestra:

Verdi, that master of inspiration and melody, has sacrificed himself to the false gods of musical algebra. Am I to believe my ears? He has 'wagnerised' [his score]! What has assured the success of the works of the master (it is not Wagner to whom I refer) are precisely those qualities that are missing from *Don Carlos* . . . an initial spark, the spontaneity of the conception, the powerful originality of the rhythms, the art of allowing [ideas] to develop without overwhelming them with choral and orchestral masses . . . Have pity, next time, be Verdi and avoid being Wagner.[85]

We can leave the rebuttal to Verdi:

So then, I am an almost perfect Wagnerian. But if the critics had paid a little more attention they would have seen that there were the same intentions in the trio in *Ernani*, in the sleepwalking scene in *Macbeth*, and in many other pieces of mine. But the question is not whether *Don Carlos* is composed to this or that system, but whether the music is good or bad. That question is clear and simple and, above all, the right one to ask.[86]

Performances elsewhere

The best of the Italians' grand operas not only held the stage in Paris and in other Francophone or Gallophile opera centres (from Marseilles, Lyons and Bordeaux to Brussels, Amsterdam, Ghent, New Orleans and elsewhere), but spread throughout the operatic world in Italian translation: the principal Italian cities plus Dresden, Barcelona, St Petersburg, London, Malta, Algiers, Cape Town, Constantinople, Mexico City, Havana, Buenos Aires, New York and Sydney.[87]

Il nuovo Mosè and *L'assedio di Corinto* supplanted Rossini's originals (*Mosè in Egitto* and *Maometto II*), even in Italy. In writing *Guillaume Tell* Rossini and his publisher had Luigi Balocchi, resident librettist of the Théâtre Italien, prepare an Italian translation. While it was used for the Dresden première (1831) and published in Vienna in the Artaria piano-vocal score, Calisto Bassi's translation (Lucca and Florence, 1831) became the standard one, an unfortunate choice since Balocchi's more closely matches Rossini's melodies. *Poliuto* was eventually given in Naples in 1848, after Donizetti's death; earlier *I martiri* made the rounds in Iberian peninsular theatres, again in Bassi's translation from the French. Several operas were subjected to bizarre transformations to meet censorship requirements. As Austria was a powerful political force in Italy, *Guillaume Tell* became *Vallace* for the 1836 Milan première: instead of the valiant Swiss fighting Austrian oppressors we have the Scots in just revolt against the English. *La favorita* in Francesco Jannetti's translation for Lucca (1841) and performed elsewhere was also deformed: references to the Pope and the Church were removed, and new and dramatically ridiculous family relationships, introduced. Donizetti disliked this version, but there was little he could do.[88] Again without the author's permission, the indefatigable Bassi transported *La favorita* to Syria during the Crusades for Milan (1843)!

Verdi's *Gerusalemme* never achieved the popularity of *I Lombardi*, for complex reasons.[89] By the time of *Les Vêpres siciliennes* and *Don Carlos* the legal situation in Italy was in the process of change: the Risorgimento and unification meant that authors' rights were greatly improved, and Verdi wanted to make sure that these two operas would be performed there. He and Scribe recognised that the Neapolitan revolt would not pass muster; the librettist, who noted the Low Countries original in *Le Duc d'Albe*, suggested another move, this time to Lisbon in 1640 under Spanish domination.[90] Verdi approved, reviewed his colleague's proposed changes, retaining the tragic ending, and suggested a new name for the heroine: *Giovanna de Guzman*. The task of translation was entrusted to Ettore Caimi, although the composer was sanguine ('I feel sympathy for all the bad translations that are around because it is impossible to make a good one.'[91]) The result, as Budden notes, 'is in fact one of the worst ever perpetrated'. Frequently the opera lost its ballet, a concession to Italian taste. (The original setting and translated title, *I vespri siciliani*, were adopted from 1861 on and some, though far from all, of Caimi's lapses removed.)

For *Don Carlo* (translated by Achille de Lauzières) Verdi took a more active role in trying to control what was presented in Italian theatres.[92] He wanted it performed in its entirety, with an exceptional cast and an augmented orchestra. The Italian première in Bologna (1867) did not conform; in Rome (1868) the text was altered for the censor (the Grand Inquisiteur became a Gran Cancelliere [chancellor]); in Naples (1871), unauthorised cuts did not prevent a cool reception. This prompted Verdi to revise the score for the following season. Two more extensively revised Italian versions followed: one in four acts in collaboration with Du Locle (via Charles Nuitter as intermediary), Italian translation by Lauzières and Angelo Zanardini (1884), and the other in five acts (1886), in which the Fontainebleau act of Paris was reintroduced, albeit abbreviated. Of all the grand operas by Italians, *Don Carlos* is the only one to exist in an Italian version, or better, versions, supervised by the composer in collaboration with a librettist of the French original.[93]

Yet, for *Don Carlos*, and even more so for *Les Vêpres siciliennes*, *Guillaume Tell* and *La Favorite*, the original versions in French are to be preferred from an aesthetic point of view. Even transformed operas, such as *Le Siège de Corinthe*, *Moïse*, *Les Martyrs* and *Jérusalem*, merit performance in French, rather than in (re)translation into Italian, for Rossini, Donizetti and Verdi worked closely with their librettists and with the Opéra administrations to create viable – and successful – grand operas. Modern critical and performing editions of several have permitted their recent revival to audiences' acclaim. May these grand operas in French, though with an Italian accent, soon form part of the standard nineteenth-century repertory at leading opera houses.

15 After 1850 at the Paris Opéra: institution and repertory

STEVEN HUEBNER

Late grand opera: Massenet's *Le Cid*

In his review of the world première of Jules Massenet's *Le Cid* (1885) at the Opéra, the critic Victor Wilder took the composer to task for smothering Corneille's tragedy 'with all the spices customarily used to season that indigestible dish called grand opera'.[1] Wilder listed the ingredients he detected: religious scene, formal ballet ('for the enjoyment of *abonnés* [subscribers] who arrive late'), Moorish dancing girls in a military camp, the fantastic apparition of St James, warrior chorus 'in the manner of the *Marseillaise*', and 'inevitable' procession. Characteristically meticulous about the latter, the libretto lists its participants: six *seigneurs*, six ladies in waiting, six pages for the king, six pages for the Infante, two officers, eight Moorish chieftains . . . and on it goes. 'What more could the most exacting *abonné* want?' asked Wilder, 'A cardinal, perhaps?' A swipe at Halévy's *La Juive*, premièred fifty years before at the same house, highlighted the generic colours of Massenet's work.

Besides spectacle, Wilder might also have noted Massenet's skill at creating rapid action sequences and manipulating the sharp contrasts and spatial effects essential to grand opera. One instance is the scene in Act II where Chimène discovers that her beloved Rodrigue has killed her father, the Comte de Gormas. Here events from the opera's literary antecedents (Guillén de Castro's *Las Mocedades del Cid* and its latter reworking by Pierre Corneille as *Le Cid*) are considerably compressed and melodramatically embellished. After Rodrigue kills the Count, the general population of Burgos floods the stage (entering as divided choral groups in typical grand opera fashion). Rodrigue's father Don Diègue publicly demonstrates gratitude to his son for avenging an earlier affront from the Comte de Gormas. Then Chimène voices her anguish. She runs among bystanders to find the murderer, stopping abruptly in her tracks before Rodrigue: 'It's him! Rodrigue! . . . him! . . . him!' – the last emitted *sans voix* low in her tessitura as she faints. After her final utterance the curtain falls slowly to a reiteration of a distant Requiem, which has punctuated the whole scene. The entire sequence after the duel – surely as gripping as the best moments in the grand operas of Meyerbeer, Halévy, and Verdi – lasts a mere seven minutes in performance.

Another fixture of French grand opera which might have irritated Wilder is a large ensemble where most of the principals appear together with the chorus at the end of an act and where private intrigue conjoins a well-articulated public dimension in the plot. Examples of such ensembles continued to appear for many years after the mid-century, in Gounod's *La Nonne sanglante* (Opéra, 1854), Félicien David's *Herculanum* (Opéra, 1859), Ambroise Thomas's *Hamlet* (Opéra, 1868) and *Françoise de Rimini* (Opéra, 1882), and Massenet's own *Le Roi de Lahore* (Opéra, 1877) and *Hérodiade* (Théâtre de la Monnaie, 1881), to name just a few. In *Le Cid*, this episode brings down the second act curtain after Chimène and Don Diègue plead their cases before king and populace. Once again the chorus is divided, with friends of the deceased Count and partisans of Don Diègue voicing their respective positions and the larger crowd (marked simply 'la foule') distinguished along the same lines. The entreaties of Chimène and Don Diègue lead to a large slow section modelled on an old-fashioned Italianate *concertato* movement: Rodrigue begins with a doleful G minor strain that is taken up by Chimène (a remnant of Rossini's pseudo-canons at moments of stupefaction), the other principals add counterpoint as needed, and various parts of the chorus contribute to the texture with brusque exclamations. The movement becomes progressively more homophonic, turns to the major mode, and works its way to the soprano's high note. Massenet shapes this culmination in a particularly striking fashion, as shown in Example 15.1. After an impressive dominant preparation (bars 1–3), the music drives to the soprano's B♭, at first giving the impression that the melodic zenith of the *concertato* will coincide with a return to the minor mode. But, in place of a conventional resolution of the bass C♯ up by a semitone in bar 4, Massenet lets it slip down to C♮ and B♮ while unexpectedly cranking up the melodic zenith *on the weak beat* of the climactic bar to B♮ (harmonised by dominant of the submediant). The music then wends its way to the cadence, where the turn to the minor mode promised by the soprano's high B♭ is realised. In short, in place of a more routine realisation (a soldering of bar 3 to bar 6, for example) the vocal shift up to B♮ makes for a thrilling conclusion. Well-worn as the *concertato* was by 1885, then, it still sparked Massenet's creative imagination.

Notwithstanding these continuities, much separated *Le Cid* from classical grand opera of the second quarter of the century. By borrowing from Guillén de Castro, Massenet's librettists (a triumvirate of Louis Gallet, Edouard Blau, and that prolific wordsmith of the boulevard theatres, Adolphe d'Ennery) emphasised the element of heroic romance in Corneille's play, which put it at some remove from most of the historical

Example 15.1 Massenet, *Le Cid*, Act II, finale: opposing groups include three separately notated choral ensembles: the Count's friends; Diègue's friends; and the crowd.

dramas by Meyerbeer and Halévy.[2] An accounting of the differences would certainly include wholesale importation of substantial passages from a literary classic. The combination of Corneille's own words with theatrical techniques derived from boulevard *mélodrame* and Spanish musical idioms attests to the longevity of the eclectic muse at the Opéra. Quotations from famous literature seem like elements in a giant collage or like attaching 'authentic' baubles to a nineteenth-century product.[3] Not all contemporaries were happy about this. One early critic observed that 'on a sentence that is too famous even the best recitative has the effect of a parody, just as the most sumptuous fabric would become an object of derision on a beautiful statue'.[4] On the other hand (and more charitably) one should not assume *a priori* that famous quotations are always aesthetically ungratifying in the new generic habitat. A different environment may sometimes yield greater theatrical impact, as at the moment after the hostile encounter between Don Diègue and the Count in Act I when Massenet's Don Diègue *speaks* 'Rodrigue, as-tu du cœur?' with no orchestral accompaniment. That one of the most famous lines in French literature stands naked in the wake of the earlier loud ceremonial music and Don Diègue's forceful remonstrance produces a chilling effect.

By the time of *Le Cid* the practice of adapting classics of world literature for the boulevard and operatic stage was decades old. Gounod's *Faust* (Théâtre-Lyrique, 1859; Opéra, 1869) travelled to the opera house from the boulevard stage, absorbing direct citations from the Goethe play *en route*.[5] That composer's *Polyeucte* (Opéra, 1878) also contains passages from the antecedent play by Corneille (in contrast to *Les Martyrs*, the earlier adaptation of the same play by Donizetti) and Ambroise Thomas's *Hamlet* (Opéra, 1868) borrows liberally from Shakespeare ('To be, or not to be, – that is the question' becomes 'Etre ou ne pas être! ô mystère!'). The latter's *Françoise de Rimini* does these works one better by actually having Dante appear on stage during a prologue in hell and in a final apotheosis.

With a large amount of local colour added to the mix, *Le Cid* seems to occupy a space somewhere between a literary monument and a big-budget Hollywood film adaptation shot on location. It had been typical enough of the Opéra production machine for several decades to fashion details of stage sets after real places: for example, the colonnades at the monastery of Las Huelgas served as models for those in the gallery of the second tableau in Massenet's opera.[6] And musical local colour in grand opera had long contributed to this aspect of Romantic theatre, which was discussed in Chapter 4. It is the scale and variety of local colour that is particularly impressive in *Le Cid*; its ballet, for example, is not merely generically Spanish but made up of dances from different regions of the peninsula (it became one of the most frequently excerpted parts of the opera). To what extent should a work such as *Le Cid* be taken, on the one hand, as an expression of a location and its history, and, on the other, as a reworking of a cornerstone in the French literary heritage? That Massenet carefully segregates the Spanish musical idioms from the discourse of his main characters would seem to suggest that local colour remains purely decorative. Such a position, however, does not account for the way such music enhances the overwhelming aesthetic impact of accurate, colourful, and elaborate sets. For instance, following the scene with the off-stage Requiem, which takes place on a street at night, the next tableau (II.2) opens to a broad view of the *grande place* in Burgos in

Figure 25 The soprano Emmy Destinn (Ema Destinnová, 1878–1930) as Verdi's Aida: collector's photographic portrait published in Berlin *c*. 1908, from which elaborate details of costuming are visible. Destinn's career began in Berlin, where she sang grand opera, especially *Les Huguenots*, Wagner and Verdi roles, and was Strauss's first Salome. She was also a writer, and appeared in silent films. A fervent Czech patriot, Destinn was interned during the Great War and finally honoured by a state funeral.

full sunlight. The crowd is present once again, now singing and dancing to Spanish rhythms. Thus, when the King appears he seems to stand not only for power and authority but for Spain as a separate sphere. Here the familiar ceremonial dimension of grand opera combines with local colour in the shift from a dark location with relatively limited indications of geographical specificity to a *grande place* suffused with a sense of the milieu. Chimène then comes running on with a threefold iteration of 'Justice!' (dousing the F major of the Spanish music with dark E♭'s and G♭'s). The preceding local colour makes her plea stand out in *greater relief* than neutral ceremonial music (appropriate to the appearance of a king, or even a cardinal) might have done because it results in a more pronounced shift from the localised and specific to a situation that makes a claim for universal empathy transcending milieu (apposite to the perceived cultural significance of Corneille's *grand siècle* classic).

The poster for the première, with its prominent dancing *almée*, also carried a promise of Massenet's well-publicised adroitness at depicting the feminine. A belly dancer, especially one whose garments are folded with erotic intent, does not usually recall Corneille to mind (see Fig. 26). Massenet's vocal writing has regularly been described as sensuous and charming by critics, adjectives not readily applicable to the style of Meyerbeer, Halévy or Auber.[7] Although the melodic language of *Le Cid* generally does not assume the voluptuous turns of phrase heard often in an opera such as *Hérodiade*, the love music is not without a certain nervous frisson (e.g., the sinuous syllabic arpeggios in Chimène's appeal to the Infante in Act I, 'Laissez le doute dans mon âme').[8] The newly naturalistic approach to prosody prevalent in the post-Gounod generation of French composers often contributes to an intimate ambience. So too does thematic recall, as during the well-known *air* 'Pleurez! pleurez mes yeux!' ('Weep! weep, my eyes') when Chimène declaims naturalistically above a slow clarinet melody that (we remember) represents her love for Rodrigue. (This procedure was used successfully by Gounod on many occasions.) As she remembers Don Rodrigue's earlier words, the orchestra becomes a sounding-board for her memory, a projection of *his* expressive voice. Her rapid declamation then evolves into a lyrical legato phrase when she joins his 'voice' by doubling the orchestra, an obvious emblem of her inability to reject him. Massenet's skill at shifting between declamation and cantabile singing within the lyrical sections of numbers, at changing tempos frequently for expressive effect, and at giving a leading role first to the orchestra and then to the voice, seems to mirror minute fluctuations of the soul. To be sure, intimate moments and thematic recall also occur in the grand operas of Meyerbeer, Halévy and others. The point is that techniques available in the second half of the century allowed an even *wider* gap between musical realisations of the public and private worlds represented on stage; the private could be rendered with great textural fluidity and nuance in the context of a genre that continued to incorporate processions and four-square choruses. The same capacity might be claimed of the larger chromatic palette employed by late nineteenth-century composers. In the first scene of *Le Cid*, a triadic march melody with diatonic walking bass and fanfares accompanies the initial public appearance of Rodrigue and contrasts sharply with the side-slipping harmonies that prepare the first hearing of the recurring love

Figure 26 Poster by Georges Clairin (1843–1919) for the première of Jules Massenet's *Le Cid* at the Paris Opéra, 30 November 1885.

melody. 'In a sort of ecstasy' he describes Chimène as 'Ange ou femme' (Angel or woman), after the harmonies have opened from B♭ major to G♭ major via a linking passage centred around D major harmony.

Defining the genre

Despite all these differences, *Le Cid* describes a fairly close orbit around classical examples of grand opera compared with many other works conceived for the Opéra after 1850. Musical and poetic style had obviously evolved, but a collection of practices associated with the genre was still in place. It is important to bear in mind that definition of the generic parameters of grand opera in France, by contrast with the rest of Europe, continued to be entwined with the institutional conventions of its founding theatre. The persistence of such conventions – some much older than grand opera, like a requirement for spectacle and ballet – should not in every case be equated with the persistence of grand opera itself. Identification of French works written after 1850 as grand operas (the term rarely appeared on scores and librettos) is less interesting than demonstrating the continuing presence of features associated with the genre. Because some of these features were institutional in France, specific evocation of the genre would seem to require a *network* of mutually reinforcing musical and dramaturgical characteristics built up from a common premise. Nestor Roqueplan, a director of the Opéra at mid-century, continued a well-grounded tradition by articulating that premise as 'faire grand' (doing great things).[9] (As a man of his century he noted that 'to make things bigger is a form of progress' as well as a manifestation of erudition and skill.) In grand opera doing great things meant an aesthetic of monumentality achieved through the allotment of considerable weight – scenic, dramaturgical and musical – to the public and political side of the plot, although conventionally fused with an equally well-elaborated private dimension.[10] Massenet's *Thaïs* (Opéra, 1894) provides an example of some of the issues involved in defining the genre during this period. He drafted the work for the Opéra-Comique as a vehicle for the soprano Sybil Sanderson, but when she contracted with the Opéra he adjusted his work by adding the ballet 'La Tentation' to the score.[11] But the intimate subject of *Thaïs* (styled *comédie lyrique* by the composer)[12] can scarcely be perceived as monumental in any respect, so much so that the conservative critic Charles Darcours remarked that the work 'does not always have the fullness of treatment ['ampleur de facture'] appropriate to the frame of the Opéra'.[13] The Opéra did, however, spend much money on the première. Thus, the ballet and splendour of the first production of *Thaïs* seem to be characteristics *shared* with grand opera more than *derivative* of that genre. Such common ground between works as different as *Thaïs* and *Le Cid* seems the result of obeisance to the practices of an institution more than adherence to a genre.

Although the line between the shared and the derivative is fluid, this distinction does provide a rough index of relative proximity to a core of classical examples as well as a gauge of value judgements in the critical climate at the *fin de siècle*. One might frame this problem as a series of questions. When can we speak of fundamental premises shared between two works, thus enhancing the critical plausibility of describing the relationship as derivative? How do we define 'fundamental'? Is it a matter of shared ingredients being numerous and significant enough? How numerous, how significant?[14]

Answers will be inflected by the goals and premises of the critical project at hand, perceptions of authorial intent, and considerations of social context and reception history. Rare, for example, was the composer in the second half of the century who publicly tarred his or her own grand opera with the brush of derivativeness. Such explicit avowals would hardly serve the cause of self-promotion. For charges of derivativeness were usually laid in a negative spirit with attendant implications of stagnation and/or pandering to the market. The career of Emmanuel Chabrier is instructive in this regard. In the early 1880s he had two opera projects on the stocks, *Les Muscadins* (libretto by Armand Silvestre) and *Gwendoline* (libretto by Catulle Mendès). He made it clear to acquaintances which he preferred. Mendès's legendary plot allowed him much greater musical freedom, whereas Silvestre's was a *drame à la Dumas père* with 'patriots, chauvinistic songs, and, well yes, four-square phrases at bottom',[15] and with 'traitors, love, light-heartedness, darkness'[16] – all characteristics of historical grand opera. Chabrier certainly talked about *Les Muscadins* as if it were a derivative project. The main attraction for him was that it actually had a chance to be staged, which speaks volumes for the conservative orientation of the Opéra as an institution in the early 1880s (in the end, however, it never saw the boards). *Gwendoline* (Théâtre de la Monnaie, 1886; Opéra, 1893), because of its *explicitly* symbolic libretto rooted in legend, may be said to derive very little from grand opera and few of Chabrier's contemporaries assumed that generic connection. Yet it shares with the grand opera a spectacular conclusion where ships are set on fire, as well as a conflict between private love and public politics. Like Amonasro in *Aida*, Gwendoline's father asks her to betray her lover for the sake of her country; but Chabrier pointedly avoids *Marseillaise*-like choruses, processions, and the conservative musical syntax he felt they required.

It was with a condemnation of derivative impulse that Victor Wilder capped his list of the spectacular accoutrements in *Le Cid*:

> In all good faith, can M. Massenet believe that the score of his *Cid* is superior to *Les Huguenots*, *Guillaume Tell*, or *Le Prophète*? No, of course not. Well, then, why condemn oneself to pour a work into a mould that has already produced consummate exemplars?

The verdict of Alfred Bruneau on Massenet's opera was similar. In 1900 he even equated it with Emile Paladilhe's *Patrie!* (Opéra, 1886) as 'an opera with a distinctly Meyerbeerian appearance'.[17] With hindsight, such attacks against Massenet seem somewhat overstated. For *Patrie!* illustrates a much greater degree of indebtedness to classical grand opera than *Le Cid*.

Based on a popular *mélodrame* by Victorien Sardou, Paladilhe's work is set during the Spanish occupation of Flanders during the sixteenth century. It provides a vivid *in situ* illustration of the cause that the Marquis de Posa espouses in Verdi's *Don Carlos*. The Flemish patriots Rysoor and Karloo seek to cast off the yoke of oppression. Karloo is the lover of Dolores, Rysoor's wife. Rysoor, for his part, ignores this affront to his honour because of his higher patriotic mission. Attempting to protect her lover, Dolores reveals the conspiracy to the Duke of Alba, who does not heed the appeals for clemency of his daughter Rafaele. At the end Karloo kills Dolores because of her betrayal and joins his compatriots in an *auto-da-fé*. Admittedly, this is more the world of Sardou than D'Ennery or Scribe: adultery is played out more explicitly than it would have been forty years before and Dolores does not feel the moral compunction of, say, an Amélie (a reluctant adulteress in Auber's *Gustave III*). Rysoor cuts a figure of baritonal civic idealism just as high-minded as Posa, but his relationship with his tenor brother-at-arms follows a different path to that of the tenor and baritone in *Don Carlos*. Folded into the work are a judgement scene, conspiracy chorus, prayers, distant revelling against dark foreground action, processions, an episode where Dolores witnesses insurrection plans from behind a tapestry (just like Valentine in *Les Huguenots*), and a duet for the two lovers where the tenor Karloo is drawn away by the desperate cries of his expiring co-conspirators (also redolent of Meyerbeer's opera). Owing to Sardou's literary inclinations, the links of *Patrie!* to boulevard *mélodrame* – that seed-bed of so many grand opera dramaturgical techniques – are even stronger than those of *Le Cid*. Another difference between the two works is that whereas Paladilhe accords considerable musical weight to several characters (as Meyerbeer and Halévy usually did), Massenet's opera centres on the two lovers. *Patrie!* achieved a total of seventy-two performances (after revivals in 1900 and 1907) and a solid record on provincial stages. It had a better run in Paris than *Don Carlos* in its day. If there was a swan-song for the historical drama side of the genre, this was it. *Le Cid* also did reasonably well, becoming the first opera premièred at the Palais Garnier (that is, after 1875) to attain 100 performances (in 1905). Both works bravely made their way while other unalloyed grand operas rapidly faded from the Opéra repertory: although *Les Huguenots* would continue to be staged until the 1930s, *Le Prophète* enjoyed a final burst of popularity between 1898 and 1908 after years of neglect, and *Robert le Diable* and *La Juive* were not performed for several decades after 1893.[18]

The Wagner factor

A major reason for the precipitous decline of grand opera performances at the Opéra was the proliferation of Wagner's works on that stage after the tumultuous *Lohengrin* première in 1891.[19] (Table 15.1 compares the

Table 15.1 *Number of performances of Wagner operas and classical grand operas 1890–1910 at the Paris Opéra*

Year	90	91	92	93	94	95	96	97	98	99	00	01	02	03	04	05	06	07	08	09	10
Wagner																					
Lohengrin	–	36	38	23	15	11	11	15	10	9	7	17	12	18	8	5	3	8	12	13	14
Die Walküre	–	–	–	45	23	10	11	–	7	7	12	6	11	2	7	8	5	18	5	15	9
Tannhäuser	–	–	–	–	–	33	19	7	7	16	16	16	6	15	13	11	14	8	15	8	13
Die Meistersinger	–	–	–	–	–	–	–	15	27	6	7	5	5	–	5	–	10	–	–	4	–
Siegfried	–	–	–	–	–	–	–	–	–	–	–	–	20	4	5	–	–	–	–	–	–
Tristan und Isolde	–	–	–	–	–	–	–	–	–	–	–	–	–	–	5	23	5	8	6	2	4
Götterdämmerung	–	–	–	–	–	–	–	–	–	–	–	–	–	–	–	–	–	–	14	7	3
Das Rheingold	–	–	–	–	–	–	–	–	–	–	–	–	–	–	–	–	–	–	–	11	4
Meyerbeer																					
Les Huguenots	14	5	8	11	1	–	–	24	20	9	20	16	10	13	12	8	16	3	10	3	5
Le Prophète	4	–	3	–	–	–	–	–	28	25	10	4	–	6	5	7	12	3	3	–	–
L'Africaine	14	7	12	3	–	–	–	–	–	–	–	–	13	–	–	–	–	–	–	–	–
Robert le Diable	–	–	–	–	–	–	–	–	–	–	–	–	–	–	–	–	–	–	–	–	–
Rossini																					
Guillaume Tell	4	6	7	–	–	–	–	–	–	16	9	8	8	7	6	3	10	2	5	2	1
Halévy																					
La Juive	6	5	5	9	–	–	–	–	–	–	–	–	–	–	–	–	–	–	–	–	–

number of Wagner performances to those of classical grand opera in the period from 1890 to 1910.) Whether contemporaneous critics accentuated the traditional or more novel elements in works such as *Le Cid* or *Patrie!* depended on critical perspectives that were most often decisively shaped by attitudes towards Wagner, particularly in the decade of the 1880s when the great battles for stagings of his work were fought in Paris.[20] Whereas, as Anselm Gerhard has noted, works written for the Opéra could legitimately claim to be the site of the most progressive music dramaturgy in Europe in the second quarter of the century, any such claim rang increasingly hollow as the century progressed.[21]

To be sure, Gounod created a new current in the third quarter of the century, one sometimes perceived as adaptable to grand opera and exhibiting at least a potential to renew it. Support for a genre that had attained considerable international prestige by 1850 was particularly important to the subsequent upstart Napoleonic régime preoccupied with demonstrating legitimacy. But by the 1870s the Wagnerian line of criticism and composition slowly positioned itself as antithetical to a genre that had run its course. And by the time of Wilder and Bruneau (Wagnerians both) this viewpoint had become commonplace. The belittling epithet 'petite musique en grand' ('small music writ large' – Louis de Fourcaud on Thomas's *Françoise de Rimini* in 1882[22]) well summarises the belligerence of an entire phalanx of critics in the 1880s. 'Doing great things' was a sham. Anti-Wagnerians, however, continued to rally behind late grand operas such as *Le Cid* and *Patrie!* as a bulwark against newer trends. The conservative Oscar Comettant found much solace in Massenet's score:

> The first thing that I have the duty to note here is that *Le Cid* is not a Wagnerian score . . . no *mélodie infinie*, in other words those long vocal emissions without rhythm, and consequently without any form, horribly monotonous . . . In *Le Cid* the singers sing, which is quite something. Although the orchestra, admirably treated with all the resources of modern art, always powerfully contributes with all the lavishness of a richly coloured and brilliantly harmonised instrumentation to the expression of the emotions that grip the actor on the stage, it never substitutes itself for him . . .[23]

Comettant clearly felt that one could be modern and write grand opera at the same time, that the genre was still capable of renewal, and that lists of derivative elements were irrelevant at best. In 1886, Arthur Pougin cast the issues in the following terms with reference to *Patrie!*:

> At a time when all of Italy prepares to cheer passionately the new *Otello* that Verdi will offer to audiences at La Scala, at a time when a series of performances of *Lohengrin* will encourage Wagnerians and their

> reinforcements to march, it pleases me to see one of ours, a Frenchman,
> plant the flag of our national art on the highest point of the horizon and,
> with the help of a powerful and virile work, prove that this art is as
> courageous and alive as ever![24]

Thus did a genre much celebrated for its cosmopolitanism in the second quarter of the century[25] – and by extension the cosmopolitanism of Paris itself – become a *point d'appui* in the more parochial nationalist debate following the defeat of 1870. Grand opera in Paris quite simply became the domain of French composers: *Don Carlos* was the last work written for the house by a foreigner in the nineteenth century.[26] And the defenders of grand opera celebrated its national characteristics. For example, in a 1906 survey of music history, the respected critic Camille Bellaigue noted that theatrical *savoir faire*, putatively a product of French genius, lay at the heart of grand opera and had made it a truly national genre: 'the *mise-en-scène* in our national grand opera is the equivalent of dialogue in opéra comique, that other equally French genre', in providing divertissement and a respite from a continual unfolding of music.[27]

Given the centrality of the Opéra as an institution it is not surprising to find heightened sensitivities to nationalism at the *fin de siècle* reflected in debates about its repertory. The political importance of the Palais Garnier was symbolically enshrined in the urban landscape: it had been conceived as a jewel in Haussmann's Paris, to be connected eventually by the splendid avenue that bears its name to the Tuileries Palace of Napoleon III. The palace (once a wing of the Louvre) was burned to the ground during the 1871 Commune as the Second Empire gave way to the Third Republic – but subscriptions continued to be coveted among elites of the aristocracy and *haute bourgeoisie*. Audiences at the house in the last two decades of the century were generally just as well-heeled as thirty years before.[28] By referring to exacting and tardy *abonnés*, Wilder hinted at the very real influence of this group behind the scenes, in his review of *Le Cid* cited at the beginning of this chapter. (With *abonnés* arriving late at performances for most of the century, social practice reinforced the sense of patchwork in the genre itself; attacks on lateness signalled a realignment between the artist and society.) Symptomatic of the *abonnés*' preference for familiar fare – and, even more, of an architectural project conceived by Charles Garnier with classical grand opera in mind – was that no new work inaugurated the Palais Garnier on 5 January 1875, but rather a gala of established pieces: the overtures to *La Muette de Portici* and *Guillaume Tell*, the first two acts of *La Juive*, the 'Consecration of the swords' from *Les Huguenots*, and *La Source*, the 1866 ballet by Delibes and Minkus.[29] Over a quarter century later, Romain Rolland characterised the house as having become 'more than ever an ostentatious salon, a bit faded, where the audience is more interested in itself than in the performance' and followed all tastes 'as long as they are thirty years old'.[30] While traditional political relationships in French society changed during the Republic and mass consumerism rapidly transformed the economy, the Opéra still provided the illusion – some might even say an oasis – of court life from a previous era. Small wonder, then, that *Patrie!* was deemed a *succès d'abonnés* (a 'hit' with the subscribers); such was their impact on the administration that they could momentarily sustain a very old-fashioned new work on the boards, a familiar bond with the past.

Now, as Nietzsche and many others have pointed out, there was *also* material aplenty in Wagner's operas to nourish the reactionary elements of society at the *fin de siècle*. A sociological account of the shift in taste to Wagner among *abonnés* might begin by observing that during the Orleanist régime historical opera had provided a cathartic experience derived from boulevard theatre (e.g., when melodramatic paragons of virtue such as Valentine or Fidès were crushed by unsavoury political developments), one made appropriate to refined taste because of the complexity of Opéra productions as well as the novelty and sophistication of their musical dramaturgy.[31] In effect, the lyrical dimension of opera turned middle-brow boulevard *mélodrame* into a fundamentally more 'poetic' experience. By the Third Republic, however, grand opera, like spoken *mélodrame* itself, became more shopworn, its 'poetry' more routine. With a surfeit of parliamentary intrigue fertilised by a burgeoning and scandal-hungry popular press,[32] the supposed time-lessness of myth became ever more credible as an aesthetic choice among Opéra elites, a new plateau of refined taste, privilege and 'poetry' within a society-at-large increasingly preoccupied with materialism and superficial sensationalism. Nevertheless, there was also the inescapable attachment to tradition, anxiety in the face of change. If nostalgia thus competed with escapism, they almost crossed paths in the close proximity of the premières of *Patrie!* (1886) and *Lohengrin* (1891). Not to mention that *Lohengrin* represented a safe choice inasmuch as it shared several elements with grand opera, as we shall see in Chapter 16.

There were other issues at stake. From the perspective of the republican régime – not necessarily coextensive with that of the *abonnés* taken as a group, though not necessarily in binary opposition to it[33] – the politically apposite images in *Patrie!*, such as its projection of civic duty or negative portrayal of a Catholic power,[34] were eventually superseded by the aura of artistic progress that the works of Wagner still represented until 1900 in France (and Paladilhe did not). That the authority of a privileged group of *abonnés* was destabilised by Wagnerian discourse about the integrity of the artist harmonised well enough with republican intensification of longstanding attempts to democratise the institution. Such initiatives were naturally couched in rhetoric about social equality before Art, instead of about privilege and rarefied taste.[35] It was a compromise that the *abonnés* presumably accepted because of other factors and also, arguably, because recognition of the creator's integrity within the opera house itself became a mark of social distinction. In other words: historians would do well to consider just at what period it became gauche to arrive late for the ballet. An exclusive atmosphere was maintained: 'family performances' with reduced ticket prices seem rarely to have occurred on Fridays, the most popular subscription day, and *abonnés* of long standing on Mondays, Wednesdays, and Fridays showed little interest when a new subscription series was opened on Saturdays.[36] The tide turned in Wagner's favour at the Opéra only when his works had become part of mainstream high taste all over Europe, when they no longer presented an aesthetic or political risk, when a sufficient mass of upper-class listeners and *abonnés* had responded favourably to his music at Parisian concert societies, and when, in an era that privileged progress, the Opéra as an institution (and the wider republican cultural apparatus it represented) risked appearing hopelessly antediluvian by giving in to the minority *revanchard* elements opposed to Wagner performances on nationalist principle. The introduction of Wagner into the Opéra repertory in 1891 brought with it a significant modification in the *cahier des charges*, the contract that directors undertook with the State: whereas the *cahier* of 1884 and most previous ones had still required directors to commission 'grand opera, with recitatives, in one or several acts, with or without ballet' (the genre was obviously *very* loosely defined here), the new clause replaced this with 'all types of opera', adopting the phrase '*drame lyrique*' – a generic designation with a distinctly Wagnerian colour.[37]

A brief tour

Practices associated with grand opera, then, flourished at the Opéra almost until the end of the century, be they understood as derivative or merely shared, and with varying commitment to renewal. Most major French composers after 1850 continued to aspire to a success at the Opéra. They all fell woefully short of that goal, generally producing works that did not survive past fifty performances at a time when Meyerbeer's operas had each chalked up hundreds.

Charles Gounod essayed no fewer than five world premières at the Opéra in this period: *Sapho* (1851; revised 1884), *La Nonne sanglante* (1854), *La Reine de Saba* (1862), *Polyeucte* (1878), *Le Tribut de Zamora* (1881). That the doors of the house were thrown open to him so many times bears eloquent witness to his towering status during the third quarter of the century, a

position achieved largely through the reputation of works premièred on
other stages. Nonetheless, despite the failures, Gounod's style opened up a
range of intimate expression through finally chiselled prosodic detail that
left its mark on a host of composers, like the Paladilhe of *Patrie!*[38] Gounod's
music was praised as especially French-sounding, not in the light manner
of Auber, but in its approach to the lyrical moment (after some notoriously
wrong-headed initial assessments by conservative critics as 'Wagnerian').
But even as nationalist issues became more profiled in the press, celebrations
of Gounod's French qualities did little to generate popular or critical success
for his grand operas, though, of course, *Faust* became a mainstay at the
Opéra, having been supplied with recitatives and a ballet.

The two Gounod works in which an effort to renew the genre seems most
evident are *La Reine de Saba* and *Polyeucte*. The first of these highlights a
tenor hero, Adoniram, master architect to the biblical King Solomon, who
woos the Queen of Sheba from under the king's nose and acts elsewhere with
flagrant *lèse-majesté*. Gounod knew *Tannhäuser* by the time he composed
this work and may have been sufficiently impressed by the theme of the
forward-looking artist against society to translate it to the grand opera stage
(but without expatiating on the nature of love as in Wagner's opera). Like
Tannhäuser, Adoniram has a trial of his own to undergo when a great casting
he attempts ends in a disastrous explosion of molten metal. Whatever its
relation to Wagner's work, the actions of Gounod's hero seem consonant
with Wagnerian initiatives to buttress the authority of the artist/composer.
In developing this premise, *La Reine de Saba* broke one of the main bonds
connecting grand opera to boulevard *mélodrame*: virtue is difficult to locate
in its characters, and villainy (be it in an individual or society) is weakly articulated. Idealistic baritones like Posa and Rysoor found few enough friends
among critics; high-minded tenors like Adoniram had an even rougher time
of it. Amidst the ballets, marches and fanfares there is much talk (and musical projection) in *La Reine de Saba* of the mysterious origins of Adoniram
and the mystically predestined nature of his relationship with the Queen –
themes unusual in grand opera before that time – but neither character is
truly persecuted. Nor do any of the other characters generate much sympathy. Contemporary critics were baffled.[39]

Polyeucte is about another 'great man', another protagonist amenable to
the doctrine of 'doing great things' in both the realm of ideas and scenography. The hero is now a Christian martyr at the outer reaches of the declining
Roman Empire. The responsiveness of the chord that Polyeucte's mission
struck within the devout Gounod is equal in volume to the unresponsiveness
the theme found with the composer's contemporaries. The central massed
tableau is a baptism scene for Polyeucte, with religious march and prayer – a
Gounodian corrective to the darker depictions of Catholicism in works such

as *Les Huguenots* and *Don Carlos*. In the last act, Polyeucte's wife Pauline takes up the new faith and joins him in the fatal arena accompanied by frenzied shouts of 'Aux lions les chrétiens!' ('Throw the Christians to the lions!') The stakes are similar in the scene between Valentine and Raoul at the end of *Les Huguenots* ('Toi, tu maudis mon culte! Moi! j'adopte le tien!' ('You, you condemn my religion! I! I convert to yours!')), feral teeth replacing gunshots. Whereas Meyerbeer's scene throws into relief the irony of murder in the name of Faith, Gounod's depicts the transformative power of Christianity within a decadent world order. Good strong melodramatic situations were supplanted by a proselytising inclination baldly out of step with contemporaneous republican initiatives to separate Church and State. In its obvious aim to create musical and scenic contrasts between the pagan and Christian, Gounod's opera looked backward to Félicien David's *Herculanum* (1859), but in that work, as in *Robert le Diable*, a sharper contrast is drawn between good and evil *per se*, in contradistinction to Gounod's 'misguided' and 'saved'. Satan even puts in a few appearances in David's opera. Set at the foot of Vesuvius in CE 79, *Herculanum* effects a striking conflation of morality play and classical setting; the volcano erupts at the end in a spectacular Old-Testament-like retribution against the wicked instead of as an extension of a political parable as in the more familiar *La Muette de Portici*.

Religious themes continued, but the devil took subtler forms. In Massenet's *Hérodiade* the soprano Salomé joins the tenor John the Baptist in a *Liebestod* enveloped by the Gospel. But Valentine–Raoul and Pauline–Polyeucte transcend physical desire in a way that Massenet's characters do not: in *Hérodiade* faith and flesh commingle – and (scandalously) not only in the soprano. And whereas the third corner in the love triangle of Gounod's opera (Pauline's erstwhile pagan lover Sévère) magnanimously does not stand in the way of the couple, Massenet's Hérode seeks revenge by executing the Christian heretic/rival-in-love. All of this was tawdry from the Gounodian perspective, but there can be no doubt about which makes for better theatre. Massenet was expert at blending traditional melodramatic themes with sensuous ones: Salomé may not be chaste, but like the typical persecuted melodramatic protagonist she has been unjustly expelled from her society, even from her family. Following conventional boulevard theatrical fashion, she finally recognises her own mother Hérodiade at the end. And she indefatigably longs for purity.

If Gounod had a real competitor at the box-office among his French colleagues during the Second Empire it was Ambroise Thomas. *Hamlet* proved to be more enduring than any of Gounod's works for the Opéra stage, and the most popular piece premièred there in the second half of the nineteenth century. It was kept afloat internationally by a succession of prima donnas in the role of Ophélie, from Christine Nilsson to Nellie Melba, as well as a number of great baritones in the title role. Shakespeare's protagonist made for another 'great' figure, but in altogether different ways from Adoniram and Polyeucte, and in ways that did not lend themselves well to grand opera. For although male indecision was a common enough phenomenon in the repertory, how could Hamlet's existential dilemma provide suitable entertainment at the Palais Garnier? The nature of the literary source suggests that if grand opera is invoked as a model at all it would be more for shared elements than for derivative dramaturgy. *Hamlet* stands at further remove from a core of classical examples than other works we have surveyed because of a confluence of two features: its overwhelming focus on the baritone and soprano leading roles (resembling *Le Cid* in this respect) and its *relatively* contained public–political dimension (unlike *Le Cid*). But Shakespeare still had to be accommodated to the exigencies of the house and its patrons. Thomas begins with Gertrude's marriage to Claudius (a *fait accompli* in the Shakespeare) in order to create a rousing opening number with fanfares and march, and the festivities continue to sound from off stage as a foil to Hamlet's first encounter with the ghost of his father. At the end, Shakespeare's pile of bodies is avoided: only Claudius falls to Hamlet's sword and Hamlet is proclaimed King of Denmark by the people and the ghost (at a final un-Shakespearean appearance). A fine touch of irony accompanies a quick final curtain when a collective 'Vive Hamlet' juxtaposes his 'Mon âme est dans la tombe, hélas! et je suis Roi!' ('My soul is entombed, alas! and I am king'). Ophélie's role, rather small in the Shakespeare, is greatly expanded over the source. Hamlet's alienation from her – that conventional grand opera foundering of love on politics – becomes cinched and melodramatically legible when he comes to believe (unlike in Shakespeare's play) that her father Polonius was implicated in the murder. Ballet and mad-scene take place in a country setting in Act IV. True to the Opéra's tradition for scenic variety, this substantial pastoral episode (complete with *danse villageoise*) provides the requisite contrast to the dour walls of Elsinore.

One of the ironies of Camille Saint-Saëns's career is that *Samson et Dalila*, which would prove to be his greatest operatic success, was premièred relatively early on in 1877 and followed by nine operas that scored lukewarm successes at best. Four of the pre-1900 fall within the generic sphere of grand opera: *Etienne Marcel* (Grand-Théâtre, Lyon, 1879), *Henry VIII* (Opéra, 1883), *Ascanio* (Opéra, 1890) and *Frédégonde* (Opéra, 1895). *Etienne Marcel* and *Frédégonde* are closest to the classical core. The latter, first drafted in part by Ernest Guiraud and completed by Saint-Saëns (he composed the last two acts from scratch), is set in sixth-century Merovingian Gaul and traces the enmity between the two queens Frédégonde and Brunehaut.[40]

The events of *Etienne Marcel* centre around a bourgeois and popular rebellion in Paris following the defeat of the French at the Battle of Poitiers
in 1356. Like Masaniello's sister in *La Muette de Portici*, ringleader Etienne
Marcel's daughter falls in love with an adherent to the ruling régime and,
like Masaniello once again, he ultimately loses control of a popular rebellion
that he initiated (but for different reasons than in *La Muette*). Conspiracy
plans, off-stage religious service, calling the curfew and cloak-and-dagger
episodes, all in a pre-Bourbon Parisian setting, bring *Les Huguenots* readily
to mind.

Politics play a smaller role in *Henry VIII*, although the central massed
tableau does condense Henry's break with the Catholic Church, reinforced
by a mob to which the king has given leave to confront the Papal Legate.
Much greater weight is given over to representation of the personal tragedy
of Catherine d'Aragon, the ascendance of Anne de Boleyn, and the general
cruelty of Henry. *Ascanio*, even further removed from the grand opera core,
follows the career of the sculptor Benvenuto Cellini in France, to which he
repaired following the escapades in Rome depicted in Berlioz's opera. Like
Benvenuto Cellini it contains many lighter episodes interspersed with cloak-
and-dagger action; and like Adoniram in *La Reine de Saba*, the haughty
Benvenuto is shown to deal on equal footing with aristocracy. He must even
execute a difficult casting of a giant reliquary. Public and political issues,
however, are subordinate to a complex intrigue in which Scozzone (mezzo
soprano) loves Benvenuto (baritone), who loves Colombe d'Estourville
(soprano), who loves Benvenuto's young protégé Ascanio (tenor), who is
loved by the evil Duchesse d'Estampes (soprano dramatique), who is mistress to the king. Such entanglements belong to the comedic mode, as does
Benvenuto's Hans Sachs-like gesture finally to endorse the two young lovers.
Nonetheless, the presence of royalty supplies a certain degree of grandeur
with ceremonial choruses and divertissement – what scene could stir the
patriotic French heart of an *abonné* more than the sight of Emperor Charles
V as guest of François I at Fontainebleau? – and a magnificent crowd scene
occurs when Benvenuto enlists the mob to help resolve a disputed claim to a
luxurious residence. And for shock value the conclusion – suddenly hijacked
away from comedy – surely finds few equals even by the standards of the
grisly grand opera fare of boiling cauldrons, exploding palaces, and ritual
entombment: the machinations of Duchesse d'Estampes lead Scozzone to
enclose herself in the reliquary and suffocate to death. At the very end, the
artist's genius is celebrated in a joyful chorus, Colombe and Ascanio set out
to live happily ever after . . . and Scozzone's cold and lifeless body tumbles
out when Benvenuto tears open the door of the reliquary.

What these operas all have in common is meticulous attention to historical local colour in stage sets, presentation of characters, and Saint-Saëns's

skilful musical pastiche of older styles. As a critic, Saint-Saëns vigorously defended historical settings against Wagnerian theorising about the dramatic efficacy of myth and legend.[41] Although such a defence should not be understood as completely synonymous with a defence of grand opera itself, it was obviously in tune with that genre. 'History and Myth in *drame lyrique*', the title of his main article on the subject,[42] sends out conflicting signals: on the one hand, *drame lyrique* was a generic designation for works written after the Wagnerian revolution; on the other, history was the stuff of so many grand operas. Saint-Saëns called all four of his historical works 'opéra' and, more important, his enthusiasm for historical subjects fitted into a larger nationalist programme to which he repeatedly returned in his writing.[43] Therefore, it is not surprising to read an unfashionable defence of *Les Huguenots* in the same article:

> after *Robert le Diable* there appeared *Les Huguenots*, which for a
> half-century was the glory of historical opera; even today, now that some
> of the tradition has been lost and the performances are inferior to those of
> yesteryear, this memorable work still gives off surprising brilliance, like a
> setting sun. How could the generations that admired it be wrong! And
> should we rail against such a successful work because Robert Schumann,
> who knew nothing about the theatre, denied its worth? It is surprising that
> the judgement of Schumann has not been contrasted with that of Berlioz
> and the enthusiasm exhibited for *Les Huguenots* in his famous
> orchestration treatise.[44]

With the value of Berlioz's stock on the rise among Wagnerians and nationalists at the *fin de siècle*, to invoke his name in defence of Meyerbeer made a clever critical strategy. In an article on Meyerbeer in the same collection Saint-Saëns reminded his readers how he had successfully raised musical standards in a period of decadent Italian influence, had initiated many musical procedures taken for granted by later composers, and (despite what the Wagnerians said) had always remained a musician of integrity.[45]

Saint-Saëns implicitly asked his readers to question whether historical grand opera had completely depleted itself with Meyerbeer (as Wilder suggested in his review of *Le Cid*). Historical characters, he argued, were intrinsically more compelling than mythological ones who had never existed. Whereas figures from myth owed their aesthetic appeal entirely to music, real historical figures could find their considerable stature even more enhanced because music 'penetrated to the deeps of the soul'. But he supplied his best answer in the works. In the case of *Etienne Marcel*, a *bona fide* grand opera, Saint-Saëns might well have argued that the aesthetic value of his characters was augmented precisely because of a close connection to recent political events: a rebellion in Paris, a revolutionary vanguard in the face of weakened central authority and a quick collapse of demagogues inevitably engaged memories of the Paris Commune of 1871. Overtones from contemporary political events were felt in previous grand operas as well – *Le Prophète* was a conspicuous example, coming as it did after the Revolutions of 1848 – but the connection seems particularly strong in *Etienne Marcel*, a further step taken on the road to the twentieth-century drama-documentary. The important point in Saint-Saëns's aesthetics was that such a setting did not entail a sacrifice of poetic depth. To achieve that depth Saint-Saëns readily fused number opera with more modern musical strategies. His historical operas are all more leitmotivic than *Samson et Dalila*, contain a seamless flow between numbers, loosen traditional formal groundplans, apply the lessons of Gounod's melodic style with a richer chromatic vocabulary, and display the remarkably dexterous orchestration of a respected composer of symphonies and symphonic poems (and a much better hand in this respect than Massenet). As syntheses between old and new musical procedures in the period 1875–90, Saint-Saëns historical operas are brilliantly conceived and may even be defended as viable attempts at generic renewal. But Wagnerians and modernists were deeply suspicious of compromise and readjusted the measuring rod of artistic renewal at the *fin de siècle*. In the midst of their vituperations – which Saint-Saëns bore as much as Massenet did – it became easy to lose sight that Saint-Saëns was one of the most gifted musicians of his century. Today, Meyerbeer's grand operas get revived much more frequently. One suspects an on-going privileging of progress in this – Meyerbeer was avant-garde in his day, whereas Saint-Saëns was not – for it is not at all certain that Saint-Saëns's historical operas are theatrically, vocally or compositionally inferior to those of Meyerbeer.

Notwithstanding Saint-Saëns's appeals, grand opera did not completely eschew myth and legend, as is shown by works such as Halévy's *Le Juif errant* (see p. 248) and Gounod's *La Nonne sanglante*. Perhaps the most exceptional of these efforts, if only for its intersection with Wagnerian source material, was Ernest Reyer's *Sigurd* (Théâtre de la Monnaie, 1884). Reyer's work was first conceived in the mid-1860s but only performed at the Opéra in 1885. *Sigurd* roughly follows the essential outlines of the *Götterdämmerung* plot, but its genetic history shows that successive Opéra administrations were nervous about the Teutonic setting and that the composer and his librettists progressively reduced the fantastic elements (for example, a prologue showing Odin and Brunehild in heaven) and reinforced its connection with *real* history by giving Attila a role in the fall of Gunther's régime.[46] The processions and divertissements of the Opéra are still in place: the fateful wedding of Gunther and Brunehild motivates some on-stage jousting as well as the appearance of a barque bedecked with flowers (just like the wedding cortege in the third act of *Les Huguenots*). Sigurd's rescue of the Valkryie is preceded by ghoulish apparitions in the manner of *Robert le Diable* (and *Der Freischütz*). The concluding elevation to paradise for Brunehild and Sigurd had antecedents in *La Nonne sanglante* and *Le Juif errrant*. Despite such shared elements with the grand opera tradition, *Sigurd* was generally championed by Wagnerians, not so much for its setting as for Reyer's relative boldness in avoiding certain stereotypical vocal and formal conventions and in extending a leitmotivic web across the entire work at a very early date.

Boldness also characterises Berlioz's *Les Troyens*, composed just a few years before *Sigurd* (largely between 1856 and 1858) and much admired by Reyer. (Indeed, it is highly probable that Berlioz's opera stimulated Reyer to try his hand at epic – with much different literary matter and using leitmotif to project that mode.) *Les Troyens* did not have good fortune in Berlioz's own day, receiving a truncated première at the Théâtre Lyrique in 1863 and still presented in two parts when it returned to Paris in the 1890s (as *Les Troyens à Carthage* at the Opéra-Comique in 1892 and *La Prise de Troie* at the Opéra in 1899). Yet in contrast to a massive legacy of works conceived for the Opéra now relegated to the repertorial wilderness, *Les Troyens* is to-day attended by the greatest cultural prestige. Unlike most other composers, Berlioz actually styled his work *grand opéra*, something of an irony since the work can only be positioned at some distance from the classical core, even further than *Ascanio*, *Hamlet* or *Sigurd*. When Alfred Bruneau suggested in 1900 (with nationalist intent) that Berlioz had taken up the mantle of Gluck to countervail the style and dramaturgy of Rossini and Meyerbeer, he was echoing a well-established position among French critics.[47] The 'grand' part of Berlioz's designation does, however, refer to an aesthetic of monu-mentality which *Les Troyens* exhibited more than any opera written before that time. Such monumentality is synonymous with the weight of History, as Paul Robinson has observed.[48] Aeneas is no ineffective leader caught up in a web of historical forces: an illustration, as so many grand operas were, of a nineteenth-century bourgeois (and partially aristocratic) predicament where self-reliance, freedom of choice and social mobility came up against the machines of the State, capitalist economy, and the conformist and po-tentially dangerous mentality of the masses. Rather, Berlioz's protagonist is a Hegelian World-Historical individual entirely consumed by a higher public mission. His first encounter with Dido in Act III, as queen and leader of her country, occurs after her Carthaginian realm has been grandiosely depicted. It follows upon a no less grandiosely delineated fall of Troy. Great historical forces come together: significantly, Aeneas first acts in Dido's presence not as a lover, but as a hero who will save her kingdom. Dido has little future with him for reasons having to do not with garden-variety power politics and conspiracies, but with destiny and the decline and fall of civilisations. At her suicide she even transcends her own plot role as the woman spurned

Figure 27 Photograph published in *L'Illustration* on 7 October 1899 of set-builders constructing the wooden horse for *Les Troyens*: the Parisian première of Acts I and II would take place on 15 November 1899 at the Opéra. Louise Goldberg has shown that not until 1921 did the Paris Opéra perform the work as a whole (in 'condensed form'). But the (complete) opera inaugurated the new Opéra Bastille on 17 March 1990, conducted by Myung-Whun Chung. See Kemp, *Les Troyens*, 157, for a discussion of sources concerning the appearance of the horse on stage.

and prophesies the glory of Rome. In short, the public dimension consumes a much greater part of the entire fabric than in classical grand opera which, for all its *grandeur*, places considerable weight on the interaction of characters. Little place exists in the world of *Les Troyens* for the sudden changes of plot direction of the boulevard theatre, changes that often function to set the plight of the individual in relief against politics and society. In place of a continuously evolving interplay among several characters, a host of players revolves about the constant figure of Aeneas.

Because of his radically different dramaturgical premise, Berlioz could dip at will into musical procedures associated with grand opera with little risk of being charged with derivativeness. For the *Marche Troyenne* at the end

of Act I he manipulates the off-stage effect so favoured by grand opera composers with great compositional virtuosity by placing three hidden groups
at different distances from the stage (and the listeners in the hall). According
to Berlioz's final instructions for the scene, the great horse seems to move
gradually closer, but it never actually appears: an off-stage effect to end all
off-stage effects. One suspects that this would have been just as unthink-
able to Meyerbeer with the same situation under pen as it has been to most
producers of *Les Troyens* for over a century. In his last version of the *mise-
en-scène* for the Marche, Berlioz avoids spectacle when it is most expected.
This strategy removes attention from the horse as a material object to the
idea represented by the horse – to Fate, to hubris, to catastrophe and to later
triumph out of ashes. Conceived in this way, then, the passage is doubly
ironic: first, in the context of an aesthetic of monumentality and, second, in
the use of a heroic march that is ultimately enlisted for triumphant purposes
at a moment of impending doom.

The *Ottetto et Double Chœur* occurring just before is another episode that
closely adheres to grand opera practice. Here Berlioz plays on the convention
of the *concertato* ensemble discussed above in relation to *Le Cid*. Whereas
normally such a movement occurs as a reaction to an event that happens
before everyone's eyes, here it is spawned by Aeneas's report of Laocoön's
off-stage death so that, once again, an idea prevails over material stage
action. Like so many other *concertato* ensembles, the movement begins
with imitative entries, but they unfold in a completely idiosyncratic way:
Berlioz twice transposes a long chromatic subject downwards by whole-
step (producing a modulatory scheme from F♯ minor to E minor to D
minor, leading to a cadence in C). A collective cry 'Horreur!' on a chord a
tritone away from the tonic (coloured by magnificent trombone pedal notes)
punctuates each rendition of the subject (the first statement is shown in
Ex. 15.2a). In this way a local level expressive effect mirrors the tonal course
of the entire bizarre fugal exposition. As in other *concertato* movements,
the second half is given over to a lyrical phrase that the soprano carries to
a gigantic climax. Underneath this, the chorus and principals continue to
stutter in disbelief, thereby producing a layered effect of two superimposed
textures. The movement ends with ominous muttering and a final *fortissimo*
articulation of the word 'horreur' that had punctuated its first section, but
now on the tonic chord (instead of on the sharpened fourth degree of the
scale) so as to produce a long-term musical resolution (Ex. 15.2b).

Many similar enrichments and redefinitions of conventional practice fill
Les Troyens. The important point for our purposes is that musical procedures which pre-date grand opera are *also* plentiful and treated with
just as much imagination. Cassandra's first recitative begins with double-
dotted rhythms appropriate to a high character in eighteenth-century opera

Example 15.2a Berlioz, *Les Troyens*, Act I, no. 8, 'Ottetto et Double chœur', opening: 'Appalling punishment! Mysterious horror!'

(Ex. 15.3). But one would be hard pressed to find a similar harmonic range in Gluck, or chords coloured by stopped horn notes as well as flutes, clarinet and oboes in their lowest registers. Dido is introduced in Act III by a *chant national* over a stately, archaic walking bass, the passive and glorious recipient of Carthaginian praise (Ex. 5.1, p. 77). After she ignites the ire of her subjects for the neighbouring war-lord Iarbas in her subsequent *air*, they suddenly explode in the same march, now metrically reinterpreted and taken at double speed, 'con fuoco' and without walking bass. In this way, the *chant national*, first static and ceremonial, becomes a kinetic response to a political predicament. A point of State seems implied: patriotism as not only a matter of lyrical effusion but of action. Once again one would be hard pressed to find this in the eighteenth-century literature. Berlioz's original idea for a closing tableau in which Dido prophesied the French

Example 15.2b Berlioz, *Les Troyens*, Act I, no. 8, conclusion: 'Victim of divine anger, eaten alive by those hideous monsters!'

empire in Africa suggests a Baroque-like conceit of celebrating the grandeur of monarchy. The final version still shows an apotheosis where Roman legions escort an emperor accompanied by 'poets and artists'. For a listener to make the leap from such a cultivated Roman emperor to Napoleon III would be consistent with the entire history of the Opéra, an institution subsidised massively by the State throughout its history (and connected to what had been Napoleon's palace by a newly created boulevard, as we have observed). Do Berlioz's artists and poets – like Gounod's Adoniram and Saint-Saëns's (and Berlioz's own) Benvenuto – deal as equals with monarchs? Perhaps, to judge by Berlioz's own self-image and the dedication of the score 'to the *divine* Virgil' (emphasis added).[49] Artistic pretensions of this sort were certainly not characteristic of the *ancien régime*. Also in tune with his own century is Berlioz's suggestion of History as a dialectical process, through a closing musical juxtaposition of Carthaginian imprecations with the *Marche Troyenne*. As much as Rome is celebrated at the conclusion of *Les Troyens*, the last passage reminds listeners that, even after the catastrophic events depicted in the opera, the final synthesis would still be hard won.

Berlioz's opera thus draws explicitly upon a substantial portion of the Paris Opéra's musical heritage up to the Second Empire and not merely upon specific musical and scenographic techniques of grand opera. Although Berlioz's contemporaries detected more Gluck and Spontini than

Example 15.3 Berlioz, *Les Troyens*, Act I, no. 2: Cassandre's recitative and air, 'The Greeks have disappeared!'

mature grand opera, Meyerbeer, Halévy and company cannot be completely discounted as influences. In this respect *Les Troyens* encapsulates a century or more of a great operatic tradition. Berlioz distilled an ideal from a range of practices at the house, to the point that, as Ian Kemp astutely remarked, 'it seems the Opéra was created for *Les Troyens* rather than vice versa'.[50] Institution and musical practice seem synonymous: certain conventions are not merely derived from Gluck or grand opera but rather generated by an independent spirit with deep empathy for a tradition. *Les Troyens* shares features with grand opera because the genre is an organic part of that tradition. But Berlioz's opera transcends that genre completely, as it transcends Gluck's operas. And for all Berlioz's utterly sincere reverence for Virgil, it is hard to conceive of a more nationalistic project. As a compendium of Opéra practices, his work is inseparable from the greatness of France as a nation. Few critics will deny that the grand operas defended by nationalistic and conservative critics in face of the Wagnerian wave at the *fin de siècle* sound feeble beside Berlioz's astounding accomplishment.

PART FOUR

Transformations of grand opera

16 Richard Wagner and the legacy of French grand opera

THOMAS GREY

In his 'Reminiscences of Auber' (1871), Richard Wagner recalled he had occasionally met the elder composer over ices at the Café Tortoni back in 1860, at the time the revised *Tannhäuser* was in rehearsal at the Paris Opéra. On one occasion, when Auber was asking after these preparations, Wagner explained to him something of the nature of the opera. Auber 'gleefully rubbed his hands together' and replied, 'Ah, so there will be spectacle; it will be a success, then, never fear!'[1] Wagner recounts the anecdote with the irony of hindsight, of course, since the Paris *Tannhäuser* production of the following March (1861) turned out to be a legendary fiasco. Auber naively assumed that *Tannhäuser* was cut from the familiar cloth of Parisian grand opera, and that French audiences would respond favourably to such elements as the fleshy ballet-pantomime with its nymphs and satyrs, the procession of pilgrims through a 'Romantic' landscape of changing seasonal hues, the hunting party at the end of Act I, and the ceremonial entry of the Thuringian nobles to the song-contest at the court of Landgrave Hermann in Act II. It was by no means an unreasonable assumption. Granted, Wagner had updated the score (the opening 'Bacchanale' and the scene between Tannhäuser and Venus in Act I, particularly) with touches of the advanced chromaticism and the sequential-developmental style of *Tristan und Isolde*, quite at odds with the comfortable phraseology of much grand opera. But when *Tannhäuser* was originally composed, in 1845, Wagner's experience of French grand opera was still relatively fresh, and its impact still considerable. Even in the 1861 version of *Tannhäuser*, the roots of the 'music drama' in classic grand operas of the not-so-distant past – the works of Meyerbeer, Halévy, and the original prototype of the genre, Auber's *La Muette de Portici* (1828) – remain palpable.

By the time he wrote his 'Reminiscences of Auber' in 1871, Wagner was able to revisit his youthful enthusiasm for *La Muette de Portici* with a relatively open mind, praising almost unreservedly a work that had profoundly influenced his beginnings as an opera composer. Now Auber had passed on, as had Rossini (1868), Meyerbeer (1864), and Halévy (1862). The recent defeat of France by Prussia, the unification of the German states and the incipient plans for a Wagner festival-theatre in Bayreuth also made it easier for the composer to put aside, for the moment, his old animus against things Parisian, rooted in the *Tannhäuser* fiasco of 1861, but even more in the failure of his first attempt to 'conquer' the French capital during an extended sojourn there in 1839–42. The ghosts of French grand opera that had long haunted Wagner's memory could now be put to rest. Yet the spirit of the genre lived on: as much in Verdi's newly premièred *Aida* as in Wagner's own *Götterdämmerung*, whose long-deferred composition was only now being undertaken. Wagner's confrontation with French grand opera – a deeply conflicted one, artistically and psychologically – was a life-long affair.

Early encounters with grand opera: the road to *Rienzi*

If the Viennese instrumental classics and Weber's operas were the formative influences of Wagner's musical childhood and school-days, French grand opera was that of his coming-of-age as a dramatic composer in the 1830s. He was later fond of representing the period of his second and third operas – *Das Liebesverbot* (1834–35) and *Rienzi* (1838–40) – as a sowing of aesthetic wild oats, a prolonged musical adolescence he could look back on with bemused indulgence. During these years Wagner was swept up in the rebellious, hedonistic values of the 'Young Germans' who rejected the tradition of German idealism, especially the ubiquitous influence of Hegelian metaphysics, in favour of a creed of sensuous immediacy, anti-authoritarian politics, and 'freedom of expression'. The first experience of French grand opera, even as produced in the German provinces, made a vivid and lasting impression.

La Muette de Portici, he recalls in the 'Reminiscences of Auber', 'took us all by surprise as something entirely new'. (As usual, Wagner speaks for 'everyone'.) Comparing it with Rossini's and Jouy's *Guillaume Tell* (1829), to the latter's disadvantage, he elaborates on the revolutionary impact of the Auber–Scribe collaboration:

> [S]uch a vivid operatic subject was a complete novelty – the first real drama in five acts with all the attributes of a genuine tragedy, down to the actual tragic ending. This [latter] fact alone caused a great stir, I recall . . . [E]ach of these five acts presented a drastic picture of the greatest vivacity, in which arias and duets in the conventional operatic sense were scarcely to be detected any more, or at least – with the exception of the prima donna's aria in the first act [Elvira: 'Plaisirs du rang suprême / A celui que j'aimais'] – no longer had this effect. Now it was the entire act, as a larger ensemble, that gripped one and carried one away.[2]

Described in these terms, it is easy to trace the genealogy of Wagnerian 'music drama' back to the earliest grand opera.

Rossini's *Guillaume Tell* was never in Wagner's repertory as a conductor in the 1830s or 1840s, and there is no evidence that he ever saw it staged. *La Muette de Portici*, on the other hand, played a prominent role in his early professional career. The twenty-year-old Richard rehearsed *La Muette* as choral répétiteur for his older brother Albert in Würzburg; later he took up the work on his own as conductor in Magdeburg in 1834–36, and again in Riga in 1837–38.[3] In Würzburg he and Albert also attempted to stage Meyerbeer's *Robert le Diable* (presumably in a much scaled-down version). The combined influence of these early grand operas, with their vigorous dramatic character (and *Charakteristik*), together with comic operas of Auber (*Le Maçon, Fra Diavolo*), Hérold's *Zampa*, and Italian operas of Rossini, Bellini and Paër resulted in the ambitious, deliberately cosmopolitan effort of Wagner's second opera, *Das Liebesverbot*.[4]

Das Liebesverbot ('The Ban on Love') was composed in the course of 1835 to a libretto sketched the preceding summer, based on Shakespeare's *Measure for Measure*. As a comic opera in two (lengthy) acts, it could be seen to take Rossini's comedies or Mozart's *Don Giovanni* as a point of orientation. On closer inspection, however, the influence of French grand opera is already in evidence (for one thing, *Das Liebesverbot* is essentially through-composed). *Measure for Measure* is only marginally a comedy: the threat of execution facing Claudio for his breach of a severe legislation suppressing any form of sexual licence gives the drama a serious underpinning. While Wagner infuses his operatic version with a larger quantity of comic business than found in the original play, it is more a *semiseria* work than a comic one, and of distinctly 'grand' proportions at that.[5] Transposing the action from Shakespeare's rather abstractly conceived Renaissance Vienna to Palermo, Wagner not only underscored the contrast between a healthy Mediterranean sensualism and the prudish 'northern' hypocrisy of the German viceroy Friedrich (Shakespeare's Angelo), in the spirit of 'Young German' moral rebellion; he also sought to emulate the sunny, southern 'local colour' of the choral-ensemble tableaux, *chœurs dansés* and ballet movements in *La Muette*, with its Neapolitan setting, and the picturesque Sicilian ambience of *Zampa* and *Robert le Diable*.

It was above all the lively musical 'stage pictures' of these recent French operas that opened up new horizons to Wagner (in 'Reminiscences of Auber' he speaks of the birth of a 'picturesque' or theatrically 'sculpted' music).[6] The animated D major Carnival scene that opens the Act II finale of *Das Liebesverbot*, for example, takes a clear cue from the 'market chorus' (also in D: see Ex. 17.1a, p. 356) in Act III of *La Muette*.[7] The 'naturalistically' fragmented antiphonal exchanges of the insurrection chorus at the end of this act are later echoed – and much extended – in many of Wagner's choral scenes up through *Lohengrin*, and beyond. Even more far-reaching was the impact of the accompanied pantomime of Auber's mute heroine, Fenella, on Wagner's conception of leitmotif as orchestrally embodied gesture.[8]

Solo and duet numbers in *Das Liebesverbot* nearly all aspire to the scope and weight of grand opera. March rhythms and extensive phrase repetitions in the Isabella–Luzio duet in Act I, for example, anticipate the idiom of *Rienzi*, as does much of the Isabella–Claudio duet, when she tests the mettle of her imprisoned brother at the opening of Act II. (Indeed, the march rhythms that pervade *Rienzi*, like its four-square phraseology infused with expressive appoggiaturas and mode-mixture, can be traced to Auber's score, and to Spontini, by way of *Das Liebesverbot*.) And while the dramaturgy and basic musical material of the two finales are essentially comic in nature, their massively extended scope – 177 and 109 pages of vocal score, respectively – seems to vie with the most extravagant of grand opera finales (*Rienzi*'s included). With its interminable cadential extensions, the *stretta* of the Act I finale almost gives the impression of a deliberate parody, though in fact it only reflects the young composer's uninhibited ambitions.

Unrealised 'Parisian' projects

A single chaotic and drastically under-rehearsed quasi-performance of *Das Liebesverbot* attempted in Magdeburg on 29 March 1836 did nothing to advance its author's reputation. That the performance happened at all offers an early proof of Wagner's indomitable determination (and charisma). It must also have made very clear to him the extreme disparity between his aspirations as an opera composer and the limited means available to him as a provincial music director. But since Giacomo Meyerbeer had now succeeded in establishing himself as the leading light of the Paris Opéra with *Robert le Diable* (1831) and *Les Huguenots* (1836), Richard Wagner saw no reason why he should not follow suit.

Indeed, he was already thinking along these lines within a year or two of his initial decision to pursue an operatic career path in the early 1830s. 'My plan is now quite firmly and unshakably fixed', he wrote to his young friend and confidant, Theodor Apel, in October 1834, almost immediately upon securing his first real position as director of Heinrich Bethmann's travelling opera troupe (on whom he was to inflict the *Liebesverbot* débâcle). With the money and reputation he fantasised winning through performances of *Das Liebesverbot* across Germany, once his first opera, *Die Feen*, had paved the way, he and Apel would settle for a time in Italy, starting in the spring of 1836. 'In Italy I'll compose an Italian opera, or maybe several, depending on how it goes; then once we're tanned and vigorous, we'll turn to France, and in Paris I'll compose a French opera, and God only knows where I'll be

after that point! *Who* I'll be, that I know; – no longer a German philistine.'[9]
Of course, things did not go so smoothly as imagined by the optimistic
twenty-one-year-old, and the Italian phase of the plan was soon dropped.
(After Meyerbeer and Otto Nicolai, the century-long tradition of German
composers polishing their lyrico-dramatic skills in Italy was in any case
growing obsolete.) But the cosmopolitan impulse did not abandon Wagner:
within a couple of years he was laying the groundwork for his campaign to
conquer Paris, the operatic capital of the nineteenth century.

Thus in the summer months of 1836 Wagner sketched an operatic scenario 'in five acts, following the opulent French design'.[10] Like *Rienzi*, afterwards, the project was based on a recent historical novel, in this case one by
Heinrich König entitled *Die hohe Braut*, set against the post-revolutionary
conflicts between France and Italy in Savoy and the French Riviera. A scenario was sent off to none other than the leading librettist of French opera,
Eugène Scribe, with the naive request that he work out a full-length French
libretto on this plan. The young German would then set it to music and,
with Scribe's assistance, have it produced at the Opéra. Wagner was evidently
unaware, as Robert Gutman points out, of the high price-tag attached to
Scribe's services.[11] Presumably he was ready to share some of the projected
profits from this scheme with the obliging Scribe.[12]

Despite the relatively 'modern', historically precise setting in Italian-
occupied Nice of 1793 and some contemporary military references, most of
Die hohe Braut as Wagner adapted it could just as well transpire in any
of the medieval or Renaissance settings favoured by grand opera. (The
text contains no concrete allusion to the French Revolution or its political aftermath.) The heroine, Bianca, is the daughter of the proud and ambitious Marchese Malvi, who has affianced her to a similarly proud and
unscrupulous nobleman, Duke Rivoli. Bianca loves a commoner, Giuseppe,
who is tempted into conspiracy against the Italian régime by Sormano, a
groundskeeper for Rivoli who married the Duke's sister, Giovanna, in secret.
When Rivoli discovered this, the pair was punished and separately exiled.
Disguised as an itinerant singer under the name Brigitta, Giovanna eventually drowns herself in despair. This story convinces Giuseppe to join in the
revolt against the Marchese and Rivoli.

The element of popular uprising against a corrupt nobility, staged in
picturesque surroundings (here, the *alpes maritimes*), recalls both *Guillaume Tell* and *La Muette de Portici*. In acquiescing to marry the hated
Rivoli in order to save Giuseppe, Bianca resembles Caterina Cornaro, heroine of Halévy's *La Reine de Chypre*, a work Wagner would get to know all
too well through producing various arrangements of the score for Maurice
Schlesinger in Paris, between the time he drafted the *Hohe Braut* scenario
and working up a full libretto later in Dresden. (In both operas the wedding

ceremony is drastically interrupted, following one of grand opera's most familiar gambits.) Bianca's determination to rescue her true love, Giuseppe, when he is imprisoned by the Duke, recalls of course Beethoven's Leonora and the whole rescue-opera genre (but also Isabella in *Das Liebesverbot*). The detail that the high-born Bianca and the commoner Giuseppe have in fact been nursed by the same woman in their infancy represents a variant of a theme that held some deep fascination for Wagner: a devotion between brother and sister that either rivals an amorous relationship (Isabella–Luzio, Rienzi–Irene) or becomes one (Siegmund–Sieglinde).

Another unrealised plan for a historical opera in the 'grand' Parisian manner, *Die Sarazenin* (*The Saracen Woman*) (sketched soon after Wagner returned to Germany in 1842), also broached the motif of ambiguously construed sibling love. Here the heir to the Hohenstaufen dynasty in early medieval Sicily, Manfred (son of Friedrich Barbarossa), falls in love with the mysterious, visionary woman of the title, who turns out to be his half-sister.[13] The project was put aside in favour of *Tannhäuser* before reaching fruition as a full libretto text. While Wagner did briefly contemplate working up the Norse fairy-tale saga material of *Wieland der Schmied* (*Wieland the Smith*) for the stage of the Paris Opéra in the early months of 1850, and while *Tannhäuser* was of course later adapted for the Opéra (with limited success), *Rienzi* was to be his only completed essay in the genre of Parisian grand opera in its relatively 'pure' form.

Rienzi: a grand opera for the Germans

Rienzi was conceived as Wagner's ticket to international success *via* Paris. While eking out a tenuous living as music director in far-off Riga he de-cided on Bulwer-Lytton's recently published historical novel, *Rienzi, Last of the Roman Tribunes* (1835), as a promising vehicle for the grand opera he longed to create, and determined to execute this project on such a 'recklessly' lavish scale that its only hope of production would be with a major opera company – ideally the Paris Opéra.[14] (*Rienzi* did eventu-ally succeed in launching Wagner's career at home in Germany, when the Dresden Court Opera mounted a deluxe production in Gottfried Semper's new, elegant theatre in the autumn of 1842, with two of Germany's leading operatic talents of the day, the dramatic soprano Wilhelmine Schröder-Devrient and the proto-Heldentenor Joseph Tichatscheck.)

The idea for *Rienzi* originated in the summer of 1837, and composition began a year later in Riga. Wagner was all the while thinking of this project as the one that would catapult him from the obscurity of this outpost beyond the furthest frontiers of East Prussia into the limelight of the French capital.

By the time he first set foot in France, at Boulogne-sur-mer in August 1839 (where Meyerbeer happened to be summering at the time), he had a complete libretto and the music of Acts I and II fully drafted. Orchestration of these first two acts was completed while at Boulogne, and Wagner took the opportunity to show his work-in-progress to Meyerbeer, who was favourably impressed by what he saw. Thus began the brief and strained 'friendship' between Wagner and the figure he would go on to vilify as the virtual antichrist of modern operatic culture. Over the next year-and-a-half in Paris he plunged ahead with the massive *Rienzi* score, completing Acts III to V plus the overture between 15 February and 19 November 1840. During that time Meyerbeer certainly made some honest efforts to help his younger compatriot, although whether he could have secured Wagner a commission for the Paris Opéra itself remains doubtful.

Also difficult to assess is just what impact Wagner's operatic experiences in Paris had on the remainder of his own grand opera score. In his auto-biographical writings the composer was wont to stress the reorientation to German music (and especially the Beethovenian legacy of 'absolute music') he underwent during these years – partly in reaction against the culture-industry of Parisian opera and other genres of musical entertainment, but also as a response to performances by the Société des Concerts du Conservatoire and to the music of Berlioz. On the other hand, he did attend some (if not many) performances at the Opéra, including the première of Halévy's *La Reine de Chypre*, which he reported for the Dresden *Abendzeitung* as well as discussing it within a more general essay on 'Halévy and the French Opera' for the *Revue et gazette musicale*. Furthermore, he became intimately acquainted with Halévy's score (as mentioned) and that of Donizetti's *La Favorite*, premièred a year earlier (December 1840), in producing piano-vocal scores of both works for the publisher Maurice Schlesinger, along with various other instrumental arrangements of excerpts from both scores.[15] Yet all this work came after *Rienzi* had been completed, apart from various cuts and revisions at the time of the Dresden première, and it is hardly likely to have influenced his work on the *Flying Dutchman*, mostly carried out in the summer of 1841, which belonged to an 'entirely different genre', as Wagner himself stressed.[16]

Rienzi is a strange amalgam of youthful enthusiasm – even inspiration – and overblown grandiloquence. The unchecked ambition of the score (even judged in terms of sheer dimensions) and its tendency to 'harangue' the listener into submission are qualities characteristic of the composer at all stages of his evolution. They also have something to do with Wagner's strong self-identification with the opera's hero: a charismatic demagogue with a messianic sense of his own mission, similarly fired by a vivid remembrance of past injustices which he is determined to avenge. (Rienzi's young brother has been killed as a bystander in the skirmishes of the feuding Roman nobility.) Rienzi is in some part a victim of the fickle mob, the common people of Rome who abandon him when his magnanimity towards the corrupt nobility ends in bloodshed, and when the Church itself turns against him. But his ultimate demise in the burning Capitol is construed as an act of heroic martyrdom, Rienzi and his sister Irene sacrificing themselves to Rienzi's noble vision of a free republic. A century later, when *Rienzi* was all but forgotten by most Wagnerians, the opera still had a fervent champion in Adolf Hitler. No less than Wagner, Hitler surely perceived the figure of Rienzi as affirming the ultimate heroism of his own reckless pursuit of a messianically construed 'mission', as well as justifying suspicion of any ally who did not share in this vision with absolute, unquestioning faith.[17]

While even later in life he maintained that he had been genuinely inspired by the subject of *Rienzi*, Wagner never thought to conceal his outright emulation of French grand opera models here, or his goal of achieving first and foremost an effective, even overwhelming musical-theatrical spectacle:

> 'Grand opera', with all its scenic and musical display, its effect-laden and massively scaled musical passions stood before me [as a model]; not simply to imitate it, but to outdo all previous examples of it through a reckless outlay of means, that was my artistic ambition . . . The grand opera constituted, in artistic terms, the spectacles through which I regarded the *Rienzi* material . . . I saw it only in the shape of 'five acts', with five brilliant 'finales', with hymns, processions and the musical clash of arms.[18]

Not without a certain touch of casuistry, however, Wagner reconciles this pragmatic goal (in same 1852 text) with his then recently formulated principles of operatic reform. He reports approaching the score with an abstract (musical) intention of creating duets and trios according to contemporary fashion; it was only because the dramatic text had been conceived 'operatically' from the outset that he responded with appropriately traditional (if, indeed, expanded) operatic forms. Similarly with regard to the ballet:

> [B]y no means did I have to concoct the pretext for a ballet from my material; but with the eyes of an opera composer I perceived a natural opportunity for one in the festival that Rienzi prepares for the populace, and in which he is to have performed for them a drastic scene from ancient history: this was the history of Lucretia and the subsequent expulsion of the Tarquin kings from Rome. In every aspect of my enterprise I was guided solely by the nature of the material, although that material had been selected strictly according to the grand opera form that continued to govern my imagination.[19]

This circular mode of rationalisation could be applied to the traces of grand opera present throughout the rest of Wagner's oeuvre: because the material had originally been filtered through a grand-operatic lens (even in *Götterdämmerung* or *Parsifal*, to some extent), the 'effects' and dramaturgy of grand opera remained a legitimate means of realising it.[20]

Despite typical (post-Wagnerian) perceptions of grand opera as tending towards the bloated and static, *Rienzi* proves how well the form succeeds – even at its most 'bloated' dimensions – in generating a dynamic, propulsive sense of drama, if a musically stylised one. There is no doubt that Wagner's appreciative comments on this aspect of *La Juive* and *Les Huguenots* in the articles written during the Paris years were entirely sincere, as was his praise for the cosmopolitan, 'universal' stylistic synthesis achieved in these works (see n. 22 below). It is the mission, he maintains, of a new Franco-German school (Halévy, Meyerbeer, and now Wagner) to take the 'thin' but malleable framework of Italian opera and nourish it, 'bulk it up' dramatically and musically, to produce the international heavyweight cultural champion that is modern grand opera. Hence Wagner's awestruck admiration for the 'gigantic, almost oppressive expansion of forms' conjoined with the 'most pleasing proportions' in Meyerbeer's operas, the ingeniously calculated organisation and pacing of his ensembles. His praise for the celebrated 'Consecration of the swords' in Act IV of *Les Huguenots* (cf. p. 203) reflects precisely the kind of thing he strove to realise in his own *Rienzi*:

> Just consider how the composer has succeeded in maintaining a continuous intensification of excitement [*fortwährende Steigerung*] throughout this tremendously extended number, never lapsing for a moment, but arriving, after a furiously impassioned outburst, at the highest fever pitch, the very ideal of fanatical expression![21]

Wagner must surely have had the 'Consecration of the swords' scene in mind when composing the Trio and Chorus (no. 11) that opens Act IV of *Rienzi*, a nocturnal conspiracy between the disaffected Roman magistrates (Cecco and Baroncelli) and Adriano with the aim of stirring up a public mutiny against Rienzi's leadership.[22] The same ideal of gradual 'intensification of excitement' continues to provide a fundamental structuring principle throughout Wagner's later works.

Whatever we wish to make of *Rienzi* within the composer's own oeuvre, the fact remains – one that ought to be acknowledged more often than it is – that it is one of very few original German adaptations of the French grand opera type dating from the 1830s and 1840s, and perhaps the only successful one. (Franz Lachner's *Catarina Cornaro* of 1841, to a translation of the libretto by J. H. V. de Saint-Georges for Halévy's *La Reine de Chypre*, is among the few other examples, though stylistically closer to Donizetti's operas.) The sprawling central acts (II and III) demonstrate how Wagner maximised the element of grandiose spectacle, integrated into a dramaturgy of political conspiracy, clemency, betrayal and revenge. Act II is the most heavily infused with ceremonial grandeur, while both acts (but especially Act III) exemplify how much Wagner learned from the likes of Spontini, Halévy and Meyerbeer with respect to broadening the formal outlines of musical numbers to encompass extended, complex, contrasted actions and emotions.

Acts II and III of *Rienzi* each consist of only three designated numbers: in each act a central number is framed by an ensemble introduction and a 'grand finale'. In Act II this central number is the trio with chorus in which Adriano confronts his father and the other conspiring patricians; in Act III it is Adriano's solo scene and aria portraying his distress at having to choose between filial loyalty, on one hand, and his love for Irene and devotion to her brother's noble cause, on the other. Apart from Rienzi's famous 'prayer' at the beginning of Act V ('Allmächt'ger Vater, blick' herab!'), Adriano's scene in Act III is the only solo aria of the score, and in any case the only one that constitutes a complete scene-complex with dramatic recitative, cantabile and cabaletta (the latter dramatically compressed into just a few phrases, following his agitated response to the bells signalling the plebeians' uprising against the treacherous nobles).

The second act is dominated by ceremonial spectacle, with its leisurely paced choral procession of the 'Heralds of Peace' at the opening and enormous public celebrations embedded in the finale (the pantomime narration of the rape of Lucretia, followed by a sequence of military games and dances). A complete performance of the pantomime music, including its own interior dance of Lucretia's attendants, plus the full ballet music would last upwards of forty minutes, bringing an uncut performance of the second-act finale alone to nearly an hour's length.[23] This pairing of narrative pantomime and ballet was probably modelled on the similar medieval divertissement-cum-tournament in *La Juive*, also detectable in some of the musical and orchestrational detail; the mix of sacred and secular pomp celebrating Rienzi's first victory for the Roman people in the first-act finale likewise bears traces of the analogous finale in Halévy's opera. The characteristic march-ductus elsewhere in the Act II finale and pervading Act III suggests Spontini, on the other hand, harmonically and melodically updated.

Though culminating in a rousing march-theme for the title character ('Ihr Römer auf! Greift zu den Waffen!'), the freely constructed ensemble-introduction to Act III (composed after Wagner had arrived in Paris) already exhibits traces of the texturally differentiated treatment of the chorus, at moments of dramatic excitement, as a collection of individualised subgroups that one finds in *Tannhäuser*, *Lohengrin* and later *Die Meistersinger*. The choral voices join in unison or block-chords only when crying out for Rienzi, alternately beseeching his leadership and accusing him of betraying their trust. The elaborate interaction of on- and off-stage chorus during the unseen battle between the popular Roman militia and the outlaw nobles at the centre of the finale might well have been suggested by Meyerbeer's portrayal of the St Bartholomew's Eve Massacre in the last act of *Les Huguenots*. There Meyerbeer intercuts the music of the bloodthirsty Catholic posse with the Protestant women singing the Lutheran chorale 'Seigneur, rempart et seul soutien' (see p. 205). In Wagner's finale, the women's chorus invoking the protection of the Virgin is intercut with fragments of the preceding 'battle hymn' to diminished harmonies. Whereas the Huguenot chorale in Meyerbeer is finally silenced by the Catholics, Rienzi's troops prevail and return to the stage with a triumphant reprise of their battle-hymn ('Santo Spirito, cavaliere – Auf, Römer, auf, für Herd und für Altäre'), taken directly from the German translation of Bulwer-Lytton's novel. Their return initiates a further phase of the finale, with choral laments for the fallen, prior to a big *stretta* for chorus and soloists ('Ertönet Freudenlieder'). The dimensions are wholly incommensurate with Meyerbeer's taut, brutal finale, and again indicative of Wagner's aim to outstrip the competition with an opera bigger, louder and longer than anything seen before.[24]

Between grand opera and music drama: *Tannhäuser* and *Lohengrin*

Although it was conceived and executed while Wagner was still in Paris, his next opera after *Rienzi – Der fliegende Holländer* – marked a conscious withdrawal from the ambition to create a 'grand opera' in the French manner. Yet initially he had conceived the 'Dutchman' plan as an alternative project *for* Paris: when he realised that a full-length commission for the Opéra was not about to come his way, he turned his thoughts to a 'curtain raiser in one or two acts', of the kind often featured in a double-bill with a ballet performance (see Table 6.1, p. 94). (Originally, the 'Dutchman' project was planned as a single act in three scenes.) This might explain why, despite the more modest dimensions of *Der fliegende Holländer*, the opera called for some relatively extravagant scenic effects – especially those involving the Dutchman's ship, the storms in Acts I and III, and the uncanny 'singing-contest' between the crews of Daland's ship and the Norwegians during the second of these storm sequences. Even within the scaled-down dimensions of this 'dramatic ballad', the composer evidently hoped to capitalise on the unparalleled stage equipment of the Opéra.

After his return to Germany, however, and his decision to pursue subjects from medieval Germanic epic romances and legend, Wagner neither forgot what he had learned from French grand opera, nor abandoned his earlier belief that a successful renaissance of German opera would require composers to absorb the lessons of Italian vocalism along with the sophisticated interactions of Scribean dramaturgy, a vivid *mise-en-scène*, the orchestral panache of composers like Berlioz and Meyerbeer, and the broad musical-scenic construction pioneered in French opera from *Guillaume Tell* and *La Muette* down to the present.

Tannhäuser and *Lohengrin* are habitually grouped with *Der fliegende Holländer* under the rubric of Wagner's 'Romantic operas', suggesting a culmination of the genre of 'German Romantic opera', a genre up until then rather meagrely represented by Weber's *Der Freischütz* and *Euryanthe* and the works of Marschner and Spohr. But in fact *Tannhäuser* and *Lohengrin* represent precisely the synthesis of operatic idioms Wagner had been advocating throughout the 1830s up to the time of *Rienzi*.[25] One of the latter's first enthusiastic critics – the twenty-one-year-old Eduard Hanslick – had no doubts on this front, however. 'I am of the firm opinion', Hanslick wrote in the *Wiener Allgemeine Musik-Zeitung* in 1846, 'that it is the finest thing achieved in grand opera in the last twelve years, that it is the most significant dramatic creation since *Les Huguenots*, and that it is just as epoch-making in its time as were *Les Huguenots*, *Der Freischütz*, and *Don Giovanni*, each for its respective period of musical history'.[26] Hanslick thus places *Rienzi*, appropriately, on the threshold between the historical grand opera of Meyerbeer and some as yet unlabelled new phase of the genre: in fact, the very 'music drama' of which Hanslick would become a notoriously outspoken opponent within another dozen years.

Tannhäuser and *Lohengrin* are the first of Wagner's operas (and among the first of any) to dispense with the formal division of acts into traditional numbers; within individual acts, the only division is according to 'scene'. Of the two, however, only *Lohengrin* (completed 1848) moves significantly away from the structures of grand opera, which are often replaced by more-or-less continuous series of smaller musical and rhetorical units (of the sort Wagner provisionally named 'poetic-musical periods' in *Opera and Drama*).[27] In *Tannhäuser* (completed 1845), on the other hand, it is easy enough to recognise many of the basic structural lineaments of grand opera, in which a scene-based musical dramaturgy had in any case already come to prevail over smaller structural divisions. Thus, for example, Act II of *Tannhäuser* begins with a solo 'scene and aria' for Elisabeth ('Dich teure Halle'), often excerpted as such. This is followed by a scene and duet for Elisabeth and Tannhäuser that would not be out of place, in formal terms, in any contemporary French opera, moving through a variety of accompanied recitative and *arioso* phases into a concluding duo-Allegro ('Gepriesen sei die Stunde') in which the reunited pair express their happiness. (The melodic cut of this last passage is clearly German, however, in the manner of Weber,

Marschner and Wagner's own early works.) The familiar 'Entry of the Guests' to the Wartburg is of course a classic grand-operatic procession, introducing the episode of the Minnesängers' contest at the centre of the drama. This song contest occupies the position of the politically sanctioned wedding procession or other ceremony typical of most grand opera – going back to such ancestral works as Spontini's *Olympie* – which is then radically disrupted. Thus Tannhäuser's scornful response to Wolfram's and Bitterolf's songs, and his own song praising Venus and the pleasures of the flesh, form the crux that ties together the two legendary sources of the opera (the Tannhäuser–Venus legend and the song contest) as well as the *coup de théâtre* that precipitates a multi-partite *concertato* finale as 'grand' as anything written for the stage of the Académie Royale de Musique. The *stretta* to the finale acquires a distinctive German accent through the up-tempo chorale-prelude idiom touched off by the Landgraf's reference to pilgrims readying themselves for the journey to Rome. The rhythmic convolutions of the ensuing ensemble and men's chorus are a characteristic Wagnerian touch, enlivening a basically homophonic texture with a 'naturalistic' sense of a large crowd of people all speaking at once.

Lohengrin was written at a time (the poem in 1845, the music between 1846 and 1848) when the first ideas for a radical reform of the operatic genre were beginning to germinate in Wagner's mind, but before he attempted to formulate these ideas in writing. All the same, *Lohengrin* remains decisively shaped by the example of French grand opera in numerous points of musical dramaturgy – above all in its second act, which, as in *Tannhäuser*, preserves the outlines of the large central acts (mostly the second and third) of the traditional five-act type.

In its broad contours, Act II of *Lohengrin* could easily be reimagined through the formal lens of Eugène Scribe and his musical collaborators. The opening scene, in which Ortrud and Friedrich von Telramund brood over the latter's defeat in the trial-by-combat with Elsa's still-unknown champion, would be a 'scene and duet', beginning darkly (as does the scene Wagner composed), and moving through recitative-based discussion of the couple's plight towards a cantabile lament over that situation, to a rousing, fast-tempo conclusion in which both figures swear to be avenged for this shameful defeat. Scene 2 again suggests the 'scene and duet' type (which was, after all, the mainstay of grand opera dramaturgy), pitting the unwary heroine, Elsa, against her scheming antagonist, Ortrud. The last three scenes, as numbered in the libretto, would constitute the 'grand finale': the public celebration of Elsa's betrothal to the new 'Protector of Brabant' (as Lohengrin proposes to be called instead of 'Duke', in the progressive, post-feudal spirit of 1848). In the hypothetical 'Scribean' redaction, these nuptials would likely be graced by a picturesque ballet sequence, incorporating perhaps a pantomime jousting match *à la Juive*, or else a series of Flemish peasant dances, culminating in some general hymn of praise and good wishes for the noble couple. Next would come the cue for Ortrud to interrupt, with her charges – or rather insinuations – of sorcery. A grandiose *largo concertato* movement would encompass the multiple responses to this interruption: the general shock of the courtiers and the townspeople, the stunned indignation of Elsa and Lohengrin, with smugly insidious asides from Ortrud and Telramund regarding the success of Ortrud's machinations. Then some formal retort from Lohengrin and/or King Henry would, without resolving the dilemma, initiate a final *stretta* in several accelerating phases, in which the whole assembled cast and chorus expressed their respective feelings of outrage, dismay, confusion and satisfaction.

The traces of this hypothetical 'grand opera' second act to *Lohengrin* are certainly present in the work as Wagner composed it – considerably attenuated, but by no means effaced. The first scene of Act II is one of the opera's most structurally 'advanced' ones, anticipating the through-composed dramatic dialogue of the later music dramas, bound together by a network of nascent 'leitmotifs' (here the various serpentine figures associated with Ortrud and her evil schemes). The scene is anchored by more formally structured 'pillars' (Friedrich's raging *arioso*, 'Durch dich musst' ich verlieren' and his hushed, conspiratorial duo with Ortrud at the end); but these have shrunken to mere vestiges of the solo and duo numbers that would have figured here in a conventional operatic realisation of the drama. The following scene works in a similar way. Ortrud's vehement F♯ minor invocation of the pagan gods ('Entweihte Götter!') at the centre and a short G major duo at the end of the scene ('Ha! dieser Stolz' / 'Lass' mich dich lehren') provide structural pillars around which a more free-flowing dramatic dialogue between Elsa and Ortrud adheres.

The considerable remainder of the act could all be construed as a large, freely developed grand opera finale. The marked contrast between the private nocturnal colloquies of the preceding scenes (1 and 2) and the public assembly that begins with scene 3, announced by reiterated fanfares off stage and through the orchestra, is wholly characteristic, down to the extended dominant pedal and string arpeggiations that accompany the accumulating masses as day breaks. (An ongoing counterpoint between on- or off-stage music and the pit orchestra, thus between different levels of dramatic 'reality' or consciousness, is something *Lohengrin* shares with Meyerbeer's operas, especially the near-contemporary *Le Prophète*.) Scenes 4 and 5 of Act II, following the assembly of the Brabantine people in scene 3, constitute a veritable apotheosis of one of grand opera's most durable gambits: the interrupted wedding ceremony.

La Muette de Portici and *La Juive* provide examples of this scenario which were intimately familiar to Wagner. Another work he knew well, from his labours in arranging the score, was Halévy's *La Reine de Chypre*, involving not one but two interrupted nuptials (see Chapter 13). The wedding of the young patrician Catarina Cornaro to her true love, Gérard de Coucy, in the first act is suddenly thwarted by the political schemes of the Venetian oligarchy; then in Act IV, the celebration of Catarina's politically arranged marriage to Lusignan, the French ruler of Cyprus, is in turn cut short by Gérard, bent on revenge. In *Lohengrin* Wagner did Saint-Georges and Halévy one better, concentrating the two interruptions into a *single* finale. Just as the chorus reaches an especially impressive cadence in E♭ and Elsa starts to ascend the steps of the church, the solemn and dignified procession to the Minster ('Gesegnet soll sie schreiten') is broken off by violent recriminations from Ortrud, casting off the mock contrition and abnegation she had assumed in the preceding scene. Lohengrin and the king arrive and try to put matters right. Eventually the procession begins anew, now in C major, but again at a deliberate and stately pace. This time it is Friedrich who interrupts, after a mere twelve bars of procession, lodging a formal charge against Lohengrin of foul play by means of magic.

However, it is not merely Friedrich's vehement accusation that precipitates the broad contemplative ensemble of general consternation, as would normally be the case with such an operatic *coup de théâtre*. Rather, Wagner infuses it with a further level of psychological tension by building it around Elsa's momentary irresolution when tempted to pose the 'forbidden question' as to Lohengrin's identity and origin. Harmonically, this slow ensemble-tableau ('Welch ein Geheimniss muss der Held bewahren?' / 'In wildem Brüten darf ich sie gewahren') works up to an impressive slow burn, moving several times from C minor to C major by way of circuitous chromatic detours. The whole ensemble is shot through with the snaky diminished contours of Ortrud's motifs, introduced at the beginning of the act. When Elsa at last resolves *not* to pose the question, Lohengrin and the chorus breath a large C major sigh of relief, and the stately music of the 'Procession to the Minster' is at last resumed. There is no frantic *stretta* here. Closure comes instead when the expansive cadential gesture Ortrud had interrupted some twenty-five minutes earlier (there in E♭) returns (now in C) to be completed, with a blaze of trumpets on and off stage (although the motif of the 'forbidden question' casts an ominous shadow even here).

This second act of *Lohengrin* seems to distil the dramaturgy of grand-operatic processional to a kind of essence. Despite the fanfares that greet the dawn, there is otherwise no loud marching, flag-waving or military pomp. In place of the visual spectacle of his models, Wagner 'interiorises' the dramaturgy of procession-and-interruption, focusing attention more than ever on the psychological dilemma of the protagonists and its musical expression.[28]

The dialectics of grand opera and music drama

Shortly after the article 'Judaism in Music' was published in the *Neue Zeitschrift für Musik*, under the pseudonym 'R. Freigedank', Wagner responded to a query from Franz Liszt regarding his presumed authorship of the piece. The letter is revealing, particularly in the way it articulates Wagner's animus towards Meyerbeer as a projection of the privations and humiliations endured in Paris during the years 1839–42. Increasingly, he felt compelled to define his own creative identity in complete opposition to Meyerbeer:

> I cannot exist as an artist in my own eyes or in those of my friends, I cannot think or feel anything without sensing in Meyerbeer my total antithesis, a contrast I am driven loudly to proclaim by the genuine despair that I feel whenever I encounter . . . the mistaken view that I have something in common with Meyerbeer. With all that I want and I feel, I cannot appear before any of these friends . . . until . . . I distance myself completely from this vague image with which so many people still associate me. This is a necessary act if my mature self is to be fully born.[29]

Wagner concludes by congratulating himself for having performed this act 'with such zeal', thereby rendering a great service to many others too timid or deferential to speak their mind in this way.

Wagner would go on to attack Meyerbeer at still greater length, and by name, in Part I of *Opera and Drama*, the longest of the theoretical tracts written during his early years of exile in Zurich. In his two preceding publications (*Art and Revolution* and *The Artwork of the Future*) he had set out the historical, philosophical and ethical grounds for a newly reformed musical drama that would edify modern society in a manner analogous to ancient Greek tragedy in its day. In *Opera and Drama* he tried to describe – if in an immensely prolix and roundabout way that betrayed his own perplexity on the matter – the kind of thing this new musical drama would be. Its musical realisation would be grounded in the very nature of myth and drama, tapping deep into the individual and collective national psyche, while the Meyerbeer–Scribe operas, on the other hand, are criticised as a shameless, aesthetically bankrupt concession to the appetites of the modern urban bourgeoisie, trading on external, unmotivated 'effect', or rather what Wagner famously called 'effects without causes' ('Wirkungen ohne Ursache'). His example of such operatic 'effect' for its own sake is the electric-light sunrise and march-like hymn celebrating the resolve of the false prophet, John of Leyden, to march against the city of Münster in Act III of *Le Prophète*.[30]

If the polarity between Meyerbeerian *Effekt* and Wagnerian *Wirkung* is scarcely as fundamental as implied in *Opera and Drama*, there *was* perhaps a genuinely dialectical quality to Wagner's confrontation with grand opera, in which the genre was gradually 'sublated' (in Hegelian terms) within the music drama – raised to a new, 'higher level' rather than summarily rejected, as Wagner would like to pretend. The 'desperation' that drove him to denounce Meyerbeer and French grand opera is thus closely bound up with the birth-pangs of the later works. If the next work he would go on to compose, *Das Rheingold*, is in many ways the antithesis of grand opera, the later *Ring* operas are rather a synthesis of these opposites, especially *Götterdämmerung*.

At the time of the above-quoted letter to Liszt, Wagner was on the point of augmenting the libretto he had drafted in late 1848 for a 'grand romantic opera', *Siegfried's Death*, with a semi-comic prefatory piece dealing with the hero's youth: *Young Siegfried*. He would soon go on to expand the project, of course, into the tetralogy of *Der Ring des Nibelungen*. But since the early text for *Siegfried's Death* would eventually constitute, with relatively few changes, the final drama of the *Ring* cycle (retitled *Götterdämmerung*), the culminating piece of this revolutionary cycle remains, paradoxically, the one most overtly grounded in the dramaturgy and aesthetics of the abominated Meyerbeerian model.

As Wagner worked 'backwards' from the last *Ring* drama (*Siegfried's Death/Götterdämmerung*) towards the first (*Das Rheingold*) he did progressively implement the critique of traditional operatic practice set out in *Opera and Drama*. Visual display 'for its own sake', ceremonial grandeur, ballet (whether integrated or wholly gratuitous), and the operatic chorus in any form play no part in *Rheingold*, *Walküre* or *Siegfried*. One could argue, however, that even these 'music dramas' benefited as much from Wagner's early absorption of the grand opera genre as they did from his more recent critique of it. The broadly paced musical designs of scenes such as that between Siegmund and Sieglinde in Act I of *Die Walküre* (following Hunding's exit), or between Brünnhilde and Siegmund in Act II (the so-called 'Annunciation of Death' scene) exhibit, in a newly fluid dramatic way, the same kind of carefully calibrated intensification Wagner had admired in the 'Consecration of the swords' scene of *Les Huguenots* or the subsequent 'grand duo' of Raoul and Valentine.[31] In particular, the great love scenes between Siegmund and Sieglinde and between Tristan and Isolde, can be seen as Wagnerian transformations of the 'grand duo' in Act IV of

Scribe's and Meyerbeer's opera: love scenes in which the expression of a socially or politically proscribed attraction transpires under the threat of discovery and punishment, thus heightening the dramatic moment and its musical expression. The end of Act I of *Tristan*, from the drinking of the love-potion, likewise resembles the situation of the Raoul–Valentine duet in this respect. Like the Siegmund–Sieglinde love scene in Act I of *Walküre*, it involves the mutual confession of an 'impossible' yet irresistible passion that finally overwhelms the hesitation of the lovers to reveal their true feelings.

It seems appropriate, in a sense, that the final *Ring* drama should reveal the Wagnerian music drama's living roots in French grand opera.[32] Between drafting the libretto of *Siegfried's Death* in 1848 and completing the score of *Götterdämmerung* in 1874 Wagner did make various cuts and adjustments to the text, but without expunging any of the tell-tale signs of an original grand opera influenced conception. Thus in Act I of both versions of the text, Siegfried and Gunther greet each other in parallel verses ('Begrüße froh, o Held' / 'Nicht Land noch Leute biete ich'), and the scene culminates in an oath-swearing duet of a wholly 'operatic' cut ('Blühenden Lebens labendes Blut'). Acts II and III conclude with classic central-act and final-act gambits of grand opera: the interrupted (and resumed) royal wedding, and the spectacular cataclysm, respectively. Rather than being disguised in the final composition, one might say that each is subjected to the ultimate Wagnerian 'apotheosis'.

The dramatic events in the latter half of Act II, from Hagen's noisy gathering of the vassals to the resumption of the wedding-train just before the curtain falls, could all find their counterpart in the libretti of Jouy, Scribe, Saint-Georges or their successors, despite the primitive Germanic-tribal colouring of the action and setting. In Wagner's realisation, however, the familiar paradigms are thrillingly transformed. The summoning of the vassals (linked to the scene's conclusion by iterations of the semitone motif associated with the plot to murder Siegfried) embeds its C major jubilation within all manner of chromatic inflections and modulations, reflecting the ambiguity of 'grim Hagen's' orders and the dark undertones of his intentions.

The *coup de théâtre* of the interruption is actually diffused across a series of actions and gestures. Before uttering a word, Brünnhilde casts a pall over the proceedings by the brooding motivic fragments that accompany her, and the shocked orchestral outburst when she perceives Siegfried as Gutrune's bridegroom. When she finally articulates her charge that this same Siegfried is her own disloyal spouse, the accusation does not send chorus and soloists into a broad *largo concertato* expressing shock and disbelief; instead, a dialogic exchange builds across a series of increasingly violent outbursts and towards the pair of oaths in which Siegfried and Brünnhilde contest each other's word of honour ('Helle Wehr! Heilige Waffe!'). Believing to have diffused the tense situation, Siegfried initiates the C major music of the wedding train that will bring down the final curtain. In the meantime, however, while he temporarily absents himself, Brünnhilde and Gunther are drawn into a 'revenge' trio with Hagen growing out of fragmentary recollections of Siegfried's oaths in this and the previous act. This revenge trio forms the fierce musical climax to the act when all three voices combine, or rather collide, in their invocations to the higher powers of Wotan or (for Hagen) Alberich. When Siegfried, Gutrune and the wedding-train reappear, Wagner dispenses with the chorus entirely. True to the theories of *Opera and Drama*, the orchestra usurps the role of chorus in this brief, concentrated conclusion, miming both the strains of general celebration and the dissonant undertones of conspiracy in a piece of breathtaking dramatic-gestural counterpoint.

The conclusion of *Götterdämmerung*, and of the whole *Ring* cycle, takes the catastrophic final tableau of French grand opera – the volcanic eruption of *La Muette*, the explosion of the Münster palace in *Le Prophète*, the destruction of Pompeii ending Félicien David's *Herculanum* (1859) or the Last Judgement ending Halévy's *Le Juif errant* (cf. p. 255) – to new, and undeniably effective, extremes.[33] Originally, in *Siegfried's Death*, the final scene was less extreme: the flames of Siegfried's funeral pyre consumed only his body and Brünnhilde's, with no sympathetic conflagration up in Valhalla. The Rhine merely swelled its waters enough to allow the Rhine-maidens to rise up in the background and grasp the Ring and Tarnhelm from the ashes of the pyre, enticing the covetous Hagen to his doom. It was only in the final redaction of the text, as set to music, that these events were augmented to suggest a universal apocalypse encompassing the downfall of the gods and the symbolic purgation of humankind by fire and water – this well *after* Wagner had castigated Meyerbeer for his alleged operatic 'effects without causes'. The conflagration of Valhalla was of course a result of Wagner's deliberations over the fate of Wotan and the gods, and the whole vexed question of what is signified by the *Ring*'s conclusion. In a sense, though, it also represents his capitulation to the imperative of grand-operatic dramaturgy inherent in this ending, in terms of both music and spectacle. In both regards he sought a maximum 'effect' as the most fitting way to conclude his sprawling mythic-allegorical epic. The musical cataclysm and catharsis that accompany Brünnhilde's (and Valhalla's) immolation are a direct response to the stage spectacle prescribed in the text. The *dramatic* 'cause' of these effects is rather less obvious. Wagner, it would seem, had never really abandoned the impulse behind his *Rienzi*: 'not simply to imitate' grand opera, as he had put it, but 'outdo all previous examples through a reckless outlay of means'.[34]

The later music dramas (*Tristan, Die Meistersinger, Parsifal*)

In those works drafted entirely *after* the period of *Opera and Drama* the traces of grand opera are sometimes fainter than in *Götterdämmerung*, but rarely absent altogether. ('Right up to *Parsifal*', Robert Gutman maintains, 'Wagner's aesthetic remained that of the Rue Le Peletier'.[35]) *Tristan und Isolde* comes perhaps the closest (after *Rheingold*) to presenting an 'antithesis' of the genre, while *Die Meistersinger von Nürnberg*, though a comedy, is clearly indebted to grand opera in its extensive ensemble and choral writing (here brought to a new and unsurpassed peak of complexity) and in the mingling of drama, song and spectacle in its concluding scene. With its transcendental pretensions, complexly layered symbolism and modern psychological dimensions (in the character of Kundry), *Parsifal* would seem to distance itself almost as far as *Tristan* from traditional products of the Opéra. Yet the memory of the *corps de ballet* lives on in the Flower Maidens (whose seductive mission in Act II is not unlike that of the nuns in Act III of *Robert le Diable*), and the solemn processionals of the Grail Knights in Acts I and III are yet another metamorphosis of familiar grand opera ingredients.

   Even in *Tristan*, Wagner's most 'uncompromising' music drama, a basic element of grand opera dramaturgy is ingeniously transformed. From the moment that the two recalcitrant lovers imbibe the love potion at the climax of Act I, through to the close of the act, Wagner reinterprets the pointed juxtaposition of private (amorous) and public (political) spheres so fundamental to many classic operatic finales, cutting rapidly between the passionate, overflowing chromaticism of Tristan's and Isolde's rapturous exchanges and the bluff, hearty music heralding their reception in Cornwall. The wordless, orchestrally pantomimed reaction of Tristan and Isolde to the potion – as they wait for its effect, and discover their proud defences suddenly vanishing – replaces the large 'contemplative ensemble' that would normally occupy this critical juncture. In this instance, the public figures (all characters on stage except Brangäne, Isolde and Tristan) remain oblivious to the 'shock' that has struck these three. Rather than a slow ensemble and *stretta* enacting public response to a shocking private disclosure, the conclusion of the act is propelled by its double perspective, the rapid shifting between private passions and public events. The second act of *Tristan* did offer Wagner opportunities for sumptuous grand-operatic display, which (as he sardonically remarked in the 1872 essay 'On the Term "Music Drama" ') he passed up altogether.

He might easily have composed, for example, 'a brilliant courtly ball, during which the unfortunate pair of lovers could have lost themselves at an opportune moment in some leafy bower, where their discovery could provoke a suitably scandalous impression and everything else that follows'[36] – in other words, a broadly paced ensemble of dismay and stupefaction, followed by violent public recriminations and lively expressions of distress on the part of the discovered lovers. Instead, as in much of *Götterdämmerung*, he realised what was, in essence, a stock operatic situation in a drastically new and different manner.

With the appearance of *Die Meistersinger* just a few years after the première of *Tristan*, the 'startled disciples' of the revolutionary master beheld a 'historical opera in the manner of Meyerbeer' (as Robert Gutman put it).[37] While the claim is more than a little exaggerated, there is certainly some truth to Gutman's related claim that the dramatic structure of *Die Meistersinger* resembles Eugène Scribe's 'well-made' plays and librettos (the opéras comiques more than the five-act historical operas, one should probably add). As was noted from the start, there is a return to many familiar requisites of pre-Wagnerian opera: 'distinct arias, marches, choruses, a rousing crescendo finale, a ballet and elaborate ensembles topped by – *horribile dictu!* – a quintet!' Beautiful as it was, says Gutman (invoking the iconography of Walther's prize song), this new aesthetic paradise 'strangely resembled [Wagner's] old descriptions of hell' – i.e. the Parisian operatic spectacles so vigorously denounced in *Opera and Drama*.

In realising the plan for *Die Meistersinger*, one which dated back to 1845, Wagner was naturally aware of its residual 'operatic' qualities, which did not conform to the theories of *Opera and Drama* (bound up as those were with the conception of the *Ring*). Yet to look at virtually any one of those instances of 'operatic form' cited by Gutman, as actually realised in *Die Meistersinger* (with the exception, perhaps, of the Apprentices' Dance in Act III), is to see how here, scarcely less than in *Götterdämmerung*, it has been transformed through the self-conscious, reflective lens of the 'music dramatist'. The 'Prize Song', an aria of sorts, is also a realistic piece of 'natural song' that we hear 'composed' and revised in the course of the opera. The sunny C major march music of the Nuremberg masters is never contained in any single 'number', nor is it limited to a single scene, but infuses even the smallest recesses of the score as a Wagnerian 'leitmotif'. The consistent integration of the chorus into the stage action is again something that would not have been possible without the lessons learned from Auber, Halévy and Meyerbeer (and Scribe). But the nocturnal brawl that closes Act II takes the busy, sometimes mechanical, finale-*strettas* of French opera and of *Rienzi* to undreamt-of levels of textural complexity, drawing especially on the kind of 'naturalistic' fragmentation of choral writing Wagner had long experimented with. And the quiet, moonlit conclusion of the act, as the puzzled night-watchman turns the corner to find the scene suddenly deserted, is a thoroughly novel touch.

Designated as it was to 'consecrate' the stage of the art-temple at Bayreuth, *Parsifal* should by rights be the furthest removed of Wagner's works from the 'corrupt', commercialised urban entertainment that he, and others, criticised in Parisian grand opera. In some ways the two are, indeed, worlds apart. The hovering, ethereal, nearly a-pulsatile music that evokes the mysteries of the Grail and its rituals is a true antithesis of the jaunty beat of those marches, *chœurs dansés* and lively ensembles that typically bring down the curtain of a grand opera. It is impossible to imagine any of the celebrated prima donnas of the Salle Le Peletier in the 1830s and 1840s (or beyond) entertaining the remotest notion of a part like Kundry, despite her role as an exotic seductress in Act II. The fragmentary outbursts that constitute much of her character in Act I and the near-silence to which she is reduced in Act III could not be further from the roles that established the reputations of singers like Cinti-Damoreau, Falcon, Dorus-Gras, Teresa Stoltz, Miolan-Carvalho or Christine Nilsson. (There is, on the other hand, a distant resemblance to Auber's and Scribe's mute heroine, Fenella – a part once interpreted by Wagner's first wife, Minna.)

In other respects, however, even *Parsifal* is indebted to Wagner's earlier initiation into the world of Meyerbeer and Scribe: the central role of liturgical ceremony as a form of *couleur local*, for instance, the deployment of instruments and voices off stage and on to develop a more realistic and imposing sense of theatrical space, or the elaborately painted 'cyclorama' that Wagner himself designed to illustrate the journey from the forest of Monsalvat into the temple itself in Acts I and III – inspired possibly by techniques he had witnessed in Parisian theatres some forty years earlier.[38] The collapse of Klingsor's magic castle at the curtain of Act II could even recall the *opéras féeries* of the very first decades of the century, not to mention the machinery of 'enchanted palaces' going back to the eighteenth century and beyond.

Critics have often sought to separate the modern, philosophical Wagner, as composer and dramatist, from Wagner the stage-designer, still beholden to antiquated notions of Romantic stage 'realism'. Yet the ways in which he remained true to the early ideals of grand opera were critical to his success in capturing the imagination of audiences in his own day, and probably now, as well. The popular, spectacular element of grand opera derived, in many points, from techniques pioneered in the Parisian 'boulevard theatres' of the 1810s and 1820s, elevating a form of urban mass entertainment to 'higher' ends (or pretensions) under the aegis of the official Opéra.[39] If Wagnerian music drama continued the process of elevating such music-theatrical spectacle (in terms of aesthetic pretension, but also in terms of genuine 'technical' sophistication), this populist genealogy is appropriate to the social ideals of Wagnerian theory, which claimed to bring its edifying messages to a broadly defined *Volk*, like the theatre of the ancient Greeks. In reaching this 'universal' audience, Wagner did not scorn to apply lessons learned from a repertory that had made such an impact on him as an enthusiastic and impressionable youth.

17 Grand opera in Russia: fragments of an unwritten history

MARINA FROLOVA-WALKER

This reminded Nikolai Andreyevich [Rimsky-Korsakov] of an incident which he related to me as follows: There was a run-through of *Snegurochka*. Evidently Napravnik didn't care for it very much, because while he was listening to it he thought of nothing except how he could make every conceivable cut. It was terribly long, he claimed. Rimsky-Korsakov ended, saying 'When I protested that in fact they do put on long operas, and cited *Les Huguenots* as a case in point, he couldn't take any more, and in ill temper he declared categorically that my argument didn't prove anything since *Les Huguenots* is a living work while my *Snegurochka* is just – dead.' V. YASTREBTSEV, *REMINISCENCES OF RIMSKY-KORSAKOV*

The familiar story of Russian opera in the nineteenth century begins in 1836, when the first performance of Glinka's *A Life for the Tsar* inaugurated Russian nationalism in music, and at the same time gave Russia its first all-sung opera. After this brief flash, two dark decades followed, when Russian audiences were distracted by the superficial brilliance of Italian opera, until a succession of powerful operas by Musorgsky, Borodin, Rimsky-Korsakov and Tchaikovsky established Russia as a nation with a great operatic culture of its own. Such was the account provided by Soviet writers, and such is the account that has largely been accepted in the West. But this conflicts violently with events on the Russian stage during the nineteenth century, when many operas left out of the account enjoyed commercial success and critical prestige and, conversely, the operas figuring in the account were often failures in their earlier productions. The present canon of nineteenth-century Russian opera certainly owes little to the perceptions of nineteenth-century Russian audiences, critics and musicians.

In the received account we are told that *A Life for the Tsar* was an unprecedented work, the first true Russian opera; accordingly, nothing preceding *A Life* was of artistic significance for the generations of composers following Glinka. Contemporary audiences, however, were well aware of the debt Glinka's opera owed to its predecessors, and indeed a number of earlier operas continued to enjoy more revivals and longer runs than *A Life*: there was, for example, *Askold's Tomb* (Moscow, 1835) by Alexey Verstovsky (condemned by later critics as vulgar and pseudo-Russian), and *Ivan Susanin* (St Petersburg, 1815) by the resident Italian, Catterino Cavos. The continued success of *Ivan Susanin* is particularly telling: the plot which Cavos had chosen was reused by Glinka in *A Life*, but *Ivan Susanin* was evidently not supplanted in the public's affections by its later rival.[1] While *A Life* did not acquire its present prestige for a couple of generations, its initial production was certainly received well; this much cannot be said of Rimsky-Korsakov's or Tchaikovsky's operas, most of which failed badly – in a number of cases, initial production runs were curtailed after only a handful of performances. These facts could hardly be imagined on the basis of the received account. In fact, the Russian operas favoured by the public during the second half of the century were written by composers who do not even figure in the received account: there was Alexander Serov, whose *Judith* (St Petersburg, 1863) and *Rogneda* (St Petersburg, 1865) enjoyed great success, and Anton Rubinstein's *Demon* (St Petersburg, 1875), which broke box-office records in Russia.[2] Even at the time when these operas entered the repertory, however, there were already critics whose conception of Russian nationalism prompted their automatic hostility – chief among these was Vladimir Stasov (1824–1906), the ideologist and propagandist for 'The Five', whose ideas and tastes posthumously shaped Soviet histories of Russian music.[3]

Although the restrictive environment of Soviet scholarship left no room for challenging this narrative, one scholar, Abram Gozenpud, provides us with more than enough information to see how remote it was from nineteenth-century events and perceptions. Gozenpud compiled a seven-volume history of opera in nineteenth-century Russia, based on a lifetime's work in opera house and newspaper archives;[4] while the standard narrative necessarily provided the framework for these volumes, Gozenpud was nevertheless under no obligation to exclude a vast amount of information which fell outside its scope so that readers who are aware of his circumstances are able to draw their own conclusions.[5] It was sufficient for Gozenpud to declare from time to time that this material was of marginal importance, with disclaimers such as the following:

> Although operas by Russian composers did not stir up so much enthusiasm as *Lucia* [*di Lammermoor*] or *Fenella* [*La Muette de Portici*], and although some of them even fell out of the repertory for a time, their influence nevertheless proved immeasurably more profound in the end.[6]

While Gozenpud has therefore provided invaluable and comprehensive primary research, it is left to us to draw the necessary inferences, and to begin comparing the works of Russian composers to the many French, Italian and German operas which we now know were familiar to them and their audiences, for we can no longer take at face value the claims for a pristine Russian national music asserted by nineteenth-century nationalist composers, and then endorsed in the official Soviet history of Russian music. We must now begin to construct a new historical narrative, of which the present essay attempts to piece together a part, by investigating the impact of the French grand opera tradition on Russia.

Reception of French grand opera in Russia

Nikolai Gogol suggested in his 'Notes from Saint Petersburg, 1836' that it was the 'lively and colourful' *La Muette de Portici* (Russian title *Fenella*) and the 'wild' *Robert le Diable* 'saturated with infernal pleasures' which made opera the talk of the town (for a public which now stretched from duchesses to shopkeepers).[7] During the 1830s and early 1840s, the social hierarchy of the audience seating-plan became established: the dress circle and first circle were occupied by the *beau monde*, the second circle by more senior civil servants and prosperous merchants, the third by junior civil servants, the fourth by the household servants of the aristocracy, and the top gallery was open to anyone else who wished to attend.[8] *Fenella* was one of the earliest productions given by St Petersburg's resident German company; it received its Russian première in January 1834 (though in Italian) in the Aleksandrinskiy Theatre and reached a record one hundred performances by mid-1836, the gripes of some critics notwithstanding. Auber's music, however, might not have been *Fenella*'s greatest attraction, for every account of the production bore witness to the astonishing spectacle of Vesuvius erupting in the final scene of the opera.

Shortly after *Fenella* came the St Petersburg production of *Robert le Diable*, a scrupulous replica of the Paris production in every detail of its staging, which apparently made an even stronger impression on the public. This time the opera was sung in Russian: see Table 17.1. The set-designer A. Roller reproduced Ciceri's original sets, and the celebrated Marie Taglioni again danced the role of Hélène, amid Gothic moonlit effects described in an earlier chapter (p. 71). The cloister scene inspired poems and novellas, and even prose reviews were effusive, as the following extract from a review by Apollon Grigoryev bears witness:

> Here the wandering lights shone on the coffins, and to monotonously gloomy sounds the lids started to burst . . . Here they are, the daughters of sin and seduction, enticing, passionate, shameless . . . Now some leaping, possessed, infernal sounds flow . . . They have all gathered together, those light, airy shadows, they want to live and enjoy life's pleasures . . . But they are waiting for someone . . . And here, to the sounds of the possessed, frenzied music it was she, rushing across the stage, the supreme priestess of pleasure . . . Oh look, look how beautiful she is, how naked, how nobly shameless, how her every movement exudes languor and longing. Yes! This is art, an art that has sacrificed all false modesty – this is the apotheosis of passion, the apotheosis of longing. There is frenzy in her eyes, desire in every movement. Look at her pleadings as she implores Robert, how avidly she gulps from a goblet, how tenderly and voluptuously she hands it [to Robert]. And then, to the longing sounds of the cello, to this bacchanalian yet tender, charming and delicately debauching music, look how she now

floats in a sea of sweet dreams, now rushing to Robert's chest with the fire
of desire, now beckoning and calling, now locked in a mad, frenzied
kiss . . . But the infernal sounds leap again . . . Spirits burst out of the abyss.
Your hour has come, airy shadows! And she, the queen of the shadows,
look how desperately she tries to free herself from the claws of the demons,
wriggling like a snake, but all in vain. Your hour has come, your sentence
has been passed, O priestess of passions![9]

Although this production of *Robert* was the first grand opera to be tackled
by a Russian company, the reviewers found the Russian singers more than
adequate. The young bass Osip Petrov (best remembered as Glinka's first
Susanin and Ruslan) was a striking Bertram in make-up that rendered him
unrecognisable; his acting was a work of 'genius', according to Serov's in-
formers, 'better even than Levasseur, for whom this role was written'.[10] This
success notwithstanding, Russian singers were soon eclipsed by Giovanni
Rubini and Pauline Viardot-Garcia, the stars of the Italian opera company
that settled in Russia in 1843, whose international reputation and adulation
by Russian audiences enabled them to command much larger fees. During
the 1840s, *Robert* and *Fenella* proved to be the only productions able to rival
Italian opera, which continued to draw by far the larger audiences.

Although the public favoured Italian opera, French grand opera always
enjoyed the special attentions of the censor – given the character of the genre,
the scenarios inevitably worked their way round to unacceptable scenes of
unrest among the masses, or some manner of political upheaval. Even sung
in Italian, *La Muette de Portici*, for example, was allowed on the stage only
after the plot had been heavily revised, under the new title *Fenella*; reporting
the completion of an acceptable version, Alexander Gedeonov, the director
of the Imperial theatres, wrote to a court minister that 'the libretto is now
completely different from the original, and the title . . . (too well known in
the annals of unrest) has been changed'.[11]

But even this degree of revision could prove insufficient when a Russian-
language production of a grand opera was proposed; thus in 1857 *La Muette*
had to undergo a further transformation, from *Fenella* into *Palermskiye ban-
ditï* (*The Bandits of Palermo*), which obliterated any features of the plot that
might conceivably stimulate the imaginations of the politically excitable.
In the case of Rossini's *Guillaume Tell*, the existing plot was evidently too
robust to admit any degree of adaptation, so the original music was accommodated to an entirely unconnected story, based on Walter Scott's novel
Anne of Geierstein; in this guise, it was presented to the Russian public in
1838/9 under the title *Karl Smelïy* (*Carl the Brave*). *Les Huguenots* was more
fortunate in receiving some concert performances – the lack of staging removed the political sting, the censor decided; but in 1850, when a staged
production was mooted, the censor was roused into action once more, and

Table 17.1 *Principal grand opera productions in St Petersburg (St.P.) and Moscow (M.), 1834–70*

Date	Title	Location	Company
1834, January	Fenella (=La Muette de Portici)	St.P.	German (in Italian)
1834, February	Robert le Diable	M.	German
1834, December	Robert le Diable	St.P.	Russian (in Russian)
1837	La Juive	St.P.	German
1838/9	Carl the Brave (=Guillaume Tell)	St.P.	Russian
1840	Les Huguenots	St.P.	German (concert performance)
1849	Fenella	M.	Russian (in Italian)
1849	Carl the Brave	M.	Russian
1850	The Guelphs and the Ghibellines (=Les Huguenots)	St.P.	Italian
1850	Le Prophète (fragments)	St.P.	concert performance
1853	The Siege of Ghent (=Le Prophète)	St.P.	Italian
1857	The Bandits of Palermo	St.P.	Russian (in Russian)
1857	(=La Muette de Portici)		
1859	La Juive	St.P.	Russian (in Russian)
1862	Les Huguenots	St.P.	Russian (in Russian)
1863	The Bandits of Palermo	M.	Italian
	Le Prophète	M.	Italian
1865	La Juive	M.	Russian and German in collaboration
1866	L'Africaine	St.P.	Italian
1869	John of Leyden (=Le Prophète)	St.P.	Russian

Note: This table covers a period when the two Imperial opera companies (in St Petersburg and Moscow) faced tough foreign competition. The foreigners were often resident in Russia for many years, and received substantial support from the Russian court. Among them was the permanent Italian company which established itself in Russia in 1843, commanding such prominent soloists as Rubini and Viardot-Garcia; the Court so favoured this company that in 1845 it was granted exclusive use of the St Petersburg Grand Theatre. The resident Russian company it displaced moved to Moscow for several years and, when it eventually returned, had to be content with the less prestigious Theatre-Circus building (replaced, on the same site, by the Mariinsky Theatre building in 1860). Much the same occurred in Moscow during the 1860s: the Grand Theatre was allocated to the Moscow branch of the same Italian company for up to five nights a week during the 1860s, leaving the Russian company with just one night a week.[12]

so the story was moved to medieval Italy as *Gvel'fi i gibellinï* (*The Guelphs and the Ghibellines*).

Le Prophète was first staged by St Petersburg's Italian company in 1853, under the title *Osada Genta* (*The Siege of Ghent*).[13] A curious incident at one of the performances, recounted by Anton Rubinstein, demonstrates that the impulse for censorship was not merely the whimsy of over-zealous officials, but came from the top: the Tsar himself approached the singer who had played John of Leyden, and asked him for the crown he had worn on stage; the Tsar took hold of the cross atop the crown and snapped it off, then without comment handed it back to the singer.[14] The next version of *Le Prophète* was given by the Russian company in 1869, now under the title of *Ioann Leydenskiy* (*John of Leyden*); according to Cui, it was a significant improvement on the version which the Italian company had been permitted to perform.[15] The censor's interference notwithstanding, these 1850s productions represent the high tide of Meyerbeer's Russian fame; his works began to receive performances in the provincial theatres such as Odessa or Kiev during the following decades, and were received warmly, but enthusiasm for Meyerbeer never ran so high again in the two capitals. In 1869 Cui noted that *Robert le Diable* could only fill the house to one third of capacity; in contrast, there were still reports of violent altercations over tickets for revivals of *La Sonnambula*.[16] By the 1880s, the public's idols were Verdi and Gounod,[17] but even though interest in Meyerbeer had waned a great deal, we would do well to remember that his operas were still able to command audiences well in excess of those for any operas by Russian composers, as our epigraph attests – Russian opera-goers evidently lacked the nationalist fervour they are supposed to have nurtured, according to the standard narrative.

The influence of French grand opera on Russian composers

The very foundation-stones of the standard narrative – Glinka's *A Life for the Tsar* (1836) and *Ruslan and Lyudmila* (1841) – display the unmistakable influence of French grand opera, and in particular Meyerbeer.[18] Even Stasov conceded on one occasion that *Robert* had firmly established the precedent of historical subject matter and appropriate local colour before Glinka had penned the first bars of *A Life*.[19] Neither of Glinka's operas, however, can be called a grand opera in the Parisian sense. *A Life* does have prominent choral and ballet music and is endowed with the requisite historical subject matter. Notwithstanding this, it appears that Glinka was not straining to emulate grand opera, since he chose to preserve the contours of his received plot (from Cavos's *Ivan Susanin*, as mentioned at the outset) rather than adopt the typical complications of a grand opera love-intrigue: the lovers do not span any dangerous religious or national divide, but they are used instead as a symbol of the opera's political conflict – as soon as Russia is wedded to her legitimate tsar, the lovers can also marry. *Ruslan*, by contrast, *does* display all the external features of grand opera: it is in five acts, with two substantial divertissements (one with an on-stage band); it also calls for frequent changes of scenery with striking contrasts of setting: a luxurious palace, a hermit's cave, a sombre battlefield, an Oriental harem, a magic garden. But instead of writing a true grand opera, Glinka employed these French conventions to update a different genre, namely that of magic opera, which had thrived in Russia from the time of Ferdinand Kauer's Viennese masterpiece, *Das Donauweibchen*, at the beginning of the century. In order to make sense of this, we should remember that Glinka was not a follower, but a contemporary of Meyerbeer (the two were friends during the 1850s); he was not working in the shadow of Meyerbeer, but followed an independent course, adopting or rejecting French innovations as he saw fit. In some respects, Glinka anticipated the French: for example, the musical contrast between the two opposing sides in *A Life for the Tsar* is maintained with far greater consistency than in *Les Huguenots*, and the Oriental colour of *Ruslan and Lyudmila* is much more prominent and richly varied than that found in *L'Africaine*. Glinka expressed some reservations about Meyerbeer's style, likening his operas to paintings where all the details are painted with such precision that no space is left for the spectator's imagination;[20] and in his *Notes on Orchestration*, Glinka cautioned his readers against Meyerbeer's 'abuse' of orchestral effects.[21]

The staging of Glinka's operas benefited greatly from the precedents set by the earlier productions of *Fenella* and *Robert le Diable*. The splendour of the sets was much remarked upon following the première of *A Life for the Tsar* at the new Bolshoi Theatre in St Petersburg (the theatre's inaugural performance). Roller, who had reproduced *Robert*'s original French sets in 1834, now drew upon his newly acquired expertise in designing the set for the final scene: the backdrop depicted a crowd gathered outside the Kremlin, while in front of this there were several layers of moving cardboard figures to extend the appearance of the crowd represented in the backdrop; finally, in front of this diorama was the real crowd, formed by the choir on stage. The resulting illusion made the onlooker imagine a crowd immensely greater than the stage could possibly accommodate, as one of the witnesses recalled: 'In the finale, the set of the Kremlin was magnificent: the crowd merged with the faces painted on the set, continuing, it seemed, into infinity.'[22] Most later Russian operatic productions did not enjoy these advantages: budgets were tight, and different operas had to make the best of the same old sets and costumes. The historical recreations and lavish production standards of *A Life for the Tsar* remained exceptional. Thirty years later, Stasov complained that the sets of Serov's *Rogneda* were historically anachronistic (the action takes place in tenth-century Russia), and he regretted that Russian theatres were slow to follow the example of their French and German counterparts (he mentions the Russian productions of *Robert*, *Les Huguenots*, *Tannhäuser* and *Lohengrin* as worthy exceptions). But Stasov was also able to note that the French preference for historical accuracy was beginning to take root in Russian practices: for although *Rogneda*'s sets proved unsatisfactory in this respect, an archaeologist had been consulted on the design of furniture, accessories and costumes.[23]

Glinka's stance towards the culture of grand opera – neither a whole-hearted embrace, nor a reaction against it – was also adopted by The Five, his self-proclaimed legatees. Their operatic values were formed under the influence of Stasov and Cui, both of whom expressed a mixture of admiration and loathing for Meyerbeer, without finally settling on one or the other attitude. Stasov never forgot the production of *Robert le Diable*, one of the great musical epiphanies of his youth, and he always believed that its final act proved that Meyerbeer was a truly great artist.[24] Stasov also lavished his praises on *Les Huguenots*, while Cui valued *Le Prophète* most highly. But Stasov and Cui also regarded the composition of operas as a high artistic calling, whose function was to educate and enlighten rather than merely entertain; indeed, for Stasov, the very fact that an opera enjoyed great popularity cast *prima facie* doubts over its artistic value. Meyerbeer obviously fared badly on both counts; Stasov and Cui thought that he lacked firm artistic convictions, and would trade anything for the sake of the acclaim of the crowd. Nevertheless, Stasov and The Five always granted that Meyerbeer even at his nadir was still superior to the Italians. Their model of an uncompromisingly noble opera was Schumann's *Genoveva* (1850), which fell as far short of Meyerbeer's success as Meyerbeer fell short of its highmindedness. In Russia, *Genoveva* never even reached the stage, such was its reputation as a box-office failure, although a concert performance was finally given in 1894. Cui's comments on Meyerbeer in a review of 1864 is representative of their attitude:

> Unthinking worship of Meyerbeer seems strange today: his music is too coarse, and devoid of poetry, as are the feelings he expresses; but if it were not for him, the public would have been even less willing than they are to attend operas by Schumann and Wagner, where we see the extreme expression of the contemporary operatic trend. Meyerbeer did not move the art forward . . . But he did manage to shift public tastes, which had frozen since Rossini . . . so that a need for drama in operatic music was felt.[25]

The deprecation of Meyerbeer took on tactical importance in the mid-1860s, when Alexander Serov, whom The Five counted as their ideological opponent by this time, composed *Judith* and *Rogneda*; both operas enjoyed great success, and both embraced the grand opera tradition unreservedly. This must have suggested double standards on Serov's part to anyone familiar with the same composer's music criticism, for here he had upheld Wagner as his operatic ideal, and expressed only contempt for Meyerbeer; now it seemed that Serov could toss these sentiments aside for the sake of box-office earnings. This gave Stasov a juicy bone to gnaw on:

> Just like Meyerbeer, he thinks only of effects calculated to please the crudest tastes. Just like Meyerbeer, he is inclined to create music of the most vacuous and trivial kind. And just like Meyerbeer, he has no gift for giving expression to the transports, sensations, joys and tears of the soul. He has no gift for representing the merest psychological detail, no gift

sufficient for creating even a single real character. In his undiscriminating eclecticism, he is ready to undertake the portrayal of all nations and epochs alike . . . We now have our own 'annals of time' wondrously expressed in music. We have our own conspiracies . . . feasts, marches, hunts, hymns! Naturally, we will soon likewise have our own simulated fires on stage, skeleton dances, resurrections from the grave and ice skating, and then we really will have no further cause to envy European music.[26]

Worse, since *Rogneda* was drawn from Russian history, Stasov believed that Serov might come to be seen as the true representative of Russian national music; this threatened to undermine Stasov's own plans to cultivate The Five as the artistic conduit for his own version of musical nationalism – they had still not produced any significant works, but Stasov was already presenting them in his journalistic writings as the 'New Russian School'. To fend off this potential disaster, Stasov had to insinuate that *Rogneda* was merely pseudo-national:

> In the whole of *Rogneda* there is just as much true Russianness, just as much of old pagan Russia, as there was of true Italianness in *Fenella*, Swissness in *Guillaume Tell* . . . or old Germanness in Gounod's *Faust*.[27]

The young composers of The Five were hardly likely, then, to contemplate the composition of a true grand opera, but, as we mentioned, they allowed themselves some latitude in adopting elements from this tradition – historical subjects, orientalism and even balletic episodes – because of the precedent set by Glinka, who was beyond criticism as far as they were concerned. The operas of Musorgsky, Borodin and Rimsky-Korsakov nevertheless demonstrate that they learned much from grand opera, and they even ventured to adopt elements which cannot be traced back to Glinka.

These vestiges of the grand opera tradition are perhaps most glaring in Musorgsky, precisely because he otherwise pushed The Five's operatic aesthetics further than his colleagues. Initially, it appears, he was quite comfortable with the French genre, for he began sketches for a grand opera of his own, based upon Flaubert's novel *Salammbô* (1862). This he abandoned for a new operatic project that was utterly remote from grand opera aesthetics: his *Marriage* (1868), a word-for-word setting of the Gogol comedy. Musorgsky took The Five's quest for operatic 'truth' to its extreme, refusing to shoehorn the play's contours into any pre-existing operatic forms, and even attempting to imitate the natural intonations of spoken Russian. Although the rest of The Five were notionally committed to such ideals, they found Musorgsky's new work-in-progress too extreme, and offered no encouragement. After the completion of scenes from Act I, Musorgsky himself decided to abandon the project (it would have been recorded as the first ever prose opera); however, the experience of working within

Marriage's rigorous aesthetic eventually proved fruitful in the first version of *Boris Godunov* (1869), which contains much the same operatic 'truth' in its many declamatory scenes. Nevertheless, the new work is in verse rather than prose, following the libretto's source, which was Pushkin's drama (1831) of the same name: see Appendix on p. 364. Musorgsky also cut and adapted the Pushkin text, which was much too lengthy to set in its entirety (a lesson he had no doubt learnt from *Marriage*). There are also various choruses, and even a grand tableau in the fullest grand opera manner, namely the Coronation Scene. Still, these elements do not signal a wholesale retreat from the aesthetic of *Marriage*; elsewhere in *Boris*, choruses have no ceremonial character and contain varying degrees of declamation and dialogue and are therefore far removed from grand opera.

The first version of *Boris* was evidently too daunting for the directorate of the Imperial Theatres, which rejected it early in 1871, in spite of the obvious attractions of the Coronation Scene. For two years, Musorgsky worked upon major revisions in order to ensure the opera's eventual performance. The resulting second version makes large concessions towards the grand opera style which the directorate evidently wished to see; it was duly accepted, and performed in 1874. There was a whole new act, set in Poland, which fully embraced the grand opera manner: the brilliance of the Polish court is conveyed through polonaises and mazurkas, allowing Musorgsky to introduce ballet and local colour. Several elements of Pushkin's plot were reinstated, all tilting the new version further towards grand opera. The political intrigue was made more complicated through the introduction of Marina Mniszek, who forms an alliance with the Pretender; this in turn provides a love intrigue, which was altogether absent from the first version, culminating in a lush duet between Marina and the Pretender (the Fountain Scene). Boris's central monologue (Act II) is present in both versions, but Musorgsky's first attempt seems stilted beside the gripping directness of the new version, an improvement facilitated by a looser paraphrase of Pushkin, which relaxes the formal prosody of the original for a more fragmented, psychologically realistic presentation. Musorgsky also included more set pieces in the opera, and, most importantly, added a final crowd scene (the Kromï Scene) resembling the finale of *Les Huguenots* which likewise depicts a violent mob on the rampage. Musorgsky was, of course, fully aware that the second version of *Boris* represented a major retreat not only from *Marriage*, but also from the first version, and he tried to justify himself thus: 'The *Marriage* is a study for a small stage . . . For the grand stage, it was necessary that the speeches of the characters . . . should have been conveyed to the audience in bold relief.'[28]

In his next opera, *Khovanshchina*, Musorgsky moved still further towards grand opera. There was no literary source, and Musorgsky's plot shadows

Les Huguenots, incorporating a similar religious conflict, an intrigue of forbidden love, a death scene for the lovers, now united on one side of the conflict, and the two sides brought together in musical counterpoint at the end. Musorgsky's terminal decline prevented him from finishing *Khovanshchina*, but Rimsky-Korsakov, who composed the standard completed version (1886), evidently sympathised with the work's grand opera tendencies, and closed the drama with a spectacular sacrificial fire that consumes the Old Believers – perhaps the most unashamed grand opera type of finale in the Russian repertory.

The characteristic grand opera motif of love across a political, religious, or ethnic divide also figures prominently in historical operas by other members of The Five, in Rimsky-Korsakov's *Maid of Pskov* (1873, rev. 1895) and Borodin's *Prince Igor* (1890), for example, the latter including spectacular scenes of solar eclipse and conflagration. However, it was a collectively composed opera-ballet, *Mlada*, which would have resembled a grand opera more closely than any other work issuing from The Five. Musorgsky, Rimsky-Korsakov, Borodin and Cui decided to embark on this curious project in the early 1870s: each of the four composers was to contribute one act, and the court ballet composer Minkus was to provide the music for balletic interludes. The opera was commissioned by its librettist, Stepan Gedeonov, director of the Imperial Theatres (and son of Alexander). Gedeonov constructed his story around the device of a silent heroine, played by a ballerina, evidently hoping to capitalise on Auber's *La Muette de Portici*, which had by this time enjoyed four successful decades in Russia. The heroine, Mlada, has been poisoned before the opera's plot begins, but her ghost appears periodically, dancing.[29] Only Minkus, Cui and Rimsky-Korsakov had produced anything substantial before Gedeonov lost his directorship, and so there could no longer be any guarantee of a lavish and well-promoted production (or indeed of any production at all). The project was therefore abandoned; Minkus soon expanded his work into a full-scale ballet, and a decade later, Rimsky-Korsakov composed music for the remaining acts of Gedeonov's libretto for his own version of *Mlada* (see Table 17.2). Although the subject matter is legendary rather than historical, the abundance of non-dramatic, decorative elements brings *Mlada* very close to grand opera. This is especially true of the Market Scene, which occupies the whole of Act II and was allocated to Rimsky-Korsakov in the original plan; Rimsky-Korsakov rose to the occasion with a crowd scene that would have been an impressive set piece in any grand opera. The music is constructed from a multitude of different elements: first Rimsky-Korsakov builds up a polyphony of hawkers' cries, then he successively introduces a bard's song, a courtly procession, a pagan ritual, and a multi-ethnic divertissement. It thus offers a great variety of entertaining spectacles, which are suddenly interrupted by a dramatic stroke:

Table 17.2 *The principal productions of grand operas by Russian composers*

1847	Moscow	Dargomïzhsky, *Esmeralda*
1851	St Petersburg	Dargomïzhsky, *Esmeralda*
1860	St Petersburg	Dütsch, *Kroatka* (*The Croatian*)
1863	St Petersburg	Serov, *Yudif* (*Judith*)
1865	Moscow	Serov, *Yudif*
	St Petersburg	Serov, *Rogneda*
1868	Moscow	Serov, *Rogneda*
1877	St Petersburg	Rubinstein, *Makkavei* (*The Maccabees*)
1881	St Petersburg	Tchaikovsky, *Orleanskaya deva* (*The Maid of Orleans*)
1883	Moscow	Rubinstein, *Makkavei*
1884	St Petersburg and Moscow	Tchaikovsky, *Mazeppa*
	St Petersburg (Italian Company)	Rubinstein, *Neron* (*Nero*)
1890	St Petersburg	Borodin (and others), *Prince Igor*
1892	St Petersburg	Rimsky-Korsakov, *Mlada*
1902	St Petersburg	Rimsky-Korsakov, *Servilia*

the appearance of Mlada's ghost. Rimsky-Korsakov considered the Market Scene of *Mlada* such a success that he used the same formula in both *Sadko* (1897/8) and *Legend of the Invisible City of Kitezh* (1907). Interestingly, the *Sadko* version points us to the Market Chorus of *La Muette de Portici* as the original source of inspiration, for there is clearly some musical kinship between the 'hustle and bustle' themes of the two operas (Ex. 17.1a and 1b). In addition, Auber's idea of stating the theme in different keys to ensure unity in variety is also adopted by Rimsky-Korsakov. And from *La Muette*, through *Mlada*, *Sadko* and *Legend of the Invisible City of Kitezh*, we can trace this appropriation from grand opera through successive decades of Russian national epic operas up to Prokofiev's *War and Peace* (1952): the grand opera-derived crowd scene became the characteristic centrepiece of these Russian works, and the French origins were eventually (and conveniently) forgotten.

Three case-studies: *Rogneda*, *The Maid of Orleans* and *Servilia*

The first Russian operas to follow the French grand opera model wholeheartedly appeared in the 1850s, but if their creators thought they would inherit the massive public following of *Fenella* and *Robert le Diable*, they must have been disappointed. Alexander Dargomïzhsky's *Esmeralda* (1847), an opera in four acts making use of very large forces, took forty rehearsals to prepare, yet lasted only nine performances. Otto Dütsch's *Kroatka* (*The Croatian*, 1860) was a little more successful, assisted, no doubt, by the substantial extracts from Liszt's *Hungarian Rhapsodies* which appear unacknowledged in the score. It was not until the arrival of Serov's two operas, *Judith* and *Rogneda*, that critics first spoke of a 'Russian Meyerbeer' (although this was

Example 17.1a Auber, *La Muette de Portici*, Act III: market scene.

sometimes only a backhanded compliment, for the reasons we noted above). Indeed, *Rogneda* in particular seems to fit the definition of a grand opera: it is written in five acts and features the struggle of Christianity with paganism in the early eleventh century (though the plot does not make any pretence at historical authenticity), and proceeds through an array of spectacular scenes: supernatural fortune-telling and a sacrificial rite in Act I, Christian chorales and a royal hunt in Act II, a dream-scene in Act III, a storm in Act IV, and finally a public trial and more chorales in Act V. But beyond the spectacular grand façade, we must admit, there is absolutely no convincing drama, and in fact hardly any dramatic action at all. Some of the events (an abduction, a struggle between Prince Vladimir and a bear) take place off-stage, and others which had been forecast do not take place at all: Rogneda plans to murder her adulterous husband, but fails when he is alerted to her intentions by a dream; he wishes to kill her in revenge, but their son pleads for her life; instead, he decides she must stand trial, but in the middle of the process he relents and forgives her, which brings the trial to a halt. Stripped of various inconsequential scenes and characters, the story boils down to two instances of Christian mercy, one triggered by the other, which is hardly a grand opera intrigue. This near-total lack of drama is particularly astonishing in Serov, since the composer, in his capacity as a critic, had complained that there was too little dramatic tension in Meyerbeer; while dramatic

Example 17.1b Rimsky-Korsakov, *Sadko*, Tableau IV, opening.

tension may not be Meyerbeer's supreme artistic virtue, nothing approaching the torpor of *Rogneda* is to be found in his operas. But its apparently obvious shortcomings notwithstanding, *Rogneda* enjoyed unprecedented success for a Russian opera, remaining an essential repertory work for several decades (long enough for the earlier Soviet music historians to be fully aware that they were changing the historical record). In fact, *Rogneda*'s success was not mysterious: it drew heavily upon the tradition inaugurated by Verstovsky's 'Slavic' operas (all but one with spoken dialogue) which were based on plots similar to *Rogneda*'s, and such operas had enjoyed a large following, particularly because they always featured a number of popular Russian melodies.[30] Serov inherited and exploited this easy-going Russianness, but he imported the spectacular elements from grand opera, and used a rich palette of the most modern harmonic and orchestral effects; evidently, Russian audiences found the combination irresistible.

Anton Rubinstein was alone among Russian composers in enjoying an international operatic career; accordingly, he had no compunction about drawing from the grand opera tradition, unlike some of his compatriots. *The Maccabees* (1877) is particularly Meyerbeerian in style, as is his *Nero* (1884), which was in fact written for the Paris Opéra (although in the end it was not produced there).[31] Tchaikovsky hoped to emulate Rubinstein in this respect, and accordingly wrote both text and music for his own grand opera, *The Maid of Orleans* (1881), taking *Le Prophète* as his model. Joan of Arc was a convenient counterpart to John of Leyden: both were acclaimed as prophets, and led their armies to victory, only to be denounced and betrayed; Tchaikovsky even added a counterpart to Fidès, namely Thibaut, Joan's father, who reluctantly brings about the protagonist's downfall in following a duty that overrides parental ties.[32] As Meyerbeer did in *Le Prophète*, Tchaikovsky begins his opera with a pastoral scene (in Joan's home village); Act I ends with Joan's calling, delivered by a choir of angels, while Meyerbeer had ended his Act II with John's parallel calling. Tchaikovsky's four-act structure conflates Acts I and II of Meyerbeer's five-act structure, but thereafter the two operas follow the same pattern. Tchaikovsky's Act II contains a divertissement, like Meyerbeer's equivalent Act III, while Tchaikovsky's Act III takes place in the shadow of Rouen Cathedral in parallel with Meyerbeer's Act IV set in the shadow of Münster Cathedral; similarly Thibaut publicly challenges Joan at this juncture, as Fidès had challenged John. The final acts of both operas lead to the punishment of the abandoned prophet, ending with a purging fire. Here we can see the superiority of Scribe's plot, for John's fatally flawed grandeur made him an appropriate tragic protagonist, whereas Joan's downfall is unconvincingly justified by the device of an ill-considered affair with Lionel, a Burgundian knight (perhaps Tchaikovsky failed to see that a protagonist who engages the audience's complete sympathy is ultimately a dramatic liability in a tragedy).

In terms of spectacle, however, Tchaikovsky easily rivals Meyerbeer, placing a large-scale choral finale at the end of each act (even that of Act I, where the angels make up the crowd). His orchestra is expanded first by off-stage trumpets, then by on-stage brass band and organ. Russian critics often scoffed at the fact that Tchaikovsky unabashedly used Meyerbeerian 'coarse' orchestral effects, but here they appear in the most appropriate context. Regarding style, *The Maid* is certainly no pastiche, since it is written within the boundaries of Tchaikovsky's mature style; nevertheless, there are some

Example 17.2 Tchaikovsky, *The Maid of Orleans*, theme of Joan's hymn in the overture.

discernible influences, such as the strong Meyerbeerian rhythms of the march of Act III scene 2, or the very French noble pathos of Joan's hymn ('Vï sonmï angelov nebesnïkh', 'Ye hosts of heavenly angels', Ex. 17.2). The opera appeared to be a success at the beginning of its first run, in St Petersburg, but it was soon in difficulties when the prima donna became ill and was unable to appear for the remainder of the run; in her absence, the critics also began to look askance at the second-hand sets, and criticised other shortcomings of the production. Although a Prague production followed three years later, Tchaikovsky's hopes that *The Maid* would provide him with international celebrity were left unfulfilled.

In contrast to Tchaikovsky, Rimsky-Korsakov tried to keep as much distance as possible between himself and Western operatic types during most of his career, in accordance with Stasov's doctrines. But around 1890 he began to confide privately in others that he believed Russian nationalist music was spent as a creative force; his thoughts soon became manifest in his deeds as he began to pastiche, assimilate and experiment with the very operatic styles, forms and genres which he had earlier avoided. His opera *Servilia* (1902) is based on a play by Lev Mey, whose works he had used before; this time, however, the particular drama he chose was of a type that he would have shunned had he still counted himself a disciple of Stasov. The story is from Roman history, set in the reign of Nero in CE 67, and each of the five acts reads like a catalogue of grand opera characteristics. Rimsky-Korsakov was evidently at ease with all these features, having abandoned his Stasovian scruples, and he exploited them fully in creating his own grand opera. Act I opens with a market-place scene; amid the hawkers' cries, we notice a political conspiracy is brewing. A solemn Roman procession is followed by the first conflict between a Christian preacher and the pagan Romans. As the preacher is taken to prison, Act I ends with a chorale-like theme. Act II, in the baths, develops a complicated political intrigue further, off-setting it with a divertissement featuring the 'exotic' Mixolydian mode; the act ends with a fire (in the bath house!) and all flee. Act III develops the love intrigue, although this is, of course, embroiled within the political part of the plot; then after a grand love-duet for the main characters, Servilia and Valerius, it is announced that the conspirators – among them Servilia's father, a senator – are to face trial on charges of conspiracy. Act IV offers us the supernatural when Servilia, distraught over the sudden disappearance of Valerius, has a sorceress conjure up a ghost to discover her beloved's whereabouts; a rival for Servilia's hand persuades her that Valerius is dead, and in her despair she turns to the Christian faith. Act V begins with the trial of the conspirators, which is interrupted by the appearance of Valerius; he wishes to marry Servilia, but he is now too late, for she has already taken a vow of celibacy. Unable to bear the conflict between her earthly and heavenly ties, she expires. This causes Valerius to convert to Christianity on the spot, and the opera ends with a Credo.

Appearances, as above, are however deceptive. Although the plot and large-scale structure belong to the world of grand opera, the musical construction of each act is post-Wagnerian: there are no clearly delineated numbers, but an almost continuous flow of music leavened with leitmotifs. And what style did Rimsky-Korsakov think appropriate for such a mongrel work? The idioms of 1830s Italian opera, filtered through the harmonies of Liszt and Wagner. The love-duet, for example, is at first blatantly Italianate, with its sweet chromatic appoggiaturas, its vocal writing in parallel sixths and thirds, and its generous repetitions to assist the least attentive of listeners; then in the middle section we are presented with major third

Example 17.3 Rimsky-Korsakov, *Servilia*, Act III, duo of Servilia and Valerius.

key-relationships, pointing just as clearly to Liszt's influence (Ex. 17.3). Unfortunately, Rimsky-Korsakov does not succeed in working the miracle needed to make this strange amalgam artistically convincing, for too often the different styles only undermine each other's strengths. Rimsky-Korsakov was doubtless well able to endow *Servilia*'s marches, processions, and public prayers with the monumentality expected of grand opera, but this cannot be done without grand opera's closed, static forms and impressive stage tableaux; instead, Rimsky-Korsakov's commitment to Wagnerian continuity, pacing and dynamism curtails such numbers before they can make their effect felt, and they are often violently interrupted for the sake of the ongoing drama. Audiences, confronted with scenes which at first seemed to be following the familiar conventions of grand opera, found their expectations confounded; as Rimsky-Korsakov complained, 'the listeners like well-defined, strongly emphasised endings, and they aren't sufficiently grown-up to understand the point of an ensemble that is interrupted for dramatic purposes'.[33]

Both the St Petersburg and Moscow productions of *Servilia* enjoyed only a *succès d'estime*; they survived for seven and six performances respectively. Some critics pointed out that *Servilia* was ill-equipped to compete with the production of Rubinstein's *Nero* which was already running at the time; for in contrast to *Servilia*, Rubinstein's Roman-history opera, set in the same period, provided audiences with more accessible music and fulfilled all expectations of monumentality, and grand spectacle too. The budgetary restraints on the *Servilia* production in Moscow led to the recycling of sets from *Nero*. Even Rimsky-Korsakov's own fame worked against him, for he was now belatedly established in the public's perception as the great composer of nationalist operas; the public now found that he had abandoned everything that they had admired in his work, and this added to their puzzlement and frustration. Although *Servilia* proved to be a liability for the theatres which produced it, and a great disappointment for its composer, it is certainly an interesting case for historians: it stands as probably the last work which we could call a Russian grand opera, and its composer self-consciously presents the genre not as a living artistic model, but as a museum piece, serving as a stimulus for his own interest in detached historicising (an interest he was to pass on, with greater effect, to his pupil Stravinsky).

Many Russian composers thus aspired to recognition in the West, even those who routinely indulged in nationalist, anti-Western rhetoric for domestic consumption. But the hour of recognition did not come until the beginning of the next century, when Diaghilev presented his Saisons Russes in Paris. In 1907, his concerts included extracts from *Boris Godunov*, which generated sufficient interest to win him an invitation to produce the entire work at the Paris Opéra. Chaliapin, in the title role, said that this prestigious opportunity would be 'a test of Russian maturity and originality, a test that we had to pass before the eyes of Europe'.[34] Diaghilev, on receiving the commission, said,

> It was always Tchaikovsky's dream to see his work staged at the Grand Opéra . . . What trouble Rubinstein took in the hope of seeing his *Nero* in Paris, and how many strings were pulled [in vain] for the sake of Serov's *Judith*. But the French would hear nothing about Russian composers . . . Yet today, they turn to me of their own accord . . .[35]

The impact of *Boris* on the Paris audience was comparable to that of *La Muette de Portici* and *Robert le Diable* on Russian audiences three generations earlier. Ironically, perhaps, it was also the magnificence of the production's spectacles that ensured success for *Boris*. Musorgsky's opera had never enjoyed such lavish staging in Russia, but the success of Diaghilev's previous ventures in Paris enabled him to guess that the packaging of the opera in bright, modern, exotic garb would prove a triumph. Paris was conquered by the sparkling robes of bishops and metropolitans, by the illusion of falling snow, and by the gaudy boldness of the sets which had at first outraged the Opéra's directorate. Chaliapin, who sang the role of Boris, became an international legend overnight. Was this a vindication of Stasov's vision for Russian nationalist opera? Perhaps not: Musorgsky's intentions might have been roundly Stasovian, but the production which thrilled Parisian audiences was a brilliantly executed study in exoticism and above all in the very grand opera populism which Stasov had denounced.

Appendix 17.1 *History and Literature in Tsarist Russia*

	Events		History and Literature
1801	Accession of Tsar Alexander I	1820	Pushkin: *Ruslan and Lyudmila*
		1822–31	Pushkin: *Yevgeny Onegin*
1825	Accession of Tsar Nicholas I	1829–41	Mikhail Lermontov: *The Demon* (source of Rubinstein's opera)
		1831	Pushkin: *Boris Godunov*
		1833	Mikhail Zagoskin: *Askold's Tomb* (source of Verstovsky's opera)
		1834	Pushkin: *The Queen of Spades*
		1835	Pushkin: *The Golden Cockerel*
1837	Death of Pushkin		
1839	Pulkovo stellar observatory built		
1841	Death of Lermontov	1841	Shevchenko: *Haydamaki*, on the peasant rebellions of the eighteenth century
		1842	Gogol: *Dead Souls*
1845–49	Meetings of the Petrashevsky radicals (including Dostoyevsky)	1845	Shevchenko: *Yeretik*, on the fifteenth-century Hussites; *Testament*
		1850	Turgenev: *Diary of a Superfluous Man*
		1852–55	Alexander Herzen: *My Past and Thoughts*
1852	Deaths of Gogol and of Basil Zhukovsky	1852	Turgenev: *Sportsman's Sketches*
1854–55	Crimean War		
1855	Accession of Tsar Alexander II, who will inaugurate 'the Great Reforms'	1856	Peter Shchebalsky: *The Regency of Tsarevna Sophia*
1857	Death of Glinka	1859	Ostrovsky: *The Storm*
1858	Provincial committees set up to consider serfs' emancipation	1859	Afanasy Shchapov: *History of the Schism*
1860	Censor permits publication of Archpriest Avvakum's autobiography (used in Musorgsky: *Khovanshchina*)		
1861	Emancipation of about 52 million serf peasants	1861	Nikolai Ustrialov: *History of the Reign of Peter the Great*

Year		Year	
1861	Various civil disturbances begin	1862	Ivan Filippov: *History of the Vigodsk Old Believers' Monastery*
1863	Polish rebellion: Russia reasserts control	1864	Sergei Solovyov: *History of Russia*
1864	Laws on modernisation of local government; reform of the legal system initiated	1866	Dostoyevsky: *Crime and Punishment*
1866	Censor permits public performance of Pushkin's drama *Boris Godunov*; assassination attempt on Tsar	1866–70	Alexei Tolstoy's trilogy: *Death of Ivan the Terrible*; *Tsar Fedor Ivanovitch*; *Tsar Boris*
1870	Laws on municipal reform	1869	Lev Tolstoy: *War and Peace*
1872	Musorgsky completes second version of *Boris Godunov*	1870	Nikolai Kostomarov: article on the Old Believers
1873	The 'populist crusade' fails	1871	Kostomarov: *The Personality of Tsar Ivan Vasilievich*
1874	Musorgsky writes: 'History is my nocturnal friend'	1873	Ostrovsky: *Snegurochka*
1874	Reform of the military services	1874	Kostomarov: *The Investigation into the Murder of the Crown Prince Dimitry*
1876	Revolutionary 'Land and Freedom' society founded	1874	Kostomarov: *The Empress Sof'ya* (source for Musorgsky, *Khovanshchina*)
1881	Assassination of Tsar Alexander II; accession of Alexander III; death of Musorgsky; death of Dostoyevsky	1877	Lev Tolstoy: *Anna Karenina*
1883	Death of Turgenev		
1884	Counter-reform of universities		
1893	Death of Tchaikovsky		
1894	Accession of Tsar Nicholas II		

18 Grand opera among the Czechs

JAN SMACZNY

On 28 March 1884 Fibich's *The Bride of Messina* (*Nevěsta Messinská* – designated a 'tragic opera', but a music drama in all but name)[1] was premièred in the nearly new Czech National Theatre, recently risen phoenix-like from the devastating fire of 1881 that had closed it only days after its long-awaited opening (see Fig. 28 opposite).[2] Two days later there was a performance of Dvořák's four-act, grand opera *Dimitrij*, which had been premièred two years before in the latter days of the old Provisional Theatre.[3] *The Bride of Messina* limped on for five performances in 1884 and a further two in 1885 to dwindling houses; by contrast, Dvořák's *Dimitrij*, which had run for fifteen performances in 1882 and 1883, was given twenty times in its revised version over a two-year period and by the end of the century was one of the most frequently performed of all non-comic Czech operas.[4] The fact that *Dimitrij* filled the theatre while *The Bride of Messina* gradually emptied it tells us much about contemporary taste. Few if any Czech operas from the national revival (dating, loosely speaking, from the opening of the Prague Provisional Theatre on 18 November 1862) were more ideologically conceived than Fibich's *Bride*.[5] The libretto was by Otakar Hostinský, one of Prague's foremost musical theoreticians and academics, a fine amateur artist, a man of letters and a well-known writer on aesthetics;[6] the music was by the most evidently intellectual Czech composer of the day, the husband of one of the National Theatre company's most respected singers, Betty Fibichová, and the darling of Prague's Czech-speaking chattering classes. Fibich and Hostinský's aim had been to compose what was effectively a Czech equivalent of Wagner's mature music dramas: the plot, based on Schiller's eponymous play, observes the unities, the tone is elevated and sombre, the score, apart from an impressive funeral march, was virtually unexcerpt-ably through-composed; to enhance the solemn intent, Fibich consciously eschewed 'irrelevant' flights of melodic fancy and ensembles, though not choruses. By contrast, and the contrast was certainly not lost on Hostinský,[7] Dvořák's *Dimitrij*, which is discussed in detail below, was an old-fashioned, full-blown grand opera (albeit lacking a fifth act) adhering to many of the features which had defined the genre: impressive crowd scenes often involv-ing opposing political forces and sung in double chorus; lyrical set pieces; extended duets including two for the central pair of lovers, Dimitrij and

Figure 28 View from the 'standing stalls' within the new National Theatre, Prague, drawn by Bohumir Roubalík and reproduced in F. Šubert's sumptuous book about the theatre (*Národní divadlo v Praze*) in 1881. Above the proscenium arch can be read 'NÁROD SOBĚ!': 'THE NATION TO ITSELF!'

Xenie (II.4, IV.2), the second of which is colossal; exciting finales and a ballet.

Although it is tempting to put the contrasting fates of the two operas down simply to a disparity in quality between the two scores, the situation is more complex – *The Bride of Messina* may not have been a box-office smash, but it was admired by critics and received enough performances in its early days to qualify for reasonable attention as part of the National Theatre canon. Nevertheless, the audience for opera that had developed in the Provisional Theatre had a taste for the popular, and no Czech opera was less overtly popular in tone than *The Bride of Messina*. Just as Smetana's high-minded, exquisitely lyrical third opera *Dalibor* (1868) never really won the sympathy of Provisional Theatre audiences[8] (unlike the populist, rabble-rousing *Brandenburgers in Bohemia* (*Braniboři v Čechách*), premièred only two years earlier), *The Bride of Messina*, so well designed to raise the tone of operatic taste, could not compete with a work that clearly fulfilled the expectations of the existing audience for Czech opera in Prague. *Dimitrij* was seen as old-fashioned by the more progressive critical establishment,[9] and excoriated for this quality in some later histories;[10] but Dvořák's and his librettist's frank adherence to grand opera convention in *Dimitrij* proved that the genre still struck a genuine chord with audiences and critics: while Hostinský retrospectively noted its archaic qualities, contemporary reaction dwelt on the fact that the work was one of the most 'carefully prepared' of premières and that it marked the start of a 'golden age' in Dvořák's output.[11]

French grand opera in the Czech lands

The foundations for audience sympathy with the medium and manner of grand opera were firmly established in the Czech lands in the 1830s, though an interest in French opera generally was already present some twenty years earlier as indicated by relatively early débuts for Spontini's *La Vestale*, in German, in Brno on 19 December 1811 (Paris première: 15 December 1807),[12] and of Méhul's *Joseph* in Prague, again in German, on 26 September 1813 (Paris première: 17 February 1807); it is also interesting to note that a performance of *Joseph* in a Czech translation, by J. K. Chmelenský,[13] was given for the first time in the Estates Theatre in Prague on 17 November 1824, a relative rarity this early in the century, and it went on, with Cherubini's *Les Deux journées* (1800), to become something of a favourite.[14] Although performances of opera in Czech were virtually unknown in the Moravian capital Brno,[15] largely owing to its proximity to Vienna, the city often gave a home to a première of a French grand opera in the Czech lands before Prague. Rossini's *Tell* was given in Brno in German on 24 November 1830,

Table 18.1 *Grand operas in Prague*

Year	Event
1829	Prague première of *La Muette de Portici*, in German
1844	Plans are laid for a Czech theatre built in stone
1852	Plot of land purchased for Czech theatre
1862	18 Nov.: opening of Provisional Theatre (PT)
1863	1 March: PT première of *La Muette de Portici*
1864	6 Jan., 30 Oct., 29 Nov.: PT premières of *La Juive*, *Les Huguenots* and *Robert le Diable*
1865	19 Oct.: PT première of Šebor's *The Templars in Moravia*
1866	5 Jan.: PT première of Smetana's *The Brandenburgers in Bohemia*
	Sept.: Smetana takes over as PT musical director
	14 Dec.: PT première of *Guillaume Tell*
1867	6 July: PT première of *Faust*: 115 performances given; the most frequently performed non-comic opera
1868	4 Jan., 27 Sept.: PT premières of Bendl's *Lejla* and Šebor's *The Hussite Bride*
1869	26 Jan., 29 Aug.: PT premières of *Gustave III* and *Roméo et Juliette*
1870	18 Sept.: PT première of Bendl's *Břetislav*
1875	5 Dec.: PT première of *Le Prophète*
1876	17 April: PT première of Dvořák's *Vanda*
1877	8 Dec.: PT première of *L'Africaine*
1881	1 June: first opening of National Theatre (NT)
	12 Aug.: NT burned down
1882	8 Oct.: PT première of Dvořák's *Dimitrij*
1883	18 Nov.: reopening of NT
1884	28 March: NT première of Fibich's *The Bride of Messina*
1894	7 Nov.: NT première of recomposed version of Dvořák's *Dimitrij*
1896	12 Feb.: NT première of Fibich's *Hedý*
1904	25 March: NT première of Dvořák's *Armida*

only five months after its Viennese première, and more than a month before Prague (30 December; Paris première, 3 August 1829), while Meyerbeer's *Robert le Diable* was given in German in Brno on 23 August 1834, fourteen months after Vienna and nearly a year before Prague (24 July 1835; Paris première, 21 November 1831); Halévy's *La Juive* was given in Brno in German on 6 March 1837, fifteen months after Vienna and over a year before its Prague première (25 July 1838; Paris première, 23 February 1835);[16] Auber's *La Muette de Portici*, one of the most popular operas among the Czechs in Prague in the 1860s and 1870s, and with a respectable performing history in the National Theatre up to the turn of the century, was given in Prague in German as early as 30 July 1829, hardly a year and a half after its notorious première (29 February 1828).

Though grand opera in Czech was undoubtedly popular among audiences in Prague from the 1830s, the opportunities for hearing it, despite the interest of Czech-speaking cultured circles, were decidedly limited before the opening of the Provisional Theatre in 1862. Given the political circumstances consequent on the Habsburg victory at the Battle of the White Mountain in 1620, among which were the suppression and dispersal of native Czech nobility, it is no surprise to find that the cultural institutions of Prague, as they developed a bourgeois cultural identity in the early

nineteenth century, were dominated by the city's German-speaking majority. The dominance of German-language performances in the Estates,
formerly the Nostitz, Theatre,[17] meant that Czech-language renditions of
standard repertory, not at all unpopular among many of the German company's singers whose first language was Czech, tended to be heard only on
Sunday afternoons and then only between 4 and 6 pm.[18] Moreover, owing
to constraints over sets and productions, they could only choose repertory
that was already being performed in the Estates Theatre. There were no real
high points for opera in Czech or, indeed, Czech opera in the first half of the
nineteenth century after the première of František Škroup's Singspiel *The
Tinker* (*Dráteník*) in 1826; performances increased briefly in the mid-1840s
with the stimulus of the New Theatre in Rose Street established by Johann
August Stöger; the situation was exacerbated by government reaction to
the Revolution of 1848 with increased censorship and a general tendency to
impede performances in Czech. Though labouring under considerable gov-
ernmental disapproval, the efforts of the Czech community to open a Czech
theatre eventually paid off after some eighteen years in the preparation.[19]

Grand opera in the Provisional Theatre (1862–83)

Towards the end of his life Dvořák enunciated his belief that opera was 'the
most suitable form for the nation'.[20] To an extent this comment may be
read as an indication of an affinity with the libertarian tendencies of grand
opera. The Czechs, after all, were a nation in the thrall of empire and their
composers often set out to construct an operatic image of themselves as
a people oppressed (see below). Three of Dvořák's eleven operas, *Vanda*,
Dimitrij and *Armida*, are full-scale grand operas, the first two dealing with
overtly political material and the third with religion. Moreover, shortly
before making his signal statement on the value of opera for the nation,
he seems to have reacquired an enthusiasm for grand opera, in particular
Meyerbeer's *Les Huguenots*, as the tenor Otakar Mařák recounted:

> We were studying *Les Huguenots* and, after
> one piano rehearsal, as I was leaving the theatre
> Dvořák stopped me [and said]: 'I heard some Meyerbeerian
> strains, I am looking forward to it'. At the first
> performance Kovařovic came to me in my dressing room
> in the interval and said that Dvořák was hunting for me,
> that he was very enthusiastic about it and must tell me. . .[21]

Dvořák's knowledge of French grand opera dates from near the beginning
of his professional career. In fact, it grew at the same pace as the repertory
of the Provisional Theatre since he was a founder member of its orchestra

in 1862 and remained in post as its principal viola player until the summer season of 1871.

Smetana made much of an apparent bias towards Italian operatic repertory on the part of the first musical director of the Provisional Theatre, Jan Maýr.[22] But, as John Tyrrell points out, practical considerations concerning the small size of the theatre, orchestra and chorus would have tended to favour smaller-scale Italian opera,[23] and to assume that a limited repertory dominated during Maýr's tenure, from November 1862 to September 1866, would be a distortion. The first opera to be given in the theatre was, in fact, Cherubini's *Les Deux journées* on 20 November 1862, two days after the official opening (one of the embarrassments for the new establishment was that there was no adequate Czech repertory with which to open the theatre). The first Czech opera staged was František Škroup's modest but locally significant *The Tinker*, given nearly three weeks later on 8 December. Apart from Conradin Kreutzer's *Das Nachtlager von Granada*, Köck's *Kriegsheimkehr* and Mozart's *Die Zauberflöte*, the repertory in the first few weeks of the Provisional Theatre under Maýr did indeed appear to be dominated by Italian opera: Bellini (*I Capuleti ed i Montecchi*), Donizetti (*Lucrezia Borgia*), Verdi (*Il trovatore*) and Rossini (*Otello* and *Il barbiere di Siviglia*). French grand opera made its début with the classic of the genre, Auber's *La Muette de Portici*, on 1 March 1863. An indication of its status was that it was given three times in succession and seven times in total that year, more than any other single opera. League tables at their crudest can be misleading, particularly where the fate of grand opera in Prague is concerned, since in the first full year of production the honours were more or less equally divided between Italian (twenty-three performances) and French opera (twenty-two performances); but out of the twenty-two only seven were of grand opera, all *La Muette*, the rest being comedies or other genres such as Halévy's *L'Eclair*, Meyerbeer's *Dinorah*, Auber's *La Neige* and Offenbach's *Orphée aux enfers*. However, on the back of the evident popularity of *La Muette*, Maýr was able to introduce other classics of the grand opera repertory in fairly short order: Halévy's *La Juive* (6 January 1864), Meyerbeer's *Les Huguenots* and *Robert le Diable* (30 October; 29 November 1864) as well as Glinka's *A Life for the Tsar* (29 August 1866). By the end of his three-and-a-half-year tenure as director, Maýr had clocked up sixty-one performances of grand opera out of a total of 474 operatic performances, hardly a negligible figure.[24]

A considerable part of the appeal of grand opera was its routine inclusion of divertissement and dance. Prague audiences showed a fascination for these elements equal to their Parisian counterparts earlier in the century. Guest dancers were popular, the pattern being set early in the history of the Provisional Theatre with the appearance on 13 December 1862 of the Spanish ballerina, Marcellina Olivera, who gave three performances of an assortment of dances before the end of the year. At the first performance of Auber's *La Muette* in March 1863 a major attraction was the portrayal of the part of Fenella by the company's prima ballerina, Marie Hentz; for performances during the rest of the year her name was printed in bigger letters on the posters than those of her singing colleagues. The clear success of ballet in attracting audiences was a feature not lost on composers: there are ballets or dance elements in the majority of Smetana's operas and all of Dvořák's, apart from the one-acter, *The Stubborn Lovers* (*Tvrdé palice*). Although Dvořák's ballets were often quite extended they never achieved the proportions of Josef Rozkošný's 'Ballet of the four seasons' in *Popelka* (premièred 1885) which occupies some 376 pages of full score, most of the second act of the opera.

When Smetana took over as musical director at the end of September 1866, he both maintained the grand opera repertory, including two new productions of *La Juive* and one of *Les Huguenots*, and extended it with Rossini's *Guillaume Tell* (14 December 1866), Glinka's *Ruslan and Lyudmila* (16 February 1867), Moniuszko's *Halka* (28 February 1868), Auber's *Gustave III* (26 January 1869) and Gounod's *Roméo et Juliette* (29 August 1869). But his most significant introduction into the repertory was Gounod's *Faust* (6 July 1867) which was given in total 115 times before the theatre finally closed in 1883; not only did it receive the most performances of any serious opera in the Provisional Theatre, but it had a major influence on Czech opera composers as diverse as Rozkošný and Dvořák. After Smetana's enforced retirement as conductor, owing to the rapid onset of deafness in the summer of 1874, there was no perceptible falling off in performances of grand opera, despite the return of Maýr as musical director, until the first opening of the National Theatre in 1881. In addition to retaining existing repertory, he introduced Meyerbeer's *Le Prophète* (5 December 1875) and *L'Africaine* (8 December 1877).

Smetana's ambitions for opera in the Provisional Theatre were inevitably affected by commercial concerns. The theatre administration, whose renewable contract was usually limited to six years, was on the whole unsentimental about commercial imperatives and was certainly unafraid to introduce theatrical turns which, although inimical to high operatic standards, nevertheless found favour with the public. Words failed Smetana when, as critic of *Národní listy*, he was forced to endure the finale of Vaccai's *Giulietta e Romeo* tacked on to the end of *Don Giovanni*, 'by popular request' according to Maýr.[25] But Smetana reserved his most withering sarcasm for the astonishing Juliano Donato. This one-legged Spanish acrobatic dancer – he had lost his leg in a previous incarnation as a toreador – was hugely popular and appeared between the acts of numerous operas in Prague in 1864 including *La Juive* and *La Muette*. In a review of *La Juive* in which Donato had loomed

large – his name was also printed larger than that of any other artist on theatre posters, or even that of the composer – Smetana suggested that lighter
repertory, such as Rossini's *Il barbiere*, might provide a more suitable frame
for his talents.

The question for the management was not so much 'what kind of opera
was best suited to raising taste among audiences?' as 'what kind of repertory would bring them in to the theatre?' Audiences were far from high-
minded and had a taste for the sensational which the management was
quite happy to accommodate. Spectacles such as *Life in Dreams* (*Život ve
snách*), described as a 'grand-fantastic play with singing, dancing and gym-
nastic performances'[26] were extremely popular. Unfortunately this taste
for the spectacular was not well served in performances of grand opera
in the Provisional Theatre. Standards were not good. Speaking as an orchestral musician, Dvořák remarked: 'The [dance] band in which I played
was engaged as the nucleus of an orchestra of thirty-six, and I must leave
you to imagine how we dance-music players got on during our opening
season . . .'.[27] Smetana, too, frequently drew attention to the inadequacies
of the orchestral accompaniment to grand opera.

Even in a theatre whose resources were a fraction of the size of those
at the Paris Opéra, grand opera could not be denied; yet the stage space of
the Provisional Theatre was far too small for such mainstays of grand opera
as crowd scenes, marches, riots and conflicts, a limitation which proved a
constant problem. In his theatrical memoirs printed in 1903, the conductor
Adolf Čech noted that the triumphal march in the fourth act of Dvořák's
first grand opera, *Vanda*, had to be much reduced owing to the small size
of the stage.[28] Nor was set design able to compensate. In the early years
of the Provisional Theatre the sets hardly rose above the rudimentary, and
many stood duty for more than one opera. The management frequently
drew attention to new lighting effects, notably at the first performance of
Les Huguenots on 30 October 1864, but other grand operas were very poorly
served by the theatre's threadbare resources. Once again *Vanda* was a victim,
with its third act, including a conjuration scene, having to be scrapped owing
to inadequate staging after the première in 1876.

There was, however, a paradox: for all the difficulties over performance,
grand opera as a model might well have seemed the ideal solution for the
nascent Czech repertory in the early days of the Provisional Theatre. The fact
that there was no real native repertory of any substance was made painfully
obvious by the first 'new' Czech opera to be given in the theatre, Skuherský's
Vladimír, bohův zvolenec (*Vladimír, God's Chosen*) on 29 September 1863;
it was, in fact, a new Czech version of an opera originally written in German (*Der Apostat*). In order to stimulate suitable contributions from Czech
composers, an opera contest had been announced by Count Jan Harrach on

10 February 1861. While he did not specify any particular models from other operatic traditions, the prescription for serious opera was that it should be based on the history of the lands of the Czech crown. Given the potential for constructing the Czech people as political victims against the background of Austrian domination, grand opera might well have seemed an inevitability. And in many ways the winning entry, Smetana and Karel Sabina's *The Brandenburgers in Bohemia*, approached the conventions and political thrust of grand opera very closely.[29] Set in the troubled late thirteenth century, when Bohemia was dominated by invading Brandenburgers, there is a major role for the Czech people in the shape of the chorus.[30] The very opening words delivered by the Czech knight Oldřich Rokycanský, as John Tyrrell has pointed out, have all the characteristic ring of righteous political indignation:

> But I say to you it is no longer possible to suffer
> foreign troops here. We must seize our arms and
> expel the Brandenburgers from our homeland; they
> destroy our country, abuse our language and under
> their sword the nation is ruined.[31]

The response of Volfram Olbramovič, a Prague worthy, 'it doesn't seem so terrible to me', rams home the message of the dangers of domestic complacency. Though set in a remote time, and with Germans rather than Austrians as the invader, the implications for Czechs as subjects of the Habsburg crown would have been clear. Willing to help those in trouble, but still ready to assert their rights, the chorus, led by Jíra, 'the king of beggars', is the very embodiment of the aspirations of the common folk of Prague and at the time was seen as a distinct manifestation of the proletariat.[32] The message would have struck home with an opera audience that was, in accordance with the wishes of those who had built the Provisional Theatre, not limited to the prosperous middle classes. The transformation of Prague from a primarily German-speaking city to a majority Czech-speaking city by the end of the nineteenth century (by 1900 barely 10 per cent of the population of Prague were first-language German speakers) was effected largely by a burgeoning industrial revolution. Since serfdom had been abolished in Austria and the lands of the Czech crown by Josef II in 1781, a large, rural Czech-speaking population could supply Prague with a new working class. Country people and those who had recently departed the countryside made up an appreciable part of the audience, as Figure 28 clearly shows.

Apart from the effective rabble-rousing nature of some of the choruses in *The Brandenburgers in Bohemia*, grand operatic features include a ballet for the townsfolk in Act I and two affecting prayer scenes, one for women soloists and chorus in the same act and another for the dispossessed of the countryside at the start of Act II. To an extent, even the outward structure of *The Brandenburgers in Bohemia* approaches grand opera: although it is nominally in three acts there is a major scene change at the start of scene 7 after a clear cadence and double bar in the largish first act, and two more in the second act. Other factors, however, weigh against *The Brandenburgers in Bohemia* as a Czech grand opera: the finales do not have the breadth associated with grand opera and there is no second, opposing chorus to represent the German invader; this exigency was prompted by a censorship nervy about the staging of national squabbles. Additionally, like Smetana's first comedy, *The Bartered Bride* (*Prodaná nevěsta*), *The Brandenburgers in Bohemia* was an eclectic work. Smetana cast his net wide in assembling his musical language in his earlier operas and there is much that echoes Italian opera and also Weber.

Two major contributors to the Provisional Theatre repertory, Karel Šebor and Karel Bendl, were prepared to embrace the externals of grand opera rather more wholeheartedly than Smetana, though with less politically explicit material. Šebor's *The Templars in Moravia* (*Templáři na Moravě*; first performed in the Provisional Theatre on 19 October 1865, some thirteen weeks before the première of *The Brandenburgers in Bohemia*), was the first newly composed opera to a Czech text staged in the Provisional Theatre. To a libretto by Sabina, *The Templars in Moravia*, although disposed across only three acts rather than five, owes a great deal to grand opera in general and Meyerbeer in particular. Šebor had little difficulty with characterisation or atmosphere. His harmonic palette, as shown by the impressive prelude, was richly chromatic. If his melodic accent is slightly limited by a tendency towards four-square phrasing, it could be distinctive, as the B minor Balláda from the opera shows.[33] The Meyerbeerian impulse is clearest in the ceremonial scenes, notably the double chorus of knights and templars in the opening sequence, and various marches. Although Šebor's next opera, *Drahomíra* (premièred in the Provisional Theatre on 20 September 1867) was susceptible to treatment as a grand opera, and includes a ballet, it has a more Italianate quality than *The Templars in Moravia*. Šebor returned, however, to the conventions of grand opera in his next work for the Provisional Theatre, *The Hussite Bride* (*Nevěsta husitská*), described at its first performance on 27 September 1868 as a 'grand national opera'.[34] Although it was originally written to a German text, Šebor's word-setting in the Czech adaptation is commendably flexible and mostly idiomatic, while the melodic writing is, if anything, more appealing than in his previous two operas. A clear success, *The Hussite Bride* received twenty-three performances in the Provisional Theatre and a further sixteen in the National Theatre up to 1900. Its historical setting, at the end of the Hussite wars in the early fifteenth century, would have had a strong resonance for Czechs who were beginning to see the Hussites' conflicts with the forces of Austrian Catholicism as a

symbol of their present political situation. An important musical symbol
was the Hussite war song 'Ye who are warriors of God' ('Ktož jsú boží bo-
jovníci') which, in this opera, Šebor was the first modern composer to use[35]
and which was subsequently employed by nearly all Czech composers of significance when touching this particular vein of national political sentiment.
Šebor's subsequent operatic career, with the 'fantastic-romantic' four acter,
Blanka (1870) and the national comedy, *The Frustrated Wedding* (*Zmařená
svatba*, 1879), not only showed a move away from grand opera, but also
marked a decline in his operatic fortunes.

The first whole-hearted Czech grand opera, however, was by Šebor's
senior of five years, Karel Bendl. *Lejla*, premièred in four acts but later revised and published in five,[36] was given for the first time in the Provisional
Theatre on 4 January 1868 to considerable public acclaim. In total, fifteen
performances were given in the lifetime of the Provisional Theatre including
two new productions, the second of which (24 September 1874) was of the
revised five-act version, and it maintained a respectable showing of ten performances (four more were given in the later 1890s) when revived in 1891
during the centenary celebrations of Leopold II's crowning as King of the
Bohemians. Krásnohorská's libretto was set in 1491 at the siege of Granada
and offered many opportunities for exotic colouring:[37] there is an extensive
dance with 'sword-play' for the Spanish victors at the end of Act IV scene 5
and Bendl's Muezzin is far more inclined to floridity than Dvořák's in Act I
of *Armida* (see below). Other grand operatic features include military music
for the Spaniards and Moors, impressive large-scale choruses, a prayer scene
for Torquemada and his monks invoking God's help in the Spaniards' struggle, and impressive finales. Bendl's personal musical style inclined towards
Mendelssohn, though in the opera there is the clear influence of Gounod.
Meyerbeer was also a potent presence; as Milan Pospíšil points out, Zorajda's
Act II Baláda from *Lejla* is extraordinarily close to the danced chorus 'Jeunes
beautés' from the second act of *Les Huguenots*.[38] Bendl continued in grand-
operatic vein in his second opera, *Břetislav* (premièred in the Provisional
Theatre on 18 September 1870 and taken off after only four performances),
although the subject was now much closer to home: taken from medieval
Czech history, the libretto, once again in five acts, deals with events leading
up to the coronation of Břetislav, one of Bohemia's signal monarchs. The
main reason for the opera's lack of popularity seems to have been its uncon-
vincing overall structure in which the coronation takes place in the central
act. There were nevertheless opportunities for considerable pomp, including a celebratory march in Act III and a prayer scene dominating the last act
as the protagonists gather around the coffin of Břetislav's father, Oldřich.

After the failure of *Břetislav*, Bendl abandoned grand opera, instead
pursuing a somewhat chameleon-like operatic career which ranged from

national comedy to *verismo*. As Smetana's influence increased, in fact, grand opera seemed to lose its attractions for Czech composers. After the eclectic tendencies of *The Brandenburgers in Bohemia* and *The Bartered Bride*, Smetana pursued a more uniform direction of a modernist nature: by comparison with his first two operas, *Dalibor* (1868), his third opera, avoids ensembles, is relatively through-composed and makes use of motivic transformation. Consequently, it was identified and excoriated by contemporary critics as Wagnerian,[39] although its Wagnerisms are rather more in the means than the manner. His next opera, the slightly more Wagnerian 'ceremonial' opera *Libuše*, was designed for the National Theatre but composed long before it opened (see n. 5): despite a nod in the direction of divertissement with the reapers' chorus in the second act, and a sequence of prophetic spectacles as the climax of the third, it was also remote from the aesthetic of grand opera. Albeit based on Czech historic mythology, *Libuše* (eventually premièred on 11 June 1881) did not really deal in national conflict beyond the disagreement of royal brothers and male *angst* about the status of a woman as leader.

While Smetana grew rapidly away from the aesthetic of grand opera in holistic terms, he was not beyond the influence of its compositional style. His admiration for Meyerbeer was genuine and it emerges strongly when Rarach conjures up devils during the 'hellish dance' in the third act of his last completed opera, *The Devil's Wall* (*Čertova stěna*, 1882); more specifically the debt is to the 'Valse infernale' from the third act of *Robert le Diable*, with which it shares both metre and key. But something of Smetana's problems with grand opera can be gleaned from a letter written to J. F. Frič in 1879 rejecting the latter's epic five-act libretto on the subject of the wandering Jew, *Ahasver* (Ahasuerus). After protesting that he had not had the opportunity to 'show the public the level of Czech-Slavonic dramatic music that I have in spirit created because *Libuše*, supreme in that direction, has not been given', and that he must devote himself to developing a style for Czech historical subjects, meaning that such cosmopolitan fare as *Ahasver* must wait, Smetana added: 'I am also worried by [the libretto's] excessive division into five acts. That is employed by the French and only for material gain since 3 per cent of takings are paid per act, thus the composer gets 15 per cent for the entire opera. From the aesthetic standpoint of opera, only three-act opera can be justified and countenanced.'[40] Thus for Smetana the objections were ideological, moral and aesthetic. Against this background, his suggestion that Frič approach Dvořák or Fibich, for their 'strength . . . freshness and youth' seems a touch waspish.

That Smetana should suggest Fibich might seem puzzling given the Wagnerian propensities of *The Bride of Messina*, but, when Smetana was writing, only one of Fibich's operas, the rather Weber-like, three-act romantic opera *Bukovín*, had been premièred (1874). Certainly there was to be a hint of grand-operatic aesthetic in his second opera, *Blaník* – based on Czech mythical history and including a certain amount of ceremonial chivalry – but this was not premièred in Prague until 1881. In the 1880s Fibich pursued a more Wagnerian path – there were already echoes of *Lohengrin* in *Blaník* – with the music drama *The Bride of Messina*; this Wagnerian tendency culminated in a three-night melodrama cycle *Hippodamie*. The only time Fibich appeared to unbend towards grand opera was in the four-act opera, *Hedy* (premièred in 1896; based on the Haidée episode in Byron's *Don Juan*) which includes an extensive ballet divertissement in the third act.

Dvořák, on the other hand, along with being fresh and energetic, had already thrown his hat into the ring with *Vanda* (premièred 17 April 1876), the only Czech grand opera of the mid-1870s. In five acts, the opera is based on the legend of the Polish princess Vanda who swears to lay down her life for the victory of her country against the invading Germans. Coinciding with Dvořák's pan-slavist interests, the 1870s were, somewhat exceptionally, a time when the Czechs felt a certain sympathy for their northern neighbours. While the libretto, with its clear differentiation between virtuous Poles and duplicitous German invaders, would be taken as a sympathy vote for fellow Slavs, it could as easily be read as an allegory of the Czech situation *vis-à-vis* the Austrians; it also avoided difficulties with the censor.[41] Moreover, the depiction of the Poles as primarily peace-loving, pastoral and musical accords well with the Herderian ideal that underpinned the philosophical basis of the Czech national revival.[42]

Dvořák's score for *Vanda* is one of his most lyrically beautiful. The opera's reputation as a failure is unjustified, though asserted in many commentaries;[43] although critical reaction at its première was minimal, owing both to a dispute between Prague's Czech-speaking political factions and to its limited performance history, no less an authority than Hostinský stated that it contained 'interesting and impressive features' and he deplored the fact that it was not included in the National Theatre's commemorative cycle of Dvořák's operas of 1901.[44] Although the libretto is poorly structured with a damagingly repetitive second act, it gave Dvořák the opportunity to write some fine large-scale set pieces. The finale of Act I, including Vanda's coronation and fateful oath to give her life for her country, is impressive. There is also a conjuration scene in Act III, a prayer and an extensive victory march in Act IV. While the choral writing is highly effective, there is little attempt to use it to represent opposing forces in the fourth-act battle. Vanda's farewell and suicide at the end of Act V is succeeded by an impressive, meditative final chorus. The influence of Meyerbeer is apparent in the first-act finale, and in the conjuration scene of Act III – also including a choral ballet – but it governs more in the externals of structure: for example, there is a *romance* for Slavoj in the first act, but the idiom is entirely Dvořák's. Gounod's *Faust* is also an influence: in temperament and treatment, Dvořák's fourth-act victory march is close to the equivalent soldiers' march in *Faust*. Bendl's *Lejla*, given a new production the year before Dvořák composed *Vanda*, is also a potent presence: the start of Bendl's second act clearly had an impact on the same place in Dvořák's score, and the rhetoric of Bendl's Torquemada is close to that of the high priest in *Vanda*; indeed, Torquemada's prayer for victory may well have been the progenitor of the High Priest's invocation in the corresponding place in *Vanda*.

Dimitrij

Dvořák put the experience he had gained in *Vanda* to good use in his second grand opera, *Dimitrij* (1882, subsequently revised). The pan-slavist dimension is strong in Marie Červinková-Riegrová's libretto, by far the best Dvořák had set to date. But, like *Vanda*, it could be read as a reflection of the Czech political situation, this time with the Poles as invaders and the Russians as the violated party. Effectively a sequel to Musorgsky's *Boris Godunov*, the opera opens with the arrival of the impostor Dimitrij at the head of a Polish army. The libretto gave Dvořák unprecedented opportunity to write for opposing choral forces, very effectively composed from the start, depicting the wavering factions which make up the Muscovite crowd. The most impressive handling of massed opposing forces is in the magnificently structured brawl between the Russians and victorious Poles, the climax of the second act's celebratory choral ballet. Equally impressive, though in a different way, is the concerted conclusion of the opera: Marfa, the widow of Ivan the Terrible, is asked to swear that Dimitrij is her son – much of the opera has hinged on her acknowledging his legitimacy although she knows he is a false pretender. Dvořák supplies what is effectively a *pezzo concertato*, a radiant quintet for the main protagonists and chorus. Dimitrij himself brings the dénouement to a climax by telling Marfa and the crowd that he does not want the throne by deceit, and is shot by Prince Šujský; shocked calls for God's mercy conclude. As with the inspired handling of Dimitrij's entry into Moscow and his greeting of the Kremlin in Act I, Dvořák shows himself able to transform atmosphere rapidly and convincingly.

Dimitrij's relationships with the Polish Princess Marina and the Russian Xenie and his own supposed mother (Marfa) energise much of the plot of the opera, as well as providing in the case of Xenie the opportunity for one of Dvořák's most effective love scenes. Apart from emotional interest, Dimitrij's relationship with the women embodies political weight since he moves from one power base to another, from the Poles to the Russians.

His abandoning of Marina for Xenie, the daughter of Boris Godunov, and magnanimity in pardoning Šujský, validate him in the eyes of the Russians: hence the sympathy and horror of the crowd when he is killed.

Despite a successful première, *Dimitrij* was revised (prompted in the first instance by Hanslick) and in 1894, after the failure of a Vienna performance two years earlier, substantially rewritten. Dvořák kept the four-act structure, but seemed intent on Wagnerising the work: the exquisite concluding quintet was removed and the prelude to its fourth act rendered gloomily portentous. Dvořák's uncertainty of hand in this much-revised version neutered the potency and freshness of the original and has confused the opera's sources, leading, in part consequence, to the opera's relatively limited stage history in the twentieth century.[45] *Dimitrij*'s claim as the greatest Czech grand opera is well founded, nevertheless. While maintaining the externals of grand opera, Dvořák managed to invest Červinková-Riegrová's magnificently structured libretto with music that is characteristic and effective dramatically. The ensembles and broad choruses allowed Dvořák to exploit the full range of his melodic ability, although he kept a perceptibly symphonic grip on the handling of recurrent motifs.

Grand opera in the National Theatre (1883–1904)

By contrast with the Provisional Theatre era, grand opera had a less sustained presence in the National Theatre. The arrival of Wagner (his works were never performed in the Provisional Theatre), the massive popularity of *Carmen* and eventually *verismo* repertory, spearheaded by twenty-eight performances of *Cavalleria rusticana* in 1891 alone, inevitably squeezed grand opera. The two most frequently performed grand operas between 1883 and 1900 were *Faust* and *Dimitrij*, given seventy-four and fifty-seven times respectively. There was also an increase in performances of native opera: *The Bartered Bride* was performed a dizzying 241 times and *Dalibor* and *Libuše* also did well.[46] *La Muette de Portici*, which introduced Provisional Theatre audiences to grand opera, faded during the 1890s with only two performances in 1895 and 1898 and a single one in 1899. Apart from *Faust* the most successful grand opera was Rossini's *Guillaume Tell* with performances nearly every year until 1903. Meyerbeer continued in the repertory, although apart from a few outings for *Le Prophète* in the early 1900s his presence was secured by performances of *Les Huguenots*.

Where Czech grand opera was concerned, *Dimitrij* was not quite the end of the story. As noted above, Dvořák rediscovered Meyerbeer in late maturity; nor was he as susceptible to fashion as his contemporaries. Where they turned to realism in the 1890s, Dvořák wrote fairy-tale operas,

The Devil and Kate (*Čert a Káča*) and *Rusalka*. His last opera, however, marked a return to an earlier love: *Armida*, based on a libretto by the Czechs' most distinguished living poet, Jaroslav Vrchlický, was a full-blown, old-fashioned grand opera, the text originally written in 1888 for Karel Kovařovic who did not get much beyond the first act.

Although he had high hopes for repeating the success of *Rusalka* – he was writing for the same leading lady, Růžena Maturová – Dvořák had considerable difficulty with *Armida*. A sincere and devout Roman Catholic, Dvořák should surely have been expected to respond well to this tale of Christian virtue overcoming pagan wiles; Vrchlický's libretto was derived from the story of Rinaldo and Armida in Tasso's *Gerusalemme liberata* with an uplifting end, imported from the combat of Tancredi and Clorinda, which effects a swelling, hymn-like choral conclusion over the dead, but baptised, heroine. Nevertheless, Dvořák's manuscript sketch, in contrast to that of *Rusalka*, strongly suggests uncertainty. In getting to grips with *Armida*, Dvořák seems to have leaned on *Vanda* – the opera had been in his mind since it was considered, and rejected, from the 1901 cycle of his operas. Both grand operas have a central female role and the depiction of Armida is often close to that of Vanda; there are also melodic similarities between Vanda and Slavoj's first-act duet and that for the lovers in the second act of the later opera. But the closest resemblance lies in the conclusions to both operas: lamenting a dead heroine, they are the same in structure and motivic treatment.[47] The solos for Armida in the first and second acts, inspired by Maturová, are attractive and affecting, but the central duet with Rinaldo, in the second act, while certainly beautiful, is hardly, by later nineteenth-century lights, erotic. The main problem with *Armida* is that there is very little theatrical dynamism in Vrchlický's libretto, by contrast with Červinková-Riegrová's *Dimitrij*. There is plenty of stately ceremonial – choruses for pilgrims and crusaders, fanfares and proclamations – but little of the exciting conflict and resolution that made *Dimitrij* so effective. The only genuine double-chorus writing ends the second act as Rinaldo and Armida escape the crusaders' camp on a chariot drawn by dragons! The finales are musically and dramatically convincing but the steady tread of ornamental set pieces, including a third-act choral ballet, generates precious little heat. Like Rimsky-Korsakov's *Servilia* (see the previous chapter), *Armida* was an opera out of time and tune with contemporary taste (the public response to the première was puzzled but respectful). More damagingly, while the libretto gave Dvořák the opportunities for eclecticism he relished, it did not balance them with a convincing dramatic thread.

The grand-operatic eclecticism that liberated Dvořák's muse was inimical to those, like Nejedlý, who later sought to construct the development of Czech opera in terms of modernism and consistency. Grand opera is not to be found in twentieth-century Czech repertory, but various aspects of its aesthetic lived on for example in the dance and divertissement in Janáček's *Excursions of Mr Brouček* (*Výlety páně Broučkovy*) and *The Cunning Little Vixen* (*Příhody Lišky Bystroušky*). They are also to be found in abundance in Martinů's last opera, *The Greek Passion* (*Řecké pašije*, completed in 1959): four acts, exotic colouring, opposed political forces (prosperous villagers against refugees), religious scenes (the libretto is based on Kazantzakis's *Christ Recrucified*, a retelling of the Passion in early twentieth-century Greece), a divertissement during a peasant wedding in Act IV and even a conjuration scene in the shape of a nightmare sequence in the third act. There is no evidence that Martinů consciously thought he was reproducing the conventions of grand opera when he fashioned the libretto and wrote the score, but for a composer who passionately avoided ideologically driven music drama and welcomed theatrical variety, it is perhaps unsurprising that a resurgence of the grand opera aesthetic should occur.

19 Italian opera

FIAMMA NICOLODI

Grand opera and *opera-ballo*

The formative phase of post-Verdian grand opera spanned more than twenty years. Among its earliest notable works was *Mefistofele* by Arrigo Boito (1868): provocative and iconoclastic, this opera swept away many rules or 'formulas' (as its composer disparagingly called them) of traditional opera. This explains why its first performance at La Scala, Milan was a complete failure. However, Italian assimilation of French grand opera had already matured as a result of three factors: aesthetic discussions in the press, vigorous publishing and promotion policies by the firms of Ricordi and Lucca, and various theatre managements open to new European products. This assimilation can be traced back several decades. The writing of 'grand operas' continued into the early 1890s, as shown in Table 19.1. The last of these works are contemporary with the first attempts at a new genre, one which was to be an antithesis in many (but not all) of its attributes: '*verismo*' opera. *Verismo*'s dramatic norms were instead based on narrative concision, unobtrusive structure and the absence of dance.

Among the last Italian grand operas were *Cristoforo Colombo* (1892) by Alberto Franchetti, based on the adventures of the discoverer of the New World; and *I Medici* (1893) by Ruggero Leoncavallo, actually the first part of an unfinished operatic trilogy on the Italian Renaissance entitled, with deliberate Wagnerian echoes, *Crepusculum*.[1] In *Cristoforo Colombo* the grandiose scale, with crowd scenes, dances and *pezzi concertati*[2] in Acts III and IV, was prompted by a particular festive occasion: the 400th anniversary of the discovery of America. It reveals, however, a utopian rather than a triumphal spirit: indeed, the message of brotherhood between races and peoples was commonly found in many works at the end of the century. *I Medici* was conceived by Leoncavallo as an epic 'national poem', something imbued with 'Italian-ness' (*Italianità*). It was also an early example of the aestheticising taste for citing 'ancient' music: there are citations of late sixteenth-century dances by Fabritio Caroso, while the libretto was inspired by Renaissance poetry, referring to *ballate* by Angelo Poliziano (1454–94) and *canzoni a ballo* and other poetry by Lorenzo the Magnificent (1449–92).[3]

An 'obituary' of grand opera published in 1898 by the Turin critic and composer Ippolito Valetta referred to *verismo* opera as the opposite pole of

Table 19.1 *List of operas discussed in Chapter 19*

Title	Librettist	Composer	Genre	Date of première
Romeo e Giulietta (4)	Marco Marcello	Filippo Marchetti	dramma lirico	1865
Mefistofele (prol., 5)	Arrigo Boito	Arrigo Boito	opera	1868
Ruy Blas (4)	Carlo D'Ormeville	Marchetti	dramma lirico	1869
Il Guarany (4)	Antonio Scalvini and D'Ormeville	António Carlos Gomes	opera-ballo	1870
Fosca (4)	Antonio Ghislanzoni	Gomes	melodramma	1873, rev. 1878
I Lituani (prol., 3)	Ghislanzoni	Amilcare Ponchielli	dramma lirico	1874, rev. 1875
Salvator Rosa (4)	Ghislanzoni	Gomes	dramma lirico	1874
Mefistofele (prol., 4, epilogue)	Boito	Boito	opera	1875
Gustavo Wasa (4)	D'Ormeville	Marchetti	dramma lirico	1875
La Gioconda (4)	Boito	Ponchielli	dramma lirico	1876 rev. 1876, 1877, 1879, 1880
Maria Tudor (4)	Emilio Praga, Boito and Angelo Zanardini	Gomes	dramma lirico	1879
Don Giovanni d'Austria (4)	D'Ormeville	Marchetti	dramma lirico	1880
Il figliuol prodigo (4)	Zanardini	Ponchielli	melodramma	1880
Elda (4)	D'Ormeville	Alfredo Catalani	dramma fantastico	1880 rev. 1890 (q.v.)
Dejanice (4)	Zanardini	Catalani	dramma lirico	1883
Le villi (1, rev. 2)	Ferdinando Fontana	Giacomo Puccini	leggenda drammatica, rev. as opera-ballo	1884
Marion Delorme (5)	E. Golisciani	Ponchielli	dramma	1885
Asrael (4)	Fontana	Alberto Franchetti	leggenda	1888
Lo schiavo (4)	Rodolfo Paravicini	Gomes	dramma lirico	1889
Loreley (3) [see *Elda*, above]	D'Ormeville, Zanardini	Catalani	azione romantica	1890
Cristoforo Colombo (4)	Luigi Illica	Franchetti	dramma lirico	1892 rev. (3) 1923
I Medici (4)	Ruggero Leoncavallo	Ruggero Leoncavallo	azione storica	1893

a genre now judged to be outmoded. It offers a good standpoint from which to view grand opera's demise:

> Public interest is flagging. Long, inflated operas with dances and grand marches, descents into Hell and more or less fantastic apotheoses are no longer regarded as valuable on the theatrical stock-market. A performance of two hours or so is perfect enough. One is no longer ordinarily obliged to suffer those five long acts, in the course of which every visual and mechanical device must pass before the astonished eye of the spectator.[4]

In order that confusion over the terms 'grand opera' (seldom used in Italy) and its Italian version *opera-ballo* (literally, opera with dance) may be avoided, a brief clarification of terms is needed. In comparison with French grand opera, the corresponding Italian genre shows some differences, attributable to the influence both of French music-theatre and of Wagnerian music drama.[5] It does not display a preference for historical subjects but, rather, offers a variety of themes, drawn equally from legend and from history, to which were added fantastic make-believe and magic at the end of the century. The commonly used term *opera-ballo* highlights precisely the component not found in traditional Italian opera: dance integrated within the action. Dance was demanded in one or more divertissements among the set pieces but did not necessarily tend towards the grandiose. On the other hand, Italian grand opera, drawing on historical dramas and constructed on a grand scale, did not consider dance an essential requirement, even if it contained large choral and ensemble scenes with at least one *pezzo concertato*, elaborate scenery, and 'characteristic' pieces to the full[6] – in other words, adhering to all the other components of French grand opera. To cite an example, *Fosca* (1873) by Antônio Carlos Gomes, may be seen as the direct antecedent of Amilcare Ponchielli's *La Gioconda* (1876), on account of the emotional extremes traversed by the protagonist. It utilises many of the formal and constituent elements of grand opera: a picturesque setting, some 'characteristic' pieces such as the second-act wedding march accompanied by organ, many (if not prominent) choral episodes, a *pezzo concertato* in the finale to Act II, and so on. Even then, it cannot be regarded as an *opera-ballo* since it contains no dance. The same might be said for *Don Giovanni d'Austria* (1880) by Filippo Marchetti: a grand opera, but not an 'opera with dance'. *Romeo e Giulietta* (1865), also by Marchetti, is called *opera-ballo* in several editions published by Lucca, but simply on account of one piece in $\frac{6}{8}$ indicated as a 'Ballabile' (i.e. 'suitable for dancing'). Other editions omit this Act I 'Ballabile' in favour of a Gb major 'Valzer' (Waltz) especially written for the tenor Italo Campanini (but without the explicit participation of the *corps de ballet*). Whether or not it may be seen as an 'opera with dance', *Romeo e Giulietta* is not, however, a grand opera, since it lacks the specific requirements of the genre such as local colour and an imposing setting. On the other hand Marchetti's *Gustavo Wasa* (1875) may justifiably be considered as both a grand opera and an *opera-ballo* on account of its 'Ballabile' in Act III, as well as its marches, hymns, popular songs, ballads, ensembles and *pezzi concertati*.

This range of differences from French grand opera reflects, on the one hand, cultural issues specific to Italy, such as the reluctance to welcome balletic episodes, and, on the other hand, the creative approaches of individual composers; for example, Marchetti's style was always felt to be intimate rather than monumental.

In general, application of the adjective 'grand' to post-Verdian opera by both public and composers (even if it never appears in the scores) requires a variety of elements variously mixed together. (Fuller details of works mentioned below may be found in Table 19.1.) First there was a structure on a substantial scale, usually in four acts. Exceptions are Boito's *Mefistofele* in its 1868 version (prologue and five acts) as well as its 1875 version (prologue, four acts and epilogue); and Franchetti's *Cristoforo Colombo* (four acts and an epilogue). Secondly there were large choral and ensemble scenes with at least one musically elaborate *pezzo concertato*, usually positioned in Act III but occasionally found in Act II (as in Gomes's *Il Guarany*, 1870). Thirdly there was a subject based on history, but also, as we have seen, possibly derived from legend or fantasy. There would be elaborate scenery and 'characteristic' pieces. The inclusion and design of divertissements was variable: for example a short divertissement occurs in *Ruy Blas*, Act III, whereas lengthy ones are found in *I Lituani, La Gioconda, Il figliuol prodigo* and *Il Guarany*. For purely orchestral dances, we have the 'Bacchanal' in *Maria Tudor* and the 'Saturnal' in *Il figliuol prodigo*, both in Act III. A symphonic–vocal type of divertissement is represented by the 'Ballabile delle Almee' in *Il figliuol prodigo*, Act II. Such episodes may be either dramatically related to the action or (as in the majority of cases) purely ornamental; or else completely absent (*Don Giovanni d'Austria, Marion Delorme*).

But combinations of different operatic types (e.g., *opera-ballo*, *verismo* and symbolist opera) are frequently found in Italian opera and often occur out of apparent chronological order. Yet even when novelty was introduced there was a structured adherence to tradition. Thus if *opera-ballo* came to an end at the close of the nineteenth century, this does not mean that some of its components were not present in opera after 1900. This is particularly the case in those *verismo* operas based on historical subjects, with their corresponding emphasis on more flexible vocal styles, leading towards the abandonment of closed forms. In turn, *verismo* elements were anticipated in earlier grand operas, particularly those containing exaggerated, immoderate or otherwise eccentric characters or gestures. Although the device was not new, the number of suicides on stage increases: Fosca poisons herself, following in the footsteps of Sélika in Meyerbeer's *L'Africaine*; Corrado in *I Lituani* drinks a 'poisonous substance'; Gioconda and Dejanice stab themselves to death. We also find fits of violence: in *Fosca*, Act III scene 4, 'pirates *brutally* drag Delia across the rocks, leaving her alone and bewildered'; Maria Tudor, called 'Bloody Mary', 'grabs her rival by the arm' and 'drags her by force', as in the original play by Victor Hugo (1833). In *La Gioconda*, Act IV, Barnaba spies on Gioconda while she prays, and later, when she feigns self-adornment for his benefit, he reveals (in an aside) his craving lust. The increasing emphasis on violence, cruelty and morbid extremities – masochistic, sadistic and voyeuristic – shifts the concept of 'shock' typical of grand opera from external action (as in the French model) to the inner psyche. It also disrupts that process of audience-identification with the character on stage that was the aesthetic basis of early nineteenth-century opera.[7]

Such characters and actions are far removed from the tragic dimensions of traditional opera with its moral code based on the archaic values of father, family and religion. They display states of emotional excitement and pathological sensuality also found in late nineteenth-century 'positivist' studies on the human psyche and on behaviour.[8] Stereotypes of treacherous, dissolute individuals are to be found in certain baritone characters who do not just limit themselves to the pursuit of evil, but threaten the female protagonist by means of devious manoeuvres. Examples include the pirate Cambro in *Fosca*, Philip II of Spain in *Don Giovanni d'Austria*, the Assyrian adventurer Amenofi in *Il figliuol prodigo*, and the satanic Barnaba who, in the *grand guignolesque* finale of *La Gioconda*, rages at the already dead protagonist, shouting in her ear that he has drowned her mother. Not surprisingly, neither Scribe's libretto *Le Fils prodigue* (see Chapter 10) nor Victor Hugo's play *Angelo, tyran de Padoue*, from which these two libretti are derived, contains any trace of such actions. Fosca, Gioconda and Dejanice are *femmes fatales* and sinners after the style of the *maudite* literature favoured by the *Scapigliatura*, the bohemian circle of writers (including Boito) and other artists active in Milan in the 1860s and 1870s, who 'exhibited a taste for morbid and macabre subjects'.[9] Undecided whether (or how) they should kill their rivals, or else themselves as an act of sacrifice for their beloveds, they reveal more complex psychological states and neuroses than were known to the monolithic heroines of earlier opera. The excesses of the text are rarely matched in the music, though exceptions do occur. It would be left to *verismo* to exploit violent, exaggerated musical gestures, such as the stabbing opening bars of the aria 'Suicidio' in *La Gioconda*, Act IV, with anacruses and a *fortissimo* descending octave leap, sustained by hammerblows on strings and horns over a chord of F$\sharp$ minor. *Verismo*

Table 19.2 *Sources of Italian operas*

Opera	Source
Il Guarany (1870)	José Martiniano de Alencar, *O Guarani* (1857)
I Lituani (1874)	Adam Bernard Mickiewicz, *Konrad Wallenrod* (1827)
Salvator Rosa (1874)	Eugène de Mirecourt, *Masaniello* (1851)
La Gioconda (1876)	Victor Hugo, *Angélo, tyran de Padoue* (1835)
Maria Tudor (1879)	Hugo, *Marie Tudor* (1833)
Il figliuol prodigo (1880)	Eugène Scribe, *L'Enfant prodigue* (1850)
Le villi (1884)	Alphonse Karr, *Les Willis* (1852)
Marion Delorme (1885)	Hugo, *Marion Delorme* (1831)
Lo schiavo (1889)	Alfredo d'Escragnolle de Taunay, *Scenas de viagem* (1868) and *La Retraite de Laguna* (1871)

would also reintroduce certain theatrical effects used by its predecessors, as in the 'quasi parlato' phrase 'Enrico mi fai ribrezzo!' uttered by Margherita before her death in the third act of *Mefistofele*, or the 'suppressed shout of anger' of Barnaba in the final moments of *La Gioconda*.

Grand opera continued in Italy along three different paths. The first comprised works by French composers performed in Italian theatres and circulated in Italian versions by the two principal music publishers. Lucca published *Roberto il diavolo*, *Gli Ugonotti* and *L'Africana* by Meyerbeer, *L'ebrea* (*La Juive*) by Halévy and *Faust* by Gounod, while Ricordi published *La muta di Portici* by Auber and *Il profeta* by Meyerbeer. The second group comprised works by Italian composers initially staged abroad, usually in Paris, and revived for the Italian stage in reworked forms. These include Rossini's *Mosè* and *Guglielmo Tell* (originally *Moïse et Pharaon* and *Guillaume Tell*); Donizetti's *La Favorita*, *Poliuto* and *Don Sebastiano* (originally *La Favorite*, *Polyeucte* and *Dom Sébastien*); and Verdi's *La forza del destino* (originally written for St Petersburg), *I vespri siciliani* and *Don Carlos* (written for Paris), and *Aida* (originally for Cairo). In the third group were works belonging to the genre of *opera-ballo* by Italian composers originally intended for the Italian stages, of which the best known were shown earlier in Table 19.1. We can see their predominantly non-Italian literary origins from the selection in Table 19.2.

All the Italian works in Table 19.2 were inspired by the Paris operas of Meyerbeer and others, which were still performed in the early twentieth century. But they were not themselves performed at the Paris Opéra, with one exception, *Mefistofele* in 1912.[10] These works enjoyed an immense success in their time in Italy, for all that they are little known today. They appeared late compared with their French counterparts, and coincided with the strong French spirit of nationalism emerging after 1870, which contrasted with the cosmopolitanism that had predominated within that country until the middle of the nineteenth century.[11]

Performance history

1840 saw the first appearance in Italy of grand opera, with Meyerbeer's *Robert le Diable*. Between then and the end of the century, when the taste for the genre died out, its fortunes involved a shift away from an elitist public towards the social pretensions of the post-unification middle classes. The bourgeoisie sought social advancement by way of cultural discourse and exchange, and also by looking beyond their own geographical boundaries. The genre achieved success not only with the public at large, but also with musicians, some of whom were committed followers of Meyerbeer (though not all admitted it), including Verdi, Boito, Ponchielli and Gomes. Performed in Italian, as was the practice at the time, Meyerbeer's grand operas became the first non-Italian genre ever to establish itself fully in the repertory of Italian theatres, precisely at the time (during the 1850s) when one could start to speak of a regular operatic repertory. (Almost no Italian opera before *La sonnambula* and *Norma* (both 1831) had constituted any sort of 'repertory'.) Grand opera in Italy was praised on account of its masterly fusion of the historical and the dramatic, the proper balance between unity and variety, and the universality of its message: in 1864 the writer Filippi would refer to Meyerbeer's works as 'an encyclopaedia of euphony'.[12] They sparked off debates centred on the categories and attributes of Romantic music, whether the 'philosophical', the supernatural, the 'fantastic' or the colouristic, that had begun with the Italian premières of Rossini's *Guglielmo Tell* in Lucca and Florence (1831), and of Auber's *La muta di Portici* in Trieste (1832).

Florence in fact staged the Italian premières of three Meyerbeer grand operas: *Roberto il diavolo* on 26 December 1840, *Gli Ugonotti* (but with the title *Gli Anglicani*) on 26 December 1841, and *Il profeta* on 26 December 1852. In the course of the 1850s interest in the genre spread through other cities. For example, *L'Ebrea* (*La Juive*) by Halévy was performed at the Teatro Carlo Felice in Genoa in 1858; Gounod's *Faust* was given at La Scala, Milan in 1862; Meyerbeer's *L'Africana* was staged at the Teatro Comunale in Bologna in 1865; and Massenet's *Re di Lahore*, described on the bill-boards as an '*opera-ballo*' and partially adapted to Italian taste by the composer himself, was staged at the Teatro Regio, Turin, in 1878. The Italian peninsula, set apart from Europe by both cultural and geographical differences, also revealed an internal diversity as regards musical reception, with north-central Italy more sensitive to northern European innovations – grand opera included – and south-central Italy (from Rome downward) being slower to follow the trend. In the twenty years between 1860 and 1879 the grand operas of Meyerbeer prompted rave responses in the chief theatres of northern Italy (thirty-one different productions, not counting revivals), while the interest demonstrated in the south was less developed.[13]

Together with a lack of uniform reception that is attributable to geo-graphical factors, any history of *opera-ballo* must take into account certain norms in regard to performance practices in Italy. Being less aware of the incorporation of dance into traditional operatic forms, and being more accustomed to the provision of a dance at the conclusion of an opera, the Italian approach was casual. It made no attempt to preserve the unity of form present in some works. In the performance history of grand opera (which for the most part has yet to be written), several constant factors emerge. If a work's first performance was more or less faithful to its original de-sign, subsequent performances often experienced alterations. Complete acts (along with their divertissements) were often dropped in favour of dances in a different style or with different dramatic content, patched together by musicians who specialised in choreography.[14] Arbitrary approaches, wholly detrimental to the original dances, were often adapted in the period 1850–60 and did not completely disappear in succeeding decades. Indeed, the alterations characteristic of provincial theatres (those without a *corps de ballet* or a competent choreographer) also became evident in some leading houses. In the 1870 and 1890 seasons at the Fenice in Venice, isolated acts of *Roberto il diavolo* were presented along with the ballet *Brahma* (music by Costantino Dall'Argine, choreography by Ippolito Monplaisir). In 1871, entire acts of both *Gli Ugonotti* by Meyerbeer and *Ruy Blas* by Marchetti were lost to the ballet *La Camargo* (again with Dall'Argine's music and Monplaisir's choreography). In 1875, only the first three acts of Gomes's *Il Guarany* were performed, so as to make room for the ballet *Satanella* (music by the ballet composers F. L. Hertel and Cesare Pugni, choreography by Paul Taglioni adapted by José Mendez). In that same Venetian season, *Satanella* was seen also alongside Donizetti's *Poliuto*.[15] Both theatre direc-tors and operatic composers were well aware of the Italian public's scant interest in the divertissements of *opera-ballo*, which had become obligatory extras. Their presence gave rise to at least two celebrated examples, the tri-umphal ballet in *Aida*, Act II scene 2, and the 'Dance of the Hours' in *La Gioconda*, Act III scene 6. Yet there was no compunction in dropping them if necessary. As early as the second La Scala performance of *La Gioconda*, Ponchielli saw several of his ballet movements cut out;[16] and aware of the choreographical difficulties involved in his most monumental work, *Il figli-uol prodigo*, he retained the second-act dances but made those in the third act optional and replaceable by a chorus.

In the second half of the nineteenth century the experience of hearing grand opera coincided with a maturing of Italian musical taste and a growing interest in symphonic and chamber music. During the 1860s the Società del Quartetto and the first symphony orchestras were formed. Within theatres, performance standards increased in terms of both music and staging. The modern figure of the conductor was established in this period, bringing together the previously separate roles of musical director and concert-master, and this produced great advantages with regard to coherence and teamwork. Similarly, the duties of the choreographer 'for the dance music' ('per i ballabili') of an opera became separated from those of the choreographer 'for the ballets' ('per i balli'). The figure of the 'stage director' emerged, similar to today's *régisseur*, with responsibility for the visual aspects of the performance, the organisation of crowd scenes, and so on.[17]

The workings of the theatre industry during this period contributed to the demise of the impresario in favour of the economically powerful figure of the publisher, whose position was consolidated by a new law concerning authors' rights promulgated on 25 June 1865.[18] The opera composer of the late nineteenth century was influenced by market forces, which led him to write works that would have public appeal. If an opera proved unsuccessful, then its most contentious passages were rewritten in accordance with the advice of the critics, and in the light of its reception in the theatre. For example, as already noted, the too forward-looking first version of *Mefistofele* was an utter failure in 1868; its morality was considered decadent,[19] and its score was felt to be characterised by anti-vocal melodic complexity and an over-enthusiasm for 'symphonic' effects. Therefore the composer-librettist provided a more acceptable second version in 1875, whose central focus on the love elements restored the themes and styles more typical of Romantic opera (e.g., Faust was cast as a tenor, not a baritone as in 1868). Ponchielli rewrote *I Lituani* twice (Milan, 1874 and 1875), and after the Milanese première of *La Gioconda* in 1876, he altered that opera no fewer than four times (Venice, 1876; Rome, 1877; Genoa, 1879; Milan, 1880). The Brazilian composer Gomes, active in Italy where he had studied at the Milan Conservatoire, produced two separate vocal-score editions of *Fosca* (Milan, 1873 and 1878) and considered altering the unsuccessful *Maria Tudor* (Milan, 1879) through the addition of cabalettas.[20]

Stylistic aspects

Those aspects of *opera-ballo* which might have met with the approval of a more informed public can be broken down into seven categories. The first was effective orchestration. This might involve using solo instruments, for example the bassoon in the Prelude to Act IV of *Ruy Blas*, the viola in the Prelude to Act IV of *Fosca*, or the oboe in the overture to *Lo schiavo*. But it could extend to symphonic music sometimes provided as an introduction, such as the two-part overture to *I Lituani* which has an Allegro con fuoco in sonata form, or else to descriptive character-pieces. For the latter, examples include the 'intermezzi' which were normally situated towards the opening of the penultimate act of a five-act work:[21] there was the 'Pastorale' in *Il figliuol prodigo*, in F major, $^6_8$, inspired by the land of Judea, and the local colour of *Lo schiavo*, Act IV scene 4, representing a Brazilian dawn complete with bird-songs, blazes of trumpets and cannon-shots, anticipating the triumphant 'Inno del sole' (Hymn to the sun) in Mascagni's *Iris* (1898).

Second was the use of more free-flowing, discursive musical forms avoiding cadential articulations in favour of the more active conversational style with which Verdi had already experimented. Third was the use of declamation, which opens up and expands musical numbers. One example is the 'tumult' scene in *La Gioconda* Act I, in which the sound-level increases as the characters arrive on stage and the musical tempo accelerates; this is almost completely built up in 'parlante' (spoken) style, with the orchestra providing thematic support for the vocal line.[22] The fourth element was harmonic subtlety originating in more frequent chromatic modulations and enharmonic passages. A case in point is the Act I duet for Cristopher Columbus and Queen Isabella in Franchetti's *Cristoforo Colombo*, based on tonal ambiguity between the use of sharp keys in the orchestra and flat ones in the voices. Fifth was the combination of high and low styles (polystylism).

Sixth in our list of stylistic aspects of *opera-ballo* was the structural unity obtained by using recurring motifs. Of this the most extensive example, deriving from its careful dramatic design, is to be found in *Mefistofele*. The luminous tonality of E major for the chorus of Celestial Hosts in the prologue recurs at two crucial points in the drama, at the deaths of Margherita and of Faust, respectively at the centre and at the conclusion of the opera. The signifying force of recurring themes in general was not developed in the Wagnerian manner, but originated instead in the graphic or pictorial techniques of French opera. Recurring motifs might symbolise, pre-announce or recall one or more characters, objects, feelings or events. Examples of the first are the rhythmically threatening motif of Barnaba in *La Gioconda*, and the rugged, diatonic theme of the pirates heard in the Prelude to *Fosca*. As for objects, one could mention the rosary of La Cieca in *La Gioconda*. Musical motifs of feeling were most commonly associated with 'love', as 'L'amo come il fulgor del creato' ('I love him as the splendour of all Creation') in *La Gioconda*, Act II scene 7 and Act III scene 2, or as in 'O dolce voluttà' ('Oh sweet voluptuousness') in *Ruy Blas*, Act III. And as for motifs representing events, we have the death of the tenor hero as anticipated in the Andante, E major, $^3_4$ section of the overture to *I Lituani*.

Opera-ballo, finally, saw the incorporation of self-contained numbers within increasingly lengthy scenes. Publishers continued to print the latter separately, simply for commercial reasons, compensating for the

conventional final cadence by means of imaginative titles such as
'Baptism Scene' (Scena del Battesimo) (*Il Guarany*), 'Chorus of Accusation'
(Invettiva-Coro) (*Fosca*), 'Ironic Short Scene' (Scenetta dell'ironia) (*Maria
Tudor*), 'Grand Gambling Scene' (Gran scena del giuoco) or 'Snakecharmer's
Scene' (Scena dell'ammaliatore di serpenti) (*Il figliuol prodigo*).

Cultured listeners doubtless appreciated more experimental aspects
as well, such as the stereophonic effects of the 'Prologue in Heaven' in
Mefistofele, whose fanfares and choruses emanate from different theatrical spaces, creating a sonic representation of the angelic hierarchy; or the
chorus of soldiers and women whose voices fade into a *pianissimo* at the
conclusion of a fierce battle near the start of Act III of *I Lituani*. The less
informed public, however, might have concentrated on the simpler, more
easily remembered elements. In the second half of the nineteenth century
the latter type of public attended the theatre frequently, partly as a result
of various practical policies: price controls promoted by theatre managers
and local councils; enlargement of auditoria (in the principal theatres the
last row of boxes was dismantled in order to make way for the more popular
'gallery'); and building of multifunctional and reasonably priced theatres.
The middle- and lower-middle-class public looked for a more immediate
type of involvement.

Six main features might particularly have attracted them. First was the
suppleness of the melodic line, achieved by regular, symmetrical phrase-
structures. This was a dominant feature of the *opera-ballo*, notwithstanding
the orchestral enrichments introduced by some composers. Second were
scenic effects, such as the burning and sinking of the ship Hecate in *La
Gioconda*, Act II, or the exploding of the castle and the church at the end of
Il Guarany and *Salvator Rosa*, both of which recall the finale of *Le Prophète*.
Third were the *coups de théâtre*: for example, in the third act of *La Gioconda*,
during festive celebrations in a hall in the Ca' d'Oro, Alvise shows his guests
the lifeless body of his wife Laura, laid out on a catafalque. Fourth was
highly dramatic expression, projected over the footlights in powerful declamation, for example in monologues where singers were able to model their
interpretation on the acting styles of contemporary spoken theatre.[23] Fifth
was the abundant presence of 'characteristic pieces' and 'stage music', iden-
tifiable by their clearly historical or geographical 'colouring', which aided
the process of popular acculturation and is evident in so many operas of
post-unification Italy.[24] And sixth was the presence of lively dance rhythms
(the waltz, *galop*, or mazurka) even outside those parts of the score specifically intended for choreography; such music diverted listeners with echoes
of operetta and 'light' or popular music. We see an abundance of waltzes
in Puccini's *Le villi*, and in the 'Saturnal' of *Il figliuol prodigo* the Allegro
is a *galop* in $\frac{2}{4}$, followed by a waltz marked Molto moderato. The 'Passo

delle freccie' (Dance of the Arrows) of *Il Guarany* contains an Allegretto in the form of a triple-time mazurka, while the *canzonetta* 'Mia piccirella' from *Salvator Rosa* could be mistaken for a Neapolitan street-song, and the recurring theme from *Ruy Blas*, 'O dolce voluttà', appears to be a homage to the waltz-king Johann Strauss.[25]

Vocal forms

Wavering between respect for tradition and desire for innovation, the Italian composers of grand opera modified past forms, adopting a number of solutions already put forward by Verdi to place the vocal numbers within increasingly large-scale scenes. Among the ensembles, great importance was accorded to the multi-sectional central finale, deploying soloists, supporting singers and chorus, which remained the point of greatest musical and scenic impact: witness the grand scale and variety of effects in the finales of *Il Guarany* (Act II), *Maria Tudor* (Act III), *I Lituani* (Act II), *La Gioconda* (Act III) and *Il figliuol prodigo* (Act III). In his finales Ponchielli was the inventor of a highly effective idea: the repetition of a theme already sung by the tenor or soprano in the cantabile section, but now with full orchestra, *fortissimo*, at the end of the whole ensemble. Made popular in *La Gioconda*, this peroration effect, calculated more for musical reasons than for dramatic ones, may well have influenced a long line of opera composers of the 'Giovane scuola' (Young School): Mascagni in *Cavalleria rusticana*, Leoncavallo in *I pagliacci*, Puccini in *Le villi, Edgar, Manon Lescaut, La bohème, Tosca, Madama Butterfly* and *Turandot*, and Cilea in *Adriana Lecouvreur*.

Ensembles for four or more voices were definitely rare (for exceptions see the quartets in *Ruy Blas*, Act I, *Fosca*, Act IV, *Salvator Rosa*, Act IV and *Don Giovanni d'Austria*, Act II, and the quintet in *Ruy Blas*, Act II). However, the structure of duets and trios became more varied. In order to conform and adapt to the dramatic content, they sometimes broke off midway, as with the duet between Pery and Gonzales in *Il Guarany*, Act II or that between Salvatore and Masaniello in *Salvator Rosa*, Act III. Sometimes they continued without a pause into the contrasting *tempo d'attacco* of the following scene, as when the tense duet between Laura and Alvise passes through a short recitative into the joyful 'Serenata' in *La Gioconda*, Act III. Other duets transformed the usual cantabile section into a *parlante* style, entrusting the thematic passages to the orchestra. This occurs in the Andante cantabile, G major, $\frac{4}{4}$, 'Contro il poter sovrano', during the 'Dialogo' in *Salvator Rosa*, Act I scene 8. Sometimes they consisted of only two sections, *tempo d'attacco*–cantabile, or cantabile–cabaletta; or included cabalettas that incorporated the chorus. Some repeated the cabaletta at the expense of the cantabile (which was omitted), as in the duet 'O grido di quest' anima' between Enzo and Barnaba in *La Gioconda*, Act I.

Cabalettas, if used, also reveal some innovative ways of avoiding outworn conventions, even if they remain melodically expansive moments in which the voices move in thirds, sixths or octaves. The final section of the piece was rarely repeated; two exceptions to this are (once again) 'O grido di quest'anima', and the duet 'L'accento dell'amor' between Isabella and Salvatore in Act II of *Salvator Rosa*. Final sections did not even necessarily retain the fast tempo of the traditional cabaletta: in the duet 'Lontano, lontano, lontano' in Act III of *Mefistofele* the tempo remains Adagio, while in the Act II duet of *La Gioconda*, 'Laggiù nelle nebbie remote' (which is modelled on the aforementioned piece), we have a lulling Andante in $\frac{9}{8}$ time.

For the most part, vocal solos conformed either to the shorter structure of the instrumental *Lied* form, ABA[1], or to that of the ballad, popular song or *romance* in strophic form. An example of ABA[1] form can be seen in *Mefistofele*, Act I: Faust's 'Larghetto' 'Dai campi, dai prati' in F major, $\frac{3}{4}$, with the middle section in the relative minor followed by a shortened reprise. (Ex. 19.1) Other solos follow some kind of continuous form. Great success was enjoyed by the bipartite structure initiated by Verdi, in which the first, agitated section in a minor key was followed by a more expansive second part in the tonic key or the relative major. Such examples include 'E da tre mesi io soffro' from *I Lituani*, Act III, 'Suicidio' from *La Gioconda*, Act IV, and 'Del corteo funeral' from *Il figliuol prodigo*, Act III.

Dramatic elements

In its dramatic use of the orchestra, grand opera continued to employ the gestural formulas of early nineteenth-century opera which were well known to the Italian public – tremolos and diminished sevenths to convey fear, horror, shock; high violins or the dotted rhythms of the funeral march for either a sublime or a mundane death; and agitated staccato figures to indicate conspiracies or uprisings. However, the range of dynamic and expressive instructions became more varied and exhilarating, seen for example in *I Lituani*: 'allargando', 'animando il tempo', 'cantando con espressione', 'affrettando con calore', 'stringendo', 'incalzando', 'con anima', and so on.

The subjects dramatised in *opera-ballo*, in keeping with those of the early nineteenth century, were influenced both by the literature of northern European Romanticism (Scott, Schiller, Byron, Hugo) and by its Italian counterpart (Francesco Domenico Guerrazzi (1804–73), Tommaso Grossi (1790–1853) and Defendente Sacchi (1796–1840)). The same subjects were also given visual expression by a school of painters whose standard-bearer

Example 19.1 Boito, *Mefistofele*, Act I: 'Dai campi, dai prati': 'I return from the fields, from the meadows flooded by night, and from quiet paths: I am filled with deep calm, and sacred mystery.'

was Francesco Hayez (1791–1882). Historical subjects were preferred, albeit deviating from history by reason of the Romantic accretions that were usually found in such librettos. As the nationalistic themes dear to the Risorgimento – crusades, foreign invasions of Italy – disappeared, so too did the music soften its patriotic fervour. Gomes's *Salvator Rosa* is to some extent an exception to this, being based on an episode in the life of the eponymous painter who joins his friend Masaniello in the Neapolitan insurrection against the Spanish régime. (See Chapter 9 for Auber's treatment of this historical event.) Here the martial overtones of the duet in Act I scene 4 and the fervour of the second-act 'March and Chorus' (supplemented by a stage band) strongly recall the politics of the 1848 Revolution. Nevertheless, post-Verdian Italian opera differs from French grand opera in that the latter is richer in socio-political implications, and also in religious conflicts which impinge upon individual faith, as well as in the juxtaposition of public and private.[26] Italian works, on the other hand, prefer to utilise history as a neutral, interchangeable back-drop. History is useful only to fuel the passions of the love-triangle, to create the space necessary for the inclusion of vigorous choruses and ensembles (including parades, marches, processions, conspiracies and uprisings) and to allow for the introduction of lavish scenery and costumes.

Ricordi published the *disposizioni sceniche* (staging-manuals) for *I Lituani*, *Salvator Rosa*, *Mefistofele*, *La Gioconda* and *Cristoforo Colombo*, and Lucca issued a similar publication for *Il Guarany*, furnished with advice to producers by Gomes himself.[27] These were based on the French *livrets de mise-en-scène*, described earlier in Chapter 4. It had been very different in 1836, when Giuseppe Mazzini was deploring the currently limited and vague use of the 'historical dimension', one which he favoured, by contrast, as a useful means of providing individuality and allowing music to communicate on the level of truth and social purpose.[28] But *opera-ballo* abounds with generic 'characteristic' pieces on the French model. Amongst these we find a 'Madrigal', an unaccompanied chorus in the second act of *Maria Tudor* sung by singers from Avignon; a 'Brindisi' in *I Lituani* and another in *Il figliuol prodigo*, each in Act II, conceived in the traditional style of the drinking-song; and a 'Ballata' (ballad) for mezzo-soprano in the second act of *Ruy Blas*, set in the form of a strophic aria with a Spanish flavour in A minor/major, reminiscent of Eboli's 'Chanson du voile' (Veil Song) in Verdi's *Don Carlos*. The Venetian lagoon which provides the setting for *La Gioconda* is musically painted with the colours of its second-act 'Marinaresca e Barcarola' (Sailors' Song and Barcarolle), while the second-act tarantella of *Salvator Rosa* signifies Naples. This brilliantly rhythmic dance is also found in *La Muette de Portici* by Auber (set – not by chance – in the same city, in the same year, 1647) as well as in Verdi's *Les Vêpres siciliennes*.

Using a coloratura soprano or mezzo-soprano for 'page' roles *en travesti*, a tradition so successfully continued by Verdi with the part of Oscar in *Un ballo in maschera* (1859), goes back to French grand opera, as in the role of Jemmy in Rossini's *Guillaume Tell*, or Urbain in Meyerbeer's *Les Huguenots*. Such light, high roles, focusing on virtuoso embellishment, compensated for the general lack of vocal virtuosity in the second half of the nineteenth century.[29] Thus they lighten the tone of otherwise ponderous works. For example, lively, festive elements are present in Gennariello's 'Canzonetta' 'Mia piccirella' in the first act of *Salvator Rosa*: because of its mandoline accompaniment (actually played on a harp) it is referred to in Act IV as a 'Serenata'. The novice monk Pablo's 'Ballata' in Marchetti's *Don Giovanni d'Austria* and the narrative 'Canzone' for Lelio in the third act of Ponchielli's *Marion Delorme* are similar responses to this tradition.

Following the success of Meyerbeer's *L'Africaine* as *L'Africana* in Bologna in 1865, and also that of *Aida*, exoticism once again became fashionable. Recent colonial exploits provided interesting and unusual settings: in 1885 Italy had begun its own 'dash for Africa'. Such settings sometimes even included pagan ceremonies and blood-curdling rituals, such as the cannibalism of the Indian tribe Aimoré in *Il Guarany*, Act III scene 3, or the torture of an old Indian by Spanish soldiers in *Cristoforo Colombo*, Act III scene 1. But in general the subject matter was faithful neither to history nor to the principle of verisimilitude. As Catalani confessed to his librettist Ghislanzoni, in a judgement with which many other composers would have concurred, his priority with regard to exotic settings was emotional expression: 'in my opinion all countries are good', wrote Catalani, 'it isn't that I don't give importance to local colour: on the contrary. But I put it in second place. True, human passions: this is what really matters!'[30]

Less than on authentic folklore sources, then, musical exoticism was based on pictorial musical ingredients tinged with generalised 'modal' or 'Iberian' colours, using normal generic forms. Ponchielli portrays the land of Judea in *Il figliuol prodigo* by a pentatonic motif above a bare fifth pedal,[31] while the adventuress Nefte strikes up a 'Ballata' in the first act which sounds more Spanish than Assyrian. The principal musical motif of *Il Guarany* has a modal flavour which can be heard at the opening of the 'Grand March and Bacchanal of the Indians' ('Gran Marcia–Baccanale indiano': see Ex. 19.2) and in the 'Invocation of the Aimoré' ('Invocazione degli Aimoré'), both in Act III. This opera, set in Brazil in 1560, has for its subject the love of a white woman for the noble savage Pery, and is also based on the conflict between rival ethnic groups, depicted in a manichean fashion. But these groups each also contain their opposites: the Indian tribes count among their number the civilised Guarany people plus the primitive Aimoré, while the Europeans comprise both good Portuguese and evil Spanish mercenaries.

Example 19.2 Antônio Carlos Gomes, *Il Guarany*, Act III, 'Gran marcia – Baccanale indiano'.

Exotic or archaic instruments were in general rarely used – they would become more common in the 'aesthetic' theatre of the early twentieth century – but one should note the eccentric appearance of *inubie*[32] and *maracá*; these bellicose instruments from South America occur in both operas by Gomes on Brazilian subjects, *Il Guarany* and *Lo schiavo*.

The evocative power of local colour is better demonstrated in the primarily decorative divertissements in *opera-ballo*, where one is able to distinguish four categories of dance. The first is formed of those stylised dances referring to specific national types. Examples of this are the 'Chorea' (a Greek dance) in *Mefistofele*, Act IV; the 'Dance of the Greek Slaves' and the 'Dance of the Andalusian Slaves' in the second act of *I Lituani*; and the aforementioned tarantella in *Salvator Rosa*. The second category comprises bacchanales or 'Saturnales', dances of an orgiastic or tribal nature: examples are the 'Grand March and Bacchanal of the Indians' in *Il Guarany*, the Bacchanal in *Maria Tudor*, and the 'Sacred Orgy' and *Saturnale* in *Il figliuol prodigo*, all found in the third act of their respective operas. The next group comprises those dances associated with exotic rituals: examples are the 'Wild Dance' ('Passo selvaggio') and 'Dance of the arrows' ('Passo delle freccie') in the third act of *Il Guarany*. Lastly, one can find dances of allegorical character, referring to the time of day, as in the third-act 'Dance of the Hours' in *La Gioconda*, or to the seasons, for example 'The Four Seasons' in Verdi's *I vespri siciliani*.[33]

In the ballets, music, choreography, lighting, scenery and costumes all vie to contribute to the effect, and the presence of ballerinas could create an extra element of visual seduction. Although the dances in *Il Guarany* left the public cold at the première (they were judged 'cacophonic', partly as a result of poor performance[34]), choreographic episodes devised by Angelo Zanardini met with great – and above all erotic – enthusiasm on the part of the audience. These included the 'Ballabile dell'etère', or dance of the courtesans, in the third act of Catalani's *Dejanice*, where 'a group of very beautiful young girls shrouded in multi-coloured floating veils enters and presents the most voluptuous dancing', after which 'the courtesans abandon themselves to a frenetic dance'. The same librettist placed dances in the Temple of Ilia in Ponchielli's *Il figliuol prodigo* in Act III: 'Priests and priestesses, Assyrian youths and courtesans linger on the side steps. Female dancers in voluptuous attitudes and poses surround them.' These were derived, if in much simplified fashion, from the more daring scenes in *L'Enfant prodigue* written by Scribe for Auber, which were considered permissive even by the French.[35]

No works are based on classical mythology, the mainstay of opera of preceding centuries. Instead, the *opera-ballo* made use of legendary and fantastic elements alongside historical themes: they were frequently presented in terms of ambivalent dualities (human/divine, angelic/diabolical) which can easily be identified with the Decadent movement. To this group of operas belong Boito's 'operatic legend' *Mefistofele* (derived from Goethe's *Faust* as well as from other sources), Catalani's 'fantastic opera' *Elda* (1880) set 'on the banks of the Rhine, about the year 1300', whose protagonist is the Loreley (celebrated by Heine, amongst others), and Puccini's *Le villi* (1884), on the theme of the spirits of betrayed girls (i.e. the Wilis, popular with the Romantics and the Scapigliati). Earlier, in 1874, Ghislanzoni and Ponchielli had also made use of this theme, including an artificial 'Chorus of Wilis' in the finale of *I Lituani*.

The chronological spread of subjects covered in the *opera-ballo* was as extensive as its geographical one. It spanned the period from ancient biblical times to the seventeenth century. *Il figliuol prodigo* re-creates the biblical world and depicts the pastoral setting of Judea and the sinful Nineveh; *Dejanice* is set in Syracuse 'Four hundred years before the Christian Era'; *I Lituani* is located in the early Middle Ages in Germany; *Fosca*'s setting alternates between Venice and the Pirate Haven at Pirano (Istria) in 944; *Gustavo Wasa* takes place in Stockholm in the first half of the sixteenth century; in *Maria Tudor* the heroine lives out her unhappy love for her favourite Fabiani in the London of 1554; both *Don Giovanni d'Austria* and *Ruy Blas* are set in Spain (respectively in 1557 and 1698); *La Gioconda* is set in seventeenth-century Venice; and in *Marion Delorme* the eponymous heroine resides in the France of 1638.

Librettos and poetry

The librettists specialising in grand opera (see Table 19.1 above) counted amongst their ranks three of the poets most in demand amongst the

Scapigliati in Milan: Arrigo Boito (whose *La Gioconda* was written under
the pseudonym Tobia Gorrio), Antonio Ghislanzoni and Emilio Praga.[36]
Angelo Zanardini was in addition a well-known translator of foreign operas
(Wagner's *Ring*, Bizet's *Carmen*, Massenet's *Le Roi de Lahore* and *Herodiade*,
Saint-Saëns' *Samson et Dalila*). Carlo D'Ormeville was a versatile individual
who combined the roles of dramatist, stage manager and theatrical agent.
Their verses in some cases tend to resemble prose, in a manner quite unlike
that of earlier librettos. They were inclined to juxtapose different metres in
the same piece (i.e. polymetre), which was also a characteristic of the first
Italian verse translations of the grand operas of Meyerbeer.[37] All this was
particularly exceptional in a context where, traditionally, there had always
been a close matching between poetic and musical structures, with the latter
determined by the former.

Symptomatic of all this was a tendency towards variety in operatic monologues, forcing composers to break away from standard forms. Mefistofele's
first-act aria in F minor, 'Son lo spirito', is given a two-part musical structure by Boito, with three sub-sections to each part (ABC/A'B'C'). But in the
libretto this same monologue is made up of three sections, as shown below:
first a quatrain of eight-syllable lines (*ottonari piani* and *tronchi*[38]), then a
quatrain of *ottonari* plus a four-syllable line, and lastly a sequence of mixed-
length lines (*piani* and *sdruccioli*[39]) ending with an odd six-syllable line. The
music ignores the metre in order to create greater fluidity, slowing down
the pace and also breaking the link between poetic and musical structure.
Not for nothing does the end of the music's A section fail to coincide with
the first quatrain of text, instead ending on the antepenultimate syllable of
line 5:

(A) Sono lo Spirito che nega	8 syllables [t = *tronco*]
sempre, tutto; l'astro, il fior.	8t
Il mio ghigno e la mia bega	8
turban gli ozi al Crëator.	8t
Voglio il Nulla e del Cre-(B) ato	8
la ruina universal.	8t
E'atmosfera mia vital	8t
cio che chiamasi peccato,	8
Morte e Mal!	4t
(C) Rido e avvento – questa sillaba:	8 [s = *sdrucciolo*]
'No'.	1
Struggo, tento,	4
ruggo, sibilo,	4s
'No'.	1
Mordo, invischio,	4s
fischio! fischio! fischio!	6

This monologue has no precedent in the poetics of the earlier nineteenth-
century libretto, and its contrivances (internal rhymes, alliteration, etc.)
prefigure many passages in the same author's later *Falstaff* in 1893. Boito
also exploits the sonic and gestural implications of the whistle (*fischio*),

which are explicit in the stage direction at the end of the aria: '[Mefistofele] whistles forcefully, with his fingers between his lips'. Finally, there is the punning use of the tritone (the old *diabolus in musica*), an omnipresent motto in the opera, which also underlines the word 'fischio' whenever it is pronounced by the devil.

In general, one can see that in this period composers did away with clear-cut musical forms, preferring instead to articulate more clearly dramatic situations, in ways that contrast with mid-century opera. Likewise, poetic forms tend to allow for flexibility within traditionally metrical frameworks, also adding unexpected variations. These permit the melody to break the bounds of fixed musical cadences and symmetrical phrase-structures.

The middle- and lower-middle-class public, emerging from the unification of Italy, had thus found a type of theatre perfectly suited to its social aspirations: old-fashioned, but not too much so; innovative, but not too radical.

Translated by Deirdre O'Grady and Tim Carter

20 Grand opera in Britain and the Americas

SARAH HIBBERD

Introduction

Britain and the Americas, lacking any significant and continuous native operatic traditions, depended upon foreign opera for much of the nineteenth century. Although Italian opera (and to a certain extent French opéra comique) often formed the basis of the repertory, German and serious French opera became increasingly popular in certain areas of Britain and the Americas in response to local circumstances: the nationality of immigrant populations, the tastes of a ruling élite, the experiences of local impresarios and the impact of political events.

In the 1830s the phenomenal popularity of grand opera – works such as Auber's *La Muette de Portici* (1828) and *Gustave III* (1833), Meyerbeer's *Robert le Diable* (1831) and *Les Huguenots* (1836), Halévy's *La Juive* (1835) – spread quickly throughout Europe and across the Channel. In London such works were translated into Italian or English and performed in a variety of faithful productions and pirate adaptations. From Europe they were exported to the East coast of America, often by English impresarios. Travelling troupes in America incorporated occasional grand operas into their still largely Italian repertories, and took them across the continent from where they entered Central and South America and were absorbed – to a lesser extent – into the repertories of local companies. Celebrated singers who had performed these operas in Paris brought to new audiences the roles for which they had become known.

This chapter examines the way in which grand operas were adapted and received. It also attempts to determine the sort of influence grand opera had, and the degree to which new traditions developed in Britain and the Americas. Although one can point to characteristic elements of grand opera – the historical subjects and melodramatic plots, the grand scale (usually five acts) and large forces, the spectacular visual effects, the integration of private and public dimensions of the drama, the (usually) tragic ending – the overriding characteristic of the genre is its tendency to synthesise.[1] Tracing the specific influences of a fluid, eclectic and imprecise genre is problematic and arguably a pointless task. Yet the enormous popularity of French grand opera (and its legacy in the works of Wagner and Verdi and others) suggests that we should broaden the context in which we understand English-language and Latin American opera of the second half of the nineteenth century.

Given the enormous number of permanent and travelling opera companies in existence in Britain and the Americas during the nineteenth century, and the widely differing local circumstances, a comprehensive survey of grand opera in these areas is beyond the scope of this chapter. Moreover, there has been little research into the subject on which to draw. The focus, therefore, is on larger cities, on places where grand opera was particularly popular (notably London), and on locations where primary research has been carried out, with a view to examining interesting – rather than representative – examples. Conclusions about the influence of grand opera are necessarily tentative, and based on the brief examination of some of the (few) works for which scores and librettos are readily available. The enormous popularity of grand opera in the English-speaking world, however, suggests that this is an area ripe for further research.

Britain

Performances of French grand opera

In London productions of grand operas could be seen at three main theatres (see Table 20.1).[2] Performances at Her Majesty's Theatre (known as the King's Theatre before 1837) were in Italian, those at Covent Garden were in English in the 1830s and early 1840s, then in Italian from 1847, and those at Drury Lane were in English. English burlettas and parodies of operas were also staged at such popular theatres as the Adelphi.[3] The translation of operas was often a requirement written into a theatre's licence, but it was also linked to historical practices. Essentially, Italian was a language associated with cultivation, while English was more generally linked to the popular, less-educated classes. For much of the century French and German operas appeared in their original language only when performed by visiting foreign troupes.

In this system, then, grand operas were routinely translated into Italian or English and adapted for performance, and they became popular in these versions, with theatres vying to stage the first production. For example, the London première of Meyerbeer's *Robert le Diable* (1831) was intended for the King's Theatre in 1832, where it was to be performed (in Italian) by the cast of the Paris Opéra production. But the great excitement awaiting the opera prompted a rush of adaptations in English which in fact preceded its 'authentic' performance at the King's Theatre.

Such intense rivalry for the same works inevitably had financial implications. When Alfred Bunn gained control of the two patent theatres in the

Table 20.1 *Repertory of London theatres*

Theatre (and company)	Repertory
Adelphi	In 1831 it housed the Lyceum's company. Its repertory consisted of spoken drama and burlettas and parodies of operas. It occasionally hosted seasons of the Carl Rosa Company (founded in 1875).
Covent Garden (patent theatre) Companies: the Playhouse at the Theatre Royal until 1846, then the Royal Italian Opera until 1892, then the Royal Opera.	Henry Bishop was musical director from 1810 to 1824; his English adaptations of opera (and those of Michael Lacy) were an important part of the repertory into the 1830s. Opera was performed in English translation under the management of Alfred Bunn, Charles Macready and others in the 1830s, with a growing focus on French repertory. In 1847 it reopened as the Royal Italian Opera, performing all works in Italian. Under the direction of Frederick Gye (1848–77) grand opera became an important feature of the repertory and continued to be so under the management of Augustus Harris (1887–96) and until World War I.
Drury Lane (patent theatre) Company: the Theatre Royal	Thomas Cooke was the principal director in the 1820s, adapting foreign operas in English, in the style of Bishop; Alfred Bunn became manager in the 1830s and 1840s. Between 1835 and 1847 the repertory was mainly English opera. Her Majesty's seasons transferred there in 1868–77 (following a fire). Under the management of Augustus Harris (1879–96) it was famed for its spectacular productions of foreign works, its performances of Wagner, and the annual (English) seasons of the Carl Rosa Company. Opera disappeared from the repertory after Harris's death.
Her Majesty's (King's Theatre until 1837)	Under the management of Pierre Laporte in the 1830s, Benjamin Lumley in the 1840s and 1850s and J. H. Mapleson (sporadically) in the 1860s, 1870s and 1880s, its repertory consisted chiefly of Italian opera and French operas of the post-grand opera generation (Bizet, Gounod). The theatre also hosted the visits of the Carl Rosa Company, Angelo Neumann's Wagner company and, in 1886, a French opera season.
Lyceum	Known as the English Opera House during the years 1816–30 and (following destruction and rebuilding after a fire) 1834–43, it then increasingly mounted spoken drama, and temporarily housed other companies and visiting troupes.

mid-1830s, he combined the companies in order to improve their financial positions and assigned distinct genres to each: ballet and spectacle at Covent Garden; tragedy, comedy, farce – including English opera – at Drury Lane. (Italian opera continued to be performed at Her Majesty's.) But in 1843 the patent monopoly was abolished and any theatre could apply for a licence to perform anything. The ensuing competition for Italian opera led to the disintegration of the Covent Garden playhouse within a year, although it continued to host concert series, and the visit in 1845 of a touring Belgian opera company which performed *Guillaume Tell*, *Les Huguenots* and *La Muette de Portici*.[4]

Following the closure of the playhouse, however, dissatisfied singers from Her Majesty's took the opportunity to turn the empty theatre into a dedicated opera house, and in 1847 the new Royal Italian Opera opened at Covent Garden. Although both houses initially staged a conservative repertory of ballet and contemporary Italian opera, the arrival of Frederick Gye at

Covent Garden in 1848 led to the emergence of a distinct, French-dominated repertory, and superior artistic standards at that theatre. Audience loyalties gradually shifted to the new company; the lesser aristocracy and liberals in particular were attracted, and a large section of the upper aristocracy followed Queen Victoria in her preference for German and French operas. The repertories were quite distinct: Covent Garden focused on French and some Italian repertory while Her Majesty's focused almost exclusively on contemporary Italian opera.[5]

Singers were fundamental to the repertory at each theatre.[6] At Covent Garden a core of fifteen to twenty singers returned annually through the 1850s and beyond, and Gye shaped the repertory around their individual talents.[7] This extended to the point that the French repertory suffered in 1852 when Pauline Viardot was unavailable, but benefited from the engagement of such singers as Marie Battu and Pauline Lucca in the 1860s.[8] While the usual star-system continued at Her Majesty's, at Covent Garden an ensemble of top-class performers was maintained, a particularly important requirement for grand operas, which featured large numbers of principal singers.

Drury Lane
During the first decades of the nineteenth century Henry Rowley Bishop (1786–1855) was the most important stage composer and arranger in London. His reworkings of operas for Drury Lane included two versions of Rossini's *Guillaume Tell* (1830, 1838) and one of Meyerbeer's *Robert le Diable* (1832).[9]

In spite of the routine complaints of the critics, it appears that such adaptations often remained remarkably close to the original. Great success was anticipated for *Robert le Diable*, which was adapted for at least three different theatres in 1832.[10] Bishop's version for Drury Lane, *The Demon, or The Mystic Branch*, proves an interesting starting point for our consideration of the nature of adaptations of grand operas in London.

At Drury Lane in 1832 (English) spoken dialogue was required by the theatre's licence, replacing recitative. In the case of *The Demon* this appears to have been the main divergence from the authentic text premièred in Paris the previous year.[11] Bishop used the music of all but four of the twenty-four numbers in *Robert*, and the spoken dialogue followed the recitative closely. Some minor harmonic variants and other small changes were the only other differences from the published vocal score (1832). However, Bishop and his collaborators (Thomas Cooke, Richard Hughes and Montague Corri) only had a vocal score to work from, and had to orchestrate the opera themselves.[12]

In spite of this relative fidelity to Meyerbeer's score, many critics received Bishop's adaptation as a travesty of the original.[13] Ignaz Moscheles, for example, claimed: 'in that piece of patchwork, *The Demon*, Meyerbeer's best intentions [were] utterly destroyed; fine scenery and ignorant listeners could alone save this performance from complete failure . . . there was no Meyerbeer in it'.[14] In contrast, Bishop's adaptation of *Guillaume Tell* as *Hofer, the Tell of the Tyrol* (1830), in partnership with Planché, had been more radical. Not only had Tell been replaced by another popular, legendary revolutionary, Andreas Hofer (1767–1810), but the score was also substantially altered.[15] Intriguingly, scenes of melodrama frequently replaced sung numbers and recitative. The English love of pantomime, spectacle and instrumental music perhaps helps to account for an important aspect of the appeal of grand opera.[16] Remarkably, given the reaction to *The Demon*, few critics objected to the substantial alterations of *Hofer*, and a number thought the adaptation an improvement on Rossini's more usual fare. Yet it would seem that faithful adaptations were becoming increasingly popular – perhaps because audiences were becoming more familiar with foreign repertory. In 1838 Bishop made a second adaptation of *Tell* for Drury Lane that was much closer to the original. Although Alfred Bunn noted that 'four hours and a half, even of Rossini, are too much for your cockney', it achieved considerable success.[17]

It would seem, on the evidence of *The Demon* and *Guillaume Tell*, that the scale of grand operas and their often complicated plots were not necessarily viewed as a problem at Drury Lane – although replacing recitative with spoken dialogue would certainly have shortened a work, and there are examples of other works that were cut more severely.[18] This doubtless provoked the French review of *Le Lac des fées* at Drury Lane quoted in Chapter 10 (p. 187). Furthermore, it would seem that such adaptations were often more popular than performances of the 'original' work by visiting companies. For example, critical reaction to the production of *Robert* by the original Paris cast at the King's Theatre later in the season illustrates English disgust with the authentic *mise-en-scène*. The Earl of Mount Edgcumbe, famously prudish, was horrified: 'the sight of the resurrection of a whole convent of nuns, who rise from their graves, and begin dancing like so many bacchantes, is revolting'; another critic declared it 'the apotheosis of blasphemy, indecency, and absurdity'.[19] Meyerbeer realised immediately on arrival that 'the performances in Covent Garden and Drury Lane have discredited the music of *Robert* in such a way that no one has much hope for [our] production at the Italian Opera', and his performers were forced by the Lord Chamberlain to perform in Italian.[20] London taste dictated in 1835 that Drury Lane give *La Juive* a happy ending (see the closing section of Chapter 13, and n. 59). But *The Harmonicon* had noted that 'the English give their sanction to the verdict pronounced in favour of the work [*Robert le Diable*] by a great and very critical nation [France]'.[21] Indeed, in adaptations tailored for the English palate, grand operas came to be widely admired by London audiences.

Covent Garden

Michael Lacy's rival adaptation of *Robert le Diable* as *The Fiend Father* helped to popularise opera at Covent Garden. Less faithful to the original, it was nevertheless well crafted and performed, and met with critical and public acclaim. The following year James Robinson Planché (the librettist of Weber's *Oberon*, 1826) reworked Auber's *Gustave III* (1833), and it enjoyed a lavish production just six months after its Paris première. Structural changes were made, as was to become usual in adaptations of grand operas at Covent Garden: it was reduced from five acts to three by omitting ensemble numbers and ballet music, and fundamental changes were made to the plot to satisfy the censor. Most significantly, the king's passion for Amélie, the wife of his close friend Ankastrœm – the pivot of the entire story – was seen as morally inappropriate. The role of lover was instead given to a new character, lieutenant-colonel Lillienhorn, and the role of the king was turned into a speaking part.[22] Moreover, Ankastrœm was recast as an ex-captain of the guards rather than as prime minister; the king is indeed assassinated, but the political thrust of the opera is thereby diffused.[23] Its combined effect of adultery, betrayal and regicide had to be tempered for London audiences, yet in spite of this dilution it was a huge success. The commentator J. E. Cox approved of Planché's 'anglicised' plot, and the critic for *The Athenæum* claimed that the staging 'surpassed not only in grandeur, but in chasteness and elegance, all that had ever been beheld either on our own or on the Parisian stage'.[24]

In spite of the popularity of *Gustavus the Third*, it was not until the arrival of Frederick Gye in 1848 that grand opera enjoyed consistent success at Covent Garden.[25] Partly in response to competition with Her Majesty's, and partly as a reaction to the precarious economic climate of opera production in the 1850s, Gye sought out successful Italian and French works on frequent visits to the Continent, and introduced them to the London stage.[26] Over a third of the new operas introduced in the first seven years of his directorship were French operas, performed in Italian; they included *Le Prophète* (1849), *La Juive* (1850) and *Benvenuto Cellini* (1853). During the early 1850s and again in the 1860s, performances of French opera at Covent Garden eclipsed those of Italian. Judging from his diary entries, it seems that Gye's interest in grand opera, and his reasons for establishing the genre at Covent Garden, were founded upon his belief that such operas embraced a particular aesthetic that appealed to London as much as Parisian audiences. *The Athenæum* described this: if Meyerbeer's melodies are sometimes thought to be 'trivial' or 'staccato' and his structures as 'ungainly', his colour and dramatic effects are highly praised by the English, and far more successful than Verdi's 'queer and harsh' music or Wagner's 'bizarre devices' that are appreciated only in Dresden. In sum 'grand opera is particularly congenial to the taste of the wide English public.'[27] They enjoyed the prevalence of melody and of dramatic tableaux, and Gye recognised the importance of good performers.

Yet in the moral climate of Victorian England certain subjects were still viewed controversially. For example, the 1847 production of *Roberto il diavolo* at Covent Garden reworked the ballet of debauched nuns that had so shocked Mount Edgcumbe. According to the printed libretto (though what happened in performance is unclear), the whole scene is condensed, the nuns are referred to simply as 'phantoms', and nowhere in the stage directions are they described as seducing Robert; rather, 'he finds himself surrounded by the Phantoms who impede his progress. They point out where lies the talisman, which he seizes, and breaking through the circle which they form round him, he departs.' This presumably satisfied religious decorum as far as the censor was concerned. The profound social divisions forming the mainspring of *Les Huguenots* could not originally be contemplated for public display in London. Planché claimed that he had visited Meyerbeer in Paris soon after the opera's première, and that the composer had agreed as follows: 'if you will . . . make such alterations in the catastrophe as may be necessary . . . to ensure its safety in London, I will recompose the last act for the English stage, direct the rehearsals, and conduct the opera for the first three nights'. But Planché apparently realised that no alteration would 'render the subject eligible for performance in England under the existing circumstances', and his plans to stage the work were abandoned.[28]

In addition to changes made in the interests of morality and politics, a structural affinity with Italian opera was apparently sought in the adaptation of grand operas.[29] In contrast to Bishop's relatively faithful adaptation of *Robert le Diable* for Drury Lane, versions staged under Gye's directorship of Covent Garden generally involved extensive reorganisation and abridgement, more in line with Planché's *Gustavus*. Although grand effects were retained, complicated ensembles and arias were simplified and rearranged (or omitted altogether) and minor characters were written out.

This is illustrated most strikingly in *Gli Ugonotti* (1848): Acts I and II were merged, Acts III and V were compressed, only Act IV remained intact; the performance time was reduced from four hours to three. The structure was simplified, and the focus fell on the principal soloists rather than the crowds.[30] For example, the Introduction – an expansive set-piece consisting of complex ensembles, choruses and solos – was reduced to a single, short ensemble, and the chorus was omitted from the Act I finale. In addition, the soprano role of the page Urbain was transposed for the contralto Marietta Alboni. These and other changes were based largely on (authorised) alterations made for the 1842 Berlin production, which illustrates how Meyerbeer actively recognised a need to adapt his works for their environment. He appears to have viewed such changes not as revisions, but simply as alternatives to be used when necessary.[31]

Contemporary perception of adaptations varied wildly, to the extent that apparently authentic versions were condemned while completely reworked operas were praised for their sympathetic alterations. For example, Charles Gruneisen was apparently outraged by the production of *Roberto il diavolo* at Her Majesty's in 1847, where he noticed Mendelssohn 'writhing in torture at the scandalous treatment of Meyerbeer's work', and he described its revival the following year as 'a base act of vandalism'.[32] Yet he admired the more heavily reworked staging of *Les Huguenots* for Covent Garden. It seems that Gruneisen (even taking into account his bias) and other commentators felt that the preservation of the spirit of a work was more important than its faithful reproduction.

By the end of the century, many of the same adaptations of Meyerbeer and others, made in the 1830s and 1840s, were still being performed with few changes. Shaw noted in 1891 that 'the present Covent Garden version of [*Les Huguenots*] is the result of a music-butchery perpetrated half a century ago . . . in accordance with the taste of that Rossinian period, the whistleable tunes were retained, and the dramatic music sacrificed'.[33] He suggested changes to bring the work into line with modern practices: first a few cuts, such as the 'silly ballet' of bathers in Act II, and then the restoration of certain elements such as the unaccompanied episode in the scene of the oath-taking. However, some fuller versions were already being performed before Shaw's time. The 1863 libretto of Manfredo Maggioni's adaptation of *Masaniello* for Covent Garden, for example, has five acts and is a near-complete version of Auber's opera.[34]

Towards a British grand opera

In 1834 Samuel James Arnold (re)opened the English Opera House at the Lyceum, for 'the presentation of English operas and the encouragement of indigenous musical talent'.[35] The theatre was leased to the flamboyant French conductor Louis Jullien in 1847–48 for the 'Royal Academy of Music, English Grand Opera', where foreign operas in English translation were performed, as well as new indigenous works. But the season was mismanaged and Jullien went bankrupt. His impetuosity and lack of practical expertise are described by Berlioz, who recorded in his *Mémoires* how Jullien proposed to produce *Robert le Diable* in just six days, without the necessary music, translation, costumes or scenery.[36] Although the venture as a whole failed, it was followed by a series of similarly short-lived enterprises.[37] The failure of such promising projects has been ascribed above all to the upper classes and their preference for – and patronage of – Italian opera.[38] Ultimately, artistic and financial rewards were to be gained from foreign rather than English opera.

Little attempt was made to create a distinctive English genre. Composers and authors tended to borrow the plots of foreign operas and to absorb aspects of the musical language of contemporary (mainly Italian) composers without developing an individual style. Such works consisted of spoken dialogue with melodically and harmonically straightforward music. However, during the 1830s the dramatic function of the music gradually began to evolve under the influence of Weber – whose *Der Freischütz* had achieved astonishing success in London – and French opera. Ensembles and arias became more extended and were used to propel the action forward, while the dramatic climax of an opera was frequently set partly or entirely to music.[39]

John Barnett (1802–90), who based *The Mountain Sylph* (1834) on the ballet *La Sylphide*, here produced the first opera to integrate music successfully into the drama in this way. Its use of melodramatic delivery and recurrent motifs in the Act I finale was indebted to the Wolf's Glen scene in *Der Freischütz*, and perhaps even to *Robert le Diable*.[40] The influence of grand opera is more evident in his later opera for Drury Lane, *Fair Rosamond* (1837). George Biddlecombe has noted specific similarities between the dramatic situation in the Act III finale and that of the Act I finale of *La Muette* (during a public ceremony the identity of the unwitting mistress's lover is revealed); the resulting musical correspondences include an anthem in *Fair Rosamond* that recalls Auber's prayer before the finale.[41] The use of ballet movements in Act IV and large choral tableaux in the finales is also clearly inspired by French models.

The Irishman Michael William Balfe (1808–70) is generally viewed as the only composer of English opera of any distinction in the 1830s and 1840s. His works, and those of his contemporaries, have been criticised for their lowbrow, popular appeal, use of popular song forms, frequent 'degeneration' into pantomime and Italianate melodies. Yet the same qualities can equally be found in grand opera, which so comprehensively combined such 'low' theatre techniques as *mélodrame* and vaudeville, with those from opera. Indeed, Balfe's light, Italianate style frequently recalls that of Auber, and his ballet movements and large choral scenes again suggest French inspiration.[42] Biddlecombe has identified stylistic examples of the influence of grand opera,[43] suggesting, for instance, that the choral scenes in *Joan of Arc* (1837) recall the imposing manner of Auber's and Meyerbeer's works. Furthermore, Balfe's most celebrated opera, *The Bohemian Girl* (1843), while clearly combining the traditions of English ballad opera and Italian opera, also draws on French models. Its use of an apparently authentic fifteenth-century Hussite melody was surely inspired by similar evocations of local colour in grand opera, such as Meyerbeer's use of 'Ein' feste Burg' in *Les Huguenots*. Furthermore, Auber's use of the *galop* in *Gustave III* presumably inspired Balfe's use of the dance as a ballet movement in Act I of his opera.

In the 1840s Balfe had more direct experience with French opera. He wrote a *grand opéra* for the Paris Opéra, *L'Etoile de Séville* (1845), and a new grand opera for London: for this, Alfred Bunn adapted Saint-Georges's libretto for Halévy's *La Reine de Chypre* as *The Daughter of St Mark* (a 'grand opera seria') which had a spectacular production at Drury Lane in 1844. Although in only three acts (and with a more positive ending), it retains many key elements of the original work: the interrupted wedding ceremony, barcarole, melodramatic music accompanying action, processions and divertissements, a patriotic duet, prominent use of the chorus and the simple juxtaposition of contrasting moods. Moreover, Biddlecombe has demonstrated that Balfe followed Halévy's setting of the text in specific ways: the duets in Act I (Adolphe and Catarina) and Act III (Adolphe and Lusignano) were originally identical in design to their French equivalents, although some material was later omitted.[44]

Balfe's contemporary Edward Loder (1813–65), who studied with Ferdinand Ries in Frankfurt in 1826–28, shows similar influences in his operas written for the English Opera House. And his *Raymond and Agnes* (1855, Royal Theatre, Manchester), based on an episode from Matthew Lewis's *The Monk*, makes use of thematic recurrence and melodrama and involves a mute woman reminiscent of Auber's *La Muette*, albeit Weber was probably a more direct influence on him than Auber.[45]

Other composers active in London in the 1830s included Mendelssohn, who was keenly interested in dramatic music from an early age and was involved in two projected operas for London – neither of which was completed.[46] Mendelssohn's appreciation of the requirements of serious opera in London in the mid-1830s is shown in a letter to Planché:

> [I aim to compose] a kind of historical opera; serious but not *tragical* – at least, not with a tragic end: but as for dangers, fears, and all sorts of passions, I cannot have too much of them. I should also like it to have some persons, if not comical, yet of *a gay and lively* character in it; and last, not least, I wish for as *many choruses*, and as active ones, as you may possibly bring in. I should like to have a whole people, or the most different classes of society and of feelings, to express in my choruses, and to have them as a kind of model, I should say a subject between *Fidelio* and *Les Deux journées* of Cherubini would suit me most.[47]

In particular, Mendelssohn had a view of the kind of history he wanted; not only should it 'provide a lively background to the whole', but it should also 'in reminding us of history . . . [at] the same time *remind us of our present time*'; furthermore, 'every act of the opera [should have] its own effects, its own poetical point which comes to issue in the finale'.[48] This particular blend, familiar from Scribe's grand opera librettos, characterised most English operas written before the 1880s, and even later.

Some advances had been made by the 1860s. William Wallace's three-act *Lurline* (1860) is representative, and also illustrates Weber's continuing influence: it is based on the German legend of Undine, and includes spirits, naiads and a gnome in the cast, and spells and drinking-songs in the score. It also features large scene-complexes (particularly at the end of Act II), expansive orchestral effects, a fluid movement between duets, ensembles and choral passages and presents opposing choruses as well as ballets and a choral prayer. In some ways it recalls Auber's quasi-grand opera *Le Lac des fées* (1839) (see Chapter 10), which had been successful in London.

It was not, however, until the 1880s that anything resembling Meyerbeerian grand opera was created. Charles Villiers Stanford's three-act *The Veiled Prophet of Khorassan* (1877–79), first performed in Hanover in 1881 (as *Der verschleierte Prophet*), comes close to the spectacular and political works of the July Monarchy.[49] Adapted from a Persian tale from Thomas Moore's *Lalla Rookh* (1817), the opera opens with a procession that is interrupted by a report of the outbreak of war. A private love story is set against the public dimension of the fighting (though the two elements are not fully integrated), and various other ingredients common to grand opera are prominent: local colour, ballet and a dream sequence in a divertissement, prominent choruses, sometimes in opposition, and the stark juxtaposition of good and evil. The harmonic language is more advanced than the Rossini–Weber-derived language of Balfe and Wallace, but there are still many (closed) solo airs and duets.

After a command performance of his cantata *The Golden Legend*, Arthur Sullivan noted in his diary that Queen Victoria had said to him 'You ought to write a grand opera, you would do it so well!' Indeed in *Ivanhoe* (1891, Royal English Opera House), remembered as the 'only' English grand opera, Sullivan was apparently aiming, 'in the tradition of Gluck and Wagner' (and therefore of French grand opera too) at 'opera as drama'.[50] Yet, the work foundered on its grandness. Expense was spared neither for the complex staging nor for the performance (with an orchestra of sixty-three, a chorus of seventy-two and two hundred people on stage for the tournament scene). Its generally favourable critical reception was arguably disingenuous: Shaw described it as 'a good novel turned into the very silliest sort of sham "grand opera"', and financial problems caused the theatre to close soon after.[51] *Ivanhoe* has been criticised for lack of unity in its panorama of events, and generally forgotten.

Perhaps the largest issue with which British opera was faced at the end of the century was the legacy of Wagner. The advance of Wagnerism undermined the status of Balfe and his contemporaries, as public demand turned away from melodic charm in favour of dramatic effectiveness and cohesion.[52] Finding a means of reconciling elements of Italian, German and French styles proved to be a recurring difficulty. A number of composers attempted to combine Wagnerian (or at least German symphonic) syntax with the eclectic approach of grand opera, and their works often had their premières (and success) in Germany rather than Britain. But the grand and ancient mythological plots of many operas tended to be let down, in the opinion of critics, by their musical execution. Frederick Corder's first opera, *Le Morte d'Arthur* (1879, Brighton), in four acts, had little success. Frederick Cowen's *Harold, or The Norman Conquest* (1895, Covent Garden) was apparently an unsatisfactory combination of lyrical number opera and quasi-Wagnerian synthesis.

Some composers were influenced by late nineteenth-century French composers. Shaw mentions George Fox, whose *Nydia* (1892) was based on E. G. Bulwer-Lytton's *Last Days of Pompeii*.[53] Although the music reminded Shaw of *Carmen*, many aspects of the opera recall the enduring influence of *La Muette*.[54] *Nydia* appears to illustrate particularly clearly the combined inspiration of grand opera and more modern musical influences that characterised most serious English opera of the time. Judging from Shaw's criticism it would also seem to exemplify the common failure to combine 'grand' subjects with suitable music. In his survey of English operas of the period, Nigel Burton notes a similar mismatch of styles, suggesting that Cowen's *Thogrim* (1890, Drury Lane) 'is neither a romantic, nor a lyric, nor a grand opera; there are elements of all three about it, but they are at war with each other'; in harmonic terms the opera 'does not advance beyond the Wagner of 1848'.[55] Stephen Banfield makes a similar point about Alexander Mackenzie's *Guillem the Troubadour* (1886, Drury Lane): the composer has failed to 'seize musico-dramatic opportunities', and the music is accordingly too slight for the drama and the conception.[56]

North America

Performances of French grand opera

From 1835 to mid-century, English opera was at the centre of theatrical life in the larger cities of America such as New York, Philadelphia and Boston, performed by visiting English singers and American troupes.[57] Indeed, until well into the 1840s American theatres operated as minor outposts of the London cultural sphere.[58] French and Italian operas were occasionally

Figure 29 The rebuilt theatre at Niblo's Garden, New York, shown on 24 February 1855 in
Ballou's Pictorial Drawing-Room Companion. Act II scene 4 of *La Muette de Portici* is in progress,
Fenella explaining in mime to Masaniello (with iconic Phrygian cap) the tale of her ill-fated
love affair. William Niblo of Ireland (1789–1875) first built his fashionable public garden and
theatre in 1829, putting on all manner of good quality entertainments, opera (including some
Meyerbeer) and concerts at reasonable prices. New Yorkers could also have seen opera at the
Italian Opera House (1833–35), Palmo's Opera House (1844–48), the Astor Place Opera House
(1847–52) and the Academy of Music (from 1854).

performed, frequently in English, with actors speaking some of the roles.
Although these works were generally cut and modified, partly to suit local
taste, partly because of the limitations of the theatre companies, this did not
prevent more difficult and demanding works (including *Robert le Diable*,
Guillaume Tell and *La Juive*) from being performed.

Gradually, non-English influences began to be felt more keenly on the
East coast. First, Italian companies became increasingly popular. Then, in
1843, the Théâtre d'Orléans from New Orleans brought comic French opera
and Donizetti to Niblo's theatre in New York. Two years later the company
returned and established grand opera at the heart of its repertory: *Guillaume
Tell*, *Robert le Diable*, *La Juive*, *La Muette de Portici* and *Les Huguenots*. The
performances were apparently far superior to those of the visiting English
companies that New York was used to, the seats were cheap, and the visit was
an enormous success. The arrival of large numbers of European emigrants

further influenced the cultural growth. Following the 1848 Revolutions in Europe an influx of German refugees settled first on the East coast and later in the Midwest.[59] After about 1855, other Europeans came to America in increasing numbers. Large opera houses were built, Italian (and later German) opera gradually replaced English-language opera, and numerous European singers toured the country.[60] All serious opera was known as 'grand opera' – whether by Auber or Meyerbeer, or by Verdi or Wagner – and it became popular with permanent and travelling companies who tailored their repertories to the available singers.[61] But it was only towards the end of the nineteenth century that American composers attempted to establish a national genre of serious opera, by which time the influence of grand opera had been filtered through more popular German, French and Italian models. Nevertheless, a fascination with grand themes emerged, with spectacular stagings reminiscent of July Monarchy opera.

New York

In New York and other cities on the East coast operas tended to be performed in Italian translation; as an imported British tradition this affirmed the perceived cultural superiority of opera in Italian. As Edith Wharton noted memorably in *The Age of Innocence*, with regard to a performance of Gounod's *Faust* at the Academy of Music: 'She [Marguerite] sang, of course, "*M'ama!*" and not "*he loves me*", since an unalterable law of the musical world required that the German text of French operas sung by Swedish artists should be translated into Italian for the clearer understanding of English-speaking audiences'.[62]

Although there was no permanent troupe until the 1880s, there were several important impresarios active in the city, and travelling companies and local troupes regularly performed. Italian opera dominated the repertory at the Academy of Music (the only venue dedicated to concerts and operas between 1854 and 1883) until the 1870s, but rivalry between two German-born conductors, Theodore Thomas and Leopold Damrosch, led to the active promotion of Wagner and other non-Italian composers. This culminated in 1884 with Damrosch's appointment as director of the Metropolitan Opera (which had opened the previous year) and a season of German-language opera.[63] He recruited singers and players from Europe, and so as not to alienate large sections of the opera-going public he included Italian and French operas (sung in German) alongside those of Wagner. Damrosch died just before the end of the season, but under the musical directorship of Anton Seidl the Metropolitan Opera continued with its programme of German-language opera. French grand operas, perceived as being closer to the Wagnerian aesthetic than Italian works, were frequently performed with success at this time. *Les Huguenots*, *Guillaume Tell*, *La Muette* and

La Juive, as well as Goldmark's grand opera *Die Königin von Saba* – all sung in German – were particularly popular throughout the 1880s and 1890s.[64]

San Francisco and New Orleans

In other parts of America grand opera's fortunes were similarly mixed. In general, Italian and English opera formed the core of most repertories. But the diversity of San Francisco's population (owing largely to the influx of immigrants following the 1849 gold rush in the neighbouring foothills of Sierra Nevada) inspired more adventurous programming.[65] Grand opera arrived in the city in the 1850s, but was not particularly popular, in spite of a certain amount of public curiosity. The travelling Bishop and Bochsa Company's productions in English of *La Muette* (1854) and *Robert le Diable* (1855), for example, had only modest success. A performance of *La Muette* in French, with Anna Bishop as Elvire, attracted a better house and was favourably received, but it was not repeated, perhaps because of the illness of another cast member. Similarly, although the first-night performance of *Robert le Diable* sold out and people were turned away from the doors, by the fourth performance the house was only half full.[66] It seems likely that the special effects created in the Paris productions of these works were well beyond the resources of the troupe, and there were no reports in San Francisco of the sorts of imaginative use of lighting that took place in Paris. This must surely have contributed to the lack of enduring success of these early grand operas.

The city in which the genre had a most sustained presence in the nineteenth century was New Orleans, owing in large part to its historical links with France.[67] A remarkable number of grand operas received their American premières in New Orleans, and many foreign singers performed there and returned home without visiting any other part of the country.

Robert le Diable was performed as early as 1834, and was the focus of rivalry between the American and French theatres in the city. James Caldwell secured the première, in English, at his Camp Street theatre with an orchestra of only fifteen players. It featured marvellous scenery and, to ensure good audiences, numbers were inserted into the opera performed by the minstrel 'Daddy' Rice, then at the height of his fame.[68] Six weeks later John Davis presented *Robert* in French at the Théâtre d'Orléans. Although the orchestra was larger and the production featured a greater number of dancers and chorus members, the singing, scenery and costumes were judged inferior by some critics. The opera was performed fifteen times in three months at the two theatres.

The Théâtre d'Orléans expanded and Davis took his company on important and influential tours of the North East of America (mentioned above). The company – which depended on the support of the Creole French population – introduced grand opera into the heart of its repertory, while Caldwell focused on Italian repertory. *La Muette* and *Robert* continued to be popular, and in 1839 Davis's company staged the American première of *Les Huguenots*. The first night audience was apparently not prepared for what seemed 'strange melodies' and 'lush instrumentation'. Nor were they used to giving sustained attention for what turned out to be five hours. Indeed a 'numbed bewilderment' rather than enthusiasm was apparently most in evidence at the first two performances.[69] Yet the demand for extra instruments and spectacular scenery meant that the production of such an opera was an impressive achievement, and the financial investment was presumably rewarded, as grand operas were staged with increasing success at the Théâtre d'Orléans and (from 1859) at its successor the French Opera House.

Towards an American grand opera

It was not until mid-century that American composers began to emerge, notably in and around New England. Even then, the Civil War disrupted much established musical culture and many composers went to Europe (usually Germany) to study. Inevitably, the few American operas written in the nineteenth century were based on European – usually Italian and German – models.

William Fry's *Leonora* (1845, Arthur Seguin's troupe, Philadelphia) is often described as the first American grand opera. In fact it drew on Italian models, and some of his other operas reveal more clearly the themes of French grand opera. *Aurelia the Vestal* (1841), for example, deals with the rise of Christianity and the clash of rival religions in the time of Constantine the Great, and features a large-scale ballet, although its musical syntax is still largely Italian.[70] In New Orleans, it has been argued, the programming of French operas acted as a disincentive for local composers to write new operas at all.[71] Although some new works were produced, they were usually in the French (mostly comic) tradition, written by Frenchmen. Eugène Prévost, for example, whose *La Esmeralda* (1840) was a favourite in the city, wrote mainly opéras comiques. The determined effort to keep opera as a cultural tie to France, and a tendency to import talent, surely contributed to this reluctance to write distinctive indigenous operas.

By the time American opera gained its own momentum towards the end of the century, grand opera's moment had passed; more obvious influences were Wagner, Realism and early modernism. For example, Walter Damrosch's first opera, *The Scarlet Letter* (1896, Boston), combined a score strongly influenced by Wagner with a naturalist plot (after Nathaniel Hawthorne) which focused on intense personal emotion. Following its

Boston première one critic noted that its score was 'heavy enough to suit the gods of Valhalla', and the incongruity of German music with an American plot was defined as its main fault.[72]

A more convincing example of an American grand opera – though its score demonstrated further obvious Wagnerian influences – was John Knowles Paine's *Azara* (1883–98; never performed). The plot centres on a classic conflict between Christians and Muslims, with the requisite opposing choruses, and a private story is set against the political background (although the two spheres are never truly integrated). It has a number of features characteristic of French grand opera, including a divertissement in which three Moorish dances provide local colour, a tragic finale with concluding choral prayer and recurring musical themes (rather than leitmotifs). Moreover, the use of pantomime and melodrama, and passages of orchestral music to accompany gestures, are reminiscent of *La Muette*.

One of the most highly publicised American operas was Victor Herbert's *Natoma* (1911, Philadelphia), set in 1820s California.[73] Herbert had ridiculed the pretensions of (French) grand opera – 'a bastard art which appalled the intelligence of all thinking people' – but he also admired its expressive power, 'its incredible eloquence in presenting human conflict'. His own modernistic opera, he claimed, would be 'a continuous logical and well knit stream of orchestral development of the dramatic action, but not [employing] the modernist methods of Strauss and Debussy'.[74] This blend of national history and a European style of music continued to characterise most American operas until World War I.

It was only in the last decades of the century, when Wagner became popular, that French grand opera was performed regularly in New York. But the enormous popularity of Wagner, linked to the fact that the major American opera composers were of German extraction, or had studied in Germany, ensured that grand opera had a mainly indirect influence on native opera.

Latin America

During the nineteenth century Italian opera dominated the repertories of Latin American opera companies and visiting troupes. Grand opera was rarely seen. The emergent tradition of native serious opera, closely linked to the expression of national independence, was consequently derived largely from Italian models, and only indirectly from French grand opera – and Wagner.[75] A number of composers travelled to Europe and experienced Wagner's music at first hand.

The 1870s in Italy saw the popularity of *opera-ballo*, the Italian equivalent of grand opera (see Chapter 19).[76] The emphasis in these works was on spectacle and history, though they did not tackle the historico-political confrontation favoured in grand opera. Wagner's dramas were increasingly seen as an intensification of the Meyerbeerian aesthetic and *Lohengrin* in particular helped to point the way forward for Italian opera in a post-fioritura period of development.[77] The influences of such Italian operas by Franchetti, Leoncavallo and others were seen in the compositions of Latin American musicians at the end of the century.

Brazil

When Pedro II became emperor of Brazil (1831–89) and political stability was established, Rio de Janeiro emerged as an important centre in Latin America for opera. Pedro was the grandson of Franz I of Austria, and he emulated the European courts, even protecting Italian opera between 1844 and 1856. Unsurprisingly, the repertory was dominated by Italian works. But those of Meyerbeer were occasionally performed, for example at the Teatro Dom Pedro II where Toscanini made his world début as a conductor with *Aida* in 1886; during the rest of the season he conducted occasional performances of *Les Huguenots* and *La Favorite* in a repertory dominated by the works of Verdi and Wagner.[78]

Native Brazilian opera began to emerge around the middle of the century. One of its most important figures was Antônio Carlos Gomes (1836–96); however, although his works were staged with success in Brazil, the majority received their premières in Italy, where Gomes lived from the mid-1860s. Though his operas often deal with national subjects their musical language is clearly derived from Donizetti and Verdi, and they are generally considered within the history of Italian rather than Brazilian opera (see Chapter 19 for a contextual discussion of five of his operas). *Il Guarany* (1870, Milan), an *opera-ballo* with emphasis on spectacle, includes the stylised music and dancing of Aimoré Indians: see Ex. 19.2 (p. 399).

Other Brazilian composers, many of whom had studied in Europe, modelled their serious works on Italian and German operas. For example, Leopoldo Miguéz (1850–1902) studied with Franchetti in Oporto, and visited Brussels in the early 1880s where he became acquainted with the music of Wagner, whose influence can be seen in *Os saldunes* (1901, Rio de Janeiro, in Italian), set during Caesar's campaign in Gaul. Similarly, Francisco Braga (1868–1945) studied at the Paris Conservatoire under Massenet and visited Bayreuth; these influences are apparent in his one-act opera, *Jupira* (1900, Rio de Janeiro, in Italian).

Argentina and elsewhere

In 1852–54 Prosper Fleuriet's company of French singers and orchestra went back and forth from Montevideo to Buenos Aires bringing to Uruguay and Argentina the first performances of a range of French operas, including *La Favorite* and *Guillaume Tell*.[79] Grand operas continued to be heard at the Teatro de la Victoria in Buenos Aires in the 1850s, and the Teatro Colón, Argentina's major theatre until 1888, also included grand opera in its repertory.

Native Argentinian operas tended to combine Italianate musical style with national history. Arturo Berutti (1858–1938), for example, acknowledged as the first nationalist Argentinian composer, studied in Leipzig and lived for a short time in Italy; his lyric dramas *Pampa* (1897) and *Yupanki* (1899), dealing with gauchos and Incas respectively, are essentially Italianate works (bearing the influence of Wagner via Italy) that draw on South American history.

In other parts of Latin America, the dominance of Italian opera was also seen and native works tended to develop models from Donizetti, Verdi, Leoncavallo and others. For example, the Mexican composer Cenobio Paniagua y Vasques (1821–82) set a libretto on a Huguenot theme by Felice Romani, *Catalina di Guisa* (1859), combining Italianate musical style with the epic quality of grand opera.

Conclusion

It is evident that French grand opera, adapted variously, was performed and enjoyed in Britain and the Americas during the major part of the nineteenth century. Grand opera's reliance on spectacular effects and large numbers of talented performers meant that it necessarily fared better in the repertories of permanent professional companies (notably at Covent Garden in London, at the Metropolitan Opera in New York, and at the Colón in Buenos Aires), but was also given in those of smaller troupes. It seems that the genre was admired for some of the reasons it was admired in Paris: the importance to the drama of visual effects, its Italianate lyricism, eclectic influences and epic qualities.

The genre's immediate success in London, as witnessed by the competing productions of *Robert le Diable* only months after the opera's première in Paris, and its continuing popularity throughout the century, are striking. But its radical political and sexual themes were often eliminated, and the resulting adaptations remain to be researched further. By the time that English serious opera was emerging in the 1880s there was still a fascination with grand themes, occasionally drawn from national history, but native composers tended to model their scores on early Wagner or on such later nineteenth-century French composers as Bizet and Saint-Saëns.

Contemporary and modern critics alike have been disappointed by the failure of British composers to develop the musico-dramatic possibilities of the librettos in the manner of grand opera.

In America grand opera was performed less frequently than it was in London. An important pocket of enthusiasm for the genre was New Orleans, where it was performed more consistently than anywhere else in North America. At the end of the century, following the opening of the Metropolitan Opera in New York, French grand opera (sung in German) became an important part of a repertory dominated by Wagner. In this context it is not surprising to find that serious American operas tended to deal with large themes – frequently drawn from national legends – in a musical style modelled on Wagner.

In Latin America, purely French grand opera was seen less often: Italian and Spanish opera dominated the repertories of most companies. Thus, native attempts at opera tended to be modelled on Italian works, emulating the eclectic nature of *opera-ballo*.

By the end of the nineteenth century, when examples of native grand opera were emerging in Britain and the Americas, it is difficult to distinguish the influence of Meyerbeer from that of later composers (not to mention the continuing sway of Weber and Rossini). However, the legacy of grand opera – its scale and spectacle, historical subjects and musical eclecticism – which more immediately influenced Verdi and Wagner, consequently served as the foundation for a host of national operas such as Stanford's *The Veiled Prophet*, Paine's *Azara* and Berutti's *Pampa*.

Notes

1 Introduction

1 The situation in German opera in these decades is comprehensively discussed by John Warrack in his magisterial *German Opera: From the Beginnings to Wagner* (Cambridge: Cambridge University Press, 2001).

2 *The Diaries of Giacomo Meyerbeer*, I (1791–1839), and II (1840–49), trans., ed. and annotated by Robert Ignatius Letellier (Madison: Fairleigh Dickinson University Press, 1999, 2001); Hector Berlioz, *La Critique musicale 1823–1863*, ed. H. Robert Cohen (vol. I only), and Yves Gérard (Paris: Buchet/Chastel, 1996–): I (1823–24) (1996); II (1835–36) (1998); III (1837–38) (2001).

3 Anselm Gerhard, 'Die französische "Grand Opéra" in der Forschung seit 1945', *Acta Musicologica*, 59/3 (1988), 220–70.

4 Jürgen Schläder, *Das Opernduett: Ein Szenentypus des 19. Jahrhunderts und seine Vorgeschichte* (Tübingen: Niemeyer, 1995).

5 Carl Dahlhaus, *Nineteenth-Century Music* (Berkeley: University of California Press, 1989); *Realism in 19th-Century Music* (Cambridge: Cambridge University Press, 1985).

6 Hervé Lacombe, 'Définitions des genres lyriques dans les dictionnaires français du XIXe siècle', in *Le Théâtre Lyrique en France au XIXe siècle*, ed. Paul Prévost (Metz: Serpenoise, 1995), 297–334.

7 'The best actors in the world, either for tragedy, comedy, history, pastoral, pastoral-comical, historical-pastoral, tragical-historical, tragical-comical-historical-pastoral, scene individable, or poem unlimited.' *Hamlet*, II. 2.

8 [Pierre-Jean-Baptiste Nougaret], *De l'art du théâtre en général*, 2 vols. (Paris: Cailleau, 1768), II, 214, 223, 226. My thanks to Herbert Schneider for pointing this out.

9 Jérôme-Joseph de Momigny, 'Opéra', in *Encyclopédie méthodique: Musique*, vol. II (Paris: Veuve Agasse, 1818; repr. New York, 1971), 220–41. The article gives a historical account of 'OPERA (GRAND)' from Lully (1632–87) to Spontini (*b.* 1774), divided into five 'schools'.

10 F. W. J. Hemmings, 'The Licensing System, 1814–1864' and 'The State-Supported Theatres in the Nineteenth Century', in *Theatre and State in France 1760–1905*

(Cambridge: Cambridge University Press, 1994), 160–92.

11 Lacombe, 'Définitions des genres lyriques', 309.

12 David Kimbell, *Verdi in the Age of Italian Romanticism* (Cambridge: Cambridge University Press, 1981).

13 Karin Pendle, *Eugène Scribe and French Opera of the Nineteenth Century* (Ann Arbor: UMI, 1979); *eadem*, 'The Boulevard Theaters and Continuity in French Opera of the 19th Century', in *Music in Paris in the Eighteen-Thirties*, ed. Peter Bloom (Stuyvesant, NY: Pendragon, 1987), 509–35.

14 D. G. Charlton, 'The French Romantic Movement', in *The French Romantics*, ed. Charlton, 2 vols. (Cambridge: Cambridge University Press, 1984), I, 1–32, here 17.

15 Mark Everist, 'Meyerbeer's *Il crociato in Egitto*: Mélodrame, Opera, Orientalism', *Cambridge Opera Journal*, 8/3 (1996), 215–50, here 247–8.

16 Théodore de Lajarte, *Bibliothèque musicale du Théâtre de l'Opéra: catalogue historique*, 2 vols. (Paris: Librairie des bibliophiles, 1878). Catel's oriental *Les Bayadères* (1810), seen up to 1828, was the only comparable success (140 performances); all other successful, long-running Paris Opéra productions were ballets of various sorts.

17 Lajarte, *Bibliothèque musicale du Théâtre de l'Opéra*, II, 69. See also his 'Spontini: *La Vestale* et *Fernand Cortez*', *Le Ménestrel*, 40, 2303–7 (6, 13, 20, 27 September and 4 October 1874).

18 Lajarte, 'Spontini: *La Vestale* et *Fernand Cortez*', *Le Ménestrel*, 40, 2305 (20 September 1874), 329. This document has been identified as Paris, Archives nationales, AJ^{13}.92, dossier 470: Nicole Wild, *Décors et costumes du XIXe siècle. Tome I: Opéra de Paris* (Paris: Bibliothèque nationale, 1987), 108. It was a report from Mitoire as *garde-magasin des Menus-Plaisirs* to the Director of the Opéra. Costume designs from the same production are seen in *New Grove/2*, X, 290.

19 *Journal de Paris*, 169 (9 March 1798), 704. The production was at the Opéra-Comique, however.

20 [Hector Berlioz], 'Le *Requiem* des Invalides . . .', *Journal des débats*, 9 August 1835, in *Hector Berlioz. Critique musicale*, II,

247–54, here 252. He goes on to say how effective the choral use of bass voices was in *Robert le Diable*.

21 Moline de Saint-Yon, 'Avant-propos', *Ipsiboé, Opéra en quatre actes* (Paris: Roullet, 1824), [i]. There is no critical literature on this work, adapted from a contemporary novel of the same name by vicomte d'Arlincourt, which has its own ironic preface (2nd edn, Paris: Béchet, 1823).

22 Sieghart Döhring, 'Giacomo Meyerbeer and the Opera of the Nineteenth Century', website 'Meyerbeer Fan Club', http://www.meyerbeer.com/sieghart.htm, 1–8 [4], accessed on 26 March 1999.

23 Peter Brooks, *The Melodramatic Imagination* (New Haven: Yale University Press, 1995 [1976]), esp. 90–3. We mentioned earlier Karin Pendle's work in this area.

24 [Anon.], 'Sur les pièces à décorations', in *Courier des spectacles*, 718 (21 pluviôse VII/9 February, 1799), 2–3.

25 See Thierry Delcourt, 'De Mehmed II à Mahomet II, le vrai paysage historique', *L'Avant-scène opéra*, 81 (*Le Siège de Corinthe*, 1985), 4–7.

26 Janet Lynn Johnson, 'The Théâtre Italien and Opera and Theatrical Life in Restoration Paris, 1818–1827', dissertation, University of Chicago (1988), 63, 67.

27 My translation from Edouard Robert's *Observations sur le Théâtre Royal Italien* (Paris, 1832), reproduced in Johnson, *ibid.*, 47.

28 Scott L. Balthazar, 'Aspects of form in the Ottocento Libretto', *Cambridge Opera Journal*, 7/1 (1995), 23–35.

29 As in Metastasio's *Demofoonte* the central couple have a young child already, born and raised in secret.

30 At least from Monsigny and Sedaine's *Le Déserteur* (1769), a pioneering work in this, as in so much else; presumed infidelity causes Alexis, like an anti-hero, to desert the army knowing that deserters are routinely shot. Act II and much of Act III are set in a prison. Type 2 operas succeeding *Le Déserteur* include 'tyrant' and other 'rescue' operas under the Revolution.

31 Dahlhaus, *Nineteenth-Century Music*, 128.

32 Hemmings, *Theatre and State in France*, 208.

33 Douglas Johnson, 'Historians', in *The French Romantics*, ed. Charlton, II, 274–307, here 290.

34 Stendhal, *Vie de Rossini*, translated and annotated by Richard Coe as *Life of Rossini*, rev. edn (London: Calder & Boyars, 1970; John Calder, 1985), 60–2.

35 Ludwig Finscher, 'Aubers *La Muette de Portici* und die Anfänge der Grand-opéra', in *Festschrift Heinz Becker*, ed. Jürgen Schläder and Reinhold Quandt (Laaber: Laaber-Verlag, 1982), 87–105.

36 Scott, *Rob Roy*, Chapter 4.

37 *Rob Roy*, Chapter 9. A 'pie' is a book of ecclesiastical rules; a 'graile' a book of antiphons; and a 'portuasse' a portable breviary.

38 Jane Fulcher, *The Nation's Image: French Grand Opera as Politics and Politicized Art* (Cambridge: Cambridge University Press, 1987); Anselm Gerhard, 'Großstadt und Große Oper: Motive der "Grand Opéra" in Verdis *Les Vêpres siciliennes* und ausgewählten Pariser Opern von Rossini und Meyerbeer', dissertation, Technische Universität, Berlin (1985).

39 Fulcher, *The Nation's Image*, 170. This view was severely contested by Anselm Gerhard in a review of the same book within *Neue Zeitschrift für Musik*, 149 (1988), Heft 3, 57–8.

40 *The Cambridge Urban History of Britain*, ed. D. M. Palliser, Peter Clark and M. J. Daunton, 3 vols. (Cambridge: Cambridge University Press, 2000, 2001).

41 Adrien Richer, *Essai sur les grands événements par les petits causes, tiré de l'histoire*, 2 vols. (Geneva: Hardy, 1758–9), mentioned in Gerhard, *Urbanization*, 311.

42 In actual history Péronne was being invaded by a lieutenant of Charles V of Spain. But this simply shows that the librettist wished to reflect modern times through opera realistically, using 'historical' material.

43 Alessandro Manzoni, 'Lettre de M. Manzoni à M. C*** sur l'unité de tems et de lieu dans la tragédie', in *Opere di Alessandro Manzoni*, 6 vols. (Florence: Fratelli Batelli, 1828), I, 142–239, here 145–6, 155ff., 188ff.

44 For example, Steven Huebner's review in *Nineteenth-Century Music*, 18/2 (1994), 168–74.

45 Mary Ann Smart, 'Mourning the Duc d'Orléans: Donizetti's *Dom Sébastien* and the Political Meanings of Grand Opera', in *Reading Critics Reading*, ed. Smart and Roger Parker (Oxford: Oxford University Press, 2001), 188–212.

46 Heather Hadlock, 'The Career of Cherubino, or the Trouser Role Grows Up', in *Siren Songs: Representations of Gender and Sexuality in Opera*, ed. Mary Ann Smart (Princeton: Princeton University Press, 2000), 73.

47 Austin Caswell (ed.), *Embellished Opera Arias* (Madison, WI: A–R Editions, 1989); Will Crutchfield, 'Ornamentation' §2 and §3

in *Grove Opera* (see additional publications in the bibliography to this article).

48 Mary Ann Smart, 'The Lost Voice of Rosine Stoltz', *Cambridge Opera Journal*, 6/1 (1994), 31–50.

49 Alan Armstrong, 'Gilbert-Louis Duprez and Gustave Roger in the Composition of Meyerbeer's *Le Prophète*', *Cambridge Opera Journal*, 8/2 (1996), 147–65.

50 Robert Ignatius Letellier, 'History, Myth and Music in a Theme of Exploration: Some Reflections on the Musico-Dramatic Language of *L'Africaine*', in *Meyerbeer und das europäische Musiktheater*, ed. Sieghart Döhring and Arnold Jacobshagen (Laaber: Laaber-Verlag, 1998); Gabriela Cruz, 'Laughing at History: the Third Act of Meyerbeer's *L'Africaine*', *Cambridge Opera Journal*, 11/1 (1999), 31–76.

51 James Parakilas, 'The Soldier and the Exotic: Operatic Variations on a Theme of Racial Encounter', *Opera Quarterly*, 10 (1993), 33–56.

52 Cormac Newark, 'Ceremony, Celebration and Spectacle in *La Juive*', in *Reading Critics Reading*, ed. Smart and Parker, 155–87. Diana Hallman's book on this composer is imminent at the time of writing.

53 Sarah Hibberd, 'Magnetism, Muteness, Magic: *Spectacle* and the Parisian Lyric Stage, c.1830', dissertation, University of Southampton (1998).

54 Dominique Leroy, *Histoire des arts du spectacle en France* (Paris: L'Harmattan, 1990); Yves Ozanam, 'Recherches sur l'Académie royale de Musique (Opéra Français) sous la seconde Restauration', dissertation, 3 vols., Paris: Ecole des Chartes (1981).

55 John Duncan Drysdale, 'Louis Véron and the Finances of the *Académie Royale de Musique*, 1827 to 1835', dissertation, University of Southampton (2000).

56 Source: Herbert Schneider, *Chronologisch-thematisches Verzeichnis sämtlicher Werke von Daniel François Esprit Auber (AWV)*, 2 vols. (Hildesheim: Georg Olms, 1994), I, 203ff.

57 Jean-Louis Tamvaco, *Les Cancans de l'Opéra. Chroniques de l'Académie Royale de Musique et du théâtre, à Paris sous les deux Restaurations*, 2 vols. (Paris: CNRS Editions, 2000).

58 Adrienne Simpson, *Opera's Farthest Frontier: A History of Professional Opera in New Zealand* (Birkenhead, Auckland: Reed, 1996).

59 *La Muette de Portici* was presented in 1853–54 at the San Giacomo theatre in Corfu, as was *Robert le Diable*. Information kindly provided by Kostas Kardamis.

2 The 'machine' and the state

1 It is customary to distinguish the Paris 'Opéra' (sometimes 'Grand Opéra'), meaning the company and its theatre building, from 'opera' or 'grand opera' as an art form; the same applies to the 'Opéra-Comique' and 'opéra comique'. See the Abbreviations (p. xvii) for more detailed aspects of nomenclature. Government departments etc. are referred to in this chapter by transparent translations.

2 'Public interest' here refers to the important concept of 'intérêt général' in French law, which includes the notion of the common good.

3 Hervé Lacombe, 'De la différentiation des genres: Réflexion sur la notion de genre lyrique français au début du XIXe siècle', *Revue de musicologie*, 84/2 (1998), 247–62.

4 The secondary theatres were the Théâtre du Vaudeville, the Théâtre des Variétés, the Théâtre de la Gaîté, and the Théâtre de l'Ambigu-Comique: Nicole Wild, *Dictionnaire des théâtres parisiens au XIXe siècle: Les théâtres et la musique* (Paris: Aux Amateurs de livres, 1989).

5 One bears the title *Sur l'Opéra, et sur les dangers auxquels il vient d'échapper* ['Concerning the Opéra and the Perils it has just Escaped'] and another is *Lettre sur l'Opéra et sur les dangers auxquels il n'a pas encore échappé, adressé à l'auteur d'un écrit sur l'Opéra et sur le danger auquel il vient d'échapper* ['Letter on the Opéra and the Perils from which it has not yet Escaped, Addressed to the Author of a Pamphlet on the Opéra and the Peril from which it has just Escaped'].

6 He was partly criticising what in French is called 'déclamation', an ancient and important term defined in various dictionaries. Louis de Cahusac in the great *Encyclopédie, ou dictionnaire raisonné*, ed. Denis Diderot and Jean le Rond D'Alembert (Paris: Briasson, 1751–65), IV, called it 'the sung expression of emotion conveyed by the words'.

7 However, the Staging Committee ceased to function in the same way after 1831.

8 Scholarly investigation is possible thanks to the sources in the Opéra library (Bibliothèque-musée de l'Opéra) and the Archives nationales, Paris, and also to three fundamental studies: Yves Ozanam, 'Recherches sur l'Académie royale de musique sous la seconde Restauration (1815–1830)', dissertation, Paris: Ecole des Chartes (1981); Anne-Sophie Cras, 'L'Exploitation de l'Opéra sous la monarchie de Juillet', dissertation, Paris: Ecole des Chartes (1996); and Viviane

Deschamps, 'Histoire de l'administration de l'Opéra de Paris (Second Empire-Troisième République)', dissertation, Université de Paris IV (Sorbonne) (1987). The Archives nationales hold most of the records of the Opéra censorship (F^{21}.989), together with the librettos submitted for censorship (F^{18}).

9 However, it is extremely difficult to be sure about the social composition of the audience. See Steven Huebner's interesting study 'Opera Audiences in Paris, 1830–1870', *Music & Letters*, 70/2 (May 1989), 206–25, and Anselm Gerhard, *The Urbanization of Opera. Music Theater in Paris in the Nineteenth Century* (Chicago: University of Chicago Press, 1998), 25–33.

10 Véron's strategies are detailed in John Duncan Drysdale, 'Louis Véron and the Finances of the *Académie Royale de Musique*, 1827 to 1835', dissertation, University of Southampton (2000).

11 Dominique Leroy, *Histoire des arts du spectacle en France* (Paris: L'Harmattan, 1990).

12 Gentil has now been shown to be the author of an unofficial backstage diary of the Opéra from 1836 to 1848: Jean-Louis Tamvaco, *Les Cancans de l'Opéra. Chroniques de l'Académie Royale de Musique et du théâtre, à Paris sous les deux Restaurations*, 2 vols. (Paris: CNRS Editions, 2000).

13 O. Krakovitch, *Hugo censuré: La liberté au théâtre au XIXe siècle* (Paris: Calmann-Lévy, 1985).

14 'Art becomes political less through the express desire of the authorities than by its reception by the public in a given context': Olivier Bara, 'Une révolution manquée? *Masaniello* face à la censure', in *Le Théâtre de l'Opéra-Comique sous la Restauration* (Hildesheim: G. Olms, 2001), 259–80, here 264–5.

15 The opera house on the rue Le Peletier, designed by François Debret, was built in 1821. A full description with illustrations is in Jean Gourret, *Histoire des salles de l'Opéra de Paris* (Paris: Trédaniel, 1985), 141–62.

16 The ball scene was a favourite in the 1830s, and staged on its own as 'Le nouveau bal masqué de Gustave III': Tamvaco, *Les Cancans de l'Opéra*, vol. II *passim*.

17 The comparison with the modern cinema is obvious: H. Lacombe, 'Opéra et produits dérivés. Le cas du théâtre lyrique français au XIXe siècle', in *Histoire des industries culturelles XIXe –XXe siècles*, ed. Jacques Marseilles and Patrick Eveno, actes de colloque (Paris-Sorbonne, 5–6 December 2001) (Paris: Association pour le Développement de l'Histoire Economique, 2002), 431–43.

18 'Opéra', in *Grand Dictionnaire du XIXe siècle*, ed. Pierre Larousse, 15 vols. (Paris: Larousse et Boyer, 1866–76), XI, 1361.

19 Gerhard, *Urbanization*.

20 See Louis Pinto, *Pierre Bourdieu et la théorie du monde social* (Paris: Albin Michel, 1998), 153–65.

3 Fictions and librettos

1 W. H. Auden, 'Notes on Music and Opera', in *The Dyer's Hand and Other Essays* (London: Faber & Faber, 1963), 473.

2 Pierre-Augustin Caron de Beaumarchais, *The Barber of Seville or the Futile Precaution*, trans. Gilbert Pestureau, Ann Wakefield and Gavin Witt (Lewiston, NY: The Edward Mellen Press, 1997), 2. Subsequent translations into English are my own, unless otherwise stated, as here. Joseph Addison, *The Spectator*, Wednesday 21 March 1711.

3 Anselm Gerhard describes the events of the 1830 performance in Brussels of *La Muette de Portici* as 'the revolutionary effect of this anti-revolutionary opera'. See his magisterial account, *The Urbanization of Opera: Music Theater in Paris in the Nineteenth Century* (Chicago: University of Chicago Press, 1998), 131.

4 In Herbert Lindenberger's words, 'the dual authorship that marks most of operatic history reveals tensions as well as possibilities foreign to other major forms of art': *Opera: The Extravagant Art* (Ithaca: Cornell University Press, 1984), 115.

5 Meyerbeer's letter to Scribe from Berlin, editorially dated 21 April 1846, cited in Heinz and Gudrun Becker, *Giacomo Meyerbeer: A Life in Letters*, trans. Mark Violette (London: Helm, 1989), 106.

6 Brian Trowell, 'Libretto', in *Grove Opera*, II, 1194–5. Gerhard charts the historical shifts in this hierarchy as 'the primacy of the literary element' wanes after around 1830 with the displacement of the *tragédie lyrique* model, still promoted in 1825 by Victor-Joseph Etienne de Jouy (*Urbanization*, 40).

7 Louis-Désiré Véron, *Mémoires d'un bourgeois de Paris*, 6 vols. (Paris: Gonet, 1853–55), III, 252. See Chapter 10, p. 170, below for the continuation of this quotation.

8 Didier van Mœre, 'Les échos de la presse', *L'Avant-scène opéra*, 118 (*Guillaume Tell*, 1989), 148.

9 Stendhal, *Life of Rossini* (1824), trans. Richard N. Coe, abridged in *The Essence of Opera*, ed. Ulrich Weisstein (New York: Norton, 1969), 191–200, here 195.

10 Théophile Gautier, *Histoire de l'art dramatique en France depuis vingt-cinq ans*, 6 vols. (Paris: Hetzel, 1859), I, 17.

11 *Ibid.*, I, 113–14.

12 To visualise the scale of Scribe's output one need only consult his *Œuvres complètes* in 76 vols. (Paris: Dentu, 1874–85); Series III, entitled *Opéras–Ballets*, contains within its six volumes thirty-seven separate works, including those which could be classed under the rubric of grand opera.

13 Jean-Alexandre Ménétrier, 'L'Amour triste: Fromental Halévy et son temps', *L'Avant-scène opéra*, 100 (*La Juive*, 1987), 4–12, here 8.

14 Scribe was, in J.-G. Prod'homme's words, 'the principal artisan': *L'Opéra (1669–1925)* (Paris: Delagrave, 1925), 39, and Jacques Bonnaure calls him 'the well named Scribe': 'Monsieur Scribe ou le romantisme du juste milieu', *L'Avant-scène opéra*, 100 (*La Juive*, 1987), 88–93, here 88.

15 Karin Pendle, *Eugène Scribe and French Opera of the Nineteenth Century* (Ann Arbor: UMI Press, 1979), 1.

16 *New Grove/*2, XXIII, 13.

17 Patrick J. Smith, *A Historical Study of the Opera Libretto* (New York: Schirmer, 1970), 211.

18 Cited in Brander Matthews, *French Dramatists of the Nineteenth Century* (New York: Scribner, 1881), 88.

19 F. W. J. Hemmings argues that 'no one ever suggested that Scribe exploited other men's work unfairly . . . On the contrary, he erred rather in giving credit where credit was barely due': *The Theatre Industry in Nineteenth-Century France* (Cambridge: Cambridge University Press, 1993), 249. Léon Halévy's account of his brother's career stresses the 'abnegation' and 'disinterestedness' of Scribe, so much so that the former prefers the term 'coopérateur' rather than '*collaborateur*': *F. Halévy. Sa vie et ses œuvres*, 2nd edn (Paris: Heugel, 1863), 24–5, Halévy's emphasis.

20 It is for such reasons that one must be attentive to the differences between the versions which librettists such as Scribe might include in their own published works and the actual versions employed in opera productions themselves: see Chapter 10 below.

21 Gerhard observes 'grand opéra's tendency to discount the public's knowledge of literature, just as the "modern cultural industry" does: it was no longer necessary for the audience at an opera to be familiar with classical mythology or to have read the libretto beforehand in order to follow the action': *Urbanization*, 23.

22 See Smith, *Historical Study*, 219, and Gerhard, *Urbanization*, 136–9, for references to Stephen S. Stanton, 'English Drama and the French Well-Made Play', dissertation, Columbia University (1955).

23 *New Grove/*2, XXIII, 14.

24 Although Gerhard reminds us that before the twentieth century Rossini's opera *Le Siège de Corinthe* (1826) was seen as a revolutionary turning-point in the history of the opera which antedated Auber's work (*Urbanization*, 70).

25 Cormac Newark, 'Ceremony, Celebration, and Spectacle in *La Juive*', in *Reading Critics Reading*, ed. Roger Parker and Mary Ann Smart (Oxford: Oxford University Press, 2001), 155–87, here 160.

26 A process detailed by Mark Everist, 'The Name of the Rose: Meyerbeer's *opéra comique, Robert le Diable*', *Revue de Musicologie*, 80/2 (1994), 210–50.

27 Scribe's authenticating footnote cites Voltaire's *Essai sur les mœurs*, chapter CXXXII, as a source of historical chronology.

28 This has been criticised at a dramatic level as 'one of the great weaknesses of the work' as 'we are never confronted with the major decision makers': Jean-Michel Brègue, 'Loin de Mérimée et du grand opéra historique', *L'Avant-scène opéra*, 76 (*Robert le Diable*, 1985), 9–19, here 14.

29 Roland Barthes, *S/Z* (Paris: Seuil, 1970), 108; Barthes's emphasis.

30 Prosper Mérimée, *Théâtre de Clara Gazul, Romans et nouvelles*, ed. Jean Mallion and Pierre Salomon (Paris: Gallimard, 1978), 259.

31 Pendle, *Eugène Scribe*, 5. Even the gaps in characterisation are construed in Pendle's praise of this 'ideal scaffolding for music' as a space into which 'the music would be able to expand, expressing qualities of spirit and emotion absent from Scribe's stick-men' (*ibid.*, 11).

32 Jerome Mitchell, *The Walter Scott Operas* (Tuscaloosa, AL: University of Alabama Press, 1977), 358–9.

33 Pendle (*Eugène Scribe*, 397) stresses this interrogation of the revolutionary spirit: 'If the Catholics are oversensitive and treacherous in *Les Huguenots*, the Protestants are self-righteous and gullible. In *Le Prophète* the three Anabaptist conspirators are just as wicked as the nobles against whom they are fighting. So too in *La Muette de Portici*, fanatics take over an originally idealistic revolution against a tyrannical ruler.'

34 George Jellinek, *History through the Opera Glass: From the Rise of Caesar to the Fall of Napoleon* (New York: Pro/Am Music Resources, 1994), 154.

35 See Edward Said, *Orientalism* (Harmondsworth: Penguin, 1985 [1978]).

36 *L'Africaine*, music by G. Meyerbeer, words by E. Scribe (Sydney: Gibbs, 1866), 14.

37 'For Scribe', as Helene Koon and Richard Switzer write, 'history is not a book of lessons, but a metaphor for the present': *Eugène Scribe* (Boston: Twayne, 1980), 110. However, the absurd potential of trying to reconstruct history from opera can be gauged from Jellinek's *History through the Opera Glass*.

38 Herbert Lindenberger, *Historical Drama: The Relation of Literature and Reality* (Chicago: Chicago University Press, 1975), 6.

39 Gary Schmidgall, *Literature as Opera* (New York: Oxford University Press, 1977), 11.

40 David Charlton, 'On the Nature of "Grand Opera" ', in *Berlioz: 'Les Troyens'*, ed. Ian Kemp (Cambridge: Cambridge University Press, 1988), 94–105, here 104. The methods of cultural history come to the fore in Jane Fulcher's analysis of the ruses in the discourse of state power and opera's response to it. See her *The Nation's Image: French Grand Opera As Politics and Politicized Art* (Cambridge: Cambridge University Press, 1987).

41 Amongst many other less well known sources, as Gerhard reminds us (*Urbanization*, 94).

42 *Le Courrier des théâtres*, 5 August 1829.

43 Suzanne Citron, *Le mythe national* (Paris: Editions ouvrières, 1987), 162. As we shall see, Berlioz would revivify this Trojan myth.

44 Lindenberger, *Historical Drama*, 61.

45 Citron, *Le mythe national*, 99.

46 Hector Berlioz, *Selected Letters*, ed. Hugh Macdonald, trans. R. Nichols (London: Faber & Faber, 1995), 362. To his son, Louis Berlioz, from Paris, 24 January 1858. See also David Cairns, *Berlioz: Servitude and Greatness 1832–1869* (London: Allen Lane, 1999), 630–1.

47 Berlioz, *Selected Letters*, 345. To Toussaint Bennet, from Paris, 11 June 1856. In a letter to Princess Carolyne Sayn-Wittgenstein from Baden-Baden, 12 August 1856, Berlioz confesses: 'I'm nothing but a marauder . . . I've stolen a bunch of flowers to make a bed for music, and pray God it's not asphyxiated by the perfumes' (346).

48 For an analysis of melodrama's components, see Peter Brooks, *The Melodramatic Imagination* (New Haven: Yale University Press, 1995 [1976]).

49 Scribe, *Œuvres complètes*, ser. III, vol. VI, 73–5.

50 This 'perfect marriage' is the third of 'four basic approaches to melodramaturgy' usefully identified by Ulrich Weisstein in his introduction to *The Essence of Opera*, 1–10. Previously, the classical and neoclassical identified with Gluck saw music as 'a modest handmaiden', whereas 'the Romantic theory of opera . . . celebrates the triumph of music over drama'. Subsequently, 'the founders of Epic Opera [such as Stravinsky, Brecht and Berg] were determined to provide equal but separate facilities for music and drama' (*ibid.*, 5–6).

51 Edward Bulwer Lytton, *Rienzi, The Last of the Roman Tribunes* (London: Saunders and Otley, 1840), xiv. Lytton's use of footnotes to authenticate sources and historical references suggests the pervasion of an impulse also common to grand opera.

52 Bulwer Lytton, *Rienzi*, 538. More generally, Herbert Lindenberger argues: 'By the nineteenth century the historical process rather than the heroic individual had become the chief carrier of heroic action. When the writer can no longer conceive of a properly heroic hero, the historical process can assume the magnitude appropriate to heroism' (*Historical Drama*, 63–4).

4 The spectacle of the past in grand opera

1 David Lowenthal, *The Past is a Foreign Country* (Cambridge: Cambridge University Press, 1985), 394.

2 Pierre Peyronnet, *La Mise en scène au XVIIIe siècle* (Paris: Nizet, 1974), 101–6.

3 Beaumont Newhall, *Daguerre* (New York: Winter House, 1971), 10.

4 Victor Hugo, 'Préface de Cromwell', in *Œuvres Complètes*, ed. Jean-Pierre Reynaud, 7 vols. (Paris: Robert Laffont, 1985, 1987), XII (Critique), 19.

5 In the first decade of the century, opera in a neoclassical mode did not entirely lack for audiences. Fontenelle's *Hécube* received forty-three performances between 1800 and 1808, Kreutzer's *Astynax* forty-six between 1801 and 1816, and Steibelt's *Le Retour de Zéphire* sixty-five between 1801 and 1821. Furthermore, some works of a more modern tendency found their way into the Opéra's repertory. *Les Mystères d'Isis*, based on Mozart's *Die Zauberflöte*, received 134 performances between 1801 and 1827 and Le Sueur's *Ossian ou Les Bardes* a respectable sixty-five between 1804 and 1811. And even in the first decade of the century, works that anticipated grand opera, such as Spontini's *La Vestale* (1807), *Fernand Cortez* (1809) and Catel's *Les Bayadères* (1810) began to emerge:

Théodore de Lajarte, *Bibliothèque musicale du Théâtre de l'Opéra* (Paris: Librairie des Bibliophiles, 1878).

6 Patrick Barbier, *A l'Opéra au temps de Rossini et Balzac, Paris: 1800–1850* (Paris: Hachette, 1987), 49; Eng. trans. as *Opera in Paris, 1800–1850: A Lively History* (Portland, OR: Amadeus Press, 1995).

7 Quoted in Barry V. Daniels, 'Ciceri and Daguerre: Set Designers for the Paris Opéra, 1820–1822', *Theatre Survey*, 22/1 (1981), 69–90, here 82. The Paris Opéra historical staging collection is catalogued in Nicole Wild, *Décors et costumes du XIXe siècle. Tome I: Opéra de Paris* and *Tome II: Théâtres et décorateurs* (Paris: Bibliothèque nationale, 1987, 1993). Vol. II contains convenient biographies of all the designers mentioned in the present chapter.

8 Jane Fulcher. *The Nation's Image: French Grand Opera as Politics and Politicized Art* (Cambridge: Cambridge University Press, 1987), 18.

9 The given name 'Henri' (not Edmond as traditionally found) has been determined by Jean-Louis Tamvaco in a new biography and list of Duponchel's productions within his *Les Cancans de l'Opéra. Chroniques de l'Académie Royale de Musique et du théâtre, à Paris sous les deux restaurations*, 2 vols. (Paris: CNRS Editions, 2000), II, 963–70. Duponchel (see Table 2.2, p. 27) had various titles at the Opéra, 1829–49: *Inspecteur du matériel de la scène* (1829–31); *Directeur de la scène* (1831–35); *Directeur de la mise-en-scène* (1840–41) as well as sole *Directeur* (1835–39) and joint *Directeur* (1839 and 1847–49): Wild, *Dictionnaire des théâtres parisiens au XIXe siècle* (Paris: Aux Amateurs de livres, 1989), 306–7, 316.

10 Jean-Pierre Moynet, *L'envers du théâtre* [1873], trans. Allan S. Jackson and M. Glen Wilson, ed. Marvin Carlson as *French Theatrical Production in the Nineteenth Century* (New York: SUNY at Binghamton, 1976), 1, 16. Moynet therefore writes retrospectively for the most part.

11 Facsimile reproductions of twenty-two *livrets scéniques* are in H. Robert Cohen (ed.), *The Original Staging Manuals for Twelve Parisian Operatic Premières*, and *The Original Staging Manuals for Ten Parisian Operatic Premières*, Musical Life in 19th-Century France III and VI (Stuyvesant, NY: Pendragon Press, 1991, 1998). Several unpublished in-house *livrets scéniques* survive: Rossini, *Guillaume Tell*, ed. M. Elizabeth C. Bartlet, Edizione Critica delle Opera di Gioachino Rossini, sezione prima–opere teatrali, 39 (Pesaro: Fondazione Rossini, 1992–94), critical commentary, II.

12 Catherine Join-Dieterle, *Les Décors de scène de l'Opéra de Paris à l'époque romantique* (Paris: Picard, 1988), 30.

13 Théophile Gautier, *Histoire de l'art dramatique en France*, 5 vols. (Leipzig: Hetzel, 1859), II, 85.

14 John Duncan Drysdale, 'Louis Véron and the Finances of the *Académie Royale de Musique*, 1827 to 1835', dissertation, University of Southampton (2000); Join-Dieterle, *Les Décors de scène*, 198; Bartlet, 'Staging French *Grand Opéra*: Rossini's *Guillaume Tell* (1829)', in *Gioachino Rossini, 1792–1992: il testo e la scena: Convegno internazionale di studi, Pesaro, 24–28 giugno 1992*, ed. Paolo Fabbri (Pesaro: Fondazione Rossini, 1994), 623–48.

15 Marie-Antoinette Allevy, *La Mise en scène en France dans la première moitié du XIXe siècle* (Paris: Droz, 1938), 55. Details in following section from Wild, *Décors et costumes*, II.

16 These are most readily available in Join-Dieterle, *Les Décors de scène*. See Wild, *Décors et costumes*, for the most advanced research on attributing the work of scene-painters.

17 Gautier, *Histoire de l'art dramatique*, II, 49.

18 Gösta M. Bergman, *Lighting in the Theatre* (Stockholm: Almqvist & Wiksell, 1977), 256–7.

19 Carl Baermann, diary entry for Paris, 2 January 1839: Robert Ignatius Letellier (ed. and trans.), *The Diaries of Giacomo Meyerbeer*, Vol. 1: *1791–1839* (Madison: Fairleigh Dickinson University Press, 1999), 525.

20 See *livret scénique* for the first production of *La Juive*: Cohen (ed.), *Staging Manuals for Twelve Premières*, 141. There is a detailed examination of the movements of stage personnel in relation to scenery and *livret de mise-en-scène* in *La Juive*, by Karin Pendle and Stephen Wilkins: 'Paradise Found: The Salle Le Peletier and French Grand Opera', in *Opera in Context: Essays on Historical Staging from the Late Renaissance to the Time of Puccini*, ed. Mark A. Radice (Portland, OR: Amadeus Press, 1998), 171–207, here 190–8. Considerations of processions by Cormac Newark and Mary Ann Smart are in Roger Parker and Smart (eds.), *Reading Critics Reading: Opera and Ballet Criticism in France from the Revolution to 1848* (Oxford: Oxford University Press, 2001), 184–7, 206–12.

21 Not only was *La Muette de Portici* chosen to initiate a revolution in The Netherlands in 1830, it sparked unrest in Frankfurt am Main in 1831. See Chapter 9 below and Anselm Gerhard, *The Urbanization of Opera: Music Theater in Paris in the Nineteenth Century*

(Chicago: University of Chicago Press, 1998), 127–34.

22 Richard Wagner, 'Reminiscences of Auber', in *Prose Works*, ed. and trans. W. A. Ellis, 8 vols. (London: Kegan Paul, 1892–99, rep. University of Nebraska Press, 1996), V (*Actors and Singers*), 41. See on this topic Pendle and Wilkins, '*La Muette de Portici* and the Scenic-Musical Tableaux', in *Opera in Context*, ed. Radice, 184–90.

23 Gerhard, *Urbanization*, 87–9, analyses the unusual predominance of chorus and the lack of formal numbers for soloists in *Guillaume Tell*. He also questions the use of the term 'tableau' as it implies no movement, mentioning Michael Walter's alternative term 'Großszene' (99–100). Pendle and Wilkins, 'Paradise Found', 184–5, use 'scenic-musical tableau' and 'musico-dramatic-scenic tableau'.

24 *Revue des Deux-Mondes*, as quoted by Catherine Join-Dieterle, '*Robert le Diable*: le premier opéra romantique', *Romantisme*, 28–29 (1980), 147–66, here 152. On the same opera see Rebecca S. Wilberg, 'The *Mise en scène* at the Paris Opéra–Salle Le Peletier (1821–1873) and the Staging of the First French Grand Opera: Meyerbeer's *Robert le Diable*', dissertation, Brigham Young University (1990).

5 The chorus

1 On the roles of the chorus in French opera in the decades before the French Revolution, see Arnold Jacobshagen, *Der Chor in der französischen Oper des späten Ancien Régime* (Frankfurt: Peter Lang, 1997).

2 The Paris Opéra chorus and its role under the Terror are the subjects of M. Elizabeth C. Bartlet, 'The New Repertory of the Opéra during the Reign of Terror: Revolutionary Rhetoric and Operatic Consequences', in *Music and the French Revolution*, ed. Malcolm Boyd (Cambridge: Cambridge University Press, 1992), 107–56.

3 On the size of the chorus at the Paris Opéra see Chapter 2 above, also Karin Pendle and Stephen Wilkins, 'Paradise Found: The Salle Le Peletier and French Grand Opera, in *Opera in Context: Essays on Historical Staging from the Late Renaissance to the Time of Puccini*, ed. Mark A. Radice (Portland, OR: Amadeus Press, 1998), 171–207, here 346 n. 25; also Hugh Macdonald, 'Music and Opera', in *The French Romantics*, ed. D. G. Charlton, 2 vols. (Cambridge: Cambridge University Press, 1984), II, 352–81, here 360. The comparable figures on German and Russian houses are in Christoph-Hellmut Mahling, *Studien zur*

Geschichte des Opernchors (Trossingen and Wolfenbüttel: Editio Intermusica, 1962), App. 5; and on Italian houses in John Rosselli, *The Opera Industry in Italy from Cimarosa to Verdi: The Role of the Impresario* (Cambridge: Cambridge University Press, 1984), 57, table 2.

4 Pendle and Wilkins, 'Paradise Found', 182–3.

5 See sources cited in n. 3.

6 On the role of the chorus throughout nineteenth-century opera as an embodiment of the political power of the people, see James Parakilas, 'Political Representation and the Chorus in Nineteenth-Century Opera', *19th-Century Music*, 16/2 (1992), 181–202.

7 David Charlton, 'The Nineteenth Century: France', in *The Oxford Illustrated History of Opera*, ed. Roger Parker (Oxford: Oxford University Press, 1994), 122–68, here 143.

8 Gaetano Donizetti, letter of 16 March 1835 to Antonio Dolci, no. 160 in Guido Zavadini, *Donizetti: Vita, Musiche, Epistolario* (Bergamo: Istituto Italiano d'Arti Grafiche, 1948), 369.

9 For some phrases of Jewish chant that could have served as models for Halévy's Seder music, see Charlton, 'Romantic Opera: 1830–1850', in *Romanticism (1830–1890)*, ed. Gerald Abraham, New Oxford History of Music, IX (Oxford: Oxford University Press, 1990), 85–139, here 103.

10 On the Old Believer song that Musorgsky turned into the chorus 'Gospod' moy' in *Khovanshchina* see Vladimir Morosan, 'Folk and Chant Elements in Musorgsky's Choral Writing', in *Musorgsky: In Memoriam, 1881–1981*, ed. Malcolm Hamrick Brown (Ann Arbor: UMI Research Press, 1982), 95–133, here 127.

6 Dance and dancers

My thanks to Lisa Arkin and Joan Erdman for offering information about character-dance and Indian dance, respectively.

1 Richard Wagner, 'Cultural Decadence of the Nineteenth Century', in *Prose Works*, ed. and trans. W. A. Ellis, 8 vols. (London: Kegan Paul, 1892–99), III, 351–2.

2 See Carol Marsh, 'Lumberjacks and Turkish Slaves', *Choreologica*, 2 (1995), 37–45; Ivor Guest, *The Ballet of the Enlightenment* (London: Dance Books, 1996), 1–11; Bruce Alan Brown, *Gluck and the French Theatre in Vienna* (Oxford: Oxford University Press, 1991), 143–93 and 282–357; Kathleen Kuzmick Hansell, 'Opera and Ballet at the Regio Teatro of Milan, 1771–1776: A Musical and Social History', dissertation, University of California at Berkeley (1980), esp. Chapters 9,

10 and Epilogue; Gerhard Croll, 'Gasparo Angiolini', in *International Encyclopedia of Dance*, ed. Selma Jeanne Cohen (Oxford: Oxford University Press, 1998), I, 87–9; Hansell, 'Jean-Georges Noverre', *International Encyclopedia of Dance*, IV, 694–700; Rebecca Harris-Warrick, 'Ballet', in *New Grove/2*.
3 Music for ballet-pantomimes at the Opéra often consisted of arrangements until the 1820s, and generally speaking was not free of borrowings until the 1840s. The term 'ballet-pantomime' was commonly used in the nineteenth century for what had been called the 'ballet d'action' in the eighteenth century.
4 The years of the reign of Louis-Philippe, 1830–48, are known as the July Monarchy.
5 See Giannandrea Poesio, 'Blasis, the Italian Ballo, and the Male Sylph', in *Rethinking the Sylph*, ed. Lynn Garafola (Hanover, NH: Wesleyan University Press, 1997), 131–41. On the Parisian stage, the *danseur* was frequently replaced by a *danseuse en travesti*. See Lynn Garafola, 'The Travesty Dancer in Nineteenth-Century Ballet', *Dance Research Journal*, 17/2 and 18/1 (Fall 1985, Spring 1986), 35–40.
6 See Lisa C. Arkin and Marian Smith, 'National Dance in the Romantic Ballet', in *Rethinking the Sylph*, 11–68. In the present chapter, the term 'character' dance is used to mean folk-derived or 'national' dance. ('National dance' was the nineteenth-century term.) Particularly in past centuries, the term could include rustic dance, dances by older characters and dances that show a character's occupation (e.g., shoemaker, baker, sailor). Today's term 'character role' is not the same (meaning non-danced roles for older characters).
7 By F. Taglioni, Schmidt and Auber, St Petersburg, 1838. Not to be confused with *La Gipsy* (1839) in Paris.
8 *La Presse*, 2 October 1837, trans. in Ivor Guest (ed.), *Gautier on Dance* (London: Dance Books, 1986), 19. Eduard Julius Friedrich Bendemann (1811–89) painted his *Jeremiah on the Ruins of Jerusalem* in 1834.
9 Théophile Gautier, *La Presse*, 7 March 1841, trans. in Ivor Guest, *The Romantic Ballet in Paris* (London, 1966; 2nd edn 1980), 204.
10 Gautier, trans. Guest in *Romantic Ballet in Paris*, 180.
11 Henrik Lundgren, 'Lucile Grahn', in *International Encyclopedia of Dance*, III, 222–4; 'Lucile Grahn', in *The Concise Oxford Dictionary of Ballet*, 2nd edn, ed. Horst Koegler (Oxford: Oxford University Press, 1982), 183.

12 See Ivor Guest, *Jules Perrot, Master of the Romantic Ballet* (London: Dance Books, 1984), 35, 47, 51. In flamenco, the term 'zapateado' refers to the technique by which rhythmic and counter-rhythmic patterns are 'made by any part of the shoe (*zapato*), including stamps (*golpes*); soft, brushing steps (*escobillas*); rhythmic heel beats (*taconeo*) and whatever toe–heel sound combinations the dancer can make with his or her shoes. The *zapateado* is also a particular dance in $^6_8$ time in which this technique is used. It is the only flamenco dance traditionally performed without arm movements': Matteo [Matteo Marcellus Vittucci] with Carola Goya, *The Language of Spanish Dance* (Norman: University of Oklahoma Press, 1990), 267.
13 *La Charte de 1830*, 18 April 1837, trans. Guest in 'Théophile Gautier on Spanish Dancing', *Dance Chronicle*, 10/1 (1987), 17.
14 *La Presse*, 28 July 1839, trans. *ibid.*, 10/1 (1987), 31.
15 Auguste Baron, *Lettres et entretiens sur la danse* (Paris: Dondey-Dupré, 1824), 282. All translations in this chapter are mine unless otherwise indicated.
16 Johann Gottfried von Herder, *Sämtliche Werke*, 33 vols. (Berlin: B. Suphan, 1877–1913), XVIII, 248, trans. in Frederick M. Barnard, *Herder's Social and Political Thought: From Enlightenment to Nationalism* (Oxford: Oxford University Press, 1965), 61. See also Arkin and Smith, 'National Dance in the Romantic Ballet', 32–4.
17 *La France musicale*, 30 June 1839, supplément, 369.
18 Pietro Lichtenthal, *Dictionnaire de musique*, trans. and ed. Dominique Mondo (Paris: Troupenas, 1839), I, 115–16 [orig. *Dizionario e Bibliografia della Musica* (Milan: A. Fontana, 1826)]. Lichtenthal was writing of dance music within the ballet-pantomime, but the same dictum applied to dance music within opera.
19 *La Tentation* (words by Edmond Cavé and Henri Duponchel, music by Halévy and Gide, choreography by Coralli) was first performed on 12 March 1832, and referred to in some official correspondence as a 'ballet mixed with singing'. 'Bayadère' was the French term for the Hindu temple dancer who was called, in South India, a 'devadasi', or 'servant of a god'. Such dancers danced their devotion to the Hindu god of whatever temple they were dedicated to, for life. From this dance, eventually, in the 1920s and 1930s came what is now called 'Bharata Natyam' (Indian dance).

20 See Emilio Sala, *L'Opera Senza Canto. Il Mélo Romantico e l'Invenzione della Collonna Sonora* (Venice: Marsilio, 1995), and Sarah Hibberd, 'Magnetism, Muteness, Magic: *Spectacle* and the Parisian Lyric Stage c.1830', dissertation, University of Southampton (1998).

21 *Le Ménestrel*, 23 March 1834, trans. Maribeth Clark, in 'Understanding French Grand Opera through Dance', dissertation, University of Pennsylvania (1998), 180. The quadrille was a balletic, technically challenging form of popular dance which may be seen as a precursor to American square dance.

22 Unnamed journalist quoted in 'Julien, Louis-Antoine', in *Biographie universelle des musiciens et bibliographie générale de la musique* ed. François-Joseph Fétis, 2nd edn (Paris, 1894; repr. Brussels, 1963), IV, 454, trans. Clark in 'Understanding French Grand Opera', 220–21.

23 *Le Constitutionnel*, date unspecified, trans. in Guest, *Romantic Ballet in Paris*, 131.

24 *Vert-Vert*, 24 December 1834. In this review *Las Treias* and *lo Chibalet* were described as having been danced by 'a large number of young men uniformly costumed like shepherds after the manner of Watteau'. See also François Gasnault, *Guinguettes et lorettes. Bals publics et danse sociale à Paris entre 1830 et 1870* (Paris: Aubier, 1986), 74.

25 'Chronique de l'Académie royale de musique', Paris, Bibliothèque-musée de l'Opéra, MS Rés. 658, III, no. 77, 273–82.

26 Gautier, *La Presse*, 1 July 1844, trans. in Guest, *Gautier on Dance*, 141.

27 Tracy C. Davis, *Actresses as Working Women* (London: Routledge, 1991), 133–5. 'Wilis' (see Chapter 10, n. 51) were nocturnal ghosts of female virgins bent on killing men by dancing them to death. Giselle is an exceptional example because she forgives her betrayer and protects him from her sister Wilis.

28 Charles de Boigne, *Petits Mémoires de l'Opéra* (Paris: Librairie Nouvelle, 1857), 132, trans. Cyril Beaumont in *Complete Book of Ballets* (New York: Garden City, 1941), 121. See also Lisa Arkin, 'The Context of Exoticism in Fanny Elssler's *Cachucha*', *Dance Chronicle*, 17/3 (1994), 316, 318. The cachucha was in $^3_8$ time, for couples or for a soloist.

29 Nestor Roqueplan (as 'Jules Vernières'), 'Les Coulisses de l'Opéra', in *La Revue de Paris* (1836), repr. in Martine Kahane, *Le Foyer de la danse* (Paris: Musée d'Orsay/Bibliothèque Nationale, 1988), 5–6. See also Susan Leigh Foster, 'The Ballerina's Phallic Pointe', in

Corporealities: Dancing Knowledge, Culture and Power, ed. Foster (London: Routledge, 1996), 1–24.

30 See Chapter 2 regarding payment details. Kahane refers to 'prostitution légère' in *Le Foyer de la danse*, 8, 13. See also Felicia M. McCarren, 'The Female Form: Gautier, Mallarmé and Céline Writing Dance', dissertation, Stanford University (1992).

31 Julie Daubié, *La Femme pauvre au XIX*^{e} *siècle* (Paris: Thorin, 1869), quoted by Susan Trites Free in 'Dance of the Demi-monde: Paris Opera Ballet Dance and Dancers in the Social Imagination of the Second Empire', M. F. A. dissertation, York University, Canada (1986), 42–3.

7 Roles, reputations, shadows: singers at the Opéra, 1828–1849

1 *Revue et gazette musicale*, 18 and 21 February 1841; this anecdote is taken from the second instalment. Early in 1841 Loewe was thought to be on the verge of signing a contract at the Opéra, and consequently her strengths and weaknesses were hotly debated in the press. The rumoured contract never materialised, and Loewe had to wait a few years to make her name in Italy by creating the prima donna roles in Verdi's *Ernani* (1844) and *Attila* (1846).

2 Chamisso, *Peter Schlemihl's wundersame Geschichte* (Munich: Winkler Verlag, 1982). Schlemihl also appears as a secondary character in E. T. A. Hoffmann's 'A New Year's Eve Adventure'.

3 Berlioz, *Memoirs*, trans. David Cairns (London: Panther Arts, 1970), 399.

4 The episode is recounted in numerous biographies; see for example, Corneille Cantinjou, *Les Adieux de Mme Stoltz* (Paris: Brettau, 1847), 22.

5 On the vogue for mute characters in *mélodrame*, see Peter Brooks, *The Melodramatic Imagination: Balzac, Henry James and the Mode of Excess* (New Haven: Yale University Press, 1976; repr. 1995); and Sarah Hibberd, 'Magnetism, Muteness, Magic: *Spectacle* and the Parisian Lyric Stage c.1830', dissertation, University of Southampton (1998).

6 See Austin Caswell, 'Mme Cinti-Damoreau and the Embellishment of Italian Opera in Paris: 1820–45', *Journal of the American Musicological Society*, 28 (1975), 459–92. According to one report, Rossini himself found Cinti-Damoreau's style too Italianate for the grand opera seriousness of *Le Siège de Corinthe*. An 1826 letter quotes him as saying that Cinti-Damoreau was ill-suited for the role of Pamyra, and, indeed, for tragic parts

generally, that she would shine only in the score's few virtuosic passages. Letter from Frederick Duplantys to Sosthène de la Rochefoucauld, 1 August 1826; Paris, Archives nationales, O/3/1676, Opéra 1826.

7 De Boigne's remark was made in the context of an unfavourable comparison with Cornélie Falcon: 'Dorus-Gras sings as an instrument plays; Mlle Falcon sang with her soul as much as with her voice': *Petits mémoires de l'Opéra* (Paris: Librairie nouvelle, 1857), 163.

8 Léon and Marie Escudier, *Etudes biographiques sur les chanteurs contemporains* (Paris: J. Tessier, 1840), 199.

9 According to Jules Janin, quoted in Barthelémy Braud, *Une reine du chant: Cornélie Falcon* (Paris: Peyriller, Roucher et Ganion, 1913), 9–10.

10 For an exhaustive account of this debut, see Charles Bouvet, *Cornélie Falcon* (Paris: Félix Alcan, 1927), 24–48.

11 Louis Véron, *Mémoires d'un bourgeois de Paris*, cited in Braud, *Une reine du chant*, 20; and Patrick Barbier, *Opera in Paris, 1800–1850: A Lively History* (Portland, OR: Amadeus Press, 1995), 154. As points of comparison, Anselm Gerhard reports that Henri Duponchel made 12,000 francs a year as director of the Opéra, Meyerbeer was paid 24,000 francs by Maurice Schlesinger for the publication rights to *Les Huguenots*, and Eugène Scribe's annual income ranged between 100,000 and 180,000: *The Urbanization of Opera: Music Theater in Paris in the Nineteenth Century* (Chicago: University of Chicago Press, 1998), 37–8. But these figures can be contradictory and unreliable: Gerhard reports that Cinti-Damoreau's salary in the 1830s 'never exceeded' 60,000 per year (38), while Barbier (154) has her at 15,000.

12 Named for Louise-Rosalie Dugazon (1755–1821), who sang at the Opéra-Comique from 1769 to 1804 and created the role of Nina in Dalayrac's *Nina, ou la Folle par amour*, as well as several roles in operas by Grétry and Méhul.

13 Quoted in Bouvet, *Cornélie Falcon*, 39.

14 I am indebted to Benjamin Walton for this insight about Falcon's break. See his 'Falcon, Cornélie', in *New Grove/2*.

15 Quoted in Paul Achard, 'Le 125ᵉ anniversaire de Cornélie Falcon', an unattributed article (but from 1939) included in Falcon's *Dossier d'artiste* at Paris, Bibliothèque-musée de l'Opéra.

16 Charles de Boigne offers a poignant account of that failed comeback in *Petits mémoires de l'Opéra*, 202–3.

17 Margaret Miner has traced the theme of prohibition on women's singing through the fantastic tales published in the *feuilletons* of the period; see her 'Phantoms of Genius: Women and the Fantastic in the Opera-House Mystery', *19th-Century Music*, 18/2 (1994), 121–35.

18 Bellaigue's account is quoted in Bouvet, *Cornélie Falcon*, 140–2.

19 Meyerbeer's letter (1 January 1837) is quoted in Quicherat, *Adolphe Nourrit: Sa vie, son talent, son caractère, sa correspondance*, 3 vols. (Paris: Hachette, 1867), III, 370. On the complicated question of how Meyerbeer's opera became '*our Huguenots*', see Steven Huebner, 'Huguenots, Les', *Grove Opera*, II, 765. Halévy outlines the genesis of 'Rachel, quand du Seigneur' in his *Derniers souvenirs et portraits* (Paris: Michel Lévy frères, 1863), 167.

20 See Quicherat, *Adolphe Nourrit*; and Henry Pleasants, ed., *The Great Tenor Tragedy: The Last Days of Adolphe Nourrit as told (mostly) by himself* (Portland, OR: Amadeus Press, 1995).

21 Berlioz tells this story in satirical terms in the sixth of his 'Evenings with the Orchestra', 'How a Tenor Revolves around the Public'; *Evenings with the Orchestra*, trans. Jacques Barzun (Chicago: University of Chicago Press, 1973), 64–75.

22 John Rosselli has shown, however, that several other tenors in the 1820s and 1830s were working towards singing high notes from the chest: *Singers of Italian Opera* (Cambridge: Cambridge University Press, 1992), 176–8.

23 L. and M. Escudier, *Etudes biographiques*, 169–70; Halévy, *Derniers souvenirs*, 152. A fascinating comparison of Nourrit and Duprez in the role of Masaniello has recently been made available, written by Berlioz: *Critique musicale*, ed. Yves Gérard (in progress: Paris: Buchet/Chastel), III, 281–2 [8 October 1837].

24 For an account of Duprez's introduction of the *ut de poitrine* into *Guillaume Tell*, beginning with a performance in Lucca in 1831, see his *Souvenirs d'un chanteur* (Paris: Calmann-Lévy, 1880); excerpts reprinted in *Voix d'Opéra: Ecrits de chanteurs du XIXe siècle* (Paris: Editions Michel Maule, 1988), 77–9 and 131–3. Duprez claimed that 'Amis, amis' had not been performed in Paris since Nourrit cut it after the opera's second performance, but Elizabeth Bartlet has shown this and some of Duprez's other claims for his own importance to be false or exaggerated. See Rossini, *Guillaume Tell*, ed. M. Elizabeth C. Bartlet (Pesaro: Fondazione Rossini, 1992),

xliii–xliv. According to at least one account, Rossini himself was appalled by the sound of Duprez's high C; see Edmond Michotte, 'An Evening at Rossini's in Beau-Séjour (Passy)', in *Richard Wagner's Visit to Rossini and An Evening at Rossini's Beau-Séjour (Passy) 1858*, trans. and ed. Herbert Weinstock (London: Quartet Books, 1968), 98–9.

25 J.-M. Mayan, *Les Guèpes du théâtre* (Paris: Bonvalot-Jouve, 1906), 152.

26 Choron's pedagogical style is outlined in J. Adrien de La Fage, *Eloge de Choron* (Paris: Comptoirs des Imprimeurs Uris, 1843). Complaints about the Conservatoire's training are found in the unreliable (but highly entertaining) manuscript purporting to be the memoirs of a woman employed backstage at the Opéra as a dresser but actually by its *contrôleur de matériel*, Louis Gentil: 'Le Conservatoire et l'Opéra' [1837] in Jean-Louis Tamvaco, *Les Cancans de l'Opéra. Chroniques de l'Académie Royale de Musique et du théâtre, à Paris sous les deux Restaurations*, 2 vols. (Paris: CNRS Editions, 2000), I, 355–6.

27 Choron's reading method is laid out in his treatise *Méthode pour apprendre en même temps à lire et à écrire* and described in La Fage, *Eloge de Choron*, 21.

28 Duprez himself described Nourrit's 'reciting' of recitative: *Souvenirs d'un chanteur*, as excerpted and translated in Pleasants, ed., *The Great Tenor Tragedy*, 160. On Duprez's innovations with recitative, see also Karin and Eugen Ott, ' "Nur von grossen Sängern lernt man sangbar und vortheilhaft für die Menschenstimme schreiben": Stil und Technik des Meyerbeer-Gesangs', in *Meyerbeer und das europäische Musiktheater*, ed. Sieghart Döhring and Arnold Jacobshagen (Laaber: Laaber-Verlag, 1999), 231–49, here 247.

29 Halévy, *Derniers souvenirs*, 199–200.

30 For a more detailed evaluation of these accusations and of Stoltz's career in general, see my 'The Lost Voice of Rosine Stoltz', *Cambridge Opera Journal*, 6/1 (1994), 31–50.

31 Letter to Michele Accursi, January 1842: *Studi donizettiani*, 1 (1962), 80.

32 On the genesis of *La Favorite* and Stoltz's contribution, see Rebecca Harris-Warrick, 'Introduzione storica', *Gaetano Donizetti–La Favorite* (Milan and Bergamo: Ricordi, 1997), xix–xxiv.

33 Liszt, 'Pauline Viardot-Garcia', *Neue Zeitschrift für Musik*, 50/5 (28 January 1859), 49–54.

34 The phrase is from L. and M. Escudier, *Etudes biographiques*, 36.

35 One version of the tale appears in M. Sterling Mackinlay, *Garcia: The Centenarian and his Times* (New York: Da Capo Press, 1976 [1908]), 132.

36 On the Berlioz–Viardot collaboration on *Orphée*, see Joel-Marie Fauquet, 'Berlioz's Version of Gluck's *Orphée*', in *Berlioz Studies*, ed. Peter Bloom (Cambridge: Cambridge University Press, 1992), 189–253. See also Berlioz's reviews of the two Gluck revivals, translated in *The Art of Singing and Other Essays (A Travers Chants)* by Elizabeth Csicsery-Rónay (Bloomington: Indiana University Press, 1994), 71–81 and 136–47.

37 Thorough discussions of Viardot's relationships with contemporary composers and other artists can be found in Gustave Dulong, *Pauline Viardot, tragédienne lyrique* (Paris: Association des amis d'Ivan Tourgueniev, Pauline Viardot, et Maria Malibran, 1987); and April Fitzlyon, *The Price of Genius: A Life of Pauline Viardot* (London: John Calder, 1964).

38 An indication of the esteem in which Viardot was held as a composer is her inclusion in the collaborative cantata, *Contes mystiques* (1890), which also includes movements by Fauré, Augusta Holmès, Massenet, Saint-Saëns and Widor. A recent and assertive recording of three of Viardot's songs by Cecilia Bartoli (another successful Rosina and Cenerentola) gives a good idea of what Viardot might have sounded like singing them herself (*Chant d'Amour*, London 452 667–2). Ten of Viardot's songs are included in Pauline Duchambge, Loïsa Puget, Pauline Viardot and Jane Vien, *Anthology of Songs* (New York: Da Capo Press, 1988).

39 Saint-Saëns, 'Pauline Viardot', in *Musical Memories*, trans. Edwin Gile Rich (London: John Murray, 1921), 145.

40 Viardot inspired an amazing number of fictional portraits, including George Sand's *Consuelo*, veiled depictions in Ivan Turgenev's *Smoke* and *A Month in the Country*, and George Eliot's verse drama *Armgart*. On the Sand and Turgenev works, see Fitzlyon, *The Price of Genius*, 113–19, 254–6, and 399–402; on Eliot, see Susan J. Leonardi and Rebecca A. Pope, *The Diva's Mouth: Body, Voice, Prima Donna Politics* (New Brunswick, NJ: Rutgers University Press, 1996), 73–82.

41 Nearly the unique exception is the cabaletta in the Act V prison scene, a number whose bravura style Berlioz lamented as completely unsuitable for 'an old woman, weighed down by care': *Journal des Débats*, 20 April 1849; repr. in *Hector Berlioz: Les*

Musiciens et la musique (Paris: Calmann-Levy, 1903), 106–27, here 114.

42 Heinz and Gudrun Becker, *Giacomo Meyerbeer: A Life in Letters* (London: Christopher Helm, 1989), 125. The special 'Meyerbeer' clause in Viardot's contract, mentioned in Chapter 2, p. 29, shows that no fixed upper limit was placed on her payments, which Meyerbeer 'arbitrated amicably' with her.

43 Interestingly, Viardot's own vocal treatise, published in a modern edition as *Gesangsunterricht (Une heure d'étude)* (Berlin: Bote and G. Bock, n.d.) includes several exercises designed to develop control of detached articulations.

44 E. Dannreuther, 'Azucena is Fidès in Romany', *Oxford History of Music*, 2nd edn (London, 1932), 63; cited in Julian Budden, *The Operas of Verdi*, 3 vols. (London: Cassell, 1978), II, 68.

8 Directing grand opera: *Rienzi* and *Guillaume Tell* at the Vienna State Opera

1 Hans Keller, *Criticism*, ed. Julian Hogg (London: Faber, 1987), 17–45.

2 The Act III 'Ballet Pantomime' given before the assembled and feasting grandees at the Council of Konstanz. A scenic infidel fortress is about to be attacked by men-at-arms when it suddenly changes into a tasteful gothic edifice, surrounded by gracious ballerinas.

3 The sequence is published in *Rienzi, der Letzte der Tribunen*, ed. Reinhard Strohm and Egon Voss, *Sämtliche Werke*, Band 3/V: 'Anhang und kritischer Bericht' (Mainz: B. Schott's Söhne, 1991), 24–40.

9 La Muette and her context

1 For example, *La Muette* was staged in Paris on 4 August 1830 in a benefit performance for the victims of the July uprising, in which, by public demand, the patriotic fishermen's chorus was replaced by the *Marseillaise*. And at a performance on 25 August, in the presence of Louis-Philippe, Nourrit sang the *Parisienne* and the *Marseillaise*, dressed in the uniform of the national guard.

2 However, rather than prompting a spontaneous uprising, as has often been believed, it seems that the opera was selected beforehand to launch the revolt. And in spite of its apparent political significance, the king of The Netherlands insisted on its performance later the same month. See Sonia Slatin, 'Opera and Revolution: *La Muette de Portici* and the Belgian Revolution of 1830

Revisited', *Journal of Musicological Research*, 3 (1979), 45–62.

3 Richard Wagner, 'Reminiscences of Auber' [1871], in *Prose Works*, ed. and trans. W. A. Ellis, 8 vols. (London, 1892–99; repr. New York, 1966), V, 35–55, here 53.

4 Jane Fulcher, '*La Muette de Portici* and the New Politics of Opera', *The Nation's Image: French Grand Opera as Politics and Politicized Art* (Cambridge: Cambridge University Press, 1987), 11–46.

5 For a discussion of the political situation in France at this time, see G. de Bertier de Sauvigny, *La Restauration* (Paris: Flammarion, 1955), esp. 409–23.

6 On Wednesday 23 April, for example, *La Muette de Portici* was at the Opéra, *Deux mots* at the Opéra-Comique, *Yelva* at the Gymnase-Dramatique, *Les Immortels* at the Variétés, *La Muette de la forêt* at the Gaîté and *La Muette* at the Luxembourg. For details about these works, see my ' "N'étourdissant jamais l'oreille": *La Muette de Portici* and Traditions of Mime', in 'Magnetism, Muteness, Magic: *Spectacle* and the Parisian Lyric Stage c.1830', dissertation, University of Southampton (1998), 109–52.

7 See, for example, John Warrack, 'The Influence of French Grand Opera on Wagner', in *Music in Paris in the Eighteen-Thirties*, ed. Peter Bloom (Stuyvesant, NY: Pendragon, 1987), 575–87; Emilio Sala, 'Verdi and the Parisian Boulevard Theatre', *Cambridge Opera Journal*, 7/3 (1995), 185–205; and Herbert Schneider, '*La Muette de Portici*', *Grove Opera*. There also appears to be a conscious evocation of Fenella's final scene in Donizetti's *Adelia* (1840): the orchestral panic that accompanies Fenella's mounting despair in *La Muette* here introduces Adelia's mad scene at the end of the opera in a striking internalising of gesture and movement.

8 *La Pandore*, 1748 (3 March 1828), 2. Translations in this chapter are my own, unless otherwise stated.

9 See Anselm Gerhard's edition of the *Essai*: 'Victor-Joseph Etienne de Jouy: *Essai sur l'opéra français*', *Bollettino del Centro rossiniano di studi*, 1–3 [bound as one] (1987), 63–91. Jouy wrote the libretto for P.-F. L. Aimon's five-act opera *Velléda, ou les Gauloises* (unperformed) in 1813, and was working on the libretto for *Guillaume Tell* at the same time as Scribe and Delavigne were preparing *La Muette*. For a discussion of the creation of *Tell* see Gerhard, ' "Sortire dalle vie comuni": Wie Rossini einem Akademiker den *Guillaume Tell* verdarb', in *Oper als Text: romantische Beiträge*

zur Libretto-Forschung, ed. Albert Gier (Heidelberg: Winter, 1986), 185–219.

10 Gerhard, 'Jouy: *Essai*', 70.

11 A comprehensive list of *Masaniello* literature is given in Jean R. Mongrédien, 'Variations sur un thème – Masaniello: Du héros de l'histoire à celui de *La Muette de Portici*', *Jahrbuch für Opernforschung* (1985), 90–160. Contrary to the claims of a number of modern commentators, the story does not appear to have been adapted for the secondary Parisian theatres in the 1820s.

12 See Karin Pendle, *Eugène Scribe and French Opera of the Nineteenth Century* (Ann Arbor: UMI Research Press, 1979), 413.

13 But it is deafness rather than muteness which proves to be the most significant affliction of Scott's Fenella: other characters talk of their innermost secrets in her presence, and are forced to mime to make her understand; she relies on facial grimaces and trembling to communicate emotion. This is a reversal of the situation in the opera, where only Fenella mimes.

14 This undated text exists only as a sixteen-page fragment entitled *Masaniello* (Paris: Boulé, n.d.) at Bibliothèque nationale, $Y^2p - 117(1)$. In a presumably earlier version of 1822, *Masaniello, ou Huit jours à Naples*, Defauconpret focuses simply on Masaniello's relationship with his wife. Although there seems to be no copy of this 1822 version extant in French, a report of it appears in Pierre Larousse, *Grand dictionnaire universel du XIXe siècle*. Herbert Schneider and Nicole Wild also mention a Spanish translation of the novel by D. F. de P. Fors de Casamayor (Barcelona, 1844) in '*La Muette de Portici*': *Kritische Ausgabe des Librettos und Dokumentation ihrer ersten Inszenierung* (Tübingen: Stauffenburg, 1993), 1–2.

15 In the play, entitled *Masaniello, the Fisherman of Naples* (with incidental music by Henry Bishop), the drama centres on Masaniello's guilt: he dines with the Spaniards, and Lorina follows him, disguised as a man, and attacks him when she sees him declaring his love to Olympia. Masaniello kills his attacker, only realising it is Lorina when it is too late. This guilt follows him throughout the rest of the play, and it is the reason that he drifts in and out of sanity. Meanwhile the people (independently) come to trust the duplicitous Spanish duke, and turn against Masaniello. The play concludes with him being shot and killed by the mob.

16 Four versions of the libretto, together with variants between the sources for each version, are reproduced in Schneider and Wild, '*La Muette de Portici*'.

17 Other ironic moments were essayed in earlier, more complicated, versions of the text, notably with regard to the possibility that Alphonse and Fenella could be together after all. The first draft concludes with a double misunderstanding: Alphonse declares he will marry Fenella, but when Elvire and the procession arrive, Fenella runs to her boat to allow the authorised wedding to take place. Alphonse decides he will leave Elvire and go to fight for his country in order to forget; Fenella sees him taking Elvire's hand and, believing they are happy, leaps into the sea while the chorus celebrates the (apparently) joyful union, oblivious of Fenella's sad end.

18 Scott Balthazar has written of the similar move in nineteenth-century Italian opera, by which plots were driven by unity of action (rather than by a rigid upholding of all three of the Aristotelian Unities), as set out by Alessandro Manzoni in his *Lettre à M. C*** sur l'unité de temps et de lieu dans la tragédie*, published in Paris in 1823. This shift had the effect of cutting out extraneous material and focusing more clearly, in the case of Italian opera, on love-triangles. Although the action in *La Muette* too can be reduced to the triangle of Fenella–Alphonse–Elvire, this leaves the important public dimension out of the equation. See Balthazar, 'Aspects of Form in the Ottocento Libretto', *Cambridge Opera Journal*, 7/1 (1995), 23–35.

19 This has particular dramatic resonance in a year (1827) when sleepwalking scenes were infiltrating many works, from Rouget de Lisle and Chelard's opera *Macbeth* and Scribe, Delavigne and Hérold's ballet *La Somnambule* at the Opéra, to a host of works at the secondary theatres. As I have discussed elsewhere, the visual aspect of such trance scenes were more appropriate to French drama of the time than the vocal aspects that were to become so popular in the visually similar mad scenes of Italian opera. Here the two dimensions are combined. See my ' "Dormez donc, mes chères amours": *La Somnambule* and Representations of Trance', in 'Magnetism, Muteness, Magic', 70–108.

20 Public interest tended to revolve either around congenitally deaf (and therefore mute) people, with the emphasis on their deafness and how other people could communicate with them (as seen in *Peveril of the Peak*, for example), or with temporary muteness caused by shock or emotion (as commonly depicted in *mélodrame*).

21 Nina's madness has been examined in some detail in relation to psychiatric theory and practice of the period. See Patrick Taïeb, 'De la composition du *Délire* (1799) au pamphlet anti-dilettante: Une étude des concéptions esthétiques de H.-M. Berton', *Revue de musicologie*, 78 (1992), 67–107; Stefano Castelvecchi, 'From *Nina* to *Nina*: Psychodrama, Absorption and Sentiment in the 1780s', *Cambridge Opera Journal*, 8/2 (1996), 91–112.

22 The Opéra's literary jury suggested the authors might insert a logical explanation for Fenella's muteness early in the opera. But Scribe and Delavigne decided to ignore this recommendation, and the gap remains in the opera: Alphonse simply states to Lorenzo, 'Speech snatched from her lips by a terrible event has left her defenceless against her unfaithful lover'. For the full exchange about the lack of explanation of Fenella's muteness, see the censors' report (Paris, Archives nationales, O³ 1724) and the accompanying letter from Auger to La Rochefoucauld, 24 October 1825, in Schneider and Wild, '*La Muette de Portici*', 195–6.

23 Anselm Gerhard, *The Urbanization of Opera: Music Theater in Paris in the Nineteenth Century* (Chicago: University of Chicago Press, 1998), 145.

24 Schneider and Wild, '*La Muette de Portici*', report the lengths of the four drafts as follows: 44 pages, 36 pages, 48 pages (unfinished) and 56 pages. (Although the final version is not included here, it differs only slightly from the fourth draft, and is comparable in length.) There is, in other words, very little expansion from the first (three-act) version to the final one, because cutting and reordering are the more significant changes.

25 Gerhard, *Urbanization*, 134.

26 See Marian Smith, 'Ballet-Pantomime and Silent Language', *Ballet and Opera in the Age of 'Giselle'* (Princeton: Princeton University Press, 2000), 97–123. Singers used gesture, though not in the extensive way that dancers did.

27 Peter Brooks gives an account of the expressive potential of melodrama in *The Melodramatic Imagination: Balzac, Henry James, Melodrama, and the Mode of Excess* (New Haven: Yale University Press, 1976; 2nd edn 1995).

28 The play was still being performed at the Théâtre Français and the Court in the 1820s, and was mentioned regularly in press reviews of theatre works featuring mutes. There is a vast literature on the work of the Abbé de l'Epée and the subsequent education of deaf-mutes. For a history and a detailed bibliography, see Harlan Lane, *When the Mind Hears: A History of the Deaf* (New York: Random House, 1984).

29 Emilio Sala terms this device an expressive 'short circuit', in ' "Que ses gestes parlants ont de grâce et de charmes": Motivi "mélo" nella "Muette de Portici" ', in *Atti del XIV Congresso della Società internazionale di musicologia: Trasmissione e recezione delle forme di cultura musicale*, ed. Angelo Pompilio, Lorenzo Bianconi, F. Alberto Gallo and Donatella Restani (Turin: EDT, 1990), I, 504–20.

30 This legibility is achieved in a variety of ways involving written notes, pictures and off-stage communication never witnessed by the audience; only in Scribe's *Yelva* is detailed mimed narrative (like that of Fenella) employed, and it relies heavily on the use of musical quotation to clarify the gestures. The unquestioned legibility of Fenella's gestures was satirised in the parody *La Muette du Porte Bercy*. In the first act the mute tries to indicate, as did Fenella to Elvire, that she has no voice; the stage instructions suggest: 'She points to her mouth, wanting to show that she is mute . . . She indicates that it is not hunger which torments her: she cannot speak . . . She indicates that she is not suffering from toothache: she is lacking speech.' The principal function of pantomime here is to show how mime is an unclear and tedious means of communication.

31 *La Pandore*, 1682 (28 December 1827), 3.

32 *Moniteur Universel*, 62 (2 March 1828), 260.

33 *Le Ménestrel*, 8/8 (25 January 1863), 59–60.

34 Smith, *Ballet and Opera*, 129.

35 For example, as Emilio Sala has shown (with illustrations), there is a clear similarity between the music that accompanies Fenella as she explains to Elvire that her despair is caused by love, and a passage in Pixérécourt's *mélodrame La Muette de la forêt* when the mute and the father of her lover try to escape from their captors. In both passages a dotted figure rises sequentially over a series of repeated triplet chords, suggesting tension and hesitation. See Sala, ' "Que ses gestes parlants ont de grâce et de charmes" ', and *L'opera senza canto: Il mélo romantico e l'invenzione della colonna sonora* (Venice: Marsilio, 1995), 182–3. Whether or not this was a conscious allusion by Auber, it illustrates his absorption of melodramatic techniques in musical depiction of emotion.

36 See, for example, Gerhard, *Urbanization*, 146.

37 Allusions to other works are suggested more subtly: Fenella's escape from her prison window, accompanied by a descending scale, is also found in *Deux mots*; there is a similarity between the orchestral accompaniment to Fenella's leap into the lava at the end of the opera and a passage in the Wolf's Glen scene, the Act II finale to *Der Freischütz*, when Max has a vision of Agathe who, having lost her senses, is about to jump into a waterfall; finally, the D minor harmony in the Act V finale of *La Muette* recalls the finale of *Don Giovanni*. Such allusions were common currency in the secondary theatres, and it seems plausible that Auber was aware of these similarities, given their dramatic significance to the opera.

38 It has another layer of significance for us, as Auber took it from the 'Dona nobis' of a mass he had previously composed for his friend the count of Caraman; see Schneider, 'Auber', *New Grove*/2.

39 In Act I it appears in Fenella's pantomime while she is in prison, just before she thinks of a way to escape; the chorus which follows comes ahead of Fenella's identification of Alphonse as her seducer; 'Saint bien heureux' heralds the final battle between the Spanish and the Neapolitans; and Fenella's prayer precedes Masaniello's death, her loss of hope and her suicide.

40 For a description of some of the techniques of popular theatre that were absorbed into grand opera in general (and into *La Muette* in particular), see Karin Pendle, 'The Boulevard Theaters and Continuity in French Opera of the 19th Century', in *Music in Paris*, ed. Bloom, 509–35.

41 Pixérécourt's stage directions for the final scene of the play (Paris, 1827). The directions for the tableau are given in full, in English translation, in Pendle, 'The Boulevard Theaters', 532.

42 For example, Pendle notes 'one cannot but notice that Fenella throws herself into the erupting volcano to the accompaniment of a rather simple chromatic passage', *Eugene Scribe*, 412. She goes on to surmise that Auber was not capable of writing suitably dramatic music for this scene, and that Meyerbeer was the first to realise such drama musically.

43 See Solomé's *mise-en-scène* for *La Muette de Portici* in H. Robert Cohen, *The Original Staging Manuals for Twelve Parisian Operatic Premières* (Stuyvesant, NY: Pendragon, 1991), 59. However, the choral prayer was added only in August 1827 at the behest of the censors; see Schneider and Wild, '*La Muette de Portici*', 7.

44 This mechanism can be compared to the psychopathology of hysteria where 'the energy attached to an idea that has been repressed returns converted into a bodily symptom'. See Geoffrey Nowell-Smith's discussion of film melodrama, 'Minnelli and Melodrama', in *Home is Where the Heart Is: Studies in Melodrama and the Woman's Film*, ed. Christine Gledhill (London: BFI Publishing, 1987), 70–74, here 73.

45 Carl Dahlhaus reminds us of this contemporary description of Auber's style in *Nineteenth-Century Music* (Berkeley: University of California Press, 1989 [1980]), 67. He defines this quality as consisting primarily of harmonic and melodic simplicity and rhythmic clarity; the beats of the time signature are often emphasised with short, 'dry' chords (typically a quaver followed by a quaver rest).

46 Wagner, 'Reminiscences of Auber', 46.

47 See Gerhard, *Urbanization*, 134–40, and Pendle, *Eugène Scribe*, 397–403.

48 They contrast strikingly with the arias of *tragédie lyrique* in which emotion and psychological development are traced through more extended forms and with lengthy recitatives. Gerhard quotes the German critic Stefan Schütze who recognised this unusual feature of *La Muette* as early as 1830, terming it the 'principle of excitement': *Urbanization*, 133.

49 For example, see Gerhard, *Urbanization*, 134.

50 Not only did the authorities view it as posing no threat to the régime, but other commentators noted its anti-revolutionary stance. After seeing the opera in 1831, Goethe described it as a 'satire on the people': *Eckermann's Conversations with Goethe*, trans. Robert O. Moon (London: Morgan, Laird, 1951), 374. But the picturesque southern European locale brought to mind at least two contemporary revolts in which France was involved as one of the three European powers: those in Naples and Greece, uprisings that both had popular support in France.

51 For a study of representations of Marianne in the nineteenth century see Maurice Agulhon, *Marianne into Battle: Republican Imagery and Symbolism in France, 1789–1880* (Cambridge: Cambridge University Press, 1981); originally published in Paris, 1979. Agulhon illustrates how around 1830 the constitutional monarchists used revolutionary symbolism – particularly the image of Marianne – to evoke a more general idea of freedom.

52 Joan Landes suggests that the movement away from the masculine iconography of the

absolutist body politic to the female representation of the Republic was matched by a rejection of the importance of visual image, in favour of the higher (masculine) status of abstract reasoning. This view has parallels with Fenella's plight: although she indirectly initiates the revolt, the resolution of the situation is decided by Alphonse and Masaniello. See Joan Landes, 'Representing the Body Politic: The Paradox of Gender in the Graphic Politics of the French Revolution', in *Rebel Daughters: Women and the French Revolution*, ed. Sara E. Melzer and Leslie W. Rabine (New York: Oxford University Press, 1992), 15–37.
53 Wagner, 'Reminiscences of Auber', 42.
54 The information here on the performance history is largely from Alfred Loewenberg, *Annals of Opera, 1597–1940*, 2nd edn (New York: Rowman & Littlefield, 1970), 711–13.
55 The Earl of Harewood and Antony Peattie (eds.), *The New Kobbé's Opera Book* (London: Ebury, 1997), 13.

10 Scribe and Auber: constructing grand opera

1 Anselm Gerhard, 'Grand Opéra', in *Die Musik in Geschichte und Gegenwart*, ed. Ludwig Finscher, 2nd edn (Kassel, 1994–), Sachteil, III, col. 1575.
2 *Aline, Reine de Golconde, Opéra en trois Actes, Paroles de MM*rs. *Vial & Favier à Monsieur Monsigny par H. Berton* (Paris: Aux Deux Lyres, chez Mme Duhan et Compie, n.d. [1803]).
3 Bibliothèque nationale, MS n.a.fr. 22562, 663: 'Plan du *Prophète*, grand-opéra en 5 actes'.
4 Bibliothèque nationale, MS n.a.fr. 22567, 108: '*Noëma*, grand-opéra'. Cf. Meyerbeer's diary entry for 10 July 1846 in Meyerbeer, *Briefwechsel und Tagebücher*, ed. H. and G. Becker, 5 vols. (Berlin: de Gruyter, 1959–99), IV (1846–1852), 92.
5 Bibliothèque nationale MS n.a.fr. 22565, 364: '*Dom Sébastien*, grand-opéra'; MS n.a.fr. 22571, fol. 17v: '*Le Fou de Péronne*, grand opéra en 2 actes'; fol. 18, '*La Tapisserie*, grand opéra en un acte'; fol. 30: '*La Tapisserie ou Pygmalion*, grand opéra en 2 actes ou opéra comique'; MS n.a.fr. 22562, 646: 'plan de *La Fiancée de Manganni*, grand opéra'; MS 22563, 2: '*Le Comte Julien*, grand opéra en 3 actes'; MS n.a.fr. 22568, 322: '*Le Cheval de bronze*, opéra comique mise en grand opéra'.
6 Herbert Schneider (ed.), *Correspondance d'E. Scribe et de D.-F.-E. Auber* (Liège: Mardaga, 1998), 68.
7 Louis-Désiré Véron, *Mémoires d'un bourgeois de Paris*, 6 vols. (Paris: de Gonet, 1853–5).

8 Castil-Blaze, *L'Académie Impériale de Musique*, 2 vols. (Paris: Castil-Blaze, 1855), II, 252.
9 The letter is in Bibliothèque nationale, MS n.a.fr. 22551, 32.
10 'de monumentaux pots-pourris': Gilles de Van, 'Le Grand Opéra entre tragédie-lyrique et drame romantique', *Il Saggiatore musicale*, 3/2 (1996), 325–60, here 329.
11 Stephen Sadler Stanton, 'English Drama and the French Well-Made Play, 1815–1915', dissertation, Columbia University (1955), 87.
12 Scenic tableaux are basically decorative; dramatic tableaux develop a strong moment of the action and 'act tableaux' bestow a special atmosphere across a whole act. The totality of these tableaux can organically constitute a second or 'social intrigue': de Van, 'Le Grand Opéra', 339.
13 de Van, *ibid.*, 354.
14 According to de Van (*ibid.*, 333) the diorama convent scene in Act III of *Robert le Diable* has affinities with certain fairytale dramas.
15 Véron, *Mémoires*, III, 252–3.
16 Ernest Legouvé, *Soixante ans de souvenirs*, 2 vols. (Paris: Hetzel, 1886), II, 181.
17 As regards content, it is especially noteworthy that the quotations from *La Marseillaise*, which Scribe did not insert until the libretto was first printed, are absent from the score. Qualitatively and quantitatively, all other differences between the libretto and the first published score are insignificant.
18 In ensembles, words for different singers printed on the same horizontal plane are counted twice; for repeated words that are not printed out, only the line calling for the repetition is counted.
19 Cf. H. Schneider and N. Wild, '*La Muette de Portici*': *Kritische Ausgabe des Librettos und Dokumentation der ersten Inszenierung* (Tübingen: Stauffenburg, 1993).
20 Anselm Gerhard, 'Die französische "Grand Opéra" in der Forschung seit 1945', *Acta Musicologica*, 59/3 (1987), 220–70, here 241.
21 Following Gustavus III's assumption of power in 1772, he established Swedish opera, financing the court theatre and other, private, theatres, encouraging composers and drafting scenarios for operas that were worked up into librettos by a number of other hands. He planned *Gustaf Wasa* (libretto by J. H. Kellgren, music by J. H. Naumann, 1786).
22 Marked 'Pas de paysans dalécarliens'. Dalecarlia (now Dalarna), is a province in central Sweden, where Gustaf Wasa has come to seek shelter: in 1521 Dalecarlia was

influential in liberating Sweden from Danish oppression (which is the theme of the king's opera).

23 Examples include the scene in which the students express alarm before the horrors of the wild Harz Mountains (Act I, end); the fact that Zéïla, early in Act II, presents herself at the inn as a maid; Marguerite's fury at Albert's disloyalty (II.13); the toast to Zéïla and Conrad's dance with her (III, second tableau); Albert's self-inculpation (IV.3); Marguerite's warning to Albert (IV.4); Rodolphe de Cronembourg's attempted kidnapping, and a few details of Albert and Rodolphe's quarrel.

24 See Jürgen Schläder, *Das Opernduett: Ein Szenentypus des 19. Jahrhunderts und seine Vorgeschichte* (Tübingen: Niemeyer, 1995), 135, 139; Steven Huebner, 'Italianate Duets in Meyerbeer's Grand Operas', *Journal of Musicological Research*, 8 (1989), 203–58; Harold S. Powers, ' "La solita forma" and "The Uses of Convention" ', *Acta Musicologica*, 59/1 (1987), 65–90.

25 This is Powers's 'Adagio', strongly preferred to 'Cantabile': ' "La solita forma" ', 69.

26 Huebner, 'Italianate Duets', 208–9.

27 Schläder, not counting the opening recitative, finds three 'sections' and two 'in-between sections', namely bars 26–45 and 68–106 (*Das Opernduett*, 86).

28 This constitutes Schläder's first 'section' plus first 'in-between section' (*Das Opernduett*, 86).

29 'as the piece was first drafted, Alfonso was to respond to Elvira's strophe in conventional manner with a solo rendition of the same strain': Huebner, 'Italianate Duets', 247, citing the full score autograph at Paris, Bibliothèque nationale (Mus) MS 2775.

30 Noting a similar conclusion in *Robert le Diable* – Isabelle's cavatina in the holograph version of the score – Schläder speaks of 'formal deficiency' and 'the breaking of an inherited pattern', since the form is not rounded off in the D major section (*Das Opernduett*, 88–9).

31 F. Danjou noted in *La Revue musicale*, 6/14 (4 April 1839), 111, that this duet, 'Est-ce toi?', 'is curtailed, and was not liked, in spite of the talents of [Gilbert] Duprez and Mlle Nau. The duet opening Act III is one of Auber's best pieces'.

32 *La France musicale*, 1 (22 July 1838), non-paginated.

33 *La Revue musicale*, 3 (1828), 133–4.

34 Théophile Gautier, *Histoire de l'art dramatique en France depuis vingt-cinq ans* (Paris: Hetzel, 1858), 40.

35 Richard Wagner, *Ein deutscher Musiker in Paris: Novellen und Aufsätze* (1840–41) in *Über deutsches Musikwesen*, in *Sämtliche Schriften und Dichtungen*, Volks-Ausgabe, 6th edn, 16 vols. (Leipzig: Breitkopf und Härtel, [1911–14]), I, 165.

36 Nevertheless, French translations of two sources by William Coxe were published long before the opera was written: *Voyage en Pologne, Russie, Suède, et Danemark* (Geneva: Barde, Manget, 1786) and *Nouveau voyage en Danemark, Suède, Russie, Pologne et dans le Jutland, la Norwège, la Livonie, le duché de Curlande et la Prusse* (Paris: Volland, 1791).

37 John Brown, *Les Cours du Nord, ou Mémoires originaux sur les souverains de la Suède et du Danemarck depuis 1766*, French translation by J. Cohen (Paris: Bertrand, 1820). The Parisian publication of the literary works of Gustavus III only two years after they appeared in Stockholm is further proof of French interest in the tragic monarch: *Collection des écrits politiques, littéraires et dramatiques de Gustave III, roi de Suède, suivie de sa correspondance*, ed. J. B. Dechaux, 5 vols. (Stockholm: C. Delén, 1803–5); *Œuvres politiques, littéraires et dramatiques de Gustave III*, ed. J. B. Dechaux, 4 vols. (Paris: Levrault, Schoell, 1805–06).

38 See *Les Cours du Nord*, III, 108–9.

39 Cf. Anselm Gerhard, 'Grand Opéra', Sachteil, III, col. 1580.

40 Scribe, *Gustave III, ou Le Bal masqué, opéra historique en trois actes suivi d'une relation de la mort de Gustave III extraite de l'ouvrage de M. Coxe sur la Suède* (Paris: Jonas, 1833), 83–7; also separately printed in Scribe, *Relation de la mort de Gustave III, suivie d'une analyse de la pièce* (Brest: De Come et Bonetbeau, 1837), which is listed under William Coxe in the Bibliothèque nationale's *Catalogue générale*. The text is not found in Scribe, *Œuvres*, in most editions of the libretto of *Gustave III* or in translations of it.

41 *Cours du Nord*, III, 157–8, reporting that the superstitious Gustavus III frequented the aged Mademoiselle Arvedsen, renowned in Stockholm as a 'sibyl' (or fortune-teller).

42 Louis-Désiré Véron, *Paris en 1860: Les Théâtres de Paris depuis 1806 jusqu'en 1860* (Paris: Bourdilliat, 1860), 126.

43 Véron, *Mémoires*, III, 247–9.

44 *Correspondance d'E. Scribe et de D.-F.-E. Auber*, 113.

45 Stefan Kunze, 'Fest und Ball in Verdis Opern', in *Die 'Couleur locale' in der Oper des 19. Jahrhunderts*, ed. Heinz Becker (Regensburg: Bosse, 1976), 269–78.

46 *Ibid.*, 273.

47 Cf. Herbert Schneider, 'Verdis Parlante und seine französischen Vorbilder', in *Traditionen–Neuansätze: Für Anna Amalie Abert (1906–1996)*, ed. Klaus Hortschansky (Tutzing: Schneider, 1997), 519–40.

48 *La France musicale*, 2 (1839), 217–18.

49 *La Fille de l'air, féerie en 3 actes mêlée de chants et de danses . . . par MM.* Cogniard frères et Raymond, musique de M. Adolphe, décors de MM. Devoir et Pourchet, Théâtre des Folies-Dramatiques, 3 août 1837 [Paris: no publisher, 1837].

50 *La Fille de l'air*, 3.

51 'The Wilis are the souls of humans who died of love . . . at midnight they come out from their coffins and dance under the light of the moon in graveyards or near ruins . . . Those who are tormented by the pangs of love find amidst these phantoms the image of their loved one . . . Then, soon caught up in the fascination of their dances, they join in and finally forfeit their lives among these treacherous illusions': *Les Filles de l'air*, 21.

52 T. Gautier puts 'Burgmann', but presumably means Hans Burgkmair; on the other hand he does not mention Lochner, who was active in Cologne.

53 Gautier, *Histoire de l'art dramatique*, 240.

54 *Ibid.*, 243. The ballet was choreographed by Jean Coralli.

55 According to Karin Pendle (*Eugène Scribe and French Opera of the Nineteenth Century* (Ann Arbor: UMI Research Press, 1979), 383) the action is purely fantastic. Consequently, this 'five-act work [is] in no sense a grand opera'; Auber himself called it simply 'opéra'.

56 Gautier, *Histoire de l'art dramatique*, 238.

57 Of all Auber's grand operas, *La Muette de Portici* was the only one for which a full staging-manual was published; in fact it was the first opera for which this was done.

58 *La France musicale*, 2 (1839), 218.

59 *La Revue et gazette musicale de Paris*, 6 (1839), 161.

60 Gautier, *Histoire de l'art dramatique*, 237.

61 *Ibid.*, 242.

62 For complete lists of librettos, scores and smaller arrangements issued in various countries for all Auber's operas, see Herbert Schneider, *Chronologisch-thematisches Verzeichnis sämtlicher Werke von Daniel François Esprit Auber*, 2 vols. (Hildesheim: Olms, 1994).

63 *Le Ménestrel*, 6/50 (10 November 1839), unpaginated.

64 *La Revue et gazette musicale de Paris*, 10 (1843), 80.

65 Véron, *Les Théâtres de Paris*, 111–12.

66 *La Revue et gazette musicale*, 17 (8 December 1850), 401.

67 *La Revue et gazette musicale*, 17 (15 December 1850), 410.

11 Meyerbeer: *Robert le Diable* and *Les Huguenots*

1 J. P. Eckermann, *Conversations with Goethe*, trans. J. Oxenford, ed. J. K. Moorhead, Everyman's Library (London: Dent, 1970), 291–2 (12 February 1829). Goethe felt that only the composer of *Don Giovanni* would have been able to cope with the 'awful and repulsive passages' in *Faust*, and it was, of course, before *Robert le Diable* that he made his comment about Meyerbeer. Earlier, on 29 January 1827 (*ibid.*, 162), Goethe remarked that *Faust* could be set to music only by a composer 'who, like Meyerbeer, has lived long in Italy, so that he combines his German nature with the Italian style and manner'.

2 See Mark Everist, 'The Name of the Rose: Meyerbeer's opéra-comique *Robert le Diable*', *Revue de musicologie*, 80/2 (1994), 211–50. Scribe's first sketches for the work date back to winter 1825–26.

3 It is important to note in passing that Véron's first actual production as director was a French version of Weber's *Euryanthe* (as *Euriante*) arranged by Castil-Blaze, in April 1831: Everist, 'Translating Weber's *Euryanthe*: German Romanticism at the Dawn of French Grand Opéra', *Revue de musicologie*, 87/1 (2001), 67–104.

4 Knud Arne Jürgensen, 'The "Ballet of the Nuns" from *Robert le Diable* and its Revival', in *Meyerbeer und das europäische Musiktheater*, ed. Sieghart Döhring and Arnold Jacobshagen (Laaber: Laaber-Verlag, 1998), 73–86, here 76.

5 See Paul Bénichou, *Le Temps des prophètes: Doctrines de l'âge romantique* (Paris: Gallimard, 1977).

6 *Oeuvres de Saint-Simon et d'Enfantin*, 47 vols. (Paris: Dentu, 1865–78; repr. Aalen: Zeller, 1963–64), XXIII, 160. This and other theories are discussed in Ralph P. Locke, *Music, Musicians and the Saint-Simonians* (Chicago: University of Chicago Press, 1986).

7 Matthias Brzoska, *Die Idee des Gesamtkunstwerks in der Musiknovellistik der Julimonarchie*, Thurnauer Schriften zum Musiktheater, 14 (Laaber: Laaber-Verlag, 1995), 165.

8 Joseph d'Ortigue, *Le Balcon de l'opéra* (Paris: Renduel, 1833), 122–3.

9 *Revue musicale*, 5/42 (26 November 1831), 336.

10 Karin Pendle, *Eugène Scribe and French Opera of the Nineteenth Century* (Ann Arbor: UMI Research Press, 1979); also Christopher Smith, 'Scribe', *Grove Opera*.

11 Meyerbeer, it appears, deserves credit for the hero's indecision in this ultimate test, which was added at the final rehearsals. In a printed libretto held by the Bibliothèque nationale (Thb. 878) with a version of the text anterior to the usual score, Robert seems to have opted for Alice, rather than his father. At the end of the trio, Robert 'taking Alice's hand' says to her 'Come', whereas in the final version, Robert remains standing between Alice and Bertram, who *both* say 'Come' to him.

12 Heinrich Heine, *Über die französische Bühne. Vertraute Briefe an August Lewald, 9. Brief* [1837], ed. Christoph Trilse (Berlin: Henschel, 1971). Heine forms part of Sandy Petrey's related study of Robert's character: '*Robert le diable* and Louis-Philippe the King', in *Reading Critics Reading*, ed. Roger Parker and Mary Ann Smart (Oxford: Oxford University Press, 2001), 136–54, here 146.

13 The entire text of *Gambara*, translated by Clara Bell and James Waring, is available on website 'Meyerbeer Fan Club', www.meyerbeer.com/Balzacs%20Meyerbeer.htm, accessed on 22 Feb. 2002.

14 Pendle, *Eugène Scribe*; Smith, 'Scribe'.

15 Sieghart Döhring and Sabine Henze-Döhring, *Oper und Musikdrama im 19ten Jahrhundert*, Handbuch der musikalischen Gattungen, 13 (Laaber: Laaber-Verlag, 1997). The acts have one tableau (stage set) each, except Acts III and V, which contain two each. A tableau can contain any number of scenes (defined by entrances and exits).

16 This aria, which originally included a metaphysical explanation of the fallen angel's fatherly love, supposedly imposed on him as a penitence by Divine Providence, was unfortunately much shortened shortly before the première: see libretto, in Bibliothèque nationale, Thb. 878, and Döhring, '*Robert le Diable*' in *Pipers Enzyklopädie des Musiktheaters*, ed. Carl Dahlhaus and Sieghart Döhring, 7 vols. (Munich: Piper, 1986–97), IV, 126.

17 Jürgensen (see 'The "Ballet of the Nuns"', 80–3) was at least able to reconstruct the step sequence of Taglioni's choreography.

18 Hector Berlioz, 'De l'instrumentation de *Robert le Diable*', *Gazette musicale de Paris*, 12 July 1835, 229–32; ed. Yves Gérard in *Hector Berlioz. Critique musicale*, II (Paris: Buchet/Chastel, 1998), 209–16, here 214.

19 Taglioni's choreography for *Robert le Diable* is the start of Romantic ballet, to be exemplified later by *La Sylphide* (1832) and *Giselle* (1841): see Chapter 6 Appendix 1, above.

20 Anselm Gerhard, 'Giacomo Meyerbeer et le thriller avant la lettre: Choc et *suspense* dans le cinquième acte des *Huguenots*', in *Le Théâtre lyrique en France au XIXe siècle*, ed. Paul Prévost (Metz: Serpenoise, 1995), 107–18.

21 Robert Ignatius Letellier (ed.), *The Diaries of Giacomo Meyerbeer* Vol. 1: *1791–1839* (Madison: Fairleigh Dickinson University Press, 1999), 420, 439.

22 *Ibid.*, 439–42.

23 Giacomo Meyerbeer, *Briefwechsel und Tagebücher*, ed. Heinz Becker *et al.*, 5 vols. (Berlin: de Gruyter, 1959–99), II, 232.

24 Döhring, '*Les Huguenots*', in *Pipers*, IV, 155.

25 Heinz Becker, 'Der Marcel von Meyerbeer: Anmerkungen zur Entstehungsgeschichte der *Hugenotten*', *Jahrbuch des Staatlichen Instituts für Musikforschung* (1979–80), 79–100.

26 Letter to Scribe, 2 July 1834: *Briefwechsel*, II, 376.

27 The vocal score with piano reduction edited by R. Zimmermann and B. Böhmel (Leipzig: Peters, 1973) restores many of the Act III cuts; the original material is in Paris, Bibliothèque de l'Opéra.

28 Joseph d'Ortigue, *Palingénésie musicale* (Paris: La France Catholique, 1833), 221: see Brzoska, *Die Idee*, 154.

29 Carl Dahlhaus, *Nineteenth-Century Music* (Berkeley: University of California Press, 1989 [1980]), 12–15.

30 Letter to Minna Meyerbeer, 15 September 1835: *Briefwechsel*, II, 481.

31 Letter to Minna Meyerbeer, 6 March 1836: *ibid.*, 511–12.

12 Meyerbeer: *Le Prophète* and *L'Africaine*

1 Giacomo Meyerbeer, *Briefwechsel und Tagebücher*, ed. Heinz Becker *et al.*, 5 vols. (Berlin: Walter de Gruyter, 1959–99), II, 527.

2 Unless otherwise identified, information on the compositional history of *Le Prophète* comes from Alan Armstrong, 'Meyerbeer's "Le Prophète": A History of its Composition and Early Performances', dissertation, Ohio State University (1990). I am also grateful to Professor Armstrong for putting at my disposal microfilms of some of the sources on which his dissertation is based. Meyerbeer's fragmentary French comments on the 1836 scenario are printed in his *Briefwechsel und*

Tagebücher, III, 19–20. This document is dated and partly completed by five pages of unpublished preliminary notes in a pocket diary that Meyerbeer used only from 26 November through to the end of the year (Staatsbibliothek zu Berlin, Preussischer Kulturbesitz, N. Mus. Nachl. 97, V/270).

3 Further information on the compositional history of *L'Africaine* can be found in John H. Roberts, 'The Genesis of Meyerbeer's *L'Africaine*', dissertation, University of California, Berkeley (1977).

4 The libretto published at the time of the first performance and reproduced in subsequent editions of Scribe's collected works is a literary text that includes some material from previous versions along with variants produced solely for publication.

5 The original production book is reprinted in *The Original Staging Manuals for Twelve Parisian Operatic Premieres*, ed. H. Robert Cohen (Stuyvesant, NY: Pendragon Press, 1991), 151–82.

6 See, for example, his *Briefwechsel und Tagebücher*, III, 399.

7 Hector Berlioz, *Correspondance générale*, ed. Pierre Citron (Paris: Flammarion, 1972–), III, 624.

8 Georg Joseph Vogler, *Betrachtungen der Mannheimer Tonschule* [Mannheim, 1778–81], 4 vols. (rpt. Hildesheim: G. Olms, 1974), III, 178.

9 Henri Blaze de Bury, *Meyerbeer et son temps* (Paris: Michel Levy, 1865), 182.

10 The heroine, for example, is poisoned at her wedding by her husband's mistress, buried alive in the belief she has died of plague, delivered from her tomb by grave-robbers, and shot by her husband, who mistakes her for a ghost; she then drags herself bleeding through the snow while he dies of plague, clutching his mistress to ensure she will not escape the same fate. See also Gilles de Van's comments on *Guido* and other late grand opera librettos by Scribe in his 'Le Grand Opéra entre tragédie lyrique et drame romantique', *Il Saggiatore Musicale*, 3/2 (1996), 325–60, here 355–8.

11 Paul Bonnefon, 'Scribe sous la Monarchie de Juillet d'après des documents inédits', *Revue d'histoire littéraire de la France*, 28 (1921), 96.

12 Meyerbeer, *Briefwechsel und Tagebücher*, III, 19.

13 See, for example, the quotation from Fétis in Meyerbeer, *Briefwechsel und Tagebücher*, IV, 626.

14 Meyerbeer, *Briefwechsel und Tagebücher*, V, 529.

15 The Handelian style is still more obvious in the original version of the *couplets*, where the semiquaver passages now sung syllabically are melismatic. Armstrong suggests that Levasseur could no longer negotiate such coloratura ('Meyerbeer's "Le Prophète" ', 317).

16 See an unpublished letter of Meyerbeer to his wife Minna, 18 October 1839 (Staatsbibliothek zu Berlin, Preussischer Kulturbesitz, N. Mus. Nachl. 97, H/122) and his *Briefwechsel und Tagebücher*, III, 245, 255. The melody of 'Roi du ciel' – which Meyerbeer reports working on while studying *Alexander's Feast* – could have been suggested by the air and chorus 'Happy pair' in that ode, and the passage beginning 'le paysan et sa cabane' in the *Trio bouffe* may echo the air 'Heroes, when with glory burning' in *Joshua*.

17 Meyerbeer, *Briefwechsel und Tagebücher*, III, 315.

18 Armstrong, 'Meyerbeer's "Le Prophète" ', 40.

19 Gustave Roger, *Le Carnet d'un ténor* (Paris: Paul Ollendorff, 1880), 191.

20 For an overview of these revisions, see Alan Armstrong, 'Gilbert-Louis Duprez and Gustave Roger in the Composition of Meyerbeer's *Le Prophète*', *Cambridge Opera Journal*, 8/2 (1996), 147–65.

21 The complete prayer, 'Eternel, Dieu sauveur', appears in many vocal scores and has been included in some recent recordings.

22 Bibliothèque nationale, MS n.a.f. 22504, fol. 37v. Partly translated in Armstrong, 'Meyerbeer's "Le Prophète" ', 26.

23 Paul Bonnefon, 'Les Métamorphoses d'un opéra: lettres inédites de Eugène Scribe', *Revue des Deux Mondes*, 41 (1917), no. 5, 880–2.

24 These notes are partially preserved in Bibliothèque nationale, MS n.a.f. 22504, fols. 68–81r. Although they are in the hand of two copyists, the content leaves little room for doubt that they came from Pillet.

25 Bibliothèque nationale, MS, n.a.f. 22504, fol. 49v.

26 Meyerbeer, *Briefwechsel und Tagebücher*, III, 207.

27 This statement is based on *The Diaries of Giacomo Meyerbeer*, ed. Robert Ignatius Letellier, II (London: Associated University Presses, 2001) rather than on the German edition, which is incomplete for this period.

28 See Armstrong, 'Meyerbeer's "Le Prophète" ', 136–41.

29 This scene is transcribed in full in Armstrong, 'Meyerbeer's "Le Prophète" ', 1367–74.

30 For an analysis of this overture, see Anselm Gerhard, 'Religiöse Aura und militärisches Gepränge: Meyerbeers Ouvertüren und das Problem der rein instrumentalen Form', in *Meyerbeer und das europäische Musiktheater*, ed. Sieghart Döhring and Arnold Jacobshagen (Laaber: Laaber-Verlag, 1998), 203–8. The complete overture is transcribed in Armstrong, 'Meyerbeer's "Le Prophète"', 511–641.

31 Armstrong, 'Meyerbeer's "Le Prophète"', 366.

32 Some of the music was physically removed from the main autograph score and currently must be reconstructed from the original performing material in the Bibliothèque de l'Opéra in Paris. It is possible, however, that the missing autograph fragments, which formed part of the Meyerbeer *Nachlass* that disappeared at the end of World War II, will eventually be recovered.

33 Roberts had access only to the autograph of Act V but Acts I–IV have since come to light in the Biblioteka Jagiellońska in Crakow.

34 Giacomo Meyerbeer, *Deuxième partie de l'opéra en cinq actes L'Africaine* (Paris: Brandus & Dufour, 1865).

35 The score is part of the missing *Nachlass* cited in n. 32. The principal numbers Meyerbeer seems to have reused were the choruses 'Debout, matelots', 'O grand Saint Dominique', and 'Il faut du vin' at the beginning of Act III, the final chorus of Act III, and portions of the Inès–Sélika duet and Sélika's solo scene in Act V.

36 Meyerbeer, *Briefwechsel und Tagebücher*, V, 96.

37 Julian Budden, *The Operas of Verdi*, 3 vols. (London: Cassell, 1973–81), III, 392.

38 Roberts, 'Genesis', 110–11.

39 On contemporary response to this ritornello, see Gabriela Gomes da Cruz, 'Giacomo Meyerbeer's *L'Africaine* and the End of Grand Opera', dissertation, Princeton University (1999), 333–7.

40 See *ibid.*, 81–2.

41 The ballet scenario is transcribed in Roberts, 'Genesis', 85.

42 *Ibid.*, 111.

43 For additional background on the ballad of Adamastor, see Gabriela Cruz, 'Laughing at History: The Third Act of Meyerbeer's *L'Africaine*', *Cambridge Opera Journal*, 11/1 (1999), 31–76.

13 The grand operas of Fromental Halévy

1 'Halévy et *La Reine de Chypre*', *Revue et gazette musicale de Paris*, 9/9 (27 February 1842), 75–8, here 76. Subsequent articles appeared in issue 11 (13 March), 100–02; issue 17 (24 April), 179–80; issue 18 (1 May), 187–8.

2 *Revue des Deux Mondes*, 29 January 1842, 140.

3 Seemingly involving the functions of both a *répétiteur* and performance accompanist: Nicole Wild, *Dictionnaire des théâtres parisiens au XIXᵉ siècle* (Paris: Aux amateurs de livres, 1989), 206.

4 Entering the Conservatoire at nearly ten years old, he went on to become a protégé of Cherubini, winner of the Prix de Rome in 1819 and instructor and professor in several posts: *répétiteur* of solfège in 1813, adjunct professor in 1818, professor of harmony and accompaniment in 1827 and of counterpoint and fugue in 1833. In 1840 he attained the honoured post of professor of composition. As the Opéra's third-ranked *chef de chant*, he worked primarily with the chorus and, as premier *chef*, with soloists: Wild, *Dictionnaire*, 312–13, notes that the positions of *chef de chant* and *chef de chœur* were not clearly designated until *c.* 1840.

5 Léon Halévy, *F. Halévy: sa vie et ses œuvres* (Paris: Heugel, 1862), 23–5, claimed that Scribe wrote little beyond the 'first draft', although he approved all subsequent textual changes.

6 F. Halévy, *Derniers souvenirs et portraits* (Paris: Michel Lévy Frères, 1863), 166–7; Stéphane Wolff, *L'Opéra au palais Garnier (1875–1962): Les Œuvres, les interprètes* (Paris: Déposé au journal *l'Entracte*, n.d.), 129.

7 Karl Leich-Galland (ed.), *Fromental Halévy, 'La Juive': dossier de presse parisienne (1835)* (Saarbrücken: Lucie Galland, 1988), 50–1.

8 William L. Crosten, *French Grand Opera: An Art and a Business* (New York: King's Crown Press, 1948), 73–4, 90; Karin Pendle, *Eugène Scribe and French Opera of the 19th Century* (Ann Arbor: UMI Research Press, 1977), 5; M. Elizabeth C. Bartlet, 'Grand opéra', *Grove Opera*, II, 514; Anselm Gerhard, *The Urbanization of Opera: Music Theater in Paris in the Nineteenth Century* (Chicago: University of Chicago Press, 1998), 125–7.

9 Paris, Bibliothèque nationale, MS n.a.fr. 22584, vol. I, fols. 14v–15v; vol. II, fols. 19v–20r.

10 *Ibid.*, vol. VIII, fol. 66r. Léon Halévy, *F. Halévy*, 23, reported that Scribe's original setting for *La Juive* was Goa, the capital of Portuguese India where the Inquisition was established in 1560. Konstanz, however, appears in the draft scenario: Bibliothèque nationale, MS n.a.fr. 22502, vol. XXIII.

11 This substitution was recognised by the *Constitutionnel* reviewer (25 February 1835).
12 *La Juive* was the most expensive production staged to date by the Paris Opéra, with costs estimated at 134,000 francs; its first six performances brought in 48,669.55 francs in receipts (Bibliothèque-musée de l'Opéra, RE 38). Nicole Wild, *Décors et costumes du XIXe siècle*. Tome II: *Théâtres et décorateurs* (Paris: Bibliothèque nationale, 1993), 328, notes that Lormier, 'champion of local colour and historical exactitude,' modelled his costumes after early fifteenth-century iconography of southern German soldiers and clerics. See his sketches, Bibliothèque-musée de l'Opéra, D 216 (10)-II.
13 *Le Rénovateur, Courier de l'Europe* (1 March 1835), in Leich-Galland (ed.), *Dossier*, 151.
14 Rachel's image is reproduced and discussed in Cormac Newark's 'Ceremony, Celebration, and Spectacle in *La Juive*', in *Reading Critics Reading: Opera and Ballet Criticism in France from the Revolution to 1848*, ed. Roger Parker and Mary Ann Smart (Oxford: Oxford University Press, 2001), 155–87.
15 Léon Halévy, *Résumé de l'histoire des juifs modernes* (Paris: Lecointe, 1828). Also see *L'Israélite français*, the first Jewish journal in France, co-founded by Halévy's father Elie in 1817 with the epigraph, 'tien[s] au pays, et conserve la foi' ('hold to one's country, and keep to one's faith').
16 Letter of 25 March [1859] in Marthe Galland (ed.), *Fromental Halévy: Lettres* (Heilbronn: Lucie Galland, 1999), 164–5; Karl Leich-Galland, 'Fromental Halévy et l'âge d'or de l'opéra français', *Entre le théâtre et l'histoire: La Famille Halévy (1760–1960)* (Paris: Arthème Fayard, 1996), 75, 345, n. 30; Halévy, *Derniers souvenirs*, 168. For further discussion of Halévy's Jewish identity, see Diana R. Hallman, 'The French Grand Opera *La Juive* (1835): A Socio-Historical Study', dissertation, The City University of New York, 1995), Hallman's new book on *La Juive* (see Select Bibliography), and Ruth Jordan, *Fromental Halévy: His Life and Music, 1799–1862* (London: Kahn & Averill, 1994).
17 Early versions of the libretto, including draft verse (Bibliothèque nationale MS n.a.fr. 22562) and fragments of libretto fair copies (MS n.a.fr. 22502, vol. 23, 4°), reveal Scribe's initial ideas to have Rachel converted at the end of Act V. Louis Véron, *Mémoires d'un bourgeois de Paris*, 5 vols. (Paris: Libraire Nouvelle, 1856–7), III, 181, gives the librettist the credit for deciding on Rachel's tragedy, or at least for selecting the mode of execution,

that of being thrown into a cauldron of boiling liquid – an idea which may have been borrowed from Christopher Marlowe's tragedy *The Jew of Malta* (1592). In 1818 this then-forgotten play had been revived amid great controversy by Edmund Kean at London's Drury Lane Theatre.
18 Halévy's use of the anvil was preceded in French opera by Rodolphe Kreutzer's *Abel* (1810, rev. 1823), associated with demons and destruction in Act II and in Act III with Cain. Auber incorporated it in *Le Maçon* (1825). Wagner's later use of anvils to represent the Nibelungen workers as well as a force of greed and malevolence in *Der Ring des Nibelungen* may have a subtextual link with Eléazar in *La Juive*, as the Nibelungen are forgers of gold, and may have represented Jewish capitalists.
19 Karl Leich-Galland, '*La Juive*: commentaire musical et littéraire', *L'Avant-scène opéra*, 100 (*La Juive*, 1987), 57.
20 Hugh Macdonald, 'Grandest of the Grand', notes to the 1989 Philips recording of *La Juive* (CD 420 190–2).
21 A. Z. Idelsohn, *Jewish Music in its Historical Development* (New York: Henry Holt, 1929), 473.
22 The libretto was used in translation for at least three other operas: Franz Lachner's successful *Catharina Cornaro* (Munich, 1841), Donizetti's *Caterina Cornaro* (Naples: San Carlo, 1844) and Balfe's *The Daughter of St Mark* (London: Drury Lane, 1844): see Chapter 20, p. 412.
23 *Revue et gazette musicale*, 5/11 (18 March 1838), 113–16, here 114.
24 *Ibid.*, 5/10 (11 March 1838), 105–7, here 106. Léon Halévy, *F. Halévy*, 26, claimed to have written the words to this *romance*.
25 *Revue et gazette musicale*, 5/11, 115. See Halévy, *F. Halévy*, 31. During the rehearsal period, Duprez, whose arrival at the Opéra sparked Nourrit's fateful departure, took over the role of Guido intended for Nourrit. The role of Ginevra also changed hands in early stages, from the vocally troubled Falcon to Dorus-Gras.
26 *Revue et gazette musicale*, 5/13 (1 April 1838), 137–41, here 141.
27 Pierre Larousse (ed.), *Grand Dictionnaire universel du XIXe siècle* (Geneva: Slatkine, 1982), XIII/2, 883 (reprint of Paris edn, 1866–79). There are at least two orchestral motifs connected with the idea of Venetian power and influence.
28 See n. 1: translations are in *Wagner: Prose Works*, ed. and trans. W. A. Ellis, 8 vols. (London, 1892–99; repr. New York, 1969), VIII, 175–200. Katharine Ellis, *Music Criticism*

in Nineteenth-Century France: La Revue et Gazette musicale de Paris, 1834–1880 (Cambridge: Cambridge University Press, 1995), 194, emphasises that Wagner's 'hyperbolic' praise of Halévy's music was motivated by his own self-interest. Although his commentary may have been affected by a need to curry favour with the publisher as well as the Opéra establishment, aspects of his own operas, as well as his later commentary, suggest an admiration that was more than superficial.

29 *La Démence de Charles VI* (Paris: Jules Didot l'aîné, n.d.); Henri Blanchard, *Revue et gazette musicale de Paris*, 10/12 (19 March 1843), 99–102. Although the names of both librettists appear on librettos and scores of *Charles VI*, press reports and other sources mention Casimir Delavigne as the primary librettist.

30 David H. Pinkney, *Decisive Years in France: 1840–1847* (Princeton: Princeton University Press, 1986), 130–2.

31 As noted in *La Gazette de France* (17 March 1843).

32 Paris, Archives nationales, AJ¹³ 205: copyist libretto with censors' markings.

33 *La Gazette de France* (17 March 1843), 1. In Schlesinger's unheeded request for reimbursement for the pulped libretto copies he reminds Pillet that the censors' authorisation had given him the go-ahead for the original printing (letter dated 3 May 1843: Archives nationales, AJ¹³ 183, folder, 'Ouvrages/Charles VI').

34 Blanchard, *Revue et gazette musicale*, 10/12 (19 March 1843), 99, reports that the censor requested replacement of the words 'Guerre aux tyrans' by 'Vive le roi'. The issue of 5 March 1843 notes that the censors' 'mutilations' included the omission of a chorus ending with the refrain 'Mort aux Anglais'.

35 'Charles VI', Larousse, *Grand Dictionnaire*, III, 127. The chorus was included among six *chants* published in an anthology of national songs by Brandus; arrangements include *Chant national de l'Opéra Charles VI de F. Halévy pour le piano par Stephen Heller*, Op. 48, No. 1 (Paris: Mᶜᵉ. Schlesinger, n.d.).

36 As pointed out in *Le Constitutionnel* (17 March 1843).

37 'Revue des théâtres', *Le Papillon* (April 1843).

38 *Mélodie: Théâtres lyriques, critique, nouvelles*, 1/34 (18 March 1843), 1.

39 Wagner's *Der fliegende Holländer* (1842) may be a loose adaptation of the myth. French approaches are discussed in Frank Paul

Bowman, 'Illuminism, Utopia, Mythology', in *The French Romantics*, ed. D. G. Charlton, 2 vols. (Cambridge: Cambridge University Press, 1984), I, 76–112, here 103–4.

40 Paul Smith [Edouard Monnais], 'Théâtre du Grand Opera: Le Juif Errant', *Revue et gazette musicale de Paris*, 19/17 (25 April 1852), 130.

41 *Ibid.*, 131.

42 *Le Constitutionnel* (22 March 1858), cited in Karl Leich-Galland, '*La Magicienne* (1858), dernier grand opéra de Fromental Halévy: livret de Jules de Saint-Georges', paper given at the meeting of the International Musicological Society, Madrid, 7 April 1992, 2.

43 Leich-Galland, '*La Magicienne*', 2.

44 H. Berlioz, *Correspondance générale*, ed. Pierre Citron, in progress (Paris: Flammarion, 1972–), V, 551, 556; letter from Gounod to Bizet, 24 May 1858, Bibliothèque nationale, MS n.a.fr. 14346, fols. 84–86.

45 Ellis, *Music Criticism*, 191–4.

46 *Gazette musicale de Paris*, 2/41 (11 October 1835), 335.

47 *Revue des Deux Mondes*, 29 (January 1842), 141; *Mélodie: Théâtres lyriques, critique, nouvelles*, 1/35 (25 March 1843), 1.

48 'Halévy et *La Reine de Chypre*' (see nn. 1 and 28), 24 April, 179.

49 Odette's 'Ah! qu'un ciel sans nuage' in *Charles VI* fits Castil-Blaze's description of a simple, unembellished *romance*, as pointed out by Huebner, along with Gérard's square-phrased ternary *romance* set in the Romantic 'love' key of G♭ major; Rachel's passionate *romance* 'Il va venir', however, offers a completely different character for this aria type: Steven Huebner, *The Operas of Charles Gounod* (Oxford: Clarendon Press, 1990), 263. Also see his discussion of aria and ensemble treatments.

50 See Berlioz's praise of his rhythmic choices in reviews of *Guido et Ginevra* (nn. 23, 24, 26 above). Among repetitive rhythms are homorhythmic patterns in choral numbers, syncopated motifs that create intense agitation, ostinati and climax-building rhythmic crescendos.

51 Huebner, *Gounod*, 224, 229, notes that Halévy 'preferred to maintain the integrity of his main rhythmic motif', and Hugh Macdonald, *Grove Opera*, III, 1283, speaks of his 'fallible' text-setting. The composer in an undated letter to Pillet concerning a duet in *La Reine de Chypre* writes of his 'verse of ten feet [*pieds*] divided by five, which is a novelty!': Bibliothèque nationale (Mus.), *Lettres autographes*, vol. 50, no. 48.

52 William Edward Runyan, 'Orchestration in Five French Grand Operas', dissertation, Eastman School of Music (1983), 270–3.

53 *Ibid.*, 275–8.

54 As suggested in the Schlesinger orchestral score, its parts could be performed, with some exceptions, by the regular orchestra if a company did not have the resources for a second. The stage music appears as a supplement in the published orchestral score, *La Reine de Chypre: Opéra en cinq actes, paroles de M. de Saint Georges, musique de F. Halévy*, 2 vols. (Paris: Maurice Schlesinger, n.d.), II, 386, 557.

55 *Revue et gazette musicale*, 5/11 (18 March 1838), 115.

56 Malou Haine, *Adolphe Sax (1814–1894): Sa vie, son œuvre, ses instruments de musique* (Brussels: Editions de l'université, 1980), 97–8. Verdi's *Jérusalem* was the first opera to benefit.

57 On 5 January 1875 the first two acts were given, with the débuts of Gabrielle Krauss as Rachel, Pierre François Villaret as Eléazar, and Gaffiot Belval as Brogni, under the direction of Ernest Deldevez. On 8 January, the full opera was presented, with choreography by Louis Merante and *mise-en-scène* by Léon Carvalho. See 'Revue musicale – l'inauguration du nouvel opéra', *Revue des Deux Mondes*, 1 (1875), 465–70; Wolff, *L'Opéra au palais Garnier*, 129–31; Martine Kahane (ed.), *L'Ouverture du nouvel opéra, 5 janvier 1875* (Paris: Ministère de la culture et de la communication, 1986), 30, 44.

58 Alfred Loewenberg, *Annals of Opera, 1597–1940*, 2nd edn (Geneva: Societas Bibliographica, 1955), 59; *Gazette musicale de Paris*, 2/32 (9 August 1835); *Revue musicale*, 9/44 (1 November 1835); *Le Ménestrel*, 3/7 (17 January 1836), 3, and 3/24 (15 May 1836).

59 The version given on 16 November was adapted by J. R. Planché with music arranged by Thomas Simpson Cook. *Le Ménestrel*, 108 (27 December 1835), 4, reported that it was performed at Drury Lane without 'some choirs, marches and dances' and with a happy ending – the saving of Rachel. In 1850 *La Juive* was sung there in multiple languages: P. A. Fiorentino, in *Les Grands Guignols* (Paris: Michel Lévy Frères, 1872), 283, referred to it as 'La Juive des quatre nations' ('The Jewess of Four Nations') and 'la Tour de Babel' ('The Tower of Babel').

60 Gerard Fitzgerald (ed.), *Annals of the Metropolitan Opera: The Complete Chronicle of Performances and Artists*, 2 vols. (New York: Metropolitan Opera Guild; Boston: G. K. Hall, 1989), I, 11–12.

61 The role of Eléazar quickly became known as one of Caruso's most effective and favoured roles, as well as the last he performed. After suffering a haemorrhage while singing Nemorino in *L'Elisir d'amore* on 11 December 1920, he made his final career appearance in *La Juive* on Christmas Eve, 1920: Fitzgerald (ed.), *Annals*, 297.

62 See Halévy's enthusiastic description: *Fromental Halévy: Lettres*, 120–1.

63 Letter to Hippolyte Rodrigues, Paris, 10 April 1861, in *ibid.*, 194–5.

64 *Correspondance [de] George Sand*, ed. Georges Lubin, 25 vols. (Paris: Garnier Frères, 1964–91), X, 496 (16 October 1851), as cited and translated in Jordan, *Fromental Halévy*, 155.

14 From Rossini to Verdi

1 Jacques-Gabriel Prod'homme, 'Verdi's Letters to Léon Escudier', *Music & Letters*, 4 (1923), 62–70, 184–96, 375–7, here 376. See n. 2 below; also Léon Escudier, *Mes souvenirs* (Paris: Dentu, 1863). The Opéra's enormous resources, for Verdi, went with a desire to dazzle (and sell) that sometimes outweighed artistic values. 'Boutique' is also slang for a place of work, especially an unpleasant one.

2 These (as well as a special government pension – see below) permitted Rossini to retire from the stage after *Guillaume Tell* and live very well indeed. Verdi later claimed that the aggravation in dealing with the Opéra was not worth the monetary rewards. Writing to his Paris agent Léon Escudier on 20 October 1858 (after the lukewarm success of *Les Vêpres siciliennes*), he exploded: 'You're talking to me about theatre? . . . and about writing for the Opéra?!! . . . You?!! . . . Let's be open, and bear with me when I speak clearly what I feel. I am not rich enough nor poor enough to write for your leading theatre. Not poor enough to need meagre gains; not rich enough to live well in a country with very high expenses': Prod'homme, 'Lettres inédites de G. Verdi à Léon Escudier', *Rivista musicale italiana*, 35 (1928), 1–28, 171–208, 519–52, here 20. In fact the honoraria, even for Verdi (as well as contracts), were not so 'meagre', and the composer kept careful track and insisted on payment in full, as was his due. See additional examples in *I copialettere di Giuseppe Verdi*, ed. Gaetano Cesari and Alessandro Luzio (Milan: Commissione esecutiva per le onoranze a Giuseppe Verdi, 1913; repr. Bologna, 1987). Furthermore, Verdi did later write for the Opéra: his masterpiece *Don Carlos*.

3 Typically by this time French publishers negotiated with composers for a lump-sum

payment for access to the score, for permission to have arrangements made and for the rights to negotiate with publishers in other countries for distribution outside France: for letters of Troupenas to Artaria about *Guillaume Tell* see Jeffrey Kallberg, 'Marketing Rossini: sei lettere di Troupenas ad Artaria', *Bollettino del Centro rossiniano di Studi* (1980), 41–63.

4 The only other prominent Italian composer successful on the international scene and in Paris was Vincenzo Bellini. After the favourable reception of *Norma* and *La sonnambula* in Paris and the première there of *I Puritani*, Bellini was actively pursuing projects for the Opéra and the Opéra-Comique at the time of his sudden death at the age of 33 (23 September 1835).

5 For Rossini's contracts with the *maison du Roi* acting on behalf of the Opéra, see Jean-Marie Bruson, *Rossini à Paris, Musée Carnavalet, 27 octobre–31 décembre 1992* (Paris: Société des Amis du Musée Carnavalet, 1992), 56–62. Rossini knew full well what power he had: by refusing to submit the final acts of *Guillaume Tell* to the copyist in the spring of 1829, he virtually blackmailed the government into accepting his terms: *ibid.*, 64–5. For an account in English citing the correspondence, see Herbert Weinstock, *Rossini: A Biography* (New York: Knopf, 1968), 161–4. The July Revolution (1830) suspended the pension, but it was reinstated in 1835 after the composer's vigorous, even legal, appeals.

6 According to an Opéra insider, Louis Gentil (*contrôleur du matériel*), the director Duponchel sensed that Donizetti would be a successful addition to the roster of contemporary composers and persisted in spite of the opposition of the institution's *premier chef du chant*, Halévy: Jean-Louis Tamvaco, *Les Cancans de l'Opéra: chroniques de l'Académie Royale de Musique et du théâtre, à Paris sous les deux Restaurations*, 2 vols. (Paris: CNRS Editions, 2000), I, 400–01, 522. Tamvaco's annotations contain a wealth of information about singers, composers, librettists, Opéra personnel and patrons.

7 To placate Scribe, whose *Le Duc d'Albe* lost its place in the queue, the administration, with librettists Royer and Vaëz, agreed to cede him 50 per cent of the librettists' royalties, although his participation seems to have been minimal: Rebecca Harris-Warrick, 'Introduzione storica', *Gaetano Donizetti: La Favorite*, Edizione Critica delle Opere di Gaetano Donizetti, 3 (Milan: Ricordi, 1997), xix–xxii.

8 Contract for *Les Vêpres siciliennes*, 28 February 1852: *I copialettere di Verdi*, 139–40; transcribed drafts of papers for *Don Carlos*, Paris, Archives Nationales, AJ[13] 505: Ursula Günther, 'La genèse de *Don Carlos*', *Revue de musicologie*, 58 (1972), 16–64, here 31–5; 60 (1974), 87–158.

9 Julian Budden, *The Operas of Verdi*, 3 vols. (London: Cassell, 1973–81), II, 240, and Charles Osborne, *Verdi: A Life in the Theatre* (New York: Alfred A. Knopf, 1987), 184–5.

10 28 March 1827, 1: '*Urlo francese*' was a common term with Italian opera supporters to refer to the traditional French declamatory and sometimes intense vocal style.

11 Letter to Charles-Edmond Duponchel, 25 May 1828: Guido Zavadini, *Donizetti: Vita–Musiche–Epistolario* (Bergamo: Istituto Italiano d'Arti Grafiche, 1948), 471–2.

12 E.g., *Le cabinet du lecture et le cercle réunis*, 10 April 1840; *Le moniteur des théâtres*, 11 April 1840: these (in French) and other reviews are in *Le prime rappresentazioni delle opere di Donizetti nella stampa coeva*, ed. Annalisa Bini and Jeremy Commons ([Rome:] Accademia Nazionale di Santa Cecilia, 1997), 793–900, here 803–05.

13 Bibliothèque de l'Opéra, 'Registres de l'Opéra', RE 6–7.

14 Budden, *The Operas of Verdi*, II, 179–80; *I copialettere di Verdi*, 154–5 (letter to Roqueplan, 28 October 1854).

15 The plot has little to do with the famous tale in the *Arabian Nights*: Ali-Baba is an avaricious spice merchant bent on thwarting young lovers. Jules Janin in *Journal des débats* was not alone in criticising the librettist for deviating from the source: 'everything has been altered, turned upside-down; we recognise neither the spirit nor the language nor the characters nor the cave nor anything else from the tale': 24 July 1833, 1–3.

16 Berlioz thought Marliani's score 'well constructed, clear, [but] without a well defined local colour; it has neither Rossini's verve nor Bellini's melancholy but, overall, the score of *La xacarilla*, a Frenchified Italian one, is pleasing': *Journal des débats*, 1 November 1839.

17 Italian composers contributed to thirteen ballets during this period. Among the most prolific and popular composers was Cesare Pugni.

18 William Ashbrook notes another possible reason, in *Donizetti and his Operas* (Cambridge: Cambridge University Press, 1982), 149–50.

19 Though the reception at the première seemed moderate, Berlioz augured for

success: *Journal des débats*, 18 November 1848, repr. Bini and Commons (eds.), *Le prime rappresentazioni*, 1228–35.

20 Perrin's papers, Paris, Archives Nationales, AJ[13] 183, provide documentation. On 25 May 1844 the director Auguste-Eugène Vatel's representative in a letter to the Ministre de l'Intérieur protested the Opéra's plans. The minister consulted the government-sponsored Commission Spéciale des Théâtres Royaux, which ruled in the Opéra's favour, as *Othello* was to be given in translation (a weak reason, it must be noted, but then, this Commission sided generally with the Opéra). The case of *Robert Bruce* was more complicated since the Théâtre Italien's objections were focused on the music. On 7 October 1846 the minister's under-secretary asked the Opéra director for copies of the libretto and the score. Two days later Perrin replied that two copies of the libretto would be sent as soon as possible, but the score was another matter. He noted that as was the usual practice, 'the score [i.e. that submitted to the Opéra by Niedermeyer] was parcelled out to twenty or thirty copyists hard at work preparing parts for the chorus, orchestra, soloists, prompters, etc. There is no [spare] copy of the score and to make one would require several weeks during which other urgent work would have to be put on hold.' (This is further confirmation that the manuscript scores currently housed at the Opéra were prepared after the parts.) Perrin went on to say that the music was selected from Rossini operas not part of the Théâtre Italien's repertory and made the questionable claim that 'all [borrowed pieces] had been revised, cut or lengthened by Rossini himself'. He concluded that it required much effort on his part to persuade the composer to participate and that he was proud to have succeeded. On 6 November the Commission again backed the Opéra: the libretto was new and Rossini had the right to reuse his music as he saw fit.

21 Critics, as often, focused on deficiencies they perceived in the libretto and Italian composers' failure to pay enough attention to the quality of the text they set: Janin on *Othello* is representative (*Journal des débats*, 16 September 1844). *Robert Bruce* was not helped by a poor performance by Rosine Stoltz and her tantrum in response to boos: Herbert Weinstock, *Rossini, a Biography* (New York: Knopf, 1968), 238–40.

22 On 28 January 1846 the minister told the Opéra that *Lucie de Lammermoor* would be permitted on condition that it did not count towards fulfilment of conditions in the *cahier des charges* (the director's schedule: see Chapter 2): 'since this work has been given as part of standard repertory both in regional theatres for a dozen years and in Paris at the Théâtre de la Renaissance for quite some time, there will be no advantage for the [Opéra] administration to stage it': Archives nationales, AJ[13] 183. Though deemed unworthy of the Opéra, *Lucie de Lammermoor* proved to be a consistent money-earner for it.

23 David Lawton, ' "Le trouvère": Verdi's Revision of "Il trovatore" for Paris', *Studi verdiani*, 3 (1985), 79–119.

24 Having Roméo sung by Mlle Vestivali may have been problematic for a mid-nineteenth-century Parisian audience, as trouser roles for main characters were never part of the tradition at this theatre (as Rossini noted when he replaced the role of General Calbo (mezzo soprano) by that of Néoclès (tenor) in *Le Siège de Corinthe*). Gustave Héquet concluded: 'Let's be honest: Bellini's music is not from any perspective suited to French singers' customs': *L'Illustration*, 17 September 1859, 213–14. Reviewing *Sémiramis*, the same critic noted that 'translations are rarely successful at the Opéra': *ibid.*, 21 July 1860, 45–6. The singer Barbara Marchisio was cast in the role of the hero, Arsace.

25 Hans Busch, *Verdi's* Aida: *The History of an Opera in Letters and Documents* (Minneapolis: University of Minnesota Press, 1978).

26 Paologiovanni Maione and Francesca Seller, *I reali teatri di Napoli nella prima metà dell'Ottocento: studi su Domenico Barbaja* (Bellona: Santabarbara, 1994); Franco Carmelo Greco (ed.), *Il Teatro del re: San Carlo da Napoli all'Europa* (Naples: Edizione scientifiche italiane, 1987); Franco Mancini, author [vols. I and III], Agostino Ziino, Bruno Cagli, eds. [vol. II], *Il Teatro di San Carlo, 1737–1987* (Naples: Electa, 1987); Carlo Marinelli Roscioni (ed.), *Il Teatro di San Carlo*, II: *La cronologia, 1737–1987* (Naples: Guida, 1987).

27 On 3 April 1826 Rossini directed a benefit concert for the Greek patriots. By the time of the opera's première the French government had begun to be openly supportive of the Greek cause: 'No doubt, the current situation on everyone's minds about the much more recent siege and self-sacrifice added significantly to [the audience's] interest': *Journal de Paris*, 11 October 1826, 2.

28 See various opera entries in *Grove Opera*; Gerhard, *The Urbanization of Opera: Music Theater in Paris in the Nineteenth Century* (Chicago: University of Chicago Press, 1998);

on Rossini and Donizetti operas, Philip
Gossett's introductions in the *Early Romantic
Opera* series (New York: Garland, 1978–83);
on Rossini operas, P. Isotta, 'Da *Mosè* a *Moïse*',
Bolletino del Centro rossiniano di studi (1971),
97–117; Pierluigi Petrobelli, 'Balzac, Stendhal
e il *Mosè* di Rossini', *ibid.*, 205–19;
L'Avant-scène opéra, 81 (*Le Siège de Corinthe*,
1985); M. Elizabeth C. Bartlet, 'Rossini e
l'Académie Royale de Musique a Parigi',
Rossini 1792–1992: mostra storico-documentaria,
ed. Mauro Bucarelli (Perugia: Electa, 1992),
245–66; on *Les Martyrs*, see *The Donizetti
Society Journal*, 2 (1975); *L'opera teatrale di
Gaetano Donizetti: Atti del Convegno
Internazionale di Studi 1992*, ed. Francesco
Bellotto (Bergamo: Comune di Bergamo,
1993), especially the essay by Michele Girardi:
'Donizetti e il grand opéra: il caso de *Les
Martyrs*', 135–47; also Ashbrook, *Donizetti*,
148–50, 428–34; On *Jérusalem*, *Quaderni
dell'Istituto di studi verdiani*, 2 (1963); David
R. B. Kimbell, 'Verdi's First Rifacimento: *I
Lombardi* and *Jérusalem*', *Music & Letters*, 60
(1969), 1–36; Ursula Günther, 'Verdi in Paris:
Aspects of *Jérusalem* and *Les Vêpres siciliennes*',
paper read at the Fourth International Verdi
Congress, Chicago, 25 September 1974;
Arrigo Quattrocchi, 'Da Milano a Parigi:
"Jérusalem", la prima revisione di Verdi', *Studi
verdiani*, 10 (1994–95), 13–60.
29 H. Robert Cohen (ed.), *The Original
Staging Manuals for Twelve Parisian Operatic
Premières* (Stuyvesant, NY: Pendragon, 1991)
includes those for *La Favorite, Guillaume Tell*
(but for another more detailed see the critical
edition) and *Les Vêpres siciliennes*. Cohen's *The
Original Staging Manuals for Ten Parisian
Operatic Premières, 1824–1843* (Stuyvesant,
NY: Pendragon, 1998) includes those for *Dom
Sébastien, Les Martyrs, Moïse* and *Le Siège de
Corinthe*.
30 Letter of 8 April 1829: Zavadini, *Donizetti*,
494–5.
31 Translated by Günther in 'Verdi in Paris'.
32 *I copialettere di Verdi*, 59. This passage in a
letter draft dated 24 September 1848 is
crossed out, but still reflects Verdi's views:
Günther, 'Verdi in Paris', also cites it.
33 People had in mind Augustin Hapdé's
highly successful *mélodrame, Le Passage de la
Mer Rouge* (Théâtre de la Gaîté, 1817). See,
e.g., *Journal des débats*, 29 March 1827: 'The
machiniste should be ashamed of himself. In
this opera the high point of his contribution
should be the parting of the Red Sea. This was
all the easier to do since he had a model for
this complex machinery in Hapdé's

mélodrame given a few years ago at the
Théâtre de la Gaîté; all that was necessary was
to enlarge and perfect it. I must admit that
the inventor [Hapdé] has the edge. Certainly
there is a lot to be done to turn this around
in the favour of the royal theatre whose
superior financial support and larger stage
should be to its advantage.'
34 Nicole Wild, *Décors et costumes du XIXe
siècle*, I: *Opéra de Paris* (Paris: Bibliothèque
nationale, 1987), 7.
35 Only two dances appear in the Troupenas
ed. (published scores, destined for regional
theatres with more limited resources for
spectacle, e.g., ballet soloists, often omit some
dances); but Bibliothèque de l'Opéra, Mat. 19
[239 (291), the part of the ballet *répétiteur*,
indicates the following: N° 1 Rondo in A; N°
2 Pas de deux in F; N° 3 Air in B♭ [= 1er air in
Troupenas]; N° 4 Pas de trois in D [= 2^e air in
Troupenas]; N° 5 Final in G. The shelf-mark
of the Final's score is Mat. 19 [239 (317).
36 What follows is based on the copy in
Archives nationales, AJ^13 206, slightly
abbreviated.
37 E.g., review of *Le Siège de Corinthe*, *Journal
des débats*, 11 October 1826, 2.
38 *Journal des débats*, 29 March 1827, explains
these distinctions in considerable detail.
39 E.g., Léon Escudier, *La France musicale*, 12
April 1840 (in Bini and Commons (eds.), *Le
prime rappresentazioni*, 826–7), and *Le
Charivari*, 12 April 1840 (Bini and Commons
(eds.), *Le prime rappresentazioni*, 823).
40 However, extempore embellishment was
another thing: the *Journal des débats*,
reviewing *Le Siège de Corinthe*, noted
'[Pamyra's *air*] would seem [even more
touching] without the embellishments which
Mlle Cinti adds without justification' and *Le
National*, reviewing *Les Martyrs* on 12 April
1840, noted that 'Mme Dorus-Gras [as
Pauline] is, as usual, the same exceptional
cantatrice, the same incorrigible embellisher,
flinging vocal pyrotechnics at random,
whether in a festive scene or one in the
tombs': in Bini and Commons (eds.), *Le prime
rappresentazioni*, 821.
41 *Le Corsaire*, 12 April 1840: 'This is the
Rossinian style *par excellence*. Expressions of
revolt are mixed with pious hopes, blessing,
anger, rage and resignation': Bini and
Commons (eds.), *Le prime rappresentazioni*,
810).
42 Ashbrook, *Donizetti*, 427.
43 As well as the Rossini literature previously
cited, see Janet Johnson, 'The Musical
Environment in France', in *The Cambridge*

Companion to Berlioz, ed. Peter Bloom
(Cambridge: Cambridge University Press,
2000).

44 *Journal des débats*, 11 October 1826, 2.

45 See literature previously cited, plus:
Berlioz, 'Guillaume Tell', *Gazette musicale*, 1
(1834), 326–7, 336–9, 341–3, 349–51, Eng.
trans. in *Source Readings in Music History*, ed.
Oliver Strunk (New York: Norton, 1950),
808–26; *L 'Avant-scène opéra*, 118 (*Guillaume
Tell*, 1989); Richard Osborne, 'Guillaume
Tell', *Grove Opera*; M. Elizabeth C. Bartlet with
Mauro Bucarelli, *Guillaume Tell di Gioachino
Rossini: Fonti iconografiche* (Pesaro:
Fondazione Rossini, 1996).

46 Gilles de Van, 'Les sources littéraires de
Guillaume Tell de Rossini', *Chroniques
italiennes*, 29 (1992), 7–24.

47 Anselm Gerhard discovered and analysed
a manuscript copy of Jouy's original in the
Archives: ' "Sortire dalle vie comuni": Wie
Rossini einem Akademiker das Libretto
verdarb', in *Oper als Text: romanistische Beiträge
zur Libretto-Forschung*, ed. Albert Gier
(Heidelberg: Winter, 1986), 185–219; see also
Gerhard, *Urbanization*, 94–6. The critical
edition mentioned in Table 14.1 note 2
contains an edition of it (*Commento critico,
testi*, 9–105) and further brief examination in
the 'Prefazione' (I, xxiv–xxix).

48 Cf. Berlioz, 'Guillaume Tell'; Georges
Imbert de Laphalèque, *Revue de Paris*, 5/4
(August 1829), 257; Alphonse Martainville, *Le
Drapeau blanc*, 5 August 1829, 2.

49 François-Joseph Fétis, *Revue musicale*, 6/4
(1829), 43. However, the balance of the piece
is skewed as a result. This may be why the
opening section, though not consistently, was
sometimes omitted in Paris while Nourrit
sang the part. Perhaps it was felt more
dramatic to begin with the news of Tell's
emprisonment and the plea for arms. There is
no truth to the rumour that it was a result of
Nourrit's vocal difficulties.

50 For her variants elsewhere see the volume
Commento critico, within the critical edition.

51 *Le Drapeau blanc*, 5 August 1829, 2.

52 *Le Messager des chambres*, 5 August 1829, 4.

53 One measure of its enduring success are
the numerous parodies. To cite but three:
Offenbach's 'trio patriotique', 'Lorsque la
Grèce est un champ de carnage', *La Belle
Hélène* (1864) quotes Rossini's music, as the
text spoofs the original (the context being
marital discord); Stop (Louis-Pierre
Morel-Retz) in his 1849 woodcut assumed
reader's knowledge of the trio to interpret a
political commentary on French involvement

in Rome; Henriot (Henri Maigrot) relies
similarly in his, which concerns the 1894
bicycle craze in Paris: Bartlet, with Bucarelli,
Fonti iconografiche, 136–40, esp. 111–20.

54 Strunk, *Source Readings*, 821.

55 *Le Globe*, 5 August 1829, 494.

56 Berlioz, review of *La Fille du régiment*,
Journal des débats, 16 February 1840: in Bini
and Commons (eds.), *Le prime
rappresentazioni*, 777. *Lucie* was playing to
packed houses; *La Fille du régiment* became a
staple at the Opéra-Comique; *Rita* – dating
from *c.* 1841 – reached the same theatre in
1860; *L'elisir* (Paris première, 1839) became
another staple. Donizetti's measured reply
appeared in *Journal des débats*, 17 February
1840: Bini and Commons (eds.), *Le prime
rappresentazioni*, 779; Ashbrook, *Donizetti*,
146–7. The exchange prompted an amusing
caricature in *Le Charivari*, the Italian
composing two scores at the same time
(Zavadini, *Donizetti*, after 512).

57 Nicole Wild, *Dictionnaire des théâtres
parisiens au XIXᵉ siècle* (Paris: Aux amateurs de
livres, 1989), 375–8.

58 Letter to Tommaso Persico, undated but
stamped 9 May 1840: Zavadini, *Donizetti*,
513.

59 On the complex history of *L'Ange de Nisida*,
based in part on an unfinished Italian opera
entitled *Adelaide*, and its transformation into
La Favorite, see Ashbrook, *Donizetti*, 441–2,
and Harris-Warrick, 'Introduzione storica',
xiv–xxiv.

60 For further detail, see Harris-Warrick,
'Introduzione storica', xix–xxiv.

61 Several critics found this in extremely
poor taste. *Le Ménestrel*, 6 December 1840,
described it as the 'one scene which no one
will find appropriate or tasteful': Bini and
Commons (eds.), *Le prime rappresentazioni*,
943.

62 E.g., *Gazette de France*, 7 December 1840:
Bini and Commons (eds.), *Le prime
rappresentazioni*, 956–62.

63 Dumas also had in mind a real courtesan,
Marie Duplessis (pseudonym of Alphonsine
Plessis), who died of tuberculosis in her
mid-twenties. The way he framed the story,
particularly in the play version, is arguably
operatic.

64 'The dance *airs* are charming. In the first,
with an English horn solo, admirably played
by M. Verroust, a pretty melody in duet
contradicts the well-known proverb: "Do you
know of anything worse than one flute? – Yes,
two flutes." *The pas de six*, a piquant bolero,
and the Moorish ensemble, in which there is a

toned-down imitation of Algerian music, with its black drummers, triangles, tambourines, etc., is lively and of a quite original cast'; Berlioz, *Journal des débats*, 6 December 1840: in Bini and Commons (eds.), *Le prime rappresentazioni*, 933.

65 On *Guillaume Tell* see the critical edition. Verdi in *Les Vêpres siciliennes* insisted on final-act changes from Scribe before setting it, after which it still came in for criticism: Andrew Porter, '*Les Vêpres siciliennes*: New Letters from Verdi to Scribe', *19th-Century Music*, 2 (1978–79), 95–109; Anselm Gerhard, ' "Ce cinquième acte sans intérêt": preoccupazioni di Scribe e di Verdi per la drammaturgia de *Les Vêpres siciliennes*', *Studi verdiani*, 4 (1986–87), 65–86; for contemporary reviews see *Giuseppe Verdi: Les Vêpres siciliennes: dossier de presse parisienne (1855)*, ed. Hervé Gartioux, Critiques de l'Opéra Français du XIXème Siècle, 6 (Heilbronn: Lucie Galland, 1995).

66 *Le Corsaire*, 4 December 1840; *L'Echo français*, 4 December 1840; *La Quotidienne*, 7 December 1840: Bini and Commons (eds.), *Le prime rappresentazioni*, 913–14, 964. Even Berlioz had many positive as well as negative things to say: *Journal des débats*, 6 December 1840 (in Bini and Commons (eds.), *Le prime rappresentazioni*, 928–35). Harris-Warrick reminds us of the venality of the Parisian press: both praise and critiques must be treated with a certain scepticism ('Introduzione storica', xxiv–xxviii). The financial records in the 'Journal de l'Opéra' (Bibliothèque de l'Opéra, Usuels 201) strongly support the positive reviews.

67 'Write for the Opéra where performances last half a day, poor me! What a mass of music, what a quantity of notes!': letter to Opprandino Arrivabene, 30 September 1865: Annibale Alberti, *Verdi intimo: carteggio di Giuseppe Verdi con il conte Opprandino Arrivabene* (Milan: A. Mondadori, 1931), 59.

68 7 August 1850: *I copialettere di Verdi*, 104.

69 According to Scribe, Verdi insisted on this collaboration: see letter to Charles Duveyrier, 3 December 1854, in Porter, '*Les Vêpres siciliennes*: New Letters'.

70 See the Chronology: in the six years prior to *Don Carlos*, of seventeen new works nine were ballets, three were short operas (in one or two acts) – all unsuccessful – and five were longer operas (in four or five acts): Rossini's *Sémiramis*, Wagner's *Tannhäuser*, Gounod's *La Reine de Saba*, Meyerbeer's *L'Africaine* and Mermet's *Roland à Roncevaux* (only the last two remained in repertory).

71 The secondary literature on *Don Carlos* is extensive. In addition to works already cited, see *Atti del IIᵉ Congresso Internazionale di Studi Verdiani, Verona, Castelvecchio; Parma, Istituto di studi verdiani; Busseto, Villa Pallavicino, 30 luglio – 5 agosto 1969*, ed. Marcello Pavarani (Parma: Istituto di studi verdiani, 1972); Andrew Porter, 'The Making of *Don Carlos*', *Proceedings of the Royal Musical Association*, 98 (1971–72), 73–88; Ursula Günther, 'La genèse de Don Carlos, opéra en cinq actes de Giuseppe Verdi, représenté pour la première fois à Paris le 11 mars 1867', *Revue de musicologie*, 58 (1972), 16–64, and 60 (1974), 87–158; Budden, *The Operas of Verdi*, III, 3–157; Paul Robinson, '*Realpolitik*: Giuseppe Verdi's *Don Carlo*', *Opera & Ideas: From Mozart to Strauss* (New York: Harper & Row, 1985), 155–209; *L'Avant-scène opéra*, 90–91 (*Don Carlos*, 1986); Ursula Günther, 'La genèse du *Don Carlos* de Verdi: nouveaux documents', *Revue de musicologie*, 72 (1986), 104–77. See *Grove Opera*, 'Don Carlos' by Roger Parker, for an explication of the plot(s) of the original French version and subsequent revisions, as well as a brief performance history, and further bibliography. For contemporary reviews see Hervé Gartioux (ed.), *Giuseppe Verdi: Don Carlos: dossier de presse parisienne (1867)* (Heilbronn: Musik-Edition Lucie Galland, 1997).

72 Verdi to Perrin, 21 July 1865; Günther, 'La genèse' (1972), 30.

73 Budden, *The Operas of Verdi*, III, 17–21; Ursula Günther, 'Le livret français de "Don Carlos": le premier acte et sa révision par Verdi', *Atti del IIᵉ Congresso*, 90–140; *eadem*, 'La genèse' (1972), *passim*.

74 On 'triangles' see Chapter 1 above; also Andrew Porter, 'Verdi', *New Grove* /1, XIX, 654, and David Charlton, 'Verdi in Paris', in *Romanticism (1830–1890)*, ed. Gerald Abraham, New Oxford History of Music, IX (Oxford: Oxford University Press, 1990), 359.

75 Escudier to Perrin, 17 July 1865, in Günther, 'La genèse' (1972), 24. The reference to *Le Prophète* is not fortuitous: it was the outstanding success at the Opéra during Verdi's first extended stay in Paris, and taught him much about French taste.

76 Gartioux (ed.), *Giuseppe Verdi*, reveals the warm reception of this finale at the première.

77 Verdi wrote to Giulio Ricordi that the third-act finale was 'without doubt the best thing in the opera': Budden, *The Operas of Verdi*, III, 119. It was praised even by those who had grave misgivings about the opera as a whole; for example Eugène Tarbé remarked,

'This scene . . . is admirable from beginning to end. It is an immense number which will ensure in itself the immortality of *Don Carlos*; it is a stunning example of skill and inspiration . . . it presents a world in movement, seething with every passion, every pain . . .' (*Le Figaro*, 17 March 1867, in Gartioux (ed.), *Giuseppe Verdi*, 29).

78 In addition to items previously cited, see Joseph Kerman, 'Verdi's Use of Recurring Themes', in *Studies in Music History: Essays for Oliver Strunk*, ed. Harold Powers (Princeton: Princeton University Press, 1968), 495–510, and for an introduction to the French heritage, Robert T. Laudon, *Sources of the Wagnerian Synthesis: A Study of the Franco-German Tradition in Nineteenth-Century Opera* (Salzburg: Katzbichler, 1979).

79 In Act II the prayer continues with repetitions and extensions; in Act V only the opening is cited. The apparent augmentation in Act V is, in fact, a notation to make the rhythm the same: in Act II the tempo is *andante sostenuto assai* ($\downarrow = 72$), whereas in Act V it is *allegro* ($\downarrow = 144$).

80 See Frits R. Noske, 'From Idea to Sound: Philip's Monologue in Verdi's "Don Carlos"', *Studi verdiani*, 10 (1994–95), 76–92, here 78–9, and Budden, *The Operas of Verdi*, III, 120–1.

81 I.e. three short notes followed by one longer: Frits Noske, 'The Musical Figure of Death', in his *The Signifier and the Signified. Studies in the Operas of Mozart and Verdi* (The Hague: Martinus Nijhoff, 1977), 171–214, here 202ff.

82 Budden, *The Operas of Verdi*, III, 125 and his preceding analysis of this scene.

83 Giuseppina Verdi (née Strepponi) to Mauro Corticelli, 7 December 1866: Alberti, *Verdi intimo*, 113, cited in the trans. of Osborne, *Verdi*, 194.

84 Günther, 'La genèse' (1972), 49 and (1974), 129. Their progress was reported to the public, in sometimes heroic-Romantic terms: 'The composer is tall . . . with shoulders like those of Atlas . . . His appearance is proud and manly, his attitude that of a defiant opponent . . . Verdi listens . . . His sense of hearing is doubly, triply, acute. He questions everything. In this tumultuous harmony he can hear the quietest of notes. He can hear everything simultaneously: the chorus, the brass, the aria, and everything that happens on and off the stage. He stands, leaps about, valiantly spurring on all these groups, shouting in an Italian accent which gives a certain charm to

his speech' (Jules Claretie in *Le Figaro*, 17 February 1867, mostly trans. in Osborne, *Verdi*, 194–5).

85 Pierre Véron, *Le Journal amusant*, 16 March 1867, in Gartioux (ed.), *Giuseppe Verdi*, 57–8. For other examples see *ibid.* and Günther, 'Wagnerismen in Verdis *Don Carlos* von 1867?' in *Wagnerliteratur–Wagnerforschung*, ed. Carl Dahlhaus and Egon Voss (Mainz: Schott, 1985), 101–08. The assumption that Italians were masters of natural, seemingly effortless melody while Germans excelled in harmonic complications, especially evident in dominant orchestral writing, was a constant trope in French music criticism for a century.

86 Verdi to Escudier, 1 April 1867: Alberti, *Verdi intimo*, 131, trans. in Osborne, *Verdi*, 197.

87 See the entries in Alfred Loewenberg, *Annals of Opera 1597–1940*, 3rd edn, rev. Frank Walker (London: J. Calder, 1978).

88 See his letter of 26 May 1844, cited by Harris-Warrick, ed., 'Introduzione storica', *Gaetano Donizetti: La favorite*, xxix.

89 Julian Budden notes that in addition to Bassi's 'wretched translation', the resources required, even without the ballet, exceeded most Italian theatres; *I Lombardi* resonated in *Risorgimento* Italy; and, perhaps most importantly, Verdi set 'conditions which priced it out of the market'. *The Operas of Verdi*, I. *From* Oberto *to* Rigoletto (New York: Oxford University Press, 1973), 358. Still, *Gerusalemme* was given in Milan, Constantinople, Vienna, Alexandria, Algiers, Oporto, Seville, Buenos Aires, Paris and Sydney, according to Loewenberg, *Annals of Opera*, col. 831.

90 The account of the history of *Les Vêpres siciliennes* in Italy summarised here is indebted to Budden, *Operas of Verdi*, II, 238–39, which provides important corrections to Loewenberg, *Annals of Opera*, col. 918.

91 Verdi to Tito Ricordi, 6 July 1855; *ibid.*, 238, after Abbiati, *Giuseppe Verdi*, II, 297.

92 What follows is indebted to Budden, *Operas of Verdi*, III, 26–39, Günther, 'Prefazione/Vorwort', *Giuseppe Verdi: Don Carlos* [piano-vocal score], and Parker, '*Don Carlos*', *Grove Opera*. These sources detail Verdi's extensive revisions for his Italian versions.

93 Unlike the translation/minor adaptation approach of *Vêpres*: Verdi wrote no new music for *Vespri* for any Italian production. Rossini's 1840 Bologna finale for *Rodolfo di Sterlinga*, yet another transplantation of *Guillaume Tell*, was a reworking of one of his Paris revisions

for the three-act version, undertaken without the help of Bis or Jouy.

15 After 1850 at the Paris Opéra: institution and repertory

1 Review in *Gil-Blas*, 2 December 1885.

2 For a fine survey of the opera's literary sources see Jean-Claude Yon, 'Les Avatars du Cid', *L'Avant-scène opéra*, 161 (*Panurge, Le Cid*, 1994), 112–19.

3 Annegret Fauser has perceptively written of an 'aura of authenticity' produced by such passages in Thomas's *Hamlet*: 'Hamlet', in *Pipers Enzyklopädie des Musiktheaters*, ed. Carl Dahlhaus and Sieghart Döhring, 7 vols. (Munich: Piper, 1986–97), VI, 287.

4 Review by 'M.B.', *L'Indépendance*, 1 December 1885.

5 See Steven Huebner, *The Operas of Charles Gounod* (Oxford: Clarendon Press, 1990), 104–19.

6 Reported by 'Un monsieur de l'orchestre' in 'La Soirée théâtrale', *Le Figaro*, 1 December 1885.

7 On this point see my *French Opera at the Fin de Siècle: Wagnerism, Nationalism, and Style* (Oxford: Oxford University Press, 1999), 49–51.

8 Hervé Lacombe has written of the development of an intimate 'poésie d'opéra' in the music of Gounod and his successors in *Les Voies de l'opéra français au XIXᵉ siècle* (Paris: Fayard, 1997), chap. 6; trans. as *The Keys to French Opera in the Nineteenth Century* (Berkeley: University of California Press, 2001).

9 The expression 'faire grand' plays an important role in a newspaper altercation that Roqueplan had with the critic Jules Janin over Halévy's *Le Juif errant*. Their exchange was published in a widely distributed pamphlet entitled *Critique du Juif errant: Roqueplan embêté par Jules Janin* (Paris, 1852).

10 David Charlton has posited that a substantial public dimension is not an essential feature of grand opera and identified a strain of the genre 'lacking an expression of public political interest' in 'On the Nature of "Grand Opera"', in *Hector Berlioz: Les Troyens*, ed. Ian Kemp (Cambridge: Cambridge University Press, 1988), 99. But several of the works he cites in this category, for example *Gustave III* and *L'Africaine*, have a very clearly articulated public–political dimension that intersects with themes of love. In *L'Africaine*, the colonial ambitions of Portugal provide the entire *raison d'être* for the plot as well as insight into the psychology of Vasco and his ultimate rejection of Sélika. Rather than

establish two categories – the political and the apolitical – it seems preferable to think of the relative balance between public and private: within a genre that as a rule accords considerable emphasis to the public realm, some works bring this more to the foreground while others must allot less time to this realm because of very complicated private intrigues. *Robert le Diable* is, however, relatively apolitical and exceptional within the context of grand opera; indeed, some might want to question whether it is a grand opera at all. On the other hand, a defence of the relevance of the term to *Robert* might begin with Herbert Lindenberger's observation that morality plays may be understood as a subset of conspiracy plays in the sense that the devil and other nefarious forces band together 'to tempt man away from God's path': *Historical Drama: The Relation of Literature and Reality* (Chicago: University of Chicago Press, 1975), 33.

11 A full and accurate account of the genesis of *Thaïs* is Patrick Gillis, 'Thaïs dans tous ses états: Genèse et remaniements', *L'Avant-scène opéra*, 109 (*Thaïs*, 1988), 66–74.

12 For a critical perspective on this generic designation see Huebner, *French Opera*, 152–9.

13 Review of *Thaïs*, *Le Figaro*, 17 March 1894.

14 Given the complexity of opera production (and its increasing internationalisation in the nineteenth century) the delineation of sub-genres such as grand opera will always be more thorny than the same critical task applied to, say, instrumental music. Anselm Gerhard writes that 'French grand opera is not an entirely self-sufficient genre, however: although there are many differences it remains too closely connected to its French precursors for that, and above all it is bound up with Italian and German opera of its own time.' *The Urbanization of Opera: Music Theater in Paris in the Nineteenth Century* (Chicago: University of Chicago Press, 1998), 10–11. But no genre or sub-genre, even an instrumental one, stands completely independent of other genres; that grand opera is *so intimately* connected to other operatic sub-genres is *in itself* a generic characteristic and a reminder that the tools and methods of genre analysis must be specially adapted to a polyvalent genre such as opera. Gerhard also rightly points out that the metaphor of generic birth–rise–decline is inappropriate to grand opera; I would add that it would be difficult to argue its appropriateness to any generic category.

15 Letter to Edouard Moullé, dated by editors to Sept. 1881 [?]: Emmanuel Chabrier, *Correspondance*, ed. Roger Delage, Frans Durif and Thierry Bodin (Paris: Klincksieck, 1994), 138.

16 Letter to Enoch and Costallat, dated by editors to early July 1881 [?]: Chabrier, *Correspondance*, 132.

17 'Les Reprises de l'Exposition', in *La Musique française* (Paris: Bibliothèque Charpentier, 1901), 202.

18 One impediment to further performance of some of the older repertory was a fire that occurred at the Opéra warehouse on the rue Richer in January 1894. The sets for *L'Africaine*, *Le Prophète*, *Robert le Diable* and *La Juive* were destroyed, although it should also be noted that so were those of *Le Cid* and *Patrie!* which (in addition to *Le Prophète*) did have pre-World War I revivals. See Marcel Rémy, 'L'Incendie des décors de l'Opéra', *Le Guide musical*, 14 January 1894.

19 For a description and social analysis of the popularity of Wagner at the Palais Garnier in this period see André Michael Spies, *Opera, State and Society in the Third Republic, 1875–1914* (New York: P. Lang, 1998), 81–90.

20 For an overview see Huebner, *French Opera*, 11–21.

21 Gerhard, *Urbanization*, 395–6.

22 Review of *Françoise de Rimini*: *La Renaissance musicale*, 7 May 1882.

23 Review of *Le Cid*: *Le Siècle*, 1 December 1885.

24 Review of *Patrie!*, *Le Ménestrel*, 26 December 1886. Pougin refers here to a forthcoming production of *Lohengrin* at the Eden-Théâtre in Paris. A. Landely wrote in his review of how he always preferred 'heroes of Rysoor's stamp, all *élan* and spontaneity, to those rugged Siegfrieds, nurtured in the rocky lairs of misty German lands': *L'Art musical*, 31 December 1886.

25 On this point see Gerhard, *Urbanization*, 388–95.

26 *Ibid.*, 394.

27 Bellaigue, 'Le Grand Opéra Français' (article written in 1906), in *Les Epoques de la musique* (Paris: Librairie Delagrave, n.d.), 201.

28 On Opéra audiences in this period see Frédérique Patureau, *Le Palais Garnier dans la société parisienne 1875–1914* (Liège: Mardaga, 1991), 297–388. On audiences from an earlier period see Huebner, 'Opera Audiences in Paris 1830–1870', *Music & Letters*, 70/2 (May 1989), 206–25.

29 On this event see Patureau, *Le Palais Garnier*, 22–3.

30 Rolland, *Musiciens d'aujourd'hui*, 10th edn (Paris: Hachette, 1922), 223, 225.

31 Refined taste of a different sort had of course been cultivated at the Théâtre Italien.

32 Guy de Maupassant's novel *Bel-Ami* (1885) is a famous illustration of press practices in this period.

33 Arno J. Mayer's *The Persistence of the Old Regime: Europe to the Great War* (New York: Pantheon, 1981) is a masterful survey of the commingling of elites in Europe.

34 On this point see Spies, *Opera, State and Society*, 53.

35 This took the form of arranging numerous performances at reduced prices in order to make the house more accessible. For a review of these largely unsuccessful attempts see Patureau, *Le Palais Garnier*, 389–430.

36 *Ibid.*, 406–7. Friday performances were the most prestigious. In a letter of 6 January 1897 Ernest Reyer once protested to Opéra director Eugène Bertrand that his *Sigurd* had been performed on three consecutive Mondays, 'the worst day of the week', and that he wished it to be given on a forthcoming Friday, the best day, in order to demonstrate that it could still make money: Paris, Archives nationales, Papiers Bertrand, ABxix 4128.

37 *Cahiers des charges* are kept at Archives nationales, AJ^{13} 1187.

38 Huebner, *Operas of Charles Gounod*, 223–50.

39 *Ibid.*, 203.

40 The genesis of the project extends back to 1879 when Saint-Saëns requested a scenario of the subject from Louis Gallet. The latter obliged, but the project lay dormant for ten years until Ernest Guiraud requested permission from Saint-Saëns to set it. When Guiraud died, Saint-Saëns took up a project that had been his to begin with: Hugues Imbert, review of *Frédégonde*, *Le Guide musical*, 22 December 1895.

41 See Huebner, *French Opera*, 213–16.

42 Saint-Saëns, 'L'histoire et la légende dans le drame lyrique', in *Ecole Buissonnière* (Paris: Lafitte, 1913), 109–20.

43 Huebner, *French Opera*, 195–212.

44 *Ecole Buissonnière*, 115. Schumann's strong attack on *Les Huguenots* dated from 1837 where it had appeared as 'Fragmente aus Leipzig, 4' in *Neue Zeitschrift für Musik*. It can be read in Fanny Raymond Ritter (trans. and ed.), *Music and Musicians: Essays and Criticisms by Robert Schumann* (London: William Reeves, 1877), 302–7.

45 *Ibid.*, 277–300.

46 These matters are more fully treated in Huebner, *French Opera*, 178–85.

47 Bruneau, *La Musique française* (Paris: E. Fasquelle, 1901), 78. A selection of the reviews of the Théâtre-Lyrique première is *Hector Berlioz: Les Troyens à Carthage: Dossier de presse parisienne (1863)*, ed. Frank Heidlberger ([Heilbronn]: Musik-Edition Lucie Galland, 1995); even at that time critics did not discuss the work as if it were a grand opera.

48 He argues the point convincingly in *Opera and Ideas: From Mozart to Strauss* (New York: Harper and Row, 1985), 101–51.

49 On this point see Kemp, *Les Troyens*, 7, where it is suggested that in reading his libretto to the Emperor in 1858, Berlioz might have hoped that a parallel would be drawn with Virgil writing the *Aeneid* for Augustus.

50 Kemp, *Les Troyens*, 89.

16 Richard Wagner and the legacy of French grand opera

1 Richard Wagner, 'Erinnerungen an Auber', in *Sämtliche Schriften und Dichtungen* [hereafter *SSD*], 16 vols. (Leipzig, 1911–16), IX, 55.

2 *Ibid.*, 44–5.

3 For a complete list of the operas Wagner is known to have rehearsed, conducted or attended as a young man between 1833 and 1839, see T. Grey, 'Musical Background and Influences', in *The Wagner Compendium*, ed. Barry Millington (London: Thames and Hudson, 1992), 69–70.

4 His first opera, *Die Feen*, after Carlo Gozzi's fable *La Donna serpente*, had taken Weber's *Euryanthe* and the operas of Marschner as a point of departure, although it already suggested something of the young composer's susceptibility to the scope and gestures of the new grand opera manner.

5 Wagner remarks on the 'grand' aspirations of his comic opera in the course of a lengthy account of *Das Liebesverbot* in his autobiography, *Mein Leben* ('My Life'), including his rash attempt to mount a production, under the most inauspicious of circumstances, at the end of his second season as music-director in Magdeburg. 'As the work was by no means a light musical comedy [*Singspiel*] but rather, despite the airy character of the music, a grand opera [*grosse Oper*] with many large and complex ensembles, this undertaking was close to foolhardy': *My Life*, trans. Andrew Gray (Cambridge: Cambridge University Press, 1983), 112.

6 'One seemed to have virtual musical pictures before one's eyes, and the concept of a musical "picturesque" might well find a foothold here, were it not even more appropriate to see in this a happy example of theatrical "sculpture" or relief' [*theatralischen Plastik*]: *SSD*, IX, 45.

7 Karin Pendle and Stephen Wilkins describe this scene of *La Muette* (III.2) as paradigmatic of the 'animated tableau' central to the aesthetic of grand opera. See 'Paradise Found: The Salle le Peletier and French Grand Opera', in *Opera in Context: Essays on Historical Staging from the Late Renaissance to the Time of Puccini*, ed. Mark A. Radice (Portland, OR: Amadeus Press, 1998), 171–207, here 184–8.

8 Issues of gesture and motivic recurrence (and signification) from Auber to Wagner are richly explored by Mary Ann Smart in *Resonant Bodies: Music and Gesture in Nineteenth-Century Opera* (Berkeley: University of California Press, 2001), esp. Chapters 1, 5 and 6.

9 'This career plan of mine', he adds characteristically, and quite irrelevantly, 'must be yours as well': letter of 27 October 1834, in *Sämtliche Briefe*, ed. Gertrud Strobel and Werner Wolf (in progress: Leipzig: VEB Deutscher Verlag für Musik, 1967–), I, 167–8.

10 Wagner, *Eine Mitteilung an meine Freunde [1852]*: *SSD*, IV, 185. The libretto he later worked out (see below) was in four rather than five acts.

11 Robert W. Gutman, *Richard Wagner: The Man, His Mind, and His Music* (New York, 1968), 59. A libretto by Scribe, Gutman notes, commanded as much as 20,000 francs at this time.

12 To give Wagner credit however, when he later worked up the scenario into a complete libretto himself, in the summer of 1842 (in high spirits over the forthcoming Dresden première of *Rienzi*), he offered the text *gratis* to his colleague C. G. Reissiger as a goodwill gesture. When Reissiger declined the offer – Wagner supposed him to be suspicious of a gift-horse coming from this particular Greek – it was offered to the German-Bohemian composer Friedrich Kittl and eventually reached the stage in Prague, on 19 February 1848, as *Bianca und Giuseppe, oder: Die Franzosen vor Nizza*. Dieter Borchmeyer examines the *Hohe Braut* project in the context of Wagner's preoccupation with the methods and historical subjects of grand opera in the 1830s in chapter 2 of *Ahasvers Wandlungen: Richard Wagner* (Frankfurt: Suhrkamp, 2002; translation forthcoming from Princeton University Press).

13 The draft scenario for *Die Sarazenin* is given in English translation in *Richard*

Wagner's Prose Works, ed. and trans. W. A. Ellis, 8 vols. (London: Kegan Paul & Co., 1892–99), VIII, 251–76. The full libretto text (1842) of *Die hohe Braut* is included in *SSD*, XII, 136–77.

14 Cf. *My Life*, 145–6, 149–50. *Rienzi* would never reach the stage of the Opéra, but only the Théâtre Lyrique in 1869, long after Wagner had repudiated his early ambitions in this direction.

15 The details of Wagner's Parisian arrangements are found in John Deathridge, Martin Geck and Egon Voss (eds.), *Wagner Werk-Verzeichnis* (Mainz: Schott, 1986), as WWV 62 (A–F). A different 'Wagner' (Paul) was doing similar arrangements at the same time in the same place.

16 'Es ist ein ganz anderer – wie viele sagen – neuer Genre': letter of 5 Jan. 1843 to Cäcilie Avenarius: *Sämtliche Briefe*, II, 203–4.

17 Hitler's early enthusiasm for *Rienzi* is discussed by Helmuth Weinland, 'Wagner zwischen Hegel und Hitler', in *Richard Wagner zwischen Beethoven und Schönberg*, ed. Heinz-Klaus Metzger and Rainer Riehn, Musik-Konzepte, 59 (Munich: edition text + kritik, 1988), 3–30, here 15. For a somewhat more free-wheeling account of the role of the opera in Hitler's development, see the first chapter of Joachim Köhler, *Wagner's Hitler: The Prophet and his Disciple*, trans. with an introduction by Ronald Taylor (Cambridge: Polity Press, 2000).

18 *Eine Mitteilung an meine Freunde* ('A Communication to my Friends'), in *SSD*, IV, 258–9.

19 *Ibid.*, 259. Wagner describes here the extensive dramatic pantomime composed to precede the formal ballet as such. This pantomime (see Chapter 8 and n. 3 for further details) was omitted from the abbreviated full score (though it exists in the later Breitkopf & Härtel piano-vocal score), and Wagner laments its omission from staged productions, precisely because it is more dramatically integral than the ensuing ballet. The latter by itself, he admits, gives the impression of 'routine operatic spectacle' (259n.)

20 He further rationalises that the tenuousness of his career at this point forced him into compromises which, under better circumstances, he might have avoided.

21 Wagner, 'Über Meyerbeers "Huguenotten" ', *SSD*, XII, 29–30. The essay seems to have been written some time between 1837 and 1840, though it was published only posthumously.

22 The conspiracy trio in Act IV of *Rienzi* shares the C♯ minor tonality of Meyerbeer's scene and the contrasts of *sotto voce* plotting with *fortissimo* exclamations of righteous anger and revenge (requisites of any 'conspiracy scene' from that point on). These contrasts are less elaborately plotted in Wagner's score than in *Les Huguenots*, however, and the printed full score leaves out much of the faster, louder material (*molto agitato*). Helmut Weinland compares the use of a signal-bell to interrupt the reverie of the love-torn protagonists in each opera: the shift to the last phase of Adriano's Act III aria in *Rienzi* and the interruption between Raoul's Cavatine and the 'Grand Duo' of Raoul and Valentine in Act IV of *Les Huguenots* (Weinland, 'Wagner und Meyerbeer', in *Richard Wagner zwischen Beethoven und Schönberg*, 31–72, here 47–50). It is unclear how well Wagner knew the *Huguenots* score before he got to Paris in 1839. Even if the *Rienzi* libretto had been conceived without direct knowledge of Scribe's for the *Huguenots*, the composition of the last three acts (in 1840) could still have reflected the impact of Meyerbeer's musical setting. An opera that Wagner *did* encounter just before starting *Rienzi* was Spontini's *Fernand Cortez*, which Anno Mungen cites as an influence on the structure and heroic-military colouring of Wagner's opera. See A. Mungen, 'Wagner, Spontini, und die grand opéra', in *Richard Wagner und seine 'Lehrmeister'*, ed. C.-H. Mahling and K. Pfarr (Mainz: Are Edition, 1999), 129–44.

23 On the pantomime, cf. n. 19 above. Wagner noted in *Mein Leben* that at the Dresden première the first two acts alone lasted as long as a complete performance of *Der Freischütz*. With each successive act he became increasingly panic-stricken that the audience would give up and leave in exhaustion. But instead (he reports with more than a little self-congratulation), they remained to cheer him *en masse* six hours later (*My Life*, 232).

24 Of course, last-act finales in grand opera generally eschewed the broad amplifications typical of central act finales in favour of a speedy and effective denouement.

25 In addition to the already cited (posthumous) essay on Meyerbeer's *Les Huguenots* (n. 21), this ideal of a cosmopolitan operatic synthesis, specifically as a solution to the tenuous position of German Romantic opera in the international canon, was articulated at the close of the essay

'On German Music' and in the feature on 'Halévy and the French Opera', published in the *Revue et gazette musicale* in 1840 and 1842 respectively, and already in Wagner's first published article, 'On German Opera': *Zeitung für die elegante Welt*, 10 June 1834. The texts of these can be found in *SSD*, I and XII, and *Richard Wagner's Prose Works*, VII and VIII.

26 Cited from Henry Pleasants' translation in *Vienna's Golden Years of Music, 1850–1900* (New York, 1950), 24.

27 *Oper und Drama*, Part 3, section 3 (*SSD*, IV, 152–5). The passage is translated in Grey, *Wagner's Musical Prose: Texts and Contexts* (Cambridge: Cambridge University Press, 1995), 375–7.

28 One might also say, along these lines, that in *Lohengrin* the visual spectacle that had always been a defining attribute of grand opera has been transposed 'into' the music, in the guise of a special emphasis on timbral and harmonic colouring and the association of such musical 'colour' with certain characters and situations. See T. Grey, 'Wagner's *Lohengrin*: Between *grand opéra* and *Musikdrama*', in *Richard Wagner: Lohengrin*, English National Opera Guides, 47, ed. Nicholas John (London: John Calder, 1993), 24–7 (section entitled 'The Dramaturgy of Musical "Colour"').

29 Letter to Franz Liszt of 18 April 1851: *Selected Letters of Richard Wagner*, trans. and ed. Stewart Spencer and Barry Millington (New York, 1988), 222.

30 *SSD*, III, 301–6. In the original German text, Wagner distinguishes Meyerbeerian *Effekt* (using the suspiciously 'foreign' word) from a genuine effect (*Wirkung*), the latter indicating a logical, necessary consequence of a legitimate 'cause' (a plausible dramatic *raison d'être*, in this case).

31 The one concession to Meyerbeer's talent in *Opera and Drama* regards this scene – although half the credit is given to Scribe: *SSD*, III, 306.

32 George Bernard Shaw pinpointed the 'regression' to grand opera within the *Ring* cycle in the final scene of *Siegfried*: 'The rest of what you are going to see is opera, and nothing but opera': *The Perfect Wagnerite* (London: Constable, 1923; rpt. New York, 1967), 54. Paradoxically, then, it was precisely the latest parts of the cycle to be composed (Act III of *Siegfried* and all of *Götterdämmerung*) that Shaw dismissed as dramatically 'backward', despite their sophistication of compositional technique.

33 Sieghart and Sabine Henze-Döhring compare the final catastrophic scenes of *Le Prophète* and *Götterdämmerung* in their book *Oper und Musikdrama im 19. Jahrhundert* (Laaber: Laaber-Verlag, 1997), 264–8. Their enthusiasm for Meyerbeer, however, encourages what is certainly a misreading (262) of Wagner's ironising reaction to *Le Prophète* in Paris in 1850 (in a letter to Theodor Uhlig of 13 March 1850). Another letter, to Ferdinand Heine on 14 September 1850, clearly refutes the Döhrings' non-ironic reading of the Uhlig letter (if the publication of 'Judaism in Music' the preceding month were not evidence enough).

34 Cf. n. 18 above.

35 Gutman, *Richard Wagner*, 154. (The reference is to the location of the Opéra at the time Wagner knew it.) Gutman is speaking here of Wagner's theatrical aesthetic more broadly (as one of pomp, spectacle, and 'realistic' historical staging), rather than of specific issues of dramaturgy or musical style.

36 'Über die Benennung "Musikdrama"': *SSD*, IX, 307; *Richard Wagner's Prose Works*, V.

37 Gutman, *Richard Wagner*, 292.

38 *Ibid.*, 185.

39 See, for example, Pendle and Wilkins, 'Paradise Found', 171–208, here 182–3.

17 Grand opera in Russia: fragments of an unwritten history

1 Cavos's *Ivan Susanin* is not to be confused with the opera known to Soviet audiences under the same title; this latter was a politically necessitated revision of *A Life for the Tsar*, expunged of the Tsarist sympathies evident in title and plot alike.

2 There are no comprehensive performance statistics on Russian opera presently available (although see n. 4, below), but useful, if partial, information is to be found in reliable sources.

3 Stasov coined the catchphrase *moguchaya kuchka* ('Mighty Handful') in 1867 for 'The Five', later also called 'The Balakirev Circle', consisting of Alexander Borodin (1833–87), César Cui (1835–1918), Mily Balakirev (1836/7–1910), Modest Musorgsky (1839–81) and Nikolay Rimsky-Korsakov (1844–1908).

4 Abram Akimovich Gozenpud (*b.* 1908), *Muzïkal'nïy teatr v Rossii: ot istokov do Glinki* (Leningrad: GMI, 1959); *Russkiy opernïy teatr XIX-go veka*, I: *1836–56* (Leningrad: Muzïka, 1969); *Russkiy opernïy teatr XIX-go veka*, II: *1857–72* (Leningrad: Muzïka, 1971); *Russkiy opernïy teatr XIX-go veka*, III: *1873–1889* (Leningrad: Muzïka, 1973); *Russkiy opernïy*

teatr na rubezhe XIX–XX vekov i F. I. Shalyapin (1890–1904) (Leningrad: Muzïka, 1974); *Russkiy opernïy teatr mezhdu dvukh revolyutsiy, 1905–1917* (Leningrad: Muzïka, 1975); *Russkiy sovetskiy opernïy teatr, 1917–1941* (Leningrad: GMI, 1963). See his biography and selective writings listed in *New Grove/2*.

5 Unfortunately Gozenpud's work lacks the full scholarly apparatus required by present-day standards in the West; it is to be hoped that Gozenpud's research materials will be made available to scholars so that his sometimes sketchy information on sources can be supplemented (at the time of writing, Gozenpud is still alive).

6 Gozenpud, *Russkiy opernïy teatr XIX veka, 1836–56*, 305.

7 N. Gogol, 'Peterburgskiye zapiski 1836 goda', *Sobraniye sochineniy v shetsi tomakh*, VI (Moscow: Gosudarstvennoye izdatel'stvo khudozhestvennoy literaturï, 1953), 113.

8 Anonymous article 'Nechto o Bol'shom teatre', *Literaturnaya gazeta*, 39 (1844), reproduced in Gozenpud, *Russkiy opernïy teatr XIX-go veka, 1836–1856*, 38.

9 A. Grigor'yev, 'Robert-d'yavol', *Repertuar i Panteon*, 1846, vol. 13, Book 1, 255; quoted in Gozenpud, *Russkiy opernïy teatr XIX-go veka, 1836–1856*, 88.

10 Quoted in *Istoriya russkoy muzïki*, V (Moscow: Muzïka, 1988), 291.

11 Quoted in *ibid.*, 28.

12 More information on the competition between native and foreign companies can be found in Richard Taruskin's essay 'Ital'yanshchina', in *Defining Russia Musically* (Princeton: Princeton University Press, 1997), 186–236.

13 In a curious reversal of this situation after the 1917 Revolution, there was a short period when French grand operas were valued precisely for their political associations. Since no operas with Soviet subject matter existed prior to 1925, the Soviet Government considered *Fenella* suitable fare for the celebrations surrounding the first anniversary of the Revolution (produced by the former Mariinsky Theatre, now renamed GATOB). *Les Huguenots* and *Le Prophète* were also revived at the time, but with their libretti modernised for propaganda value. *Les Huguenots* thus became *The Decembrists*, set in Russia in 1825, with Saint-Bris transformed into Nicholas I.

14 Gozenpud, *Russkiy opernïy teatr XIX-go veka*, 182. If the incident occurred within two years of the première, the tsar in question was Nicholas I, but if later, then Alexander II; the date is not specified.

15 Ts. A. Kyui [C. A. Cui], 'Russkaya opera', first published in *Sankt-Peterburgskiye vedomosti*, 261 (22 September 1875), signed ***; repr. in *Izbrannïye stat'yi*, ed. Y. A. Kremlyov (Leningrad: Gosudarstvennoye musïkal' noye izdatel'stvo, 1952), 183–9, here 185.

16 Ts. A. Kyui, 'Neskol'ko vïvodov', first published in *Sankt-Peterburgskiye vedomosti*, 73 (15 March 1869), repr. in *Izbrannïye stat'yi*, 147–54, here 148.

17 V. V. Stasov, 'Tormozï novogo russkogo iskusstva', *Stat'yi o muzïke*, ed. V. Protopopov, 5 vols. (Moscow: Muzïka, 1974–80), III, 264. Stasov claimed that the Russian public now favoured *La Traviata, Il Trovatore, Aida* and *Faust*; since the last two follow many conventions of grand opera, the change owed more to the musical content than the generic framework.

18 Mikhail Ivanov, although a contemporary of Stasov, had none of the latter's fear of admitting the many foreign influences upon Russian composers; he readily declared, therefore, that Glinka 'made use of grand opera forms' in both his operas, and also saw the character of Susanin as a successor to Guillaume Tell and Masaniello. See M. M. Ivanov, *Istoriya muzïkal'nogo razvitiya Rossii v 2-kh tomakh*, 2 vols. (St Petersburg: Suvorin, 1910–12), I, 280–95.

19 Stasov, 'Iskusstvo XIX veka', *Stat'yi o muzïke*, vol. Vb, 66. For Stasov, however, *Ruslan* was always the more important of the two works; he might have been more reluctant to make a similar admission with respect to this work.

20 M. I. Zheleznov's memoirs, quoted in M. I. Glinka, *Literaturnïye proizvedeniya i perepiska*, I (Moscow: Muzïka, 1973), 423.

21 Glinka, 'Zametki ob instrumentovke', *Literaturnïye proizvedeniya i perepiska*, I, 183.

22 Gozenpud, *Russkiy opernïy teatr XIX-go veka*, 51.

23 Stasov, 'Arkheologicheskaya zametka of postanovke *Rognedï*', *Stat'yi o muzïke*, II, 65–9. Stasov went on to advise Musorgsky concerning both *Boris Godunov* and *Khovanshchina* as well as several other well-known operas.

24 Stasov, 'Iskusstvo XIX veka', *Stat'yi o muzïke*, Vb, 9–105, here 68.

25 Ts. A. Kyui [Cui], 'Muzïkal'naya deyatel'nost' Meyerbera', signed***, *Sankt-Peterburgskiye vedomosti*, 98 (25 May 1864), ed. in Kyui, *Izbrannïye stat'yi*, 23–8, here 25.

26 Stasov, 'Verit' li?', Eng. trans. by R. Taruskin in *Opera and Drama in Russia as*

Preached and Practiced in the 1860s (Ann
Arbor: UMI Research Press, 1981), 130–1.
27 Stasov, 'Verit' li?', *Stat'yi o muzïke*, II, 79.
28 Musorgsky's letter to Arseny
Golenishchev-Kutuzov, 15/27 August 1877;
see M. P. Musorgsky, *Pis'ma* (Moscow:
Muzïka, 1984), 245.
29 The idea of commissioning a collective
work also seems to have come to Gedeonov
from French soil, where the tradition of
collective composition flourished in the late
eighteenth and early nineteenth centuries; the
most extreme example was *La Marquise de
Brinvilliers* (1831), the work of no less than
nine composers including Auber, Boieldieu
and Cherubini. As it happens, *Mlada*'s plot
can also be traced to France, since it closely
resembles one of Filippo Taglioni's ballet
plots. See Gozenpud, *Russkiy opernïy teatr na
rubezhe XIX–XX vekov i F. I. Shalyapin
(1890–1904)*, 84.
30 Four of Alexey Verstovsky's six completed
operas are based on a mixture of history and
legend from the Kievan Rus era (*c.* 882–*c.*
1169), and often pivot around a conflict
between Christians and pagans; these are the
dialogue operas, *Vadim* (1832, the part of the
main character is spoken), *Askold's Tomb*
(1835), *A Waking Dream, or Churov Valley*
(1844), and the only all-sung opera,
Gromoboy (1857).
31 *Néron* was commissioned by the Paris
Opéra, as a setting of a pre-existing libretto
by Jules Barbier. For reasons that remain
obscure, it was never produced in Paris, but
instead received its première in Hamburg
(1879), when it was praised by von Bülow as a
successful example of a non-Wagnerian
opera.
32 Tchaikovsky used Zhukovsky's translation
of Schiller's drama *Die Jungfrau von Orleans*, as
well as French versions of the story by Jules
Barbier (the play *Jeanne d'Arc*, 1873) and
Auguste Mermet (the opera *Jeanne d'Arc*, to
his own libretto, Opéra, 1876). However, the
role of Thibaut in the drama is entirely
Tchaikovsky's own invention.
33 N. A. Rimsky-Korsakov, *Letopis' moyey
muzïkal'noy zhizni* (Moscow: Muzïka, 1972),
279.
34 I. S. Zil'bersheyn and V. A. Samkov (eds.),
Sergei Dyagilev i russkoye iskusstvo, I (Moscow:
Izobrazitel'noye iskusstvo, 1982), 421.
35 *Ibid.*, 205–6.

18 Grand opera among the Czechs
1 All Czech opera titles are given in English
with the Czech title following the first

citation. All genre designations are taken,
where possible, from contemporary
published vocal scores or as they were
advertised on the posters of premières.
Although the term '*zpěvohra*' (literally 'sung
play', i.e. Singspiel) was used routinely as an
alternative to 'opera' on posters and in scores,
for the purposes of this chapter '*zpěvohra*' will
be translated as 'opera'.
2 The Prague National Theatre (Královské
zemské české a národní divadlo [the Royal
Provincial Czech National Theatre]) was
open briefly from 11 to 23 June 1881 giving
five performances of Smetana's Festival
Opera *Libuše*, intended for the opening of the
theatre, and two of Meyerbeer's *Les
Huguenots*. The major part of the building
was burnt down on the night of 12 August
and the theatre reopened slightly over two
years later on 18 November 1883, to the day
the twenty-first anniversary of the opening of
the Provisional Theatre (18 November 1862).
3 This was given on 8 October 1882, a little
over a year before the theatre closed to make
way for the rebuilt National Theatre. It ran for
a spectacular, in Czech terms, five consecutive
performances followed by two more before
the end of the year: see Jan Smaczny, 'The
Daily Repertoire of the Provisional Theatre in
Prague', *Miscellanea musicologica*, 34 (1994),
9–139, here 109; the 1884 performances were
of a revised version of the opera.
4 The relative figures concerning the most
popular operas are informative: Smetana's
Dalibor (premièred 1868) was given 103
times, *Libuše* (premièred 1881), 71 and
Dimitrij, 63; in total Fibich's *The Bride of
Messina* was given sixteen times.
5 Smetana's *Libuše* was written in 1869–72 as
a coronation opera: but when Franz Joseph
turned down the Bohemian crown the opera
served to inaugurate the National Theatre. In
spite of its dignified demeanour and unique
aim as a festival opera, it was not designed
specifically as a 'reform' work.
6 An excellent digest of Hostinský's activities
is given in John Tyrrell, *Czech Opera*
(Cambridge: Cambridge University Press,
1988), 112–14.
7 When Hostinský discussed *Dimitrij* as part
of a more general survey of Dvořák's operatic
works in the context of the Czech national
revival, the question of the Smetana
succession, with Fibich as the chosen heir,
occupied much of the discussion: *Dimitrij* was
seen as being firmly in the Meyerbeer line by
comparison with works such as Smetana's
Libuše (*The Bride of Messina* is not mentioned).

His extended article is the major progenitor of the notion that the Smetana–Fibich line represented the progressives and that Dvořák was, as a composer of absolute music, the drag on the tendency. See *Antonín Dvořák ve vývoji naší dramatické hudby* (Prague, 1908), 12–15, reprinted in Boleslav Kalenský (ed.), *Antonín Dvořák: Sborník statí o jeho díle a životě* [Antonín Dvořák: A Collection of Essays about his Life and Work] (Prague: Umělecká Beseda, 1912), 208–26. Zdeněk Nejedlý, to an extent Hostinský's successor in developing the idea of a line of descent in Czech opera, considered *Dimitrij* to be Dvořák's most 'regressive' work (Zdeněk Nejedlý, *Zdenko Fibich: zakladatel scénického melodramatu* [Zdenko Fibich: The Founder of Scenic Melodrama] (Prague: Roman Nejedlý, 1901), 172.

8 In the twenty-one-year history of the Provisional Theatre, *Dalibor*, which Smetana said he considered his most important score, was given complete only fifteen times, fewer than *The Brandenburgers in Bohemia* (27), *The Bartered Bride* (116), *The Two Widows* (19), *The Kiss* (46) and *The Secret* (25); *Libuše* (11) and *The Devil's Wall* (5) had only two and four years respectively to make their mark before the second opening of the National Theatre in 1884 while *Dalibor* had fifteen (see Smaczny, 'Daily Repertoire', 137). Performances of *Dalibor* increased considerably towards the end of the nineteenth century and in the first twenty years of the twentieth (see Hana Konečná, *Soupis repertoáru Národního divadla v Praze 1881–1983* [List of Repertory of the Prague National Theatre 1881–1983] (Prague: Národní divadlo, 1983)), perhaps indicating greater sophistication among audiences. In addition, the company of the Provisional Theatre had been unable to provide a suitably heroic tenor for the title role. For a comparative table of the most frequently performed operas in the Provisional and National Theatres, see Tyrrell, *Czech Opera*, 40.

9 See Hostinský, *Antonín Dvořák*, 13.

10 See Zdeněk Nejedlý, *Dějiny opery Národního divadla* [The History of Opera in the National Theatre], 2nd edn, 2 vols. (Prague: Práce, 1949), I, 367.

11 Reviews in *Divadelní listy* [Theatre Pages], 3/36 (1882), 290 and *Dalibor*, 4/27 (1882), 214.

12 In fact *La Vestale* was enough of a favourite in Prague in the first half of the nineteenth century for the overture and an aria to feature at the head of at least two 'quodlibet'

evenings, on 14 December 1834 and 1 December 1840, for the actor Josef Grabniger and the conductor František Škroup respectively: J. Vondráček, *Dějiny českého divadla: doba předbřeznová 1824–1846* [The History of Czech Theatre: The Period Before the March Revolution 1824–1846] (Prague: Orbis, 1957), 79 and 144.

13 Josef Krasoslav Chmelenský (1800–39), also the librettist of the 'first' Czech opera, František Škroup's *The Tinker* (*Dráteník*) was, as the January 1826 edition of the Viennese *Theaterzeitung* noted, both assiduous and brisk in translating foreign operas into Czech at this stage (see Vondráček, *Dějiny*, 28–9).

14 Méhul's *Joseph* was given four times in the Provisional Theatre; though *Les Deux journées* was given only twice in the Provisional Theatre, some indication of its significance can be gauged from the fact that these were also the first two performances of any opera in the Theatre: Smaczny, 'Daily Repertoire', 11 and 115.

15 Méhul's *Joseph* was the first opera to be given complete in Czech, in Brno in 1839; even after this, opera in Czech was virtually unknown until Moravia opened its own Provisional Czech National Theatre: Tyrrell, *Czech Opera*, 57.

16 Première in Czech translation: Prague, Estates Theatre, 6 January 1854.

17 Built by Count Nostitz and opened in 1783 as the Count Nostitz National Theatre (Gräflich Nostizsches Nationaltheater), and for which Mozart wrote *Don Giovanni* and *La Clemenza di Tito*, it had various incarnations. Nostitz sold it to the Bohemian Estates in 1789 after which it was known as the Royal Theatre of the Estates (Königliches Ständestheater). For much of the nineteenth century it was the main stage for plays and opera in German, and after 1824 until the opening of the Provisional Theatre, a large number of performances in Czech took place; in 1888 it ceded its primacy for performances in German to the larger New German Theatre (Neues Deutsches Theater). After the Second World War it was known as the Smetana Theatre and from 1992 the State Opera of Prague. For a full account of Prague theatres pre-1990 see Tyrrell, *Czech Opera*, 13–59.

18 Tyrrell, *Czech Opera*, 21.

19 Otakar Nový's *Národní divadlo 1883–1983* [The National Theatre 1883–1983] (Prague: Národní divadlo, 1983) gives a lively account of the building and its precursor.

20 From an interview in the Viennese newspaper, *Die Reichswehr*, 1 March 1904;

partially reprinted in O. Šourek, *Dvořák ve vzpomínkách a dopisech* [Dvorák in Letters and Reminiscences] (Prague: Topič, 1938), 180–1.

21 From a reminiscence: Otakar Mařák, 'Mé vzpomínky na Ant. Dvořáka' [My Memories of Antonín Dvořák], *Divadlo* (1929) partially reprinted in Šourek, *Dvořák*, 177–8. The performance referred to was the première of a new production of *Les Huguenots* given on 26 April 1903 in which Mařák took the role of Raoul.

22 In numerous reviews for *Národní listy* for which Smetana wrote between May 1864 and April 1865 (reprinted in V. H. Jarka, *Kritické dílo Bedřicha Smetany* [The Critical Writings of Bedřich Smetana] (Prague: Pražská akciová tiskárna, 1948). Smetana's view is also echoed by later commentators including John Clapham in his Master Musicians study, *Smetana* (London: Dent, 1972), 34.

23 Tyrrell, *Czech Opera*, 34.

24 All figures are derived from Smaczny, 'Daily Repertoire'.

25 *Národní listy*, 16 July 1864; repr. in Jarka, *Kritické dílo*, 90–1. In fact, Smetana mistakenly described the Vaccai opera as *I Capuleti e i Montecchi*, the Bellini opera on the same subject which was in the repertory of the Provisional Theatre and whose finale, as was common throughout Europe in the nineteenth century, was replaced by that of Vaccai's opera.

26 Theatre poster of 16 October 1864 (Theatre Centre of the National Museum, Prague). On this particular occasion, the performance was enhanced by two guest acrobats from the Cirque Napoléon in Paris.

27 Interview in the *Sunday Times* (10 May 1885) repr. in David Beveridge (ed.), *Rethinking Dvořák: Views from Five Countries* (Oxford: Clarendon Press, 1996), 281–8.

28 Adolf Čech, *Z mých divadelních pamětí* [From My Theatre Memories] (Prague: Urbánek, 1903), 94.

29 See Tyrrell, *Czech Opera*, 104; also Marta Ottlová, 'K problematice české historické opery 19. století' [Towards Problems of Czech Historical Operas in the Nineteenth Century], *Hudební rozhledy*, 34 (1981), 169–72.

30 Sabina, a radical, may have been influenced by an unfinished play by J. K. Tyl called *The Expulsion of the Brandenburgers* [Zapuzení Braniborů] whose prime focus is the populace rather than individuals: Brian Large, *Smetana* (London: Faber and Faber, 1970), 146–7.

31 Tyrrell, *Czech Opera*, 1.

32 Tyrrell notes that the poet and folklorist, Karel Jaromir Erben, described the town rabble as 'communists of the basest sort': Tyrrell, *Czech Opera*, 159, quoting Petr Daněk and Jana Vysohlídová, 'Dokumenty k operní soutěži o cenu hraběte Harracha' [Documents Concerning the Operatic Prize Competition of Count Harrach], *Miscellanea musicologica*, 30 (1983), 147–75.

33 In fact, this expressive number anticipates by nearly ten years the main theme from Smetana's *Vltava*.

34 On the theatre poster (Theatre Centre of the National Museum, Prague) the description is 'vel. nár. op.' (velká národní opera). Other contemporary sources describe it as a 'grand romantic opera' (velká romantická opera): Tyrrell, *Czech Opera*, 326.

35 Tyrrell, *Czech Opera*, 135.

36 The first two acts were published in Prague in 1874, entitled 'grand opera' (veliká opera), and the remaining three in 1880. This was the first serious Czech opera to be published in vocal score and only the second after *The Bartered Bride*.

37 Much was made on the poster of new decorative sets for the first two acts.

38 Milan Pospíšil, 'Meyerbeer und die tschechische Oper des 19. Jahrhunderts', in *Meyerbeer und das europäischer Musiktheater*, ed. Sieghart Döhring and Arnold Jacobshagen (Laaber: Laaber-Verlag, 1998), 407–41.

39 Vituperative and tortured polemics surrounded the reception of *Dalibor*: John Clapham, 'The Smetana–Pivoda Controversy', *Music & Letters*, 52/4 (1971), 353–64.

40 Repr. in František Bartoš, *Smetana ve vzpomínkách a dopisech* [Smetana in Reminiscences and Letters] (Prague: Topič, 1939), 153–4. Halévy's Ahasuerus opera is discussed in Chapter 13.

41 Alan Houtchens makes this point in his excellent doctoral dissertation, 'A Critical Study of Antonín Dvořák's *Vanda*', University of California, Santa Barbara (1987), see esp. Chapter 1, sec. 4, 'Wave of Slavic Nationalism', 17–45. Additionally, both Czech librettists, Václav Beneš-Šumavský and František Zakrejs, were sympathetic to their national cause.

42 For a succinct, perceptive account of the trajectory of the Czech national revival, including a consideration of the impact of humanist philosophers such as Herder, see René Wellek (ed.), Peter Kussi (trans.), *The Meaning of Czech History, by Tomáš G. Masaryk* (Chapel Hill: University of North Carolina, 1974).

43 Alec Robertson, *Dvořák* (London: Dent, 1945), 130; Hans-Hubert Schönzeler, *Dvořák* (London: Marion Boyars, 1984), 47–8; even John Clapham, basing his judgement on Šourek, was decidedly lukewarm about the opera: *Dvořák: Musician and Craftsman* (London: Faber and Faber, 1966), 272–3.

44 Hostinský, *Antonín Dvořák*, 12. A recent recording of the opera gives some idea of the virtues of this remarkable score (*Wanda*: Prague Chamber Choir, WDR Radio Choir/ Symphony Orchestra, Cologne, cond. Gerd Albrecht: Orfeo C149 003 F).

45 A comprehensive critical edition by Milan Pospíšil still awaits publication.

46 Figures in this paragraph from Tyrrell, *Czech Opera*, 40.

47 A more detailed examination of the relationship between *Vanda* and *Armida* is in Smaczny, '*Vanda* and *Armida*, a Grand-Operatic Sisterhood', in *Rethinking Dvořák*, ed. Beveridge, 81–97.

19 Italian opera

1 *Crepuscolo* means 'twilight'; the Italian trilogy thus alludes to Wagner's *Götterdämmerung*, first performed in 1876.

2 A *pezzo concertato* (concerted piece) is defined in *Grove Opera*, III, 989, as 'A large ensemble of soloists and chorus generally to be found as the second movement of a central finale, to which it forms the lyrical climax', whether slow or fast; they sometimes begin canonically with soloists, but are sometimes choral from the start.

3 See Luca Zoppelli, '*I Medici* e Wagner', in *Ruggero Leoncavallo nel suo tempo. Atti del 1° Convegno internazionale di studi su Ruggero Leoncavallo*, ed. Jürgen Maehder and Lorenza Guiot (Milan: Sonzogno, 1993), 149–62; idem, 'The Twilight of the True Gods: *Cristoforo Colombo*, *I Medici* and the Construction of Italian History', *Cambridge Opera Journal*, 8/3 (1996), 251–69; Jürgen Maehder, '*I Medici* e l'immagine del Rinascimento italiano nella letteratura del decadentismo europeo', in *Nazionalismo e cosmopolitismo nell'opera fra '800 e '900. Atti del 3° Convegno Internazionale 'Ruggero Leoncavallo nel suo tempo*', ed. Jürgen Maehder and Lorenza Guiot (Milan: Sonzogno, 1998), 239–60; Alan Mallach, 'Alberto Franchetti e la sua opera *Cristoforo Colombo*', *Nuovo Rivista Musicale Italiana*, 26/2 (1992), 193–211.

4 Ippolito Valetta, 'Rassegna musicale', *Nuova Antologia*, 157 (16 January 1898), 360–1.

5 Marcello Conati, ' "L'oltracotata turba che s'indraca". Inforestieramenti dell'opera italiana nel secondo Ottocento', in *Musica senza aggettivi. Studi per Fedele d'Amico*, ed. Agostino Ziino, 2 vols. (Florence: Olschki, 1991), I, 345–53, here 349.

6 A 'characteristic' piece is one designed to evoke a particular geographical, historical and cultural locale, for example, by using folk-like material. See Chapter 6, 'Dance and dancers'.

7 For this reversal of perspective, see Giovanni Morelli, 'Il bello della *Gioconda*', in the programme-book for the opera given at La Scala, Milan (1997), 47–83, here 73. On *Gioconda* and Decadent opera see Maehder, 'Szenische Imagination und Stoffwahle in der italienischen Oper des Fin de siècle', in *Italienische Oper im 18. und 19. Jahrhundert*, ed. Maehder and J. Stenzl (Bern: Lang, 1994), 187–248.

8 For the ideology of the post-Verdian libretto see Luigi Baldacci, *Dopo Verdi* (1974), reissued in idem, *La musica in italiano. Libretti d'opera dell'Ottocento* (Milan: Rizzoli, 1997), 118–39.

9 See *Grove Opera*, IV, 199: '*Scapigliatura*' ('bohemianism') refers to the artists themselves, to the 'period of renewal in Italian culture' between 1860 and 1880, and also to 'a literary trend that opened the way to *verismo* while anticipating some features of the *fin-de-siècle* decadent movement'. For Boito and the Scapigliatura, see Guido Salvetti, 'La Scapigliatura milanese e il teatro d'opera', in *Il melodramma italiano dell'Ottocento. Studi e ricerche per Massimo Mila* (Turin: Einaudi, 1977), 567–604; idem, 'Dal Verdi della maturità a Giacomo Puccini', in *Musica in scena. Storia dello spettacolo musicale*, ed. Alberto Basso, 6 vols. (Turin: Unione tipografico-editrice torinese, *c.* 1995–97), II (Gli Italiani all'estero. L'opera in Italia e in Francia), 370–401; Paolo Rossini, 'Il teatro musicale di Arrigo Boito', in *Arrigo Boito, musicista e letterato*, ed. Giampiero Tintori (Milan: Nuove edizioni, 1986), 39; and, importantly, Adriana Guarnieri Corazzol, 'Scapigliatura e Décadence', in *Musica e letteratura in Italia tra Ottocento e Novecento* (Milan: Sansoni, 2000), 7–127.

10 See Anselm Gerhard, *Die Verstädterung der Oper. Paris und das Musiktheater des 19. Jahrhunderts* (Stuttgart: J. B. Metzler and Carl Ernst Poeschel, 1992); trans. as *The Urbanization of Opera: Music Theater in Paris in the Nineteenth Century* (Chicago: University of Chicago Press, 1998), esp. 402–8; Stéphane Wolff, *L'Opéra au Palais Garnier (1875–1962)* (Paris, 1962; repr. Paris: Slatkine, 1983), 147.

11 See Michael Faure, 'Du nationalisme dans les théâtres lyriques parisiens entre 1875 et 1925', in *Nazionalismo e cosmopolitismo*, ed. Maehder and Guiot (see n. 3 above), 79–97.

12 Filippo Filippi, *Meyerbeer, Studii critico-biografici* [1864], in *Musica e musicisti. Critiche. Biografie ed escursioni* (Milan: Brigola, 1876), 161. On the circulation of the first grand operas by Meyerbeer, see Fiamma Nicolodi, 'Meyerbeer e il grand-opéra a Firenze', *Quaderni di teatro*, 9/36 (May 1987), 80–98; partially abridged as 'Il grand-opéra di Meyerbeer in Italia: da fenomeno elitario a spettacolo di massa', in *Orizzonti musicali italo-europei, 1860–1980* (Rome: Bulzoni, 1990), 43–75. Especially valuable are Fabrizio Della Seta, 'L'immagine di Meyerbeer nella critica italiana dell'Ottocento e l'idea di "dramma musicale" ', in *L'opera tra Venezia e Parigi*, ed. Maria Teresa Muraro, 2 vols. (Florence: Olschki, 1988), I, 147–76; Della Seta, *Italia e Francia nell'Ottocento* (Turin: E.D.T., 1993), 277ff.; Alessandro Roccatagliati, 'Opera, opera-ballo e *grand opéra*: Commistioni stilistiche e recezione critica nell'Italia teatrale di secondo Ottocento (1860–1870)', in *Opera e libretto*, ed. Gianfranco Folena, Maria Teresa Muraro and Giovanni Morelli (Florence: Olschki, 1990), 283–349.

13 Fiamma Nicolodi, 'Les Grands Opéras de Meyerbeer en Italie', in *L'Opéra en France et en Italie (1791–1925). Une scène privilégiée d'échanges littéraires et musicaux. Actes du Colloque franco-italien (Villecroze, 16–18 oct. 1997)*, ed. Hervé Lacombe (Paris: Société française de musicologie, 2000), 87–115. For a census of the widespread appreciation of Meyerbeer throughout the theatres of Italy, see Anna Tedesco, ' "Opere a macchina". La fortuna di Giacomo Meyerbeer in Italia dal 1840 al 1870', dissertation, University of Bologna (1996–97), 19, 23 *et passim*. Also Marcello Conati, 'Quasi un mistero il silenzio italiano sui Grand-opéra di Meyerbeer', *Nuova Rivista Musicale Italiana*, 27/2 and 27/4 (April–June and October–December 1999), 157–70, 535–57.

14 Kathleen Kuzmic Hansell, 'Il ballo teatrale e l'opera italiana', in *Storia dell' opera italiana*, ed. Lorenzo Bianconi and Giorgio Pestelli, V (*La spettacolarità*) (Turin: E.D.T., 1988), 287–302.

15 Michele Girardi and Franco Rossi, *Il teatro La Fenice. Cronologia degli spettacoli 1792–1936* (Venice: Albrizzi, 1989), 246–52, 259. *Satanella*, a *ballo fantastico* in five tableaux (Berlin, 1852), was one of the German-born

Hertel's early successes, in collaboration with the Milanese composer Cesare Pugni. *Brahma* and *La Camargo* were both first seen in Milan, both in 1868.

16 From *Pungolo*, 10–11 April 1876, reproduced in *Gazzetta musicale di Milano*, 31/16 (16 April 1876), 135.

17 See Alberto Rizzuti, *Fenomeni del baraccone. Il 'Guarany' di Antônio Carlos Gomes fra donne, cavalier, armi et orrori* (Turin: Paravia, 1997), 62–3.

18 Numbered 2337; also *Testo unico* R.D. dated 19 September 1882, no. 1012.

19 Boito wrote that its protagonist 'is the incarnation of the eternal "No" in the face of Truth, Beauty and Goodness': see the 'Prologo in teatro' of *Mefistofele* (libretto, 1868 version) in *idem*, *Tutti gli scritti*, ed. Piero Nardi ([Milan]: Mondadori, 1942), 101.

20 Letter from A. C. Gomes to G. Ricordi, 9 February 1880, ed. in *Antônio Carlos Gomes. Carteggi italiani*, ed. Gaspare Nello Vetro Gomes (Milan: Nuove edizioni [*c.* 1976]), 128. See this volume particularly for Gomes, containing also Marcello Conati, 'Formazione e affermazione di Gomes nel panorama dell'opera italiana. Appunti e considerazioni', 33–77.

21 Music which, indeed, influenced the generation comprising 'la Giovane Scuola' ('Young School'): the term is discussed in *Grove Opera*, II, 428–9. It applies to composers influenced by *verismo*, for example, in Mascagni's *Cavalleria rusticana* (1890).

22 Jay Nicolaisen, *Italian Opera in Transition, 1871–1893* (Ann Arbor: UMI Research Press, 1980), 100–8, gives a thorough account of the rich treasury of forms in Italian opera in the late nineteenth century.

23 According to Gomes, enthusing about Maddalena Mariani-Masi (who created the title role in *La Gioconda)*, the latter's interpretation was as incisive as that of the famous actress Adelaide Ristori: see letter from Gomes to G. Ricordi of 7 November 1879 in *Antônio Carlos Gomes. Carteggi italiani*, 123.

24 Adriana Guarnieri Corazzol, 'Opera and Verismo: Regressive Points of View and the Artifice of Alienation', *Cambridge Opera Journal*, 5/1 (1993), 39–53.

25 For the dances in *Il figliuol prodigo*, see Renato Di Benedetto, 'I ballabili nelle opere di Amilcare Ponchielli', in *Amilcare Ponchielli 1834–1886. Saggi e ricerche nel 150° anniversario della nascita*, ed. Nino Albarosa (Casalmorano: Cassa rurale, ed artigiana di Casalmorano, 1984), 246; the reference to J. Strauss is in G. Ricordi, 'Il Teatro della Scala. *Ruy Blas*',

Gazzetta musicale di Milano, 24/15 (11 April 1869), 122.

26 David Charlton, 'On the Nature of "Grand Opera" ', in *Hector Berlioz: Les Troyens*, ed. Ian Kemp (Cambridge: Cambridge University Press, 1988), 94–105; repr. in *idem, French Opera 1730–1830: Meaning and Media* (Aldershot: Ashgate, 2000); Gilles de Van, 'Le Grand Opéra entre tragédie lyrique et drame romantique', *Il Saggiatore musicale*, 3/2 (1996), 325–60.

27 Dated 1872, the *Messa in scena* for *Il Guarany* is reproduced in Rizzuti, *Fenomeni del baraccone*, 98–152. See too Michaela Peterseil, 'Die "Disposizioni sceniche" des Verlags Ricordi. Ihre Publikation und Zielpublikum', in *Studi Verdiani*, 12 (1997), 150–5.

28 Giuseppe Mazzini, *Filosofia della musica* [1836], ed. Marcello De Angelis (Florence: Guaraldi, 1977), 61–2.

29 An exception is Cecilia's 'Polacca-sortita' in *Il Guarany*, Act I, which is preceded by trills and runs.

30 Letter from Alfredo Catalani to Antonio Ghislanzoni of 23 November 1883, reproduced in Alfredo Bonaccorsi, *Alfredo Catalani* (Turin: Arione, 1942), 13.

31 Julian Budden, *The Operas of Verdi*, 3 vols. (London: Cassell, 1973–81), III, 283.

32 The 'inubia' (here, a poetic synonym for the *membitarará*) was a war-horn made of maçaranduba wood, used by the Tupi-Guarani Indians.

33 On typologies of Italian operatic dances of the period, see G. Schüller, 'Ponchielli: *La Gioconda: Ballett*', in *Pipers Enzyklopädie des Musiktheaters*, ed. Carl Dahlhaus and Sieghart Döhring, 7 vols. (Munich: Piper, 1986–97), V, 41.

34 S. F[arina], 'Rivista milanese', *Gazzetta musicale di Milano*, 25/13 (27 March 1870), 107.

35 'How on earth has this sophisticated orgy, on the steps of the very temple of Isis, been given official authorisation? it makes one blush with embarrassment': Léon Escudier, 'Opéra. *L'Enfant prodigue*', *La Musique. Gazette de la France musicale*, 49 (8 December 1850), 373.

36 Emilio Praga had by then written the libretto of *I profughi fiamminghi* for Franco Faccio, first staged in 1863. See note 9 above concerning the *Scapigliati*.

37 Fabrizio Della Seta, 'Un aspetto della ricezione di Meyerbeer in Italia: Le traduzioni dei Grands opéras', in *Meyerbeer und das europäische Musiktheater*, ed. Sieghart Döhring and Arnold Jacobshagen (Laaber: Laaber-Verlag, 1998), 309–51.

38 *Piano*: line with final accent on the penultimate syllable (commoner in Italian prosody); *tronco*: line with final accent on the final syllable.

39 *Sdrucciolo*: line with final accent on the antepenultimate syllable.

20 Grand opera in Britain and the Americas

1 See discussions of terminology within Chapters 1 and 10.

2 London was the centre for opera in Britain in the nineteenth century. Although such cities as Birmingham, Manchester, Glasgow and Edinburgh hosted the performances of visiting opera companies, they acquired their own permanent troupes only from the end of the nineteenth century. For the establishment of permanent companies in these and other cities, see *Grove Opera* under relevant place name.

3 For further information about the licensing, management and repertory of these theatres, see Robert D. Hume and Arthur Jacobs, 'London, §II: Institutions', in *Grove Opera*, and Christina Fuhrmann, '*Adapted and Arranged for the English Stage*: Continental Operas Transformed for the English Theater, 1814–33', dissertation, University of Washington (2000). Until 1843 the King's Theatre had the legal monopoly on Italian opera, while the patent theatres Covent Garden and Drury Lane had the monopoly on 'regular' spoken drama, and French and German opera (in English) – although the authorities tended to be lenient during the nineteenth century. A useful reference work is Theodore Fenner, *Opera in London: Views of the Press, 1785–1830* (Carbondale: Southern Illinois University Press, 1994).

4 See Hume and Jacobs, 'London, §II: Institutions', 2: Theatres: *Covent Garden*.

5 For more detail on Her Majesty's and Covent Garden, see Gabriella Dideriksen, 'Repertory and Rivalry: Opera at the Second Covent Garden Theatre, 1830 to 1856', dissertation, King's College, University of London (1997), Part I.

6 Although rivalry for the grand opera repertory had diminished to an extent, spoiling tactics could be used. The tenor Ander, for example, was engaged for a high sum in 1852 to sing Arnold in *Guillaume Tell*, even though he was not rated by Gye; the main benefit was that Lumley was prevented from staging more French operas at Her Majesty's: Dideriksen, 'Repertory and Rivalry', 223–5.

7 At Covent Garden the main season ran from March or April through to the end of

August, while in Paris it ran from September through to the spring; this enabled singers to perform in both cities. During autumn and winter at Covent Garden the opera house was frequently leased to entrepreneurs; in autumn 1848, for example, Alfred Bunn ran a season of English opera (including both native works and English translations of foreign works): Harold Rosenthal, *Two Centuries of Opera at Covent Garden* (London: Putnam, 1958), 72–84.

8 These and other examples of how the repertory was moulded around the available singers are discussed in Gabriella Dideriksen and Matthew Ringel, 'Frederick Gye and "The Dreadful Business of Opera Management"', *19th-Century Music*, 19/1 (1995), 3–30; and Rosenthal, *Two Centuries of Opera*, 32–4.

9 For a detailed discussion of Bishop's adaptations of Italian and comic French operas as well as grand operas, see Fuhrmann, '*Adapted and Arranged*'.

10 These adaptations were a burletta at the Adelphi (23 January 1832), Bishop's *The Demon* at Drury Lane (20 February 1832) and Lacy's *The Fiend Father* at Covent Garden (21 February 1832). Fuhrmann ('*Adapted and Arranged*') notes that Allardyce Nicoll identified further adaptations at Sadler's Wells (13 February) and the Royal Pavilion (16 March): *A History of English Drama 1660–1900*, IV: *Early Nineteenth-Century Drama*, 2nd edn (Cambridge: Cambridge University Press, 1955), 83.

11 Rupert Ridgewell, ' "Meyerbeer's Best Intentions Utterly Destroyed"? Henry Bishop's "Robert le Diable" (London, 1832)', dissertation, Royal Holloway, University of London (1993). I am grateful to Rupert for drawing my attention to his thesis, from which most of the information concerning this adaptation is drawn.

12 Covent Garden source: Royal College of Music, MS 382, dated January 1832. Ridgewell establishes that the score to which they had access (presumably acquired from the Opéra or from Schlesinger) must have postdated the Paris première, but predated the 1832 publication: ' "Meyerbeer's Best Intentions" ', 31–2.

13 Though some critics actually criticised it for its fidelity: Fuhrmann, '*Adapted and Arranged*', 186.

14 Ignaz Moscheles, *Recent Music and Musicians: As Described in the Diaries and Correspondence of Ignaz Moscheles* (New York: Da Capo, 1970), 176; cited in Ridgewell, ' "Meyerbeer's Best Intentions" ', 3. Given the careful attention Meyerbeer paid to

orchestration, creating specific timbral effects to underline dramatic developments, it is possible that the new orchestration led Moscheles and other critics to complain about the adaptation. Examination of the new orchestration might throw light on this particular aspect of the work's reception.

15 Hofer was a Tyrolean freedom fighter who headed a successful series of peasants' revolts but was betrayed to the French, who shot him. Four numbers were cut, four more combined into two new numbers, a chorus transformed into a duet, a soprano aria transposed for bass-baritone, and several new pieces created out of the hunting-horn theme associated with the enemy, and of melodies from the overture: Fuhrmann, '*Adapted and Arranged*', 176–9.

16 Ingredients of melodrama, from plots, characters and visual effects to trouser roles, were often added to operas, and the use of pantomime 'eased audiences into an acceptance of more action-based music'. Extra scenes with special effects were often supplied, and a new tableau was added to *The Demon*: Fuhrmann, '*Adapted and Arranged*', 280, 331.

17 Alfred Bunn, *The Stage both Before and Behind the Curtain*, 3 vols. (London: R. Bentley, 1840), III, 110–11; cited in Fuhrmann, '*Adapted and Arranged*', 202–3.

18 For example, James Kenney's adaptation of *La Muette de Portici* as *Masaniello* for Drury Lane condensed some longer scenes, reordered material and added a few lines of dialogue in an effort to simplify the story and recast it in three acts. Fenella's pantomime scenes remained more or less intact. Kenney claimed that 'lopping off redundancies, and making some slight additions, giving colour and reality to the action, is all I have done for *Masaniello*': preface to printed libretto (London: E. Moxon, 1831).

19 Earl of Mount Edgcumbe, *Musical Reminiscences*, 4th edn (London: John Andrews, 1834), 216 (supplement); anonymous critic, cited in Charles Gruneisen, *Memoir of Meyerbeer* (London: T. Brettell, 1848), 14.

20 Robert Ignatius Letellier (trans. and ed.), *The Diaries of Giacomo Meyerbeer*, Vol. 1: *1791–1839* (Madison: Fairleigh Dickinson University Press, 1999), 439–40.

21 *The Harmonicon* (1832), 160; cited in [John Edmund Cox], *Musical Recollections of the Last Half-Century*, 2 vols. (London: Tinsley Brothers, 1872), I, 242.

22 Planché justified this radical change to the plot – and intensified interest in its status as a

dramatisation of actual events – by claiming that he had taken the liberty of 'vindicat[ing] the character of poor Madame Ankestrom, who was actually living at that period'; see James Robinson Planché, *Recollections and Reflections*, rev. edn (London: Sampson Low, 1901), 148. Speaking roles were common in English opera of the time.

23 See Dideriksen, 'Repertory and Rivalry', 316, for a reconstruction of the new opera.

24 Cited in [Cox], *Musical Recollections*, 281–3.

25 Information about Gye in this paragraph is drawn from Gye's newly discovered diaries, as presented in Dideriksen and Ringel, 'Frederick Gye'.

26 On his annual visits Gye made a point of attending new works and concluding contracts for operas and singers; he often had the personal involvement of composers for their works. Meyerbeer, for example, was involved in the productions of all but one of his operas for the Royal Italian Opera, and composed new music and oversaw (from Paris) alterations made for the adaptations: Dideriksen, 'Repertory and Rivalry', 204.

27 *The Athenæum*, 1083 (29 July 1848), 754–5.

28 Planché, *Recollections and Reflections*, 179. Even in 1848 censorship required that the murder of Valentine, Raoul and Marcel on stage at the end of *Les Huguenots* be omitted; instead the curtain falls as 'the murderers rush against them': see the printed libretto (London, 1849).

29 Dideriksen, 'Repertory and Rivalry', 294, 307.

30 In modern terms, adaptations of Italian operas fared better than those of French (or German) works, as adapters were guided by the conventions of Italian opera. Roberta Montemorra Marvin has shown how changes required for the censor were generally made only in the translations in the librettos, the original Italian being sung with few if any changes to the music: 'The Censorship of Verdi's Operas in Victorian London', *Music & Letters*, 82/4 (2001), 582–610.

31 The changes are detailed in *The Athenæum*, 1082 (22 July 1848), 731–2; also Dideriksen, 'Repertory and Rivalry', 300–03, 312–13; see 328–9 for a reconstruction of the new opera.

32 Gruneisen, *Memoir of Meyerbeer*, 16, 18. Gruneisen was a founding member of the Royal Italian Opera at Covent Garden, and so not an impartial observer.

33 George Bernard Shaw, *Music in London 1890–94*, 3 vols. (London: Constable, 1932), I, 199 [27 May 1891].

34 *La Muette* appears to have been a particularly popular opera with English-speaking audiences during the nineteenth century, and performed far more frequently than any of Auber's other grand operas. Herbert Schneider finds twenty-six librettos, published in Britain (eleven), America (fourteen) and Australia (one), in English, Italian and German adaptations. It was particularly popular in Britain in the 1830s, and continued to be published until 1916. Arrangements of numbers from the opera were published in England as late as 1938. See Table 1.2 and Chapter 1, n. 56.

35 See Eric Walter White, *A History of English Opera* (London: Faber, 1983), 262.

36 Berlioz was engaged as the conductor for the 1847–48 season (during the first of his five visits to London): David Cairns (ed. and trans.), *A Life of Love and Music: The Memoirs of Hector Berlioz 1803–1869* (London: Folio Society, 1987), 384.

37 See Hume and Jacobs, 'London §II: Institutions'.

38 For example, see Rosenthal, *Opera at Covent Garden*, 295; and Cairns (ed.), *A Life of Love and Music*, 454–7.

39 On the influences of French (mainly comic) opera on English musical style, see Dideriksen, 'Repertory and Rivalry', 240–55.

40 Barnett wrote the music for a two-act 'Musical Romance' by R. J. Raymond entitled *Robert the Devil! Duke of Normandy*, for Covent Garden in 1830. Based on the legend which inspired Meyerbeer's opera of 1831, it may have been influenced by Bouilly's and Dumersan's *comédie* of 1813, written for the Théâtre du Vaudeville, Paris, and by *Don Giovanni*.

41 See George Biddlecombe, *English Opera from 1834 to 1864 with Particular Reference to the Works of Michael Balfe* (New York: Garland, 1994), 83.

42 Balfe's operas naturally embody his musical influences. He studied composition and singing in Italy and pursued a short career as a singer, had a contract with the Théâtre Italien, Paris in the mid-1820s, and associated with Cherubini and Rossini: Nigel Burton, 'Balfe', *New Grove/2*.

43 Biddlecombe discusses specific influences of Rossini, Auber and Meyerbeer on Balfe's *The Bohemian Girl*: *English Opera*, 109–10.

44 Biddlecombe, *English Opera*, 115–18; other examples of similarities with Halévy's score are also discussed.

45 Dalayrac's *Deux mots* (1806, revived in Paris in the 1820s) is also based on episodes from *The Monk*, and it, together perhaps with

Weber's *Silvana*, inspired the authors of *La Muette*. Any of these works could have been known by Loder, but the coincidence of 'mute' works serves to illustrate the continuous circulation of ideas at this time and the difficulty in pinning down specific influences.

46 These were settings of Planché's libretto on the theme of Edward III's siege of Calais (1838) and (an Italian version of) Scribe's adaptation of *The Tempest* (1846–47): John Warrack, 'Mendelssohn's Operas', in *Music and Theatre: Essays in Honour of Winton Dean*, ed. Nigel Fortune (Cambridge: Cambridge University Press, 1987), 263–97. For more on *The Tempest* see Benjamin Lumley, *Reminiscences of the Opera* (London: Hurst and Blackett, 1864), 166–8. Halévy eventually set the libretto in 1850.

47 Planché, *Recollections and Reflections*, letter from Mendelssohn to Planché [1838], 202–4, cited in White, *A History of English Opera*, 272.

48 Planché, *Recollections and Reflections*, 203. Details of the dealings between librettist and composer, together with a reproduction of their letters, are provided by Planché (202–17). Later in the volume he notes that Mendelssohn did not like *Masaniello*, *Tell* or *Robert*, which perhaps helps to explain why Mendelssohn was not happy with Planché's libretto for their own 'grand opera' (227–8).

49 Although, as Stephen Banfield notes, it must have seemed old-fashioned by the time it was performed at Covent Garden in 1893: 'Stanford', in *Grove Opera*.

50 Andrew Lamb, 'Ivanhoe and the Royal English Opera', *Musical Times*, 114 (1973), 475–8. The venue was built specifically for the opera, by the impresario Richard D'Oyly Carte.

51 Shaw, *Music in London 1890–94*, I, 76 (27 April 1892). The reasons are explored in Lamb, 'Ivanhoe', 475.

52 Biddlecombe, *English Opera*, 167.

53 Shaw, *Music in London 1890–94*, I, 168–9 (18 May 1892).

54 It features a blind girl (with her own leitmotif), a lively chorus, 'Water-melons rich and rare', that recalls Auber's market chorus, and concludes with the eruption of Vesuvius and a scene 'of terror and confusion in the streets'; the hero and heroine escape in a boat with the blind girl, who leaps into the sea, to her death.

55 Nigel Burton, 'Opera: 1865–1914', in *The Romantic Age 1800–1914*, ed. Nicholas Temperley, Blackwell History of Music in Britain (Oxford: Blackwell, 1988), 342–5, here 343. Burton suggests that Cowen's

Pauline (1876, Lyceum) and Goring Thomas's *Esmeralda* (1883, Drury Lane) reveal the influences of Gounod and Ambroise Thomas (*Pauline*) and Bizet.

56 Stephen Banfield, 'The Early Music Renaissance: Mackenzie, Stanford and Smyth', *British Opera in Retrospect* (Gerrard's Cross: British Music Society, 1986), 63–8, here 64.

57 For different national schools of opera and their influences on American opera see Elsie Kirk, 'United States of America', in *Grove Opera*.

58 Katherine Preston, *Opera on the Road: Travelling Opera Troupes in the United States, 1825–60* (Urbana: University of Illinois Press, 1993), 1–6.

59 John Dizikes, *Opera in America: A Cultural History* (New Haven: Yale University Press, 1993), 231. In 1854 the Bowery theatre in New York became known as the Stadt Theater, and German theatre and opera was presented there, including performances of *Tannhäuser* and *Lohengrin* in 1859 conducted by Carl Bergmann, which attracted mainly German immigrant audiences. In 1855 a German season was mounted at Niblo's theatre, and German musicians gradually came to dominate the country's leading orchestras.

60 American and European troupes would often extend their tours into Canada. Occasional French grand operas were given (notably *Les Huguenots*), but Italian and then German operas became favoured in Canada, as in America: Helmut Kallmann, *A History of Music in Canada 1534–1914* (Toronto: University of Toronto Press, 1960).

61 One of the largest travelling troupes was Theodore Thomas's American Opera Company (1886), performing 'grand operas' sung in English by Americans, but also Mozart, Verdi, Delibes and Wagner. It disbanded after two years owing to lack of funds.

62 Edith Wharton, *The Age of Innocence* [1920] (Harmondsworth: Penguin, 1996), 2–3; cited in Pierre Degott, 'L'opéra en version traduite: L'exception de la Grande-Bretagne', *Revue de musicologie*, 85/2 (1999), 333–50, here 345–6.

63 Carl Bergmann and others had already begun to champion Wagner's music in concert halls and increasingly in opera houses, in spite of the limited enthusiasm of audiences, and there was heated philosophical debate about the composer's writings. In this climate, Italian opera came to seem old-fashioned and limited: Karen Ahlquist, 'Mrs Potiphar at the Opera: Satire, Idealism, and Cultural Authority in Post-Civil War New York', in *Music and Culture in America*,

1861–1918, ed. Michael Saffle (New York: Garland, 1998), 29–51, here 42.

64 See W. H. Seltsam, *Metropolitan Opera Annals* (New York: H. W. Wilson; Metropolitan Opera Guild, 1947).

65 Information about opera in San Francisco is from George Martin, *Verdi at the Golden Gate: Opera and San Francisco in the Gold Rush Years* (Berkeley: University of California Press, 1993), 3 and 64–94.

66 Bochsa advertised in the *Daily Alta California* for extra performers to swell the ranks of his company and the opera opened five days later: Martin, *Verdi at the Golden Gate*, 75–6.

67 Louisiana was French until 1762, then ceded to Spain. In 1800 it was returned to France, but sold to America in 1803. See Henry A. Kmen, *Music in New Orleans: The Formative Years, 1791–1841* (Baton Rouge: Louisiana State University Press, 1966); and Ronald L. Davis, *A History of Opera in the American West* (Englewood Cliffs: Prentice-Hall, 1965).

68 Acrobatics and vaudevilles were frequently added to encourage audiences at both theatres, although they were added only between acts at the French theatre.

69 Kmen, *Music in New Orleans*, 160.

70 The opera was never performed and Fry did not even try to have it staged in America, instead giving it to a singer to show around London, where it attracted no interest: Dizikes, *Opera in America*, 98–9.

71 Kmen, *Music in New Orleans*, 199–200.

72 Dizikes, *Opera in America*, 379.

73 Charles Wakefield Cadman (1881–1946) similarly attempted to ground American opera in national history, using 'authentic' American folk music. *Shanewis* (1918, New York), was based on the life of an Indian, but Cadman's idiom was essentially European and he set native melodies in conservative nineteenth-century harmonies.

74 Cited in Dizikes, *Opera in America*, 380–1.

75 The brief details here about Latin American composers are drawn from biographical entries in *Grove Opera*.

76 Also Luca Zoppelli, 'The Twilight of the True Gods: *Cristoforo Colombo*, *I Medici* and the Construction of Italian History', *Cambridge Opera Journal*, 8/3 (1996), 251–69.

77 Julian Budden, 'Wagnerian Tendencies in Italian Opera', in *Music and Theatre*, ed. Fortune, 299–332.

78 For a survey, see Robert Stevenson, 'Rio de Janeiro', in *Grove Opera*.

79 Stevenson, 'Buenos Aires', in *Grove Opera*.

Select bibliography

Note: A great deal of the literature quoted in the end-notes to this book is not in English, but is essential for closer study. This Select Bibliography omits almost all publications not in English, and also dictionary articles.

Abbate, Carolyn, and Parker, Roger (eds.), *Analyzing Opera: Verdi and Wagner* (Berkeley: University of California Press, 1989)

Armstrong, Alan, 'Meyerbeer's *Le Prophète*: A History of its Composition and Early Performances', dissertation, Ohio State University (1990)

  'Gilbert-Louis Duprez and Gustave Roger in the Composition of Meyerbeer's *Le Prophète*', *Cambridge Opera Journal*, 8/2 (1996), 147–65

Ashbrook, William, *Donizetti and His Operas* (Cambridge: Cambridge University Press, 1982)

Ault, Cecil Thomas, 'Design, Operation and Organization of Stage Machinery at the Paris Opéra (1770–1873)', dissertation, University of Michigan, Ann Arbor (1983)

Barbier, Patrick, *Opera in Paris, 1800–1850: A Lively History*, trans. Robert Luoma (Portland, OR: Amadeus Press, 1995)

Bartlet, M. Elizabeth C., *Guillaume Tell di Gioachino Rossini: Fonti Iconografiche* (Pesaro: Fondazione Rossini, 1996)

  'Staging French *Grand Opéra*: Rossini's *Guillaume Tell* (1829)', in *Gioachino Rossini, 1792–1992: il testo e la scena: Convegno internazionale di studi, Pesaro, 24–28 giugno 1992*, ed. Paolo Fabbri (Pesaro: Fondazione Rossini, 1994), 623–48

Becker, Heinz and Gudrun, *Giacomo Meyerbeer: A Life in Letters*, trans. Mark Violette (London: Helm, 1989)

Berlioz, Hector, 'Guillaume Tell', *Gazette musicale de Paris*, 1 (12, 19, 26 October and 2 November 1834), Eng. trans. in *Source Readings in Music History*, ed. Oliver Strunk (New York: W. W. Norton, 1950)

Beveridge, David (ed.), *Rethinking Dvořák: Views from Five Countries* (Oxford: Clarendon Press, 1996)

Biddlecombe, George, *English Opera from 1834 to 1864 with Particular Reference to the Works of Michael Balfe* (New York: Garland, 1994)

Bloom, Peter (ed.), *The Cambridge Companion to Berlioz* (Cambridge: Cambridge University Press, 2000)

Budden, Julian, *The Operas of Verdi*, 3 vols. (London: Cassell, 1973–81)

  'Verdi and Meyerbeer in Relation to *Les Vêpres siciliennes*', *Studi verdiani*, 1 (1982), 11–20

  'Wagnerian Tendencies in Italian Opera', in *Music and Theatre: Essays in Honour of Winton Dean*, ed. Nigel Fortune (Oxford: Oxford University Press, 1987), 299–332

Burton, Nigel, 'Opera: 1865–1914', in *The Romantic Age 1800–1914*, Blackwell
    History of Music in Britain, ed. Nicholas Temperley (Oxford: Blackwell, 1988),
    342–5

Charlton, D. G. (ed.), *The French Romantics*, 2 vols. (Cambridge: Cambridge
    University Press, 1984)

Clark, Maribeth, 'Understanding French Grand Opera through Dance',
    dissertation, University of Pennsylvania (1998)

Cohen, H. Robert, 'On the Reconstruction of the Visual Elements of French Grand
    Opéra', in *International Musicological Society. Report of the Twelfth Congress,
    Berkeley 1977*, ed. Daniel Heartz and Bonnie Wade (Kassel, 1981), 463–80

    The Original Staging Manuals for Twelve Parisian Operatic Premières (Stuyvesant,
    NY: Pendragon Press, 1991)

Commons, Jeffrey, 'An Introduction to "Il duca d'Alba" ', *Opera*, 10 (1959), 421–6

Corazzol, Adriana Guarnieri, 'Opera and Verismo: Regressive Points of View and
    the Artifice of Alienation', *Cambridge Opera Journal*, 5/1 (1993), 39–53

Cruz, Gabriela, 'Laughing at History: The Third Act of Meyerbeer's *L'Africaine*',
    Cambridge Opera Journal, 11/1 (1999), 31–76

    'Giacomo Meyerbeer's *L'Africaine* and the End of Grand Opera', dissertation,
    Princeton University (1999)

Daniels, Barry V., 'Ciceri and Daguerre: Set Designers for the Paris Opéra,
    1820–1822', *Theatre Survey*, 22/1 (1981), 69–90

Davis, Ronald L., *A History of Opera in the American West* (Englewood Cliffs:
    Prentice-Hall, 1965)

Dean, Winton, 'Donizetti's Serious Operas', *Proceedings of the Royal Musical
    Association*, 100 (1973–74), 123–41

Dideriksen, Gabriella, 'Repertory and Rivalry: Opera at the Second Covent
    Garden Theatre, 1830 to 1856', dissertation, King's College, University of
    London (1997)

Dideriksen, Gabriella, and Ringel, Matthew, 'Frederick Gye and "The Dreadful
    Business of Opera Management" ', *19th-Century Music*, 19/1 (1995), 3–30

Dizikes, John, *Opera in America: A Cultural History* (New Haven: Yale University
    Press, 1993)

Döhring, Sieghart, 'Giacomo Meyerbeer and the Opera of the Nineteenth
    Century', website 'Meyerbeer Fan Club', http://www.meyerbeer.com/
    sieghart.htm, 1–8 [4], accessed on 26 March 1999

Döhring, Sieghart, and Jacobshagen, Arnold (eds.), *Meyerbeer und das europäische
    Musiktheater* (Laaber: Laaber-Verlag, 1998)

Drysdale, John Duncan, 'Louis Véron and the Finances of the *Académie Royale de
    Musique*, 1827 to 1835', dissertation, University of Southampton (2000)

Emerson, Caryl, 'Musorgsky's Libretti on Historical Themes: From the Two
    Borises to *Khovanshchina*', in *Reading Opera*, ed. Arthur Groos and Roger
    Parker (Princeton: Princeton University Press, 1988), 235–67

Everist, Mark, 'The Name of the Rose: Meyerbeer's opéra-comique *Robert le
    Diable*', *Revue de musicologie*, 80/2 (1994), 211–50

    'Translating Weber's *Euryanthe*: German Romanticism at the Dawn of French
    Grand Opéra', *Revue de musicologie*, 87/1 (2001), 67–104

Fitzlyon, April, *The Price of Genius: A Life of Pauline Viardot* (London: John Calder, 1964)

Fuhrmann, Christina, '*Adapted and Arranged for the English Stage*: Continental Operas Transformed for the English Theater, 1814–33', dissertation, University of Washington (2000)

Fulcher, Jane, *The Nation's Image: French Grand Opera as Politics and Politicized Art* (Cambridge: Cambridge University Press, 1987)

Garafola, Lynn, 'The Travesty Dancer in Nineteenth-Century Ballet', *Dance Research Journal*, 17/2 and 18/1 (Autumn 1985, Spring 1986), 35–40

Garafola, Lynn (ed.), *Rethinking the Sylph* (Hanover: Wesleyan University Press, 1997)

Gerhard, Anselm, 'Die französische "Grand Opéra" in der Forschung seit 1945', *Acta Musicologica*, 59/3 (1987), 220–70

The Urbanization of Opera: Music Theater in Paris in the Nineteenth Century, trans. Mary Whittall (Chicago: University of Chicago Press, 1998)

Guest, Ivor, *The Romantic Ballet in Paris* (London, 1966; 2nd edn 1980)

Hallman, Diana, *Opera, Liberalism, and Antisemitism in Nineteenth-Century France: The Politics of Halévy's 'La Juive'* (Cambridge: Cambridge University Press, 2002)

Hemmings, F. W. J., *The Theatre Industry in Nineteenth-Century France* (Cambridge: Cambridge University Press, 1993)

Theatre and State in France, 1760–1905 (Cambridge: Cambridge University Press, 1994)

Hibberd, Sarah, 'Magnetism, Muteness, Magic: *Spectacle* and the Parisian Lyric Stage, c.1830', dissertation, University of Southampton (1998)

Huebner, Steven, 'Opera Audiences in Paris, 1830–1870', *Music & Letters*, 70/2 (May 1989), 206–25

'Italianate Duets in Meyerbeer's Grand Operas', *Journal of Musicological Research*, 8 (1989), 203–58

The Operas of Charles Gounod (Oxford: Clarendon Press, 1990)

French Opera at the Fin de Siècle: *Wagnerism, Nationalism, and Style* (Oxford: Oxford University Press, 1999)

Jordan, Ruth, *Fromental Halévy: His Life and Music, 1799–1862* (London: Kahn & Averill, 1994)

Kallmann, Helmut, *A History of Music in Canada 1534–1914* (Toronto: University of Toronto Press, 1960)

Kemp, Ian (ed.), *Hector Berlioz: Les Troyens* (Cambridge: Cambridge University Press, 1988)

Kimbell, David R. B., *Verdi in the Age of Italian Romanticism* (Cambridge: Cambridge University Press, 1981)

'Verdi's First Rifacimento: *I Lombardi* and *Jérusalem*', *Music & Letters*, 60 (1969), 1–36

Kmen, Henry A., *Music in New Orleans: The Formative Years, 1791–1841* (Baton Rouge: Louisiana State University Press, 1966)

Lacombe, Hervé, *The Keys to French Opera in the Nineteenth Century*, trans. Edward Schneider (Berkeley: University of California Press, 2001)

Lamb, Andrew, 'Ivanhoe and the Royal English Opera', *Musical Times*, 114 (1973), 475–8

Letellier, Robert Ignatius, *The Diaries of Giacomo Meyerbeer*, vol. I (1791–1839); vol. II (1840–49) [of 3 projected] (Madison: Fairleigh Dickinson University Press, 1999, 2001)

'The Thematic Nexus of Religion, Power, Politics and Love in the Operas of Giacomo Meyerbeer', website 'Meyerbeer Fan Club', http://www.meyerbeer.com/nexus.htm, accessed on 22 February 2002

'History, Myth and Music in a Theme of Exploration: Some Reflections on the Musico-Dramatic Language of *L'Africaine*', in Döhring and Jacobshagen (eds.), *Meyerbeer und das europäische Musiktheater* (see above); also website 'Meyerbeer Fan Club', http://www.meyerbeer.com/lafricai.htm, accessed on 22 February 2002

Libby, Dennis Albert, 'Gaspare Spontini and his French and German Operas', dissertation, Princeton University (1969)

Lindenberger, Herbert, *Historical Drama: The Relation of Literature and Reality* (Chicago: University of Chicago Press, 1975)

Lo Presti, F., '*Le duc d'Albe*: The Livret of Scribe and Duveyrier', *Donizetti Society Journal*, 5 (1984), 243–316

Martin, George, *Verdi at the Golden Gate: Opera and San Francisco in the Gold Rush Years* (Berkeley: University of California Press, 1993)

Messenger, M. F., 'Donizetti, 1840: Three "French" Operas and their Italian Counterparts', *Donizetti Society Journal*, 2 (1975), 161–77

Mitchell, Jerome, *The Walter Scott Operas* (Tuscaloosa, AL: University of Alabama Press, 1977)

Morosan, Vladimir, 'Folk and Chant Elements in Musorgsky's Choral Writing', in *Musorgsky: In Memoriam, 1881–1981*, ed. Malcolm Hamrick Brown (Ann Arbor: UMI Research Press, 1982), 95–133

Moynet, Jean-Pierre, *L'Envers du théâtre* [1873], trans. Allan S. Jackson with M. Glen Wilson and ed. Marvin Carlson as *French Theatrical Production in the Nineteenth Century* (New York: SUNY at Binghamton, 1976)

Newark, Cormac, 'Staging Grand Opéra: History and Imagination in Nineteenth-Century Paris', dissertation, University of Oxford (1999)

Nicolaisen, Jay, *Italian Opera in Transition, 1871–1893* (Ann Arbor: UMI Research Press, 1980)

Osborne, Richard, *Rossini* (London, 1986; 2/1987)

Parakilas, James, 'Political Representation and the Chorus in Nineteenth-Century Opera', *19th-Century Music*, 16/2 (1992), 181–202

Parker, Roger, *Leonora's Last Act: Essays in Verdian Discourse* (Princeton: Princeton University Press, 1997)

Parker, Roger (ed.), *The Oxford Illustrated History of Opera* (Oxford: Oxford University Press, 1994)

Parker, Roger, and Smart, Mary Ann (eds.), *Reading Critics Reading: Opera and Ballet Criticism in France from the Revolution to 1848* (Oxford: Oxford University Press, 2001)

Pendle, Karin, *Eugène Scribe and French Opera of the Nineteenth Century* (Ann Arbor: UMI Research Press, 1979)

'The Boulevard Theaters and Continuity in French Opera of the 19th Century', in *Music in Paris in the Eighteen-Thirties*, ed. Peter Bloom (Stuyvesant, NY: Pendragon Press, 1987), 509–35

Pendle, Karin, and Wilkins, Stephen, 'Paradise Found: The Salle Le Peletier and French Grand Opera', in *Opera in Context: Essays on Historical Staging from the Late Renaissance to the Time of Puccini*, ed. Mark A. Radice (Portland, OR: Amadeus Press, 1998), 171–207

Pleasants, Henry (ed.), *The Great Tenor Tragedy: The Last Days of Adolphe Nourrit as told (mostly) by himself* (Portland, OR: Amadeus Press, 1995)

Porter, Andrew, '*Les Vêpres siciliennes*: New Letters from Verdi to Scribe', *19th-Century Music*, 2 (1978–79), 95–109

Preston, Katherine, *Opera on the Road: Travelling Opera Troupes in the United States, 1825–60* (Urbana: University of Illinois Press, 1993)

Ridgewell, Rupert, ' "Meyerbeer's Best Intentions Utterly Destroyed"? Henry Bishop's *Robert le Diable* (London, 1832)', dissertation, Royal Holloway, University of London (1993)

Roberts, John H., 'The Genesis of Meyerbeer's *L'Africaine*', dissertation, University of California, Berkeley (1977)

Robinson, Paul, *Opera and Ideas: From Mozart to Strauss* (New York: Harper and Row, 1985)

Rosenthal, Harold, *Two Centuries of Opera at Covent Garden* (London: Putnam, 1958)

Rosselli, John, 'Grand Opera: Nineteenth-century Revolution and Twentieth-century Tradition', in *The Cambridge Companion to Singing*, ed. John Potter (Cambridge: Cambridge University Press, 2000), 96–108

Runyan, William Edward, 'Orchestration in Five French Grand Operas', dissertation, Eastman School of Music (1983)

Sadie, Stanley (ed.), *History of Opera*, The New Grove Handbooks in Music (Basingstoke: Macmillan, 1989)

Schneider, Herbert (ed.), *Correspondance d'E. Scribe et de D.-F.-E. Auber* (Liège: Mardaga, 1998)

Schönzeler, Hans-Hubert, *Dvořák* (London: Marion Boyars, 1984)

Schumann, Robert, 'Fragmente aus Leipzig, 4' [1837: attacking *Les Huguenots*], trans. Fanny Raymond Ritter, in *Music and Musicians: Essays and Criticisms by Robert Schumann* (London: William Reeves, 1877), 302–7

Simpson, Adrienne, *Opera's Furthest Frontier: A History of Professional Opera in New Zealand* (Birkenhead, Auk.: Reed, 1996)

Smaczny, Jan, 'The Daily Repertoire of the Provisional Theatre in Prague', *Miscellania musicologica*, 34 (1994), 9–139

Smart, Mary Ann, 'The Lost Voice of Rosine Stoltz', *Cambridge Opera Journal*, 6/1 (1994), 31–50

' "Proud, Indomitable, Irascible": Allegories of Nation in *Attila* and *Les Vêpres siciliennes*', in *Verdi's Middle Period, 1849–1859: Source Studies, Analysis, and Performance Practice*, ed. Martin Chusid (Chicago: University of Chicago Press, 1997), 227–56

Resonant Bodies: Music and Gesture in Nineteenth-Century Opera (Berkeley: University of California Press, 2001)

Smith, Marian, *Ballet and Opera in the Age of 'Giselle'* (Princeton: Princeton University Press, 2000)

Smith, Patrick J., *A Historical Study of the Opera Libretto* (New York: Schirmer, 1970)

Spies, André Michael, *Opera, State and Society in the Third Republic, 1875–1914* (New York: P. Lang, 1998)

Tamvaco, Jean-Louis, *Les Cancans de l'Opéra: Chroniques de l'Académie Royale de Musique et du théâtre, à Paris sous les deux Restaurations*, 2 vols. (Paris: CNRS Editions, 2000)

Taruskin, Richard, *Opera and Drama in Russia as Preached and Practiced in the 1860s* (Ann Arbor: UMI Research Press, 1981)

Defining Russia Musically (Princeton: Princeton University Press, 1997)

Tyrrell, John, *Czech Opera* (Cambridge: Cambridge University Press, 1988)

Walton, Benjamin, 'Romanticisms and Nationalisms in Restoration France', dissertation, University of California, Berkeley (2000)

Warrack, John, 'The Influence of French Grand Opera on Wagner', in *Music in Paris in the Eighteen-Thirties*, ed. Peter Bloom (Stuyvesant, NY: Pendragon Press, 1987), 575–87

German Opera: From the Beginnings to Wagner (Cambridge: Cambridge University Press, 2001)

Weaver, William, *Verdi: A Documentary Study* (London, 1977)

Weinstock, Herbert, *Donizetti and the World of Opera in Italy, Paris and Vienna in the First Half of the Nineteenth Century* (New York, 1963)

Wilberg, Rebecca S., 'The *Mise en scène* at the Paris Opéra – Salle Le Peletier (1821–1873) and the Staging of the First French Grand Opera: Meyerbeer's *Robert le Diable*', dissertation, Brigham Young University (1990)

Wild, Nicole, *Décors et costumes du XIXe siècle. Tome I: Opéra de Paris; Tome II: Théâtres et décorateurs* (Paris: Bibliothèque nationale, 1987, 1993)

Dictionnaire des théâtres parisiens au XIXe siècle: les théâtres et la musique (Paris: Aux amateurs de livres, 1989)

Wittmann, Michael, 'Meyerbeer and Mercadante? The Reception of Meyerbeer in Italy', *Cambridge Opera Journal*, 5/2 (1993), 115–65

Zoppelli, Luca, 'The Twilight of the True Gods: *Cristoforo Colombo, I Medici* and the Construction of Italian History', *Cambridge Opera Journal*, 8/3 (1996), 251–69

Index